i

GLEIM®

2018
EDITION

CPA Review

Business Environment & Concepts

by

Irvin N. Gleim, Ph.D., CPA, CIA, CMA, CFM

and

Garrett W. Gleim

with the assistance of
Grady M. Irwin, J.D.

Gleim Publications, Inc.
PO Box 12848
University Station
Gainesville, Florida 32604
(800) 87-GLEIM or (800) 874-5346
(352) 375-0772
Website: www.gleim.com
Email: admin@gleim.com

For updates to this 2018 edition of
CPA Review: Business Environment and Concepts

Go To: www.gleim.com/CPAupdate

Or: Email update@gleim.com with **CPA BEC 2018-1** in the subject line. You will receive our current update as a reply.

Updates are available until the next edition is published.

ISSN: 1547-8084

ISBN: 978-1-61854-079-9 *CPA Review: Auditing and Attestation*
ISBN: 978-1-61854-148-2 *CPA Review: Business Environment and Concepts*
ISBN: 978-1-61854-149-9 *CPA Review: Financial Accounting and Reporting*
ISBN: 978-1-61854-150-5 *CPA Review: Regulation*
ISBN: 978-1-61854-151-2 *CPA Exam Guide: A System for Success*

ACKNOWLEDGMENTS

Material from *Uniform CPA Examination, Selected Questions and Unofficial Answers*, Copyright © 1974-2017 by the American Institute of Certified Public Accountants, Inc., is reprinted and/or adapted with permission. Visit the AICPA's website at www.aicpa.org for more information.

The author is indebted to the Institute of Certified Management Accountants for permission to use problem materials from past CMA examinations. Questions and unofficial answers from the Certified Management Accountant Examinations, copyright by the Institute of Certified Management Accountants, are reprinted and/or adapted with permission.

The author is grateful for permission to reproduce Certified Internal Auditor Examination Questions, Copyright © 1991-2017 by The Institute of Internal Auditors, Inc.

Environmental Statement -- This book is printed on recyclable, environmentally friendly groundwood paper, sourced from certified sustainable forests and produced either TCF (totally chlorine-free) or ECF (elementally chlorine-free).

ABOUT THE AUTHORS

Irvin N. Gleim is Professor Emeritus in the Fisher School of Accounting at the University of Florida and is a member of the American Accounting Association, Academy of Legal Studies in Business, American Institute of Certified Public Accountants, Association of Government Accountants, Florida Institute of Certified Public Accountants, The Institute of Internal Auditors, and the Institute of Management Accountants. He has had articles published in the *Journal of Accountancy*, *The Accounting Review*, and *The American Business Law Journal* and is author/coauthor of numerous accounting books, aviation books, and CPE courses.

Garrett W. Gleim, B.S., CGMA, received a Bachelor of Science degree with a concentration in Accounting from the University of Pennsylvania, The Wharton School. He also holds a CPA Certificate issued by the State of Delaware. In addition to his roles as Vice President/Co-Author at Gleim Publications, Inc., and co-editor of all Gleim learning management systems, he is the inventor of multiple patents with educational applications. Outside of Gleim, he is a member of the Emergent Growth Fund I & II, where he is actively involved with entrepreneurs and start-up companies, and he serves on the boards of BACCH Labs (3D Audio Technology) and CaviDyne, LLC (OFS Technology).

REVIEWERS AND CONTRIBUTORS

Solomon E. Gonite, J.D., CPA, CIA, is a graduate of the Florida State University College of Law and the Fisher School of Accounting at the University of Florida. He has practiced as an auditor (in both the private and government sectors) and as a tax practitioner. Mr. Gonite provided substantial editorial assistance throughout the project.

William A. Hillison, Ph.D., CPA, CMA, is a Professor Emeritus of Accounting at Florida State University. His primary teaching duties included graduate and undergraduate auditing and systems courses. Dr. Hillison provided substantial editorial assistance throughout the project.

Grady M. Irwin, J.D., is a graduate of the University of Florida College of Law, and he has taught in the University of Florida College of Business. Mr. Irwin provided substantial editorial assistance throughout the project.

Michael Kustanovich, M.A., CPA, is a graduate of Ben-Gurion University of the Negev in Israel. He is a Lecturer of Accountancy in the Department of Accountancy at the University of Illinois at Urbana-Champaign. He has worked in the audit departments of KPMG and PWC and as a financial accounting lecturer in the Department of Economics of Ben-Gurion University of the Negev. Mr. Kustanovich provided substantial editorial assistance throughout the project.

Mark S. Modas, M.S.T., CPA, received a Bachelor of Arts in Accounting from Florida Atlantic University and a Master of Science in Taxation from Nova Southeastern University. He was the Sarbanes-Oxley project manager and internal audit department manager at Perry Ellis International, and the former Acting Director of Accounting and Financial Reporting for the School Board of Broward County, Florida. Mr. Modas provided substantial editorial assistance throughout the project.

Yiqian Zhao, MAcc., CIA, is a graduate from the Fisher School of Accounting at the University of Florida, and she has passed the CPA exam. Ms. Zhao participated in the technical editing of the manuscript.

A PERSONAL THANKS

This manual would not have been possible without the extraordinary effort and dedication of Jacob Bennett, Julie Cutlip, Ethan Good, Doug Green, Blaine Hatton, Fernanda Martinez, Kelsey Olson, Bree Rodriguez, Teresa Soard, Justin Stephenson, Joanne Strong, Elmer Tucker, and Candace Van Doren, who typed the entire manuscript and all revisions and drafted and laid out the diagrams, illustrations, and cover for this book.

The authors also appreciate the production and editorial assistance of Levi Bradford, Steven Critelli, Jim Harvin, Jessica Hatker, Kristen Hennen, Belea Keeney, Katie Larson, Diana León, Bernadyn Nettles, Jake Pettifor, Shane Rapp, Drew Sheppard, and Alyssa Thomas.

The authors also appreciate the critical reading assistance of Felix Chen, Corey Connell, Nathan Giron, Justin Hamilton, Nichole Hyde, Andrew Johnson, Dean Kingston, Melissa Leonard, Monica Metz, Timothy Murphy, Cristian Prieto, Crystal Quach, and Martin Salazar.

Finally, we appreciate the encouragement, support, and tolerance of our families throughout this project.

TABLE OF CONTENTS

DETAILED TABLE OF CONTENTS

PREFACE FOR CPA CANDIDATES

The purpose of this Gleim CPA Review study book is to help you prepare to pass the 2018 Business Environment and Concepts (also referred to throughout the rest of this text as Business or BEC) section of the CPA examination. Our overriding consideration is to provide a comprehensive, effective, and easy-to-use study program. This book

1. Explains how to optimize your grade by focusing on the BEC section of the CPA exam.
2. Defines the subject matter tested on the BEC section of the CPA exam.
3. Outlines all of the subject matter tested on the BEC section in 20 easy-to-use-and-complete study units.
4. Presents multiple-choice questions from recent CPA examinations to prepare you for questions in future CPA exams. Our answer explanations are presented to the immediate right of each question for your convenience. Use a piece of paper to cover our answer explanations as you study the questions.

The outline format, the spacing, and the question and answer formats in this book are designed to facilitate readability, learning, understanding, and success on the CPA exam. Our most successful candidates use the Gleim Premium CPA Review System,* which includes Gleim Instruct videos; our Access Until You Pass Guarantee; SmartAdapt technology; expertly authored books; the largest test bank of multiple-choice questions, Task-Based Simulations, and Written Communications; audio lectures; and the support of our team of accounting experts. This review book and all Gleim CPA Review materials are compatible with other CPA review materials and courses that follow the AICPA Blueprints.

To maximize the efficiency and effectiveness of your CPA review program, augment your studying with *CPA Exam Guide: A System for Success*, which has been carefully written and organized to provide important information to assist you in passing the CPA examination.

Thank you for your interest in the Gleim CPA Review materials. We deeply appreciate the thousands of letters and suggestions received from CPA, CIA, CMA, and EA candidates during the past 5 decades.

If you use the Gleim materials, we want YOUR feedback immediately after the exam and as soon as you have received your grades. The CPA exam is NONDISCLOSED, and you will sign an attestation including, "I hereby agree that I will maintain the confidentiality of the Uniform CPA Examination. In addition, I agree that I will not divulge the nature or content of any Uniform CPA Examination question or answer under any circumstance . . ." We ask only for information about our materials, i.e., the topics that need to be added, expanded, etc. Our approach has AICPA approval.

Please go to www.gleim.com/feedbackBEC to share your suggestions on how we can improve this edition.

Good Luck on the Exam,
Irvin N. Gleim
November 2017

* Visit www.gleimcpa.com or call (800) 874-5346 to order.

OPTIMIZING YOUR BUSINESS ENVIRONMENT AND CONCEPTS SCORE

UNIFORM CPA EXAMINATION

CPA Exam Section	Auditing & Attestation	Business Environment & Concepts	Financial Accounting & Reporting	Regulation
Acronym	AUD	**BEC**	FAR	REG
Exam Length	4 hours	**4 hours**	4 hours	4 hours
Testlet 1: Multiple-Choice	36 questions	**31 questions**	33 questions	38 questions
Testlet 2: Multiple-Choice	36 questions	**31 questions**	33 questions	38 questions
Testlet 3: Task-Based Simulations	2 tasks	**2 tasks**	2 tasks	2 tasks
Standardized Break	Clock stops for 15 minutes			
Testlet 4: Task-Based Simulations	3 tasks	**2 tasks**	3 tasks	3 tasks
Testlet 5: Task-Based Simulations or Written Communications	3 tasks	**3 written communications**	3 tasks	3 tasks

---

2018 CPA Exam User Interface Changes

At time of print, updates to the CPA exam user interface are slated for mid-2018. These changes affect the layout, functionality, and general appearance of all testlets. Additionally, the basic spreadsheet tool currently available in the exam will be replaced by Microsoft Excel. Learn about the new user interface by visiting www.gleim.com/CPAchanges.

Passing the CPA exam is a serious undertaking. Begin by becoming an expert in the content, formatting, and functionality of the BEC exam before you take it. The objective is no surprises on exam day. Also, you will save time and money, decrease frustration, and increase your probability of success by learning all you can about how to prepare for and take BEC.

Review *CPA Exam Guide: A System for Success* at www.gleim.com/PassCPA for a complete explanation of how to prepare for and take each section of the CPA exam. This free guide includes over 40 pages of test-taking techniques, time management strategies, and more.

More exam tactics and information, as well as breaking news and updates from the AICPA and NASBA, are available on our blog at www.gleim.com/CPAblog. Follow us on all your favorite social media networks for blog updates and other critical information.

CPA Exam Pass Rates

	Percentage of Candidates		
	2015	2016	2017
AUD	47	46	49
BEC	57	57	52
FAR	47	46	45
REG	49	49	48

The implication of these pass rates for you as a CPA candidate is that you have to be, on average, in the top 45% of all candidates to pass. The major difference between CPA candidates who pass and those who do not is their preparation program. You have access to the best CPA review material; it is up to you to use it. Even if you are enrolled in a review course that uses other materials, you will benefit with the Gleim Premium CPA Review System.

GLEIM CPA REVIEW WITH SmartAdapt

Gleim CPA Review features the most comprehensive coverage of exam content and employs the most efficient learning techniques to help you study smarter and faster. The Gleim CPA Review System is powered by SmartAdapt technology, an innovative platform that continually zeros in on your knowledge gaps when you move through the following steps for optimized CPA review:

Step 1:

Complete a Diagnostic Quiz. Based on your quiz results, our SmartAdapt technology will create a custom learning track.

Step 2:

Solidify your knowledge by studying the suggested Knowledge Transfer Outline(s) or watching the suggested Gleim Instruct video(s).

Step 3:

Focus on weak areas and perfect your question-answering techniques by taking the adaptive quizzes and simulations that SmartAdapt directs you to.

Final Review:

After completing all study units, take the Exam Rehearsal. Then, SmartAdapt will walk you through a Final Review based on your results.

To facilitate your studies, the Gleim Premium CPA Review System uses the largest test bank of CPA exam questions on the market. Our system's content and presentation precisely mimic the whole AICPA exam environment so you feel comfortable on test day.

Learning from Your Mistakes

One of the main building blocks of the Gleim studying system is that learning from questions you answer incorrectly is very important. Each question you answer incorrectly is an **opportunity** to avoid missing actual test questions on your CPA exam. Thus, you should carefully study the answer explanations provided so you understand why the original answer you chose is wrong as well as why the correct answer indicated is correct. This learning technique is the difference between passing and failing for many CPA candidates.

The Gleim Premium CPA Review System has built-in functionality for this step. After each quiz and simulation you complete, the Gleim system directs you to study why you answered questions incorrectly so you can learn how to avoid making the same errors in the future. Reasons for answering questions incorrectly include

1. Misreading the requirement (stem)
2. Not understanding what is required
3. Making a math error
4. Applying the wrong rule or concept
5. Being distracted by one or more of the answers
6. Incorrectly eliminating answers from consideration
7. Not having any knowledge of the topic tested
8. Using a poor educated guessing strategy

SUBJECT MATTER FOR BUSINESS ENVIRONMENT AND CONCEPTS

Below, we have provided the AICPA's major content areas from the Blueprint for Business Environment and Concepts (BEC). The averaged percentage of coverage for each topic is indicated.

I. (22%) Corporate Governance
II. (22%) Economic Concepts and Analysis
III. (16%) Financial Management
IV. (20%) Information Technology
V. (20%) Operations Management

Appendix A contains the Blueprint for BEC as well as cross-references to the subunits in our materials where topics are covered. Remember that we have studied and restudied the Blueprint and explain the subject matter thoroughly in our CPA Review. Accordingly, you do not need to spend time with Appendix A. Rather, it should give you confidence that Gleim CPA Review is the best review available to help you PASS the CPA exam.

The BEC section tests knowledge and skills necessary to demonstrate an understanding of the general business environment and business concepts in performing audit, attest, accounting, and review services; financial reporting; tax preparation; and other professional responsibilities as certified public accountants.

To demonstrate the knowledge and skills associated with the business environment and concepts, the following general topics will be tested:

- Internal control frameworks and enterprise risk management frameworks: (1) purpose and objectives and (2) components and principles
- Key corporate governance provisions of the Sarbanes-Oxley Act of 2002
- Impact of business cycles on industry or business operation
- Market influences on the business environment
- Transactions: (1) business reasons, (2) underlying economic substance, and (3) accounting implications
- Factors influencing a company's capital structure

- Calculation of metrics associated with the components of working capital
- Impact of business decisions on working capital
- Commonly used financial valuation and decision models
- Governance of information technology operations
- Information systems used to process and accumulate data and provide monitoring and financial reporting information
- Appropriate segregation of duties, authorization levels, and data security
- Inherent risks in disaster recovery and business continuity plans
- Business operation and use of quality control and performance measures
- Cost accounting concepts and variance analysis techniques
- Budgeting and forecasting techniques

WHICH PRONOUNCEMENTS ARE TESTED?

The following is the section of the AICPA's pronouncement policy that is relevant to the Business section:

*For all other subjects covered in the Regulation (REG) and Business Environment and Concepts (BEC) sections, materials eligible to be tested include federal laws in the window beginning six (6) months after their **effective** date, and uniform acts in the window beginning one (1) year after their adoption by a simple majority of the jurisdictions.*

AICPA's NONDISCLOSURE AGREEMENT

As part of the AICPA's nondisclosure policy and to prove each candidate's willingness to adhere to this policy, a confidentiality and break policy statement must be accepted by each candidate during the introductory screens at the beginning of each exam. Nonacceptance of this policy means the exam will be terminated and the test fees will be forfeited. This statement is reproduced here to remind all CPA candidates about the AICPA's strict policy of nondisclosure, which Gleim consistently supports and upholds.

"Policy Statement and Agreement Regarding Exam Confidentiality and the Taking of Breaks

I hereby agree that I will maintain the confidentiality of the Uniform CPA Examination. In addition, I agree that I will not:

- Divulge the nature or content of any Uniform CPA Examination question or answer under any circumstance
- Engage in any unauthorized communication during testing
- Refer to unauthorized materials or use unauthorized equipment during testing; or
- Remove or attempt to remove any Uniform CPA Examination materials, notes, or any other items from the examination room

I understand and agree that liability for test administration activities, including but not limited to the adequacy or accuracy of test materials and equipment, and the accuracy of scoring and score reporting, will be limited to score correction or test retake at no additional fee. I waive any and all right to all other claims.

I further agree to report to the AICPA any examination question disclosures, or solicitations for disclosure of which I become aware.

I affirm that I have had the opportunity to read the Candidate Bulletin and I agree to all of its terms and conditions.

I understand that breaks are only allowed between testlets. I understand that I will be asked to complete any open testlet before leaving the testing room for a break.

In addition, I understand that failure to comply with this Policy statement and Agreement may result in the invalidation of my grades, disqualification from future examinations, expulsion from the testing facility and possible civil or criminal penalties."

GLEIM CPA REVIEW ESSENTIALS

Gleim CPA Review has the following features to make studying easier:

1. **Backgrounds:** In certain instances, we have provided historical background or supplemental information. This information is intended to illuminate the topic under discussion and is set off in bordered boxes with shaded headings. This material does not need to be memorized for the exam.

Background
Because ERP software is costly and complex, it is usually installed only by the largest enterprises, although mid-size organizations are increasingly likely to buy ERP software. Major ERP packages include SAP ERP Central Component from SAP SE and Oracle e-Business Suite, PeopleSoft, and JD Edwards EnterpriseOne, all from Oracle Corp.

2. **Examples:** Illustrative examples, both hypothetical and those drawn from actual events, are set off in shaded, bordered boxes.

EXAMPLE
If the Fed requires reserves of 4% on all deposits, a bank with $10 million on deposit can create $250 million of new money [$10,000,000 × (1.0 ÷ .04)].

3. **Gleim Success Tips:** These tips supplement the core exam material by suggesting how certain topics might be presented on the exam or how you should prepare for an issue.

 Because of the legislation passed in response to major accounting scandals, Gleim believes that the AICPA will test CPA candidates on the actions required of directors and officers to meet their fiduciary duties.

4. **Memory Aids:** These mnemonic devices are designed to assist you in memorizing important concepts. For example, the following is a useful memory aid for the COSO categories of objectives:

$$O = Operations$$
$$R = Reporting$$
$$C = Compliance$$

5. **Detailed Table of Contents:** This information at the beginning of the book is a complete listing of all study units and subunits in the Gleim CPA BEC Review program. Use this list as a study aid to mark off your progress and to provide jumping-off points for review.

6. **Blueprint with Gleim Cross-References:** Appendix A contains a reprint of the AICPA Blueprint for BEC along with cross-references to the corresponding Gleim study units.

7. **Optimizing Your Score on the Task-Based Simulations (TBSs) and Written Communications (WCs):** Appendix B explains how to approach and allocate your time for the TBS and WC testlets. It also presents several example TBSs and WCs for your review.

8. **Core Concepts:** We have also provided additional study materials to supplement the Knowledge Transfer Outlines in the digital Gleim CPA Review Course. The Core Concepts, for example, are consolidated documents providing an overview of the key points of each subunit that serve as the foundation for learning. As part of your review, you should make sure that you understand each of them.

TIME BUDGETING AND QUESTION-ANSWERING TECHNIQUES FOR BEC

To begin the exam, you will enter your Launch Code on the Welcome screen. If you do not enter the correct code within 5 minutes of the screen appearing, the exam session will end.

Next, you will have an additional 5 minutes to view a brief exam introduction containing two screens: the nondisclosure policy and a section information screen. Accept the policy and then review the information screen, but be sure to click the Begin Exam button on the bottom right of the screen within the allotted 5 minutes. If you fail to do so, the exam will be terminated and you will not have the option to restart your exam.

These 10 minutes, along with the 5 minutes you may spend on a post-exam survey, are not included in the 240 minutes of exam time.

Once you complete the introductory screens and begin your exam, expect two testlets of 31 multiple-choice questions (MCQs) each, two testlets of Task-Based Simulations (each with 2 TBSs), and one testlet with three written communication (WC) tasks. You will have 240 minutes to complete the five testlets.

1.   **Budget your time so you can finish before time expires.**

   a.   Here is our suggested time allocation for BEC:

	Minutes	Start Time	
Testlet 1 (MCQ)	38*	4 hours	00 minutes
Testlet 2 (MCQ)	38*	3 hours	22 minutes
Testlet 3 (TBS)	36	2 hour	44 minutes
Break	15	Clock stops	
Testlet 4 (TBS)	36	2 hours	08 minutes
Testlet 5 (WC)	75	1 hour	32 minutes
**Extra time	17	0 hour	17 minutes
*Rounded down			

   b.   Before beginning your first MCQ testlet, prepare a Gleim Time Management plan as recommended in *CPA Exam Guide: A System for Success*.

   c.   As you work through the individual questions, monitor your time. In BEC, we suggest 38 minutes (1.25 minutes per question) for each testlet of 31 MCQs. If you answer five items in 6 minutes, you are fine, but if you spend 8 minutes on five items, you need to speed up. In the TBS testlets, spend no more than 18 minutes on each TBS. For more information on TBS time budgets, refer to Appendix B, "Optimizing Your Score on the Task-Based Simulations and Written Communications." In the fifth testlet, spend 20 minutes or less on completing each WC, then 5 minutes or less reviewing each response.

   **BEC candidates may prefer to allocate more time to the TBSs and reduce the 17 minutes of extra review time after the WCs. In this case, we suggest 20 minutes per TBS, for a total time of 40 minutes in Testlet 3 and 40 minutes in Testlet 4, leaving 9 minutes of final review after the WCs.

   Remember to allocate your budgeted extra time, as needed, to each testlet. Your goal is to answer all of the items and achieve the maximum score possible. As you practice answering TBSs and WCs in the Gleim Premium CPA Review System, you will be practicing your time management.

2. **Answer the questions in consecutive order.**

    a. Do not agonize over any one question. **Stay within your time budget.**

    b. Never leave an MCQ unanswered. Your score is based on the number of correct responses. You will not be penalized for answering incorrectly. If you are unsure about a question,

        1) Make an educated guess.

        2) Flag it for review by clicking on the flag icon at the bottom of the screen.

        3) Return to it before you submit the testlet as time allows. Remember, once you have selected the Submit Testlet option, you will no longer be able to review or change any answers in the completed testlet.

3. **Read the question carefully to discover exactly what is being asked.**

    a. Ignore the answer choices so they do not affect your precise reading of the question.

    b. Focusing on what is required allows you to

        1) Reject extraneous information
        2) Concentrate on relevant facts
        3) Proceed directly to determining the best answer

    c. **Careful!** The requirement may be an exception that features negative words.

    d. Decide the correct answer before looking at the answer choices.

4. **Read the answer choices, paying attention to small details.**

    a. Even if an answer choice appears to be correct, do not skip the remaining choices. Each choice requires consideration because you are looking for the best answer provided.

    b. **Only one answer option is the best.** In the MCQs, four answer choices are presented, and you know one of them is correct. The remaining choices are distractors and are meant to appear correct at first glance. Eliminate them as quickly as you can.

    c. Treat each answer choice like a true/false question as you analyze it.

    d. In computational MCQs, the distractor answers are carefully calculated to be the result of common mistakes. Be careful, and double-check your computations if time permits.

        1) There will be a mix of conceptual and calculation questions. When you take the exam, it may appear that more of the questions are calculation-type because they take longer and are more difficult.

5. **Click on the best answer.**

    a. You have a 25% chance of answering correctly by guessing blindly, but you can improve your odds with an educated guess.

    b. For many MCQs, you can **eliminate two answer choices with minimal effort** and increase your educated guess to a 50/50 proposition.

        1) Rule out answers that you think are incorrect.

        2) Speculate what the AICPA is looking for and/or why the question is being asked.

        3) Select the best answer or guess between equally appealing answers. Your first guess is usually the most intuitive.

6. **Do not click the Submit Testlet button until you have consulted the question status list at the bottom of each MCQ screen.**

    a. Return to flagged questions to finalize your answer choices if you have time.

    b. Verify that you have answered every question.

    c. Stay on schedule because time management is critical to exam success.

Doing well on the **task-based simulations** and **written communications** requires you to be an expert on how to approach them both from a question answering and a time allocation perspective. Refer to Appendix B, "Optimizing Your Score on the Task-Based Simulations and Written Communications," for a complete explanation of task-based simulations and how to optimize your score on each one.

HOW TO BE IN CONTROL

Remember, you must be in control to be successful during exam preparation and execution. Perhaps more importantly, control can also contribute greatly to your personal and other professional goals. Control is the process whereby you

1. Develop expectations, standards, budgets, and plans
2. Undertake activity, production, study, and learning
3. Measure the activity, production, output, and knowledge
4. Compare actual activity with expected and budgeted activity
5. Modify the activity, behavior, or study to better achieve the expected or desired outcome
6. Revise expectations and standards in light of actual experience
7. Continue the process or restart the process in the future

Exercising control will ultimately develop the confidence you need to outperform most other CPA candidates and PASS the CPA exam!

QUESTIONS ABOUT GLEIM MATERIALS

Gleim has an efficient and effective way for candidates who have purchased the Gleim Premium CPA Review System to submit an inquiry and receive a response regarding Gleim materials **directly through their course**. This system also allows you to view your Q&A session online in your Gleim Personal Classroom.

Questions regarding the information in this **introduction and/or the Gleim *CPA Exam Guide*** (study suggestions, study plans, exam specifics) may be emailed to personalcounselor@gleim.com.

Questions concerning **orders, prices, shipments, or payments** should be sent via email to customerservice@gleim.com and will be promptly handled by our competent and courteous customer service staff.

For **technical support**, you may use our automated technical support service at www.gleim.com/support, email us at support@gleim.com, or call us at (800) 874-5346.

FEEDBACK

Please fill out our online feedback form (www.gleim.com/feedbackBEC) IMMEDIATELY after you take the CPA Business section so we can adapt our material based on where candidates say we need to increase or decrease coverage. Our approach has been approved by the AICPA.

STUDY UNIT ONE
CORPORATE GOVERNANCE
STRUCTURE AND REGULATIONS

(9 pages of outline)

Accounting scandals and concerns about the functioning of financial markets have resulted in greater attention to corporate governance (i.e., the means of directing the actions of a corporation). Fundamental governance tools include (1) the governance structure, (2) regulatory requirements, (3) internal control, and (4) enterprise risk management. This study unit covers corporate governance structure and key corporate governance provisions from relevant regulatory pronouncements. Study Unit 2 covers internal control and enterprise risk management.

1.1 GOVERNANCE DOCUMENTS, ROLES, AND RESPONSIBILITIES

1. **Definition of Corporate Governance**

   a. **Governance** is a combination of people, policies, procedures, and processes (including internal control). It helps to ensure that an entity effectively and efficiently directs its activities toward meeting the objectives of its stakeholders.

      1) **Stakeholders** are persons or other entities who are affected by the activities of the entity. Examples are shareholders, employees, suppliers, customers, neighbors of the entity's facilities, and government regulators.

   b. Corporate governance can be influenced by **internal or external** sources.

      1) Corporate charters and bylaws, boards of directors, codes of ethics, and internal audit functions are internal sources.

      2) The requirements of the Securities Act of 1933 and the Securities Exchange Act of 1934 administered by the Securities and Exchange Commission (SEC) are external sources.

2. **Corporate Documents**

   a. Corporations are formed under the **laws of the state of incorporation** (very few corporations are incorporated under federal law).

   b. A corporation comes into being when the **articles of incorporation** are filed with the secretary of state of the relevant state. The secretary in turn issues a certificate of incorporation.

      1) The articles ordinarily **must** include the following:

         a) Corporation's name
         b) Number of authorized shares of stock
         c) Street address of the corporation's initial registered office
         d) Name of the registered agent at that office
         e) Name and address of each incorporator

      2) The articles also **may** contain optional provisions, such as

         a) Purpose and powers of the corporation,
         b) Internal management, and
         c) Any subject required or allowed to be addressed in the bylaws.

c.   The **bylaws** of a corporation may contain any provision for managing its business and affairs that does not conflict with the law or the articles of incorporation.

    1)   The bylaws state such matters as the authority of officers and directors, how they are selected, the lengths of their terms, their compensation, and how the decision to issue new stock will be made.

d.   **Code of Ethics**

    1)   The primary purpose of a code of ethics is to promote an ethical culture within the corporation. An ethical culture is best promoted by senior management setting the example.

    2)   Additional purposes of a code of ethics include

        a)   Communicating acceptable values to employees,

        b)   Establishing objective standards against which employees can evaluate their conduct, and

        c)   Communicating the corporation's values to outsiders.

    3)   To be effective, the code should provide for disciplinary action for violators.

3.   **Shareholders**

a.   The **common** shareholders are those who have contributed the basic capital for the corporation to carry on its business.

    1)   **Preferred** shareholders have the contractual right to receive dividends and liquidation distributions before common shareholders (hence why "preferred") but usually do not have voting rights.

b.   Generally, shareholders are permitted to act only at a meeting.

    1)   They are required to hold an annual meeting. Special meetings may be held for important purposes, such as to approve a merger or other fundamental change.

    2)   The most important acts performed by the shareholders at the annual meeting are

        a)   Amending the articles of incorporation,

        b)   Voting on any matters requiring a general vote, and

        c)   Electing or removing directors.

c.   Many states permit shareholders to change, by unanimous agreement, the provisions for corporate governance. This flexibility may allow a closely held corporation to function more nearly as a partnership without loss of corporate status.

    1)   For example, a shareholder agreement may (a) eliminate the board or restrict its powers, (b) determine who will be officers and directors, or (c) set voting requirements for directors and shareholders.

4.   **Board of Directors**

a.   All **major corporate decisions** are made or approved by the board.

    1)   Directly managing the day-to-day operations of the entity is management's responsibility. The board has an **oversight role**.

b.   The board has the following **duties**:

    1)   Selection and removal of officers

    2)   Decisions about capital structure (mix of debt and equity, consideration to be received for shares, etc.)

    3)   Adding, amending, or repealing bylaws (unless this authority is reserved to the shareholders)

    4)   Initiation of fundamental changes (mergers, acquisitions, etc.)

5) Decisions to declare and distribute dividends

6) Setting of management compensation (sometimes performed by a subcommittee called the compensation committee)

7) Coordinating audit activities (most often performed by a subcommittee called the audit committee)

8) Evaluating and managing risk (sometimes performed by a subcommittee called the risk committee)

c. If permitted by the articles or bylaws, the board may delegate authority to **committees** composed of its members or corporate officers.

1) Committees may exercise broad powers consistent with the limits of the resolutions by which they were established.

2) Every public corporation (i.e., issuer) must have an **audit committee** consisting of independent directors.

5. **Officers**

a. The corporation's officers (i.e., executive management) are responsible for carrying out the entity's **day-to-day operations**.

b. The **chief executive officer (CEO)** is directly selected by, and reports to, the board of directors.

c. The CEO in turn usually selects other executives such as the chief financial officer (CFO) and chief information officer (CIO). These executives oversee the various functional areas of the entity.

d. Officers are **agents of the corporation** and as such may enter the corporation into legally binding contracts.

6. **Fiduciary Duties**

> Because of the legislation passed in response to major accounting scandals, Gleim believes that the AICPA will test CPA candidates on the actions required of directors and officers to meet their fiduciary duties.

a. Directors and officers owe a **fiduciary duty** to the corporation to (1) act in its best interests, (2) be loyal, (3) use due diligence in discharging responsibilities, (4) be informed about information relevant to the corporation, and (5) disclose conflicts of interest. **Controlling or majority shareholders** owe similar duties.

1) The fiduciary duty of directors and officers is generally divided into the **duty of care** and the **duty of loyalty**.

b. The **duty of care** requires directors and officers to discharge their duties

1) In good faith,

2) In a manner (s)he reasonably believes to be in the best interests of the corporation, and

3) With the care that a person in a similar position would reasonably believe appropriate under similar circumstances.

4) **Reliance on others.** In exercising reasonable care, directors and officers may rely on information, reports, opinions, and statements prepared or presented by persons (an appropriate officer, employee, or specialist) whom the director **reasonably believes** to be competent in the matters presented.

a) Directors and officers also may rely on the specialized knowledge of lawyers, accountants, investment bankers, and board committees.

5) Directors and officers are expected to be **informed** about pertinent corporate information when giving advice. To exercise the required care, directors and officers should

    a) Attend relevant meetings
    b) Analyze corporate financial statements
    c) Review pertinent legal opinions
    d) Become knowledgeable about the available relevant information

c. The **duty of loyalty** requires directors and officers to take certain steps when they are involved in a conflicting-interest transaction or are presented with a corporate opportunity.

    1) **Conflicting-interest transactions.** To protect the corporation against self-dealing, directors and officers are required to make **full disclosure** of any financial interest they may have in any transaction to which they and the corporation may be a party. Directors and officers must not make a secret profit.

        a) A transaction is **not** improper merely on the grounds of a director's or officer's conflict of interest. If the transaction (1) is **fair** to the corporation or (2) has been **approved** by a majority of informed, disinterested directors or shareholders, it is not voidable and does not result in sanctions even if the director or officer makes a profit.

    2) Directors and officers may not usurp any **corporate opportunity**. They must give the corporation the right of first refusal.

EXAMPLE

Skip, a director of The Fishing Corp., learns in his corporate capacity that a state-of-the-art, deep-sea hydroplane fishing vessel is available for a bargain price. The purchase of this unique hydroplane may be a business opportunity from which the corporation could benefit. If Skip purchases the hydroplane for himself without giving the corporation the right of first refusal, he is usurping a corporate opportunity.

---

d. The **business judgment rule** protects a director or an officer from personal liability for honest mistakes of judgment if (s)he

    1) Acted in good faith;
    2) Was not motivated by fraud, conflict of interest, or illegality; and
    3) Was not grossly negligent.

        a) To avoid personal liability, directors and officers must

            i) Make informed decisions (educate themselves about the issues),
            ii) Be free from conflicts of interest, and
            iii) Have a rational basis to support their position.

        b) Furthermore, a director is entitled to rely on information provided by an officer (or professional specialist) if the director reasonably believes the officer (or specialist) has the relevant competence.

7. Internal Auditors

a. Internal auditing is an independent, objective assurance and consulting activity designed to add value and improve an organization's operations.

b. The internal audit function should assess, and make appropriate recommendations for, improving governance to achieve the following objectives:

    1) Promoting appropriate ethics and values within the organization
    2) Ensuring effective organizational performance management and accountability

3) Communicating risk and control information to appropriate areas of the organization

4) Coordinating the activities of, and communicating information among, the board, external and internal auditors, and management

8. **Corporate Governance Structure**

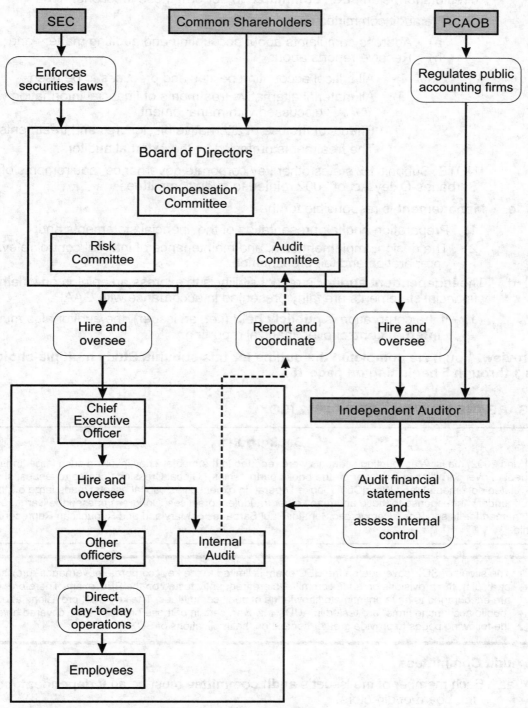

Figure 1-1

9.   **Financial Reporting**

a.   A publicly held corporation's annual report to its shareholders must contain audited financial statements and other specified information.

b.   The **board of directors** is responsible for hiring, setting the compensation for, and overseeing the work of the independent auditor. In large corporations, a group of directors forms an **audit committee** to perform these functions.

1)   The audit committee also must

a)   Address complaints about accounting and auditing matters and

b)   Receive reports about

i)   All critical accounting polices and practices to be used,

ii)   All material alternative treatments of financial information within GAAP discussed with management,

iii) Effects of the use of alternative disclosures and treatments, and

iv)   The treatments preferred by the external auditors.

NOTE: Subunit 1.2 states other key corporate governance requirements of the Sarbanes-Oxley Act of 2002 related to audit committees.

c.   **Management** is responsible for the

1)   Preparation and fair presentation of the financial statements and

2)   The design, implementation, and maintenance of internal control relevant to their preparation and fair presentation.

d.   The **independent auditor's** responsibility is to express an opinion on whether the financial statements are fairly presented in accordance with GAAP.

1)   If the corporation is **publicly held** (i.e., an issuer), the auditor also must assess **internal control** over financial reporting.

Stop and review! You have completed the outline for this subunit. Study multiple-choice questions 1 through 5 beginning on page 18.

1.2 THE SARBANES-OXLEY ACT OF 2002 (SOX)

Background

In late 2001 and 2002, massive accounting scandals were reported in the media. They involved such large firms as Enron (hid debt of over $1 billion in improper off-the-books partnerships), Global Crossing (inflated revenues; shredded accounting-related documents), and WorldCom (booked operating expenses as capital assets; made large off-the-books payments to founder). In response to these and many other fraudulent practices, Congress passed the Sarbanes-Oxley Act of 2002, named for its sponsors, Democratic Senator Paul Sarbanes of Maryland and Republican Representative Mike Oxley of Ohio.

 The scope of SOX coverage on the BEC exam is limited to the key "corporate governance" provisions. In particular, the provisions on audit committees are frequently tested on the BEC exam. Therefore, candidates are encouraged to have an intimate knowledge of audit committees. The key SOX provisions affecting "public accounting firms" are tested in AUD. However, certain of those provisions are covered below and on the following pages to provide greater context on the implications of SOX.

---

1.   **Audit Committees**

a.   Each member of the issuer's **audit committee** must be an **independent member** of the board of directors.

1)   To be independent, a director must not be affiliated with, or receive any compensation (other than for service on the board) from, the issuer.

a)   The audit committee must be comprised of **at least three** fully independent members.

    b.   At least **one** member of the audit committee must be a **financial expert**.

        1)   An issuer must **disclose** whether its audit committee has at least one financial expert.

            a)   If the audit committee lacks a financial expert, the issuer must disclose the reason(s).

        2)   To be considered a financial expert, the director must have

            a)   An understanding of generally accepted accounting principles (GAAP) and financial statements;

            b)   Experience in

                i)   The preparation or audit of financial statements of generally comparable issuers;

                ii)   The application of GAAP in connection with the accounting for estimates, accruals, and reserves;

            c)   Experience with internal accounting controls; and

            d)   An understanding of audit committee functions.

    c.   The audit committee must be **directly responsible** for appointing, compensating, and overseeing the work of the independent auditor.

        1)   The independent auditor must report directly to the audit committee, not to management.

    d.   The audit committee must also **establish procedures** for

        1)   The receipt, retention, and treatment of complaints received regarding accounting, internal control, or auditing matters and

        2)   The confidential, anonymous submission of employees' concerns regarding questionable accounting or auditing matters.

2.   **Public Company Accounting Oversight Board (PCAOB)**

    a.   The PCAOB was established to oversee the audits of public companies.

    b.   The PCAOB

        1)   Issues auditing and related standards;

        2)   Inspects and investigates accounting firms; and

        3)   Enforces compliance with its rules, professional standards, SOX, and relevant securities laws.

3.   **Public Accounting Firms**

    a.   Public accounting firms that act as independent auditors must register with the PCAOB.

    b.   A public accounting firm is **prohibited** from performing certain **nonaudit services** for an audit client.

    c.   The prohibited nonaudit services consist of the following:

        1)   Bookkeeping

        2)   Financial information systems design and implementation

        3)   Appraisal or valuation services, fairness opinions, or contribution-in-kind reports

        4)   Actuarial services

        5)   Internal audit outsourcing services

        6)   Management functions or human resources

        7)   Broker-dealer, investment advisor, or investment banking services

        8)   Legal services and expert services unrelated to the audit

    d.   A public accounting firm may perform **permitted nonaudit services** (e.g., tax services) for an audit client if those services are **preapproved by the audit committee**.

4. **Reporting -- CEO and CFO Certification**

   a. In every **annual or quarterly** filing with the SEC, the CEO and CFO must certify the following:

     1) They have reviewed the report.

     2) To the best of their knowledge, the financial statements are free of material misstatements.

     3) They are responsible for the system of internal control and have evaluated its effectiveness.

     4) They have informed the audit committee and the independent auditors of all significant control deficiencies and any fraud, whether or not material.

     5) Significant changes were (or were not) made in internal controls, including corrective actions.

5. **Reporting -- Management's Assessment of Internal Controls**

   a. The **annual** report must contain the following:

     1) A statement that management has taken responsibility for establishing and maintaining an adequate system of internal control over financial reporting

     2) The name of the internal control model, if any, used to design and assess the effectiveness of the internal control system (COSO's *Internal Control – Integrated Framework* is the most widely used model in the United States)

     3) An assessment of whether internal control over financial reporting is effective

     4) A statement that an independent public accounting firm that is registered with the PCAOB also has assessed the system

6. **Loans to Directors and Executive Officers**

   a. Although certain exceptions apply (e.g., home improvement loans and consumer credit), issuers are generally prohibited from extending **personal loans** to any director or executive officer.

7. **Code of Ethics**

   a. Issuers are required to disclose whether or not they have adopted a code of ethics for **senior financial officers**.

     1) If they have **not** adopted a code of ethics for senior financial officers, then they must also disclose the reason(s) why.

8. **Penalties**

   a. **Altering documents** could result in a fine, imprisonment of up to 20 years, or both.

   b. **Retaliating against informants** (e.g., whistleblowers) could result in a fine, imprisonment of up to 10 years, or both.

   c. Separate penalties are provided for unknowingly and knowingly **certifying noncomplying filings**.

     1) **Unknowingly** certifying filings that do not meet the requirements of SOX can result in fines of up to $1,000,000 or up to 10 years imprisonment.

     2) **Knowingly** certifying filings that do not meet the requirements of SOX can result in fines of up to $5,000,000 or up to 20 years imprisonment.

   d. If an issuer is required to prepare an **accounting restatement** because of **misconduct**, the issuer's CEO and CFO must forfeit

     1) Any bonus or other incentive-based compensation received from the issuer during the previous 12 months and

     2) Any profits received from the sale of stock of the issuer during the previous 12 months.

e. For certain violations, the SEC has the authority to prohibit persons from serving as a director or officer of any issuer.

Stop and review! You have completed the outline for this subunit. Study multiple-choice questions 6 through 17 beginning on page 19.

1.3 DODD-FRANK WALL STREET REFORM AND CONSUMER PROTECTION ACT OF 2010

1. **Background**

    a. This comprehensive legislation was enacted after the economic crisis in 2008. The act extends to, among other things, (1) the financial services industry, (2) consumer protection, (3) financial markets, (4) securities laws, (5) financial reporting and governance, and (6) broker-dealer audits.

The key corporate governance provisions are those regarding executive compensation. Therefore, candidates should focus their attention on the rules regarding executive compensation.

2. **Key Provisions**

    a. The act enlarges the scope of the SEC's authority to prosecute those who **aid and abet** securities law violations.

        1) Moreover, the legal standard for those involved is now "knowing or reckless" instead of merely knowing.

    b. Auditors of **broker-dealers** are subject to inspection by the PCAOB and possible sanctions.

        1) All broker-dealers must be audited by registered auditors.

    c. The **Financial Stability Oversight Council** was established to (1) identify, in advance, financial system risks; (2) comment to the SEC about accounting issues; and (3) report **annually** to Congress about financial market and regulatory matters.

    d. The **Bureau of Consumer Financial Protection** was established to ensure consumers are provided with understandable and timely information and protected from unfair, abusive, deceptive, or discriminating practices.

    e. Shareholders have the right to a nonbinding vote on **compensation** for specified corporate officers at least once every 3 years.

        1) The act also requires independent compensation committee members and disclosure of independent compensation committee advisors and related fees or conflicts of interest.

        2) A public company must have a **clawback policy** defining how to recover performance-based executive compensation after a financial restatement.

        3) The SEC now has the power to give shareholders with at least 3% of the voting interests access to the corporation's **proxy** procedures.

    f. The SEC may compensate whistleblowers who provide original information not obtained through audits or other investigations.

    g. **Credit rating agencies** are to be examined annually by the SEC. These agencies (1) must disclose their methods, (2) are subject to investor suits, and (3) must consent to use of their ratings in **registration statements**.

Stop and review! You have completed the outline for this subunit. Study multiple-choice questions 18 through 20 on page 23.

QUESTIONS

1.1 Governance Documents, Roles, and Responsibilities

1. Davis, a director of Active Corp., is entitled to

    A. Serve on the board of a competing business.

    B. Take sole advantage of a business opportunity that would benefit Active.

    C. Rely on information provided by a corporate officer.

    D. Unilaterally grant a corporate loan to one of Active's shareholders.

Answer (C) is correct.
REQUIRED: The action not a breach of a director's duties.
DISCUSSION: In the course of exercising good business judgment and reasonable care, a director is entitled to rely on information provided by an officer (or professional specialist) if the director reasonably believes the officer has competence in the relevant area.
Answer (A) is incorrect. Serving as a director of a competing business is a conflict of interest. Answer (B) is incorrect. Usurping a business opportunity of the corporation is a breach of the director's fiduciary duty of loyalty. Answer (D) is incorrect. A director is not an agent of the corporation, and directors authorize corporate transactions by approving resolutions as a board.

2. Which of the following provisions must a for-profit corporation include in its articles of incorporation to obtain a corporate charter?

I.   Provision for the issuance of voting stock
II.   Name of the corporation

    A. I only.

    B. II only.

    C. Both I and II.

    D. Neither I nor II.

Answer (C) is correct.
REQUIRED: The provisions a for-profit corporation must include in its articles of incorporation.
DISCUSSION: A corporation comes into being when the articles of incorporation are filed with the secretary of state of the relevant state. Among the items that the articles ordinarily must include are the corporation's name and the number of authorized shares of stock. Because the articles must include the number of authorized shares of stock, the provision for issuance of voting stock is an implicit requirement.
Answer (A) is incorrect. The name of the corporation must be included in the articles. Answer (B) is incorrect. The articles must include the number of shares authorized to be issued. Thus, provision for issuance of voting stock is an implicit requirement. Answer (D) is incorrect. Both the name of the corporation and the provision for issuance of voting stock must be included in the articles.

3. In general, which of the following must be contained in articles of incorporation?

    A. Names of states in which the corporation will be doing business.

    B. Name of the state in which the corporation will maintain its principal place of business.

    C. Names of the initial officers and their terms of office.

    D. Number of shares of stock authorized to be issued by the corporation.

Answer (D) is correct.
REQUIRED: The information required in articles of incorporation.
DISCUSSION: Articles of incorporation must contain the name of the corporation, the number of authorized shares, the address of the initial registered office of the corporation, the name of its first registered agent at that address, and the names and addresses of the incorporators. The articles may also include names and addresses of the initial directors, purpose and duration of the corporation, and any provision that may be set forth in the bylaws.
Answer (A) is incorrect. The names of states in which the corporation will be doing business need not be included in the articles. Answer (B) is incorrect. The name of the state in which the corporation will maintain its principal place of business need not be included in the articles. Answer (C) is incorrect. The names of initial officers and their terms of office need not be included in the articles.

4. The board of directors performs all of the following duties **except**

    A. Managing day-to-day operations.

    B. Selection and removal of officers.

    C. Adding or repealing bylaws.

    D. Initiation of fundamental changes.

Answer (A) is correct.
REQUIRED: The duty not performed by the board of directors.
DISCUSSION: The board of directors guides management. It does not directly manage day-to-day operations of the entity. That is management's responsibility, with the board having an oversight role. All major corporate decisions are made or approved by the board.
Answer (B) is incorrect. The board has the duty of selection and removal of officers. Answer (C) is incorrect. Adding, amending, or repealing bylaws is a duty of the board. Answer (D) is incorrect. Initiation of fundamental changes, such as mergers or acquisitions, is a duty of the board.

5. A corporate director commits a breach of duty if

- A. The director's exercise of care and skill is minimal.

- B. A contract is awarded by the company to an organization owned by the director.

- C. An interest in property is acquired by the director without prior approval of the board.

- D. The director's action, prompted by confidential information, results in an abuse of corporate opportunity.

Answer (D) is correct.
    REQUIRED: The breach of a corporate director's duty.
    DISCUSSION: Corporate directors have a fiduciary duty to provide the corporation with business opportunities that come to them in their positions as directors of the corporation. A director who personally takes such a business opportunity has breached his or her duty of loyalty.
    Answer (A) is incorrect. A director is under a duty to use good business judgment, but (s)he is not responsible for the highest standard of care and skill. Moreover, a director may reasonably rely on information from competent officers, employees, and experts. Answer (B) is incorrect. A director is not prohibited from entering into a conflicting interest transaction if it is (1) fair to the corporation or (2) approved after required disclosure by a majority of disinterested directors or of shares voted by disinterested parties. Answer (C) is incorrect. A director has no duty to report personal property investments unless they relate to corporate business.

1.2 The Sarbanes-Oxley Act of 2002 (SOX)

6. The Sarbanes-Oxley Act of 2002 limits the nonaudit services that an audit firm can provide to public company audit clients. Which of the following is most likely to be a service that an auditor may provide to a public client?

- A. Internal audit outsourcing.

- B. Legal services.

- C. Bookkeeping services.

- D. Tax compliance services.

Answer (D) is correct.
    REQUIRED: The type of service that an audit firm may provide to an audit client.
    DISCUSSION: The Sarbanes-Oxley Act prohibits audit firms from providing bookkeeping, legal, and internal auditing services, among others, to public audit clients. Audit firms may, however, provide conventional tax planning and certain other nonaudit services to public audit clients if they are preapproved by the audit committee.
    Answer (A) is incorrect. Internal audit outsourcing is a service that may not be provided to public audit clients. Answer (B) is incorrect. Legal and other expert services may not be provided to public audit clients if they do not pertain to the audit. Answer (C) is incorrect. Bookkeeping services may not be provided to public audit clients.

7. Which of the following is most likely a violation of the rules of the Public Company Accounting Oversight Board (PCAOB)?

- A. An issuer's independent auditor also performs consulting work for the issuer on the design and operation of its internal controls.

- B. An issuer offers its common shares and preferred shares on different stock exchanges.

- C. An issuer's management is not independent of its board of directors.

- D. An issuer uses the same independent auditor in 2 consecutive years.

Answer (A) is correct.
    REQUIRED: The action prohibited by SOX.
    DISCUSSION: The PCAOB prohibits a public accounting firm from performing internal auditing services for an audit client.
    Answer (B) is incorrect. The PCAOB regulates public accounting firms, not stock offerings. Answer (C) is incorrect. The PCAOB cannot dictate terms of internal corporate governance. Answer (D) is incorrect. The PCAOB's rules do not prohibit issuers from using the same independent auditor in 2 consecutive years.

8. Under the Sarbanes-Oxley Act of 2002,

- A. At least one member of the audit committee must be a financial expert.

- B. The chairman of the board of directors must be a financial expert.

- C. The audit committee must rotate at least one seat on an annual basis.

- D. All members of the audit committee must be financial experts.

Answer (A) is correct.
    REQUIRED: The SOX requirement relevant to the audit committee.
    DISCUSSION: Under the terms of SOX, at least one member of the audit committee must be a financial expert. If the audit committee lacks a financial expert, the issuer must disclose the reason(s).
    Answer (B) is incorrect. The SOX requirement regarding a financial expert does not refer to the chairman of the board. Answer (C) is incorrect. SOX imposes no requirements regarding membership rotation of the audit committee. Answer (D) is incorrect. Under the terms of SOX, only one member of the audit committee need be a financial expert.

9. When Congress passed the Sarbanes-Oxley Act of 2002, it imposed greater regulation on public companies and their auditors and required increased accountability. Which of the following is **not** a provision of the act?

A. Certain executives must certify the fair presentation of the financial statements.

B. Management must establish and document internal control procedures.

C. The act created the Public Company Accounting Oversight Board (PCAOB).

D. One of the company's officers may serve on the audit committee.

Answer (D) is correct.
REQUIRED: The choice that is not a provision of the Sarbanes-Oxley Act of 2002.
DISCUSSION: The act requires that all members of the audit committee be independent of the corporation, meaning they can receive no compensation other than what they receive for serving on the board. Thus, no officers or employees of the corporation may serve on the audit committee.
Answer (A) is incorrect. The CEO and CFO of a public company must provide a statement to accompany the audit report. This statement certifies the fair presentation of the financial statements and disclosures. However, a violation of this requirement must be knowing and intentional. Answer (B) is incorrect. Section 404 of the act requires management to establish and document internal control procedures, and to include in annual reports a report on the entity's internal control over financial reporting. Answer (C) is incorrect. The PCAOB was created by the act as a private sector, nonprofit corporation to oversee the conduct of accounting firms in the performance of financial statement audits of issuers.

10. Under the reporting requirements of Section 404 of the Sarbanes-Oxley Act of 2002, the CEO and CFO must include a statement in the annual report to the effect that

A. The system of internal control has been assessed by an independent public accounting firm that is registered with the PCAOB.

B. The system of internal control has been assessed by an independent public accounting firm that is not currently the subject of any PCAOB investigation.

C. The board of directors has taken responsibility for establishing and maintaining an adequate system of internal control over financial reporting.

D. The issuer has used the COSO model to design and assess the effectiveness of its system of internal control.

Answer (A) is correct.
REQUIRED: The statement required by Sarbanes-Oxley.
DISCUSSION: The CEO and CFO must include a statement in the annual report to the effect that the system of internal control has been assessed by an independent public accounting firm that is registered with the PCAOB.
Answer (B) is incorrect. Section 404 of SOX does not require that the independent auditor not be under investigation by the PCAOB. Answer (C) is incorrect. Section 404 of SOX requires the CEO and CFO to state that they, not the board, have taken responsibility for internal controls. Answer (D) is incorrect. Section 404 of SOX requires that if the issuer used an internal control model, it must be named; it does not have to be the COSO model.

11. Section 302 of the Sarbanes-Oxley Act of 2002 requires the CEO and CFO, in every annual or quarterly filing with the SEC, to certify all of the following **except**

A. That they have taken every practical step to correct significant control deficiencies identified in the previous audit.

B. That they have evaluated the effectiveness of the system of internal control.

C. That they have taken responsibility for the system of internal control.

D. That to the best of their knowledge, the financial statements are free of material misstatements.

Answer (A) is correct.
REQUIRED: The required certification in SEC filings by the CEO and CFO.
DISCUSSION: Whether the issuer has taken sufficient steps to correct significant control deficiencies is a matter of the auditor's professional judgment.

12. The Sarbanes-Oxley Act of 2002 imposes which of the following requirements?

    A. The board of directors must be composed entirely of independent shareholders.

    B. At least one corporate member of the audit committee must be a former partner of the independent public accounting firm.

    C. The audit committee must be composed entirely of independent members of the board.

    D. Once the audit committee has selected the independent public accounting firm, the committee must not interfere with the firm's conduct of the financial statement audit.

Answer (C) is correct.
    REQUIRED: The provision required by SOX.
    DISCUSSION: Under SOX, each member of the issuer's audit committee must be an independent member of the board of directors. To be independent, a director must not be affiliated with, or receive any compensation (other than for service on the board) from, the issuer.
    Answer (A) is incorrect. The SOX requirement regarding independent members refers to the audit committee, not the entire board. Answer (B) is incorrect. SOX does not impose a requirement regarding mandatory former employment with the independent public accounting firm. Answer (D) is incorrect. The audit committee must be directly responsible for appointing, compensating, and overseeing the work of the independent auditor.

13. An issuer's audit committee consists of its CEO and three outside board members. The issuer compensates the outside board members for their service on the board. Under the Sarbanes-Oxley Act of 2002, which of the following is a deficiency in the issuer's audit committee?

    A. Not enough audit committee members.

    B. The CEO is an audit committee member.

    C. All audit committee members are not officers in the corporation.

    D. The outside board members receive compensation for their service on the board.

Answer (B) is correct.
    REQUIRED: The identification of the violation of the Sarbanes-Oxley Act of 2002.
    DISCUSSION: Under the Sarbanes-Oxley Act of 2002, audit committee members must be independent. To be independent, members may not receive compensation from the corporation other than for their service on the board. A CEO receives compensation for services other than those performed as a board member and therefore violates the independence requirement for audit committee members.
    Answer (A) is incorrect. Under the Sarbanes-Oxley Act of 2002, the audit committee is only required to be comprised of at least three independent members. Answer (C) is incorrect. Under the Sarbanes-Oxley Act of 2002, audit committee members are not required to be officers of the issuing corporation. Answer (D) is incorrect. Under the Sarbanes-Oxley Act of 2002, audit committee members may receive compensation for their service on the board.

14. Which of the following represents a violation of the Sarbanes-Oxley Act of 2002?

  I. An issuer's audit committee decides auditor compensation without board approval.

  II. An issuer's audit committee selects the independent auditor without board approval.

  III. An issuer's audit committee delegates to management the responsibility to oversee the work of the independent auditor.

    A. I and II only.

    B. II only.

    C. III only.

    D. None of the answers are correct.

Answer (C) is correct.
    REQUIRED: The identification of the violation of the Sarbanes-Oxley Act of 2002.
    DISCUSSION: Under the Sarbanes-Oxley Act of 2002, the audit committee is directly responsible for selecting, compensating, and overseeing the work of the independent auditor.
    Answer (A) is incorrect. Under the Sarbanes-Oxley Act of 2002, the audit committee is directly responsible for selecting and compensating the independent auditor. Thus, board approval is not required. Answer (B) is incorrect. Under the Sarbanes-Oxley Act of 2002, the audit committee is directly responsible for compensating the independent auditor. Thus, board approval is not required. Answer (D) is incorrect. Under the Sarbanes-Oxley Act of 2002, the audit committee is directly responsible for overseeing the work of the independent auditor and therefore cannot delegate that responsibility to management.

15. A public accounting firm performs both audit and nonaudit services for an issuer. A violation of the Sarbanes-Oxley Act of 2002 occurs if

I.   The issuer's audit committee preapproves the nonaudit services.

II. The issuer's audit committee preapproves the audit services.

III. The issuer's board preapproves the nonaudit services.

IV. The issuer's board preapproves the audit services.

    A.   I only.

    B.   II only.

    C.   III only.

    D.   III and IV only.

Answer (D) is correct.
REQUIRED: The identification of the violation of the Sarbanes-Oxley Act of 2002.
DISCUSSION: Under the Sarbanes-Oxley Act of 2002, an issuer's audit committee must preapprove audit services and nonaudit services performed by its independent auditor.
Answer (A) is incorrect. Under the Sarbanes-Oxley Act of 2002, an issuer's audit committee must preapprove nonaudit services performed by its independent auditor. Answer (B) is incorrect. Under the Sarbanes-Oxley Act of 2002, an issuer's audit committee must preapprove audit services. Answer (C) is incorrect. Although it is a violation of the Sarbanes-Oxley Act of 2002 (SOX) for an issuer's board to preapprove nonaudit services performed by its independent auditor, it is also a violation of SOX for an issuer's board to preapprove audit services.

16. An issuer's CEO and CFO certified the company's annual filing for Year 1 pursuant to the Sarbanes-Oxley Act of 2002. However, only the CEO certified the issuer's first quarterly filing for Year 2. The issuer has

    A.   Violated SOX because the CFO did not certify the quarterly filing.

    B.   Complied with SOX because only the CEO is required to certify quarterly filings.

    C.   Complied with SOX because the CEO and CFO are only required to certify annual filings.

    D.   Violated SOX because the issuer's Chief Audit Executive did not certify the annual filing.

Answer (A) is correct.
REQUIRED: The certification requirement of the Sarbanes-Oxley Act of 2002.
DISCUSSION: Pursuant to the Sarbanes-Oxley Act of 2002, an issuer's CEO and CFO must certify quarterly and annual filings.
Answer (B) is incorrect. Pursuant to the Sarbanes-Oxley Act of 2002, an issuer's CFO must also certify quarterly filings. Answer (C) is incorrect. Pursuant to the Sarbanes-Oxley Act of 2002, an issuer's CEO and CFO must also certify quarterly filings. Answer (D) is incorrect. No provision of the Sarbanes-Oxley Act of 2002 requires an issuer's Chief Audit Executive to certify filings.

17. Which of the following will most likely call into question the expertise of an audit committee's financial expert?

    A.   Lack of understanding of generally accepted auditing standards.

    B.   Lack of understanding of fraud examination techniques.

    C.   Lack of experience with internal accounting controls.

    D.   Lack of experience with performing business valuations.

Answer (C) is correct.
REQUIRED: The identification of the lack of skill that would call into question the expertise of an audit committee's financial expert.
DISCUSSION: Under the Sarbanes-Oxley Act of 2002, an audit committee's financial expert must have–among other qualifications–experience with internal accounting controls.
Answer (A) is incorrect. Under the Sarbanes-Oxley Act of 2002, an audit committee's financial expert is not required to have an understanding of generally accepted auditing standards. However, such person must have an understanding of generally accepted accounting principles. Answer (B) is incorrect. The Sarbanes-Oxley Act of 2002 does not require an audit committee's financial expert to have an understanding of fraud examination techniques. Answer (D) is incorrect. The Sarbanes-Oxley Act of 2002 does not require an audit committee's financial expert to have experience with performing business valuations.

1.3 Dodd-Frank Wall Street Reform and Consumer Protection Act of 2010

18. Which of the following person(s) may bring a whistleblower claim under the Dodd-Frank Wall Street Reform and Consumer Protection Act of 2010?

I.   An employee of the issuer

II. An individual whose claim originates from information obtained while auditing the issuer

III. An individual whose claim originates from information obtained while investigating the issuer

    A. I only.

    B. I and II only.

    C. I and III only.

    D. I, II, and III.

Answer (A) is correct.
    REQUIRED: The person(s) who may bring a whistleblower claim under the Dodd-Frank Wall Street Reform and Consumer Protection Act of 2010.
    DISCUSSION: Under Dodd-Frank, either an employee of the issuer or any another individual(s) whose claim does not originate from information obtained during an audit or investigation of the issuer may bring a whistleblower claim.
    Answer (B) is incorrect. Under Dodd-Frank, an individual whose whistleblower claim originates from information obtained while auditing the issuer cannot bring a claim. Answer (C) is incorrect. Under Dodd-Frank, an individual whose whistleblower claim originates from information obtained while investigating the issuer cannot bring a claim. Answer (D) is incorrect. Although an employee of the issuer may bring a whistleblower claim, an individual whose claim originates from information obtained while auditing or investigating the issuer may not bring a claim.

19. Which provisions of the Dodd-Frank Wall Street Reform and Consumer Protection Act of 2010 requires an issuer to have a policy defining how to recover performance-based executive compensation?

    A. Clawback provisions.

    B. Whistleblower protection provisions.

    C. The provisions on aiding and abetting securities law violations.

    D. None of the answers are correct.

Answer (A) is correct.
    REQUIRED: The provision of the Dodd-Frank Wall Street Reform and Consumer Protection Act of 2010 on recovering performance-based executive compensation.
    DISCUSSION: Under Dodd-Frank, an issuer must have a clawback policy defining how to recover performance-based executive compensation after a financial restatement.
    Answer (B) is incorrect. Under Dodd-Frank, the whistleblower protection provisions protects whistleblowers against retaliation from their employer. Answer (C) is incorrect. Under Dodd-Frank, the provisions on aiding and abetting securities law violations expands the types of securities law violations that the SEC can prosecute. Answer (D) is incorrect. Under Dodd-Frank, an issuer must have a clawback policy defining how to recover performance-based executive compensation after a financial restatement.

20. Which of the following is **true** regarding an issuer's compensation committee under the Dodd-Frank Wall Street Reform and Consumer Protection Act of 2010?

    A. All committee members must be independent.

    B. A majority of committee members must be independent.

    C. At least one committee member must be on the audit committee.

    D. Committee advisers do not have to be disclosed.

Answer (A) is correct.
    REQUIRED: The independence requirement of a company's compensation committee under the Dodd-Frank Wall Street Reform and Consumer Protection Act of 2010.
    DISCUSSION: Under Dodd-Frank, all members of an issuer's compensation committee must be independent. Additionally, advisers to the committee must be disclosed.
    Answer (B) is incorrect. Under Dodd-Frank, all members of an issuer's compensation committee must be independent. Answer (C) is incorrect. Under Dodd-Frank, there is no requirement that an issuer's compensation committee be comprised of at least one member on the audit committee. Answer (D) is incorrect. Under Dodd-Frank, advisers to an issuer's compensation committee must be disclosed.

STUDY UNIT TWO
COSO FRAMEWORKS

(16 pages of outline)

Effective corporate governance relies heavily on effective systems of (1) internal control and (2) enterprise risk management. The Committee of Sponsoring Organizations of the Treadway Commission (COSO) has established a widely accepted framework for each system.

2.1 COSO FRAMEWORK -- INTERNAL CONTROL

1. **Overview**

   a. Although the COSO *Internal Control – Integrated Framework* is widely accepted as the standard for the design and operation of internal control systems, regulatory or legal requirements may specify another control framework or design.

   b. The COSO framework consists primarily of a definition of internal control, categories of objectives, components and related principles, and requirements of an effective system of internal control.

Background

The Watergate investigations of 1973-74 revealed that U.S. companies were bribing government officials, politicians, and political parties in foreign countries. The result was the Foreign Corrupt Practices Act of 1977. The private sector also responded by forming the National Commission on Fraudulent Financial Reporting (NCFFR) in 1985. The NCFFR is known as the Treadway Commission because James C. Treadway was its first chair.

The Treadway Commission was originally sponsored and funded by five professional accounting organizations based in the United States. This group of five became known as the Committee of Sponsoring Organizations of the Treadway Commission (COSO). The Commission recommended that this group of five organizations cooperate in creating guidance for internal control. The result was *Internal Control – Integrated Framework*, published in 1992, which was modified in 1994 and again in 2013.

The executive summary is available at https://www.coso.org/documents/990025P-Executive-Summary-final-may20.pdf.

---

2. **Definition of Internal Control**

   a. The COSO framework defines internal control as follows:

   Internal control is a process, effected by an entity's board of directors, management, and other personnel, designed to provide reasonable assurance regarding the achievement of objectives relating to operations, reporting, and compliance.

   b. Thus, internal control is

      1) Intended to **achieve** three classes of **objectives**
      2) An **ongoing process**
      3) Effected by **people** at **all** organizational **levels**, e.g., the board, management, and all other employees
      4) Able to provide **reasonable**, but not absolute, **assurance**
      5) **Adaptable** to an entity's structure

3. **Objectives**

   a. Setting objectives is a prerequisite to internal control.

   b. Objectives should be specific, measurable or observable, attainable, relevant, and time-based.

c. According to the definition of internal control, there are three categories of objectives: (1) operations, (2) reporting, and (3) compliance.

   1) **Operations Objectives**

      a) Operations objectives relate to **achieving the entity's mission**.

         i) These objectives are based more on the entity's preferences and judgments, as opposed to laws, rules, regulations, or some other authority.

         ii) Appropriate objectives include improving (a) financial performance, (b) productivity, (c) quality, (d) innovation, and (e) customer satisfaction.

      b) Operations objectives also include **safeguarding of assets**.

         i) Objectives related to protecting and preserving assets form the basis for assessing risk and developing controls to mitigate such risk.

         ii) Prevention of loss through waste, inefficiency, or bad business decisions relates to broader objectives than safeguarding of assets.

   2) **Reporting Objectives**

      a) Reporting objectives relate to the entity's preparation of **financial** and **non-financial** reports for the organization (i.e., internal users) and stakeholders (i.e., external users).

         i) The primary purpose of reporting objectives is to provide reliable, timely, and transparent information to users of reports.

      b) There are two broad categories of reporting objectives: (1) **internal reporting** objectives and (2) **external reporting** objectives.

         i) Internal reporting objectives are influenced by the preferences and judgments of the entity's management and board.

         ii) External reporting objectives are influenced by externally established laws, rules, regulations, standards, and/or frameworks.

      c) There are four sub-categories of reporting objectives.

         i) **Internal financial** reporting objectives may relate, e.g., to division-level financial reports.

         ii) **Internal nonfinancial** reporting objectives may relate, e.g., to customer satisfaction measures.

         iii) **External financial** reporting objectives may relate, e.g., to annual or interim financial statements.

         iv) **External nonfinancial** reporting objectives may relate, e.g., to internal control reports.

      d) The COSO framework treats external reporting that does not conform to any externally established authority (i.e., a law, rule, regulation, standard, and/or framework) as **external communication**.

   3) **Compliance Objectives**

      a) Compliance objectives relate to the entity's adherence to applicable laws, rules, and regulations.

         i) Examples include taxation, environmental protection, and employee relations.

      b) In contrast, compliance with **internal policies and procedures** relates to operational objectives.

        4)   The following is a useful memory aid for the COSO categories of objectives:

O = **O**perations
R = **R**eporting
C = **C**ompliance

    d.   Overlap of Objectives

        1)   An objective in one category may overlap or support an objective in another.

            a)   An example is a policy to close the monthly books by the fifth working day of the following month.

                i)   This objective applies to operations and reporting objectives.

    e.   Sub-Objectives

        1)   Entity-level objectives are linked to more specific **sub-objectives** for the entity's subunits and functions (sales, production, marketing, IT, etc.).

        2)   As conditions change, the sub-objectives must be altered to adapt to changes to the entity-level objectives.

4.   **Components of Internal Control**

    a.   Supporting the organization in its efforts to achieve objectives are the following five components of internal control:

        1)   Control environment
        2)   Risk assessment
        3)   Control activities
        4)   Information and communication
        5)   Monitoring

5.   **Control Environment**

    a.   The control environment is a set of standards, processes, and structures that pervasively affects the system of internal control. Five principles relate to the control environment:

        1)   The organization demonstrates a commitment to **integrity** and **ethical values** by (a) communicating its attitude toward integrity and ethical values, (b) establishing standards of conduct, (c) evaluating performance based on the standards, and (d) correcting deviations in a timely and consistent manner.

            a)   A written code of conduct is an element of a control environment that encourages teamwork in the pursuit of an entity's objectives.

        2)   The board demonstrates **independence** from management and exercises **oversight** of internal control.

        3)   With board oversight, management establishes structures, reporting lines, and authorities and responsibilities.

        4)   The organization demonstrates a commitment to attract, develop, and retain competent individuals in alignment with objectives.

        5)   The organization holds **individuals accountable** for their internal control responsibilities in pursuit of objectives.

    b.   The most effective way to transmit ethical behavior throughout an organization is to set the example.

6. **Risk Assessment**

    a. This process identifies and assesses risks to achieving the organization's objectives, which forms the basis for determining how risks should be managed. Four principles relate to risk assessment:

        1) The organization **specifies objectives** to enable the identification and assessment of risks.

            a) **Operations** objectives

                i)   Reflect management's choices,
                ii)   Must consider **risk tolerances**,
                iii) Include operations and financial performance goals, and
                iv)   Form a basis for committing resources.

            b) **External financial reporting** objectives

                i)   Must comply with applicable accounting standards,
                ii)   Consider materiality, and
                iii) Reflect entity activities.

            c) **External nonfinancial reporting** objectives

                i)   Must comply with externally established standards and frameworks,
                ii)   Consider the required level of precision, and
                iii) Reflect entity activities.

            d) **Internal reporting** objectives

                i)   Reflect management choices,
                ii)   Consider the required level of precision, and
                iii) Reflect entity activities.

            e) **Compliance** objectives

                i)   Reflect external laws and regulations and
                ii)   Consider **risk tolerances**.

        2) The organization **identifies all risks** (internal and external) to the achievement of its objectives across the entity and **analyzes risks** to determine how the risks should be managed.

            a) Examples of internal risk factors at the entity level include interruptions of IT systems and the quality of personnel hired.

            b) Examples of external risk factors at the entity level include technological changes and changes in customer wants.

            c) The appropriate management should analyze risks.

                i)   The analysis generally involves (a) estimating the significance of an event, (b) assessing its likelihood, and (c) considering the risk response in light of the organization's **risk tolerances**.

                ii) Inherent and residual risk (the post-response) must be considered. In general, the seriousness of a risk and its likelihood are inversely related.

            d) The **risk response** considers how each risk should be managed; whether to accept, avoid, reduce, or share the risk; and the design of controls.

        3) The organization should consider the potential for fraud in **assessing fraud risks**. It not only must consider various types of fraud but also must assess (a) incentives and pressures, (b) opportunities, and (c) attitudes and rationalizations.

        4) The organization **identifies and assesses changes** (internal and external) that could significantly affect the system of internal control and adopts appropriate controls.

            a) Risk frequently increases when (1) the organization implements change and (2) objectives differ from past performance.

7. **Control Activities**

    a. These policies and procedures help ensure that management directives to mitigate risks are carried out. Whether **automated** or **manual**, they are (1) applied at all levels of the entity, (2) within various stages of business processes, and (3) over the technology environment. They may be **preventive** or **detective**, and **segregation of duties** is usually present. Three principles relate to control activities:

        1) The organization **selects and develops control activities** that contribute to the mitigation of risks to the achievement of objectives to acceptable levels.

            a) Control activities are **integrated** with the risk assessment.

            b) Management considers how **entity-specific** factors affect control activities.

            c) Management determines which **business processes** require control activities.

            d) The entity evaluates a **mix of control activities**, of which transactional controls are the most basic and include the following controls:

                i) Authorizations and approvals
                ii) Verifications
                iii) Physical controls
                iv) Controls over standing data
                v) Reconciliations
                vi) Supervisory controls

            e) Control activities are selected and developed for application at **different levels** of the organization.

                i) **Transactional control activities** are typically applied at lower levels.
                ii) **Business performance** or **analytical reviews** are typically applied at higher levels.

            f) **Segregation of duties** divides responsibility for the recording, authorization, approval, and cash custody functions when feasible.

        2) The organization selects and develops **general control activities over technology** to support the achievement of objectives.

        3) The organization **deploys control activities** through **policies** that establish what is expected and **procedures** that put policies into action.

8. **Information and Communication**

    a. Information systems enable the organization to obtain, generate, use, and communicate information to (1) maintain accountability and (2) measure and review performance. Three principles relate to information and communication:

        1) The organization obtains or generates and uses **relevant, quality** information to support the functioning of internal control.

            a) Information can include both internal and external sources of data.
            b) Only high-quality information is appropriate.
            c) The cost and the benefit of obtaining the information are considered.

        2) The organization **internally communicates** information, including objectives and responsibilities for internal control, necessary to support the functioning of internal control.

            a) A process enables all personnel to perform their control responsibilities.
            b) Management and the board communicate.
            c) Alternative internal (and external) communication lines, e.g., hotlines, are provided.
            d) The method of internal (and external) communication depends on the timing, audience, and nature of the information.

        3) The organization **communicates with external parties** about matters affecting internal control.

           a) Relevant and timely information is communicated to shareholders, regulators, customers, etc.

           b) Input from external sources provides relevant information.

           c) External assessments are communicated to the board.

           d) Legal requirements are considered.

9. **Monitoring**

    a. Controls and their application change. Monitoring assesses the quality of internal control performance over time to ensure that controls continue to effectively manage existing risks. Two principles relate to monitoring:

        1) The organization selects, develops, and performs **ongoing or separate evaluations (or both)** to determine whether the components of internal control are present and functioning.

           a) **Ongoing** Evaluations

               i) Routine activities that are control-oriented include (a) the periodic reconciliation of operational division data with enterprise-wide financial data, (b) the presence or absence of customer complaints about billing, (c) the reports of internal and external auditors, and (d) training seminars.

           b) **Separate** Evaluations

               i) The significance of risks determines the scope and frequency of separate evaluations of internal control.

               ii) In some environments, control self-assessment is appropriate. In others, the internal audit function should perform a thorough review.

               iii) The evaluator must understand how the system should work and its objectives and must test whether the system is working as designed.

        2) The organization **evaluates and communicates control deficiencies** in a timely manner.

           a) Whether deficiency is reportable depends on its effect on the entity's ability to achieve its objectives.

               i) Reporting should be to a level of the organization with sufficient authority to correct the deficiency.

    b. An effective approach to monitoring consists of three phases: (1) establishing a foundation for monitoring, (2) designing and executing monitoring procedures, and (3) assessing and reporting results.

        1) The **foundation for monitoring** phase consists of

           a) Tone at the top,

           b) Organizational structure, and

           c) Baseline understanding of internal control effectiveness.

        2) The **design and execute** phase consists of

           a) Prioritizing risks,

           b) Identifying controls,

           c) Identifying persuasive information about controls, and

           d) Implementing monitoring procedures.

3)   The **assess and report** phase consists of

   a)   Prioritizing findings,
   b)   Reporting results to the appropriate level, and
   c)   Following up on corrective action.

c.   **Monitoring for Change Continuum**

1)   The causes of ineffective internal control systems include the following:

   a)   They are **not** properly designed or implemented.

   b)   They are properly designed and implemented but are not properly modified when **changes occur in the environment** (e.g., changes in risks, people, processes or technology) in which they operate.

   c)   They are properly designed and implemented, but **changes in their operation** cause them to be ineffective in managing or mitigating applicable risks.

2)   A solution for managing the causes of ineffective internal control systems is the **monitoring for change continuum**. The continuum has four components:

   a)   **The control baseline** is a **starting point** that includes an understanding of

      i)   The internal control system's **design** and

      ii)   Whether controls have been **implemented** to achieve the organization's internal control objectives.

   b)   **Change identification** identifies, through ongoing monitoring and separate evaluations, changes in internal control.

   c)   **Change management** evaluates the design and implementation of identified changes and establishes a **new baseline**.

   d)   **Control revalidation/update** periodically revalidates the operation of internal control in the absence of changes.

10.   **Relationship of Objectives, Components, and Organizational Structure**

a.   The COSO model may be represented by a cube with rows, slices, and columns. (1) The rows are the five components, (2) the slices are the three objectives, and (3) the columns are an entity's organizational structure.

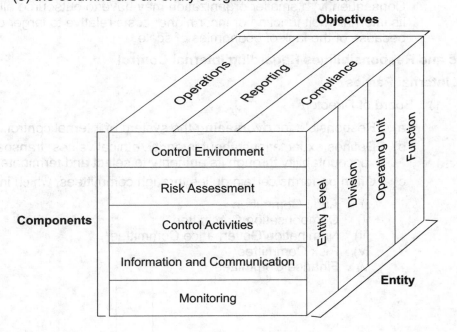

Figure 2-1

11. **Requirements for Effective Internal Control**

    a. A system of internal control is effective if it provides **reasonable assurance** of achieving an entity's objectives relating to operations, reporting, and compliance. Such a system reduces the risk(s) of not achieving those objectives to an **acceptable level**.

    b. An effective system of internal control requires that

        1) Each of the five components of internal control and relevant principles is present and functioning.

            a) **Present** refers to whether the components and relevant principles exist in the design and implementation of the system of internal control.

            b) **Functioning** refers to whether the components and relevant principles continue to exist in the operation of the system of internal control.

        2) The five components are operating together in an integrated manner.

            a) **Operating together** refers to whether all five components collectively reduce the risk of not achieving an objective to an acceptable level.

12. **Other Considerations**

    a. The use of **judgment** is required in designing, implementing, and conducting internal control and assessing its effectiveness.

    b. The use of **outsourced service providers** for certain business processes does not relieve the organization of its responsibility for the system of internal control.

    c. Although technology innovation creates opportunities and risks, the principles in the COSO framework do not change.

    d. The **organization's size** may affect how it implements internal control.

        1) Senior management of smaller organizations typically have a wider span of control and greater direct interaction with personnel than senior management of larger organizations. Larger organizations may need to rely on more formal mechanisms of control (e.g., written reports, formal meetings, or conference calls).

        2) Larger organizations have more resources than smaller organizations. Consequently, a smaller organization may have to outsource all, or parts, of its internal audit function or incur higher costs relative to larger organizations because of the lack of economies of scale.

13. **Roles and Responsibilities Regarding Internal Control**

    a. **Internal Parties**

        1) Board of Directors

            a) Responsible for **overseeing** the system of internal control.

            b) Defines expectations about integrity, ethical values, transparency, and accountability through its authority to select and terminate the CEO.

            c) Often performs certain duties through committees, which include the

                i) Audit Committee
                ii) Compensation Committee
                iii) Nomination/Governance Committee
                iv) Risk Committee
                v) Finance Committee

2) Senior Management

    a) Sets the **tone at the top** and has primary responsibility for establishing proper ethical culture.

    b) Sets objectives.

    c) Has overall responsibility for **designing**, **implementing**, and **operating** an effective system of internal control.

        i) Maintains oversight and control over the entity's risks.

        ii) Guides the development and performance of control activities at the entity level.

        iii) Assigns responsibility for establishing more specific internal controls at the different levels of the entity.

        iv) Communicates expectations.

        v) Evaluates control deficiencies.

3) Operational Management

    a) Provides the **first line of defense** for effective management of risk and control.

    b) Develops and implements control and risk management processes.

4) Business-Enabling Functions

    a) Provide the **second line of defense** for effective management of risk and control.

    b) These functions support the entity through specialized skills and include various risk management and compliance functions.

    c) Additionally, these functions are typically responsible for the ongoing monitoring of control and risk.

5) Internal Auditors

    a) Provide the **third line of defense** for effective management of risk and control.

    b) Evaluate the adequacy and effectiveness of controls in responding to risks in the entity's oversight, operations, and information systems.

    c) To remain independent, the internal audit activity cannot be responsible for selecting and executing controls.

6) Other Entity Personnel

    a) Everyone in the organization is expected to (1) competently perform his or her appropriate control activities and (2) inform those higher in the organization about ineffective control.

b. **External Parties**

1) External Auditors

    a) Independent accountants have been required to consider the auditee's system of internal control as part of their audit of the financial statements.

    b) The PCAOB also requires auditors of public companies to examine and report on internal control.

2) Legislators and Regulators

    a) The Foreign Corrupt Practices Act and the Sarbanes-Oxley Act set legal requirements regarding internal control.

3) Parties Interacting with the Entity

    a) The following are examples of control-related information received from outside sources:

        i) A major customer informs management that a sales representative attempted to arrange a kickback scheme in return for the customer's business.

        ii) A supplier reveals inventory and shipping problems by complaining about incomplete orders.

    b) Parties without a supplier or customer relationship with the entity also may provide insight into the functioning of controls.

        i) As a condition for granting a loan, a bank may require that certain ratios be kept above or below specified levels. As a result, management may need to pay closer attention to controls over cash and inventory levels than it did previously.

4) Financial Analysts, Bond Rating Agencies, and the News Media

    a) The actions of these parties can inform an entity about how it is perceived by the world at large.

5) Outsourced Service Providers

    a) Some of an entity's business functions, e.g., IT, human resources, or internal audit, may be performed by external service providers.

        i) Accordingly, the entity must understand the activities and controls related to the outsourced services and how the provider's internal control system affects the entity's system of internal control.

14. Limitations

a. Internal control only provides **reasonable assurance** of achieving objectives. It cannot provide absolute assurance because any system of internal control has the following **inherent limitations**:

1) Established objectives must be **suitable** for internal control.

    a) For example, if an entity establishes unrealistic objectives, the system of internal controls will be ineffective.

2) Human **judgment** is faulty, and controls may fail because of simple errors or mistakes.

3) Controls may fail due to **breakdowns** (e.g., employee misunderstanding, carelessness, or fatigue).

4) **Management** may inappropriately **override** internal controls, e.g., to fraudulently achieve revenue projections or hide liabilities.

5) Manual or automated controls can be circumvented by **collusion**.

6) **External events** are beyond an organization's control.

The AICPA frequently tests the inherent limitations of internal control. Be able to identify the six basic limitations.

Stop and review! You have completed the outline for this subunit. Study multiple-choice questions 1 through 10 beginning on page 41.

2.2 COSO FRAMEWORK -- ENTERPRISE RISK MANAGEMENT

1. **COSO Risk Management Framework**

    a. *Enterprise Risk Management – Integrated Framework* describes a framework that extends the COSO internal control framework to enterprise risk management (ERM).

        1) It is a basis for coordinating and integrating all of an entity's risk management activities.

2. **ERM Definition**

    a. ERM is based on key concepts applicable to many types of entities. The emphasis is on (1) the objectives of a specific entity and (2) establishing a means for evaluating the effectiveness of ERM.

        > *Enterprise risk management is a process, effected by an entity's board of directors, management, and other personnel, applied in strategy setting and across the enterprise, designed to identify potential events that may affect the entity, and manage risk to be within its risk appetite, to provide reasonable assurance regarding the achievement of entity objectives.*

3. **ERM Concepts**

    a. **Risk** is the possibility that an event will occur and negatively affect the achievement of objectives.

    b. An **opportunity** is the possibility that an event will occur and positively affect the achievement of objectives by creating or preserving value.

        1) Management plans to exploit opportunities, subject to the entity's objectives and strategies.

    c. **Inherent risk** is the risk in the absence of a risk response.

    d. **Control risk** is the risk that controls fail to manage controllable risks effectively.

    e. **Residual risk** is the risk that remains after a risk response.

    f. **Risk appetite** is the amount of risk an entity is willing to accept in pursuit of value. It reflects the entity's risk management philosophy and influences the entity's culture and operating style.

    g. **Risk tolerance** is the acceptable variation relative to the achievement of an objective.

4. **Responsibilities**

    a. Board of Directors

        1) The board has an **oversight role**. It should determine that risk management processes are in place, adequate, and effective.

        2) Directors must possess certain qualities for them to be effective.

            a) A majority of the board should be outside directors.
            b) Directors generally should have years of experience.
            c) Directors must be willing to challenge management's choices.

    b. Senior Management

        1) The CEO sets the **tone at the top** and has ultimate responsibility for ERM.

        2) Senior management should ensure that sound risk management processes are in place and functioning.

        3) Senior management also determines the entity's risk management philosophy.

    c. Risk Committee and Chief Risk Officer

        1) Larger entities may wish to establish a **risk committee** composed of directors that also includes managers.

            a) A chief risk officer (CRO) may coordinate risk management activities. The CRO is a member of, and reports to, the risk committee.

d.   Internal Auditing

1)   Internal auditors may be directed by the board to evaluate the effectiveness and contribute to the improvement of risk management processes.

2)   The internal auditors' determination of whether risk management processes are effective is a judgment resulting from the assessment that

a)   Entity objectives support and align with its mission,

b)   Significant risks are identified and assessed,

c)   Appropriate risk responses are selected that align risks and the entity's risk appetite, and

d)   Relevant risk information is captured and timely communicated across the entity.

5.   **ERM Capabilities**

a.   ERM allows management to **optimize stakeholder value** by coping effectively with uncertainty and the risks and opportunities it presents. ERM helps management to

1)   Achieve objectives,
2)   Prevent loss of reputation and resources,
3)   Report effectively, and
4)   Comply with laws and regulations.

b.   The following are the capabilities of ERM:

1)   Consideration of risk appetite and strategy

a)   Risk appetite should be considered in

i)   Evaluating strategic options,
ii)   Setting objectives, and
iii)   Developing risk management techniques.

2)   Risk response decisions

a)   ERM permits identification and selection of such responses to risk as

i)   Avoidance,
ii)   Reduction,
iii)   Sharing, and
iv)   Acceptance.

3)   Reduction of operational surprises and losses

a)   These are reduced by an improved ability to anticipate potential events and develop responses.

4)   Multiple and cross-enterprise risks

a)   Risks may affect different parts of the entity. ERM allows

i)   Effective responses to interrelated effects and
ii)   Integrated responses to multiple risks.

5)   Response to opportunities

a)   By facilitating the identification of potential events, ERM helps management to respond quickly to opportunities.

6)   Use of capital

a)   The risk information provided by ERM permits

i)   Assessment of capital needs and
ii)   Better capital allocation.

6. **Entity Objectives**

    a. Four categories of objectives apply to all entities:

    1) **Strategic** objectives align with and support the entity's mission.
    2) **Operations** objectives address effectiveness and efficiency.
    3) **Reporting** objectives apply to reliability.
    4) **Compliance** objectives relate to adherence to laws and regulations.

    b. The following is a useful memory aid for the COSO ERM categories of objectives:

    > **O** = **O**perations
    > **R** = **R**eporting
    > **C** = **C**ompliance
    > **S** = **S**trategies

    c. The categories overlap but are distinct. They relate to different needs, and different managers may be assigned responsibility for them.

    1) Safeguarding of resources is another category that may be appropriate for some entities.

    d. Strategic and operational objectives are affected by external events that the entity may not control. In contrast, reporting and compliance objectives are within the entity's control.

    1) Regardless of the category of objectives, ERM should provide reasonable assurance of achieving all objectives.

7. **Components of COSO ERM**

    a. The eight components of ERM are integrated with the management process and may mutually influence each other.

    1) The **internal environment** sets the tone of the entity and reflects its
       a) Risk management philosophy,
       b) Risk appetite,
       c) Integrity,
       d) Ethical values, and
       e) Overall environment.

    2) **Objective setting** must be completed before risk events can be identified. ERM ensures that
       a) A process is established and
       b) Objectives align with the mission and the risk appetite.

    3) **Event identification** relates to internal and external events affecting the entity. The process should consider past events (looking for trends) as well as future possibilities. It differentiates between opportunities and risks.

       a) Specific event identification methods include the following:
          i) Software is available that provides **event inventories** to be used as a starting point for event identification.
          ii) **Internal analysis** considers experience with similar risks in the past when planning a response for future occurrences.
          iii) A certain risk response may be designed for an **escalation or threshold trigger**, such as a decline in cash on hand or a price cut by a competitor.
          iv) **Facilitated workshops and interviews** take discussion groups consisting of management and other stakeholders through structured conversation and exploration of potential events.

v) **Process flow analysis** studies a single business process, such as vendor authorization and payment.

vi) **Leading event indicators** may predict adverse events. An example is avoiding debtor default by intervention upon the occurrence of a late payment.

vii) **Loss event data methodologies** can be used to build a predictive model based on past events. An example is matching workers' compensation claims against the frequency of accidents.

4) **Risk assessment** considers likelihood and impact as a basis for risk management. The assessment considers the inherent risk and the residual risk.

a) Inherent risk is the risk resulting from an activity itself. It is the risk in the absence of a risk response.

b) Residual risk is what remains after risk responses.

5) **Risk responses** should be consistent with the organization's risk tolerances and appetite.

a) Risk **avoidance** ends the activity from which the risk arises.

i) For example, the risk of having a pipeline sabotaged in an unstable region can be avoided by simply selling the pipeline.

b) Risk **retention** accepts the risk of an activity. This term is a synonym for self insurance.

c) Risk **reduction** (mitigation) lowers the level of risk associated with an activity.

i) For example, the risk of systems penetration can be reduced by maintaining a robust information security function within the organization.

d) Risk **sharing** transfers some loss potential to another party.

i) Examples are purchasing insurance, hedging, and entering into joint ventures.

e) Risk **exploitation** seeks risk to obtain a high return on investment.

6) **Control activities** are policies and procedures to ensure the effectiveness of risk responses.

7) The **information and communication** component identifies, captures, and communicates relevant and timely information.

8) **Monitoring** involves ongoing management activities or separate evaluations. The full ERM process is monitored.

b. The following is a useful memory aid for the components of COSO ERM:

C = Control activities
R = Risk assessment
I = Information and communication
M = Monitoring
E = Event identification

R = Risk responses
O = Objective setting
I = Internal environment

8. **COSO ERM Framework**

    a. The interaction of the various elements of the framework may be represented by a cube with rows, slices, and columns. (1) The rows are the eight components, (2) the slices are the four objectives, and (3) the columns are an entity's organizational structure.

COSO ERM Framework

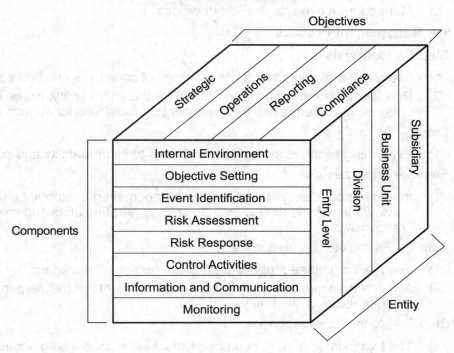

Figure 2-2

    b. Components should be **present and functioning effectively**. Thus, the components are criteria for the effectiveness of ERM.

        1) A component is present and functioning effectively if

            a) No material weaknesses exist and
            b) Risk is within the risk appetite.

        2) When ERM is effective regarding all of the objectives, the board and management have reasonable assurance that

            a) Reporting is reliable,
            b) Compliance is achieved, and
            c) They know the extent of achievement of strategic and operations objectives.

        3) The components may be applied differently in different organizations. For example, they may be applied in a less formal way in smaller organizations compared to larger organizations.

9. **ERM Limitations**

    a. Limitations of ERM result from the possibility of

        1) Faulty human judgment,
        2) Cost-benefit considerations,
        3) Simple errors or mistakes,
        4) Collusion, and
        5) Management override of ERM decisions.

10. **The Risk Management Process**

    a. Step 1 – Identify risks.

        1) Every risk that could affect achievement of objectives must be considered.
        2) Risk identification must be performed for the entire entity. Some occurrences may be inconsequential for the entity but disastrous for an individual unit.

    b. Step 2 – Assess risks.

        1) Every risk identified must be assessed as to its probability and potential effect.

    c. Step 3 – Prioritize risks.

        1) In large or complex entities, senior management may appoint a risk committee to review the risks identified by the various operating units and create a coherent response plan.

    d. Step 4 – Formulate risk responses.

        1) The risk committee proposes adequate response strategies.
        2) All personnel must be aware of the importance of the risk response appropriate to their levels of the entity.

    e. Step 5 – Monitor risk responses.

        1) The two most important sources of information for ongoing assessments of the adequacy of risk responses are

            a) Those closest to the activities. The manager of an operating unit is in the best position to monitor the effects of the chosen risk response strategies.
            b) The audit function. Operating managers may not be objective about risks, especially if they were involved in designing a response strategy. Analyzing risks and responses are normal duties of internal auditors.

    f. The following is a useful memory aid for the components of the risk management process:

I	=	**I**dentify risks
Ate	=	**A**ssess risks
Pie	=	**P**rioritize risks
For	=	**F**ormulate risk responses
Money	=	**M**onitor risk responses

Stop and review! You have completed the outline for this subunit. Study multiple-choice questions 11 through 20 beginning on page 44.

QUESTIONS

2.1 COSO Framework -- Internal Control

1. Which of the following factors are included in an entity's control environment?

A. Organizational structure, management philosophy, and monitoring.

B. Integrity and ethical values, assignment of authority, and human resource practices.

C. Competence of personnel, segregation of duties, and fraud risk assessment.

D. Risk assessment, assignment of responsibility, and human resource practices.

Answer (B) is correct.
    REQUIRED: The factors in a control environment.
    DISCUSSION: Five principles relate to the control environment. The principles are as follows: (1) the organization demonstrates a commitment to integrity and ethical values; (2) the board demonstrates independence from management and exercises oversight of internal control; (3) management establishes structures, reporting lines, and authorities and responsibilities; (4) the organization demonstrates a commitment to attract, develop, and retain competent individuals in alignment with objectives; and (5) the organization holds individuals accountable for their internal control responsibilities. Therefore, integrity and ethical values, assignment of authority, and human resource practices are factors considered in the control environment.
    Answer (A) is incorrect. Monitoring is its own component of internal control. Answer (C) is incorrect. Segregation of duties and fraud risk assessment are factors in the control activities and risk assessment components, respectively, of internal control. Answer (D) is incorrect. Risk assessment is its own component of internal control.

2. Internal control is a process designed to provide reasonable assurance regarding the achievement of objectives related to

A. Reporting.

B. Operations.

C. Compliance

D. All of the answers are correct.

Answer (D) is correct.
    REQUIRED: The true statement regarding COSO's objectives in relation to internal control.
    DISCUSSION: The COSO model for internal control establishes control objectives for operations, reporting, and compliance.
    Answer (A) is incorrect. Operations and compliance also are control objectives. Answer (B) is incorrect. Reporting and compliance also are control objectives. Answer (C) is incorrect. Reporting and operations also are control objectives.

3. Which of the following is the control component that reflects the attitude and actions of the board and management regarding the significance of control within the organization?

A. Risk assessment.

B. Control activities.

C. Control environment.

D. Monitoring.

Answer (C) is correct.
    REQUIRED: The control component that reflects the attitude and actions of the board and management regarding control.
    DISCUSSION: According to the COSO model for internal control, the control environment reflects the attitude and actions of the board and management regarding the significance of control within the organization.
    Answer (A) is incorrect. Risk assessment identifies and analyzes external or internal risks to achievement of the objectives at the activity level as well as the entity level. Answer (B) is incorrect. Control activities are the policies and procedures helping to ensure that management directives are executed and actions are taken to address risks to achievement of objectives. Answer (D) is incorrect. Monitoring is a process that assesses the quality of the system's performance over time.

4. Which of the following most likely would **not** be considered an inherent limitation of the potential effectiveness of an entity's internal control?

A. Incompatible duties.

B. Management override.

C. Faulty judgment.

D. Collusion among employees.

Answer (A) is correct.
    REQUIRED: The item not considered an inherent limitation of internal control.
    DISCUSSION: Internal control has inherent limitations. The performance of incompatible duties, however, is a failure to assign different people the functions of authorization, recording, and asset custody, not an inherent limitation of internal control. Segregation of duties is a category of control activities.
    Answer (B) is incorrect. Management establishes internal controls. Thus, it can override those controls. Answer (C) is incorrect. Human judgment in decision making may be faulty. Answer (D) is incorrect. Controls, whether manual or automated, may be circumvented by collusion among two or more people.

5. The policies and procedures helping to ensure that management directives are executed and actions are taken to address risks to achievement of objectives are best described as

- A. Risk assessments.
- B. Control environments.
- C. Control activities.
- D. Monitoring activities.

6. Internal control can provide only reasonable assurance that the entity's objectives and goals will be met efficiently and effectively. One factor limiting the likelihood of achieving those objectives is that

- A. The internal auditor's primary responsibility is the detection of fraud.
- B. The audit committee is active and independent.
- C. The cost of internal control should not exceed its benefits.
- D. Management monitors performance.

7. Which of the following statements about internal control is correct?

- A. Internal control should provide reasonable assurance that collusion among employees cannot occur.
- B. The establishment and maintenance of internal control are important responsibilities of the internal auditor.
- C. Exceptionally effective internal control is enough for the auditor to eliminate substantive procedures on a significant account balance.
- D. The cost-benefit relationship is a primary criterion that should be considered in designing internal control.

Answer (C) is correct.
  REQUIRED: The definition of control activities.
  DISCUSSION: The COSO model for internal control describes control activities as the policies and procedures helping to ensure that management directives are executed and actions are taken to address risks to achievement of objectives.
  Answer (A) is incorrect. Risk assessment identifies and analyzes external or internal risks to achievement of the objectives at the activity level as well as the entity level. Answer (B) is incorrect. The control environment reflects the attitude and actions of the board and management regarding the significance of control within the organization. Answer (D) is incorrect. Monitoring is a process that assesses the quality of the system's performance over time.

Answer (C) is correct.
  REQUIRED: The true statement about the limitation of internal control.
  DISCUSSION: A limiting factor is that the cost of internal control should not exceed the benefits that are expected to be derived. Thus, the potential loss associated with any exposure or risk is weighed against the cost to control it. Although the cost-benefit relationship is a primary criterion that should be considered in designing and implementing internal control, the precise measurement of costs and benefits usually is not possible.
  Answer (A) is incorrect. The internal audit activity's responsibility regarding controls is to evaluate effectiveness and efficiency and to promote continuous improvement. Answer (B) is incorrect. An effective governance function strengthens the control environment. Answer (D) is incorrect. Senior management's role is to oversee the establishment, administration, and assessment of the system of risk management and control processes. Among the responsibilities of the organization's line managers is the assessment of the control processes in their respective areas. Internal auditors provide varying degrees of assurance about the effectiveness of the risk management and control processes in select activities and functions of the organization.

Answer (D) is correct.
  REQUIRED: The true statement about internal control.
  DISCUSSION: Internal control reflects the quantitative and qualitative estimates and judgments of management in evaluating the cost-benefit relationship. The cost of internal control should not exceed its benefits. Although the cost-benefit relationship is a primary criterion in designing controls, precise measurement of costs and benefits is usually impossible.
  Answer (A) is incorrect. Collusion is an inherent limitation of internal control. Answer (B) is incorrect. Establishment and maintenance of internal control are responsibilities of management. Answer (C) is incorrect. Regardless of the assessed risks of material misstatement, some substantive procedures should be performed for all relevant assertions about material classes of transactions, account balances, and disclosures (AU-C 330).

8. An adequate system of internal controls is most likely to detect a fraud perpetrated by a

    A. Group of employees in collusion.

    B. Single employee.

    C. Group of managers in collusion.

    D. Single manager.

Answer (B) is correct.

    REQUIRED: The fraud most likely to be detected by an adequate system of internal controls.

    DISCUSSION: Segregation of duties and other control processes serve to prevent or detect a fraud committed by an employee acting alone. One employee may not have the ability to engage in wrongdoing or may be subject to detection by other employees in the course of performing their assigned duties. However, collusion may circumvent controls. For example, comparison of recorded accountability for assets with the assets known to be held may fail to detect fraud if persons having custody of assets collude with record keepers.

    Answer (A) is incorrect. A group has a better chance of successfully perpetrating a fraud than does an individual employee. Answer (C) is incorrect. Management can override controls. Answer (D) is incorrect. Even a single manager may be able to override controls.

9. Control activities do **not** encompass

    A. Performance reviews.

    B. Information processing.

    C. Physical controls.

    D. An internal auditing function.

Answer (D) is correct.

    REQUIRED: The item not belonging to the control activities component.

    DISCUSSION: The COSO model describes control activities as policies and procedures that help ensure that management directives are carried out. They are intended to ensure that necessary actions are taken to address risks to achieve the entity's objectives. Control activities have various objectives and are applied at various organizational and functional levels. However, an internal auditing function is part of the monitoring component.

    Answer (A) is incorrect. Performance reviews is a category of control activities. Answer (B) is incorrect. Information processing is a category of control activities. Answer (C) is incorrect. Physical controls is a category of control activities.

10. An organization's directors, management, and internal auditors all have important roles in creating a proper control environment. Senior management is primarily responsible for

    A. Establishing a proper ethical culture.

    B. Designing and operating a control system that provides reasonable assurance that established objectives and goals will be achieved.

    C. Ensuring that external and internal auditors adequately monitor the control environment.

    D. Implementing and monitoring controls designed by the board of directors.

Answer (A) is correct.

    REQUIRED: The best description of senior management's responsibility.

    DISCUSSION: The COSO model treats internal control as a process, effected by an entity's board of directors, management, and other personnel, designed to provide reasonable assurance regarding the achievement of entity objectives. The control environment component of internal control reflects the attitude and actions of the board and management regarding the significance of control within the organization. It sets the organization's tone and influences the control consciousness of its personnel. Moreover, the control environment provides discipline and structure for the achievement of the primary objectives of internal control. The control environment includes, among other elements, integrity and ethical values. Thus, standards should be effectively communicated, e.g., by management example. Management also should remove incentives and temptations for dishonest or unethical acts.

    Answer (B) is incorrect. Senior management has overall responsibility for designing, implementing, and operating an effective system of internal control. However, it is not primarily responsible for designing and operating a control system because senior management is not likely to be involved in the detailed design and day-to-day operations of a control system. Answer (C) is incorrect. Management administers risk and control processes. It cannot delegate this responsibility to the external or internal auditors. Answer (D) is incorrect. The board has oversight governance responsibilities but ordinarily does not become involved in the details of operations.

2.2 COSO Framework -- Enterprise Risk Management

11. Enterprise risk management (ERM) helps management achieve all of the following **except**

    A. Achieving objectives.

    B. Reporting on a timely basis.

    C. Preventing loss of reputation and resources.

    D. Complying with laws and regulations.

Answer (B) is correct.
    REQUIRED: The item not a purpose of ERM.
    DISCUSSION: Enterprise risk management (ERM) helps management

1. Achieve objectives
2. Prevent loss of reputation and resources
3. Report effectively
4. Comply with laws and regulations

ERM allows management to report effectively, not necessarily on a timely basis.
    Answer (A) is incorrect. ERM helps management achieve objectives. Answer (C) is incorrect. ERM helps management prevent loss of reputation and resources. Answer (D) is incorrect. ERM helps management comply with laws and regulations.

12. Management considers risk appetite for all of the following reasons **except**

    A. Evaluating strategic options.

    B. Setting objectives.

    C. Developing risk management techniques.

    D. Increasing the net present value of investments.

Answer (D) is correct.
    REQUIRED: The item not a reason for considering risk appetite.
    DISCUSSION: As described in the COSO ERM framework, risk appetite should be considered in

1. Evaluating strategic options
2. Setting related objectives
3. Developing risk management techniques

Increasing the net present value of investments is an operational objective. It would be determined after consideration of the entity's risk appetite and other strategic factors.
    Answer (A) is incorrect. Management considers risk appetite when evaluating strategic options. Answer (B) is incorrect. Management considers risk appetite when setting objectives. Answer (C) is incorrect. Management considers risk appetite when developing risk management techniques.

13. ERM allows management greater capabilities. Which of the following is **not** a capability of ERM?

    A. Reduced operational surprises and losses.

    B. Better deployment of capital.

    C. Increased productivity.

    D. Improved risk response decisions.

Answer (C) is correct.
    REQUIRED: The item not a capability of ERM.
    DISCUSSION: The following are the categories of the capabilities of ERM:

1. Risk appetite and strategy
2. Risk response decisions
3. Operational surprises and losses
4. Multiple and cross-enterprise risks
5. Opportunities
6. Deployment of capital

Although increased productivity may result from ERM, it is not directly a capability provided by ERM.
    Answer (A) is incorrect. Reduction of operational surprises and losses is a capability of ERM. Answer (B) is incorrect. Better deployment of capital is a capability of ERM. Answer (D) is incorrect. Improvement of risk response decisions is a capability of ERM.

14. The components of ERM should be present and functioning effectively. What does "present and functioning effectively" mean?

    I. No material weaknesses exist.
    II. Risk is within the risk appetite.

    A. I only.

    B. II only.

    C. Both I and II.

    D. Neither I nor II.

Answer (C) is correct.
    REQUIRED: The definition of "present and functioning effectively."
    DISCUSSION: A component is present and functioning effectively if (1) no material weaknesses exist and (2) risk is within the risk appetite.

15. Inherent risk is

A. A potential event that will adversely affect the organization.

B. Risk response risk.

C. The risk after management takes action to reduce the impact or likelihood of an adverse event.

D. The risk when management has not taken action to reduce the impact or likelihood of an adverse event.

Answer (D) is correct.
REQUIRED: The definition of inherent risk.
DISCUSSION: Inherent risk is the risk when management has not taken action to reduce the effect or likelihood of an adverse event. Thus, it is risk in the absence of a risk response.
Answer (A) is incorrect. A risk event is a potential event that will affect the entity adversely. Answer (B) is incorrect. A risk response is an action taken to reduce the impact or likelihood of an adverse event, including a control activity. Risk response risk is not meaningful in this context. Answer (C) is incorrect. The risk after management takes action to reduce the impact or likelihood of an adverse event, including control activities, in responding to a risk is residual risk.

16. Which risk response reflects a change from acceptance to sharing?

A. An insurance policy on a manufacturing plant was not renewed.

B. Management purchased insurance on previously uninsured property.

C. Management sold a manufacturing plant.

D. After employees stole numerous inventory items, management implemented mandatory background checks on all employees.

Answer (B) is correct.
REQUIRED: The risk response reflecting a change from acceptance to sharing.
DISCUSSION: The categories of risk responses under the COSO ERM model are avoidance, acceptance, reduction, and sharing. If management does not insure a building, the response is acceptance. Ordinarily, acceptance is based on a judgment that the cost of another response is excessive. However, once management purchases insurance, the risk is shared with an outside party.
Answer (A) is incorrect. Not renewing insurance represents a change from risk sharing to risk acceptance. Answer (C) is incorrect. Selling property avoids all the risks of ownership. Answer (D) is incorrect. Management originally accepted the risk of employee theft by not implementing pre-hire investigation. Conducting background checks on all employees reduces the risk of theft.

17. Enterprise risk management

A. Guarantees achievement of organizational objectives.

B. Requires establishment of risk and control activities by internal auditors.

C. Involves the identification of events with negative impacts on organizational objectives.

D. Includes selection of the best risk response for the organization.

Answer (C) is correct.
REQUIRED: The description of enterprise risk management.
DISCUSSION: Enterprise risk management (ERM) is a process, effected by an entity's board of directors, management, and other personnel, applied in strategy setting and across the enterprise, designed to identify potential events that may affect the entity, and manage risk to be within its risk appetite, to provide reasonable assurance regarding the achievement of entity objectives.
Answer (A) is incorrect. Risk management processes cannot guarantee achievement of objectives. Answer (B) is incorrect. Involvement of internal auditors in establishing control activities impairs their independence and objectivity. Answer (D) is incorrect. Enterprise risk management is concerned with selecting not the best risk response but the risk response that falls within the enterprise's risk tolerances and appetite.

18. Under the COSO's ERM framework, which of the following most accurately describes risk management responsibilities?

A. In practice, management has primary responsibility.

B. The internal audit activity has an oversight role.

C. The board provides assurance about the effectiveness of ERM.

D. The chief audit executive should serve as chief risk officer.

Answer (A) is correct.
REQUIRED: The most accurate description of ERM responsibilities.
DISCUSSION: The board has overall responsibility. However, in practice, the board delegates responsibility for ERM to senior management, which ensures that sound processes are in place and functioning.
Answer (B) is incorrect. The internal audit activity provides objective assurance that (1) ERM processes are effective and (2) key risks are managed at an acceptable level. Answer (C) is incorrect. The board has an oversight role. The board should determine that risk management processes are in place, adequate, and effective. Answer (D) is incorrect. The CAE must not be the CRO because of the impairment of independence and objectivity.

19. A recent inventory shortage at XYZ Corp., an unaffiliated supplier, contributed to production failures at OPS Corp. in the current period. To avoid future production failures because of supplier inventory shortages, the most appropriate method is for OPS to

    A. Establish an inventory control framework at XYZ.

    B. Increase the size of orders.

    C. Produce the inventory items instead of purchasing from suppliers.

    D. Inform XYZ about its risk appetite regarding supply failures.

Answer (D) is correct.
    REQUIRED: The most effective method to prevent accepting excessive risk of supplier failure.
    DISCUSSION: The risk appetite is the level of risk that an organization is willing to accept. In an enterprise risk management (ERM) system, the risk appetite is considered in (1) evaluating strategic options, (2) setting objectives, and (3) developing risk management techniques. Thus, communicating about the risk appetite with external parties is an important aspect of risk management. It allows the organization to develop strategies to work with suppliers who may have different objectives.
    Answer (A) is incorrect. OPS has no authority to establish an inventory control framework at XYZ. Answer (B) is incorrect. Increasing order size does not address the cause of supplier failures. Answer (C) is incorrect. Although in-house production will eliminate the external parties, it may not be the most cost-effective method. The external party may have cost advantages the organization does not.

20. Which of the following members of an organization has ultimate responsibility for enterprise risk management, provides leadership and direction to senior managers, and monitors the entity's overall risk activities in relation to its risk appetite?

    A. Chief risk officer.

    B. Chief executive officer.

    C. Internal auditors.

    D. Chief financial officer.

Answer (B) is correct.
    REQUIRED: The member of the organization with the stated responsibilities.
    DISCUSSION: The chief executive officer (CEO) sets the tone at the top of the organization and has ultimate responsibility for ownership of the ERM. The CEO will influence the composition and conduct of the board, provide leadership and direction to senior managers, and monitor the entity's overall risk activities in relation to its risk appetite. If any problems arise with the organization's risk appetite, the CEO will also take any measures to adjust the alignment to better suit the organization.
    Answer (A) is incorrect. The risk officer works in assigned areas of responsibility in a staff function. The work of a risk officer often extends beyond one specific area because the officer will have the necessary resources to work across many segments or divisions. Answer (C) is incorrect. The internal auditors evaluate the ERM and may provide recommendations. Answer (D) is incorrect. The CFO is subordinate to the CEO.

STUDY UNIT THREE
MICROECONOMICS

(32 pages of outline)

Microeconomics is the analysis of the behaviors of individual units within a larger economy. Specifically, microeconomics examines the factors that affect individuals' decisions about the efficient allocation of scarce resources between alternative uses. We assume the goal is to maximize profits for individual firms and to maximize satisfaction (or utility) for humans. This is a "bottom up" approach, whereas macroeconomics is a "top down" approach.

3.1 DEMAND, SUPPLY, AND EQUILIBRIUM

1. **Demand -- the Buyer's Side of the Market**

   a. Demand vs. Quantity Demanded

   1) Demand is a schedule of the amounts of a good or service that consumers are willing and able to purchase at various prices during a period of time. Quantity demanded is the amount that will be purchased at a specific price during a period of time.

   Demand Schedule

Price per Unit	Quantity Demanded
$10	0
$9	1
$8	2
$7	3
$6	4
$5	5
$4	6
$3	7
$2	8
$1	9
$0	10

   2) A demand schedule can be graphically depicted as a relationship between the prices of a commodity (on the vertical axis) and the quantity demanded at the various prices (horizontal axis), if other determinants of demand are constant.

   3) A change in quantity demanded results from a change in price; a change in demand results from factors other than price.

b. **The Law of Demand**

1) If all other factors are constant, the price of a product and the quantity demanded are inversely related. The higher (lower) the price, the lower (higher) the quantity demanded. The result is a movement **along** a demand curve.

   a) For example, as price decreases from P_1 to P_2, quantity demanded increases from Q_1 to Q_2.

Movement Along a Demand Curve

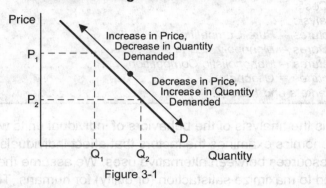

Figure 3-1

c. Factors Other than Price

1) A change in any of the determinants of demand (factors other than price) results in a **shift** of the demand curve.

Change in Demand

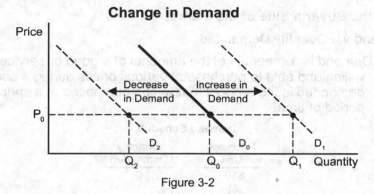

Figure 3-2

   a) A shift to the right (D_0 to D_1) indicates that more goods ($Q_1 > Q_0$) will be sold at a given price (P_0). A shift to the left (D_0 to D_2) indicates that fewer goods ($Q_2 < Q_0$) will be sold at a given price (P_0).

2) The determinants of demand are

   a) Consumer incomes

      i) Most goods are **normal goods**, that is, commodities for which demand is positively (directly) related to income (e.g., steak, new clothes, and airline travel). Thus, demand for these goods shifts to the right as incomes rise. These goods are often referred to as "more is better."

        ii)   However, a few goods are **inferior goods**, that is, commodities for which demand is negatively (inversely) related to income (e.g., potatoes, used clothing, and bus transportation). In this situation, demand shifts to the left as incomes rise. These goods are often referred to as "less is better."

        iii)   For example, as income rises, a consumer would substitute new clothing (normal goods) for used clothes (inferior goods). The opposite is also true.

   b)   Consumer taste and preference

        i)   If a product becomes more (less) popular, the demand curve shifts to the right (left).

   c)   Prices of related goods

        i)   If a price increase in Product A results in an increase in demand for Product B, Products A and B are **substitutes**. For example, when beef prices rise, the demand for chicken increases because consumers switch to chicken to maintain budgets.

        ii)   If a price increase in Product A results in a decrease in demand for Product B, Products A and B are **complements**. For example, if the price of bread increases, the demand for grape jam decreases because consumers rarely use grape jam alone.

   d)   Consumer expectations

        i)   For example, as a hurricane approaches Florida, there is an increased demand for chainsaws and power generators (their demand curves to the right) due to the expectation of a natural disaster.

   e)   Number of consumers

        i)   An increase in the number of consumers shifts the demand curve to the right (increase in demand).

        ii)   A decrease in the number of consumers shifts the demand curve to the left (decrease in demand).

2.   **Supply -- the Seller's Side of the Market**

   a.   Price vs. Quantity Supplied

       1)   Supply is a schedule of the amounts of a good that producers are willing and able to offer to the market at various prices during a specified period. Quantity supplied is the amount that will be offered at a specific price during a period.

       2)   A supply schedule can be graphically depicted as a relationship between the prices of a commodity (on the vertical axis) and the quantity offered at the various prices (horizontal axis) if other determinants of supply are constant.

       3)   A change in quantity supplied results from a change in price; a change in supply results from factors other than price.

b. **The Law of Supply**

1) If all other factors are constant, the price of a product and the quantity supplied are directly related. The higher (lower) the price, the greater (lower) the quantity supplied. The result is a movement **along** a supply curve.

Movement Along a Supply Curve

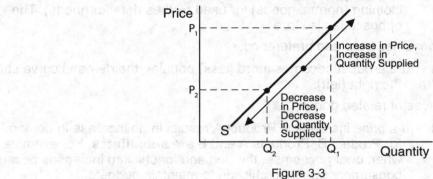

Figure 3-3

a) Thus, as price increases from P_2 to P_1, quantity supplied increases from Q_2 to Q_1.

c. **Factors Other than Price**

1) A change in any of the determinants of supply (factors other than price) results in a **shift** of the supply curve.

Change in Supply

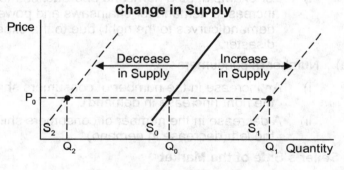

Figure 3-4

a) A shift to the right (S_0 to S_1) indicates that more goods ($Q_1 > Q_0$) will be supplied at a given price (P_0). A shift to the left (S_0 to S_2) indicates that fewer goods ($Q_2 < Q_1$) will be supplied at a given price (P_0).

2) The determinants of supply are

a) Costs of inputs

i) An increase in the costs of inputs, such as employees' wages and materials, shifts the supply curve to the left.

ii) A decrease in the costs of inputs shifts the supply curve to the right.

b) A change in efficiency of the production process

i) For example, better technology that improves the production process (e.g., automated manufacturing) shifts the supply curve to the right.

c) Expectations about price changes

i) If a product's price is expected to decrease, firms will increase supply before the decrease in price to sell as much as possible at the higher price. The supply curve shifts to the right. Production is then decreased when prices fall (law of supply affects quantity supplied).

SU 3: Microeconomics

d) Taxes and subsidies

 i) An increase in taxes or a decrease in subsidies shifts the supply curve to the left.

 ii) A decrease in taxes or an increase in subsidies shifts the supply curve to the right.

3. Market Equilibrium

a. Market demand is the sum of the individual demand curves of all buyers. Market supply is the sum of the individual supply curves of all sellers.

 1) Market equilibrium is the combination of price and quantity at which the market demand and market supply curves intersect.

Market Equilibrium

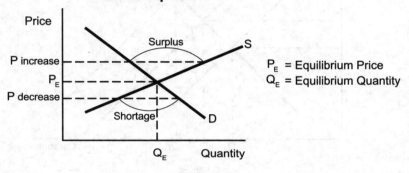

Figure 3-5

b. At the intersection of the supply and demand curves, anyone wishing to purchase economic goods at the market price can do so. Anyone offering the goods can sell everything they bring to market.

 1) **Equilibrium** is at the market-clearing price and the market-clearing quantity.

c. The market forces of supply and demand create an automatic, efficient rationing system.

 1) When the market price exceeds the equilibrium price, the quantity supplied exceeds the quantity demanded by consumers. A surplus results.

  a) The competition among sellers to eliminate excess inventories causes price cuts and lower production.

  b) As the price falls, more buyers enter the market. Eventually, the price settles at the equilibrium price, and the surplus is eliminated.

  c) Government intervention can create a market surplus. An example is a price floor for an agricultural commodity. If the price is above equilibrium, supply exceeds demand. We will discuss this further in Subunit 3.3, item 3.

 2) When the market price is lower than the equilibrium price, the quantity demanded by consumers is greater than the quantity supplied. A shortage results.

  a) Consumers compete for scarce goods by bidding up prices.

  b) As the price rises, new suppliers enter the market. Eventually, the price settles at the equilibrium price, and the shortage is eliminated.

  c) Government intervention also can create shortages. An example is a price ceiling for apartment rents. If the price is below equilibrium, demand exceeds supply. We will discuss this further in Subunit 3.3, item 2.

d.   The shift in the demand and supply curves results in various effects on equilibrium price and quantity.

1)   Shift in demand curve only

a)   When the demand curve shifts to the right (D_0 to D_1), the initial equilibrium price (P_0) and equilibrium quantity (Q_0) increase to P_1 and Q_1, respectively.

b)   When the demand curve shifts to the left (D_0 to D_2), equilibrium price (P_0) and equilibrium quantity (Q_0) decrease to P_2 and Q_2, respectively.

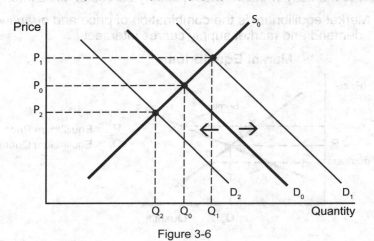

Figure 3-6

2)   Shift in supply curve only

a)   When the supply curve shifts to the right (S_0 to S_1), equilibrium price (P_0) decreases to P_1 and equilibrium quantity (Q_0) increases to Q_1.

b)   When the supply curve shifts to the left (S_0 to S_2), equilibrium price (P_0) increases to P_2 and equilibrium quantity (Q_0) decrease to Q_2.

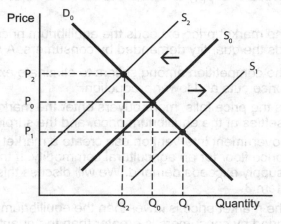

Figure 3-7

3)   Shift in both supply and demand curve towards the same direction

a)   When the demand and supply curves both shift to the left (right) and the increase (decrease) in demand equals the increase (decrease) in supply, equilibrium price (P_0) remains the same.

i)   When both shift to the left, equilibrium quantity decreases from Q_0 to Q_1.

ii) When both shift to the right, equilibrium quantity increases from Q_0 to Q_2.

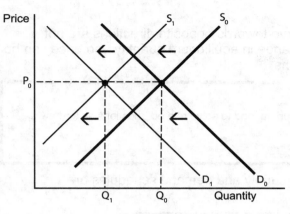

Figure 3-8

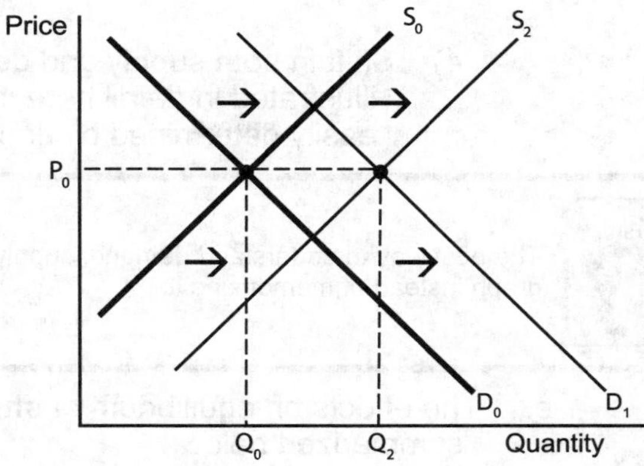

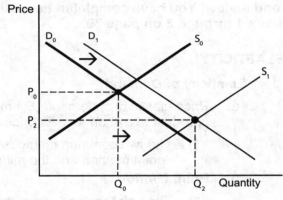

Figure 3-9

b) Rightward shift in both demand and supply curve

i) When the increase in demand is greater than the increase in supply, the equilibrium price (P_0) increases to P_1 and equilibrium quantity (Q_0) increases to Q_1.

ii) When the increase in demand is less than the increase in supply, the equilibrium price (P_0) decreases to P_2 and the equilibrium quantity (Q_0) increases to Q_2.

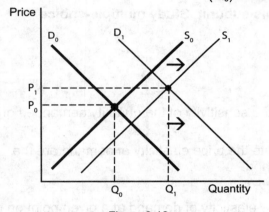

Figure 3-10

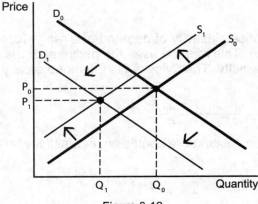

Figure 3-11

c) Leftward shift in both demand and supply curve

i) When the decrease in demand is greater than the decrease in supply, the equilibrium price (P_0) decreases to P_1 and the equilibrium quantity (Q_0) decreases to Q_1.

ii) When the decrease in demand is less than the decrease in supply, the equilibrium price (P_0) increases to P_2 and the equilibrium quantity (Q_0) decreases to Q_2.

Figure 3-12

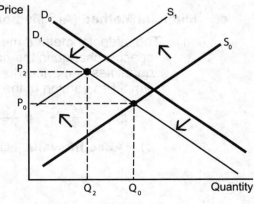

Figure 3-13

4)   Shift in both supply and demand curve towards opposite directions are not illustrated in detail here, but the change in equilibrium quantity and price can be easily determined by drawing graphs.

The best way to understand demand, supply, and equilibrium, and to solve related questions, is to draw a graph instead of memorizing it.

e.   The effects on equilibrium of **shifts** in the supply and demand schedules are summarized below:

	Demand increase (rightward shift)	Demand constant	Demand decrease (leftward shift)
Supply increase (rightward shift)	P_0 uncertain Q_0 increase	P_0 decrease Q_0 increase	P_0 decrease Q_0 uncertain
Supply constant	P_0 increase Q_0 increase	– –	P_0 decrease Q_0 decrease
Supply decrease (leftward shift)	P_0 increase Q_0 uncertain	P_0 increase Q_0 decrease	P_0 uncertain Q_0 decrease

Stop and review! You have completed the outline for this subunit. Study multiple-choice questions 1 through 3 on page 79.

3.2 ELASTICITY

1.   **Elasticity of Demand**

a.   Price elasticity of demand (E_d) measures the sensitivity of the quantity demanded of a product to a change in its price.

1)   The two common methods to calculate the price elasticity of demand are the point method and the midpoint method.

b.   **Point Method**

1)   The point method measures the price elasticity of demand at a given point on the demand curve for a specific change in the product's price.

$$\%\Delta Q = \frac{Quantity\ demanded\ \textbf{after}\ the\ change\ -\ Quantity\ demanded\ \textbf{before}\ the\ change}{Quantity\ demanded\ \textbf{before}\ the\ change}$$

$$\%\Delta P = \frac{Price\ \textbf{after}\ the\ change\ -\ Price\ \textbf{before}\ the\ change}{Price\ \textbf{before}\ the\ change}$$

$$E_d = \frac{Percentage\ change\ in\ quantity\ demanded}{Percentage\ change\ in\ price} = \frac{\%\Delta Q}{\%\Delta P}$$

c.   **Midpoint Method (Arc Method)**

1)   The midpoint method measures the price elasticity of demand of a range for a specific change in the product's price. This method uses the midpoint of the quantities and prices to measure elasticity. The following is the algebraically simplified version of the formula:

$$E_d = \frac{\%\Delta Q}{\%\Delta P} = \frac{(Q_1 - Q_2) \div (Q_1 + Q_2)}{(P_1 - P_2) \div (P_1 + P_2)}$$

a)   **Absolute value** is used when calculating the coefficient of elasticity.

EXAMPLE

Roxy's Ice Cream Shoppe sells 100 quarts of chocolate a day at $6 each. If it lowers the price to $3 per quart, it will sell 300 quarts a day.

Point Method

$$\%\,\Delta\,Q \;=\; \frac{300-100}{100} \;=\; 2 \;=\; 200\%$$

$$\%\,\Delta\,P \;=\; \frac{3-6}{6} \;=\; 0.5 \;=\; 50\%$$

$$E_d \;=\; \frac{\%\,\Delta\,Q}{\%\,\Delta\,P} \;=\; \frac{200\%}{50\%} \;=\; 4$$

The elasticity absolute value of 4 indicates that the specific change of the product's price by 50% (from $6 to $3) will increase the demand for the product by 200% (from Q = 100 to Q = 300).

Midpoint (Arc) Method

	Num.	Denom.		Num.	Denom.		Num.	Denom.		Elasticity
$E_d =$	$\dfrac{(100-300)}{(100+300)}$	$\div$	$\dfrac{(\$6-\$3)}{(\$6+\$3)}$	$=$	$\dfrac{200}{400}$	$\div$	$\dfrac{\$3}{\$9}$	$=$	$0.500 \div 0.333 =$	**1.50**

The elasticity absolute value of 1.5 indicates that the range on the demand curve between P = 6 and P = 3 is relatively elastic.

---

    d.   When the demand elasticity coefficient is

        1) **Greater than one**, demand is in a **relatively elastic** range. The percentage change in the quantity demanded is higher than the percentage change in the price.

$$\%\Delta Q \;>\; \%\Delta P$$

            a)   For example, a 10% decline in the price of ice cream results in a 20% increase in ice cream demanded.

        2) **Equal to one**, demand has **unitary elasticity** (usually a very limited range). The percentage change in the quantity demanded is equal to the percentage change in the price.

$$\%\Delta Q \;=\; \%\Delta P$$

        3) **Less than one**, demand is in a **relatively inelastic** range. The percentage change in the quantity demanded is lower than the percentage change in the price.

$$\%\Delta Q \;<\; \%\Delta P$$

            a)   For example, a 20% decline in the price of ice cream results in a 10% increase in ice cream demanded.

        4) **Infinite**, demand is **perfectly elastic** (depicted as a horizontal line).

            a)   In pure competition, the number of firms is so great that one cannot influence the market price. The demand curve faced by a single seller in such a market is perfectly elastic (although the demand curve for the market as a whole has the normal downward slope).

EXAMPLE

Consumers will buy a farmer's total output of soybeans at the market price but will buy none at a slightly higher price. Moreover, the farmer cannot sell below the market price without incurring losses.

---

        5) **Equal to zero**, demand is **perfectly inelastic** (depicted as a vertical line).

            a)   Some consumers' need for a certain product is so high that they will pay whatever price the market sets. The number of these consumers is limited, and the amount they desire is relatively fixed.

EXAMPLE

Drug addiction tends to result in demand that is unresponsive to price changes. Existing buyers (addicts) are not driven out of the market by a rise in price, and no new buyers are induced to enter the market by a reduction in price.

    e.   The price elasticity of demand of a product can be affected by the availability of substitute products in the market.

        1)   As more substitute products become available, the demand for the product becomes more elastic. A small increase in the product's price causes a proportionally larger decrease in the quantity demanded because substitutes are available.

        2)   As fewer substitute products become available in the market, the demand for the product becomes more inelastic.

    f.   Price elasticity of demand is useful for determining how a change in the price of a product will affect total revenue (Quantity × Price).

        1)   If the product demand is price elastic, as price **increases**, the percentage decrease in the quantity demanded is greater than the percentage increase in price. Thus, total revenue decreases.

        2)   If the product demand is price unitary elastic, as price **increases**, the percentage decrease in the quantity demanded is equal to the percentage increase in price. Thus, total revenue stays the same.

        3)   If product demand is price inelastic, as price **increases**, the percentage decrease in the quantity demanded is less than the percentage increase in the price. Thus, total revenue increases.

Effect on Total Revenue

	Elastic Range	Unitary Elasticity	Inelastic Range
Price increase	Decrease	No change	Increase
Price decrease	Increase	No change	Decrease

2.   **Elasticity of Supply**

    a.   Price elasticity of supply (E_s) measures the sensitivity of the quantity supplied of a product to a change in its price.

$$E_s = \frac{Percentage\ change\ in\ quantity\ supplied}{Percentage\ change\ in\ price}$$

        1)   The same formulas used in the calculation of price elasticity of demand are used to calculate the price elasticity of supply.

        2)   When the supply elasticity coefficient is

            a)   **Greater than one**, supply is in a **relatively elastic** range. The percentage change in the quantity supplied is higher than the percentage change in the price.

$$\%\Delta Q \quad > \quad \%\Delta P$$

            b)   **Equal to one**, supply has **unitary elasticity** (usually a very limited range). The percentage change in the quantity supplied is equal to the percentage change in the price.

$$\%\Delta Q \quad = \quad \%\Delta P$$

c)   **Less than one**, supply is in a **relatively inelastic** range. The percentage change in the quantity supplied is lower than the percentage change in the price.

$$\%\Delta Q \ < \ \%\Delta P$$

d)   **Infinite**, supply is **perfectly elastic** (depicted as a horizontal line).

e)   **Equal to zero**, supply is **perfectly inelastic** (depicted as a vertical line).

   i)   A perfectly inelastic supply curve indicates that, in the very short run, a seller cannot change the quantity supplied.

EXAMPLE

A farmer offering a perishable good with no means of storage must sell the entire crop regardless of the price buyers offer. The farmer cannot offer a larger quantity because the harvest has ended for the season.

Stop and review! You have completed the outline for this subunit. Study multiple-choice questions 4 through 6 on page 80.

3.3 GOVERNMENT ACTION IN THE MARKET

1.   **Price Controls**

   a.   Price controls are attempts by government to remedy perceived imbalances of power between economic actors, i.e., sellers and buyers in the marketplace.

2.   **Price Ceilings**

   a.   To keep essential goods and services affordable to all, sellers sometimes are forced to charge below the equilibrium price.

   b.   Shortages result because the market is unwilling to supply all that is demanded at the (government-mandated) artificially low price.

Price Ceiling and Resulting Shortage

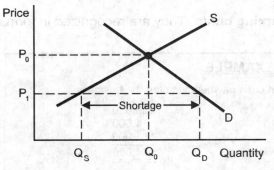

P_0 = Initial equilibrium price

Q_0 = Initial equilibrium quantity

P_1 = Artificial ceiling set by government (price not allowed to rise above this ceiling)

Q_S = Quantity supplied at P_1

Q_D = Quantity demanded at P_1

$Q_D - Q_S$ = Amount of shortage

Figure 3-14

   c.   Rent controls and usury laws are examples.

3. **Price Floors**

    a. To compensate certain suppliers perceived to be treated adversely by market forces, buyers sometimes are required to pay above the equilibrium price for certain products or services.

    b. Surpluses result because sellers are encouraged by the artificially high price to produce more than the market is willing to buy.

Price Floor and Resulting Surplus

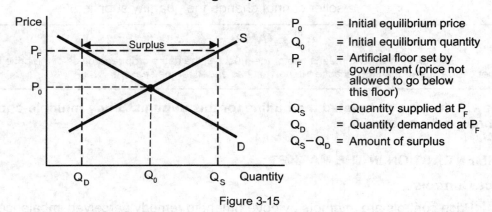

P_0	= Initial equilibrium price
Q_0	= Initial equilibrium quantity
P_F	= Artificial floor set by government (price not allowed to go below this floor)
Q_S	= Quantity supplied at P_F
Q_D	= Quantity demanded at P_F
$Q_S - Q_D$	= Amount of surplus

Figure 3-15

    c. Price supports for agricultural products and minimum wage legislation are examples.

Stop and review! You have completed the outline for this subunit. Study multiple-choice questions 7 through 9 beginning on page 80.

3.4 PROFITS AND COSTS

1. **Explicit vs. Implicit Costs**

    a. **Explicit costs** require actual cash payments. For this reason, they also are known as out-of-pocket or outlay costs.

        1) Explicit costs are **accounting costs**. They are recognized in formal accounting records.

EXAMPLE

An entrepreneur opening a gift shop has to make certain cash payments to start the business.

Inventory	$59,000
Rent	4,000
Utilities	1,000
Total explicit costs	**$64,000**

---

b. **Implicit costs** are not recognized in formal accounting records.

1) An implicit cost is an **opportunity cost**, i.e., the maximum benefit forgone by using a scarce resource for a given purpose instead of the next-best alternative.

2) To measure the true economic success or failure of the venture, the entrepreneur in the example on the previous page must consider more than the explicit costs in the accounting records.

a) The entrepreneur's opportunity costs often are important implicit costs. For example, (s)he could have worked for another firm rather than open the gift shop.

b) Startup costs are resources that could have been invested in financial instruments.

c) A **normal profit** is an implicit cost.

EXAMPLE

The normal profit is the income that the entrepreneur could have earned by applying his or her skill in another venture.

Salary forgone	$35,000
Investment income forgone	3,600
Total implicit costs	**$38,600**

---

c. **Economic costs** are total costs (explicit and implicit).

1) The standard for an economic decision is whether the revenues from the venture cover all costs, both explicit and implicit.

EXAMPLE

Economic costs = Total costs
= Explicit costs + Implicit costs
= $64,000 + $38,600
= **$102,600**

---

2. **Accounting vs. Economic Profit**

a. **Accounting profits** are earned when the income of an organization exceeds its expenses.

EXAMPLE

After the first year of operation, the gift shop owner made an accounting profit.

Sales revenue	$100,000
Explicit costs	(64,000)
Accounting profit	**$ 36,000**

---

b.   **Economic profits** are earned when the income of an organization exceeds its economic costs. They are not earned until the income exceeds not only costs recorded in the accounting records but also its implicit costs. Economic profit also is called pure profit.

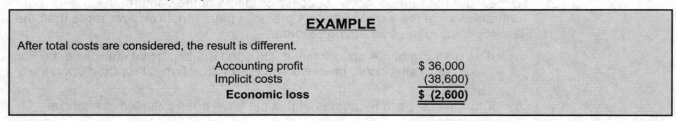

EXAMPLE

After total costs are considered, the result is different.

Accounting profit	$ 36,000
Implicit costs	(38,600)
Economic loss	**$ (2,600)**

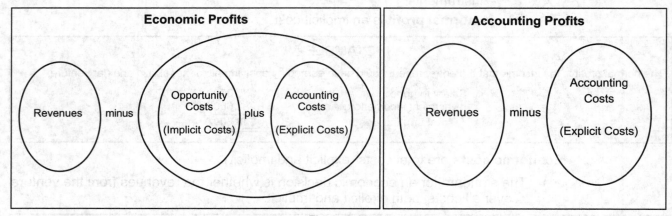

Figure 3-16

1)   **Normal profit** occurs when total revenue equals total costs (explicit and implicit), that is, when economic profit equals zero.

3.   Short- vs. Long-Run Costs

a.   The **short run** is a period so brief that a firm cannot vary its fixed costs. Thus, Short-run costs = Variable costs + Fixed costs.

b.   The **long run** is a period long enough that all inputs, including those incurred as fixed costs, can be varied. Thus, Long-run costs = Variable costs.

1)   Investment in new, more productive equipment results in higher total fixed costs but may result in lower total and per-unit variable costs.

Stop and review! You have completed the outline for this subunit. Study multiple-choice questions 10 through 12 beginning on page 81.

3.5 MARGINAL ANALYSIS

1.   **Marginal Analysis**

a.   Marginal analysis allows economic decisions to be made based on projecting the results of varying the levels of resource consumption and output production.

1)   **Total product** is the entire production of a good or service for a given period.

2)   **Marginal product** is the additional output obtained by adding one extra unit of input. It is calculated by dividing the change in total output at a given input by the change in inputs.

b.   As inputs are added to a process, each additional unit of input results in increased production. However, past the point of diminishing marginal returns, the increase is smaller with each unit. That is, the benefit of adding input units decreases.

1)   This principle is the **law of diminishing returns**.
2)   Eventually, so many inputs enter the process that it becomes inefficient, and total output actually decreases. This is the point of negative marginal returns.

a)   EXAMPLE: Too many cooks in the kitchen get in the way of each other and slow production.

EXAMPLE

The table below reflects the changes in total product and marginal product as additional units of input are added to the production process.

Units of Input	Total Product	Marginal Product
1	2	2
2	6	4
3	12	6
4	20	8
5	29	9
6	**39**	**10**
7	48	9
8	56	8
9	62	6
10	66	4
11	68	2
12	66	−2

At the sixth unit of input, marginal product peaks and then begins to decrease. This is the point of diminishing marginal returns. When the twelfth unit is added, the production process is receiving so much input that the efficiency of the process is actually decreased, and total output also decreases.

---

c.   These relationships can be depicted graphically as follows:

Marginal Returns

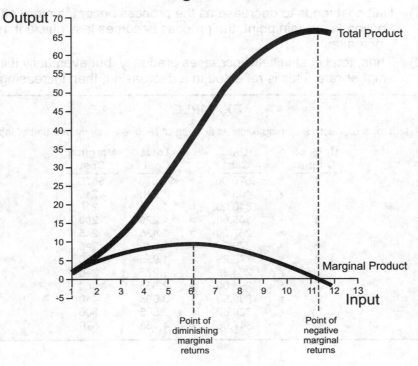

Figure 3-17

2. **Marginal Revenue**

    a. Marginal revenue is the additional (incremental) revenue produced by generating one additional unit of output. It is the difference in total revenue at each level of output.

        1) If the product is sold in a competitive market (the seller does not have monopoly power), the seller must reduce its price to sell additional units.

        2) Thus, as total revenue increases with the sale of each additional unit, it increases by a smaller amount. The result is constantly decreasing marginal revenue.

EXAMPLE

A company has the following revenue data for one of its products:

Units of Output		Unit Price		Total Revenue	Marginal Revenue
1	×	$580	=	$ 580	$580
2	×	575	=	1,150	570
3	×	570	=	1,710	560
4	×	565	=	2,260	550
5	×	560	=	2,800	540
6	×	555	=	3,330	530
7	×	550	=	3,850	520
8	×	545	=	4,360	510
9	×	540	=	4,860	500
10	×	535	=	5,350	490
11	×	530	=	5,830	480
12	×	525	=	6,300	470

---

    b. Revenue by itself cannot determine the proper level of output. Cost also must be considered.

3. **Marginal Cost**

    a. Marginal cost is the additional (incremental) cost incurred by generating one additional unit of output. It is the difference in total cost at each level of output.

        1) Unit cost tends to decrease as the process becomes more efficient. However, beyond a certain point, the process becomes less efficient, and unit cost increases.

        2) Thus, total cost initially increases gradually, but eventually it increases at a higher rate. This is reflected in a decreasing, then increasing, of marginal cost.

EXAMPLE

The following are cost data for a product, assuming each unit of output requires exactly one unit of input:

Units of Output		Unit Cost		Total Cost	Marginal Cost
1	×	$570.00	=	$ 570	$570
2	×	405.00	=	810	240
3	×	340.00	=	1,020	210
4	×	**305.00**	=	**1,220**	**200**
5	×	287.00	=	1,435	215
6	×	279.17	=	1,675	240
7	×	279.29	=	1,955	280
8	×	284.38	=	2,275	320
9	×	295.00	=	2,655	380
10	×	309.50	=	3,095	440
11	×	326.82	=	3,595	500
12	×	347.08	=	4,165	570

4. Profit Maximization

a. The firm's goal is to maximize profits, not revenues. Thus, marginal revenue must be compared with marginal cost to determine the point of profit maximization.

   1) Profit maximization occurs at the output at which **marginal revenue equals marginal cost**. Beyond this point, increasing production results in costs so high that total profit is diminished.

EXAMPLE

Comparing marginal revenue and marginal cost data allows determination of the point of profit maximization.

Units of Output	Marginal Revenue		Marginal Cost		Marginal Profit	Total Revenue		Total Cost		Total Profit
1	$580	–	$570	=	$ 10	$ 580	–	$ 570	=	$ 10
2	570	–	240	=	330	1,150	–	810	=	340
3	560	–	210	=	350	1,710	–	1,020	=	690
4	550	–	200	=	350	2,260	–	1,220	=	1,040
5	540	–	215	=	325	2,800	–	1,435	=	1,365
6	530	–	240	=	290	3,330	–	1,675	=	1,655
7	520	–	280	=	240	3,850	–	1,955	=	1,895
8	510	–	320	=	190	4,360	–	2,275	=	2,085
9	500	–	380	=	120	4,860	–	2,655	=	2,205
10	**490**	–	**440**	=	**50**	**5,350**	–	**3,095**	=	**2,255**
11	480	–	500	=	(20)	5,830	–	3,595	=	2,235
12	470	–	570	=	(100)	6,300	–	4,165	=	2,135

Beyond an output of 10 units, marginal profit is negative. By definition, this output is the point of highest total profit.

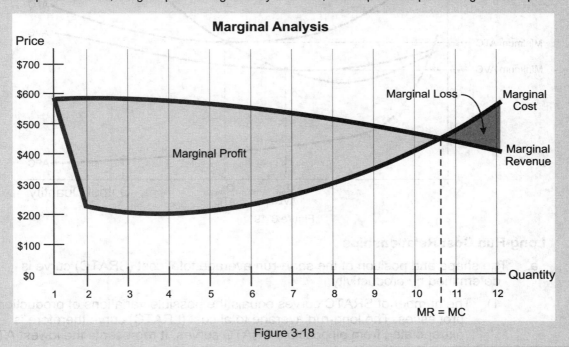

Figure 3-18

5.   **Average Total Cost (ATC) and Marginal Cost (MC)**

   a.   Total costs of production (TC) equals the sum of total fixed costs (FC) and total variable costs (VC).

$$TC = FC + VC$$

   b.   Average total cost (ATC = TC ÷ Q) equals the sum of average fixed costs (AFC = FC ÷ Q) and average variable costs (AVC = VC ÷ Q).

   c.   An increase in fixed costs results in the following:

   1)   An increase in FC and AFC
   2)   An increase in TC and ATC
   3)   No effect on VC or AVC

   d.   The marginal cost curve (MC = ΔTC ÷ ΔQ) always intersects the ATC curve and the AVC curve at their minimum points.

Cost Relationships in the Short Run

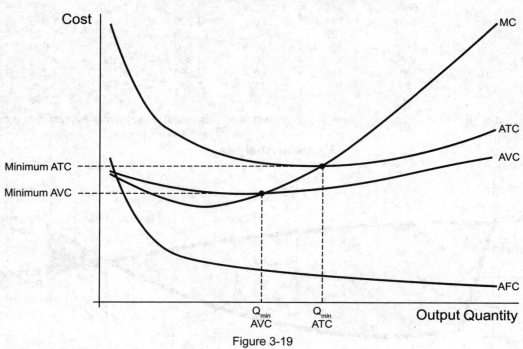

Figure 3-19

6.   **Long-Run Cost Relationships**

   a.   The shape and position of the short-run average total cost (SRATC) curve is determined by productivity.

   1)   The number of SRATC curves equals the possible variations of production processes. The long-run average total cost (LRATC) curve therefore is extrapolated from all possible SRATC curves. It represents the lowest ATC for any output that can be produced.

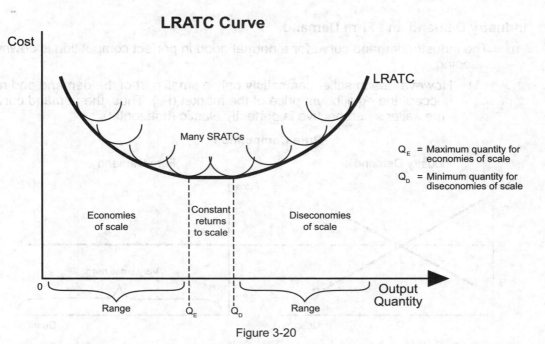

Figure 3-20

b.   The LRATC curve derives its shape from the phenomenon of economies and diseconomies of scale.

1)   **Economies of scale** (increasing returns to scale). Initially, as production increases, average costs of production tend to decline and the marginal cost of production tends to decrease. Some of the reasons are

a)   Increased specialization and division of labor,
b)   Better use and specialization of management, and
c)   Use of more efficient machinery and equipment.

2)   **Constant returns to scale.** For a certain range of output, an increase in production results in no change in average costs and marginal cost of production does not change as output changes.

3)   **Diseconomies of scale** (decreasing returns to scale). Eventually, as output continues to increase, the marginal cost of production tends to increase.

a)   The most frequent reason for diseconomies of scale is the difficulty of managing a large-scale entity.

Stop and review! You have completed the outline for this subunit. Study multiple-choice questions 13 through 15 beginning on page 82.

3.6   MARKET STRUCTURES -- PURE COMPETITION

1.   **Defining Characteristics**

a.   A very large number of buyers and sellers act independently. Examples are the stock market and agricultural markets.

b.   The product is homogeneous or standardized. Thus, the product of one seller is a perfect substitute for that of any other. The only basis for competition is price.

c.   Each seller produces an immaterial amount of the industry's total output and thus cannot influence the market price.

d.   No barriers to entry or exit from the market exist.

e.   Every seller or buyer has perfect information.

1)   Pure competition exists only in theory. However, the model is useful for understanding basic economic concepts. It also provides a standard of comparison with real-world markets.

2. **Industry Demand and Firm Demand**

    a. The industry demand curve for a normal good in perfect competition is downward sloping.

        1) However, each seller can satisfy only a small part of the demand and must accept the equilibrium price of the market (P_0). Thus, the demand curve from the seller's perspective is perfectly elastic (horizontal).

Pure Competition

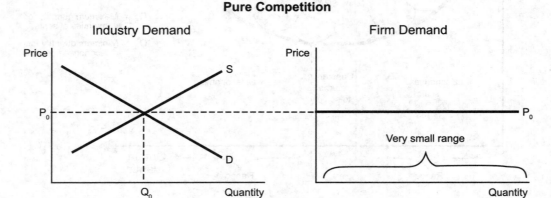

Figure 3-21

        2) The small segment of the industry's demand curve occupied by each seller necessarily is at the point of market equilibrium.

        3) Sellers in perfect competition therefore are price takers because they must sell at the market price.

EXAMPLE

The seller's perfectly elastic demand curve means that marginal revenue, average revenue, and market price are equal.

Units of Output		Unit Price (Average Revenue)		Total Revenue	Marginal Revenue
1	×	$960	=	$ 960	$960
2	×	960	=	1,920	960
3	×	960	=	2,880	960
4	×	960	=	3,840	960
5	×	960	=	4,800	960
6	×	960	=	5,760	960
7	×	960	=	6,720	960
8	×	960	=	7,680	960

---

3. **Short-Run Profit Maximization in Pure Competition**

    a. In the short run, a seller should produce (continue to operate) when it can earn a profit or incur a loss smaller than fixed costs. This is because short-run costs include both variable costs and fixed costs (costs incurred even if a firm closes). Thus, a firm could lose less money by continually operating instead of shutting down.

        1) If the revenue drops below the average variable cost, the seller should shut down instead of continually operating.

	Revenue	Variable cost	Fixed cost	Shut down	Operating
				Loss	
Scenario A	$10	($4)	($8)	($8)	**($2)**
Scenario B	$10	($10)	($2)	($2)	($2)
Scenario C	$10	($14)	($2)	**($2)**	($6)

a)   In scenario A, the revenue is above the variable cost. The seller would incur a loss of $8 if shut down and incur a loss of only $2 if (s)he chose to **continue operating**.

b)   In scenario B, the revenue is equal to variable cost. The seller would incur a loss of $2 whether (s)he chose to operate or shut down.

c)   In scenario C, the revenue is below the variable cost. The seller would incur a loss of $6 if (s)he chose to operate and incur a loss of only $2 if (s)he chose to **shut down**.

b.   For all market structures, a seller that does not close should produce the output at which marginal revenue equals marginal cost **(MR = MC)**.

EXAMPLE

If the next unit of output adds more in revenue (MR) than in cost (MC), the seller increases total profit or decreases total losses. For a purely competitive seller, price equals MC is the same as MR equals MC. MR equals MC at an output of 7 units in the table below.

Units of Output	Revenue		Cost		Profit	
	Total	Marginal	Total	Marginal	Total	Marginal
1	$ 960	$960	$1,800	$1,800	$(840)	$(840)
2	1,920	960	2,500	700	(580)	260
3	2,880	960	3,100	600	(220)	360
4	3,840	960	3,600	500	240	460
5	4,800	960	4,200	600	600	360
6	5,760	960	4,980	780	780	180
7	**6,720**	**960**	**5,940**	**960**	**780**	**0**
8	7,680	960	7,060	1,120	620	(160)

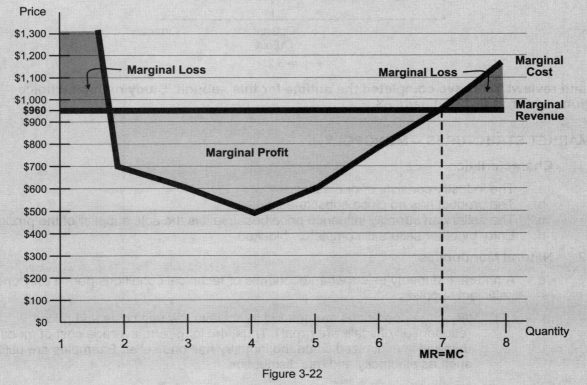

Figure 3-22

4.   **Long-Run Equilibrium in Pure Competition**

a.   Because sellers are earning a normal profit, the industry attracts new entrants.

1)   New competitors move the supply curve to the right, thus lowering the price.

2)   The lower price results in losses for sellers with high costs, and the sellers leave the market. The exit of the sellers shifts the supply curve to the left.

3)   The output generated by the industry returns to the previous level, and the price can rise again. Equilibrium is restored. Thus, in the long run, economic profit is zero.

b.   The surviving sellers have the lowest average total cost. Price and quantity are at the intersection of the MR and MC curves.

Long-Run Equilibrium for a Purely Competitive Firm

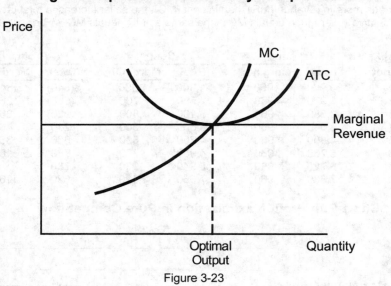

Figure 3-23

Stop and review! You have completed the outline for this subunit. Study multiple-choice questions 16 through 18 on page 83.

3.7 MARKET STRUCTURES -- MONOPOLY

1.   **Characteristics**

a.   The industry consists of one seller.

b.   The product has no close substitutes.

c.   The seller can strongly influence price because it is the sole supplier of the product.

d.   Entry by other sellers is completely blocked.

2.   **Natural Monopolies**

a.   A natural monopoly exists when economic or technical conditions permit only one efficient supplier.

1)   Very large operations are needed to achieve low unit costs and prices (economies of scale are great). Thus, the long-term average cost of meeting demand is minimized when the industry has one seller. Examples are utilities, such as electricity and gas distribution.

3. **Pricing Power**

   a. Economists use two terms to describe a monopolist's pricing behavior:

      1) A **price maker** sets prices as high as it wants because it is not limited by competition.

      2) A **price searcher** does not set prices arbitrarily high but seeks the price that maximizes its profits.

4. **Demand**

   a. Unlike the horizontal firm demand curve in pure competition covered in Subunit 3.6, the demand curve is downward sloping because a monopolist can sell more units only by lowering price.

      1) Furthermore, the monopolist's demand curve is the industry's demand curve, not a small part as in pure competition.

      2) A monopolist's price decrease affects all the units sold, not just the additional unit(s). Thus, a monopolist's marginal revenue curve is below the demand curve.

      3) A monopolist's marginal revenue continuously decreases as output increases. Total revenue decreases if marginal revenue is less than $0.

EXAMPLE

Units of Output		Unit Price (Average Revenue)		Total Revenue	Marginal Revenue
1	×	$960	=	$ 960	$960
2	×	910	=	1,820	860
3	×	860	=	2,580	760
4	×	810	=	3,240	660
5	×	760	=	3,800	560
6	×	710	=	4,260	460
7	×	660	=	4,620	360
8	×	610	=	4,880	260

---

5. **Profit Maximization**

   a. Unlike a firm in pure competition, the monopolist can set output at the level at which profits are maximized **(MR = MC)**.

      1) The corresponding price is based on a downward-sloping demand curve.

         a) Monopoly does **not** result in the highest possible price, and the monopolist does **not** produce at the lowest average total cost.

EXAMPLE

Price Searching for a Monopolist

Units of Output	Selling Price per Unit	Revenue Total	Revenue Marginal	Cost Total	Cost Marginal	Profit Total	Profit Marginal
1	$960	$ 960	$960	$ 800	$800	$ 160	$ 160
2	910	1,820	860	1,480	680	340	180
3	860	2,580	760	1,980	500	600	260
4	810	3,240	660	2,320	340	920	320
5	**760**	**3,800**	**560**	**2,800**	**480**	**1,000**	**80**
6	710	4,260	460	3,480	680	780	(220)
7	660	4,620	360	4,420	940	200	(580)
8	610	4,880	260	5,720	1,300	(840)	(1,040)

The monopolist produces 5 units and sells them at $760 each.

6.   **Economic Consequences**

    a.   Given sufficiently low costs and adequate demand, a monopolist earns an economic profit in the long run. In the graph below, D_M is the industry demand curve, and MC is the industry supply curve. (The monopolist is the industry.)

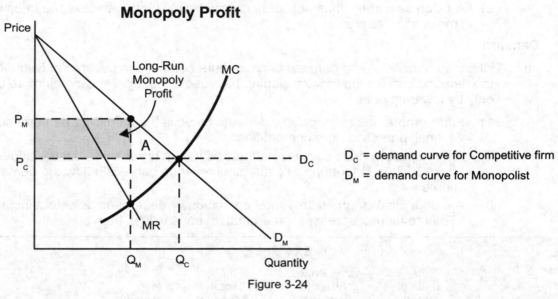

Monopoly Profit

D_C = demand curve for Competitive firm

D_M = demand curve for Monopolist

Figure 3-24

    b.   In a purely competitive industry, the market price and quantity are P_C and Q_C, respectively.

        1)   However, a monopolist restricts output to the profit-maximizing level (Q_M for MR = MC). The resulting price is therefore P_M. MR for the monopolist is less than price, and the MR curve is below the demand curve.

            a)   Accordingly, output is lower ($Q_M < Q_C$), and prices are higher ($P_M > P_C$) than under pure competition.

    c.   Allocation of resources is not efficient because fewer resources are used in the production process than is justified by society's interests.

Stop and review! You have completed the outline for this subunit. Study multiple-choice questions 19 and 20 on page 84.

3.8 MARKET STRUCTURES -- MONOPOLISTIC COMPETITION

1. **Characteristics**

    a. The industry has a large number of firms. The number is fewer than in pure competition, but it suffices to prevent firms from colluding to restrict output and fix prices.

    b. Products are **differentiated**. In pure competition, products are standardized, so price is the only basis for competition. In monopolistic competition, products can be differentiated on a basis other than price, such as quality, brands, and styles. Thus, advertising may be crucial.

    c. Few **barriers** to entry and exit exist. Because firms tend not to be large, great economies of scale do **not** exist. The cost of product differentiation is the most significant barrier to entry.

2. **Short-Run Profit Maximization**

    a. Profit is maximized when MR equals MC. The price is the point on the demand curve corresponding to this quantity.

Short-Run Profits in Monopolistic Competition

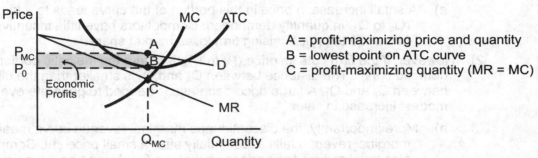

A = profit-maximizing price and quantity
B = lowest point on ATC curve
C = profit-maximizing quantity (MR = MC)

Figure 3-25

1) If the profit-maximizing price (P_{MC}) is higher than the minimum average total cost, the firm earns an **economic profit** in the short run.

2) If the profit-maximizing price (P_{MC}) is lower than the minimum average total cost, the firm incurs a loss in the short run and leaves the industry in the long run.

3. **Long-Run Equilibrium**

    a. In the long run, the economic profit of all firms is $0 because firms will enter a profitable industry and leave an unprofitable one.

    1) In a profitable monopolistically competitive industry, the possibility of earning economic profits attracts new entrants.

    2) The presence of new firms requires all firms to differentiate their products further, increasing average total costs.

    3) Higher costs eliminate the economic profits that attracted the new entrants. The firms least able to absorb the higher costs leave the market.

    4) The remaining firms now have higher costs and steady demand. The economic profits generated earlier are replaced with normal profits.

Stop and review! You have completed the outline for this subunit. Study multiple-choice questions 21 and 22 beginning on page 84.

3.9 MARKET STRUCTURES -- OLIGOPOLY

1. **Characteristics**

   a.   The industry has few large firms. Firms operating in an oligopoly are mutually aware and mutually interdependent. Their decisions as to price, advertising, etc., are significantly dependent on the actions of the other firms.

   b.   Products can be differentiated (e.g., autos) or standardized (e.g., steel).

   c.   Each firm sets price and production level after considering mutual interdependence.

   d.   Entry is difficult because of barriers that can be natural, e.g., an absolute cost advantage, or created, e.g., ongoing advertising or ownership of patents.

2. **Industry Demand**

   a.   The price rigidity normally found in oligopolistic markets can be explained in part by the **kinked demand curve** theory. Its essence is that firms will follow a price decrease by a competitor but not a price increase. This is based on the assumption that a firm in an oligopoly strives to protect existing market shares.

   1)   If price and quantity for the industry are at P_0 and Q_0, a firm that raises its price will move into the elastic portion of the demand curve (P_0 to P_1).

   a)   A small increase in price in this portion of the curve leads to a large decline (Q_0 to Q_1) in quantity demanded. Competitors have little incentive to follow, so the price-raising firm loses market share.

   2)   However, if the firm cuts its price (P_0 to P_2), it enters the inelastic portion of the demand curve. The distance between Q_0 and Q_2 is smaller than the difference between Q_0 and Q_1. A large price decrease is needed to generate even a modest increase in sales.

   a)   More importantly, the discontinuous marginal revenue curve means that marginal revenue falls substantially after a small price cut. Competitors also must reduce their prices so that the first firm gains no market share.

   3)   Price and quantity therefore tend to remain at point A on the demand curve.

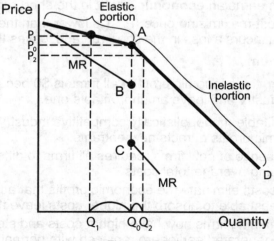

Figure 3-26

b.   To avoid the hazards of the kinked demand curve, price leadership is typical in oligopolistic industries.

1)   Price changes are announced first by a major firm in the industry. After the industry leader has acted, other firms match its price.

3.   **Cartels**

a.   A cartel is a group of oligopolistic firms that agree to set prices. This practice is illegal except in international markets.

1)   The economic effects are similar to those of a monopoly. Each firm restricts output, charges a higher price, and earns the maximum profit.

2)   Thus, each firm in effect becomes a monopolist, but only because it is colluding with other members of the cartel.

b.   Cohesion of the cartel is maintained only if the members maintain their agreed-upon prices and production quotas.

1)   A cartel fails if one member attempts either to increase profits by producing more or to increase market share by cutting prices.

4.   **Boycotts**

a.   A boycott is a concerted effort to avoid doing business with a particular supplier, forcing a leftward shift in the demand curve for that supplier.

1)   Usually, the motivation is moral or ethical rather than purely economic.

5.   **Game Theory**

a.   Game theory is an interactive decision tool used to study strategic behavior.

1)   For example, oligopolistic firms are mutually aware and interdependent. Many of their decisions, such as pricing, depend on the actions of competitor firms.

2)   Accordingly, game theory, with its analysis of rules, strategies, and payoffs, can be used to understand rivalries of many kinds, whether or not economic.

Characteristics of Different Market Structures

	Number of sellers	Barriers to entry and exit	Product nature	Sellers' control over price	Long-run profitability	Firm's elasticity of demand	Examples
Pure Competition	Many	No barrier	Homogeneous	Price taker	Zero	Perfectly elastic	Stock market
Monopoly	One	Completely blocked	Unique	Has control	Positive	Inelastic	Utilities
Monopolistic Competition	A large number of firms (but fewer than in pure competition)	Few barriers	Differentiated	Has control	Zero	Highly elastic	Restaurants, hotels
Oligopoly	Few large firms	High barriers	Differentiated or standardized	Has control (mutually interdependent)	Positive (less than monopoly)	Elastic portion and inelastic portion	Auto makers, steel

Stop and review! You have completed the outline for this subunit. Study multiple-choice questions 23 and 24 on page 85.

3.10 RESOURCE MARKETS AND LABOR

1. **Resource Planning**

    a. Resource planning is essential because profit maximization requires production of the optimal output at the least cost. The resources used in production (e.g., labor and materials) are acquired in markets.

        1) Resource markets also can be structured as pure competition, monopoly, monopolistic competition, and oligopoly.

    b. **Derived** demand is the demand for the **inputs** to production (factors), e.g., lumber, derived from the demand for the **outputs** (final goods), e.g., a house.

2. **Factors Affecting Demand for Resources**

    a. Demand for the final product that the resource produces. An increase (decrease) in the demand for the final output will also increase (decrease) the demand for resources.

    b. Productivity of the resource. As the productivity of an input increases, input price decreases, thereby demand for it increases. Productivity increases when

        1) The proportions of the combination of the resource with other resources shift.
        2) Technical improvements are made in those combining resources.
        3) Technical improvements are made in the resource itself.

    c. Prices of other resources.

        1) If the price of a resource that can substitute for another resource decreases, the demand for the second resource decreases. This result is the **substitution** effect.

            a) For example, as the price of answering machines decreases, answering machines are substituted for telephone operators, and the demand curve for telephone operators shifts to the left.

        2) If two resources are **complements**, a decrease in the price of one causes an increase in the demand for the other.

            a) For example, as the price of computers decreases, the demand curve for computer technicians shifts to the right.

3. **Elasticity of Resource Demand**

    a. The elasticity of resource demand applies to movements along, not the shift of, a demand curve. The elasticity of demand for a resource is directly related to the

        1) Elasticity of demand for the final product. Thus, if the demand for t-shirts becomes more elastic, the demand for cotton becomes more elastic.
        2) Availability of resource substitutes. For example, as more rayon becomes available, the demand for cotton becomes more elastic.
        3) Proportion of total production cost represented by the resource. For example, if cotton is a large proportion of the total cost of blended fabric, an increase in the price of cotton significantly increases the total cost. Accordingly, the firm's demand for cotton becomes more elastic. In this instance, the blend of the fabric would shift to have more lower-cost material and less higher-cost material.

4. **Wage Determination**

    a. A wage is the amount paid to the factor of production (labor) that includes the efforts of blue-collar and white-collar workers, professionals, and small business owners. The term "wage" customarily relates to amounts paid per unit of time.

    b. **Nominal wages** are the amounts paid (and received) without adjustments for inflation. **Real wages** represent the actual purchasing power (goods and services) of nominal wages after adjusting for inflation.

    c. Real wages are determined by the productivity (real output ÷ hours worked) of labor.

        1) As productivity increases, the demand for labor also increases. Given a certain supply, greater demand results in a higher average real wage.

5. **Labor Supply and Demand in a Competitive Market**

    a. Many firms are competing for a large number of equally skilled workers who provide their services independently, so neither firms nor workers can affect the market rate for labor. Thus, both firms and workers are necessarily price takers.

    b. Market demand for labor is the total of the individual firms' demand curves, i.e., their marginal revenue product (MRP) curves.

    c. The market supply curve has a positive slope because, given little unemployment, firms must raise wages to hire additional workers.

        1) The upward slope reflects the need of firms to match the opportunity costs of workers, such as wages paid in employment alternatives or greater leisure.

    d. The wage rate and the level of employment in the market are determined by the intersection of the market labor demand curve and the market labor supply curve, i.e., labor market equilibrium.

    e. Each firm must accept the market wage rate as determined by the point of labor market equilibrium. Thus, the supply curve for labor facing a single firm is perfectly elastic, and marginal resource cost (MRC) is therefore the same for all amounts of labor hired.

Supply and Demand for Labor in a Purely Competitive Resource Market

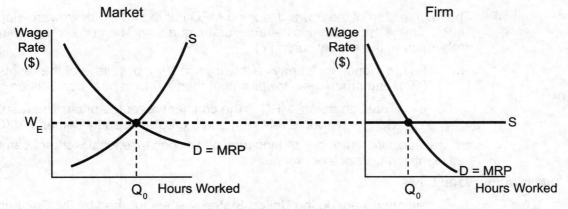

Figure 3-27

6.   **Labor Supply and Demand in a Monopsony**

    a.   In some labor markets, workers have the option of only a single employer.

        1)   A market in which all sellers must sell to a single buyer is a **monopsony**.

    b.   For a monopsonist, the marginal resource cost exceeds the current rate for the resource.

        1)   The reason is that, given an upward-sloping supply curve, additional units of the resource can be obtained only by paying a higher rate for all resource units (labor hours).

            a)   In contrast, a firm in perfect competition pays a constant amount per unit because its consumption is not great enough to influence the rate.

        2)   For example, if the first worker may be hired at a rate of $10, but the second must be paid $11, the MRC is $12 ($11 + $1 increase for the first worker), given the need to pay both the same amount to avoid worker dissatisfaction.

        3)   To maximize its profits, a buyer of resources in a monopsony uses resources until MRP equals MRC.

**Supply and Demand for Labor in
a Monopsony Resource Market**

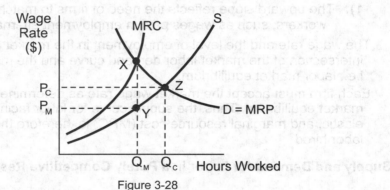

Figure 3-28

        4)   The intersection of the upward-sloping MRC curve and the downward-sloping MRP curve (X) determines the equilibrium quantity. The price is determined by reference to the supply curve (Y).

            a)   Thus, a monopsonist pays a lower price (P_M), buys less of the resource (Q_M), and produces a lower output than a firm in pure competition.

                i)   For such a firm, MRC is the constant resource price. The result is a higher resource rate (P_C) and a greater quantity demanded (Q_C).

    c.   Low-cost transportation reduces monopsony power because local workers can travel more efficiently to distant labor markets.

7.   **Minimum Wage Laws**

    a.   The federal minimum wage in the United States was established by the Fair Labor Standards Act of 1938. The intent was to provide all workers with a level of pay high enough to avoid poverty by setting a price floor for wages.

    b.   Against the Minimum Wage

        1)   Because a wage rate above equilibrium is established by law, unemployment is increased. It would be far better for people with marginal skills to have work at some level of pay than to be idle.

        2)   The higher labor cost may drive some firms out of business.

    c.   For the Minimum Wage

       1)   Because many labor markets are monopsonies, minimum wage laws raise pay without increasing unemployment.

       2)   The minimum wage may improve productivity.

           a)   Because firms cannot pay a substandard wage no matter how menial the task, employers may be encouraged to move workers into productive activities.

           b)   A minimum wage may reduce employee turnover, allowing the retention of experienced workers.

8.   **General Pricing Approaches**

    a.   **Cost-Based Pricing**

       1)   This process begins with a cost determination followed by setting a price that will recover the value chain costs and provide the desired return on investment.

       2)   When an industry is characterized by significant product differentiation, e.g., the automobile industry, cost-based and market-based pricing approaches are combined.

           a)   Basing prices on cost assumes that costs can be correctly determined. Thus, cost-behavior patterns, cost traceability, and cost drivers become important determinants of profitability.

       3)   A cost-plus price equals the cost plus a markup. Cost may be defined in many ways. Most companies use either absorption manufacturing cost or total cost when calculating the price. Variable costs may be used as the basis for cost, but then fixed costs must be covered by the markup.

    b.   **Market-Based Pricing**

       1)   This approach involves basing prices on the product's perceived value and competitors' actions rather than on the seller's cost. Nonprice variables in the marketing mix augment the perceived value. Market comparables, which are assets with similar characteristics, are used to estimate the price of a product.

           a)   For example, a cup of coffee may have a higher price at an expensive restaurant than at a fast-food outlet.

       2)   Market-based pricing is typical when many competitors exist, and the product is undifferentiated, as in many commodities markets, e.g., agricultural products or natural gas.

    c.   **Competition-Based Pricing**

       1)   Going-rate pricing bases price largely on competitors' prices.
       2)   Sealed-bid pricing bases price on the perception of competitors' prices.

    d.   **New Product Pricing**

       1)   **Price skimming** sets an introductory price relatively high to (a) attract buyers who are not concerned about price and (b) recover research and development costs.

       2)   **Penetration pricing** sets an introductory price relatively low to gain deep market penetration quickly.

    e.   **Pricing by Intermediaries**

       1)   Using markups tied closely to the price paid for a product
       2)   Using markdowns -- a reduction in the original price set on a product

      f.   **Price Adjustments**

          1)   Geographical Pricing

              a)   FOB-origin pricing charges each customer its actual freight costs.

              b)   A seller that uses uniform delivered pricing charges the same price, inclusive of shipping, to all customers regardless of their location.

                   i)   This policy is easy to administer, permits the company to advertise one price nationwide, and facilitates marketing to faraway customers.

              c)   **Zone pricing** sets differential freight charges for customers on the basis of their location. Customers are not charged actual average freight costs.

          2)   Discounts and Allowances

              a)   Cash discounts encourage prompt payment, improve cash flows, and avoid bad debts.

              b)   Quantity discounts encourage large volume purchases.

              c)   Trade (functional) discounts are offered to other members of the marketing channel for performing certain services, such as selling.

              d)   Seasonal discounts are offered for sales out of season. They help smooth production.

              e)   Allowances (e.g., trade-in and promotional allowances) reduce list prices.

          3)   **Discriminatory pricing** adjusts for differences among customers, the forms of a product, or locations.

          4)   **Promotional pricing** temporarily reduces prices below list or even cost to stimulate sales.

          5)   **Value pricing** involves redesigning products to improve quality without raising prices or offering the same quality at lower prices.

          6)   **International pricing** adjusts prices to local conditions.

      g.   **Illegal Pricing**

          1)   Certain pricing tactics are illegal. For example, pricing products below cost to harm competitors (predatory pricing) is illegal.

              a)   The U.S. Supreme Court has held that a price is predatory if (1) it is below an appropriate measure of costs, and (2) the seller has a reasonable prospect of recovering its losses in the future through higher prices or greater market share.

          2)   Price discrimination among customers also is illegal. Pricing is illegal if it has the effect of lessening competition.

          3)   Another improper form of pricing is collusive pricing. Conspiracies to restrict output and set artificially high prices violate antitrust laws.

          4)   Still another inappropriate pricing tactic is selling below cost in other countries (dumping), which may trigger retaliatory tariffs and other sanctions.

      h.   **Target pricing** is the expected market price for a product or service, given knowledge of consumers' perceptions of value and competitors' responses.

Stop and review! You have completed the outline for this subunit. Study multiple-choice questions 25 and 26 on page 86.

QUESTIONS

3.1 Demand, Supply, and Equilibrium

1. If the average household income increases and there is relatively little change in the price of a normal good, then the

- A. Supply curve will shift to the left.
- B. Quantity demanded will move farther down the demand curve.
- C. Demand will shift to the left.
- D. Demand curve will shift to the right.

Answer (D) is correct.
    REQUIRED: The result of an increase in income given little change in the price of a normal good.
    DISCUSSION: The demand schedule is a relationship between the prices of a product and the quantity demanded at each price, holding other determinants of the quantity demanded constant. A movement along an existing demand curve occurs when the price is changed. A shift in the curve itself occurs when any of the determinants changes. Such shifts can be caused by a change in the tastes and preferences of consumers toward a product, for example, as a result of a successful advertising campaign, an increase in consumer income (if a product is a normal good), or changes in the prices of substitute or complementary products. An increase in consumer income would shift the demand curve to the right and result in greater consumption of the product at each price.
    Answer (A) is incorrect. The increase in income shifts the demand, not the supply, curve. Answer (B) is incorrect. Moving down an existing demand curve is the effect of a lower price. The change in income shifts the economy to a new demand curve. Answer (C) is incorrect. A shift to the left means that consumers will buy fewer products at each price. This leftward shift in response to increased income is characteristic of an inferior good, not a normal good. The demand for inferior goods is inversely related to income. Hamburger is an inferior good, and steak is a normal good.

2. The demand curve for a normal good is

- A. Upward sloping because firms produce more at higher prices.
- B. Upward sloping because higher-priced goods are of higher quality.
- C. Vertical.
- D. Downward sloping because of the income and substitution effects of price changes.

Answer (D) is correct.
    REQUIRED: The true statement about the demand curve for a normal good.
    DISCUSSION: The demand curve for a normal good is downward sloping to the right. At high prices, the amount demanded is relatively low. As prices decrease, the amount demanded increases. The substitution effect is the change in the cost of a good relative to others that will cause a cheaper good to be substituted for more expensive ones. The income effect is the change in purchasing power experienced by consumers as a result of a price change (real income increases or decreases). Both of these effects cause the price of a product and the quantity demanded to be inversely related.
    Answer (A) is incorrect. An upward-sloping demand curve suggests that consumers purchase more of a product if its price is raised. Answer (B) is incorrect. An upward-sloping demand curve suggests that consumers purchase more of a product if its price is raised. Answer (C) is incorrect. A vertical demand curve signifies that the quantity demanded does not change with price.

3. The situation depicted in the graph below could be caused by

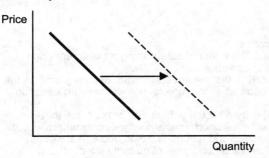

- A. A price cut by all producers.
- B. A price hike by all producers.
- C. A rise in the country's population.
- D. An improvement in manufacturers' productivity.

Answer (C) is correct.
    REQUIRED: The possible cause of a rightward demand curve shift.
    DISCUSSION: A downward-sloping curve relating price to quantity depicts the demand schedule for a normal good. When a country's population grows, producers can sell more of their products at every price level. This is depicted as a rightward shift in the demand curve.
    Answer (A) is incorrect. A price cut by all producers would be depicted as a downward movement along a fixed curve. Answer (B) is incorrect. A price hike by all producers would be depicted as an upward movement along a fixed curve. Answer (D) is incorrect. An improvement in manufacturers' productivity would be depicted by a shift in the (upward-sloping) supply curve, not the (downward-sloping) demand curve.

3.2 Elasticity

4. If the coefficient of elasticity is zero, then the consumer demand for the product is said to be

    A. Perfectly inelastic.

    B. Perfectly elastic.

    C. Unit inelastic.

    D. Unit elastic.

Answer (A) is correct.
    REQUIRED: The applicable term when the coefficient of elasticity is zero.
    DISCUSSION: When the coefficient of elasticity (percentage change in quantity ÷ percentage change in price) is less than one, demand is inelastic. When the coefficient is zero, demand is perfectly inelastic.
    Answer (B) is incorrect. Demand is perfectly elastic when the coefficient is infinite. Answer (C) is incorrect. "Unitary inelasticity" is not a meaningful term in this context. Answer (D) is incorrect. Unitary elasticity exists when the coefficient is exactly one.

5. As the price for a particular product changes, the quantity of the product demanded changes according to the following schedule.

Total Quantity Demanded	Price per Unit
100	$50
150	45
200	40
225	35
230	30
232	25

Using the arc method, the price elasticity of demand for this product when the price decreases from $50 to $45 is

    A. 0.20

    B. 10.00

    C. 0.10

    D. 3.80

Answer (D) is correct.
    REQUIRED: The price elasticity of demand using the arc method.
    DISCUSSION: A product's price elasticity of demand is measured as the percentage change in quantity demanded divided by the percentage change in price. When price falls from $50 to $45, the coefficient is 3.8, calculated as follows:

$$E_d = [(150 - 100) \div (150 + 100)] \div [(\$50 - \$45) \div (\$50 + \$45)]$$
$$= (50 \div 250) \div (\$5 \div \$95)$$
$$= 20.0\% \div 5.26\%$$
$$= 3.8$$

    Answer (A) is incorrect. The figure of 0.20 equals the 10% decline in price divided by the 50% change in quantity demanded. Answer (B) is incorrect. The figure of 10.00 assumes a 5% change in price. It also does not calculate the change over the sum of the endpoints of the range. Answer (C) is incorrect. The figure of 0.10 is the percentage change in price.

6. Last week, the quantity of apples demanded fell by 6%. If this was a result of a 10% price increase, what is the price elasticity of demand for apples?

    A. 1.67

    B. 1.06

    C. 0.16

    D. 0.60

Answer (D) is correct.
    REQUIRED: The price elasticity of demand.
    DISCUSSION: The price elasticity of demand is calculated by dividing the percentage change in quantity demanded by the percentage change in price. Thus, the change in quantity of 6% divided by the 10% price increase produces an elasticity of 0.6.
    Answer (A) is incorrect. The inverse of the elasticity is 1.67. Answer (B) is incorrect. Adding the 6% quantity decline to 1 results in 1.06. Answer (C) is incorrect. The price elasticity of demand is found by dividing the 6% quantity decline by the 10% price increase, not by adding them.

3.3 Government Action in the Market

7. If a rent control law in a competitive housing market establishes a maximum or ceiling rent that is above the market or equilibrium rent,

    A. The law has no effect on the rental market.

    B. A surplus of rental housing units will result.

    C. Supply will decrease as price increases.

    D. Demand will increase as price increases.

Answer (A) is correct.
    REQUIRED: The effect of establishing a maximum price above the equilibrium price.
    DISCUSSION: If the market equilibrium price is less than the maximum rent allowed, a rent control law will have no effect on the market.
    Answer (B) is incorrect. If a minimum or floor rent that is above the market equilibrium rent is charged, consumers would demand less housing and a surplus would occur. Answer (C) is incorrect. Price is a determinant of quantity supplied, not supply. Answer (D) is incorrect. Price is a determinant of quantity demanded, not demand.

8. A government price support program will

A. Lead to surpluses.

B. Lead to shortages.

C. Improve the rationing function of prices.

D. Encourage firms to leave the industry.

Answer (A) is correct.
    REQUIRED: The effect of a government price support program.
    DISCUSSION: A government price support program, which sets a price higher than the market price, will cause producers to supply more goods than can be absorbed by the market. The effect will be surpluses because the amount supplied will exceed the amount demanded. In these cases, the government must buy up the surplus and either destroy it or seek other distribution channels; both are highly inefficient outcomes.
    Answer (B) is incorrect. No shortages will occur. Suppliers will be induced by the higher-than-equilibrium price to produce more than the amount demanded. Answer (C) is incorrect. No rationing would occur. Consumers will be able to buy all they desire because supply will exceed demand. Answer (D) is incorrect. Firms will be encouraged to enter the industry by the availability of greater revenue than that provided by consumer demand. In fact, price support programs are often designed with the intention of keeping marginal firms from leaving the industry.

9. Government price regulations in competitive markets that set maximum or ceiling prices below the equilibrium price will in the short run

A. Cause demand to decrease.

B. Cause supply to increase.

C. Create shortages of that product.

D. Produce a surplus of the product.

Answer (C) is correct.
    REQUIRED: The short-run effect of price ceilings that are below the equilibrium price.
    DISCUSSION: A price ceiling lower than the equilibrium price causes shortages to develop. The artificially low price results in an amount supplied less than that at the equilibrium price. It also causes consumers to demand more of the commodity than at the equilibrium price.
    Answer (A) is incorrect. The amount demanded will increase as a result of the artificially low price. Answer (B) is incorrect. The amount supplied will decline as a result of the artificially low price. Answer (D) is incorrect. Surpluses do not occur as a result of price ceilings regardless of whether they are above or below the equilibrium price.

3.4 Profits and Costs

10. A corporation's net income as presented on its income statement is usually

A. More than its economic profits because opportunity costs are not considered in calculating net income.

B. More than its economic profits because economists do not consider interest payments to be costs.

C. Equal to its economic profits.

D. Less than its economic profits because accountants include labor costs, while economists exclude labor costs.

Answer (A) is correct.
    REQUIRED: The true statement about a corporation's net income.
    DISCUSSION: Economic (pure) profit equals total revenue minus economic costs. Economic costs are defined by economists as total costs, which are the sum of outlay costs, and opportunity costs, which are the values of productive resources in their best alternative uses. The return sufficient to induce the entrepreneur to remain in business (normal profit) is an implicit (opportunity) cost. Net income as computed under generally accepted accounting principles considers only explicit costs, not such implicit costs as normal profit and the opportunity costs associated with not using assets for alternative purposes. Thus, net income will be higher than economic profit because the former fails to include a deduction for opportunity costs, for example, the salary forgone by an entrepreneur who chooses to be self-employed.
    Answer (B) is incorrect. Both economists and accountants treat interest as a cost. Answer (C) is incorrect. Economic profits will be less than net income. Answer (D) is incorrect. Economic profits will be less than net income.

11. A normal profit is

    A. The same as an economic profit.

    B. The same as the accountant's bottom line.

    C. An explicit or out-of-pocket cost.

    D. A cost of resources from an economic perspective.

Answer (D) is correct.
    REQUIRED: The true statement about normal profit.
    DISCUSSION: Normal profit is the level of profit necessary to induce entrepreneurs to enter and remain in the market. Economists view this profit as an implicit cost of economic activity.
    Answer (A) is incorrect. Economic (pure) profit is the residual return in excess of normal profit. Economic profit equals accounting profit minus implicit costs. Normal profit occurs when total revenue equals total costs (explicit and implicit), that is, when economic profit equals zero. Answer (B) is incorrect. Accounting profit is the excess of total revenue over explicit costs (out-of-pocket payments to outsiders). Answer (C) is incorrect. A normal profit is an implicit cost.

12. In the economic theory of production and cost, the short run is defined to be a production process

    A. That spans a time period of less than 1 year in length.

    B. In which there is insufficient time to vary the amount of all inputs.

    C. That is subject to economies of scale.

    D. That always produces economic profits.

Answer (B) is correct.
    REQUIRED: The short run in the economic theory of production and cost.
    DISCUSSION: The short run is defined as a period so brief that a firm has insufficient time to vary the amount of all inputs. Thus, the quantity of one or more inputs is fixed. The long run is a period long enough that all inputs, including plant capacity, can be varied.
    Answer (A) is incorrect. The short run can be more or less than a year depending upon a firm's ability to change its inputs. Answer (C) is incorrect. Economies of scale are associated with the long run. Answer (D) is incorrect. Economic profits may be earned, either in the long or short run, when a firm earns more than the profits needed for it to remain in operation.

3.5 Marginal Analysis

13. Because of economies of scale, as output from production expands,

    A. The short-run average cost of production decreases.

    B. The long-run average cost of production increases.

    C. The long-run total cost decreases.

    D. The slope of the demand curve increases.

Answer (A) is correct.
    REQUIRED: The effect of economies of scale.
    DISCUSSION: When a firm experiences economies of scale, the average unit cost of production decreases as production increases. This phenomenon is attributable to spreading fixed costs over a greater number of units of output. Both the short-run and long-run average costs are lower because of economies of scale.
    Answer (B) is incorrect. Long-run unit production costs decline with economies of scale. Answer (C) is incorrect. Total costs increase with increased production; only the average cost per unit declines. Answer (D) is incorrect. Changes in the supply curve do not affect the demand curve.

14. When long-run average cost is declining over a range of increasing output, the firm is experiencing

    A. Increasing fixed costs.

    B. Technological efficiency.

    C. Decreasing returns.

    D. Economies of scale.

Answer (D) is correct.
    REQUIRED: The condition experienced when long-run average cost declines over a range of increasing output.
    DISCUSSION: When long-run average cost declines as output increases, the firm is experiencing economies of scale. Average cost falls when marginal cost is below it and rises when marginal cost is above it. Average cost reaches its minimum when it equals marginal cost. Some of the reasons for this phenomenon are increased specialization and division of labor, better use and specialization of management, and use of more efficient machinery and equipment.
    Answer (A) is incorrect. An increase in fixed costs could cause average costs to increase. Also, by definition, all long-run costs are variable. Answer (B) is incorrect. Technological efficiency refers to the ratio of physical output of a given technology and the maximum output that is possible. An increase in technological efficiency is only one of the ways that economies of scale can occur. Answer (C) is incorrect. A decline in average cost means the firm is experiencing increasing returns, not decreasing returns.

15. Because of the existence of economies of scale, business firms may find that

   A. Each additional unit of labor is less efficient than the previous unit.

   B. As more labor is added to a factory, increases in output will diminish in the short run.

   C. Increasing the size of a factory will result in lower average costs.

   D. Increasing the size of a factory will result in lower total costs.

Answer (C) is correct.
   REQUIRED: The true statement about economies of scale.
   DISCUSSION: As most firms expand output, average costs of production initially tend to decline. The reasons for this include increased specialization and division of labor, better use and specialization of management, and use of more efficient machinery and equipment. Consequently, increasing the size of a factory often results in lower average costs.
   Answer (A) is incorrect. Economies of scale refer to the savings in costs as production increases; less efficient labor would lead to higher costs. Answer (B) is incorrect. Output should increase, although average productivity may or may not change. Answer (D) is incorrect. Increasing factory size will normally increase total costs but result in lower average costs.

3.6 Market Structures -- Pure Competition

16. Which one of the following is **not** a key assumption of perfect competition?

   A. Firms sell a homogeneous product.

   B. Customers are indifferent about which firm they buy from.

   C. The level of a firm's output is small relative to the industry's total output.

   D. Each firm can price its product above the industry price.

Answer (D) is correct.
   REQUIRED: The assumption not made about perfect competition.
   DISCUSSION: Perfect competition is characterized by a market structure with many buyers and sellers acting independently, a homogeneous or standardized product, free entry into and exit from the market, perfect information, no control over the industry price, and the absence of nonprice competition. Moreover, customers are indifferent about which firm they buy from because price is the only difference between one seller and the next.
   Answer (A) is incorrect. A homogeneous product is a key assumption of perfect competition. Answer (B) is incorrect. Customer indifference regarding choice of seller is a key assumption of perfect competition. Answer (C) is incorrect. Small firm output relative to the industry is a key assumption of perfect competition.

17. Mr. Smith is hired as a consultant to a firm in a perfectly competitive industry. At the current output level the price is $20, the average variable cost is $15, average total cost is $22, and marginal cost is $20. In order to maximize profits in the short-run, Mr. Smith will recommend that the firm should

   A. Not change output.

   B. Decrease production.

   C. Increase production.

   D. Shut down.

Answer (A) is correct.
   REQUIRED: The action a firm should take when marginal cost equals selling price.
   DISCUSSION: For profit maximization, a firm operating under pure competition should produce the level of output at which price is equal to marginal cost. Since price and marginal cost are both $20, the firm is already at its profit-maximizing position.
   Answer (B) is incorrect. A firm should not decrease output when price is at least equal to marginal cost. Answer (C) is incorrect. There is no incentive to increase production when marginal cost is equal to selling price. Answer (D) is incorrect. A firm should not shut down as long as price exceeds variable cost; any excess of price over variable cost provides a contribution toward the coverage of fixed costs.

18. All of the following are true about perfect competition **except** that

   A. There is free market entry without large capital costs for entry.

   B. There are many firms participating in the market.

   C. In the long run, an increase in profit will have no effect on the number of firms in the market.

   D. Firms are price takers.

Answer (C) is correct.
   REQUIRED: The false statement about perfect competition.
   DISCUSSION: Perfect competition assumes a large number of buyers and sellers that act independently, a homogeneous or standardized product, free entry into and exit from the market, perfect information, no nonprice competition, no control over prices (sellers are price takers rather than price setters), and an equilibrium price equal to the average total cost. Given free entry into the market and perfect information, an increase in profits in the industry will attract new firms. This will have the long-run effect of reducing the price to the level at which no economic profits are earned.
   Answer (A) is incorrect. An absence of barriers to entry is a characteristic of pure competition. Answer (B) is incorrect. A large number of firms is a characteristic of pure competition. Answer (D) is incorrect. Firms in pure competition must accept the market price.

3.7   Market Structures -- Monopoly

19. A characteristic of a monopoly is that

    A. A monopoly will produce when marginal revenue is equal to marginal cost.

    B. There is a unique relationship between the market price and the quantity supplied.

    C. In optimizing profits, a monopoly will increase its supply curve to where the demand curve becomes inelastic.

    D. There are multiple prices for the product to the consumer.

Answer (A) is correct.

REQUIRED: The characteristic of a monopoly.

DISCUSSION: A monopoly consists of a single firm with a unique product. Such a firm has significant price control. For profit maximization, it increases production until its marginal revenue equals its marginal cost. In a monopoly, price will be higher and output lower than in perfect competition.

Answer (B) is incorrect. The monopolist is in control of the quantity supplied. Thus, the supply can be limited to produce the profit-maximizing price. Answer (C) is incorrect. To optimize profits, a monopoly will produce at the point when its marginal revenue equals its marginal cost. Answer (D) is incorrect. There is only one price when a monopoly exists.

20. Any business firm that has the ability to control the price of the product it sells

    A. Faces a downward-sloping demand curve.

    B. Has a supply curve that is horizontal.

    C. Has a demand curve that is horizontal.

    D. Will sell all output produced.

Answer (A) is correct.

REQUIRED: The true statement about a business firm with the ability to control the price of its product.

DISCUSSION: A firm that can control the price of its product is a monopolist. In a monopoly, the industry demand curve is also the firm's demand curve. The demand curve is downward-sloping since the lower the price, the higher the demand for a product.

Answer (B) is incorrect. A horizontal supply curve implies that the company will produce any quantity of output at the constant price. The ability to control one's price implies a changing price level. Answer (C) is incorrect. A horizontal demand curve implies an unchanging price. Answer (D) is incorrect. The firm will not be able to sell all of its output if it sets the price higher than what consumers were willing to pay. Also, a monopolist's incentive is not to sell the maximum that can be produced, but to sell the amount that maximizes profits.

3.8   Market Structures -- Monopolistic Competition

21. All of the following are characteristics of monopolistic competition **except** that

    A. The firms sell a homogeneous product.

    B. The firms tend not to recognize the reaction of competitors when determining prices.

    C. Individual firms have some control over the price of the product.

    D. The consumer demand curve is highly elastic.

Answer (A) is correct.

REQUIRED: The item not a characteristic of monopolistic competition.

DISCUSSION: Monopolistic competition assumes a large number of firms with differentiated (heterogeneous) products and relatively easy entry into the market. Sellers have some price control because of product differentiation. Monopolistic competition is characterized by nonprice competition, such as advertising, service after the sale, and emphasis on trademark quality. In the short run, firms equate marginal revenue and marginal cost. In the long run, firms tend to earn normal (not economic) profits, and price exceeds marginal cost, resulting in an underallocation of resources. Firms produce less than the ideal output, and the industry is populated by too many firms that are too small in size. Price is higher and output less than in pure competition.

Answer (B) is incorrect. Responses to competitors' actions are unnecessary if products are sufficiently differentiated to make price competition meaningless. Answer (C) is incorrect. Product differentiation permits some price control. Answer (D) is incorrect. The availability of close substitutes makes the product demand curve elastic.

22. Entry into monopolistic competition is

A. Blocked.

B. Difficult, with significant obstacles.

C. Rare, as significant capital is required.

D. Relatively easy, with only a few obstacles.

Answer (D) is correct.
REQUIRED: The true statement about entry into monopolistic competition.
DISCUSSION: Monopolistic competition is characterized by the existence of a large number of firms, differentiated products, relative ease of entry, some control of price by the firms, and significant nonprice competition (e.g., by advertising). Entry into monopolistic competition is more difficult than entry into pure competition, but it is relatively easy compared with entry into a monopoly.
Answer (A) is incorrect. Entry is possible and relatively easy. Blocked entry is typical of monopoly. Answer (B) is incorrect. Difficult entry is typical of oligopoly. Answer (C) is incorrect. Given the large number of firms, most are likely to be small, with correspondingly low economies of scale and capital needs.

3.9 Market Structures -- Oligopoly

23. The distinguishing characteristic of oligopolistic markets is

A. A single seller of a homogeneous product with no close substitute.

B. A single seller of a heterogeneous product with no close substitute.

C. Lack of entry and exit barriers in the industry.

D. Mutual interdependence of firm pricing and output decisions.

Answer (D) is correct.
REQUIRED: The distinguishing characteristic of oligopolistic markets.
DISCUSSION: The oligopoly model is much less specific than the other market structures, but there are typically few firms in the industry. Thus, the decisions of rival firms do not go unnoticed. Products can be either differentiated or standardized. Prices tend to be rigid (sticky) because of the interdependence among firms. Entry is difficult because of either natural or created barriers. Price leadership is typical in oligopolistic industries. Under price leadership, price changes are announced first by a major firm. Once the industry leader has spoken, other firms in the industry match the price charged by the leader. The mutual interdependence of the firms influences both pricing and output decisions.
Answer (A) is incorrect. Oligopolies contain several firms; a single seller is characteristic of a monopoly. Answer (B) is incorrect. Oligopolies contain several firms; a single seller is characteristic of a monopoly. Answer (C) is incorrect. Oligopolies are typified by barriers to entry; that is the reason the industry has only a few firms.

24. An oligopolist faces a "kinked" demand curve. This terminology indicates that

A. When an oligopolist lowers its price, the other firms in the oligopoly will match the price reduction, but if the oligopolist raises its price, the other firms will ignore the price change.

B. An oligopolist faces a non-linear demand for its product, and price changes will have little effect on demand for that product.

C. An oligopolist can sell its product at any price but, after the "saturation point," another oligopolist will lower its price and therefore shift the demand curve to the left.

D. Consumers have no effect on the demand curve, and an oligopolist can shape the curve to optimize its own efficiency.

Answer (A) is correct.
REQUIRED: The meaning of an oligopolist's kinked demand curve.
DISCUSSION: An oligopoly consists of a few firms. Thus, the decisions of rivals do not go unnoticed. Prices tend to be rigid (sticky) because of the interdependence among firms. Because competitors respond only to certain price changes by one of the firms in an oligopolistic industry, the demand curve for an oligopolist tends to be kinked. Price decreases are usually matched by price decreases, but price increases are often not followed. If other firms do not match a lower price, a price decrease by an oligopolist would capture more of the market. If other firms match the price decrease, less of the market will be captured.
Answer (B) is incorrect. Price changes will have an effect on demand for an oligopolist's product. Answer (C) is incorrect. An oligopolist must essentially match the price of other firms in the industry. A change in price does not shift the demand curve. Answer (D) is incorrect. An oligopolist cannot shape its demand curve.

3.10 Resource Markets and Labor

25. Derived demand can best be described as

    A. The demand derived purely from the market structure of a particular industry.

    B. The demand for a final product generated by the demand for a complementary good.

    C. The demand for an input generated by the demand for the final product.

    D. The demand for a final product generated by an abundant supply of inputs.

Answer (C) is correct.
REQUIRED: The definition of derived demand.
DISCUSSION: Derived demand is the demand for the inputs to the production process (sometimes called factors) derived from the demand for the outputs of the process (i.e., final goods).
Answer (A) is incorrect. Derived demand is the demand for an input generated by the demand for the final product. Answer (B) is incorrect. The demand for complementary goods is not properly referred to as derived demand. Answer (D) is incorrect. Demand for a final product based on the supply of its inputs is not a meaningful economic concept.

26. The amounts paid to laborers are

    A. Real wages.

    B. Nominal wages.

    C. Productivity wages.

    D. Minimum wages.

Answer (B) is correct.
REQUIRED: The term for wages actually paid to laborers.
DISCUSSION: Nominal wages are the amounts actually paid (and received), while real wages represent the purchasing power of goods and services that can be acquired by the nominal wages. The level of real wages is determined by the productivity of labor. As productivity increases, the demand for labor also increases.
Answer (A) is incorrect. Real wages represent the purchasing power of the wages paid. Answer (C) is incorrect. Productivity wages is a nonsense term. Answer (D) is incorrect. A minimum wage is established by law. It is a nominal wage, but all amounts paid to laborers are not minimum wages.

STUDY UNIT FOUR
MACROECONOMICS

(26 pages of outline)

Macroeconomics is the study of how the aggregate economy behaves as a whole. The focus is primarily on forecasting national income by examining predictable patterns and trends and their influence on each other. Gross domestic product, employment/unemployment, inflation, and other factors are the primary target variables for governments who use monetary and fiscal policy tools to achieve their goals of growth, full employment, and stable prices. Fiscal policies of spending and taxation are the primary tools of governmental bodies (Subunits 4.4 through 4.6). Monetary policy is the tool of the Federal Reserve (Subunits 4.8 and 4.9). This is a "top down" approach.

4.1 GDP -- EXPENDITURES APPROACH

1. **Measuring an Economy's Aggregate Output**

    a. **Gross domestic product (GDP)** is the principal measure of national economic performance.

       1) U.S. GDP measures the total market value of all final goods and services produced within the boundaries of the U.S. by domestic- or foreign-owned sources during a specified period (usually a year).

       2) A visual depiction of annual GDP is below.

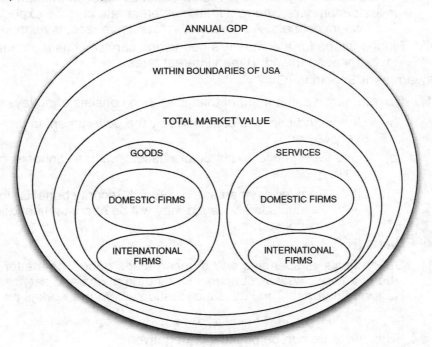

Figure 4-1

3) GDP is calculated without regard to the ownership of productive resources. Thus, the value of the output of a U.S.-owned factory abroad is excluded, but the output of a foreign-owned factory in the U.S. is included.

b. The three methods of measuring GDP are (1) the expenditures approach (described below), (2) the income approach (described in the next subunit), and (3) the production approach (described below).

1) The production approach calculates GDP by estimating the gross value added within the country.

a) GDP is the sum of the final uses of the goods and services (ignoring intermediate uses, i.e., cost of materials and supplies) measured at the purchasers' prices minus the value of goods and services imported.

2. **Expenditures Approach**

a. The expenditures approach, the simplest of the three methods, calculates GDP as the sum of all expenditures within the economy.

$$Gross\ domestic\ product\ (GDP)\ =\ C\ +\ I\ +\ G\ +\ NX$$

b. Consumer Spending (C)

1) This measure is by far the largest component of GDP. Its most important determinant is personal incomes.

2) Changes in incomes do not affect GDP dollar-for-dollar. For every additional dollar consumers receive in income, some portion is spent, and the remainder is saved.

c. Investment Spending (I)

1) Business investments create jobs and income. Examples are purchases of equipment and machinery, construction (including construction of leased residences), and changes in inventory.

2) Business investment is by far the most volatile component. Investment reflects the level of optimism about future demand, and business optimism is subject to wide and sudden variations.

3) Investment demand has an inverse relationship with the real market interest rate. To determine whether to invest or deposit money in the banking system, the investor compares the real market interest rate and the expected rate of return from the investment. As the interest rate decreases, investment increases.

4) Final demand for a company's goods and services has more influence on investment spending (I) than interest rates.

d. Government Spending (G)

1) Government's component of total spending consists of outlays for

a) Goods and services consumed by the government in providing public services and

b) Long-lived public infrastructure assets, such as schools, bridges, and military bases.

i) Transfer payments (e.g., Social Security benefits) to its citizens are not included because they will be spent on final goods and services by consumers.

e. Net Exports (NX)

1) GDP reflects all spending on American-made goods, no matter who purchases them, and excludes American spending on goods and services produced abroad (imports). The key is the location where the work is performed.

$$Net\ exports\ (NX)\ =\ Exports\ (X)\ -\ Imports\ (M)$$

This measure can be positive or negative.

f.   The following is a useful memory aid for the expenditures approach:

Creativity   = **C**onsumer spending
Increases   = **I**nvestment spending
Greenland's = **G**overnment spending
Net   = **N**et
e**X**ports   = E**x**ports

EXAMPLE

Expenditures Approach

	In Billions
Consumption by households (C)	$6,000
Investment by businesses (I)	1,200
Government purchases (G)	2,020
Net exports (NX)	(400)
Gross domestic product (GDP)	**$8,820**

---

g.   A change in any of the four expenditure functions causes equilibrium GDP to rise or fall.

1)   Consumer spending (C). If consumers increase their spending, for example, because they expect higher incomes or lower taxes, the consumption function shifts upward to reflect greater national output (e.g., autos purchased for personal use).

2)   Investment spending (I). If businesses increase their spending on productive assets, for example, because new technology is available or real interest rates are lower, the investment function shifts upward to reflect greater national output (e.g., autos purchased for taxi companies).

3)   Government spending (G). If government increases its spending, for example, because of increased defense spending, the government function shifts upward to reflect greater national output (e.g., autos purchased by the military).

4)   Net exports (NX). If American firms sell more products abroad, the net exports function shifts upward to reflect greater national output. If exports eventually exceed imports, this measure will be positive (e.g., autos sold to foreigners).

Stop and review! You have completed the outline for this subunit. Study multiple-choice questions 1 and 2 on page 113.

4.2 GDP -- INCOME APPROACH

1.   **Components of the Income Approach**

a.   The income approach determines the same total GDP as the expenditures approach. But the income calculation is more complex.

GDP Calculation -- Income Approach

	In Billions
Salaries and wages	$ x,xxx
Rents	x,xxx
Interest	x,xxx
Proprietor and partnership incomes	x,xxx
Corporate profits	x,xxx
National income	$xx,xxx
Indirect business taxes	x,xxx
Net foreign factor income	x,xxx
Net domestic product	$xx,xxx
Capital consumption allowance	x,xxx
Gross domestic product	$xx,xxx

b.   The income approach also produces two intermediate measures that are significant: national income and net domestic product.

1)   **National income (NI)** is all income generated by U.S.-owned resources, no matter where located. Employee compensation is by far the largest component.

a)   The following is a useful memory aid for national income:

Scholarly = Salaries and wages
Research = Rents
Interests = Interest
Promote = Proprietor and partnership incomes
Competition = Corporate profits

2)   **Net domestic product (NDP)** measures income generated in the U.S., regardless of the ownership of the productive resources. It is the sum of NI and the following two items:

a)   Indirect business taxes (sales taxes, excise taxes, etc.), are collected by businesses and transmitted to some level of government.

b)   Net foreign-factor income is the excess of (1) income generated in the U.S. from foreign-owned resources over (2) income generated in other countries from U.S.-owned resources.

i)   The following is a useful memory aid for net domestic product:

I = Indirect
Bought = Business
Two = Taxes
Nets = Net
For = Foreign
Fishing = Factor
Income = Income

3)   **GDP** is calculated by adding to NDP an allowance for the capital stock consumed or lost in the process of generating income. Thus, GDP equals NDP plus a capital consumption allowance (GDP = NDP + Depreciation of capital).

EXAMPLE

	In Billions
Salaries and wages	$3,200
Rents	500
Interest	500
Proprietor and partnership incomes	200
Corporate profits	2,400
National income	**$6,800**
Indirect business taxes	320
Net foreign factor income	200
Net domestic product	**$7,320**
Capital consumption allowance	1,500
Gross domestic product	**$8,820**

---

2.   **Other Income Measures**

a.   **Personal income (PI)** is all income received by individuals.

b.   **Disposable income (DI)** is the after-tax income of individuals.

EXAMPLE	
	In Billions
National income (NI)	**$6,800**
Social Security contributions	(600)
Corporate income taxes	(100)
Undistributed corporate profits	(100)
Transfer payments	1,400
Personal income (PI)	**$7,400**
Personal taxes	(1,600)
Disposable income (DI)	**$5,800**

3. **Graphical Depiction**

Flow of National Income (NI)

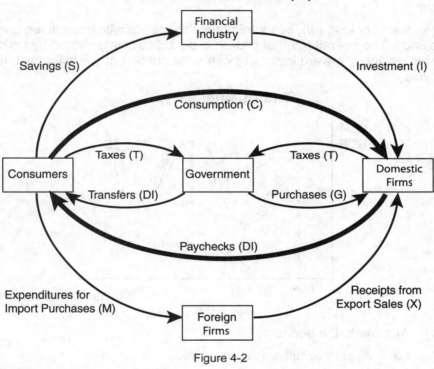

Figure 4-2

4. **Limitations of GDP**

a. Calculating GDP requires aggregating an enormous amount of data, some of which may be difficult to acquire, such as information from privately held entities.

b. Because GDP is calculated in current-year dollars, it is a monetary measure. Thus, comparing GDP over time requires adjustment for changes in the general price level.

c. GDP includes only final goods and services. Much economic activity involves the trading of intermediate goods, such as when a manufacturer buys materials.

   1) The exchange of intermediate goods is not included in GDP to avoid double-counting some goods.

d. Increases in GDP often involve environmental damage such as noise, congestion, or pollution. This cost is not considered in the calculation of GDP.

e. Some economic activity occurs as a result of disasters. For example, after a hurricane, sales by home improvement stores increase. This benefit is reflected in GDP, but the financial loss of the customers is not included in GDP.

f. Some economic activity, especially in developing countries, occurs in the underground economy, which is not captured in GDP.

g. The value of leisure time to its consumers is not included in GDP.

5.   **Price Level Accounting**

a.   **Nominal GDP.** The basic GDP calculation includes the total market value of all final goods and services in current dollars.

b.   **Real GDP.** To facilitate year-to-year comparisons, nominal GDP is adjusted for changes in the general price level so that it can be reported in constant dollars.

$$Real\ GDP = \frac{Nominal\ GDP}{Price\ index\ (in\ hundredths)}$$

Stop and review! You have completed the outline for this subunit. Study multiple-choice questions 3 through 5 beginning on page 113.

4.3 BUSINESS CYCLES

1.   **Overview**

a.   Over the very long run, economic growth in capitalistic economies has not been steady. The overall trend of growth is periodically interrupted by periods of instability. This tendency toward instability within the context of overall growth is the business cycle.

The Business Cycle

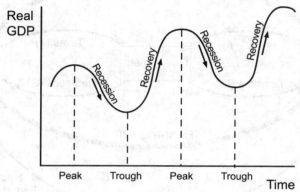

Figure 4-3

1)   At a **peak**, the economy is

a)   At or near full employment and

b)   At or near maximum output for the current level of resources and technology.

2)   A **recession** (contraction) is a period during which real GDP falls and unemployment rises.

a)   If the recession is severe enough, prices fall and the phase is considered a **depression**.

3)   In a **trough**, economic activity reaches its lowest point.

4)   During a **recovery** (expansion), output and employment rise. Eventually, the price level also rises.

In addition to identifying the phases of the business cycle, a candidate should be able to assess the business cycle's effects on an entity's operations and its industry.

b. Possible Causes of Recessions or Troughs

1) When consumer confidence declines, i.e., when consumers become pessimistic about the future, they spend less. Unsold inventory increases, and businesses respond by reducing production and laying off workers.

2) A miscalculation in fiscal or monetary policy by the government may suffice to cause a recession or a trough.

3) Often a major default triggers a cascade of confidences leading to reduced lending and consumption.

c. Economists use leading economic indicators to forecast future economic trends. Lagging indicators report past economic activity.

1) The best-known sets of economic indicators are those prepared by The Conference Board, a private research group.

2) These indicators in isolation are not meaningful. It is the composite index that has predictive uses. This index has historically been valuable but not infallible.

2. **Leading Economic Indicators**

a. A change in any of the following indicators suggests a future change in real GDP in the same direction:

1) The average workweek for manufacturing workers
2) New orders for consumer goods
3) New orders for nondefense capital goods
4) Building permits for houses
5) Stock prices
6) The money supply growth rate
7) The spread between short- and long-term interest rates (yield curve)
8) Consumer expectations

b. A change in either of the following indicators suggests a future change in real GDP in the opposite direction:

1) Initial claims for unemployment insurance. An increase in unemployment slows business activity.

2) Vendor performance. Slower deliveries by vendors (low vendor performance) indicate higher demand (high GDP) because vendors are not fast enough to adjust output with changing demands. In an economic downturn, vendors with slack time are holding excess inventory and thereby make faster deliveries (high vendor performance).

 You do not need to memorize all of the leading economic indicators. If one of these economic indicators is in the stem of a multiple-choice question, you need to understand how it may affect future growth or contraction of the economy. A written communication question on economic indicators may be required, but your response should be acceptable if you can remember some of them. Most accounting majors should have acquired the necessary knowledge from course work and coverage of business news, e.g., stock prices (such as the S&P 500 and the Dow Jones Industrial Average), unemployment claims, and interest rates.

Stop and review! You have completed the outline for this subunit. Study multiple-choice questions 6 and 7 on page 114.

4.4 AGGREGATE DEMAND AND AGGREGATE SUPPLY

1. **Aggregate Supply and Demand Curve**

    a. The aggregate demand is a schedule reflecting all the goods and services that consumers are willing and able to buy at various price levels. The curve reflects the inverse relationship between the price level and real GDP. Rising prices reduce demand.

Aggregate Demand Curve

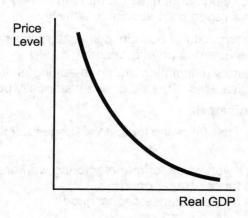

Figure 4-4

1) Aggregate demand is downward sloping.

    a) **Wealth effect.** As the price level rises, consumers' purchasing power decreases, thereby decreasing consumption expenditure and aggregate demand.

    b) **Interest rate effect.** As the price level rises, consumers are forced to spend a greater portion of their income on consumption and savings are therefore reduced. A rise in price level also induces a rise in interest rates, causing the cost of borrowing to increase. Thus, people are less able to invest while paying higher interest rates. The decrease in investment reduces aggregate demand.

    c) **Exchange rate effect.** As the increasing price level increases the interest rate, the demand for that country's currency rises, and the domestic currency value rises. Thus, exports decrease and imports increase, resulting in decreasing net exports and decreasing aggregate demand.

2) No distinction is made between a short-run and long-run aggregate demand curve.

b. Aggregate supply is a schedule reflecting all the goods and services an economy is willing and able to produce at various price levels.

Aggregate Supply

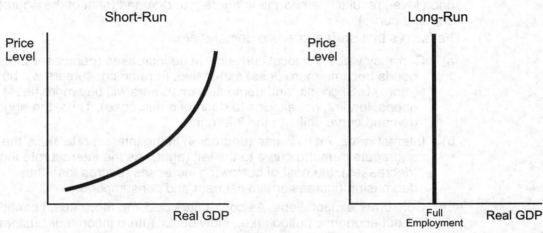

Figure 4-5

1) In the **short run**, changes in the price level induce firms to adjust their output to earn additional profits. The higher (lower) the price level, firms are more (less) willing to produce goods.

   a) **Sticky wage effect.** Firms are slow to adjust wages. Input prices (e.g., labor, natural resources) rise slower than final goods prices. If prices rise relative to costs, hiring more workers will increase profitability. Thus, firms choose to hire more workers, and more workers produce more output.

   b) As profit rises, more firms are in business, fewer firms will choose shutdown, and the production thereby increases.

2) In the **long run**, assuming full employment, any change in the price level is matched by a change in wages (and other input prices). Thus, firms' real profits do not change, and no additional output is produced.

   a) Because the change in the price level has no long-term effect on output produced, the long-run aggregate supply curve is a vertical line at the level of full-employment GDP.

2.   **Shifts in Aggregate Supply and Demand**

   a.   Shifts in Aggregate Demand

      1)   A change in any of the determinants of aggregate demand (factors other than price level) results in a change in aggregate demand (shift of the aggregate demand curve).

      2)   The factors that **shift** aggregate demand are

         a)   Currency value. As local currency value increases (decreases), domestic goods become more (less) expensive. Foreign consumers will buy less (more) U.S. goods, and domestic consumers will buy more (less) foreign goods, leading net exports to decrease (increase). Thus, the aggregate demand curve shifts to the left (right).

         b)   Interest rates. An increase (decrease) in the interest rate shifts the aggregate demand curve to the left (right). As the interest rate increases (decreases), the cost of borrowing increases (decreases), thus decreasing (increasing) investment and consumption.

         c)   Consumer expectations. As consumers become more (less) confident about economic outlook (i.e., individuals' future income or businesses' future profit will increase), they will increase (decrease) spending and consumption, thus increasing (decreasing) aggregate demand.

         d)   World economy. If domestic real GDP increases faster (slower) than foreign GDP, net exports will fall (rise), shifting aggregate demand to the left (right).

         e)   Government purchases. As the government increases (decreases) spending, aggregate demand will increase (decrease).

         f)   Taxes. As taxes increase (decrease), consumers are less (more) willing to spend. Aggregate demand thus shifts to the left (right).

   b.   Shifts in Short-Run Aggregate Supply

      1)   A change in any of the determinants of aggregate supply (factors other than price level) results in a change in aggregate supply (shift of the short-run aggregate supply curve). The factors that **shift** short-run aggregate supply are

         a)   Input costs. As input costs increase (decrease), aggregate supply shifts to the left (right).

         b)   Nominal wage. As nominal wage increases (decreases), aggregate supply shifts to the left (right).

      2)   A change in productivity results in a change in the long-run aggregate supply (shift of the long-run aggregate supply curve).

         a)   **Productivity** is usually measured by worker productivity, that is, the total real GDP produced during the year divided by the total number of hours worked in the economy. The more a worker can produce in an hour of work, the more productive (s)he is.

       b)   Productivity depends on three factors:

           i)   Amount of capital. The more an economy has invested in plant and machinery, the higher its productivity (more automation = higher productivity).

          ii)   State of technology. The more technologically advanced an economy's plants and machinery, the higher its productivity.

         iii)   Workforce education level. The more educated and trained an economy's workers, the higher its productivity.

       c)   As productivity increases (decreases), long-run aggregate supply (LRAS) shifts to the right (left).

> Long-run aggregate supply (LRAS) is determined solely by factors of production (e.g., amount of capital, state of technology, workforce education level). Short-run aggregate supply (SRAS) assumes that productivity is fixed. For example, in the short run, a new factory cannot be built, but utilization of existing factors of production can affect SRAS (e.g., input costs, nominal wage).

3.   **Business Fluctuation and Economic Growth**

    a.   Aggregate Demand Fluctuation

       1)   In the short run, when aggregate demand shifts to the right, real GDP increases, leading to a recovery or a peak. If an **expansion** occurs (graph on left below), wages and prices of resources will rise, shifting the short-run aggregate supply (SRAS) to the left. Thus, in the long run, a right shift of the aggregate demand only causes an increase in price level.

       2)   In the short run, when aggregate demand shifts to the left, real GDP decreases, leading to a recession or even a trough. If a **recession** occurs (graph on right below), wages and prices of resources will also fall, shifting the SRAS to the right. Thus, in the long run, a left shift of the aggregate demand only causes a decrease in the price level.

Expansion   **Recession**

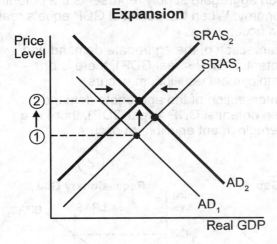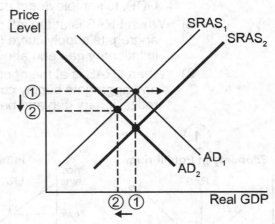

Figure 4-6

    b.   SRAS fluctuation

        1)   Supply shock. When SRAS shifts to the left, the price level rises and real GDP decreases. This is called **stagflation**, which occurs when inflation and recession occur at the same time. For example, when oil price greatly increases, it could cause a recession and a higher price level. This is also called a **supply shock**.

        2)   Automatic mechanism. When a supply shock occurs (graph on left below), an auto mechanism follows (graph on right below). As unemployment rises and output falls, workers are willing to accept lower wages. Thus, SRAS shifts to the right, and equilibrium moves back to the original point.

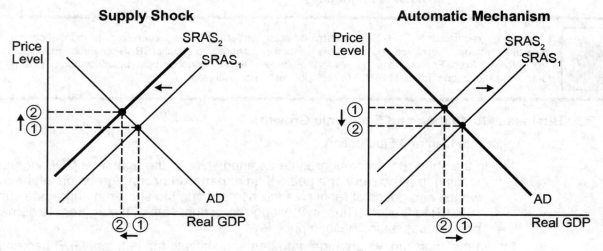

Figure 4-7

    c.   Economy in Equilibrium. The following three points correspond to Figure 4-8.

        1)   An economy is in equilibrium at the intersection of the aggregate demand and aggregate supply curves. Long-run aggregate supply represents the potential output (potential GDP) of the economy. When the potential GDP equals real GDP, full-employment equilibrium occurs.

        2)   When LRAS is at the left of the intersection of the aggregate demand and aggregate supply curve (when potential GDP < real GDP), there is an inflationary gap and above full-employment equilibrium occurs.

        3)   When LRAS is at the right of the intersection of the aggregate demand and aggregate supply curve (when potential GDP > real GDP), there is a recessionary gap and below full-employment equilibrium occurs.

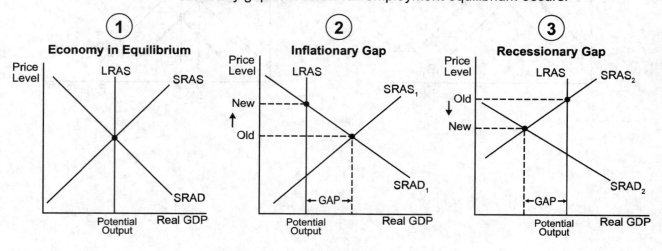

Figure 4-8

d. Economic Growth and Prosperity

1) Economic growth is the increase of economy capacity to produce output.

2) The change in real per capita GDP over a period of time is one way to measure economic growth and the accompanying improvement in the standard of living.

   a) If real GDP (adjusted for inflation) rises at a faster rate than the population, the economy has an improved standard of living.

3) **Growth** is a macroeconomic goal.

   a) When an economy grows, workers ordinarily earn higher real wages and have access to a greater variety and quantity of goods and services. Thus, the standard of living rises.

4) The rightward shift of long-term aggregate supply leads to economic growth.

   a) As productivity increases, LRAS shifts to the right. Increased productivity generates additional income for workers and businesses. Additional income shifts the aggregate demand curve to the right.

5) Growth is the increase in real GDP from Q_0 to Q_1.

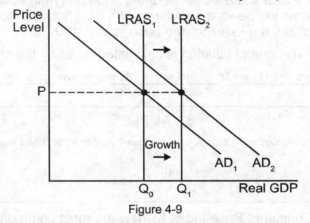

Figure 4-9

In the long run, the economy is in potential GDP level. All existing factors of production are employed. At this stage, economy can only be improved if LRAS shifts to the right (i.e., productivity improves). Remember that a shift of LRAS leads to economic growth. Shifts of SRAS and aggregate demand cause business fluctuation.

Stop and review! You have completed the outline for this subunit. Study multiple-choice questions 8 and 9 on page 115.

4.5 INFLATION

1.   **Overview**

The AICPA has tested topics related to inflation on recent CPA exams. Multiple-choice questions have asked how inflation is measured and inflation's effects on the economy.

a.   Inflation is a sustained increase in the general level of prices. The reported rate of inflation is therefore an average of the increase across all prices in the economy. But this definition does not sufficiently explain all the effects of inflation.

   1)   The value of any unit of money (e.g., the U.S. dollar) is measured by the goods and services that can be acquired in exchange for it. This measure is money's purchasing power. Inflation decreases purchasing power.

b.   The percentage rate of inflation is calculated using a price index.

   1)   A **price index** is a measure of the price of a market basket of goods and services in one year compared with the price in a designated base year. By definition, the index for the base year is 100.

   a)   The rate of inflation is calculated by using the change in the index.

$$\frac{\text{Current-year price index} - \text{Prior-year price index}}{\text{Prior-year price index}}$$

EXAMPLE

If the price index of the market basket was 10% higher than the base year in Year 3 and was 15% higher in Year 4, the inflation rate for Year 4 is

$$\frac{115 - 110}{110} = 4.55\%$$

   2)   The Consumer Price Index (CPI) is the most common price index for adjusting nominal GDP. It measures changes in the general price level by a pricing of items on a typical urban household shopping list.

$$CPI = \frac{\text{Cost of market basket in current year}}{\text{Cost of market basket in base year}} \times 100$$

Background

The CPI is computed monthly by the Bureau of Labor Statistics (an agency of the U.S. Department of Labor). According to the agency's website (www.bls.gov/cpi/), prices for the goods and services used to calculate the CPI are collected in 87 urban areas throughout the country and from about 23,000 retail and service establishments. Data on rents are collected from about 50,000 landlords or tenants. The base period for the CPI (i.e., the period for which the index equaled 100) is the period 1982-1984.

   a)   The CPI also is a relevant tool in business analysis. For example, rising prices can reduce the purchasing power and profit of a business.

   b)   To compare two monetary amounts in constant dollars, they must be deflated using the appropriate price index. The difference then must be divided by the prior period's amount.

EXAMPLE

A law firm is analyzing its revenue history. This year's billings were $1,080,000, and last year's were $950,000. This year's CPI is 115, and last year's was 107.

	Nominal Dollars		CPI		Constant Dollars
This year's billings:	$1,080,000	÷	1.15	=	$939,130
Last year's billings:	950,000	÷	1.07	=	887,850
Difference	$ 130,000				$ 51,280

Thus, nominal billings increased by 13.7% ($130,000 ÷ $950,000). But after adjusting for inflation, they increased by only 5.8% ($51,280 ÷ $887,850).

---

2. **Real Income vs. Nominal Income**

    a. Nominal income is the money received by a consumer as wages, interest, rent, and profits. For example, a worker might have an annual salary, and therefore a nominal income, of $64,000.

    b. Real income is the purchasing power of the income received. It is nominal income adjusted for inflation. Purchasing power relates directly to the consumer's standard of living.

    c. Real income decreases when the rate of increase in nominal income is less than the inflation rate.

3. **Macroeconomic Effects of Inflation**

    a. Unexpected inflation can cause economic chaos.
    b. The efficiency of economic relationships relies on stable pricing.

4. **Effects on Financial Reporting**

    a. In financial reporting, the principal effects of inflation are on inventory, cost of goods sold, and equipment and depreciation.

        1) In a last-in, first-out (LIFO) inventory accounting system, the most recently purchased goods are expensed first. In a period of rapidly rising prices, LIFO increases cost of goods sold and decreases operating income, thereby decreasing income tax liability.

            a) If the entity uses first-in, first-out (FIFO) inventory accounting, cost of goods sold consists of lower inventory costs, thereby increasing operating income.

        2) The depreciable base of a long-lived asset is its historical cost. During a period of rising prices, depreciation expense is lower at historical cost than if it were stated in terms of replacement cost. Reported operating income is higher in the current period, but replacing such assets as they are retired is more expensive.

5.   **Two Types of Inflation**

    a.   **Demand-pull inflation** is caused by an excess of demand over supply.

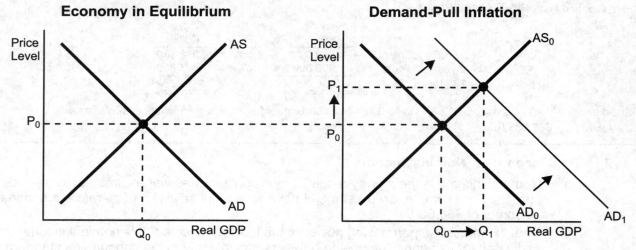

Figure 4-10

        1)   If the economy cannot produce enough to meet demand, the prices of existing goods increase.

EXAMPLE

The economy of Spain during the Age of Exploration was almost wrecked by the influx of gold and silver from the Western Hemisphere. The sudden infusion of wealth moved the aggregate demand curve to the right. Because this change was not accompanied by an increase in the goods available, the aggregate supply curve remained fixed, and demand-pull inflation resulted. The effect was to increase the prices of existing goods. This historical example demonstrates the principle that the value of money is derived from the wealth that underlies it.

---

        2)   In modern times, demand-pull inflation occurs when an economy approaches full employment and demand continues to increase.

    b.   **Cost-push inflation** is caused by increased per-unit production costs that are passed on to consumers as higher prices.

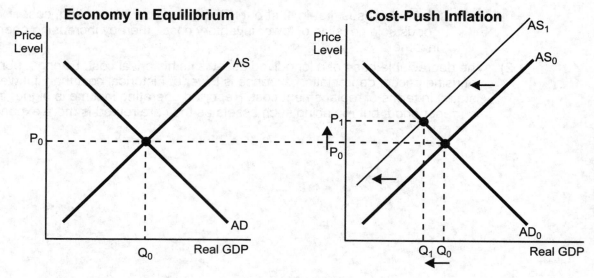

Figure 4-11

        1)   Increases in materials costs are the principal cause, particularly when they occur suddenly in the form of a **supply shock**.

EXAMPLE

The fourth war between the Arab nations and Israel began in October 1973. While the Soviet Union supplied aid to the Arab countries, the United States aided the Israelis. In retaliation, the Organization of Petroleum Exporting Countries (OPEC) declared an embargo of oil shipments to the U.S. The supply curve for petroleum suddenly shifted far to the left.

The price of petroleum products skyrocketed, and the quantity available plummeted. U.S. automobile drivers sometimes waited in line for hours to buy gasoline at much higher prices than they were accustomed to. Because the U.S. economy is dependent on petroleum products, the increase in production costs for practically everything had a severe effect on the country. In macroeconomic terms, the result was stagflation, in which slow economic growth is accompanied by high inflation, an unprecedented condition.

OPEC ended the embargo in March 1974, but the economic effects were felt in the U.S. for years afterward.

---

6. **Deflation**

    a. Deflation is a sustained decrease in the general price level. It is caused by conditions that are the opposite of those causing demand-pull and cost-push inflation.

        1) A decrease in demand not accompanied by a decrease in supply causes a leftward shift of the aggregate demand curve. Firms sell inventory even if they incur losses. Prices and output fall.

        2) An increase in output not accompanied by an increase in demand causes a rightward shift of the aggregate supply curve. Prices fall.

Stop and review! You have completed the outline for this subunit. Study multiple-choice questions 10 and 11 on page 115.

4.6 UNEMPLOYMENT

1. **Overview**

    a. Unemployment is the failure of an economy to employ fully its labor force. The **unemployment rate** is stated in percentage terms.

$$\frac{Number\ of\ unemployed}{Size\ of\ labor\ force} \times 100$$

Background

The unemployment rate is based on the Current Population Survey, a monthly survey of households conducted by the U.S. Census Bureau on behalf of the Bureau of Labor Statistics (www.bls.gov/cps).

---

    b. The **labor force** (the equation's denominator) includes all individuals **except** those who are (1) under the age of 16; (2) incarcerated or institutionalized; (3) homemakers, full-time students, and retirees; and (4) discouraged workers (who are unemployed and able to work but are not actively seeking work).

        1) Among those included in the labor force, no distinction is made between full- and part-time workers. They are considered equally employed.

    c. The number of unemployed (the equation's numerator) consists of those who are willing and able to work and are seeking employment.

    d. The official statistics can be distorted by

        1) Workers who falsely claim to be seeking work or

        2) Those unemployed in the underground economy (e.g., cash-only basis workers).

2.   **Three Types of Unemployment**

    a.   **Frictional unemployment** is the amount of unemployment caused by the normal workings of the labor market.

        1)   This group can include those (a) moving to another location, (b) stopping work temporarily to obtain further education and training, and (c) who are between jobs.

        2)   This definition acknowledges that normal unemployment exists at any given time in a dynamic economy.

    b.   **Structural unemployment** results when

        1)   The composition of the workforce does not match the need. It can be a result of changes in consumer demand or technology.

            a)   The computer revolution has drastically changed the skills required for many jobs and completely eliminated others.

        2)   The available jobs are not in the location where unemployed workers live.

    c.   **Cyclical unemployment** is directly related to the level of an economy's output. It is likely to occur in the recession phase of the business cycle. For this reason, it is sometimes called **deficient-demand unemployment**.

        1)   As consumers spend less, firms reduce production and lay off workers.

        2)   The Great Depression of the 1930's was a period of low prices, low demand, and extremely low industrial output. During the worst of this period, as much as 25% of the American labor force was unemployed.

3.   **Full Employment**

    a.   The **natural rate of unemployment** consists of frictional and structural unemployment combined (cyclical unemployment is omitted).

        1)   Economists consider the economy to be at **full employment** when the economy is at the natural rate of unemployment. Thus, full employment is **not** "100% employment."

        2)   The rate varies over time because of demographic and institutional changes in the economy.

    b.   The economy's potential output is the real (i.e., inflation-adjusted) domestic output, or potential national income, that could be achieved if the economy sustained full employment.

4.   **Macroeconomic Effects of Unemployment**

    a.   Lost value to the economy is the primary economic cost of unemployment. The goods not produced and services not provided by idle workers can never be regained.

        1)   This loss is called the **GDP gap**. (GDP, or gross domestic product, is a measure of national output, covered in Subunit 4.1.)

    b.   Unemployment has social costs, including loss of skills, personal and family stress, violence and other crime, and social upheaval.

5. **Inflation and Unemployment**

    a. The inverse relationship between inflation and unemployment can be described using the Phillips Curve.

    b. When the unemployment rate is low, firms have to pay higher wages to attract workers, thereby increasing labor costs and product prices. Thus, the lower (higher) the unemployment rate, the higher (lower) the inflation.

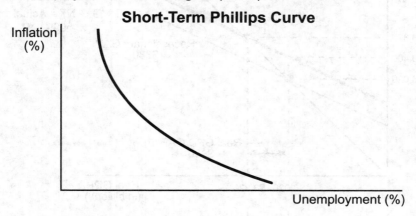

Figure 4-12

        1) The Phillips curve applies only in the short-term.

        2) In the long-term, inflationary policies do not decrease unemployment.

Stop and review! You have completed the outline for this subunit. Study multiple-choice question 12 on page 116.

4.7 DEMAND MANAGEMENT THROUGH FISCAL POLICY

1. **Overview**

    a. Government affects the economy through its fiscal and monetary policies.

        1) Fiscal policy is the use of taxation and expenditures to reach macroeconomic objectives, taking in revenues (taxes) and making purchases (the annual expenditures).

        2) Monetary policy is covered in Subunit 4.9.

    b. Fiscal policies can be discretionary or nondiscretionary.

        1) **Discretionary** fiscal policy involves spending that is under the control of individuals within the government, such as contracting for new weapons systems.

        2) **Nondiscretionary** fiscal policy is enacted in law. Certain outlays, e.g., Social Security, must be made regardless of their consequences or source of funding because Congress has made them a legal requirement. No individual bureaucrat or group can choose to withhold (or increase) these expenditures.

    c. The following tools of fiscal policy are used by the government:

        1) Tax policy

        2) Government spending (highway maintenance, military buildup, etc.)

        3) Transfer payments (welfare, food stamps, unemployment compensation, etc.)

2.   **Using Fiscal Policy**

a.   In the graph below, the economy's full employment output is $8.82 billion.

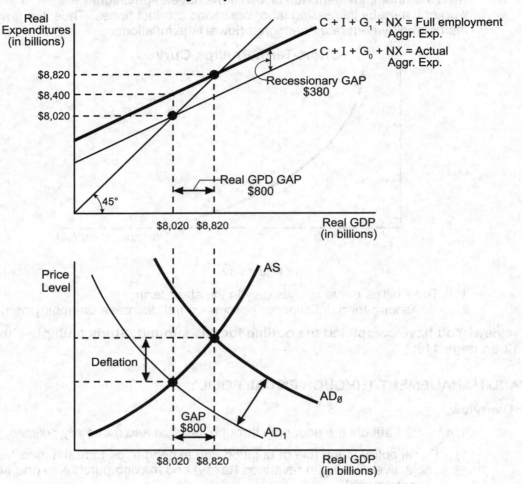

Recessionary Gap and Demand Stimulus

Figure 4-13

1)   A reduction in consumer expectations leads to a decrease in consumption, causing the aggregate demand curve to shift to the left from AD_0 to AD_1 (assuming that prices can go down).

2)   Recession and unemployment follow because real GDP decreased from $8,820 billion to $8,020 billion.

a)   The $380 billion recessionary gap causes an $800 billion negative GDP gap.

3) To promote growth and reduce unemployment, the federal government may increase its spending (G_1) by $380 billion ($G_1 = G_0$ + $380 billion).

    a) Because of the multiplier effect, an increase in government spending of $380 billion suffices to increase real GDP by $800 billion.

    b) The **multiplier effect** occurs because each dollar spent by a consumer in the economy becomes another consumer's income, and so forth. The increase in the consumption for every additional dollar consumers receive in income is the **marginal propensity to consume (MPC)**. The remainder that was not spent is saved.

        i) Spending has a cumulative effect on the economy, greater than the initial amount. The multiplier in the economy is calculated as follows:

$$Multiplier = \frac{1}{(1 - MPC)}$$

        ii) The MPC in the example is 0.525. Accordingly, the multiplier in the economy is 2.105 [1 ÷ (1 − 0.525)]. The government needs to increase its expenditures by only $380 billion to increase total GDP by $800 billion ($380 billion × 2.105).

4) The increase in government spending shifts the economy's aggregate demand curve to the right (from AD_0 to AD_1). The recessionary gap of $800 billion ($8,820 billion − $8,020 billion) is closed, unemployment is reduced, and prices increase.

3. **Issues in Fiscal Policy**

    a. **Keynesian theory** calls for expansionary fiscal policy during times of recession (to stimulate aggregate demand) and contractionary policy during an expansion (to prevent inflation).

    b. If a recessionary gap exists, the government adopts **expansionary policies**.

        1) Taxes can be decreased and transfer payments increased, giving consumers more disposable income.

        2) Government can increase its spending, increasing demand for goods and services from the private sector.

        3) Federal deficit increases under expansionary policies.

    c. An **inflationary gap** is the amount by which the economy's aggregate expenditures at the full-employment GDP exceed those necessary to achieve full-employment GDP.

    d. If an inflationary gap exists, the government adopts **contractionary policies** to reduce aggregate demand.

        1) Taxes can be increased and transfer payments decreased, giving consumers less disposable income.

        2) Government can decrease its spending, reducing demand for goods and services from the private sector.

        3) Federal deficit decreases under contractionary policies.

4.   **How Fiscal Policy Affects Aggregate Demand**

a.   In Subunit 4.4, we discussed the shift in aggregate demand in the short run. In the short run, a leftward shift of aggregate demand will decrease GDP. In the long run, the economy's automatic mechanism will shift aggregate supply to the right, eventually causing a decrease in the price level.

b.   However, this process sometimes takes a long time, and therefore, to stop the recession, the government will take action (i.e., fiscal policy) before the automatic adjustment occurs.

c.   The government's goal is to expedite the automatic adjustment before its citizens have an opportunity to vote for change.

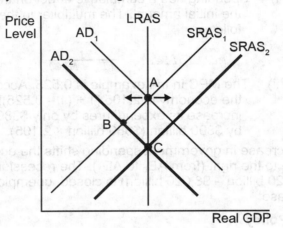

Figure 4-14

AD_1 and $SRAS_1$ originally intersect at equilibrium A. In the short run, AD_1 shifts to AD_2, moving the equilibrium from A to B. Compared to equilibrium A, B has a lower GDP level and lower price. In the long run, $SRAS_1$ shifts to $SRAS_2$, moving the equilibrium from B to C. Compared to equilibrium A, C has a lower price level, but the GDP level is the same as A's.

Stop and review! You have completed the outline for this subunit. Study multiple-choice questions 13 and 14 on page 116.

4.8 THE CREATION OF MONEY

1.   **Three Uses of Money**

a.   Medium of exchange. The existence of money greatly facilitates the free exchange of goods and services by providing a common means of valuation. Without money, all goods and services would have to be bartered, creating extraordinary inefficiencies.

b.   Unit of account. Money also provides a convenient basis for bookkeeping. Anything stated in terms of money can be easily compared.

c.   Store of value. Any society using the barter basis is subject to great inefficiencies. Many objects of great value, such as perishable food, spoil, making them worthless. The value of a unit of money is determined by the quantity of goods and services it can be exchanged for, not by its inherent characteristics.

2.   **Interest Rates**

a.   When money is borrowed, the debtor pays the lender an amount in addition to the sum that was borrowed (interest).

1)   The two major determinants of the interest rate on a loan are

a)   Overall economic conditions as reflected in the prime rate, which is the rate to the most credit-worthy customers, and

b)   The creditworthiness of the borrower.

b. Economists distinguish between real and nominal interest rates.

  1) The **nominal interest rate** is the stated rate on a loan.

  2) The **real interest rate** equals the nominal rate minus the rate of inflation that the lender expects over the life of the loan.

    a) The lender must charge this inflation premium to compensate for the purchasing power lost while the loan is at the borrower's disposal.

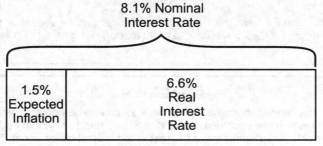

Figure 4-15

c. Misunderstandings over the difference between real and nominal interest rates can lead to distortions in the economy.

  1) For example, a loan bearing 10% interest may seem excessive to a borrower. But if inflation is 8%, the borrower is paying a real rate of only 2%.

  2) For example, a loan bearing 6% interest may seem to be a bargain. But if inflation is 1%, the borrower is actually paying 5% real interest.

3. **The Supply of Money**

a. The U.S. Federal Reserve System tracks and reports the amount of money in circulation.

  1) The metrics used by the Fed are called M1 and M2. M1 includes only the most liquid forms of money. M2 includes M1 and less-liquid forms of money.

EXAMPLE

The following is a hypothetical money supply calculation for an economy the approximate size of the U.S.:

	In Billions
Currency (paper money + coins)	$ 600
Checking accounts	700
M1 money supply	**$1,300**
Savings accounts, including money market accounts	2,900
Small time deposits (< $100,000)	1,400
Money market mutual funds	800
M2 money supply	**$6,400**

Background

Although they need not be memorized for the CPA exam, the Federal Reserve's latest Money Stock Measures are at www.federalreserve.gov/releases/h6/current/default.htm.

4.   **Banks and the Creation of Money**

a.   The example M1 money supply calculation illustrates that paper money and coins (currency) are less than half the total.

1)   The money in the economy greatly exceeds the currency in circulation because of the creation of money by banks.

EXAMPLE

A bank customer deposits $1,000, and the bank then lends $800. The depositor's statement shows that (s)he has a claim to $1,000 of cash, and the borrower has $800 of cash. Thus, $1,800 exists when only $1,000 existed previously. The bank has created $800.

Background

From its founding, the United States tended to view a central bank as an anti-democratic institution. Thus, instead of having a single central bank like many other countries, the United States has 12 regional Federal Reserve Banks. The Federal Reserve, established in 1913, is independent of the rest of the federal government. This independence, and the long terms of its members, protect the Fed's decisions from political pressures. The Board of Governors is responsible for overseeing the operations of the Federal Reserve System. The Federal Open Market Committee (FOMC) is responsible for administering monetary policy.

 In today's world, the actions taken by the Federal Reserve receive extensive media coverage. Be prepared to answer questions about policies pursued of the Federal Reserve for different economic situations.

---

5.   **Bank Reserves**

a.   Fractional reserve banking is the practice of prohibiting banks from lending all the money they receive on deposit.

b.   The required **reserve ratio** is the percentage of each dollar deposited that a bank is required to either (1) keep in its vault or (2) deposit with the Federal Reserve Bank in its district.

1)   The minimum that must be held by law is required reserves.

Background

For example, the Fed recently required medium-sized banks to keep 3% in reserve (in the vault or on deposit with the district Fed). An explanation and a complete table of the current reserve requirements are at www.federalreserve.gov/monetarypolicy/reservereq.htm.

---

a)   The amount of customer deposits that exceeds required reserves is **excess reserves**. It is from excess reserves that the bank makes loans.

2)   Fractional reserves obviously do not suffice to prevent a bank's collapse in the event customers withdraw excessive amounts. The Federal Deposit Insurance Corporation provides depositors with insurance on their deposits and examines banks for safety.

a)   The Fed has the sole authority to set minimum reserve requirements for all depository institutions, which influences the money supply.

c.   The amount of money banks potentially can create is approximated using the monetary multiplier.

$$Monetary\ multiplier\ =\ \frac{1}{Required\ reserve\ ratio}$$

1)   The money supply decreases as required reserves are raised.

Stop and review! You have completed the outline for this subunit. Study multiple-choice questions 15 through 17 on page 117.

4.9 MONETARY POLICY

1. **Goals and Tools of Monetary Policy**

   a. The Fed balances the goals of gradual, steady economic growth and price stability (manageable inflation).

      1) The Fed has three tools of monetary policy:

         a) Open-market operations

         b) The required reserve ratio

         c) The discount rate (equals the rate charged by the Fed on loans to member banks)

      2) Fiscal and monetary policy can be combined to influence aggregate demand.

   b. **Open-market operations** are the Fed's strongest tool. It can choose potential effects that are immediate and range from large to small.

      1) U.S. Treasury securities are traded on the open market. The Fed can either purchase them from, or sell them to, commercial banks.

         a) When the Fed wishes to increase the money supply, it purchases Treasury securities. It removes securities from the market and injects money.

         b) When the Fed wishes to decrease the money supply, it sells Treasury securities. It removes money from the economy and injects securities.

      2) The **Federal funds rate** is the rate banks charge each other for overnight loans.

         a) A bank's excess reserves do not have to be idle. They can be lent on a short-term basis to other banks with deficient reserves.

            i) The following graph depicts the relationship between the money supply (S_0 and S_1) and the interest rate (r):

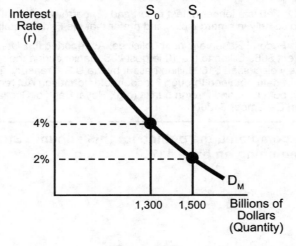

Figure 4-16

         b) When the Fed buys Treasury securities, the money supply increases and the Federal funds rate falls. When the Fed sells Treasury securities, the money supply decreases and the Federal funds rate rises.

3) The following table summarizes the effects of changes in the money supply resulting from open-market operations:

Increase Money Supply	Decrease Money Supply
1. The Fed expects a **recession**.	1. The Fed expects higher **inflation**.
2. The Fed **buys securities** on the open market.	2. The Fed **sells securities** on the open market.
3. The Fed **credits cash to reserve accounts** of banks selling securities.	3. The Fed **decreases cash in reserve accounts** of banks buying securities.
• The increase in cash **creates excess reserves**. Banks are more willing to lend.	• The decrease in cash **reduces excess reserves**. Banks are less able to lend.
• Greater availability of cash for overnight loans decreases the **Federal funds rate.**	• Lower availability of cash for overnight loans **increases the Federal funds rate.**
4. Lower interest rates stimulate investment spending by businesses.	4. Higher interest rates discourage investment spending by businesses.
5. Greater investment spending increases aggregate demand (a shift to the right), increasing real GDP and decreasing unemployment.	5. Lower investment spending decreases aggregate demand (a shift to the left), decreasing inflation.

c. Changes in the required **reserve ratio** are used less frequently. Requiring banks to retain more funds in reserve accounts reduces profits.

1) Lowering the reserve ratio increases the money supply.

a) If reserves decrease, banks have more money to lend.

2) Raising the reserve ratio decreases the money supply.

a) If reserves increase, banks have less money to lend.

d. The **discount rate** is the rate Federal Reserve banks charge for short-term loans directly to commercial banks.

1) Increasing the discount rate reduces borrowing and the money supply.

a) Banks are most likely to borrow from the Fed because of temporary shortages of reserves. If such loans are more expensive, banks are more likely to increase reserves to ensure that borrowing is unnecessary.

2) Decreasing the discount rate increases borrowing and the money supply.

Background

The widely-held belief is that (1) the Fed is a lender of last resort and (2) borrowing from the Fed is a sign of financial weakness. Thus, banks tend to do so only in emergencies and prefer that the Fed maintain their anonymity.

The direct provision of cash by the Federal Reserve is not publicized. As reported in *Bloomberg Businessweek* on August 22, 2011, the Fed quietly lent $669 billion to the 10 largest U.S. banks during the market crisis of late 2008, an amount that far exceeded the widely discussed $160 billion bailout by the U.S. Treasury. The magazine could only report this information after "compilation of data obtained through Freedom of Information Act requests, months of litigation, and an act of Congress." Including both U.S. and foreign banks (e.g., Royal Bank of Scotland, UBS AG), the Fed had $1.2 trillion in loans outstanding on December 5, 2008.

Stop and review! You have completed the outline for this subunit. Study multiple-choice questions 18 through 20 beginning on page 117.

QUESTIONS

4.1 GDP -- Expenditures Approach

1. Which of the following is **not** included in the gross domestic product (GDP)?

- A. Purchase of a new home.
- B. Investment in new computers.
- C. A doctor's fee.
- D. Purchase of common stock.

Answer (D) is correct.
REQUIRED: The transaction not included in GDP.
DISCUSSION: GDP is the value of all final goods and services produced in the U.S., whether by domestic or foreign-owned sources, during a specified period. A common stock purchase is not a new good or service. It is instead a claim to ownership of property that already exists.
Answer (A) is incorrect. A new home is a productive good and is included in GDP. Answer (B) is incorrect. An investment in productive assets is part of GDP. Answer (C) is incorrect. The doctor's services were produced during the year. His or her fee is part of GDP.

2. Which one of the following components of gross domestic product (GDP) has the greatest fluctuation from year to year?

- A. Personal consumption expenditures.
- B. Gross domestic private investment.
- C. Government spending.
- D. Net exports.

Answer (B) is correct.
REQUIRED: The component of GDP fluctuating the most from year to year.
DISCUSSION: By far the most volatile component of GDP is business investment. Investment reflects the level of businesses' optimism about future demand, and business optimism is subject to sudden variations.
Answer (A) is incorrect. Personal consumption, while the largest component of GDP, is not the most volatile. Answer (C) is incorrect. Government spending is not as volatile a component of GDP as business investment. Answer (D) is incorrect. Net exports are subject to less variability from year to year than gross domestic private investment.

4.2 GDP -- Income Approach

3. Personal income is equal to

- A. Gross domestic product minus net domestic product.
- B. Net domestic product plus transfer payments to individuals.
- C. Disposable income minus personal tax payments.
- D. Disposable income plus personal tax payments.

Answer (D) is correct.
REQUIRED: The factors calculated in personal income.
DISCUSSION: Personal income is all income received by individuals, whether earned or unearned. It equals disposable income plus taxes.
Answer (A) is incorrect. GDP minus net domestic product equals depreciation (the capital consumption allowance). Answer (B) is incorrect. Net domestic product plus transfer payments to individuals does not define a meaningful national income concept. Answer (C) is incorrect. Disposable income equals personal income minus personal income taxes. Thus, adding personal taxes to disposable income results in personal income.

4. Using the income approach, calculate the national income used to calculate GDP with the information provided below:

Interest:	$ 8,000
Salaries and wages:	50,000
Net foreign factor income:	7,000
Partnership income:	10,000
Rents:	20,000
Indirect business taxes:	1,000
Corporate profits:	25,000
Proprietor income:	4,000

- A. $107,000
- B. $117,000
- C. $118,000
- D. $124,000

Answer (B) is correct.
REQUIRED: The calculation of national income using the income approach for measuring GDP.
DISCUSSION: National income is calculated using the following formula: national income = salaries and wages + rents + interest + proprietor and partnership incomes + corporate profits. Thus, national income equals $117,000 ($50,000 + $20,000 + $8,000 + $4,000 + $10,000 + $25,000).
Answer (A) is incorrect. Proprietor and partnership income of $10,000 should be included in national income. Answer (C) is incorrect. National income does not include indirect business taxes of $1,000. Answer (D) is incorrect. The calculation of national income does not include net foreign factor income of $7,000.

5. Each of the following is a limitation of GDP's usefulness as a measure of a nation's prosperity **except**

    A. No practical means are available to compare real GDP from different time periods.

    B. GDP leaves out intermediate goods.

    C. Increases in GDP often involve environmental damage.

    D. Cash-only economic activity is not counted in GDP.

Answer (A) is correct.
    REQUIRED: The item not a limitation of GDP's usefulness as a measure of national prosperity.
    DISCUSSION: Various price indexes, such as the Bureau of Labor Statistics' Consumer Price Index and the GDP deflator, are suitable for converting nominal GDP amounts from different years to comparable amounts in terms of a base year.
    Answer (B) is incorrect. GDP includes only final goods and services. Economic activity that leads to intermediate goods is omitted. Answer (C) is incorrect. Increases in GDP often involve environmental damage, such as noise, congestion, or pollution. Answer (D) is incorrect. Unreported cash-only economic activity is not counted in GDP.

4.3 Business Cycles

6. Which of the following may provide a leading indicator of a future increase in gross domestic product?

    A. A reduction in the money supply.

    B. A decrease in the issuance of building permits.

    C. An increase in the timeliness of delivery by vendors.

    D. An increase in the average hours worked per week of production workers.

Answer (D) is correct.
    REQUIRED: The leading indicator of an increase in GDP.
    DISCUSSION: An economic indicator is highly correlated with changes in aggregate economic activity. A leading indicator changes prior to a change in the direction of the business cycle. The leading indicators included in the Conference Board's index are (1) average weekly hours worked by manufacturing workers, (2) unemployment claims, (3) consumer goods orders, (4) stock prices, (5) orders for fixed assets, (6) building permits, (7) timeliness of deliveries, (8) money supply, (9) consumer confidence, and (10) the spread between the yield on 10-year Treasury bonds and the federal funds rate. An increase in weekly hours worked by production workers is favorable for economic growth.
    Answer (A) is incorrect. A falling money supply is associated with falling GDP. Answer (B) is incorrect. A decline in the issuance of building permits signals lower expected building activity and a falling GDP. Answer (C) is incorrect. An increase in the timeliness of delivery by vendors indicates slacking business demand and a potentially falling GDP.

7. Diana has noticed that many of her coworkers at Bubble, Inc., have been laid off over the past year due to low profits. Also, prices were lowered recently due to economic conditions. Even though Diana is worried about her future at Bubble, she has noticed that employment has risen over the past month and that prices are slowly increasing. Because other companies have had the same experience, what phase of the business cycle is the economy currently in?

    A. Peak.

    B. Recession.

    C. Trough.

    D. Recovery.

Answer (D) is correct.
    REQUIRED: The phases of the business cycle.
    DISCUSSION: During a recovery, employment rises. The price level eventually also rises. Employment has been increasing in many companies, and the price level is slowly recovering.
    Answer (A) is incorrect. At a peak, the economy is at or near full employment. Answer (B) is incorrect. A recession is a period during which unemployment rises. Answer (C) is incorrect. In a trough, employment reaches its lowest point.

4.4 Aggregate Demand and Aggregate Supply

8. One of the measures economists and economic policy makers use to gauge a nation's economic growth is to calculate the change in the

   A. Money supply.

   B. Total wages.

   C. General price level.

   D. Real per capita output.

Answer (D) is correct.
   REQUIRED: The measure used by economists to gauge economic growth.
   DISCUSSION: Real per-capita output is defined as the GDP adjusted for changes in the general price level and divided by the population. It is often used to measure the standard of living.
   Answer (A) is incorrect. The change in the money supply is not a direct measure of the nation's output. Answer (B) is incorrect. The change in total wages is not a direct measure of the nation's output. Answer (C) is incorrect. The change in the general price level is not a direct measure of the nation's output.

9. Which one of the following factors would cause the aggregate supply curve shown below to shift from AS$_1$ to AS$_2$?

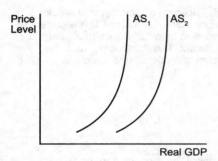

   A. An improvement in technology.

   B. A higher resource price.

   C. An increase in the expected rate of inflation.

   D. A decrease in productivity.

Answer (A) is correct.
   REQUIRED: The factor causing a rightward shift in the aggregate supply curve.
   DISCUSSION: A shift of the entire aggregate supply curve as opposed to a movement along a given curve is caused by any of three determinants of aggregate demand: a change in input prices, a change in productivity, or a change in the legal-institutional environment in which the industry operates. An improvement in technology leads to greater productivity and thus to an outward shift in aggregate supply.
   Answer (B) is incorrect. Higher resource prices lead to a leftward shift of aggregate supply. Answer (C) is incorrect. An increase in the expected rate of inflation causes consumers to purchase more goods before prices increase. This effect is represented as a movement along the aggregate demand curve. Answer (D) is incorrect. A decrease in productivity means a loss of efficiency by businesses, reflected in a leftward shift in aggregate supply.

4.5 Inflation

10. Demand-pull inflation occurs when

   A. Incomes rise suddenly.

   B. There are excessive wage increases.

   C. There are rapid increases in raw materials prices.

   D. There are substantial changes in energy prices.

Answer (A) is correct.
   REQUIRED: The cause of demand-pull inflation.
   DISCUSSION: When incomes rise suddenly, consumers demand more of everything, driving up the price level.
   Answer (B) is incorrect. Excessive wage increases result in cost-push inflation. Answer (C) is incorrect. A rapid increase in materials prices is a supply shock. It may be the cause of stagflation but not of demand-pull inflation. Answer (D) is incorrect. Changes in the prices of an important input can be increases or decreases. Thus, they do not necessarily predict inflation.

11. Assume that real gross domestic product (GDP), measured in Year 1 dollars, rose from $3,000 billion in Year 1 to $4,500 billion in Year 10. Assume also that the price index rose from 100 to 200 during the same period. The GDP for Year 1 expressed in terms of Year 10 prices is

   A. $1,500 billion.

   B. $3,000 billion.

   C. $4,500 billion.

   D. $6,000 billion.

Answer (D) is correct.
   REQUIRED: The GDP for Year 1 adjusted for inflation.
   DISCUSSION: Between Year 1 and Year 10, the price index doubled (from 100 to 200). Thus, the nominal value of Year 1 GDP ($3,000 billion) also must be doubled when restated in Year 10 terms. The Year 1 GDP in Year 10 prices is $6,000 billion.
   Answer (A) is incorrect. The amount of $1,500 billion assumes deflation rather than inflation from Year 1 to Year 10. Answer (B) is incorrect. The amount of $3,000 billion is the nominal value of the Year 1 GDP. Answer (C) is incorrect. The amount of $4,500 billion is the actual Year 10 GDP. The question asks about the restated Year 1 GDP.

4.6 Unemployment

12. The rate of unemployment caused by changes in the composition of employment opportunities over time is referred to as the

A. Frictional unemployment rate.

B. Cyclical unemployment rate.

C. Structural unemployment rate.

D. Full employment unemployment rate.

Answer (C) is correct.

REQUIRED: The rate of unemployment caused by changes in the composition of employment opportunities over time.

DISCUSSION: Economists define full employment as occurring when cyclical unemployment is zero. Thus, the natural rate of unemployment (the full employment unemployment rate) equals the sum of structural and frictional unemployment. Cyclical unemployment is caused by insufficient aggregate demand. Frictional unemployment occurs when both jobs and the workers qualified to fill them are available. This definition acknowledges that workers change jobs, are laid off, abandon paid work temporarily, etc. Structural unemployment exists when aggregate demand is sufficient to provide full employment, but the distribution of the demand does not correspond precisely to the composition of the labor force. This form of unemployment results when the required job skills or the geographic distribution of jobs change.

Answer (A) is incorrect. Frictional unemployment results from imperfections in the labor market. Answer (B) is incorrect. Cyclical unemployment is caused by a deficiency of aggregate spending. Answer (D) is incorrect. The full employment unemployment rate is the sum of frictional and structural unemployment.

4.7 Demand Management through Fiscal Policy

13. What is the recessionary gap if the economy's full-employment real gross domestic product (GDP) is $1.2 trillion and its equilibrium real GDP is $1.0 trillion?

A. $200 billion.

B. $200 billion divided by the multiplier.

C. $200 billion multiplied by the multiplier.

D. $200 billion times the reciprocal of the marginal propensity to consume (MPC).

Answer (B) is correct.

REQUIRED: The amount of the recessionary gap.

DISCUSSION: The $200 billion difference between full-employment GDP and equilibrium GDP can be eliminated by additional consumption, government spending, or exports. Because of the multiplier effect, the amount of the increase can be less than $200 billion. The amount of additional activity necessary to close the gap is ($200 billion ÷ multiplier).

Answer (A) is incorrect. The amount of $200 billion ignores the effect of the multiplier. Answer (C) is incorrect. The amount of $200 billion should be divided by the multiplier. Answer (D) is incorrect. The multiplier is based on the reciprocal of the marginal propensity to save (MPS), not the MPC.

14. If a government were to use only fiscal policy to stimulate the economy from a recession, it would

A. Raise consumer taxes and increase government spending.

B. Lower business taxes and government spending.

C. Increase the money supply and increase government spending.

D. Lower consumer taxes and increase government spending.

Answer (D) is correct.

REQUIRED: The actions taken if a government were to use only fiscal policy to stimulate the economy.

DISCUSSION: According to Keynesian economics, fiscal policy should be expansionary when the economy is in recession. Increases in government spending, decreases in taxation, or both have a stimulative effect. To achieve this effect, the increase in spending should not be matched by a tax increase, the effect of which is contractionary. Thus, deficit spending is the result of an expansionary fiscal policy.

Answer (A) is incorrect. Raising consumer taxes is contractionary. Answer (B) is incorrect. Lower government spending is contractionary. Answer (C) is incorrect. Increasing the supply of money involves monetary, not fiscal, policy.

4.8 The Creation of Money

15. The Federal Reserve System's reserve ratio is the

   A. Specified percentage of a commercial bank's deposit liabilities that must be deposited in the central bank or kept on hand.

   B. Rate that the central bank charges for loans granted to commercial banks.

   C. Ratio of excess reserves to legal reserves that are deposited in the central bank.

   D. Specified percentage of a commercial bank's demand deposits to total liabilities.

Answer (A) is correct.
   REQUIRED: The definition of the reserve ratio.
   DISCUSSION: The reserve ratio is the percentage of the customer deposits that banks must keep on hand or deposit with the Fed. These deposits are required by law to ensure the soundness of the bank and also serve as a tool for monetary policy. Accordingly, changes in the reserve ratio affect the money supply.
   Answer (B) is incorrect. The discount rate is the rate the Fed charges for loans to commercial banks. Answer (C) is incorrect. Excess reserves are amounts in excess of the reserve requirement. Answer (D) is incorrect. The reserve ratio is the ratio of required reserves to demand deposits.

16. A bank with a reserve ratio of 20% and reserves of $1,000,000 can increase its total demand deposits by

   A. $5,000,000

   B. $1,000,000

   C. $800,000

   D. $200,000

Answer (A) is correct.
   REQUIRED: The amount by which a bank can increase its total demand deposits given the reserve ratio and the amount of reserves.
   DISCUSSION: The amount of new money a bank can create equals actual reserves times the monetary multiplier (or divided by the required reserve ratio). This bank therefore can increase total demand deposits by $5,000,000 ($1,000,000 ÷ 0.2).
   Answer (B) is incorrect. Reserves need to be only 20% of deposits. Accordingly, an increase in reserves supports a 500% increase in deposits. Answer (C) is incorrect. The amount of $800,000 equals the increase in net lendable funds, assuming a $1,000,000 increase in deposits. Answer (D) is incorrect. The reserve is 20% of deposits, not the reverse.

17. The money supply in a nation's economy will decrease following

   A. Open-market purchases by the nation's central bank.

   B. A decrease in the discount rate.

   C. An increase in the reserve ratio.

   D. A decrease in the margin requirement.

Answer (C) is correct.
   REQUIRED: The item that causes a decrease in the money supply.
   DISCUSSION: The reserve ratio is the minimum percentage of its deposits that a bank must keep on deposit with the Federal Reserve or in its vault. When the reserve ratio increases, banks must maintain larger reserves, and less money is available for lending and investment. Consequently, the money supply decreases.
   Answer (A) is incorrect. Open-market purchases by the central bank increase the money supply by increasing commercial banks' reserves. Answer (B) is incorrect. A decrease in the rate charged to member banks for loans by the Federal Reserve (the discount rate) increases the money supply by increasing bank reserves. Answer (D) is incorrect. A decrease in the margin requirement decreases the minimum down payment that purchasers of stock must make. This credit control affects the stock market and has no direct impact on the money supply.

4.9 Monetary Policy

18. All of the following actions are valid tools that the Federal Reserve Bank uses to control the supply of money **except**

   A. Buying government securities.

   B. Selling government securities.

   C. Changing the reserve ratio.

   D. Printing money when the level of M1 appears low.

Answer (D) is correct.
   REQUIRED: The item that is not a valid tool of the Fed in controlling the money supply.
   DISCUSSION: The amount of money to print is a decision for the Department of the Treasury (an executive branch agency), not the Federal Reserve (an independent agency). Moreover, paper currency and coins make up only about half of the M1 money supply. The Fed has other, more complex tools for implementing monetary policy.
   Answer (A) is incorrect. Buying government securities is one method the Fed uses to control the money supply. Answer (B) is incorrect. Selling government securities is one method the Fed uses to control the money supply. Answer (C) is incorrect. Changing the reserve ratio is one method the Fed uses to control the money supply.

19. The primary mechanism of monetary control of the Federal Reserve System is

   A. Changing the discount rate.

   B. Conducting open market operations.

   C. Changing reserve requirements.

   D. Using moral persuasion.

Answer (B) is correct.
REQUIRED: The primary mechanism of monetary control used by the Fed.
DISCUSSION: Open market operations (buying and selling government securities) are the primary means used by the Fed to control the money supply. Fed purchases are expansionary. They increase bank reserves and the money supply. Fed sales are contractional. If money is paid into the Federal Reserve, bank reserves are reduced, and the money supply decreases.
Answer (A) is incorrect. Changing the discount rate is a less important tool of monetary policy. Answer (C) is incorrect. Changing reserve requirements is a less important tool of monetary policy. Answer (D) is incorrect. Moral persuasion is not a means of controlling the money supply.

20. Which of the following results could be expected from an open market operation of the Federal Reserve?

   A. A sale of securities would lower interest rates.

   B. A purchase of securities would raise interest rates.

   C. A purchase of securities would lower security prices.

   D. A sale of securities would raise interest rates.

Answer (D) is correct.
REQUIRED: The expected result from the given open market operation.
DISCUSSION: A sale of securities removes money from the economy and reduces bank reserves. Thus, banks cannot lend as much as previously, and higher interest rates follow. Money supply and interest rates are inversely related.
Answer (A) is incorrect. A sale increases interest rates. Answer (B) is incorrect. A purchase of securities increases reserves, allows banks to make more loans, and results in lower interest rates. Answer (C) is incorrect. A purchase of securities removes securities from the economy, increasing securities prices.

 Online is better! To best prepare for the CPA exam, access **thousands** of exam-emulating MCQs and TBSs through Gleim CPA Review online courses with SmartAdapt technology. Learn more at www.gleimcpa.com or contact our team at 800.874.5346 to upgrade.

STUDY UNIT FIVE
INTERNATIONAL ECONOMICS

(12 pages of outline)

International economics describes the economic effects in productive resources and consumer preferences between nations. Due to these differences, the patterns and consequences of transactions affect trade, investment, and migration. Accordingly, international economics affects economies on the macro scale as well as business entities on the micro scale. Protectionism (or the lack of free trade) concerns government policies that impact a business entity's industry as well as the overall economy. The ability of countries to trade also affects the value of their currencies. In our global economy, the value of a nation's currency can have dramatic effects on the nation's economy as well as the business conditions for business entities operating in the respective nation.

5.1 PROTECTIONISM

1. **Overview**

   a. Even though individuals generally are benefited by free trade, governments often establish policies designed to impact the workings of the marketplace. **Protectionism** is any measure taken by a government to protect domestic producers.

2. **Forms of Protectionism**

   a. **Tariffs** are taxes imposed on imported goods.

      1) Tariffs can discourage consumption of foreign goods, raise revenue, or both.

      2) To achieve both goals, the government must set the tariff rate very carefully. The effect of tariffs also depends on the elasticity of demand and how market participants react to the tariff. If the rate is set too high, demand for the good is decreased and revenue declines.

Background

Until the income tax was enacted in 1913, the U.S. government raised most of its revenue from tariffs.

---

   b. **Import quotas** set limits on the quantity of different products that can be imported.

      1) In the short run, import quotas improve a country's balance of payments by decreasing foreign outflow payments. But the prices of domestic products increase.

         a) A country's **balance of payments** is the sum of all transactions between domestic and foreign individuals, firms, and governments.

      2) An **embargo** is a total ban on some kinds of imports. It is an extreme form of import quota.

      3) As a result of import quotas and tariffs, domestic consumers pay higher prices and consume fewer goods. However, the domestic producers are able to sell more goods. Thus, domestic consumers pay a subsidy to domestic producers.

    c.   **Domestic content rules** require that at least a portion of any imported product be constructed from parts manufactured in the importing nation.

        1)   This rule is sometimes used by capital-intensive nations (e.g., United States). Parts can be produced using idle capacity and then sent to a labor-intensive country (e.g., Philippines) for final assembly.

    d.   A **trigger price** mechanism automatically imposes a tariff barrier against unfairly cheap imports by levying a duty (tariff) on all imports below a particular reference price.

    e.   **Antidumping** rules prevent foreign producers from selling excess goods on the domestic market at less than cost to squeeze out competitors and gain control of the market. This is a form of predatory pricing.

    f.   **Repatriation** is the process of transferring money earned in a foreign location back to the domestic location.

        1)   Exchange controls by the foreign country limit foreign currency transactions and set exchange rates. The purpose is to limit the ability of a firm selling in a country to repatriate its earnings to its home country.

        2)   Tax policy can impose additional costs on earnings that are repatriated. For example, the U.S. has a worldwide corporate taxation system that taxes foreign earnings only when they are repatriated. Thus, many companies choose to keep their capital offshore to avoid high tax rates in the U.S.

    g.   Export subsidies are payments by the government to producers in certain industries in an attempt to increase exports.

        1)   A government may impose **countervailing duties** on imported goods if those goods were produced in a foreign country with the aid of a governmental subsidy. The purpose is to protect domestic producers by offsetting subsidies made by foreign governments to foreign producers.

    h.   Certain exports may require **licenses**, especially if these sales are potentially not in the interest of national security. For example, sales of technology with military applications are limited by many nations that are members of the Wassenaar Arrangement. The related U.S. legislation is the Export Administration Act of 1979.

    i.   The Export Trading Company Act of 1982 provides an alternative to reduce the trade deficit by encouraging American exports to foreign markets. The Act permits competitors to form export trading companies without regard to U.S. antitrust legislation.

3.   **Economic Effects of Tariffs and Quotas**

    a.   Workers are shifted from relatively efficient export industries into less efficient protected industries. Real wages decline as prices rise, as does total world output.

    b.   Under a tariff, the excess paid by the customer for an imported good is government revenue that can be spent for domestic purposes.

        1)   Under a quota, prices also are increased (by the induced shortage), but the excess is paid to the exporter in the foreign country.

    c.   A tariff is imposed on all importers equally. Thus, the more efficient firms can still charge lower prices.

        1)   But an import quota does not affect foreign importers equally because import licenses can be granted based on political favoritism.

4. **Arguments for Protectionism**

    a.   Reducing imports protects domestic jobs.

        1)   This argument is compelling because the costs of cheaper imports are obvious, direct, and concentrated. People lose jobs and firms go out of business. The benefits of unrestricted trade are less noticeable. Lower prices, higher wages, and more jobs in export industries are future effects.

        2)   An argument against protectionism is that many of the ill effects of job loss can be mitigated by government programs to help in displaced-worker transition. Such measures are not protectionist.

    b.   Certain industries are essential to national security.

        1)   This argument is sound for some firms. But firms only peripherally related to national defense can claim that they are crucial to national security.

        2)   The national security concern also may result in the opposite of protectionism. For example, the U.S. government forbids exports of nuclear technology and certain weapons to countries such as Cuba, Iran, and North Korea. Thus, domestic exporters are hurt by government policies.

    c.   Infant industries need protection in the early stages of development.

        1)   An extension of the infant-industry argument is the strategic trade policy argument. It states that a government should use trade barriers strategically to reduce the risk of product development by domestic firms, particularly for products involving advanced technology.

        2)   Two counterarguments are usually offered. One is that, if the firm is promising, venture capitalists will provide financing until the entity becomes profitable. Also, some firms dependent on special government protections never become self-sufficient.

    NOTE: Special-interest groups advocating one or more of these arguments are strong and well organized, and they lobby effectively for legislation that is harmful to free trade.

5. **Global Capital Flow**

    a.   The rise of high-speed electronic communications makes the flow of capital much faster than in earlier eras.

        1)   The Internet and social media also have greatly facilitated **crowdfunding**, which is the funding of a project by raising contributions from a large number of people.

    b.   Emerging-market countries can attract capital with much greater ease than before, thereby exploiting their particular **comparative advantages**. The economic balance of power can shift rapidly back and forth between developed and developing nations.

6. **Sustainability**

    a.   The sustainability movement is built upon the goal of creating a higher standard of living for the present and the future, with a focus on reducing waste, energy use, and distribution costs while protecting the environment.

    b.   As the sustainability movement has become more important to consumers, major brands are attempting to provide their products and services in a more sustainable manner and to advertise that practice to consumers.

Stop and review! You have completed the outline for this subunit. Study multiple-choice questions 1 through 8 beginning on page 130.

5.2 CURRENCY EXCHANGE RATES

 The AICPA has tested the topic of currency exchange rates on recent CPA exams. CPA candidates should have a solid understanding of currency exchange rates and the effects of globalization on the business environment.

1.   **The Market for Foreign Currency**

   a.   When an entity buys merchandise, a capital asset, or a financial instrument from another country, the seller wants to be paid in his or her domestic currency.

      1)   Thus, in general, when the demand for a country's merchandise, capital assets, and financial instruments rises, demand for its currency rises.

   b.   For international exchanges to occur, the two currencies involved must be easily converted at some prevailing exchange rate.

      1)   The exchange rate is the price of one country's currency in terms of another country's currency.

2.   **Exchange Rate Systems**

   a.   **Fixed Exchange Rate System**

      1)   In a fixed exchange rate system, the value of a country's currency in relation to another country's currency is either fixed or allowed to fluctuate only within a very narrow range. For example, the Bahamian dollar is pegged to the U.S. dollar at a 1:1 ratio.

      2)   The one significant advantage of a fixed exchange rate is that it provides predictability in international trade by eliminating uncertainty about gains and losses on exchange rate fluctuations.

EXAMPLE

Since July 1986, the Saudi government has allowed its currency to trade within an extremely narrow band surrounding the ratio of 3.75 riyals to 1 U.S. dollar. Because the U.S. buys large amounts of petroleum from Saudi Arabia, this system has the advantage of adding stability to the U.S. oil market.

---

      3)   A disadvantage is that a government can manipulate the value of its currency.

EXAMPLE

One of the complaints of authorities in the U.S. about the enormous trade deficit with China is the belief that the Chinese government has held the value of the yuan in an artificially low range to make its exports more affordable. (After years of urging by the U.S. government, China allowed its currency to rise almost 18% between 2005 and 2008. After further negotiations, China agreed in April 2012 to allow the value of the yuan to fluctuate by as much as 1.0% against the value of the dollar on any given day. This doubled the size of the previous trading band of 0.5%.)

---

   b.   **Freely Floating Exchange Rate System**

      1)   In this system, exchange rates are determined entirely by supply and demand.

         a)   The advantage is that the system tends to automatically correct any disequilibrium in the balance of payments.

         b)   The disadvantage is that a freely floating system makes a country vulnerable to economic conditions in other countries.

   c.   **Managed Float Exchange Rate System**

      1)   Under a managed float, market forces determine exchange rates until they move too far in one direction or another. The government then intervenes to maintain the currency within the broad range considered appropriate.

a)   The advantage of managed float is that it has the market-response nature of a freely floating system while allowing for government intervention when necessary.

2)   The dominant exchange rate system in use among the world's largest economies is the managed float system.

3.   **Exchange Rates and Purchasing Power**

a.   The graph below depicts the relationship between the supply of, and demand for, a foreign currency by consumers and investors who use a given domestic currency.

Exchange Rate Equilibrium

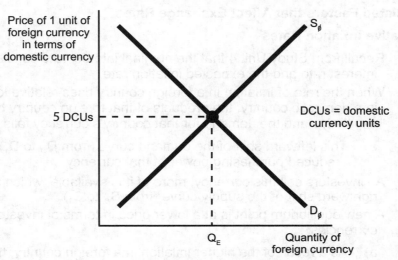

Figure 5-1

1)   The demand curve for the foreign currency is downward sloping. When that currency becomes cheaper, goods and services denominated in that currency are more affordable and domestic consumers need more of it.

2)   The supply curve for the foreign currency is upward sloping. When that currency becomes more expensive, goods and services denominated in the domestic currency become more affordable to users of the foreign currency. Thus, they inject more of their currency into the domestic market.

b.   When one currency can be exchanged for more units of another currency, the first currency **appreciates** in relation to the second currency. The second currency **depreciates** in relation to the first.

1)   This phenomenon has definite implications for international trade. The currency that appreciates has greater purchasing power. Any financial instrument denominated in that currency is more valuable (expensive).

2)   The appreciation or depreciation affects the business strategies of firms. When a firm's domestic currency depreciates, the demand for their product increases, so the firm is likely to expand operations. The opposite can also be true.

EXAMPLE

A U.S. company buys merchandise from an EU company for €1,000,000, due in 60 days. On the day of the sale, $0.795 is required to buy a single euro. By the 60th day, $0.812 is required to buy a euro. The dollar has therefore depreciated in relation to the euro, and the euro has appreciated in relation to the dollar. Accordingly, the dollar has lost purchasing power in relation to the euro. The U.S. firm needed $795,000 to pay a €1,000,000 debt on the date of sale. On the due date, it must pay $812,000, resulting in a loss of $17,000.

c. The five factors that affect currency exchange rates can be classified as three trade-related factors and two financial factors.

1) Trade-related factors

   a) Relative inflation rates
   b) Relative income levels
   c) Government intervention

2) Financial factors

   a) Relative interest rates
   b) Ease of capital flow

4. **Trade-Related Factors that Affect Exchange Rates**

a. **Relative Inflation Rates**

1) Recall from Study Unit 4 that the nominal interest rate consists of the real interest rate and the expected inflation rate.

2) When the rate of inflation in a foreign country rises relative to the rate of inflation in a domestic country, the products of that foreign country become relatively expensive and the demand for that country's currency falls.

   a) This leftward shift of the demand curve (from $D_\emptyset$ to D_1) results from the reduced purchasing power of that currency.

3) As investors sell this currency, more of it is available, which is reflected in a rightward shift of the supply curve (from $S_\emptyset$ to S_1).

4) A new equilibrium point is at a lower price in terms of investors' domestic currencies.

   a) As a result of the higher inflation in a foreign country, the domestic currency has appreciated in relation to that foreign currency. Thus, exports from the domestic country to the foreign country decrease and imports from the foreign country to the domestic country increase because the domestic goods are more expensive than the foreign goods.

Changes in Supply of and Demand for the Currency of a Foreign Country with Higher Relative Inflation

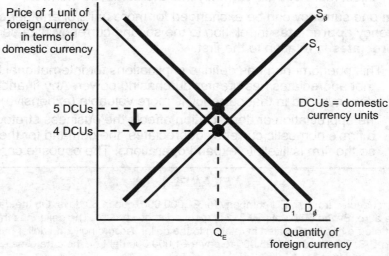

Figure 5-2

b)   The difference between the countries' inflation rates approximately equals the change in the currency exchange rate between the two countries.

   i)   For example, X has a 3% nominal inflation rate and Y has a 7% nominal rate. Because of the difference in nominal inflation rates, X's currency appreciates against Y's currency by approximately 4% (7% − 3%). This example assumes the real interest rate is constant between nations.

b.   **Relative Income Levels**

   1)   Persons with higher incomes look for new consumption opportunities in other countries, increasing the demand for those currencies and shifting the demand curve to the right.

      a)   As domestic incomes rise, the prices of foreign currencies also rise and the local currency depreciates. Thus, exports from the domestic to the foreign country increase and imports from the foreign country to the domestic country decrease.

Changes in Supply of and Demand for the Currency of a Foreign Country When Domestic Incomes Rise

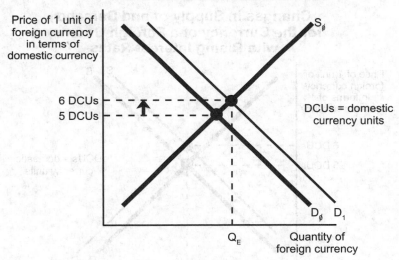

Figure 5-3

c.   **Government Intervention**

   1)   Actions by national governments, such as trade barriers and currency restrictions, complicate the process of exchange rate determination.

      a)   Trade barriers decrease imports of foreign goods and increase demand for domestic goods. Thus, domestic currency appreciates without hurting domestic producers.

         i)   However, trade barriers hurt consumers because consumers pay more for goods and ultimately have access to less diverse goods.

      b)   Currency controls limit exchange rate volatility by restricting the use of foreign currency or using a fixed exchange rate. As more people purchase domestic currency, domestic currency appreciates against foreign currency.

5.   **Financial Factors that Affect Exchange Rates**

    a.   **Relative Interest Rates**

        1)   When the interest rates in a foreign country rise relative to those of a domestic country, more investors are willing to buy the foreign country's currency to make investments and the demand for the foreign currency rises.

           a)   This rightward shift of the demand curve (from $D_\emptyset$ to D_1) results because holders of other currencies seek the higher returns available in the foreign country.

        2)   As more investors buy the high-interest country's currency to make investments, less of it is available, which is reflected in a leftward shift of the supply curve (from $S_\emptyset$ to S_1).

        3)   A new equilibrium point is at a higher price in terms of investors' domestic currencies.

           a)   An investor's domestic currency has depreciated against the currency of a foreign country with higher interest rates. Thus, exports from the domestic country to the foreign country increase and imports from the foreign country to the domestic country decrease because the domestic goods become more affordable than foreign goods.

Changes in Supply of and Demand for the Currency of a Foreign Country with Rising Interest Rates

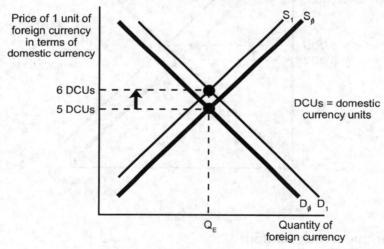

Figure 5-4

    b.   **Ease of Capital Flow**

        1)   If a country with high real interest rates removes restrictions on the cross-border movement of capital, the demand for the currency and the currency's value rises as investors seek higher returns.

           a)   As more capital flows into a country, the domestic currency supply increases because foreigners lend money to domestic firms and its citizenry. Consequently, this increase in supply reduces the currency's value. As a result, export demand rises and import demand falls. The opposite is also true.

        2)   This factor has become by far the most important of those listed.

           a)   The speed with which capital can be moved electronically and the huge amounts involved in the global economy are more significant than the effects of the trade-related factors.

6. **Graphical Depiction**

Exchange Rate Determination

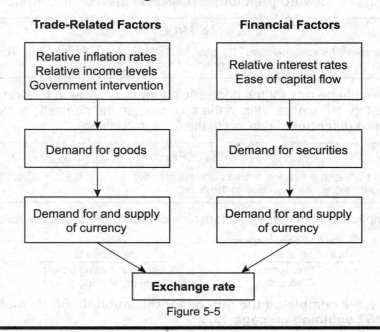

Figure 5-5

Candidates who can understand the relationship between the value of currency and financial or trade-related factors should be able to handle a variety of CPA questions. For example, when the real interest rate increases, the currency value appreciates. Also, when the real interest rate decreases, the currency value depreciates. Therefore, the real interest rate and the currency value have a direct relationship.

Trade-Related Factors that Occur in Domestic Economy	Domestic Currency Value	Foreign Currency Value*
Real interest rate	Direct	Indirect
Inflation rate	Indirect	Direct
Relative income level	Indirect	Direct
Demand for goods (or securities)	Direct	Indirect
Demand for currency	Direct	Indirect
Supply of currency	Indirect	Direct

*Assumes the foreign economy's trade-related factors are constant, i.e., are not changing.

7. **Exchange Rates**

    a. The **spot rate** is the number of units of a foreign currency that can be received today ("on the spot") in exchange for a single unit of the domestic currency.

EXAMPLE

A currency trader is willing to give 1.6 Swiss francs today in exchange for one British pound. Today's spot rate for the pound is therefore 1.6 Swiss francs, and today's spot rate for the franc is £0.625 (1 ÷ F1.6).

    b. The **forward rate** is the number of units of a foreign currency that can be received in exchange for a single unit of the domestic currency at some definite date in the future.

EXAMPLE

The currency trader contracts to provide 1.8 Swiss francs in exchange for one British pound 30 days from now. Today's 30-day forward rate for the pound is therefore 1.8 Swiss francs, and the 30-day forward rate for the franc is £0.555 (1 ÷ F1.8).

c.   If the exchange rate for the domestic currency is higher in relation to a foreign currency in the forward market than in the spot market, the domestic currency is trading at a **forward premium** in relation to the foreign currency.

EXAMPLE

The pound is currently trading at a forward premium in relation to the Swiss franc (F1.8 > F1.6). The market believes that the pound is going to appreciate in relation to the Swiss franc.

---

d.   If the exchange rate for the domestic currency is lower in relation to a foreign currency in the forward market than in the spot market, the domestic currency is trading at a **forward discount** in relation to the foreign currency.

EXAMPLE

The Swiss franc is currently trading at a forward discount in relation to the pound (£0.555 < £0.625). The market believes that the Swiss franc is going to depreciate in relation to the pound.

---

e.   The implications of these relationships can be generalized as follows:

If the domestic currency is trading at a forward	Then it is expected to
Premium	Gain purchasing power
Discount	Lose purchasing power

Stop and review! You have completed the outline for this subunit. Study multiple-choice questions 9 through 16 beginning on page 132.

5.3 GLOBALIZATION AND BUSINESS RESTRUCTURING

1.   **Impact of Globalization on the Business Environment**

a.   The business environment and decision making become increasingly complex as globalization brings capital flows, international competition, technological innovation, migration of labor and work, environmental concerns, etc.

1)   Globalization significantly increases business risks ranging from exchange rate and interest rate fluctuation to piracy in the global supply chain.

2)   Globalization increases cross-border investments and international competition. Cross-border investments face regulatory obstacles that impact trade, such as protectionism, taxation, and environmental laws.

3)   Managing a global workforce is difficult because the operations are further separated on a global scale. A related challenge is reconciling cultural and religious differences while maintaining a diverse workforce to empower global and local success.

4)   Globalization of the financial market leads to increasing mergers and acquisitions in the financial service industry. Capital flows more freely across the globe as a result.

5)   Cross-border restructuring happens more frequently as companies seek to obtain global capital, increase economies of scale, improve market share, increase geographical diversification, etc.

2.   **Restructuring in a Global Context**

a.   Forms of Business Restructuring

1)   A **merger** is the combination of two companies to form a new company (Company A + Company B = Company C).

2)   An **acquisition** is a business combination that involves the purchase of one company by another in which no new company is formed (Company A + Company B = Company A).

3) In a **joint venture**, two or more entities agree to pool their resources to achieve specific objectives. Unlike mergers or acquisitions, a joint venture forms a temporary partnership. After the specific objective is achieved, the joint venture will be dissolved or sold.

4) A **divestiture** is the partial or full disposal of a business unit through sale, exchange, closure, or bankruptcy.

b. Business Purposes for Mergers and Acquisitions

1) Fluctuation in exchange rates can influence cross-border mergers and acquisitions. Companies in countries where the currency is stronger are more likely to acquire the company in countries where the currency is weaker.

2) When a company buys out a supplier or a distributor, the company saves supply costs or shipping costs that would have been spent if the supplier or the distributor were independent from the company. This is **vertical integration**.

3) Many companies acquire or merge with competitors to gain market share and eliminate competition. This is **horizontal integration**.

4) Mergers and acquisitions might occur when an existing company acquires a company in a different industry because they seek to diversify the risks and reduce the impact of a particular industry's performance. In contrast, a company might also choose to merge with a company that focuses on a particular area to sharpen business focus.

5) Mergers and acquisitions achieve synergy. Two businesses can create greater efficiency and economies of scale by combining business activities. For example, two companies may choose to combine their IT departments or their finance departments to reduce overhead costs significantly.

c. Business Purposes for Joint Venture

1) Joint venture enables businesses to share assets, costs, expertise, and business risks.

2) The flexibility of a joint venture helps businesses avoid costly mergers, acquisitions, and transfer of ownership. Entities have the freedom to choose alliances with multiple firms and not be tied to an alliance with one firm (e.g., in the case of a merger). Ultimately, joint ventures allow open-ended and new business opportunities.

3) Like mergers and acquisitions, a joint venture helps businesses gain access to market share, obtain capital, and achieve diversification.

d. Business Purposes for Divestiture

1) Companies divest when part of the business is not performing well to prevent further loss.

2) Regulators might require companies to divest for antitrust concerns.

3) Divestiture could be a part of the bankruptcy process when a healthier company arises from the bankruptcy.

4) Companies could obtain funds by divesting part of the business to solve financial difficulties and provide much-needed liquidity.

5) Companies sometimes divest so they can focus on their prominent operations and improve core competency.

6) Companies could also divest when they believe two separate entities would be more profitable than a consolidated entity.

7) As the exchange rate for a domestic currency falls, a foreign company might purchase a subsidiary from the domestic country. Once the exchange rate in the domestic country rises, the foreign company sells the subsidiary to gain the difference between the purchase and selling price.

3.　**Culture Change in Mergers and Acquisitions**

　　a.　Organizational culture undergoes significant changes after a merger or acquisition. Four modes of acculturation can be triggered.

　　　　1)　**Integration** refers to incorporating external individuals into a workplace as equals. The members of the acquired company try to maintain their culture to a certain degree; however, they are willing to integrate into the acquirer's culture simultaneously.

　　　　2)　**Assimilation** is the abandonment of one culture in favor of another when becoming part of a new workplace. The members of the acquired company gradually abandon their culture and willingly adopt the acquiring company's culture.

　　　　3)　**Separation** occurs when the two entities distance themselves from one another culturally. The members of the acquired company try to maintain their own culture and resist adopting the acquiring company's culture.

　　　　4)　**Deculturation** refers to the loss or desertion of cultural characteristics in the workplace. The employees in the acquired company do not value their previous workplace culture, and they refuse to assimilate into the acquirer's culture.

Stop and review! You have completed the outline for this subunit. Study multiple-choice questions 17 through 20 beginning on page 134.

QUESTIONS
5.1　Protectionism

1. Which of the following is a tariff?

　A.　Licensing requirements.

　B.　Consumption taxes on imported goods.

　C.　Unreasonable standards pertaining to product quality and safety.

　D.　Domestic content rules.

Answer (B) is correct.
　REQUIRED: The example of a tariff.
　DISCUSSION: Tariffs are excise taxes on imported goods imposed either to generate revenue or protect domestic producers. Thus, consumption taxes on imported goods are tariffs.
　Answer (A) is incorrect. Licensing requirements limit exports, e.g., of militarily sensitive technology. Answer (C) is incorrect. Unreasonable standards pertaining to product quality and safety are nontariff trade barriers. Answer (D) is incorrect. Domestic content rules require that a portion of an imported good be made in the importing country.

2. The return to the home country of income earned by a domestic firm in a foreign country is

　A.　Expropriation.

　B.　Bankruptcy.

　C.　Repatriation.

　D.　Reinvestment.

Answer (C) is correct.
　REQUIRED: The return to the home country of income earned in a foreign country.
　DISCUSSION: Many firms have business operations abroad. Repatriation is conversion of funds held in a foreign country into another currency and remittance of these funds to another nation. A firm often must obtain permission from the currency exchange authorities to repatriate earnings and investments. Regulations in many nations encourage a reinvestment of earnings in the country.
　Answer (A) is incorrect. Expropriation is a foreign government's seizure (nationalization) of the assets of a business for a public purpose and for just compensation. Answer (B) is incorrect. Bankruptcy occurs when a person's liabilities exceed assets or (s)he cannot meet obligations when they are due. Answer (D) is incorrect. Reinvestment in the foreign country is a purpose of restrictions on repatriation.

3. Import restrictions for purposes of creating domestic employment

    A. Are likely to increase the number of export jobs.

    B. May lead to lower prices for consumers.

    C. Will lead to lower sales tax collections.

    D. May lead to retaliation by other countries.

Answer (D) is correct.
    REQUIRED: The true statement about the effect of import restrictions for creating domestic employment.
    DISCUSSION: Protectionism in the form of import restrictions can lead to a variety of economic and social costs, including higher prices to consumers for both domestic and imported goods, higher taxes, and retaliation by other countries.
    Answer (A) is incorrect. Export jobs may decline due to retaliation by other countries. Answer (B) is incorrect. Consumers will have to pay higher prices for the protected domestic goods and may have to pay higher prices for foreign goods as well. Answer (C) is incorrect. Depending on the price elasticity of demand for the product, sales tax revenues may or may not fall.

4. The appropriate remedy for the dumping of products by a foreign firm in the U.S. market would be to

    A. Pass "buy American" laws.

    B. Impose restrictions on U.S. exports to the offending country.

    C. Impose countervailing duties or tariffs.

    D. Deny "most favored nation" treatment to exporters of the offending country.

Answer (C) is correct.
    REQUIRED: The appropriate remedy for the dumping of products by a foreign firm in the U.S. market.
    DISCUSSION: Dumping is the practice of supporting exports by selling products at a lower price in foreign markets than in the domestic market. The result is that foreign goods can be purchased in the U.S. at a price much lower than would be charged by a U.S. manufacturer. Because dumping lowers the price of foreign goods, the appropriate remedy is for the importing nation to impose a tariff that reduces the price differential.
    Answer (A) is incorrect. The passing of laws requiring domestic sourcing could result in a decline in overall domestic consumption, higher prices, and retaliatory foreign action. Answer (B) is incorrect. A country does not benefit from restricting its exports. Answer (D) is incorrect. Denying most favored nation treatment makes trade with a country more difficult and is a more extreme remedy than necessary.

5. Which of the following results in a complete elimination of trade?

    A. Voluntary export restraints.

    B. Domestic content requirements.

    C. Embargoes.

    D. Import quotas.

Answer (C) is correct.
    REQUIRED: The item that results in a complete elimination of trade.
    DISCUSSION: An embargo is a total ban on some kinds of imports. It is an extreme form of the import quota (i.e., the quota is zero).
    Answer (A) is incorrect. A voluntary restraint can be waived. Answer (B) is incorrect. Domestic content rules require that at least a portion of the imported product be constructed from parts manufactured in the importing nation. If this requirement is met, trade is not limited. Answer (D) is incorrect. Import quotas set fixed limits on the quantity of certain goods that can be imported. They limit but do not eliminate trade.

6. Domestic content rules

    A. Tend to be imposed by capital-intensive countries.

    B. Tend to be imposed by labor-intensive countries.

    C. Exclude products not made domestically.

    D. Restrict demand for affected products.

Answer (A) is correct.
    REQUIRED: The description of domestic content rules.
    DISCUSSION: Domestic content rules require that at least a portion of any imported product be constructed from parts manufactured in the importing nation. This rule sometimes is used by capital-intensive nations. Parts can be produced using idle capacity and then sent to a labor-intensive country for final assembly.
    Answer (B) is incorrect. Labor-intensive exporters are more likely to assemble final products. Answer (C) is incorrect. Domestic content rules place limits on, but do not exclude, imports. Answer (D) is incorrect. Supply is restricted.

7. What is the most likely economic effect of tariffs and quotas?

A. Workers are shifted into more efficient export industries.

B. Tariffs but not quotas affect all importers of the affected goods equally.

C. Total world output increases.

D. The price increase is received by exporters in foreign countries.

Answer (B) is correct.
REQUIRED: The effect of tariffs and quotas.
DISCUSSION: A tariff has an equal effect on all goods on which it is applied. Import licenses, however, may be awarded based on political favoritism.
Answer (A) is incorrect. The effect is to shift workers into relatively inefficient domestic protected industries. Answer (C) is incorrect. Total world output decreases. Answer (D) is incorrect. A tariff increases the domestic government's general tax revenues.

8. Which of the following is an economic reason for government intervention in trade?

A. Maintaining spheres of influence.

B. Protecting infant industries.

C. Preserving national identity.

D. Dealing with friendly countries.

Answer (B) is correct.
REQUIRED: The best economic reason for government intervention in trade.
DISCUSSION: The infant-industry argument is that protective tariffs are needed to allow new domestic industries to become established. Once such industries reach the maturity stage in their life cycles, the tariffs supposedly can be removed.

5.2 Currency Exchange Rates

9. If the value of the U.S. dollar in foreign currency markets changes from $1 = .75 euros to $1 = .70 euros,

A. The euro has depreciated against the dollar.

B. Products imported from Europe to the U.S. will become more expensive.

C. U.S. tourists in Europe will find their dollars will buy more European products.

D. U.S. exports to Europe should decrease.

Answer (B) is correct.
REQUIRED: The effect of a depreciation in the value of the dollar.
DISCUSSION: The dollar has declined in value relative to the euro. If an American had previously wished to purchase a European product that was priced at 10 euros, the price would have been about $13.33. After the dollar's decline in value, the price of the item has increased to about $14.29. Thus, imports from Europe should decrease and exports increase.
Answer (A) is incorrect. The euro has appreciated (increased in value) relative to the dollar. Answer (C) is incorrect. Dollars will buy fewer European products. Answer (D) is incorrect. U.S. exports should increase because the euro has appreciated with respect to the dollar.

10. The U.S. dollar has a freely floating exchange rate. When the dollar has fallen considerably in relation to other currencies, the

A. Trade account in the U.S. balance of payments is neither in a deficit nor in a surplus because of the floating exchange rates.

B. Capital account in the U.S. balance of payments is neither in a deficit nor in a surplus because of the floating exchange rates.

C. Fall in the dollar's value cannot be expected to have any effect on the U.S. trade balance.

D. Cheaper dollar helps U.S. exporters of domestically produced goods.

Answer (D) is correct.
REQUIRED: The true statement about the fall in the price of the dollar relative to other currencies.
DISCUSSION: A decline in the value of the dollar relative to other currencies lowers the price of U.S. goods to foreign consumers. Thus, exporters of domestically produced goods benefit. A low value of the dollar also decreases imports by making foreign goods more expensive.
Answer (A) is incorrect. Net exports increase as a result of dollar depreciation. Answer (B) is incorrect. The capital account benefits from the cheaper dollar. Foreigners can buy more dollars with fewer yen, euros, etc. Moreover, foreign capital inflow increases because of the federal government's budget deficits. Thus, the U.S. has a net capital inflow. Answer (C) is incorrect. The fall in the dollar has a positive effect on the nation's trade deficit. Exports increase and imports decrease.

11. The spot rate for one Australian dollar is $0.92685 and the 60-day forward rate is $0.93005. Which one of the following statements is consistent with these facts?

    A. The U.S. dollar is trading at a forward discount with respect to the Australian dollar.

    B. The U.S. dollar is trading at a forward premium with respect to the Australian dollar.

    C. The U.S. dollar has lost purchasing power with respect to the Australian dollar.

    D. The U.S. dollar has gained purchasing power with respect to the Australian dollar.

Answer (A) is correct.
    REQUIRED: The conclusion about a forward exchange rate.
    DISCUSSION: The exchange rate for the Australian dollar is higher in the forward market than the spot market. The Australian dollar is therefore trading at a forward premium. Accordingly, the U.S. dollar is trading at a forward discount.
    Answer (B) is incorrect. The U.S. dollar is trading at a forward discount in relation to the Australian dollar. Answer (C) is incorrect. No conclusion about purchasing power changes can be drawn without information about past exchange rates. Answer (D) is incorrect. No conclusion about purchasing power changes can be drawn without information about past exchange rates.

12. The accompanying graph depicts the supply of and demand for U.S. dollars in terms of euros at a moment in time. Currently, the equilibrium exchange rate is $1 to 0.65 €. If inflation of the dollar exceeds that of the euro, the new equilibrium exchange rate would most likely settle at

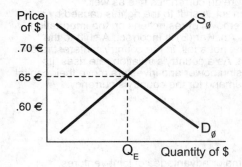

	Quantity	Price
A.	Indeterminate	0.70 €
B.	Lower than Q_E	0.70 €
C.	Higher than Q_E	0.60 €
D.	Indeterminate	0.60 €

Answer (D) is correct.
    REQUIRED: The graphic depiction of inflation of a base currency against a foreign currency.
    DISCUSSION: The graph depicts the supply of and demand for the U.S. dollar by holders of euros. When the U.S. dollar inflates faster than the euro, the U.S. dollar loses purchasing power. As the weakening U.S. dollar becomes less attractive, the demand for it falls (its demand curve shifts to the left) and the supply for it increases (its supply curve shifts to the right). A new equilibrium point is at a lower price. However, a new equilibrium quantity cannot be determined. If the supply curve shift is greater (lesser) than the demand curve shift, the new equilibrium quantity will be higher (lower); if the supply curve shift is equal to the demand curve shift, the equilibrium quantity will remain the same.
    Answer (A) is incorrect. The new equilibrium price will be lower. Answer (B) is incorrect. The new equilibrium quantity cannot be determined, and the new equilibrium price will be lower. Answer (C) is incorrect. The new equilibrium quantity cannot be determined.

13. If the U.S. dollar-peso exchange rate is $1 for 9 pesos, a product priced at 45 pesos will cost a U.S. consumer

    A. $0.20

    B. $5

    C. $45

    D. $405

Answer (B) is correct.
    REQUIRED: The price in dollars of a product for which the price is quoted in pesos.
    DISCUSSION: At a 1-for-9 rate, the price in U.S. dollars is $5, calculated by dividing 45 pesos by 9.
    Answer (A) is incorrect. The amount of $0.20 is based on an inversion of the numerator and denominator in the calculation. Answer (C) is incorrect. The amount of $45 is the price in pesos, not dollars. Answer (D) is incorrect. The amount of $405 is based on multiplying 45 and 9.

14. If the central bank of a country raises interest rates sharply, the country's currency will likely

    A. Increase in relative value.

    B. Remain unchanged in value.

    C. Decrease in relative value.

    D. Decrease sharply in value at first and then return to its initial value.

Answer (A) is correct.
    REQUIRED: The effect on a country's currency if its central bank raises interest rates sharply.
    DISCUSSION: Exchange rates fluctuate depending upon the demand for each country's currency. If a country raises its interest rates, its currency will appreciate. The demand for investment at the higher interest rates will shift the demand curve for the currency to the right. The reverse holds true for a decrease in interest rates.

15. Which one of the following statements supports the conclusion that the U.S. dollar has gained purchasing power against the Japanese yen?

    A. Inflation has recently been higher in the U.S. than in Japan.

    B. The dollar is currently trading at a premium in the forward market with respect to the yen.

    C. The yen's spot rate with respect to the dollar has just fallen.

    D. Studies recently published in the financial press have shed doubt on the interest rate parity (IRP) theory.

Answer (C) is correct.
    REQUIRED: The statement that supports the conclusion that the U.S. dollar has gained purchasing power against the Japanese yen.
    DISCUSSION: If the yen's spot rate has just fallen, more yen are required to buy a single dollar. The yen has therefore depreciated, i.e., lost purchasing power. At the same time, the dollar has gained purchasing power.
    Answer (A) is incorrect. Higher inflation in the U.S. than in Japan reflects a loss, not a gain, of the dollar's purchasing power. Answer (B) is incorrect. No conclusion can be drawn about changes in purchasing power simply from a statement about forward rates. Answer (D) is incorrect. No conclusion can be drawn about changes in purchasing power simply from evidence for or against the interest rate parity (IRP) theory.

16. A shift of the demand curve for a country's currency to the right could be caused by which of the following?

    A. A foreign government placing restrictions on the importation of the country's goods.

    B. A fall in the country's interest rates.

    C. Domestic inflation worsens.

    D. A rise in consumer incomes in another country.

Answer (D) is correct.
    REQUIRED: The condition that could cause a rise in demand for a country's currency.
    DISCUSSION: Citizens with higher incomes look for new consumption opportunities in other countries, driving up the demand for those currencies. Thus, as incomes rise in one country, the prices of foreign currencies rise as well.
    Answer (A) is incorrect. A shift to the right is caused by a foreign government's removal of restrictions on the importation of the country's goods. Answer (B) is incorrect. A shift to the right is caused by a rise, not a fall, in the country's interest rates. Answer (C) is incorrect. As a country's inflation rate rises, its currency loses purchasing power and investors move their capital elsewhere, reducing demand for the country's currency.

5.3 Globalization and Business Restructuring

17. The major advantages of joint ventures include each of the following **except**

    A. An open relationship where each company can become involved with other firms.

    B. Access to skills the second company has that the first company needs.

    C. Limited liability for the actions of the partners.

    D. Avoiding the expensive process of a formal merger.

Answer (C) is correct.
    REQUIRED: The major advantages of joint ventures.
    DISCUSSION: Limited liability does not apply to corporations in joint ventures, only to passive owners of corporations.
    Answer (A) is incorrect. Companies in joint ventures are often involved with other firms on specific projects. Answer (B) is incorrect. Access to skills the other company has is often why firms choose joint ventures. Answer (D) is incorrect. Joint ventures do reduce the regulatory burden on firms that want to work together and are usually less expensive than a formal merger.

18. Which of the following is **not** a business purpose for divestment of a part of a business?

    A. The two separate entities would be more profitable than the combined unit.

    B. The owner wants to acquire a new subsidiary and wants to avoid jealousy by the existing employees.

    C. The subsidiary requires so much effort and attention it distracts from other areas of the business.

    D. The two separate entities would be more profitable than the combined unit and the subsidiary requires so much effort and attention it distracts from other areas of the business.

Answer (B) is correct.
    REQUIRED: The business purpose that is not a reason for divestment.
    DISCUSSION: Divestiture of an old division in order to obtain a new division to avoid jealousy may not be a business purpose for the divestiture. There may be other ways to handle jealousy, such as inclusion of the older employees in the new division.
    Answer (A) is incorrect. When two separate entities would be more profitable than the combined unit indicates they should not be a combined unit. Answer (C) is incorrect. When the subsidiary requires so much effort and attention it distracts from other areas of the business is a business purpose for divestment of a part of a business as it simply costs too much to have this subsidiary and can drag down the rest of the company. Answer (D) is incorrect. Divesting a part of a business because the two separate entities would be more profitable than the combined unit or the subsidiary requires so much effort and attention it distracts from other areas of the business would qualify as a business purpose.

19. Which of the following business combinations is a vertical integration?

- A. The corner gas station buys the competitor across the street and shuts them down to increase its own market share.

- B. The corner gas station and the competitor across the street agree to set their prices at the same level.

- C. The corner gas station acquires the gasoline distributor to ensure they can get gas in times of shortages.

- D. The corner gas station starts selling fireworks during December/January and June/July.

Answer (C) is correct.
  REQUIRED: The types of vertical business combinations.
  DISCUSSION: A vertical integration is where a company acquires control through ownership of its suppliers. Because the corner gas station acquires control through ownership of the gas distributor, its supplier, this is a vertical integration.
  Answer (A) is incorrect. Because the corner gas station acquires control through ownership of its competitors, this is a horizontal merger. Answer (B) is incorrect. This is price fixing, not a business combination. Answer (D) is incorrect. This is not a combination. The gas station is simply adding a new product line.

20. When Beta Company bought Gamma Company, Beta sold off about 30% of Gamma's assets because they did not need them. Beta kept only the part of Gamma that is counter-cyclical to Beta's other business. Why did they do this?

- A. To reduce their seasonal variation in sales via diversification.

- B. To obtain financing for the merger not available from any other source.

- C. To increase their risks and magnify the impact of sales fluctuation during the year.

- D. To achieve horizontal integration.

Answer (A) is correct.
  REQUIRED: The reason behind business combinations in businesses with seasonal variation in sales.
  DISCUSSION: The company is trying to avoid the wide swings of their first business without getting distracted by Gamma's unrelated operations.
  Answer (B) is incorrect. Often assets are liquidated to reduce the cost of a combination, and financing is usually available from other sources. Answer (C) is incorrect. Gamma is trying to reduce risk by reducing losses during idle times, not add to risk by increasing the variability of revenues. Answer (D) is incorrect. Horizontal integration is where a company is trying to gain market share by acquisition and may involve shutting down competitors, neither of which are indicated here.

Online is better! To best prepare for the CPA exam, access **thousands** of exam-emulating MCQs and TBSs through Gleim CPA Review online courses with SmartAdapt technology. Learn more at www.gleimcpa.com or contact our team at 800.874.5346 to upgrade.

136

STUDY UNIT SIX
RISK RETURN PRINCIPLES

(11 pages of outline)

Every investment has an expectation of a return and some amount of risk. An investing entity can receive an adequate return on its investments while minimizing risk by quantifying and understanding the principles of risk and return.

6.1 RISK AND RETURN

1. **Rate of Return**

    a. A return is the amount received by an investor as compensation for accepting the risk of the investment.

    $$Return\ on\ investment\ =\ Amount\ received\ -\ Amount\ invested$$

    ### EXAMPLE

    An investor paid $100,000 for an investment that returned $112,000. The investor's return is $12,000 ($112,000 − $100,000).

    b. The rate of return is a percentage of the amount invested.

    $$Rate\ of\ return\ =\ \frac{Return\ on\ investment}{Amount\ invested}$$

    ### EXAMPLE

    The investor's rate of return is 12% ($12,000 ÷ $100,000).

2.   **Time Value of Money**

a.   People prefer to hold money now rather than in the future. "A dollar today is worth more than a dollar tomorrow."

b.   This principle of desiring money sooner rather than later is the basis for the concept of interest.

c.   **Interest** is the cornerstone of investment because interest represents the price charged by investors (or creditors) to permit others to use their money. Investors are willing to forgo the use of money now in exchange for a return at a later moment in time.

d.   The relationship between a dollar today and its value in the future is depicted in the graph below.

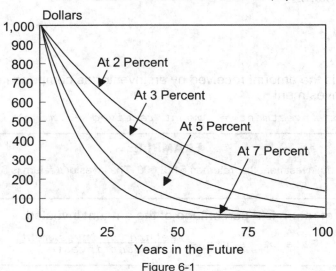

The Present Discounted Value of $1,000

Figure 6-1

e.   The formula for compound interest and present value/future value computations is

$$FV = PV \times (1 + i)^n$$

FV = Future value
PV = Present value
    i = Interest rate for the period
   n = Number of periods

EXAMPLE

Assume

        PV = $100
          i = 5% per year
          n = 2 years

The future value of the $100 held for 2 years earning 5% per year, compounded annually, is calculated as follows:

        FV = $100 × (1 + 0.05)^2
            = $110.25

3. **Simple Interest vs. Compound Interest**

   a. The interest generated by an investment can either be paid periodically in cash or added to the investment principal in a process known as **compounding**.

EXAMPLE

A mutual fund offers its investors an annual 4% return. It can be received in cash or compounded. The following tables illustrate the difference in cash flows under the two methods:

	Using Simple Interest					Using Compound Interest			
	Beginning Balance	Annual Return	Cash Disbursed	Added to Balance		Beginning Balance	Annual Return	Added to Balance	Cash Disbursed
Year 1	$10,000.00 ×	4% =	$400.00	--		$10,000.00 ×	4% =	$400.00	--
Year 2	10,000.00 ×	4% =	400.00	--		10,400.00 ×	4% =	416.00	--
Year 3	10,000.00 ×	4% =	400.00	--		10,816.00 ×	4% =	432.64	--
Year 4	10,000.00 ×	4% =	400.00	--		11,248.64 ×	4% =	449.95	--
Year 5	10,000.00 ×	4% =	400.00	--		11,698.59 ×	4% =	467.94	--

At the end of 5 years, the investor who received periodic payments had the use of $400 cash every year but has only the original $10,000 principle. An investor who chose compounding received no periodic cash flow but has a principle of $12,166.53 ($11,698.59 Year 5 beginning balance + $467.94 Year 5 return).

---

4. **Two Basic Types of Investment Risk**

   a. Based on statistical analysis of stock market data, risk can be categorized as systematic or unsystematic.

   b. All firms have **systematic risk**, also called **market risk**. Changes in the economy, such as inflation or the business cycle, affect all those in the market. Systematic risk is unavoidable.

      1) For this reason, systematic risk sometimes is called **undiversifiable risk**. Because all investments are affected, it cannot be reduced by diversification.

   c. **Unsystematic risk**, also called idiosyncratic risk or company risk, is the risk inherent in a particular investment. Thus, it is the risk of a specific firm. This type of risk is determined by the firm's industry, products, customer loyalty, degree of leverage, management competence, etc.

      1) Unsystematic risk sometimes is called **diversifiable risk**. Because individual investments are affected by the particular strengths and weaknesses of the firm, this risk can be reduced by diversification. (Item 4. in Subunit 6.2 explains diversification.)

5. **Types of Investment Risk**

   a. **Credit default risk** is the risk that the borrower will default and not be able to repay principal or interest. This risk is estimated by credit-rating agencies.

   b. **Liquidity risk** is the risk that a security cannot be sold on short notice without a loss.

   c. **Maturity risk**, also called **interest rate risk**, is the risk that an investment security will fluctuate in value between the time it was issued and its maturity date. The longer the time until maturity, the greater the degree of maturity risk. It may also be paid back before maturity.

   d. **Inflation risk** is the risk that purchasing power of the currency will decline. (Study Unit 4, Subunit 5, describes the causes and effects of inflation.)

   e. **Political risk** is the probability of loss from actions of governments, such as changes in tax laws or environmental regulations or expropriation of assets.

   f. **Exchange rate risk** is the risk of loss because of fluctuation in the relative value of a foreign currency in which the investment is payable.

g. **Business risk** (or **operations risk**) is the risk of fluctuations in earnings before interest and taxes or in operating income when the firm uses no debt, which causes cash flows to be inadequate to pay interest and principal on time.

   1) It is the risk inherent in operations that excludes **financial risk**, the risk to the shareholders of financial leverage.

   2) Business risk depends on factors such as (a) demand variability, (b) sales price variability, (c) input price variability, and (d) the amount of operating leverage.

h. **Country risk** is the overall risk of investing in a foreign country.

i. **Principal risk** (default risk) is the risk of losing the principal invested.

6. **Relationship between Risk and Return**

   a. Whether the expected return on an investment suffices to attract an investor depends on (1) its risk, (2) the risks and returns of alternative investments, (3) the investor's attitude toward risk, and (4) the investor's portfolio of investments.

      1) Most investors (and people in general) are **risk-averse**. For them, the utility of a gain is less than the disutility of a loss of the same amount. For instance, the pain of losing $1,000 is worse than the happiness gained from earning $1,000.

EXAMPLE

Risk aversion is reflected by actions of people in a casino. Many are willing to bet $1 on one of the numbers on a roulette table because the chance of a gain of multiple dollars versus the loss of $1 is acceptable. However, as the minimum amount of a bet increases (from $1 to $100 to $1,000), the number of willing casual gamblers decreases because the chance for earning hundreds or thousands of dollars versus the probability of losing $100 or $1,000 is not acceptable. Thus, risk aversion keeps many people from gambling as the minimum bet increases.

---

      a) Because of risk aversion, risky securities must have higher expected returns. These returns induce investors to accept additional risk. In the example above, if a casino were to provide better odds (i.e., a higher expected return) for higher bet amounts, more casual gamblers may be induced to place higher minimum bets.

      b) In financial and economic models, all investors are assumed to be risk averse.

   2) A **risk-neutral** investor adopts an expected value approach. (S)he regards the utility of a gain as equal to the disutility of a loss of the same amount.

      a) In the case of a casino gambler, a risk-neutral person is as willing to gamble for a high amount as a low amount (assuming the odds are commensurate with the expected value).

   3) A **risk-seeking** investor has an optimistic attitude toward risk. (S)he regards the utility of a gain as exceeding the disutility of a loss of the same amount.

      a) In the case of a casino gambler, a risk-seeking person is more willing to play roulette than craps, baccarat, or poker due to the greater risk.

      b) Some seek risk as the reward, such as sky divers.

b. The greater the risk of the investment, the higher the rate of return required by the investor. For each type of investment risk, the investor requires an additional risk premium that compensates him or her for bearing that risk.

   1) The **risk premium** is the excess of an investment's expected rate of return over the risk-free interest rate.

   2) The **risk-free rate** is the interest rate on the safest investment. In practice, the stated interest rate on U.S. Treasury bills is considered to be the risk-free interest rate.

      a) A holder of U.S. Treasury bills generally is exposed only to inflation risk. Thus, the market rate of interest on U.S. Treasury bills equals the risk-free rate of interest plus the inflation premium.

3) The **required rate of return** considers all investment risks that relate to a specific security.

EXAMPLE

Real risk-free rate	3%
Inflation premium	1%
Risk-free rate	4%
Liquidity risk premium	1%
Default risk premium	2%
Maturity risk premium	1%
Required rate of return	8%

---

7. **Investment Securities**

   a. Financial managers may select from a wide range of financial instruments to raise capital or invest.

      1) The safety of an investment and its potential return have an inverse relationship. The following is a short list of widely available investment securities:

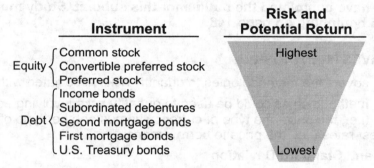

Figure 6-2

   b. The reasons for the varying risks and potential returns of these securities can be summarized as follows:

      1) Equity securities are considered riskier than debt because an entity's owners are not legally guaranteed a return.

         a) Common shareholders are the residual owners of a corporation. They are last in order of priority during liquidation, but they have the right to receive distributions of excess profits. Thus, the equity investments have a higher upside (or reward) than debt investments.

         b) Preferred shareholders usually have a higher priority than common shareholders in liquidation, but their potential returns are limited by the board of directors. They may participate in extra dividends or their shares may be converted into common stock.

      2) Issuers of debt securities are legally obligated to redeem them. Because these returns are guaranteed, their risks and returns are lower than those for equity investments.

         a) Income bonds pay a return only if the issuer is profitable.

         b) Debentures are unsecured debt securities, which means they are not collateralized.

         c) Mortgage bonds are secured (or collateralized) by real property.

         d) U.S. Treasury bonds are backed by the full faith and credit of the United States government.

      3) Precious metals (also called commodities) normally are considered a risky investment because their prices are highly volatile. During periods of high inflation, however, currency loses purchasing power rapidly, and precious metals, such as gold, may be a safe investment.

8. **Efficient Market Hypothesis (EMH)**

   a. The EMH is that the stock price can immediately and fully reflect all relevant information.

   b. Characteristics of the EMH include the following:

      1) Investors are knowledgeable.
      2) Capital market prices can reflect underlying value.
      3) Accounting changes do not influence the stock price.

   c. The EMH has three forms.

      1) The weak-form EMH is that public and non-public insider information may or may not be available to investors. The current stock price only reflects historical prices.

      2) The semi-strong form EMH is that all public information is incorporated into the current stock price.

      3) The strong-form EMH is that all information, including public information and nonpublic insider information, is incorporated into the current stock price.

Stop and review! You have completed the outline for this subunit. Study multiple-choice questions 1 through 5 beginning on page 148.

6.2 QUANTIFYING INVESTMENT RISK

1. This subunit covers the methodologies to quantify risks associated with business entities.

   a. These methodologies could be used to quantify risks involving equity prices, exchange rates (i.e., the price of a type of currency versus another type of currency), and interest rates (i.e., the price to borrow money).

2. **Probability and Standard Deviation**

   a. Probability provides a method for mathematically expressing the likelihood of possible outcomes.

   b. A **probability distribution** is the set of all possible outcomes of a decision, with a probability assigned to each outcome. For example, a simple probability distribution might be defined for the possible returns on a stock investment. A different return could be estimated for each of a limited number of possible states of the economy, and a probability could be determined for each state. Such a distribution is **discrete** because the outcomes are limited.

3. **Measures of Risk – Standard Deviation and Variance**

   a. The **expected rate of return ($\overline{R}$)** on an investment is determined using an expected value calculation. It is an average of the possible outcomes weighted according to their probabilities.

   Expected rate of return ($\overline{R}$) = $\sum$ (Possible rate of return × Probability)

EXAMPLE

A company is considering investing in the common stock of one of two firms, Xatalan Corp. and Yarmouth Co. The expected rates of return on the two securities based on the weighted averages of their probable outcomes are calculated as follows:

Xatalan Corporation Stock					Yarmouth Company Stock				
Rate of Return %		Probability %		Weighted Average	Rate of Return %		Probability %		Weighted Average
80 %	×	60%	=	48 %	30 %	×	70%	=	21 %
(50)%	×	40%	=	(20)%	(10)%	×	30%	=	(3)%
Expected rate of return ($\overline{R}$)				**28 %**	**Expected rate of return ($\overline{R}$)**				**18 %**

The expected rate of return on Xatalan stock is higher, but the risk of each investment also should be measured.

b. Risk is the probability that the actual return on an investment will differ from the expected return. One measure of risk is the standard deviation (variance's square root) of the distribution of an investment's return.

$$\textit{Standard deviation } (\sigma) = \sqrt{\sum [(R_i - \bar{R})^2 \times \textit{Probability}} = \sqrt{\textit{Variance}}$$

If: R_i = Possible rate of return
       $\bar{R}$ = Expected rate of return

1) The **standard deviation** measures the tightness of the distribution and the riskiness of the investment. In practice, the standard deviation is often annualized by multiplying weekly/monthly/quarterly returns by the square root. For example, for monthly returns, the annualized standard deviation equals the standard deviation of monthly returns multiplied by the square root of 12.

     a) A large standard deviation reflects a broadly dispersed probability distribution, meaning the range of possible returns is wide. But, the smaller the standard deviation, the tighter the probability distribution and the lower the risk.

     b) Thus, the greater the standard deviation, the riskier the investment.

Small Standard Deviation   **Large Standard Deviation**

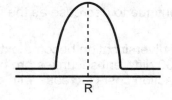 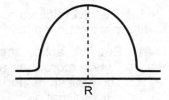

Figure 6-3

EXAMPLE

The following are the standard deviations of the returns on the investments from the previous example:

<u>**Xatalan Corporation Stock**</u>

Standard deviation (σ)   = $\sqrt{[(80\% - 28\%)^2 \times 60\%] + [(-50\% - 28\%)^2 \times 40\%]}$ $= \sqrt{40.56\%}$ =   **63.69%**

<u>**Yarmouth Company Stock**</u>

Standard deviation (σ)   = $\sqrt{[(30\% - 18\%)^2 \times 70\%] + [(-10\% - 18\%)^2 \times 30\%]}$ $= \sqrt{3.36\%}$ =   **18.33%**

The investment in Xatalan stock has a higher expected return than the investment in Yarmouth stock (28% > 18%). It also is riskier because its standard deviation is greater (63.69% > 18.33%). Accordingly, to determine which investment has the preferable risk-return tradeoff, the coefficient of variation (CV) of the expected returns on the two investments is measured.

---

c. The **coefficient of variation (CV)** is useful when the rates of return and standard deviations of two investments differ. It measures the **risk per unit of return**.

$$\textit{Coefficient of variation} = \frac{\textit{Standard deviation}}{\textit{Expected rate of return}}$$

$$CV = (\sigma) \div \bar{R}$$

The lower the ratio, the better the risk-return tradeoff.

EXAMPLE

The coefficients of variation for the expected return of the two potential investments are calculated as follows:

			Coefficient of Variation
Xatalan Corporation Stock:	$\sigma \div \bar{R}$ = 63.69% ÷ 28%	=	**2.275**
Yarmouth Company Stock:	$\sigma \div \bar{R}$ = 18.33% ÷ 18%	=	**1.018**

The investment in Yarmouth has a better risk-return tradeoff. Its coefficient of variation (CV) is lower than that of the investment in Xatalan (1.018 < 2.275).

---

4.   **Diversification**

a.   The measures presented on the previous pages relate to the risk and return for individual securities. However, few investors hold only one security.

1)   The goal of portfolio management is to hold a group of securities that provides a reasonable rate of return without the risks associated with one security.

a)   Expected portfolio **return** is the weighted average of the returns on the individual securities.

b)   Portfolio **risk** is usually less than a simple average of the standard deviations of the component securities. This is one benefit of diversification.

b.   Idiosyncratic risk (also called diversifiable risk or unsystematic risk) is associated with one investment security. Specific risk potentially can be minimized by diversification.

1)   Diversification reduces aggregate volatility.

a)   Some stocks move in the same direction as other stocks in the portfolio but by a smaller amount. Some stocks move in the opposite direction from other stocks.

b)   Thus, by combining imperfectly correlated securities into a portfolio, the risk of the group as a whole is less than the average of their standard deviations.

2)   In theory, diversifiable risk should continue to decrease as the number of different securities held increases.

a)   But, in practice, the benefits of diversification become extremely small when more than about 20 to 30 different securities are held. Moreover, commissions and other transaction costs increase with greater diversification.

c.   Market risk is the risk of the stock market as a whole. For an ideal, well-diversified portfolio, it is the only risk.

d.   The **coefficient of correlation (r)** measures the degree to which any two variables, e.g., the prices of two stocks, are related. In practice, the coefficient of correlation can be used to determine how (1) a security performs against its benchmarks or (2) securities behave against other securities within a portfolio. Investment risks can be diversified by adding negatively correlated securities to the existing portfolio.

1)   The coefficient of correlation has a range from 1.0 to −1.0 (Study Unit 7, Subunit 1, fully covers correlation).

a)   Perfect positive correlation (1.0) means that the two variables always move together.

b)   Perfect negative correlation (−1.0) means that the two variables always move in the opposite direction.

c)   If a pair of securities has a coefficient of correlation of 1.0, the risk of the two together is the same as the risk of each security by itself. If a pair of securities has a coefficient of correlation of −1.0, all specific (unsystematic) risk has been eliminated.

2)   The ideal portfolio consists of securities with a wide enough variety of coefficients of correlation that only market risk remains.

Stop and review! You have completed the outline for this subunit. Study multiple-choice questions 6 through 10 beginning on page 149.

6.3 EXPECTED VALUE

1. Expected value is a means of associating a dollar amount with each possible outcome of a probability distribution. The outcome yielding the highest expected value (which may or may not be the most likely one) is the optimal alternative.

   a. The decision is under the manager's control.
   b. The state of nature is the future event whose outcome the manager is attempting to predict.
   c. The payoff is the financial result of the combination of the manager's decision and the actual state of nature.

2. The expected value is calculated by multiplying the probability of each outcome by its payoff and adding the products. This calculation often is called a payoff table.

EXAMPLE

An investor is considering the purchase of two identically priced properties. Their value will change if a road is built.

The following are estimates that road construction will occur:

Future State of Nature (SN)	Event	Probability
SN 1	No road is ever built.	.10 = 10%
SN 2	A road is built this year.	.20 = 20%
SN 3	A road is built more than 1 year from now.	.70 = 70%
		100%

The following are estimates of the values of the properties (payoffs) for each event:

Property	SN 1	SN 2	SN 3
Bivens Tract	$10,000	$40,000	$35,000
Newnan Tract	$20,000	$50,000	$30,000

The expected value of each property is determined by multiplying the probability of each state of nature (outcome) by its payoff and adding all of the products.

		Expected Value
Bivens Tract:	.1($10,000) + .2($40,000) + .7($35,000) =	$33,500
Newnan Tract:	.1($20,000) + .2($50,000) + .7($30,000) =	$33,000

Thus, the Bivens Tract is the better investment.

---

3. A **criticism** is that expected value is based on repetitive trials, but many business decisions ultimately involve only one event.

EXAMPLE

A company wishes to launch a communications satellite. The probability of launch failure is .2, and the payoff is $0. The probability of a successful launch is .8, and the payoff is $25,000,000. The expected value is

.2($0) + .8($25,000,000) = $20,000,000

But $20,000,000 is not a possible payoff. Either the satellite orbits for $25,000,000, or it crashes for $0.

---

4. The difficulty of constructing a payoff table is the determination of all possible outcomes of decisions and their probabilities. Thus, a probability distribution must be established.

   a. The assigned probabilities may reflect prior experience with similar decisions, the results of research, or subjective estimates.

5.   Expected value is likely to be used by a decision maker who is risk neutral. However, other circumstances may cause the decision maker to be risk averse or even risk seeking.

EXAMPLE

A dealer in yachts may order 0, 1, or 2 yachts for inventory.

The dealer projects demand as follows:

Demand	Probability
0 yachts	.10 = 10%
1 yacht	.50 = 50%
2 yachts	.40 = 40%
	100%

The cost of carrying an excess yacht is $50,000, and the gain for each yacht sold is $200,000. The profit or loss resulting from each combination of decision and outcome is as follows:

				Expected Value		
Decision	State of Nature Demand = 0			Stock 0 Yachts	Stock 1 Yacht	Stock 2 Yachts
Stock 0 yachts	$ 0 × 10%	=		$0		
Stock 1 yacht	(50,000) × 10%	=			$ (5,000)	
Stock 2 yachts	(100,000) × 10%	=				$ (10,000)
	Demand = 1					
Stock 0 yachts	$ 0 × 50%	=		$0		
Stock 1 yacht	200,000 × 50%	=			$100,000	
Stock 2 yachts	150,000 × 50%	=				$ 75,000
	Demand = 2					
Stock 0 yachts	$ 0 × 40%	=		$0		
Stock 1 yacht	200,000 × 40%	=			$ 80,000	
Stock 2 yachts	400,000 × 40%	=				$160,000
All expected values				$0	$175,000	$225,000

In this example, a risk-averse decision maker may not wish to accept the risk of losing $100,000 by ordering two yachts, even though that decision has the highest expected value.

---

a.   Although exact probabilities may not be known, the use of expected value analysis forces managers to evaluate decisions logically. At the least, managers are forced to consider all outcomes of each decision.

Expected value calculations and analysis may appear difficult. However, you are simply multiplying the probability of each outcome by its payoff and summing the products. In the calculation of the net expected value or expected incremental profit from an investment, do not forget to subtract the amount of the initial investment.

Stop and review! You have completed the outline for this subunit. Study multiple-choice questions 11 through 18 beginning on page 150.

6.4 SELECTING THE FORECASTING METHOD

1.   **Various Approaches to Quantify or Understand Risk**

a.   **Sensitivity Analysis**

1)   Sensitivity analysis uses trial-and-error to determine the effects of changes in variables or assumptions on final results. It is useful in deciding whether expending additional resources to obtain better forecasts is justified.

2)   The trial-and-error method inherent in sensitivity analysis is greatly facilitated by the use of computer software.

a)   A major use of sensitivity analysis is in capital budgeting. Small changes in interest rates or payoffs can make a significant difference in the profitability of a project.

b.   **Simulation**

1)   This method is a sophisticated refinement of probability theory and sensitivity analysis. The computer is used to generate many examples of results based upon various assumptions.

2)   Project simulation is frequently expensive. Unless a project is exceptionally large and expensive, full-scale simulation is usually not worthwhile.

c.   **Monte Carlo Simulation**

1)   This method often is used in simulation to generate the individual values for a random variable.

a)   The performance of a quantitative model under uncertainty may be investigated by randomly selecting values for each of the variables in the model (based on the probability distribution of each variable) and then calculating the value of the solution.

2)   Performing this process many times produces the distribution of results from the model.

d.   **Delphi Approach**

1)   The Delphi approach solicits opinions from experts, summarizes the opinions, and feeds the summaries back to the experts (without revealing participants to each other).

a)   The process is repeated until the opinions converge on an optimal solution.

e.   **Time Series Analysis**

1)   Time series analysis (also called trend analysis) is the process of projecting future trends based on past experience. It is a regression model in which the independent variable is time.

Some of the forecasting-related questions on the CPA exam require the candidate to read about a forecasting situation and then choose the appropriate method. Thus, candidates should be as comfortable recognizing when to use the different forecasting methods as they are in working through the details of applying them.

2.   Accounting estimates often incorporate approaches that quantify risks and unknowns.

a.   Management is responsible for the process that prepares accounting estimates. It must

1)   Identify circumstances requiring accounting estimates;
2)   Understand factors affecting the accounting estimate;
3)   Accumulate relevant, sufficient, and reliable data;
4)   Predict the most likely circumstances and factors;
5)   Determine the estimate based on these predictions and other relevant factors; and
6)   Present the estimate per correct accounting principles with adequate disclosure.

b.   Management judgment includes

1)   Experience and knowledge covering events (past and current).
2)   Assumptions about expected conditions, events, etc., and changes therein.

Stop and review! You have completed the outline for this subunit. Study multiple-choice questions 19 and 20 on page 153.

QUESTIONS

6.1 Risk and Return

1. A company is evaluating its experience with five recent investments. The following data are available:

Investment	Cost of Investment	Amount Received
A	$ 8,500	$ 8,390
B	4,200	4,610
C	12,100	12,400
D	7,900	8,220
E	11,000	11,400

Rank the investments in order from highest rate of return to lowest.

- A. C, E, A, D, B.
- B. B, D, E, C, A.
- C. B, E, D, C, A.
- D. A, C, E, D, B.

Answer (B) is correct.

REQUIRED: The order of investments from highest rate of return to lowest.

DISCUSSION: Rate of return is equal to the return on an investment (the amount received minus the amount invested) divided by the amount invested. The calculation for these five investments can be performed as follows:

Investment	Cost of Investment	Amount Received	Return	Rate of Return
A	$ 8,500	$ 8,390	$(110)	(1.3%)
B	4,200	4,610	410	9.8%
C	12,100	12,400	300	2.5%
D	7,900	8,220	320	4.1%
E	11,000	11,400	400	3.6%

Answer (A) is incorrect. The ranking C, E, A, D, B is in order by amount received, not rate of return. Answer (C) is incorrect. The ranking B, E, D, C, A is in order by return, not rate of return. Answer (D) is incorrect. The ranking A, C, E, D, B is from lowest rate of return to highest.

2. Dr. G invested $10,000 in a lifetime annuity for his granddaughter Emily. The annuity is expected to yield $400 annually forever. What is the anticipated annual rate of return for the annuity?

- A. Cannot be determined without additional information.
- B. 4.0%
- C. 2.5%
- D. 8.0%

Answer (B) is correct.

REQUIRED: The annual rate of return for an annuity.

DISCUSSION: A return is the amount received by an investor as compensation for taking on the risk of the investment. The rate of return is the return stated as a percentage of the amount invested. In this case, it is 4% ($400 ÷ $10,000).

Answer (A) is incorrect. The rate of return can be calculated. Answer (C) is incorrect. Reversing the numerator and denominator, and dividing the result by 1,000, results in a rate of 2.5%. Answer (D) is incorrect. Treating the return as semi-annual rather than annual results in a rate of 8.0%.

3. Catherine & Co. has extra cash at the end of the year and is analyzing the best way to invest the funds. The company should invest in a project only if the

- A. Expected return on the project exceeds the return on investments of comparable risk.
- B. Return on investments of comparable risk exceeds the expected return on the project.
- C. Expected return on the project is equal to the return on investments of comparable risk.
- D. Return on investments of comparable risk equals the expected return on the project.

Answer (A) is correct.

REQUIRED: The rule for deciding whether to invest in a project.

DISCUSSION: Investment risk is analyzed in terms of the probability that the actual return on an investment will be lower than the expected return. Comparing a project's expected return with the return on an asset of similar risk helps determine whether the project is worth investing in. If the expected return on a project exceeds the return on an asset of comparable risk, the project should be pursued.

4. The risk of loss because of fluctuations in the relative value of foreign currencies is called

- A. Expropriation risk.
- B. Multinational beta.
- C. Exchange rate risk.
- D. Undiversifiable risk.

Answer (C) is correct.

REQUIRED: The risk of loss because of fluctuations in the relative value of foreign currencies.

DISCUSSION: When amounts to be paid or received are denominated in a foreign currency, exchange rate fluctuations may result in exchange gains or losses. For example, if a U.S. firm has a receivable fixed in terms of units of a foreign currency, a decline in the value of that currency relative to the U.S. dollar results in a foreign exchange loss.

Answer (A) is incorrect. Expropriation risk is the risk that the sovereign country in which the assets backing an investment are located will seize the assets without adequate compensation. Answer (B) is incorrect. The beta value in the capital asset pricing model for a multinational firm is the systematic risk of a given multinational firm relative to that of the market as a whole. Answer (D) is incorrect. Undiversifiable risk is risk that cannot be offset through diversification.

5. Beginning January 2, Year 1, a company deposited $50,000 in a savings account for 2 years. The account earns 10% interest, compounded annually. What amount of interest did the company earn during the 2-year period?

A. $10,500

B. $10,000

C. $5,500

D. $5,000

Answer (A) is correct.
    REQUIRED: The amount of compound interest earned during the 2-year period.
    DISCUSSION: Compounding interest is the practice of adding interest to the carrying amount of the principal rather than paying it in cash. The amount of interest earned in Year 1 ($50,000 × 10% = $5,000) was added to the principal, which was then used to calculate the amount of interest earned in Year 2 [($50,000 + $5,000) × 10% = $5,500]. The total amount of interest earned during the 2-year period was thus $10,500 ($5,000 Year 1 + $5,500 Year 2). This amount also can be calculated as follows: [($50,000 × 1.1 × 1.1) – $50,000].
    Answer (B) is incorrect. The amount of $10,000 is interest that would have been earned using simple, not compound, interest. Answer (C) is incorrect. The amount of $5,500 is the interest earned in the second year. Answer (D) is incorrect. The amount of $5,000 is the interest earned in the first year.

6.2 Quantifying Investment Risk

6. City Development, Inc., is considering a new investment project that will involve building a large office block in Frankfurt-am-Main. The firm's financial analysis department has estimated that the proposed investment has the following estimated rate of return distributions:

Rate of Return	Probability
(5%)	30%
10%	50%
20%	20%

Calculate the expected rate of return.

A. 5.5%

B. 7.5%

C. 10.5%

D. 11.7%

Answer (B) is correct.
    REQUIRED: The expected rate of return for an investment project.
    DISCUSSION: The expected rate of return on an investment can be calculated by weighting each potential rate of return by its probability of occurrence and summing the results. City Development's expected rate of return for this development is:

Rate of Return	Probability	Expected Rate of Return
(5.0)%	30.0%	(1.5)%
10.0%	50.0%	5.0%
20.0%	20.0%	4.0%
		7.5%

    Answer (A) is incorrect. The rate of 5.5% is a nonsense result. Answer (C) is incorrect. The rate of 10.5% results from improperly treating the negative 5% return as a positive number. Answer (D) is incorrect. The rate of 11.7% results from treating the negative return as a positive number and weighting the three possible results equally.

7. Russell, Inc., is evaluating four independent investment proposals. The expected returns and standard deviations for each of these proposals are presented below.

Investment Proposal	Expected Returns	Standard Deviation
I	16%	10%
II	14%	10%
III	20%	11%
IV	22%	15%

Which one of the investment proposals has the **least** risk per unit of return?

A. Investment I.

B. Investment II.

C. Investment III.

D. Investment IV.

Answer (C) is correct.
    REQUIRED: The investment proposal with the least risk per unit of return.
    DISCUSSION: The coefficient of variation (CV) measures the risk per unit of return by dividing the standard deviation (σ) by the expected return. The investment with the lowest CV has the best risk-return tradeoff. The CVs of Russell's four investment proposals can thus be calculated as follows:

	Standard Deviation		Expected Returns		Coefficient of Variation
Investment I	10%	÷	16%	=	62.5%
Investment II	10%	÷	14%	=	71.4%
Investment III	11%	÷	20%	=	55.0%
Investment IV	15%	÷	22%	=	68.2%

    Answer (A) is incorrect. The coefficient of variation for Investment I is 0.625 (10% ÷ 16%), which is not the lowest coefficient of the four. Answer (B) is incorrect. Investment II has the highest relative level of risk with a coefficient of variation of 0.714 (10% ÷ 14%). Answer (D) is incorrect. The coefficient of variation for Investment IV is 0.682 (15% ÷ 22%), which is not the lowest coefficient of the four.

8. The risk of a single stock is

A.   Interest rate risk.

B.   Unsystematic risk.

C.   Portfolio risk.

D.   Market risk.

Answer (B) is correct.
REQUIRED: The risk of a single stock.
DISCUSSION: Unsystematic risk is the risk of a single stock, but portfolio risk is the net risk of holding a portfolio of diversified securities. Portfolio risk therefore includes systematic and unsystematic risk.
Answer (A) is incorrect. Interest rate risk is the risk of changes in interest rates. Answer (C) is incorrect. Portfolio risk is the net risk of multiple securities. Answer (D) is incorrect. Market risk is systematic risk.

9. The expected rate of return for the stock of Cornhusker Enterprises is 20%, with a standard deviation of 15%. The expected rate of return for the stock of Mustang Associates is 10%, with a standard deviation of 9%. The stock with the worse risk/return relationship is

A.   Cornhusker because the return is higher.

B.   Cornhusker because the standard deviation is higher.

C.   Mustang because the standard deviation is higher.

D.   Mustang because the coefficient of variation is higher.

Answer (D) is correct.
REQUIRED: The stock with the worse risk/return relationship.
DISCUSSION: The coefficient of variation is useful when the rates of return and standard deviations of two investments differ. It measures the risk per unit of return by dividing the standard deviation by the expected return. The coefficient of variation is higher for Mustang (.09 ÷ .10 = .90) than for Cornhusker (.15 ÷ .20 = .75).
Answer (A) is incorrect. The existence of a higher return is not necessarily indicative of high risk. Answer (B) is incorrect. The level of standard deviation by itself is not enough for determining the stock's risk-return relationship. Answer (C) is incorrect. Mustang does not have the higher standard deviation.

10. If two projects are completely and positively linearly dependent (or positively related), the measure of correlation between them is

A.   0

B.   +.5

C.   +1

D.   –1

Answer (C) is correct.
REQUIRED: The measure of correlation when two projects are positively linearly dependent.
DISCUSSION: The measure of correlation when two projects are linearly dependent in a positive way is +1.
Answer (A) is incorrect. A zero correlation indicates no linear relationship. Answer (B) is incorrect. The measure +.5 does not indicate linearity. Answer (D) is incorrect. A –1 would indicate a negative correlation.

6.3 Expected Value

11. Philip Enterprises, distributor of video discs, is developing its budgeted cost of goods sold for next year. Philip has developed the following range of sales estimates and associated probabilities for the year:

Sales Estimate	Probability
$ 60,000	25%
85,000	40
100,000	35

Philip's cost of goods sold averages 80% of sales. What is the expected value of Philip's budgeted cost of goods sold?

A. $85,000

B. $84,000

C. $68,000

D. $67,200

Answer (D) is correct.
REQUIRED: The expected value of cost of goods sold.
DISCUSSION: The expected value is calculated by weighting each sales estimate by the probability of its occurrence. Consequently, the expected value of sales is $84,000 [($60,000 × .25) + ($85,000 × .40) + ($100,000 × .35)]. Cost of goods sold is therefore $67,200 ($84,000 × .80).
Answer (A) is incorrect. The amount of $85,000 is the sales estimate with the highest probability. Answer (B) is incorrect. The amount of $84,000 is the expected value of sales. Answer (C) is incorrect. The amount of $68,000 is 80% of the sales estimate with the highest probability.

12. During the past few years, Wilder Company has experienced the following average number of power outages:

Number per Month	Number of Months
0	3
1	2
2	4
3	3
	12

Each power outage results in out-of-pocket costs of $800. For $1,000 per month, Wilder can lease a generator to provide power during outages. If Wilder leases a generator in the coming year, the estimated savings (or additional expense) for the year will be

A. $(15,200)

B. $(1,267)

C. $3,200

D. $7,200

Answer (C) is correct.
   REQUIRED: The estimated savings or additional expense from leasing the generator, given expected levels of occurrence.
   DISCUSSION: Each outage costs $800, but this expense can be avoided by paying $1,000 per month ($12,000 for the year). The expected-value approach uses the probability distribution derived from past experience to determine the average expected outages per month.

$$3 \div 12 \times 0 = 0.0$$
$$2 \div 12 \times 1 = 0.16667$$
$$4 \div 12 \times 2 = 0.66667$$
$$3 \div 12 \times 3 = \underline{0.75000}$$
$$1.58334$$

The company can expect to have, on average, 1.58334 outages per month. At $800 per outage, the expected cost is $1,266.67. Thus, paying $1,000 to avoid an expense of $1,266.67 saves $266.67 per month, or $3,200 per year.
   Answer (A) is incorrect. The annual amount the company will lose without a generator is $(15,200). Answer (B) is incorrect. The monthly amount the company will lose without a generator is $(1,267). Answer (D) is incorrect. The amount saved if two outages occur per month is $7,200.

Questions 13 and 14 are based on the following information. The probabilities shown in the table below represent the estimate of sales for a new product.

Sales (Units)	Probability
0-200	15%
201-400	45%
401-600	25%
601-800	15%

---

13. What is the probability of selling between 201 and 600 units of the product?

A. 0%

B. 11.25%

C. 70%

D. 25%

Answer (C) is correct.
   REQUIRED: The probability of selling between 201 and 600 units of the new product.
   DISCUSSION: The probability of selling between 201 and 400 units is 45%, and the probability of selling between 401 and 600 units is 25%. Thus, the probability of selling between 201 and 600 units is the sum of these probabilities, or 70%.

14. Using the midpoint of each range as the best estimate for that range, what is the best estimate of the expected sales of the new product?

A. 480

B. 380

C. 400

D. 800

Answer (B) is correct.
   REQUIRED: The best estimate of the expected sales of the new product.
   DISCUSSION: The expected sales levels should be weighted by the individual probabilities of their occurrence. The midpoint of each sales level is used as the estimate for that level. Thus, sales are expected to be 380 units.

$$100 \times 15\% = 15$$
$$300 \times 45\% = 135$$
$$500 \times 25\% = 125$$
$$700 \times 15\% = \underline{105}$$
$$380$$

   Answer (A) is incorrect. The amount of 480 is based on the maximum value in each range. Answer (C) is incorrect. The maximum value in the modal range is 400. Answer (D) is incorrect. The highest estimate is 800.

15. Pongo Company's managers are attempting to value a piece of land they own. One potential occurrence is that the old road bordering the land gets paved. Another possibility is that the road does not get paved. A third outcome is that the road might be destroyed and completely replaced by a new road. Based on the following future states of nature, their probabilities, and subsequent values of the land, what is the expected value of the land?

Future States of Nature (SN)	Probability
SN 1: Current road gets paved	.5
SN 2: Road does not get paved	.4
SN 3: Current road destroyed and replaced with new road	.1

Estimates of land value under each possible future state of nature:

Value if SN 1: $200,000
Value if SN 2: $100,000
Value if SN 3: $550,000

A. $133,333

B. $195,000

C. $225,000

D. $283,333

Answer (B) is correct.

REQUIRED: The expected value of the land.

DISCUSSION: The expected value of the land is determined by multiplying the probability of each state of nature (outcome) by its payoff and adding all of the products. Thus, the land's expected value is (0.5)($200,000) + (0.4)($100,000) + (0.1)($550,000) = $195,000.

Answer (A) is incorrect. The amount of $133,333 places too much weight on the second option. Answer (C) is incorrect. The amount of $225,000 gives too much weight to the third option. Answer (D) is incorrect. The amount of $283,333 uses a simple unweighted average of the returns from the three options.

Question 16 is based on the following information. The Booster Club at Blair College sells hot dogs at home basketball games. The group has a frequency distribution of the demand for hot dogs per game and plans to apply the expected value decision rule to determine the number of hot dogs to stock.

16. The Booster Club should select the demand level that

A. Is closest to the expected demand.

B. Has the greatest probability of occurring.

C. Has the greatest expected opportunity cost.

D. Has the greatest expected monetary value.

Answer (D) is correct.

REQUIRED: The demand level that should be selected.

DISCUSSION: The Booster Club should select the demand level that maximizes profits, that is, the level with the greatest expected monetary value. This level may not include the event with the highest conditional profit because this profit may be accompanied by a low probability of occurrence. Alternatively, the event with the highest probability of occurrence may not be selected because it does not offer a high conditional profit.

Answer (A) is incorrect. Stocking an amount equal to expected demand (the sum of the products of the possible amounts demanded and their respective probabilities) does not necessarily maximize expected profits. Answer (B) is incorrect. The number of bags to stock is not necessarily the same as the amount demanded with the highest probability. The inventory decision should be based on the relation of the probability distribution to the monetary outcomes. Answer (C) is incorrect. The greatest opportunity cost is not factored into the expected value analysis.

---

17. In decision theory, those uncontrollable future events that can affect the outcome of a decision are

A. Payoffs.

B. States of nature.

C. Probabilities.

D. Nodes.

Answer (B) is correct.

REQUIRED: The term describing uncontrollable future events.

DISCUSSION: Applying decision theory requires the decision maker to develop an exhaustive list of possible future events. All possible future events that might occur must be included, even though the decision maker is likely to be uncertain about which specific events will occur. These future uncontrollable events are states of nature.

Answer (A) is incorrect. Payoffs are outcome measures such as profit or loss. Answer (C) is incorrect. Probabilities are the likelihood of occurrence of the states of nature. Answer (D) is incorrect. Nodes (junction points) are decision points.

18. A beverage stand can sell either soft drinks or coffee on any given day. If the stand sells soft drinks and the weather is hot, it will make $2,500; if the weather is cold, the profit will be $1,000. If the stand sells coffee and the weather is hot, it will make $1,900; if the weather is cold, the profit will be $2,000. The probability of cold weather on a given day at this time is 60%. The expected payoff for selling coffee is

   A. $1,360

   B. $2,200

   C. $3,900

   D. $1,960

Answer (D) is correct.
   REQUIRED: The expected payoff for selling coffee.
   DISCUSSION: The expected payoff calculation for coffee is

$$\text{Expected payoff} = \text{Prob. hot (Payoff hot)} + \text{Prob. cold (Payoff cold)}$$
$$= .4(\$1,900) + .6(\$2,000)$$
$$= \$1,960$$

   Answer (A) is incorrect. The least the company can make by selling coffee is $1,900. Answer (B) is incorrect. The most the company can make by selling coffee is $2,000. Answer (C) is incorrect. The most the company can make by selling coffee is $2,000.

6.4 Selecting the Forecasting Method

19. Through the use of decision models, managers thoroughly analyze many alternatives and decide on the best alternative for the company. Often the actual results achieved from a particular decision are not what was expected when the decision was made. In addition, an alternative that was not selected would have actually been the best decision for the company. The appropriate technique to analyze the alternatives by using expected inputs and altering them before a decision is made is

   A. Expected value analysis.

   B. Linear programming.

   C. Program evaluation review technique (PERT).

   D. Sensitivity analysis.

Answer (D) is correct.
   REQUIRED: The technique that involves altering expected inputs during the decision process.
   DISCUSSION: After a problem has been formulated into any mathematical model, it may be subjected to sensitivity analysis. Sensitivity analysis examines how the model's outcomes change as the parameters change.
   Answer (A) is incorrect. Expected value analysis is used to determine an anticipated return or cost based upon probabilities of events and their related outcomes. Answer (B) is incorrect. Linear programming optimizes a function given certain constraints. Answer (C) is incorrect. PERT is a network method used to plan and control large projects.

20. A widely used approach that managers use to recognize uncertainty about individual items and to obtain an immediate financial estimate of the consequences of possible prediction errors is

   A. Expected value analysis.

   B. Learning curve analysis.

   C. Sensitivity analysis.

   D. Regression analysis.

Answer (C) is correct.
   REQUIRED: The approach that gives an immediate financial estimate of the consequences of possible prediction errors.
   DISCUSSION: After a problem has been formulated into any mathematical model, it may be subjected to sensitivity analysis. Sensitivity analysis examines how the model's outcomes change as the parameters change.
   Answer (A) is incorrect. Expected value is the probabilistically weighted average of the outcomes of an action. Answer (B) is incorrect. Learning curve analysis quantifies how labor costs decline as employees learn their jobs through repetition. Answer (D) is incorrect. Regression, or least squares, analysis determines the average change in the dependent variable given a unit change in one or more independent variables.

STUDY UNIT SEVEN
FINANCIAL RISK MANAGEMENT

(17 pages of outline)

The complex modern organization regularly confronts financial risk. A CPA is expected to understand how to mitigate this risk through **financial risk management**. The previous study unit reviewed the basics of risk and return. This study unit continues by further reviewing how to quantify risks through linear regression, correlation analysis, and the capital asset pricing model (CAPM). The CAPM also enables a CPA to quantify how to mitigate financial risk. Typically, CPAs employ derivatives as a way to mitigate financial risk. Because firms today operate in a global economy, the AICPA usually tests candidates on how to mitigate financial risk associated with currency exchange.

7.1 CORRELATION ANALYSIS

1. **Correlation**

    a. Correlation is the strength of the linear (straight-line) relationship between two variables, expressed mathematically in terms of the **coefficient of correlation (r)** (the correlation coefficient).

    1) The coefficient r can be graphically depicted by plotting the values for the variables on a graph in the form of a scatter diagram.

    b. The value of r ranges from 1 (perfect direct relationship) to –1 (perfect inverse relationship). The closer the scatter pattern is to a straight line, the greater the absolute value of r.

    1) Perfect direct relationship ($r = 1$)

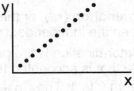

Figure 7-1

    2) Perfect inverse relationship ($r = -1$)

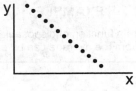

Figure 7-2

3) Strong direct relationship ($r = 0.7$)

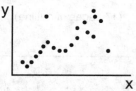

Figure 7-3

4) No linear relationship ($r = 0$)

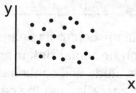

Figure 7-4

5) Non-linear relationship ($r = 0$)

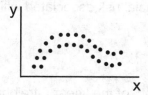

Figure 7-5

a) A coefficient of correlation of zero does not mean that the two variables are unrelated, only that any relationship cannot be expressed as a linear equation.

b) The data points in Figure 7-6 on page 157 have a strong direct relationship, implying an r value close to 1.

c. Correlation is not causation. We only know that two variables move together, but not what causes them to move.

2. **Determination**

a. The **coefficient of determination (r^2)**, or the coefficient of correlation squared, is a measure of the fit between the independent and dependent variables.

1) The coefficient of determination is the proportion of the total variation in the dependent variable that is accounted for by the independent variable.

2) The value of r^2 is from 0 to 1. The closer the value of r^2 to 1, the more useful the independent variable (x) in explaining or predicting the variation in the dependent variable (y).

EXAMPLE

A car dealership determines that new car sales are a function of disposable income with a coefficient of correlation of .8. Thus, 64% ($.8^2$) of the variation of new car sales from the average can be explained by changes in disposable income.

---

3. **Standard Error**

a. The standard error measures how well the linear equation represents the data. It is the vertical distance between the data points in a scatter diagram and the regression line.

1) The closer the data points to the regression line, the lower the standard error.

Stop and review! You have completed the outline for this subunit. Study multiple-choice questions 1 through 3 on page 172.

7.2 LINEAR REGRESSION ANALYSIS

1. **Simple Regression**

   a. Regression analysis is the process of deriving a linear equation that describes the relationship between two variables.

      1) Simple regression is used for one independent variable. Multiple regression is used for more than one.

   b. The simple regression equation is the algebraic formula for a straight line.

$$y = a + bx$$

   If: y = the dependent variable
        a = the y intercept
        b = the slope of the regression line
        x = the independent variable

      1) The best straight line that fits a set of data points is derived using calculus.

   c. Regression analysis is particularly valuable for quantifying risk in financial risk management as well as for budgeting and cost accounting purposes.

      1) One extremely common application of simple regression in a business setting is the estimation of a mixed cost function, one with a fixed component and a variable component.

      2) The y-axis intercept is the fixed portion, and the slope of the regression line is the variable portion.

EXAMPLE

A firm has performed a linear regression analysis and determined that total manufacturing costs (y) consist of fixed costs of $420,000 and variable costs of $32 per unit of output. This relationship can be stated mathematically as follows:

$$y = \$420,000 + \$32x$$

If the firm is planning to produce 12,000 units of output, its forecast for total manufacturing costs is $804,000 ($420,000 + $32 × 12,000).

EXAMPLE

The firm has collected the following observations on units of output (independent variable) and total manufacturing costs (dependent variable) to support its linear regression analysis:

	Units of Output (000s)	Actual Total Manufacturing Costs ($000s)
A	5	$620
B	8	$640
C	14	$850
D	17	$1,010

The observations are graphed as follows:

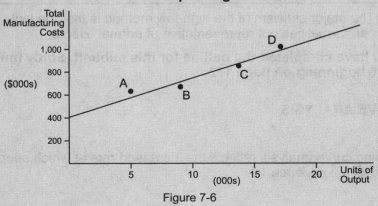

Figure 7-6

2.   **Multiple Regression**

    a.   Multiple regression is used for more than one independent variable.

        1)   Multiple regression allows a firm to identify many factors (independent variables) and weight each one according to its influence on the overall outcome.

$$y = a + b_1x_1 + b_2x_2 + b_3x_3 + b_4x_4 + etc.$$

EXAMPLE

Bond traders apply multiple regression to determine the value of bonds. Using the market trading prices of bonds, they can estimate a cost function based on the following independent variables: (1) interest rate, (2) collateral coverage, (3) pro forma coverage, (4) pro forma leverage, and (5) the term of the bonds. Valuing unpriced bonds requires knowledge of these variables and their weights of influence on the equation.

---

3.   **Aspects of Regression Analysis**

    a.   The linear relationship established for *x* and *y* is valid only across the relevant range, the range from the highest to the smallest measures in the data set. The user must identify the relevant range and ensure that projections lie within it.

        1)   In the example above, if the bonds are worth between $1 million and $100 million, the trader should not assume the same equation will produce an accurate valuation of a bond worth $1 billion or $100,000.

    b.   Regression analysis assumes that past relationships are a basis for valid projections.

    c.   Regression does not determine causality.

        1)   Although *x* and *y* move together, the apparent relationship may be caused by some other factor. For example, car wash sales volume and sunny weather are strongly correlated, but car wash sales do not cause sunny weather.

4.   **High-Low Method**

    a.   The high-low method generates a regression line using only the highest and lowest of a series of observations.

EXAMPLE

A regression equation for electricity costs can be based on the high-cost month and the low-cost month. If the lowest costs were $400 in April when production was 800 machine hours and the highest costs were $600 in September when production was 1,300 hours, the equation is determined as follows:

High month	$600	for	1,300 hours
Low month	400	for	800 hours
Increase	$200		500 hours

Because costs increased $200 for 500 additional hours, the variable cost is $.40 per machine hour ($200 ÷ 500 hours). For the low month, the total variable portion of that monthly cost is $320 ($.40 × 800 hours). Given that the total cost is $400 and $320 is variable, the remaining $80 must be a fixed cost. The regression equation is y = 80 + .4x.

---

        1)   The major criticism of the high-low method is that the high and low points may be abnormalities not representative of normal events.

Stop and review! You have completed the outline for this subunit. Study multiple-choice questions 4 through 6 beginning on page 172.

7.3 LEARNING CURVE ANALYSIS

1.   **Overview**

    a.   Learning curve analysis reflects the increased rate at which people perform tasks as they gain experience.

1)   The time required to perform a given task decreases most rapidly during the early stages of production.

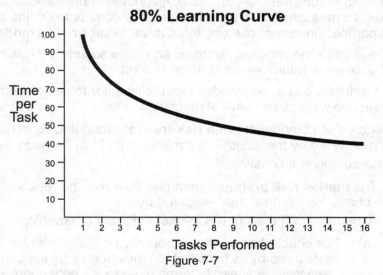

80% Learning Curve

Time per Task

Tasks Performed

Figure 7-7

b.   The curve is usually expressed as a percentage of reduced time to complete a task for each doubling of cumulative production. The most common percentage used in practice is 80%. The most common assumption is that the learning rate applies to the **cumulative average completion time per unit**.

1)   The table below is based on two assumptions: (a) the cumulative average time per unit is reduced by 20% (100% – 80%) for each doubling of production and (b) the first unit required 100 minutes.

| | | | 80% | |
Batch	Cumulative Units Produced	Total Time	Cumulative Average Time per Unit	The Learning Rate %
1 (Unit 1)	1	100	100	--
2 (Unit 2)	2	160	80 (= 100 × 80%)	80% = [160 ÷ (100 × 2)]
3 (Units 3-4)	4	256	64 (= 80 × 80%)	80% = [256 ÷ (160 × 2)]
4 (Units 5-8)	8	409.6	51.2 (= 64 × 80%)	80% = [409.6 ÷ (256 × 2)]
5 (Units 9-16)	16	655.36	40.96 (= 51.2 × 80%)	80% = [655.36 ÷ (409.6 × 2)]

GLEIM
SUCCESS TIPS
®

Candidates need to be alert to the question's requirement. The question might ask, "What is the average time per unit after two units?" From the table above, the answer is 80. The question also might be, "What is the time to produce the second unit?" The answer is 60. Because the first unit took 100 minutes, and the average for the two units is 80 minutes (a total of 160), the second unit must have taken 60 minutes. Another possible question might ask for the average time for units in a batch. In the table, the average unit time for the third batch (units 3 and 4) is 48 minutes [(256 – 160) ÷ (4 – 2)].

2.   **Limitation**

a.   The limitation of the learning curve in practice is the difficulty in knowing the shape of the learning curve.

1)   The existence of the learning curve effect is widely accepted, but the percentage to be used may not be known while the information is still useful. As a result, many simply assume an 80% learning curve and make decisions based on those results.

Stop and review! You have completed the outline for this subunit. Study multiple-choice questions 7 through 10 beginning on page 174.

7.4 CAPITAL ASSET PRICING MODEL (CAPM)

1.   Investors want to reduce their risk and take advantage of diversification by holding a portfolio of securities. To measure how a particular security contributes to the risk and return of a diversified portfolio, investors can use the **capital asset pricing model (CAPM)**.

2.   The CAPM quantifies the required return on an equity security by relating the security's level of risk to the average return available in the market.

3.   The CAPM formula is based on the idea that the investor must be compensated for an investment in two ways: time value of money and risk.

   a.   The time value component is the **risk-free rate** (denoted R_F in the formula). It is the return provided by the safest investments, e.g., U.S. Treasury securities.

   b.   The risk component consists of

      1)   The **market risk premium** (denoted $R_M - R_F$), the return provided by the market above the risk-free rate, weighted by

      2)   A measure of the security's market risk, called **beta** (β).

         a)   The effect of an individual security on the volatility of a portfolio is measured by its sensitivity to movements by the overall market. This sensitivity is stated in terms of a stock's beta coefficient (β).

         b)   Thus, the beta of the market portfolio equals 1, and the beta of U.S. Treasury securities is 0.

      3)   The **security risk premium** is $\beta(R_M - R_F)$. Thus, the required rate of return of the security is the risk-free rate of return (R_F) plus the security risk premium.

   c.   The **security market line (SML)** is the graphical representation of the relationship between the expected rate of return and market, or systematic (beta) risk.

      1)   A β of 1.0 indicates market beta. The security's return matches the market.

      2)   A β of 1.5 indicates the security will return 150% of the market return. If the market returns 10%, the security returns 15%.

      3)   A β of .8 indicates the security will return 80% of the market return. If the market returns 10%, the security returns 8%.

CAPM Formula

$$Required\ rate\ of\ return = R_F + \beta(R_M - R_F)$$

If: R_F = Risk-free rate
       R_M = Market return
       β = Measure of the systematic risk or volatility of the individual security in comparison with the market (diversified portfolio)

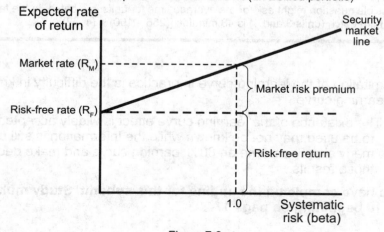

Figure 7-8

4. The market risk premium varies in direct proportion to beta. Consequently, all investments (securities) must lie on the security market line.

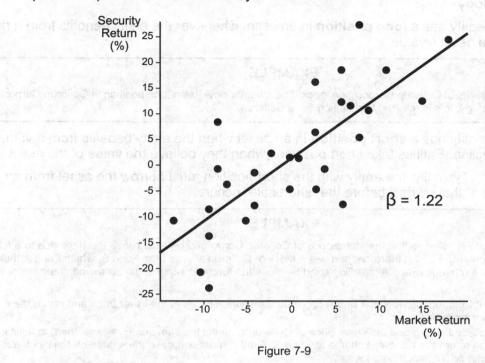

Figure 7-9

EXAMPLE

An investor is considering the purchase of a stock with a beta of 1.2. Treasury bills currently are paying 8.6%, and the average return on the market is 10.1%. (Remember, U.S. Treasuries are considered as close to a risk-free investment as can exist.) To be induced to buy this stock, the return that the investor must receive is calculated as follows:

$$\text{Required rate of return} = R_F + \beta(R_M - R_F)$$
$$= 8.6\% + 1.2(10.1\% - 8.6\%)$$
$$= 8.6\% + 1.8\%$$
$$= 10.4\%$$

Stop and review! You have completed the outline for this subunit. Study multiple-choice questions 11 through 16 beginning on page 176.

7.5 DERIVATIVES

1. **Terminology**

   a. An entity has a **long position** in an asset whenever the entity benefits from a rise in the asset's value.

EXAMPLE

An investor buys 100 shares of Collerup Corporation stock. The investor now has a long position in Collerup Corporation; in financial market terminology, this is referred to as being "long Collerup."

---

   b. An entity has a **short position** in an asset when the entity benefits from a value decline. Entities take short positions when they believe the value of the asset will fall.

   1) Typically, the entity with the short position must borrow the asset from an entity that owns it before the "short sale" occurs.

EXAMPLE

Money Management Fund A believes that the share price of Collerup Corporation will decrease (perhaps due to a future poor earnings announcement). Fund A therefore borrows a block of Collerup shares from Fund B, which Fund A then sells on the appropriate stock exchange. Fund A is selling short because the fund can replace the borrowed shares later when the share value falls.

- If the price of Collerup decreases, Fund A can repurchase the shares at the lower price and return them to Fund B, making a profit.
- If Fund A guessed wrong and the share price of Collerup remains the same or increases, then, to fulfill its obligation to return the borrowed shares to Fund B, Fund A must purchase the shares on the stock exchange (at the higher price), incurring a loss.

---

2. **Overview**

   a. A **derivative instrument** is an investment whose value is based on another asset's value, such as an option to buy shares (call option).

   1) For example, in a free and open exchange market (e.g., Stubhub), season tickets to a favorite sports team are based on the entertainment value (i.e., how well the team will perform) of the respective sports team. If the team does well, the individual tickets for future games can be sold for more money than if the team does not do well. Thus, the tickets (a derivative instrument) are based on the value of the team's performance (the underlying).

   b. The financial definition of a derivative instrument is a transaction in which each party's gain or loss is derived from some other economic event, for example, (1) the price of a given stock, (2) a foreign currency exchange rate, or (3) the price of a certain commodity.

   1) One party enters into the transaction to speculate (incur risk) and the other enters into it to hedge (avoid risk). Alternatively, two parties with opposite investments may work together to hedge each other.

   c. Derivatives are often used to hedge (or insure against) financial risks.

   d. Derivatives are a type of financial instrument, along with cash, accounts receivable, notes receivable, bonds, preferred shares, etc.

3. **Hedging**

    a. To hedge an investment, the entity takes a position in a financial instrument (usually a derivative) that is almost perfectly correlated with the original asset (the underlying) but in the opposite direction. By taking an opposite position in the derivative, the entity is able to effectively negate any changes in value to its original investment.

    b. Hedging uses offsetting commitments to minimize or avoid the effect of adverse price movements. For example, if the original investment would require the entity to make a $100 payment, the derivative investment (being used as a hedge) would pay the entity $100. Thus, the entity is effectively made whole by the derivative investment.

        1) Of course, this is how a hedge works in theory. In practice, the derivative instrument is not perfectly correlated. In a more realistic example, the entity may need to pay $102 and the derivative instrument would pay the entity $99.

    c. The overall goal of hedging is to minimize changes in total value and have the hedge act as insurance against price (or value) fluctuations.

    d. Simplified example of a hedge transaction without using technical financial terms: Your favorite sports team is playing against its rival, and you bet on the rival. If your favorite team wins, you are happy it beats its rival. If your favorite team loses, your sorrows are negated by the happiness of winning the bet.

4. **Options**

    a. A party who buys an option has bought the right to demand that the counterparty (the seller or writer of the option) buy or sell an underlying asset on or before a specified future date. The buyer holds all of the rights, and the seller has all of the obligations. The buyer pays a fee to be able to determine whether the seller buys (sells) the underlying asset from (to) the buyer.

Many CPA candidates become intimidated when studying options. A listed option is merely a standardized legal contract that requires two parties to comply with its terms. These contracts are no more complicated than the legal contract a person has with his or her cell phone carrier. Individuals pay the cell phone company money, and in return the cell phone provider is obligated to supply the individual with telephone service when the individual wants to make a phone call. Furthermore, some cell phone carriers charge on the basis of pay-as-you-go while others charge a fixed amount for a fixed amount of minutes. There are many terms associated with cell phone providers, and, similar to cell phones, options have their own terminology. The terms below and on the next page are useful for people in finance because they indicate how a contract is standardized, allowing people to communicate quickly and succinctly when discussing options.

---

        1) A **call option** gives the buyer (holder) the right to purchase (the right to call for) the underlying asset (stock, currency, commodity, etc.) at a fixed price.

        2) A **put option** gives the buyer (holder) the right to sell (the right to put onto the market) the underlying asset (stock, currency, commodity, etc.) at a fixed price.

        3) The asset that is subject to being bought or sold under the terms of the option is the **underlying**.

        4) The party buying an option is the **holder**. The seller is the **writer**.

        5) The exercise of an option is always at the discretion of the option holder (the buyer) who has, in effect, bought the right to exercise the option or not. The seller of an option has no choice. (S)he must perform if the holder chooses to exercise.

        6) An option has an expiration date after which it can no longer be exercised.

5.   **Valuing an Option**

a.   The two best-known models for valuing options are the Black-Scholes formula for call options and the binomial method. The equations are beyond the scope of this text, but some general statements can be made about the factors that affect the outcomes.

1)   **Exercise price.** The exercise price (also called "strike price") is the price at which the holder can purchase (call option) or sell (put option) the underlying asset in the option contract.

a)   Thus, an increase in the exercise price of an option results in a decrease in the value of a call option and an increase in the value of a put option.

2)   **Price of the underlying.** As the price of the underlying increases, the value of a call option also increases.

a)   The value of a put option decreases as the price of the underlying increases. Selling at the exercise price, which is at a lower-than-market price, is not advantageous.

3)   **Interest rates.** Buying a call option is similar to buying the underlying on credit. Buying the right to purchase the underlying asset (call option) is much cheaper than buying the underlying asset directly due to the cost to carry the underlying asset. The holder of the call option may invest the difference between the option premium and the price of the underlying in a savings account and receive interest income. Thus, a rise in interest rates makes call options more attractive to buyers and increases their value.

a)   Instead of receiving interest income from selling the underlying asset and investing the proceeds in a saving account, the holder of a put option needs to hold the underlying asset to deliver it under the put option. Thus, a rise in interest rates makes the put options less attractive to buyers (holders) and decreases the value of the put options.

4)   **Time until expiration.** The longer the term of an option, the greater the chance that the underlying price will change and the option will be **in-the-money**. A call option is "in-the-money" if, for example, the price of the underlying is $20 and the strike price is less than $20 (e.g., $15 or $19).

a)   Thus, when comparing two options that are similar except for time until expiration, an increase in the term of an option (both calls and puts) will result in an increase in the value of the option.

5)   **Volatility of price of the underlying.** Because the holder's loss on an option is limited to the option premium (amount paid for the option), the holder prefers greater volatility of the price of the underlying. The more volatile the price of the underlying, the greater the chance that it will change and the option will be in-the-money.

a)   An increase in the volatility of the price of the underlying results in an increase in the value of the option (both calls and puts).

b. These factors and their effects are summarized as follows:

Increase in	Value of call option	Value of put option
Exercise price of option	Decrease	Increase
Price of underlying	Increase	Decrease
Interest rates	Increase	Decrease
Time until expiration	Increase	Increase
Volatility of price of underlying	Increase	Increase

c. Intrinsic value is the value of the option today if the option is exercised today. If the intrinsic value of an option is zero, it does not mean the market value of the option is zero because the value of an option is affected by the time value of money, interest rates, and market volatility.

1) The **intrinsic value of a call option** is the amount by which the exercise price is less than the current price of the underlying.

a) If an option has a positive intrinsic value, it is in-the-money.

EXAMPLE

An investor holds call options for 200 shares of Locksley Corporation with an exercise price of $48 per share. Locksley stock is currently trading at $50 per share. The investor's options have an intrinsic value of $2 each ($50 – $48).

b) If an option has an intrinsic value of $0, it is out-of-the-money.

EXAMPLE

An investor holds call options for 200 shares of Locksley Corporation with an exercise price of $48 per share. Locksley stock is currently trading at $45 per share. The investor's options are out-of-the-money. They have no intrinsic value.

Call Contract Position

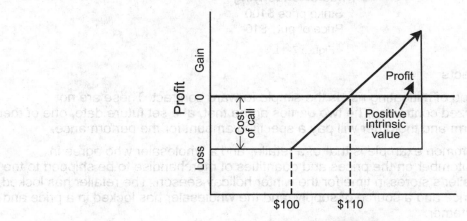

Price of Underlying
Strike price $100
Price of call $10

Figure 7-10

2)   The **intrinsic value of a put option** is the amount by which the exercise price is greater than the current price of the underlying.

a)   If an option has a positive intrinsic value, it is in-the-money.

EXAMPLE

An investor holds put options for 200 shares of Locksley Corporation with an exercise price of $48 per share. Locksley stock is currently trading at $45 per share. The investor's options have an intrinsic value of $3 each ($48 – $45).

---

b)   If an option has an intrinsic value of $0, it is out-of-the-money.

EXAMPLE

An investor holds put options for 200 shares of Locksley Corporation with an exercise price of $48 per share. Locksley stock is currently trading at $50 per share. The investor's options are out-of-the-money. They have no intrinsic value.

Put Contract Position

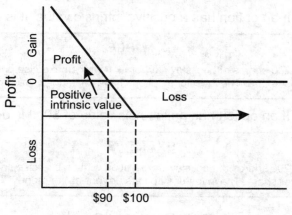

Price of Underlying
Strike price $100
Price of put $10

Figure 7-11

6.   **Forward Contracts**

a.   One method of mitigating risk is the simple forward contract. These are not standardized contracts. The two parties agree that, at a set future date, one of them will perform and the other will pay a specified amount for the performance.

1)   A common example is that of a retailer and a wholesaler who agree in September on the prices and quantities of merchandise to be shipped to the retailer's stores in time for the winter holiday season. The retailer has locked in a price and a source of supply, and the wholesaler has locked in a price and a customer.

b.   The significant difference between a forward contract and a listed option is that a contract imposes obligations to fulfill the contractual obligations (e.g., delivering bushels of wheat or foreign currency). Both parties must meet those obligations, i.e., to deliver merchandise and to pay. On the other hand, listed options do not typically require fulfilling obligations, such as delivering wheat, and they are settled based on the net closing positions. Neither forward contracts nor listed options allow nonperformance.

1)   Forward contracts are frequently used in transactions to exchange foreign currencies.

7. **Futures Contracts**

a. A futures contract is a commitment to buy or sell an asset at a fixed price during a specific future period. In contrast with a forward contract, the counterparty is unknown. In contrast, option contracts allow a choice to buy and sell.

b. Futures contracts are standardized forward contracts with predetermined quantities and dates. These standardized contracts are traded actively on futures exchanges.

   1) Forward contracts are negotiated individually between the parties on a one-by-one basis. But futures contracts are essentially commodities that are traded on an exchange, making them available to more parties.

      a) The clearinghouse matches sellers who will deliver during a given period with buyers who are seeking delivery during the same period. The clearinghouse also underwrites the contract, removing the risk of nonperformance by either party.

   2) Futures contracts are available only for standard amounts (e.g., 62,500 British pounds, 100,000 Brazilian reals, or 12,500,000 Japanese yen) and with specific settlement dates (typically the third Wednesday in March, June, September, and December).

      a) This rigidity makes them less flexible than forward contracts because forward contracts are customized for the parties.

Background

The largest market in the world for trading currency futures is the Chicago Mercantile Exchange. Information about the sizes and prices of various actively traded futures contracts is available at www.cmegroup.com/trading/fx/.

---

c. Because futures contracts are actively traded, the result is a **liquid market** in futures that permits buyers and sellers to net their positions. In contrast, forward contracts are not liquid because they are customized to meet the needs of each party and are not standardized.

d. Another distinguishing feature of futures contracts is that the market price is posted and netted to each person's account at the close of every business day. In other words, each party's gains or losses are tallied in its brokerage account. If significant losses are incurred in the brokerage account, the broker requires funds be added to the brokerage account. This practice is called **mark-to-market**.

   1) A mark-to-market provision minimizes a futures contract's chance of default because profits and losses on the contracts must be received or paid each day through a clearinghouse.

EXAMPLE

On August 1, 20X0, a firm wishes to hedge 120,000 Brazilian reals that it is contractually due to receive on November 7, 20X0. The spot rate on 8/1/20X0 is 3 USD/BRL. The firm sells a 100,000 December 20X0 Brazilian real futures contract at 2.8 USD/BRL. On November 1, 20X0, the company buys a 100,000 December 20X0 Brazilian real futures contract at 2.9 USD/BRL. The company then translates 120,000 real into U.S. dollars by selling 100,000 real on the spot market, which is trading at 2.92 USD/BRL.

$$(2.8 \text{ USD/BRL} - 2.9 \text{ USD/BRL}) \times 100,000 \text{ BRL} = \$(10,000)$$
$$120,000 \text{ BRL} \times 2.92 \text{ USD/BRL} = \$350,400$$
$$\text{Net proceeds} = \$340,400$$

$$\text{Effective exchange rate} = 340,400 \text{ USD} \div 120,000 \text{ BRL} = 2.84$$

8.   **Margin Requirements**

    a.   A **margin account** is a brokerage account in which the investor borrows money (obtains credit) from a broker to purchase securities, such as derivative instruments. The broker charges interest on the credit provided.

    b.   A **margin requirement** (set by the Federal Reserve Board's Regulation T) is the minimum down payment that the purchasers of securities must deposit in the margin account. When the margin account falls below the margin requirement, the broker informs the investor to add funds to the account. This is called a **margin call**.

Stop and review! You have completed the outline for this subunit. Study multiple-choice questions 17 through 20 beginning on page 178.

7.6 MITIGATING EXCHANGE RATE RISK

 Currency exchange is one of the biggest financial risks firms face in the global economy. The AICPA tests this area heavily on the CPA exam.

1.   **Exchange Rate Fluctuations**

    a.   Fluctuations in currency exchange rates can significantly affect a firm's profits.

    b.   The settlement date is the future date when the transaction will occur. The settlement amount is the agreed-upon amount of the transaction.

    c.   Currencies are exchanged at the spot market price. When one wires money internationally, the currency is exchanged on the spot market.

    d.   Review the example below of exchange rate and purchasing power interaction reprinted from page 123.

EXAMPLE

A U.S. company buys merchandise from an EU company for €1,000,000, due in 60 days. On the day of the sale, $0.795 is required to buy a single euro. By the 60th day, $0.812 is required to buy a euro. The dollar has therefore depreciated in relation to the euro, and the euro has appreciated in relation to the dollar. Accordingly, the dollar has lost purchasing power in relation to the euro. The U.S. firm needed $795,000 to pay a €1,000,000 debt on the date of sale. On the due date, it must pay $812,000, resulting in a loss of $17,000.

---

    e.   A firm with a **payable** denominated in a **foreign** currency wants the foreign currency to depreciate by the settlement date so that fewer units of its domestic currency are required to pay the debt.

        1)   A firm with a **payable** denominated in the **domestic** currency is indifferent to fluctuations in the exchange rate for the two currencies. The settlement amount is fixed in terms of its domestic currency.

    f.   A firm with a **receivable** denominated in a **foreign** currency wants the foreign currency to appreciate by the settlement date. When the firm converts the foreign currency into its domestic currency, the conversion results in more units of the domestic currency.

        1)   A firm with a **receivable** denominated in its **domestic** currency is indifferent to fluctuations in the exchange rate for the two currencies. The settlement amount is fixed in terms of its domestic currency.

g. These effects can be summarized in the following table:

	A Domestic Firm with Foreign Currency	
	Net Inflows	**Net Outflows**
As of the Settlement Date	**Will Experience a**	
If the domestic currency has appreciated and the foreign currency has depreciated	(Loss)	Gain
If the domestic currency has depreciated and the foreign currency has appreciated	Gain	(Loss)

2. **Exposures to Exchange Rate Risk**

   a. **Transaction exposure** is the exposure to fluctuations in exchange rates between the date a transaction is entered into and the settlement date.

   b. **Economic exposure** is the exposure to fluctuations in exchange rates resulting from overall economic conditions.

   c. **Translation exposure** is the exposure to fluctuations in exchange rates between the date a transaction is entered into and the date that financial statements denominated in another currency must be reported.

3. **Transaction Exposure**

   a. Multinational corporations enter into numerous individual cross-border transactions during a year. Each transaction is subject to exchange rate variations between the transaction date and the settlement date.

   b. To address transaction exposure, a firm must

      1) Estimate its net cash flows in each currency for affected transactions

         a) If inflows and outflows in a given currency are nearly equal, transaction exposure is minimal, even if the currency itself is volatile.

      2) Measure the potential effect of exposure in each currency

         a) A range of possible rates for each currency must be estimated, reflecting that currency's volatility.

      3) Use hedging methods to mitigate exposure to exchange rate fluctuations

4. **Hedging in Response to Transaction Exposure**

   a. Hedging and Uncertainty

      1) When hedging, some amount of possible gain is forgone to protect against potential loss.

   b. Basic Hedging Principles

      1) When a debtor is to pay a foreign currency amount at some time in the future, the risk is that the foreign currency will appreciate.

         a) If the foreign currency appreciates, more domestic currency is required to pay the debt.

      2) The hedge is to purchase the foreign currency forward to fix a definite price.

EXAMPLE

A U.S. firm knows that it will need 100,000 Canadian dollars in 60 days to pay an invoice. The firm hedges by purchasing 100,000 Canadian dollars 60 days forward. The firm is buying a guarantee that it will have C $100,000 available for use in 60 days. The 60-day forward rate for a Canadian dollar is US $0.99. Thus, for the privilege of having a guaranteed receipt of 100,000 Canadian dollars, the firm commits now to paying $99,000 in 60 days.

The counterparty to the hedge (the seller of Canadian dollars) also might be hedging, but it could be speculating or simply making a market in the instrument. The two parties are indifferent to each other's goals.

3) When a creditor is to receive a foreign currency amount at some time in the future, the risk is that the foreign currency will depreciate.

a) If the foreign currency depreciates, the creditor receives less domestic currency in the conversion.

4) The hedge is to sell the foreign currency forward to fix a definite price.

EXAMPLE

A U.S. firm knows that it will be receiving 5,000,000 pesos in 30 days from the sale of some equipment at one of its facilities in Mexico. The spot rate for a peso is $0.77, and the 30-day forward rate is $0.80. The firm wants to be certain that it can sell the pesos it will receive in 30 days for $0.80 each. The firm hedges by selling 5,000,000 pesos 30 days forward. The firm is buying a guarantee that it can sell 5,000,000 pesos in 30 days and receive $4,000,000 (5,000,000 × $0.80) in return.

The spot rate on day 30 is $0.82. Thus, the U.S. firm could have made more money by forgoing the hedge and simply waiting to convert the pesos on day 30. However, this possibility was not worth the risk that the peso might have fallen below $0.80.

The counterparty to the hedge (the buyer of pesos) also might be hedging, but it could be speculating or simply making a market in the instrument. The two parties are indifferent to each other's goals.

---

c. The following are the most common methods for addressing transaction exposure:

1) **Money Market Hedges**

a) The least complex method for hedging exchange rate risk is the money market hedge.

b) A firm with a payable denominated in a foreign currency can buy a money market instrument denominated in that currency that is timed to mature when the payable is due. Exchange rate fluctuations between the transaction date and the settlement date are avoided.

c) A firm with a receivable denominated in a foreign currency can borrow the amount and convert it to its domestic currency now, then pay the foreign loan when the receivable is collected.

2) **Forward Contracts**

a) Large corporations that have close relationships with major banks can enter into contracts for individual transactions in large amounts.

b) The bank guarantees that it will make available to the firm a given quantity of a certain currency at a definite rate at some time in the future. The price charged by the bank for this guarantee is the premium.

EXAMPLE

A large U.S. firm purchases equipment from a Korean manufacturer for 222,000,000 won, due in 90 days. The exchange rate on the date of sale is $1 to 1,110 won. The U.S. firm suspects that the won may appreciate over the next 90 days and wants to fix a forward rate of 1-to-1,110. The firm negotiates a contract in which its bank promises to deliver 222,000,000 won to the firm in 90 days for $200,000. In return for this guarantee, the firm pays the bank a 2% premium ($200,000 × 2% = $4,000).

---

c) The use of any mitigation strategy has an opportunity cost. The firm in the example above must execute its part of the contract whether or not the exchange rate with the won has fluctuated.

i) If the won falls in value or rises less than the 2% premium in relation to the dollar, the firm has incurred an economic loss on the transaction.

3) **Futures Contracts** (discussed on page 167 in the previous subunit)

4) **Currency Options** (discussed on pages 163 through 166 in the previous subunit)

5.   **Economic Exposure**

   a.   Economic exposure is the exposure to fluctuations in exchange rates resulting from overall economic conditions.

EXAMPLES

An exporter may require all of its customers to pay their invoices in the exporter's domestic currency. Thus, customers bear all the transaction risk of exchange rate variation. If the exporter's currency appreciates beyond a certain exchange rate, the exporter's products no longer will be price-competitive, and the customers will buy from local firms, reducing the exporter's cash inflows.

A manufacturer establishes operations in a low-wage country. As that country's economy strengthens, its currency appreciates and real wages increase. The manufacturer's cash outflows therefore have increased, eliminating the original cost advantage.

---

   b.   Estimating Economic Exposure

   1)   The degree of exposure can be estimated using either of two approaches:

   a)   Sensitivity of earnings. The entity prepares a pro forma income statement for operations in each country.

   b)   Sensitivity of cash flows. The entity performs a regression analysis, weighting each net cash flow by the amount of that currency in the firm's portfolio.

   2)   Next, the entity constructs multiple scenarios (performs a sensitivity analysis) using various estimated exchange rates and determines the ultimate effect of each scenario on accrual-basis earnings or cash flows.

   c.   Mitigating Economic Exposure

   1)   A high level of economic exposure may require restructuring the entity's operations using the following guidelines:

	Actions to Be Taken when Foreign Currency	
Reliance on	Inflows Are Greater	Outflows Are Greater
Sales to foreign customers	Reduce foreign sales	Increase foreign sales
Purchases from foreign suppliers	Increase foreign orders	Reduce foreign orders

6.   **Translation Exposure**

   a.   Translation exposure is the risk that a foreign subsidiary's balance sheet items and results of operations, denominated in a currency different from the parent's, will change as a result of exchange rate fluctuations.

   b.   The degree of a firm's exposure to translation risk is determined by three factors:

   1)   Proportion of Total Business Conducted by Foreign Subsidiaries

   a)   A firm with half of its revenues derived from overseas subsidiaries has a high degree of exposure to translation risk. A 100% domestic firm has none.

   b)   A 100% domestic firm with foreign customers or suppliers still has transaction and economic risk.

   2)   Locations of Foreign Subsidiaries

   a)   A firm with a subsidiary in a country with a volatile currency has more translation risk than a firm with a subsidiary in a country with a stable currency.

   3)   Applicable Accounting Method

   a)   This can be either a cash flow hedge or fair value hedge.

Stop and review! You have completed the outline for this subunit. Study multiple-choice questions 21 through 25 beginning on page 179.

QUESTIONS

7.1 Correlation Analysis

1. Correlation is a term frequently used in conjunction with regression analysis and is measured by the value of the coefficient of correlation, *r*. The best explanation of the value *r* is that it

A. Is always positive.

B. Interprets variances in terms of the independent variable.

C. Ranges in size from negative infinity to positive infinity.

D. Is a measure of the relative relationship between two variables.

Answer (D) is correct.

REQUIRED: The best explanation of the coefficient of correlation *(r)*.

DISCUSSION: The coefficient of correlation *(r)* measures the strength of the linear relationship between the dependent and independent variables. The magnitude of *r* is independent of the scales of measurement of *x* and *y*. The coefficient lies between −1.0 and +1.0. A value of zero indicates no linear relationship between the *x* and *y* variables. A value of +1.0 indicates a perfectly direct relationship, and a value of −1.0 indicates a perfectly inverse relationship.

Answer (A) is incorrect. The coefficient is negative if the relationship between the variables is inverse. Answer (B) is incorrect. The coefficient relates the two variables to each other. Answer (C) is incorrect. The size of the coefficient varies between −1.0 and +1.0.

2. The coefficient of correlation that indicates the weakest linear association between two variables is

A. −0.73

B. −0.11

C. 0.12

D. 0.35

Answer (B) is correct.

REQUIRED: The correlation coefficient that indicates the weakest linear association between two variables.

DISCUSSION: The coefficient of correlation can vary from −1 to +1. A −1 coefficient indicates a perfect negative correlation, and a +1 coefficient indicates a perfect positive correlation. A zero coefficient of correlation indicates no linear association between the variables. Thus, the coefficient of correlation that is nearest to zero indicates the weakest linear association. Of the options given in the question, the correlation coefficient that is nearest to zero is −0.11.

Answer (A) is incorrect. The coefficient of −0.73 signifies a strong negative correlation. Answer (C) is incorrect. The coefficient of 0.12 is a slightly stronger correlation. Answer (D) is incorrect. The coefficient of 0.35 is a considerably stronger correlation.

3. In regression analysis, which of the following coefficients of correlation represents the strongest linear relationship between the independent and dependent variables?

A. 1.03

B. −.02

C. −.89

D. .75

Answer (C) is correct.

REQUIRED: The correlation coefficient with the strongest relationship between independent and dependent variables.

DISCUSSION: A coefficient of −1.0 signifies a perfect inverse relationship, and a coefficient of 1.0 signifies a perfect direct relationship. Thus, the higher the absolute value of the coefficient of correlation, the stronger the linear relationship. A coefficient of −.89 suggests a very strong inverse relationship between the independent and dependent variables.

Answer (A) is incorrect. A coefficient of 1.03 is impossible. Answer (B) is incorrect. A coefficient of −.02 is very weak. Answer (D) is incorrect. A coefficient of .75 is .25 from the maximum, whereas −.89 is only .11 from the minimum.

7.2 Linear Regression Analysis

4. In the standard regression equation $y = a + bx$, the letter *b* is best described as a(n)

A. Independent variable.

B. Dependent variable.

C. Y intercept.

D. Slope of the regression line.

Answer (D) is correct.

REQUIRED: The meaning of the letter *b* in the standard regression equation.

DISCUSSION: In the standard regression equation, *b* represents the slope of the regression line. For example, in a cost determination regression, *y* equals total costs, *b* is the variable cost per unit, *x* is the number of units produced, and *a* is fixed cost.

Answer (A) is incorrect. The independent variable is *x*. Answer (B) is incorrect. The dependent variable is *y*. Answer (C) is incorrect. The y intercept is *a*.

Questions 5 and 6 are based on the following information. Jackson Co. has the following information for the first quarter of this year:

	Machine Hours	Cleaning Expense
January	2,100	$ 900
February	2,600	1,200
March	1,600	800
April	2,000	1,000

5. Using the high-low method, what is Jackson's variable cost of cleaning per machine hour?

A. $.40

B. $.48

C. $2.00

D. $2.50

Answer (A) is correct.
   REQUIRED: The variable cost in the high-low method.
   DISCUSSION: The high-low method is used to generate a regression line by basing the equation on only the highest and lowest of a series of observations. In this problem, March was the lowest and February the highest.

February	$1,200	for	2,600 hours
March	(800)	for	(1,600) hours
Increase	$ 400	for	1,000 hours

Thus, it costs $400 for 1,000 hours, or $.40 for an hour.
   Answer (B) is incorrect. The average of the cleaning expense per machine hour for the high and low months is $.48. Answer (C) is incorrect. The March machine hours divided by the March cost is $2.00. Answer (D) is incorrect. The increase in hours divided by the increase in cost is $2.50.

6. Jackson's management expects machine hours for the month of May to be 1,400 hours. What is their expected total cost for the month of May using the high-low method?

A. $560

B. $650

C. $720

D. $760

Answer (C) is correct.
   REQUIRED: The expected total cost using the high-low method.
   DISCUSSION: The expected total cost, using the high-low method, can be found as follows:

First, calculate the variable cost per machine hour.

($1,200 – $800) ÷ (2,600 hours – 1,600 hours) = $.40

Then, using the data from February (or March), calculate the expected fixed costs.

Total cost	$1,200
Less: Variable cost (2,600 hours × $.40)	(1,040)
Fixed cost	$ 160

Finally, calculate the expected total cost.

Expected total cost = Expected fixed cost + Expected variable cost
   = $160 + (1,400 hours × $.40 per hour)
   = $160 + $560
   = $720

   Answer (A) is incorrect. The variable cost is $560, not the total cost. Answer (B) is incorrect. The expected total cost for May is not $650. Answer (D) is incorrect. The expected total cost for May is not $760.

7.3 Learning Curve Analysis

7. Given demand in excess of capacity, no spoilage or waste, and full use of a constant number of assembly hours, the number of components needed for an assembly operation with an 80% learning curve should

I.   Increase for successive periods.
II. Decrease per unit of output.

   A. I only.

   B. II only.

   C. Both I and II.

   D. Neither I nor II.

Answer (A) is correct.
   REQUIRED: The movement(s) of the number of components needed.
   DISCUSSION: Learning curves reflect the increased rate at which people perform tasks as they gain experience. An 80% learning curve means that the cumulative average time required to complete a unit (or the time required to produce the last unit) declines by 20% when unit output doubles in the early stages of production. Thus, as the cumulative average time per unit (or the time to complete the last unit) declines, the number of units produced per period of time increases. As more units are produced, more components are needed for the production. The number of components per unit of output is not affected by an increase in output.
   Answer (B) is incorrect. The number of components needed per unit of output produced should remain constant, assuming no spoilage or waste. Answer (C) is incorrect. The number of components needed per unit of output produced should remain constant, assuming no spoilage or waste. Answer (D) is incorrect. The number of components needed will increase for successive periods for an assembly operation with an 80% learning curve.

Questions 8 through 10 are based on the following information. Aerosub, Inc., has developed a new product for spacecraft that includes the production of a complex part. The manufacture of this part requires a high degree of technical skill. Management believes there is a good opportunity for its technical force to learn and improve as they become accustomed to the production process. The production of the first unit requires 10,000 direct labor hours. Management projects an 80% learning curve and wants to produce a total of eight units.

---

8. After completing the first unit, the estimated total direct labor hours Aerosub will require to produce the seven additional units will be

   A. 30,960 hours.

   B. 40,960 hours.

   C. 56,000 hours.

   D. 70,000 hours.

Answer (A) is correct.
   REQUIRED: The total direct labor hours to produce seven incremental units given an 80% learning curve.
   DISCUSSION: The cumulative total hours spent on the units can be calculated as follows:

Batch	Cumulative Units Produced	Cumulative Average Labor Hours	Cumulative Total Labor Hours
1	1	10,000	10,000
2	2	8,000 (10,000 × 80%)	16,000
3	4	6,400 (8,000 × 80%)	25,600
4	8	5,120 (6,400 × 80%)	40,960

Because 40,960 hours were needed to complete eight units and 10,000 to complete the first one, units 2 through 8 needed 30,960 hours (40,960 – 10,000).
   Answer (B) is incorrect. The number of hours to complete all eight units is 40,960. Answer (C) is incorrect. The amount of 56,000 hours results from improperly multiplying the seven units by the 8,000 average labor hours consumed in producing the second batch. Answer (D) is incorrect. The amount of 70,000 hours results from improperly multiplying the seven units by the 10,000 average labor hours consumed in producing the first unit.

9. Upon completion of the eighth unit, Aerosub's cumulative direct labor hours will be

A. 29,520 hours.

B. 40,960 hours.

C. 64,000 hours.

D. 80,000 hours.

Answer (B) is correct.
REQUIRED: The cumulative direct labor hours to produce eight units given an 80% learning curve.
DISCUSSION: The underlying assumption of learning curve analysis is that workers gain productivity at a predictable rate as they gain experience with a new process. A common assumption is that the number of hours required for each doubling of output is 80% of the hours required for the previous doubling. The effects of Aerosub's projected learning curve on this product can be calculated as follows:

Batch	Cumulative Units Produced	Cumulative Average Labor Hours	Cumulative Total Labor Hours
1	1	10,000	10,000
2	2	8,000 (10,000 × 80%)	16,000
3	4	6,400 (8,000 × 80%)	25,600
4	8	5,120 (6,400 × 80%)	40,960

Answer (A) is incorrect. The amount of 29,520 hours results from improperly summing the cumulative average labor hour figures. Answer (C) is incorrect. The amount of 64,000 hours results from improperly multiplying the cumulative number of units produced by the 10,000 hours spent on the first batch, then multiplying by the learning curve percentage. Answer (D) is incorrect. The amount of 80,000 hours results from improperly multiplying the cumulative number of units produced by the 10,000 hours spent on the first batch.

10. Upon completion of the eighth unit, Aerosub's cumulative average direct labor hours required per unit of the product will be

A. 5,120 hours.

B. 6,400 hours.

C. 8,000 hours.

D. 10,000 hours.

Answer (A) is correct.
REQUIRED: The cumulative average hours given an 80% learning curve.
DISCUSSION: The underlying assumption of learning curve analysis is that workers gain productivity at a predictable rate as they gain experience with a new process. A common assumption is that the number of hours required for each doubling of output is 80% of the hours required for the previous doubling. The effects of Aerosub's projected learning curve on this product can be calculated as follows:

Batch	Cumulative Units Produced	Cumulative Average Labor Hours
1	1	10,000
2	2	8,000 (10,000 × 80%)
3	4	6,400 (8,000 × 80%)
4	8	5,120 (6,400 × 80%)

Answer (B) is incorrect. The projected number of hours after four units is 6,400. Answer (C) is incorrect. The projected number of hours after two units is 8,000. Answer (D) is incorrect. The number 10,000 results from failing to take the learning curve effect into account at all.

7.4 Capital Asset Pricing Model (CAPM)

11. If the return on the market portfolio is 10% and the risk-free rate is 5%, what is the effect on a company's required rate of return on its stock of an increase in the beta coefficient from 1.2 to 1.5?

A. 3% increase.

B. 1.5% increase.

C. No change.

D. 1.5% decrease.

Answer (B) is correct.

REQUIRED: The effect on a company's required rate of return on its stock of an increase in the beta coefficient.

DISCUSSION: The required rate of return on equity capital can be estimated with the capital asset pricing model (CAPM). CAPM consists of adding the risk-free rate (i.e., the return on government securities, denoted R_F) to the product of the beta coefficient (a measure of the issuer's risk) and the difference between the market return and the risk-free rate (denoted $R_M - R_F$, referred to as the risk premium). Below is the basic equilibrium equation for the CAPM:

$$Required\ rate\ of\ return = R_F + \beta(R_M - R_F)$$

In this situation, the risk premium is 5% (10% − 5%). Thus, the required rate of return when the beta coefficient is 1.2 is 11% [5% + (1.2 × 5%)], and the required rate when the beta coefficient is 1.5 is 12.5% [5% + (1.5 × 5%)]. This is an increase of 1.5% (12.5% − 11%).

12. The betas and expected returns for three investments being considered by Sky, Inc., are given below.

Investment	Beta	Expected Return
A	1.4	12%
B	0.8	11%
C	1.5	13%

The return on the market is 11% and the risk-free rate is 6%. If the capital asset pricing model (CAPM) is used for calculating the required rate of return, which investments should the management of Sky make?

A. B only.

B. A and C only.

C. B and C only.

D. A, B, and C.

Answer (A) is correct.

REQUIRED: The investment(s) that should be made based on the CAPM.

DISCUSSION: The required rate of return on equity capital can be estimated with the capital asset pricing model (CAPM). CAPM consists of adding the risk-free rate (i.e., the return on government securities, denoted R_F) to the product of the beta coefficient (a measure of the issuer's risk) and the difference between the market return and the risk-free rate (denoted $R_M - R_F$, referred to as the risk premium). Below is the basic equilibrium equation for the CAPM:

$$Required\ rate\ of\ return = R_F + \beta(R_M - R_F)$$

The risk premium is 5% (11% − 6%).

The CAPM can be thus applied to each of the three investments as follows:

Investment A: 6% + (1.4 × 5%) = 13.0%
Investment B: 6% + (0.8 × 5%) = 10.0%
Investment C: 6% + (1.5 × 5%) = 13.5%

These required rates of return can be compared with the expected rates to evaluate which investments should be accepted and which should be rejected.

	Required Rate		Expected Rate	Decision
Investment A:	13.0%	>	12%	Reject
Investment B:	10.0%	<	11%	Accept
Investment C:	13.5%	>	13%	Reject

Answer (B) is incorrect. The required rates of return for Investment A and Investment C exceed their expected returns. Answer (C) is incorrect. The required rate of return for Investment C exceeds its expected return. Answer (D) is incorrect. The required rates of return for Investment A and Investment C exceed their expected returns.

13. If Dexter Industries has a beta value of 1.0, then its

A. Return should equal the risk-free rate.

B. Price is relatively stable.

C. Expected return should approximate the overall market.

D. Volatility is low.

Answer (C) is correct.

REQUIRED: The result when the beta value is 1.0.

DISCUSSION: The effect of an individual security on the volatility of a portfolio is measured by its sensitivity to movements by the overall market. This sensitivity is stated in terms of a stock's beta coefficient. If the beta coefficient is 1.0, the price of that stock tends to move in the same direction and to the same degree as the overall market. The expected return can be calculated from the CAPM model formula.

$$Expected\ return = R_F + \beta\ (R_M - R_F)$$

R_F = Risk-free rate
R_M = Market return

When $\beta = 1$, expected return is equal to the market return.

Answer (A) is incorrect. Return is equal to the risk-free rate when $\beta = 0$. Answer (B) is incorrect. A beta value of 1.0 only means the price of the stock moves in concert with that of the overall market; if the market is not stable, the stock price will not be either. Answer (D) is incorrect. A beta value of 1.0 only means the price of the stock moves with that of the overall market. If the market is volatile, the stock price also will be.

14. An analyst covering Guilderland Mining Co. common stock estimates the following information for next year:

Expected return on the market portfolio	12%
Expected return on Treasury securities	5%
Expected beta of Guilderland	2.2

Using the CAPM, the analyst's estimate of next year's risk premium for Guilderland's stock is closest to

A. 7.0%

B. 10.4%

C. 15.4%

D. 21.4%

Answer (C) is correct.

REQUIRED: The expected risk-adjusted premium of a stock based on the capital asset pricing model.

DISCUSSION: According to the capital asset pricing model, the risk premium of a particular stock is the excess of the market rate of return over the risk-free rate weighted by the stock's beta coefficient. For Guilderland Mining, this calculation is

$$Stock's\ risk\ premium = 2.2 \times (12\% - 5\%)$$
$$= 2.2 \times 7\%$$
$$= 15.4\%$$

Answer (A) is incorrect. The percentage of 7.0% is the difference between the overall market rate of return and the risk-free rate. Answer (B) is incorrect. The percentage of 10.4% results from improperly subtracting the risk-free rate from the stock's risk premium. Answer (D) is incorrect. The percentage of 21.4% results from multiplying beta by market rate of return, then subtracting risk-free rate from it.

15. The common stock of Wisconsin's Finest Cheese has a beta coefficient of 1.7. The following information about overall market conditions is available:

Expected return on U.S. Treasury bonds	6%
Expected return on the market portfolio	8.5%

Using the capital asset pricing model (CAPM), what is the risk premium on the market?

A. 10.3%

B. 4.3%

C. 2.5%

D. 1.7%

Answer (C) is correct.

REQUIRED: The risk premium on the market using CAPM.

DISCUSSION: The risk premium on the market is the return on the market portfolio (8.5%) minus the risk-free return as measured by the return on U.S. Treasury securities (6%), or 2.5%.

Answer (A) is incorrect. The rate of 10.3% is the expected return on the stock. Answer (B) is incorrect. The rate of 4.3% is the risk premium on the stock, not the market. Answer (D) is incorrect. The stock's beta coefficient and the risk premium on the market are not the same in this case.

16. Using the capital asset pricing model (CAPM), the required rate of return for a firm with a beta of 1.5 when the market return is 10% and the risk-free rate is 8% is

    A. 5%

    B. 8%

    C. 10%

    D. 11%

Answer (D) is correct.
    REQUIRED: The required rate of return using the capital asset pricing model.
    DISCUSSION: The CAPM quantifies the required rate of return on a security by relating the security's level of risk to the average return available in the market. The required rate of return is calculated as follows:

$$
\begin{aligned}
\text{Required rate of return} &= R_F + \beta(R_M - R_F) \\
&= 8\% + [1.5 \times (10\% - 8\%)] \\
&= 8\% + (1.5 \times 2\%) \\
&= 11\%
\end{aligned}
$$

    Answer (A) is incorrect. The required rate of return cannot be lower than the risk-free rate. Answer (B) is incorrect. The required rate of return for the safest investments (U.S. Treasury securities) is the risk-free rate of 8%. Answer (C) is incorrect. The market return, not the required rate of return, is 10%.

7.5 Derivatives

17. Which of the following options is(are) worth exercising?

	Exercise Price	Price of Underlying Asset
Put Option A	$30	$27
Call Option B	$29	$26
Put Option C	$25	$25
Call Option D	$20	$24

    A. Options A, B, and C.

    B. Options A and B.

    C. Options A and D.

    D. Option D only.

Answer (C) is correct.
    REQUIRED: The option(s) that is(are) worth exercising.
    DISCUSSION: An option is worth exercising if its intrinsic value is positive. A call option gives the holder the right to purchase (i.e., call for) the underlying asset at a fixed price, called the exercise or strike price. The intrinsic value of a call option is the amount by which the exercise price is less than the market price of the underlying asset. Thus, the intrinsic value of call option D is positive ($24 – $20 = $4). A put option gives the holder the right to sell (i.e., put onto the market) the underlying asset at a fixed price. The intrinsic value of a put option is the amount by which the exercise price is greater than the price of the underlying asset. Thus, the intrinsic value of put option A is positive ($30 – $27 = $3).
    Answer (A) is incorrect. Because their intrinsic values are $0, options B and C are not worth exercising. Answer (B) is incorrect. The intrinsic value of call option B is $0. The holder of this option will prefer to buy the underlying asset at its market price of $26 rather than to exercise the option to buy this asset for $29. Answer (D) is incorrect. Option A is also worth exercising. Its intrinsic value ($30 – $27 = $3) is positive.

18. The use of derivatives to either hedge or speculate results in

    A. Increased risk regardless of motive.

    B. Decreased risk regardless of motive.

    C. Offsetting risk when hedging and increased risk when speculating.

    D. Offsetting risk when speculating and increased risk when hedging.

Answer (C) is correct.
    REQUIRED: The effects on risk of hedging and speculating.
    DISCUSSION: Derivatives, including options and futures, are contracts. Unlike stocks and bonds, they are not claims on business assets. A futures contract is entered into as either a speculation or a hedge. Speculation involves the assumption of risk in the hope of gaining from price movements. Hedging is the process of using offsetting commitments to minimize or avoid the effect of adverse price movements.
    Answer (A) is incorrect. Hedging decreases risk by using offsetting commitments that avoid the impact of adverse price movements. Answer (B) is incorrect. Speculation involves the assumption of risk in the hope of gaining from price movements. Answer (D) is incorrect. Speculating increases risk, while hedging offsets risk.

19. A forward contract involves a commitment today to purchase a product

    A. On a specific future date at a price to be determined some time in the future.

    B. At some time during the current day at its present price.

    C. On a specific future date at a price determined today.

    D. Only when its price increases above its current exercise price.

Answer (C) is correct.
    REQUIRED: The terms of a forward contract.
    DISCUSSION: A forward contract is an executory contract in which the parties involved agree to the terms of a purchase and a sale, but performance is deferred. Accordingly, a forward contract involves a commitment today to purchase a product on a specific future date at a price determined today.
    Answer (A) is incorrect. The price of a forward contract is determined on the day of commitment, not some time in the future. Answer (B) is incorrect. Performance is deferred in a forward contract, and the price of the product is not necessarily its present price. The price can be any price determined on the day of commitment. Answer (D) is incorrect. A forward contract is a firm commitment to purchase a product. It is not based on a contingency. Also, a forward contract does not involve an exercise price. (An exercise price is an element of an option contract.)

20. A distinguishing feature of a futures contract is that

    A. Performance is delayed.

    B. It is a hedge, not a speculation.

    C. The parties know each other.

    D. The price is marked to market each day.

Answer (D) is correct.
    REQUIRED: The distinguishing feature of a futures contract.
    DISCUSSION: A characteristic of futures contracts is that their prices are marked to market every day at the close of the day. Thus, the market price is posted at the close of business each day. A mark-to-market provision minimizes a futures contract's chance of default because profits and losses on the contracts must be received or paid each day through a clearinghouse.
    Answer (A) is incorrect. Both a forward contract and a futures contract are executory. Answer (B) is incorrect. A futures contract may be speculative. Answer (C) is incorrect. In a forward contract, the parties know each other. In a future contract, the counterparty is unknown.

7.6 Mitigating Exchange Rate Risk

21. An American importer of English clothing has contracted to pay an amount fixed in British pounds 3 months from now. If the importer worries that the U.S. dollar may depreciate sharply against the British pound in the interim, it would be well advised to

    A. Buy pounds in the forward exchange market.

    B. Sell pounds in the forward exchange market.

    C. Buy dollars in the futures market.

    D. Sell dollars in the futures market.

Answer (A) is correct.
    REQUIRED: The action to hedge a liability denominated in a foreign currency.
    DISCUSSION: The American importer should buy pounds now. If the dollar depreciates against the pound in the next 90 days, the gain on the forward exchange contract offsets the loss from having to pay more dollars to satisfy the liability.
    Answer (B) is incorrect. Selling pounds increases the risk of loss for someone who has incurred a liability. However, it is an appropriate hedge of a receivable denominated in pounds. Answer (C) is incorrect. The importer needs pounds, not dollars. Answer (D) is incorrect. Although buying pounds might be equivalent to selling dollars for pounds, this is not the best answer. This choice does not state what is received for the dollars.

22. A U.S. manufacturer sold a piece of equipment to an engineering firm in New Zealand. The New Zealand firm must pay the invoice in U.S. dollars in 30 days and would like to mitigate the risk that the New Zealand dollar will depreciate against the U.S. dollar in the meantime. The type of exchange rate risk contemplated by the New Zealand firm is known as

    A. Transition exposure.

    B. Economic exposure.

    C. Transaction exposure.

    D. Translation exposure.

Answer (C) is correct.
    REQUIRED: The type of exchange rate exposure embodied in a sale transaction.
    DISCUSSION: Transaction exposure is the exposure to fluctuations in exchange rates between the date a transaction is entered into and the settlement date.
    Answer (A) is incorrect. Transition exposure is not a meaningful term. Answer (B) is incorrect. Economic exposure is the exposure to fluctuations in exchange rates resulting from overall economic conditions. Answer (D) is incorrect. Translation exposure is the risk that a foreign subsidiary's balance sheet items and the results of operations denominated in a currency different from the parent's currency will change in value as a result of exchange rate changes.

23. A company based in West Palm Beach, Florida, is building a resort in Jamaica. The Jamaican property owners must make a progress payment of US $1 million in 30 days. The spot rate for the U.S. dollar is 88 Jamaican dollars (J $), and the 30-day forward rate is J $90. The most likely hedge in response to the transaction exposure inherent in this situation is

    A. The contractor will purchase J $88,000,000 in the spot market.

    B. The contractor will sell J $90,000,000 in the 30-day forward market.

    C. The property owners will purchase US $1,000,000 in the 30-day forward market.

    D. The property owners will sell US $1,000,000 in the 30-day forward market.

Answer (C) is correct.

REQUIRED: The most likely hedging transaction in response to a receivable/payable.

DISCUSSION: This receivable or payable is denominated in the currency of the creditor. Thus, the creditor has no incentive to hedge. The debtors (the property owners) want to hedge against the possibility that their domestic currency will depreciate against the U.S. dollar in the next 30 days. The typical mitigation strategy is to purchase the amount needed to pay the debt so that funds are available when needed.

Answer (A) is incorrect. The party on the receivable side of this transaction has no need to hedge. The debt is denominated in its domestic currency. Answer (B) is incorrect. The party on the receivable side of this transaction has no need to hedge. The debt is denominated in its domestic currency. Answer (D) is incorrect. The debtors need US $1,000,000 in 30 days to pay the invoice. Thus, they will purchase, not sell, the U.S. dollar in the forward market.

24. A company headquartered in Vancouver, British Columbia, is building a pipeline for a company in Russia. The invoice amount is due in 90 days and is denominated at 28 million rubles. The Canadian dollar is trading for 28 rubles currently and 29 rubles 90 days forward. Which of the following strategies will the Canadian firm most likely pursue in the 90-day forward market to hedge the transaction exposure inherent in this situation?

    A. Sell 29,000,000 rubles.

    B. Purchase 28,000,000 rubles.

    C. Purchase 29,000,000 rubles.

    D. Sell 28,000,000 rubles.

Answer (D) is correct.

REQUIRED: The most likely hedging transaction in response to a foreign-denominated receivable.

DISCUSSION: The Canadian company knows that it will be receiving 28,000,000 rubles in 90 days. The firm wants to ensure that it will be able to sell these rubles at that time for a certain number of Canadian dollars. The Canadian firm therefore hedges by selling 28,000,000 rubles in the 90-day forward market. The company is buying a guarantee that it will be able to sell a definite number of rubles in 90 days and receive a definite number of Canadian dollars in return, regardless of fluctuations in the exchange rate in the meantime.

Answer (A) is incorrect. The creditor firm will receive only 28 million rubles. Answer (B) is incorrect. The creditor firm wants to sell, not purchase, forward rubles. Answer (C) is incorrect. The creditor firm wants to sell, not purchase, forward rubles. Also, the firm will receive only 28 million rubles.

25. A company with significant sales in a particular foreign country has recently been subjected to extreme variations in the exchange rate with that country's currency. These variations are expected to continue. To mitigate the resulting economic exposure, a likely strategy for the company to implement would be to

    A. Reduce sales to that country.

    B. Increase sales to that country.

    C. Reduce orders from suppliers in other foreign countries.

    D. Increase orders from suppliers in other foreign countries.

Answer (A) is correct.

REQUIRED: The most likely strategy to mitigate economic exposure to exchange rate variation.

DISCUSSION: When cash inflows from a country with a volatile currency exceed cash outflows to that country, the appropriate strategy to mitigate economic exposure is to decrease sales to that country.

Answer (B) is incorrect. The appropriate strategy to mitigate this economic exposure is to decrease, not increase, sales to that country. Answer (C) is incorrect. Reducing orders from suppliers in other foreign countries will not address this economic exposure. Answer (D) is incorrect. Increasing orders from suppliers in other foreign countries will not address this economic exposure.

STUDY UNIT EIGHT
CORPORATE CAPITAL STRUCTURE

(17 pages of outline)

The balance sheet of a corporation reports the firm's resources and capital structure. Resources consist of the assets used to earn a return. The capital structure consists of the amounts contributed by creditors (Subunit 8.1) and owners (Subunit 8.2). A firm's ability to remain in business in the long run is solvency, a measurable condition (Subunit 8.3).

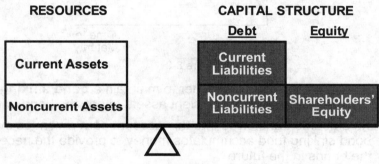

Figure 8-1

Every corporation must determine the appropriate mix of debt and equity in the capital structure. Each component has a cost that changes as economic conditions vary, and as more or less of a component is used. Finding the right mix is the subject of Subunits 8.4 and 8.5.

Background

Many terms are used in business to describe who is borrowing money and who is lending money.

Borrower	Lender
Debtor	Debtee
Payer	Payee
Issuer	Investor
	Creditor
	Holder

8.1 BONDS

1. **Overview**

   a. Bonds are the main form of long-term debt financing for corporations and governments.

      1) A bond is a formal contract to pay an amount of money (par value, maturity amount, or face amount) to the holder at a certain date (maturity date). Also, most bonds provide for a series of cash interest payments based on a specified percentage (stated rate or coupon rate) of the face amount at specified intervals.

         a) The agreement is included in a legal document called an **indenture**.

    b.   Issuing bonds requires legal and accounting work. The expense is rarely justified for bonds with maturities of less than 5 years.

        1)   In general, the longer the term of a bond, the higher the return (yield) demanded by investors to compensate for increased risk, such as the time value of money, interest rate risk, inflation, cyclical economic risk, etc.

            a)   This relationship is the **term structure of interest rates**. It is depicted by the yield curve.

Positive (Normal) Yield Curve

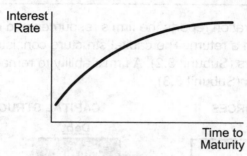

Figure 8-2

    c.   The indenture may require the issuer to maintain a **bond sinking fund**. The objective of the fund is to accumulate sufficient assets to pay the bond principal at maturity.

        1)   The amounts transferred into this account earn revenues over time. Thus, the bond sinking fund accumulates money to provide the necessary funds to repay the bonds in the future.

    d.   **Advantages of Bonds to the Issuer**

        1)   Interest paid on debt is tax deductible (referred to as a tax shield).
        2)   Control of the firm is not shared with debtholders.

    e.   **Disadvantages of Bonds to the Issuer**

        1)   Unlike returns on equity investments, the payment of interest and principal on debt is a legal obligation. If cash flow is insufficient, the firm could become insolvent.

        2)   The legal requirement to pay interest and principal increases a firm's risk and reduces its retained earnings. Since shareholders demand increased retained earnings, they are less likely to invest in the firm; thus decreasing the share price.

        3)   Bonds may require collateral, which is specific property pledged to a lender in case of default.

        4)   The amount of debt financing available to the individual firm is limited. Generally accepted standards of the investment community usually require a certain debt-equity ratio for a firm. Beyond this limit, the cost of debt may rise rapidly, or debt may not be available.

2.   **Types of Bonds**

    a.   Maturity Pattern

        1)   A **term bond** has a single maturity date at the end of its term.
        2)   A **serial bond** matures in stated amounts at regular intervals.

   b.   Valuation

   1)   **Variable (or floating) rate bonds** pay interest that is dependent on market conditions. In other words, the interest rate of the bonds changes (or floats).

   2)   **Zero-coupon or deep-discount bonds** have no stated rate of interest and require no periodic cash payments. The interest component consists entirely of the bond's discount.

   3)   **Commodity-backed bonds** are payable at prices related to a commodity such as gold.

   c.   Redemption Provisions

   1)   **Callable bonds** may be repurchased by the issuer at a specified price before maturity. When interest rates are declining, the issuer can replace high-interest debt with low-interest debt.

   a)   Call provisions allow the issuer to repurchase and retire the bonds (or other fixed-income instruments) early. They typically specify when the bond may be called and the price to be paid. Callable bonds have higher interest rates than comparable noncallable bonds.

   b)   If the sum of the interest payments avoided exceeds the premium paid to retire the debt, it is an advantage to issuers and a disadvantage to investors to call the bond.

   2)   **Convertible bonds** may be converted into equity securities of the issuer at the option of the holder under certain conditions. The ability to become equity holders is an inducement to potential investors.

   d.   Securitization

   1)   **Mortgage bonds** are backed by specific assets, usually real estate.
   2)   **Debentures** are backed by the issuer's credit, not specific assets.

   e.   Ownership

   1)   **Registered bonds** are issued in the name of the holder. Only the registered holder may receive interest and principal payments.

   2)   **Bearer bonds** are not individually registered. Interest and principal are paid to whoever presents the bond.

   f.   Priority

   1)   **Subordinated debentures** and second mortgage bonds are junior securities with claims inferior to those of senior bonds.

   g.   Repayment Provisions

   1)   **Income bonds** pay interest contingent on the issuer's profitability.
   2)   **Revenue bonds** are issued by governmental units and are payable from specific revenue sources.

3.   **Bond Ratings**

   a.   Credit-rating agencies judge the creditworthiness of bonds. The higher the rating, the more likely the firm will pay the interest and principal.

   b.   The three largest firms are Moody's, Standard & Poor's, and Fitch.

   1)   **Investment-grade bonds** are safe investments and have the lowest yields. The highest rating assigned is AAA, and the lowest investment-grade bond is BBB–. Some fiduciary organizations (such as banks and insurers) are allowed to invest only in investment-grade bonds.

   2)   **Noninvestment-grade bonds**, also called speculative-grade, high-yield, or junk bonds, have high risk. The ratings range from BB+ to DDD.

4.   **Bond Valuation**

a.   A bond issuer's main concern is the cash received from investors.

1)   This amount equals the **present value** of the cash flows from the bonds (principal at maturity and periodic interest) discounted at the market (effective) interest rate.

2)   Use of the **effective rate** ensures that the bonds' yield to maturity (ultimate rate of return to the investor) equals the rate of return in the market at the time of sale.

b.   Cash proceeds may be equal to, less than, or greater than the face amount of the bonds, depending on the relationship of the bonds' stated rate of interest to the market rate.

1)   Bonds are sold **at par** if the stated rate equals the market rate at the time of sale (present value = face amount).

2)   If the bonds' **stated rate is lower than the market rate**, periodic interest payments are lower than those currently available. Thus, the bonds are sold for less than par value (at a **discount**) so that the effective interest rate equals the market rate.

EXAMPLE

On January 1, Year 1, a firm issues 100 bonds at 6% annual interest with a face amount of $1,000 maturing in 5 years. At issuance, the market rate is 8%. The proceeds are calculated as follows:

Using PV/FV Tables

Face amount:
Present value of a single payment of
$100,000 discounted at 8% for 5 years $100,000 × .68058 = $68,058

Interest payments:
Present value of an ordinary annuity of
$6,000 discounted at 8% for 5 years $6,000 × 3.99271 =   23,956
Total proceeds $92,014

Using Formula

Face amount:

$$PV = \frac{Amount}{(1 + i)^n}$$

$$\left(\frac{\$100,000}{(1 + .08)^5}\right) = \$68,058$$

Interest payments:

$$PV = \frac{Amount_1}{(1 + r)^1} + \frac{Amount_2}{(1 + r)^2} + \cdots + \frac{Amount_n}{(1 + r)^n}$$

$$\frac{\$6,000}{(1.08)^1} + \frac{\$6,000}{(1.08)^2} + \frac{\$6,000}{(1.08)^3} + \frac{\$6,000}{(1.08)^4} + \frac{\$6,000}{(1.08)^5} = \$23,956$$

The issuer receives cash of $92,014 and records a discount on bonds payable of $7,986 ($100,000 − $92,014).

---

3)   If the bonds' **stated rate is higher than the market rate**, periodic interest payments are higher than those currently available. Thus, the bonds are sold for more than par value (at a **premium**) so that the effective interest rate equals the market rate.

EXAMPLE

On January 1, Year 1, a firm issues bonds with the same terms as those in the previous example, except that the stated rate is 8% and the effective rate is 6%. The present value of the face amount is $74,726 ($100,000 × .74726) and the present value of the interest payments is $33,699 ($8,000 × 4.21236). The issuer therefore receives cash of $108,425 ($74,726 + $33,699) and records a premium on bonds payable of $8,425.

c. The amortization of discount or premium over the term of the bonds results in a carrying amount at maturity equal to their face amount.

1) Straight-line amortization is most common; however, the effective rate method is the most accurate.

d. When bonds are traded among investors in the secondary market, the issuer is not a party to the transaction and receives no cash.

1) The price of the resold bonds is determined by a risk assessment of the issuer and the market rate of interest at the time of the trade. Accordingly, the bonds are priced to achieve a new yield.

5. **Leverage**

a. Leverage is the relative amount of fixed cost in a firm's cost structure. In other words, leverage is the amount of debt a firm has. Leverage creates risk because fixed costs must be paid, regardless of sales.

1) A firm's total leverage consists of operating leverage and financial leverage.

b. **Operating leverage** is the extent to which a firm's costs of operating are fixed. A firm's **degree of operating leverage (DOL)** is a ratio that measures the effect that given fixed operating costs have on earnings.

$$DOL = \frac{\% \text{ change in earnings before interest and taxes (EBIT)}}{\% \text{ change in sales}}$$

1) For example, if the firm's EBIT increases by 24% as a result of an increase in sales of 12%, the firm's DOL is 2 (24% ÷ 12%).

2) The DOL helps the firm determine the operating leverage that maximizes the firm's EBIT.

3) A firm with a high percentage of fixed costs is riskier than a firm in the same industry that relies more on variable costs. It generates more earnings by increasing sales.

c. **Financial leverage** is the degree of debt (fixed financial costs) in the firm's financial structure. A firm's **degree of financial leverage (DFL)** is a ratio that measures the effect that an amount of fixed financing costs has on earnings per share (EPS).

$$EPS = \frac{Net \text{ income available to common shareholders}}{Average \text{ outstanding common shares}}$$

$$DFL = \frac{\% \text{ change in earnings per share (EPS)}}{\% \text{ change in earnings before interest and taxes (EBIT)}}$$

1) For example, if the firm's EPS increases by 12% as a result of an increase in EBIT of 6%, the firm's DFL is 2 (12% ÷ 6%).

2) When a firm has a high percentage of fixed financial costs, it must accept more risk to increase its EPS.

d. **The degree of total (combined) leverage (DTL)** is the product of the degrees of operating and financial leverage.

$$DTL = DOL \times DFL = \frac{\% \text{ change in EBIT}}{\% \text{ change in sales}} \times \frac{\% \text{ change in EPS}}{\% \text{ change in EBIT}} = \frac{\% \text{ change in EPS}}{\% \text{ change in sales}}$$

1) For example, if the firm's EPS increases by 10% as a result of an increase in sales of 2%, the firm's DTL is 5 (10% ÷ 2%).

2) A firm with a higher DTL provides a higher return to investors, but it is also more risky. The risk is due to a higher likelihood of default.

6.   **Debt Covenants**

    a.   Debt covenants are restrictions imposed on a borrower by the creditor in a formal debt agreement (indenture).

    b.   The following are examples of debt covenants:

        1)   Limitations on issuing additional long-term or short-term debt
        2)   Limitations on dividend payments
        3)   Maintenance of certain financial ratios
        4)   Maintenance of specific collateral that secures the debt

    c.   The more restrictive the debt covenants, the lower the risk the borrower will not pay. The less risky the investment, the lower the interest rate on the debt (the risk premium is lower).

    d.   If the debtor violates a covenant, the debt becomes due immediately.

Stop and review! You have completed the outline for this subunit. Study multiple-choice questions 1 through 5 beginning on page 197.

8.2 EQUITY

1.   **Common Stock**

    a.   Common shareholders are the owners of the corporation. But their rights, although reasonably uniform throughout the U.S., depend on the laws of the state of incorporation.

        1)   Equity ownership involves risk because holders of common stock are not guaranteed a return and are last in priority in a liquidation. Shareholders' capital is a source of funds for payment of creditors if losses occur on liquidation.

    b.   Common shareholders ordinarily have a **preemptive right** to purchase additional stock issues in proportion to their current ownership percentages.

    c.   Common shareholders have voting rights. They select the board of directors and vote on resolutions.

    d.   **Advantages to the Corporation**

        1)   Common stock does not require a fixed dividend. Dividends are paid from profits when available.
        2)   Common stock has no fixed maturity date for repayment of capital.
        3)   The sale of common stock increases the creditworthiness of the firm by providing more capital (or money) for the corporation to use.

    e.   **Disadvantages to the Corporation**

        1)   Cash dividends on common stock are not tax-deductible and are paid from after-tax profits. This means common stockholders are double taxed: once on the corporate income and once individually on their personal dividend income. It also means that paying dividends does not decrease a corporation's net income.
        2)   New common stock sales dilute EPS available to current shareholders.
        3)   Underwriting costs (e.g., fees to issue new common stock) typically are higher for common stock than debt.
        4)   Too much equity may raise the average cost of capital of the firm above its optimal level.

f. **Common stock valuation** based on dividend payout models

1) When the dividend per share of common stock is constant and expected to be paid continuously, the price per share is calculated as follows:

$$P_0 = D \div r$$

P_0 = Current price per share
D = Dividend per share (constant)
r = Required rate of return

2) The **constant growth model** (dividend discount model) assumes that dividends per share and price per share increase at the same constant rate (which can be positive or negative). The price per share can be calculated as follows:

$$P_0 = \frac{D_0(1 + g)}{r - g} = \frac{D_1}{r - g}$$

P_0 = Current price per share
D_0 = Current dividends per share
D_1 = Dividends per share expected next year
r = Required rate of return
g = Growth rate (constant)

EXAMPLE

A firm currently pays dividends of $10 per common share. The dividends are expected to increase at a constant rate of 5% per year. If investors' required rate of return is 8%, the current market value of a common share is $350.

$$P_0 = \frac{D_0(1 + g)}{r - g} = \frac{\$10(1 + 5\%)}{8\% - 5\%} = \$350$$

---

3) The required rate of return (the cost of common stock) can be derived from the dividend growth model.

$$r = \frac{D_1}{P_0} + g$$

4) Disadvantages of the constant growth model include that it

a) Assumes the dividend growth rate is constant and is always less than the required rate of return.

b) Cannot be used to value stock price if a company does not pay dividends.

2. **Preferred Stock**

a. Preferred stock is a hybrid of debt and equity. It has a fixed payment, but dividends need not be paid.

1) Also, preferred shareholders have priority over common shareholders in bankruptcy.

b. **Advantages to the Corporation**

1) Preferred stock is equity and increases the creditworthiness of the firm.

2) Control is still held by common shareholders. (Preferred stock rarely has voting rights.)

3) Superior earnings of the firm benefit the common shareholders.

4) Preferred stock does not require periodic payments. Thus, nonpayment of dividends does not lead to bankruptcy.

c. **Disadvantages to the Corporation**

1) Cash dividends on preferred stock are not tax-deductible and are paid from after-tax profits. The result is a substantially greater cost relative to bonds because preferred stockholders also enjoy the value of ownership, whereas bondholders do not.

2) In periods of economic difficulty, accumulated unpaid dividends **(dividends in arrears)** may create managerial and financial problems for the firm.

d. **Typical Preferred Stock Provisions**

1) Priority in assets and earnings. If the firm is bankrupt, the preferred shareholders have priority over common shareholders.

2) Accumulation of dividends. If preferred dividends are cumulative, dividends in arrears must be paid before any common dividends can be paid.

3) Convertibility. Preferred stock issues may be convertible into common stock at the option of the shareholder.

4) Participation. Preferred stock may participate with common stock in excess earnings of the firm. In other words, preferred stockholders not only get their preferred dividend, but also receive common shareholder dividends on a pro-rata basis. For example, 8% participating preferred stock might pay a preferred dividend each year of 8% and, when the corporation is extremely profitable, receives an ordinary dividend equal to what the common shareholders receive.

    a) But **nonparticipating preferred stock** receives no further dividends than are required.

5) Par value. Par value is the liquidation value, and a percentage of par equals the preferred dividend.

e. **Preferred stock valuation** applies the same method used to value a bond that is described in Subunit 8.1.

1) Future cash flows associated with the security are discounted at an investor's required rate of return (market rate) used to value preferred stock.

2) The future cash flows from bonds consist of principal at maturity and periodic interest. But future cash flows from preferred stock are assumed to consist only of the estimated future annual dividends (D_p).

$$D_p = Par\ value\ of\ preferred\ stock \times Preferred\ dividend\ rate$$

3) The discount rate used is the investor's required rate of return (r).

4) Unlike a bond, which has a specific maturity date, preferred stock is assumed to be outstanding in perpetuity.

$$Preferred\ stock\ price\ (P_p) = \frac{D_p}{r}$$

    a) For example, the value of a share of preferred stock with a par value of $100 and a dividend rate of 5% to an investor with a required rate of return of 10% is $50 [($100 × 5%) ÷ 10%].

3. **Other Market-Based Measures**

a. Increasing shareholder wealth is the fundamental goal of any corporation. Two common ratios measure the degree of success toward this goal.

b. The **dividend payout ratio** measures what portion of accrual-basis earnings was actually paid out to common shareholders in the form of dividends.

$$Dividend\ payout\ ratio = \frac{Dividend\ per\ share}{Earnings\ per\ share}$$

c. The **dividend yield ratio** measures how much a company distributes to shareholders relative to its price per share.

$$Dividend\ yield = \frac{Dividend\ per\ share}{Market\ price\ per\ share}$$

4. **Initial Public Offering (IPO)**

a. A firm's first issuance of securities to the public is an IPO. The process by which a closely held corporation issues new securities to the public is called **going public**. When a firm goes public, it issues its securities on a new issue or **IPO market** (a primary market). The corporation becomes an issuer.

b.   **Advantages of Going Public**

1)   The ability to raise additional funds
2)   The establishment of the firm's value in the market
3)   An increase in the liquidity of the firm's stock

c.   **Disadvantages of Going Public**

1)   Costs of the reporting requirements of the SEC and other agencies
2)   Access to the firm's operating data by competing firms
3)   Access to net worth information of major shareholders
4)   Limitations on self-dealing by corporate insiders
5)   Pressure from outside shareholders for earnings growth
6)   Stock prices that may not accurately reflect the true net worth of the firm
7)   Loss of control by management as ownership is diversified
8)   Increased shareholder servicing costs

d.   The main differences between debt financing (payment of interest) and equity financing (payment of dividends) can be summarized as follows:

	Debt Financing	Equity Financing
Effect on control of the firm	No	Yes
Cost of issuing	Lower	Higher
Effect on net income	Yes	No
Dilution of EPS	No	Yes
Effect on solvency risk	Yes	No
Tax deductibility of payments	Yes	No

5.   **Crowdfunding** involves a number of individuals each investing, lending, or contributing small amounts of money to a business or idea to enable the business or entrepreneur to reach a funding target.

a.   Crowdfunding is advantageous because it allows small businesses and entrepreneurs to

1)   Seek alternative funding opportunities rather than conventional methods, such as bank loans,
2)   Quickly achieve financing without upfront fees, and
3)   Raise public awareness of the business or idea.

b.   However, crowdfunding may be detrimental to small businesses and entrepreneurs in some situations.

1)   Unless patented or copyrighted, many ideas can be used by others in the marketplace.
2)   Any money raised can be returned if the crowdfunding target amount is not achieved.

c.   Title III of the JOBS Act of 2012 provides an exemption under the securities laws so that companies can easily use crowdfunding to offer and sell securities. The intent is to (1) make it easier for startups and small businesses to raise capital from a wide range of potential investors and (2) provide additional investment opportunities for investors.

d.   The SEC's rule concerning crowdfunding is called Regulation Crowdfunding. In general, entrepreneurs, companies, and investors must adhere to this rule as follows:

1)   A company may raise a maximum aggregate amount of $1 million through crowdfunding offerings in a 12-month period.

2) Individual investments in all crowdfunding issuers over a 12-month period are limited as follows:

    a) If either their annual income or net worth is less than $100,000,

        i) Investment is limited to the greater of $2,000 or 5% of the lesser of their annual income or net worth.

    b) If annual income or net worth of the investor is $100,000 or more,

        i) Investment is limited to 10% of the lesser of their annual income or net worth.

    c) In addition to the limitations above, during the 12-month period, the aggregate amount of securities sold to an investor through all crowdfunding offerings may not exceed $100,000.

e. Some companies are not eligible to issue securities through crowdfunding, e.g., foreign companies, certain investment companies, and companies that have failed to comply with the reporting requirements under Regulation Crowdfunding.

f. In addition to these regulations, companies must provide certain disclosures:

    1) The price of the securities, the target crowdfunding amount, the deadline of the crowdfunding, and whether the firm will accept investments in excess of the crowdfunding target amount

    2) The company's financial condition, including

        a) Financial statements based on the company's tax returns and reviewed (or audited) by an independent CPA

        b) A description of the business and the use of the proceeds from crowdfunding

        c) Information about officers, directors, and owners of 20% or more of the company

        d) Material related-party transactions

g. Companies choosing to use crowdfunding must use a crowdfunding platform registered with the SEC. These platforms are required to provide investors with educational materials and to take certain measures to reduce the risk of fraud, such as ensuring the companies comply with the disclosures necessary under Regulation Crowdfunding.

Stop and review! You have completed the outline for this subunit. Study multiple-choice questions 6 through 10 beginning on page 199.

8.3 MEASURES OF SOLVENCY

1. **Solvency**

    a. Solvency is a firm's ability to pay its noncurrent obligations as they come due and to remain in business in the long run. It should be contrasted with liquidity.

        1) The ability to service debt from current earnings is part of the effective use of leverage.

$$Times\text{-}interest\text{-}earned\ ratio = \frac{Earnings\ before\ interest\ and\ taxes\ (EBIT)}{Interest\ expense}$$

    b. The key elements of solvency are the firm's capital structure and degree of leverage. (The degree of leverage is defined in item 5. in Subunit 8.1.)

2. **Capital Structure**

   a. A firm's capital structure includes its sources of financing, both long- and short-term. These sources are debt (external sources) and equity (internal sources).

   b. **Debt** is the creditor interest in the firm.

      1) The firm is contractually obligated to repay debtholders. The terms of repayment (timing of interest and principal) are specified in the debt agreement.

      2) If the return on debt exceeds the interest paid, debt financing is advantageous. The return is increased because interest payments on debt are tax-deductible.

      3) The disadvantage of debt is that it increases the firm's risk. Debt must be paid regardless of whether the firm is profitable.

   c. **Equity** is the ownership interest in the firm.

      1) Equity is permanent capital contributed by the firm's owners to earn a return.

      2) However, a return on equity is uncertain. Equity is a residual interest in the firm's assets. It is residual because it is a claim only to assets remaining after all debt has been paid.

      3) Periodic returns to owners of excess earnings are dividends. The firm may be contractually obligated to pay dividends to preferred shareholders but not common shareholders.

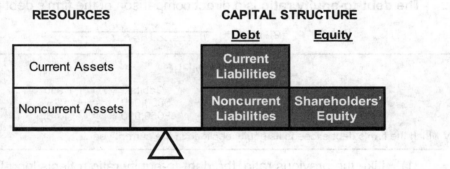

Figure 8-3

   d. Capital structure decisions affect the risk of a firm. For example, a firm with a higher percentage of debt capital is riskier than a firm with a higher percentage of equity capital.

      1) Thus, when the relative amount of debt is high, equity investors demand a higher rate of return on their investments to compensate for the additional risk of financial leverage.

      2) But a firm with a relatively larger proportion of equity capital may be able to borrow at lower rates. Debt holders accept lower interest rates in exchange for lower risk.

3.   **Capital Structure Ratios**

    a.   Capital structure ratios report the relative proportions of debt and equity in a firm's capital structure.

    b.   The **total-debt-to-total-capital ratio** measures the percentage of the firm's capital provided by creditors. This is the same formula as the **debt ratio**.

$$Total\ debt\ to\ total\ capital = \frac{Total\ debt}{Total\ capital}$$

EXAMPLE

The following are a firm's ratios for the current and prior years:

	Debt		Capital		Ratio
Current year:	$1,000,000	÷	$1,800,000	=	0.556
Prior year:	$950,000	÷	$1,600,000	=	0.594

The firm became slightly less reliant on debt during the current year. Although total debt increased, equity increased by a greater percentage. The firm is therefore less leveraged than before.

---

        1)   When total debt to total capital is low, more of the firm's capital is supplied by the shareholders. Thus, creditors prefer this ratio to be low to provide a cushion against losses.

    c.   The **debt-to-equity ratio** is a direct comparison of the firm's debt with its equity.

$$Debt\ to\ equity = \frac{Total\ debt}{Shareholders'\ equity}$$

EXAMPLE

	Debt		Capital		Ratio
Current year:	$1,000,000	÷	$800,000	=	1.25
Prior year:	$950,000	÷	$650,000	=	1.46

The amount by which the firm's debt exceeds its equity declined in the current year.

---

        1)   Like the previous ratio, the debt-to-equity ratio reflects long-term debt-payment ability. Again, a low ratio means a lower relative debt and less risk for creditors.

    d.   The **long-term-debt-to-total-equity ratio** reports long-term debt per dollar of equity.

$$Long\text{-}term\ debt\ to\ total\ equity = \frac{Long\text{-}term\ debt}{Shareholder's\ equity}$$

EXAMPLE

	Debt		Capital		Ratio
Current year:	$610,000	÷	$800,000	=	0.763
Prior year:	$675,000	÷	$650,000	=	1.038

The firm has reduced its long-term debt. It now has less than one dollar of long-term debt for every dollar of equity.

---

        1)   A firm with a low ratio has a better chance of obtaining new debt financing at a favorable rate.

Stop and review! You have completed the outline for this subunit. Study multiple-choice questions 11 and 12 on page 200.

8.4 COMPONENT COSTS OF CAPITAL

1. **Overview**

   a. Investment in corporations is with the understanding that management will use the capital to provide a return to investors.

   1) If management does not provide required rate of return, investors sell their stock on the secondary market, causing the market value of the stock to drop. Creditors then demand higher rates on the firm's debt.

   2) For this reason, investors' required rate of return (also called their opportunity cost of capital) becomes the firm's cost of capital.

   b. Equity holders demand higher returns than debt holders.

   1) Providers of equity capital are exposed to more risk than are lenders because

   a) The firm is not legally obligated to pay them a return, and
   b) In case of liquidation, creditors have priority.

   2) To compensate for this higher risk, equity investors demand a higher return, making equity financing more expensive than debt.

   c. A firm's cost of capital is used to discount the future cash flows of long-term projects the firm is considering. Potential investments with a rate of return higher than the cost of capital will increase the value of the firm and shareholders' wealth. On the other hand, potential investments with a rate of return lower than the cost of capital will decrease the value of the firm and shareholders' wealth.

2. **Component Costs of Capital**

   a. A firm's cost of capital is the required rate of return by investors on the firm's debt and equity (both preferred and common).

   b. Component cost of capital includes (1) cost of long-term debt, (2) cost of preferred stock, and (3) cost of equity (retained earnings).

   1) The component cost of **long-term debt** is the after-tax interest rate on the debt because interest payments are tax-deductible.

   $$\text{Effective rate} \times (1.0 - \text{Marginal tax rate})$$

   2) The component cost of **preferred stock** is calculated using the dividend yield ratio.

   $$R_{preferred\ stock\ (old)} = \frac{Cash\ dividend\ on\ preferred\ stock}{Market\ price\ of\ preferred\ stock}$$

   a) The market price of preferred stock upon issuance equals the net proceeds (gross proceeds − flotation costs). Flotation (issuance) costs reduce the net proceeds received, raising the cost of capital.

   i) Thus, the component cost of preferred stock also can be derived by using the following formula:

   $$R_{preferred\ stock\ (new)} = \frac{Cash\ dividend\ on\ preferred\ stock}{Preferred\ stock\ market\ price - Flotation\ costs}$$

3)   The costs of debt and preferred stock reflect the requirements of creditors and prospective purchasers of preferred shares, respectively. However, **retained earnings** (internal equity capital) already belong to the common shareholders. These earnings would be distributed to them as dividends if not retained. Accordingly, the component cost of retained earnings is the rate of return required by common shareholders.

   a)   If the firm cannot use retained earnings profitably, it should be distributed to the common shareholders as dividends so they can make their own investments.

   b)   The following is the traditional formula for cost of equity:

$$R_{common\ equity\ (basic)} = \frac{Next\ dividend\ per\ share}{Share\ price}$$

   c)   An advanced formula combines the basic formula above with the dividend growth model:

$$R_{common\ equity\ (advanced)} = \frac{Next\ dividend\ per\ share}{Share\ price} + Dividend\ growth\ rate$$

4)   The methods of calculating the cost of internal equity include the discounted cash flow approach and bond yield plus a risk premium. But the best known method is the **capital asset pricing model (CAPM)** described in Study Unit 7, Subunit 4. It quantifies the required return on an equity security by relating the security's level of risk to the average return available in the market (portfolio). The CAPM may be used to calculate the cost of equity as

$$Required\ rate\ of\ return = R_F + \beta(R_M - R_F)$$

If: R_F = Risk-free return
      R_M = Market return
      β = Measure of the systematic risk or volatility of the individual security in comparison to the market (diversified portfolio)

   a)   Beta (β) measures the volatility of an individual security's returns relative to the equity returns of the overall market. Beta is determined by plotting the returns of the individual security and the overall market return over a period of time. A regression line then is fitted to the resulting data points, and its slope is the levered equity beta.

   i)   Returns on the security are no more or less volatile than returns on the market if the slope of the regression line is 1.00.

   ii) Returns on the security are more volatile than returns on the market if the slope of the regression line is greater than 1.00.

EXAMPLE

A firm has outstanding bonds with a coupon rate of 7% and an effective rate of 5%. Its 9%, $60 par-value preferred stock currently is trading at $67.50 per share. The firm's $1 par-value common stock trades at $1.40 per share and pays a 14% dividend with 5% growth rate. The applicable tax rate is 35%.

The component costs of capital are calculated as follows:

Long-Term Debt	Preferred Equity	Common Equity
Cost = Effective rate × (1.0 − Tax rate)	Cost = Cash dividend ÷ Market price	Cost = (Next dividend ÷ Market price) + Growth rate
= 5% × (1.0 − .35)	= ($60 × 9%) ÷ $67.50	= {[$1 × 14% × (1 + 5%)] ÷ $1.40} + 5%
= 5% × .65	= $5.40 ÷ $67.50	= ($.147 ÷ $1.40) + 5%
= 3.25%	= 8%	= 15.5%

Stop and review! You have completed the outline for this subunit. Study multiple-choice questions 13 through 16 beginning on page 200.

8.5 WEIGHTED-AVERAGE COST OF CAPITAL

The weighted-average cost of capital has been tested recently using general conceptual questions and calculation questions.

1. **Weighted-Average Cost of Capital (WACC)**

   a. Corporate management usually designates a target capital structure, i.e., the proportion of each component of capital: long-term debt, preferred equity, and common equity.

   b. A firm's WACC combines the three components of capital into one composite rate of return on the combined components of capital. The weights are based on the target capital structure.

EXAMPLE

The firm has a target capital structure of 20% long-term debt, 30% preferred equity, and 50% common equity. The weighted-average cost of capital is calculated as follows:

	Target Weight		Cost of Capital		Weighted Cost
Long-term debt	20%	×	3.25%	=	0.65%
Preferred equity	30%	×	8.16%	=	2.45%
Common equity	50%	×	15.00%	=	7.50%
					10.60%

---

   c. A formula to calculate the WACC given no preferred equity is

$$WACC = \left[\left(\frac{Value_{Debt}}{Value_{Equity} + Value_{Debt}}\right) \times R_{Debt} \times (1 - R_{Tax})\right] + \left[\left(\frac{Value_{Equity}}{Value_{Equity} + Value_{Debt}}\right) \times R_{Equity}\right]$$

$$\underbrace{\hspace{4cm}}_{Debt\ Component} \quad \underbrace{\hspace{4cm}}_{Equity\ Component}$$

R_{Equity}	=	Cost of equity
R_{Debt}	=	Cost of debt
$Value_{Equity}$	=	Market value of the firm's equity
$Value_{Debt}$	=	Market value of the firm's debt
R_{Tax}	=	Corporate tax rate

EXAMPLE

The firm provides the following information:

Capital used to generate profits	
Equity	$ 300
Debt	900
	$1,200

Cost of equity	15%
Cost of debt	5%
Corporate tax rate	40%

$$WACC = \left[\frac{\$900}{\$1,200} \times 5\% \times (1 - 40\%)\right] + \frac{\$300}{\$1,200} \times 15\% = 0.06 = 6\%$$

---

d.   A formula to calculate WACC with preferred equity is

$$WACC = \frac{D}{V} \times R_d \times (1 - T) + \frac{E}{V} \times R_e + \frac{P}{V} \times R_p$$

$$\underbrace{\phantom{\frac{D}{V} \times R_d \times (1 - T)}}_{\substack{\text{Debt} \\ \text{Component}}} \underbrace{\phantom{\frac{E}{V} \times R_e}}_{\substack{\text{Equity} \\ \text{Component}}} \underbrace{\phantom{\frac{P}{V} \times R_p}}_{\substack{\text{Preferred} \\ \text{Equity} \\ \text{Component}}}$$

R_e	= Cost of equity
R_d	= Cost of debt
R_P	= Cost of preferred equity
E	= Market value of the firm's common equity
D	= Market value of the firm's debt
P	= Market value of the firm's preferred equity
T	= Corporate tax rate
V = E + D + P	= Capital used to generate profits

1)   The market values of the firm's debt, common equity, and preferred equity should reflect the targeted capital structure rather than the current capital structure.

2)   Although the WACC formula includes the market value of debt, the carrying amount may be used as a proxy. However, if the firm is in financial distress, the market value and carrying amount may differ greatly.

3)   The debt component is multiplied by $(1 - T)$ to incorporate the tax benefit of interest expense.

2.   **Optimal Capital Structure**

a.   Standard financial theory provides a model for the optimal capital structure of every firm. In accordance with this model, shareholder wealth-maximization results from **minimizing the weighted-average cost of capital**. Thus, management should **not** focus only on maximizing earnings per share. (EPS can be increased by assuming more debt, but debt increases risk.)

1)   The relevant relationships are depicted below:

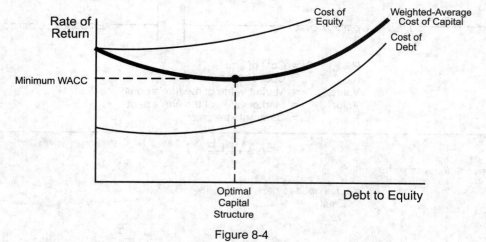

Figure 8-4

Ordinarily, firms cannot identify this optimal point precisely. Thus, they should attempt to find an optimal range for the capital structure.

3. **Modigliani-Miller and Capital Structure Irrelevance**

   a. The Modigliani-Miller theorem disagrees with the standard financial theory. It asserts that no optimal capital structure exists for a firm. Thus, whether the firm finances with all debt, all equity, or some combination is irrelevant to shareholders' wealth.

      1) The reasoning is that any increase in expected return from debt financing is exactly offset by an increase in the required rate of return on equity because of the risk related to leverage.

      2) Thus, such measures as degree of leverage and the debt-to-equity ratio should be of no use to shareholders.

   b. While many (or most) firms follow the standard financial theory and set a target or a range for the capital structure, CPAs should be aware of the Modigliani-Miller theorem and other counterarguments to the standard financial theory.

Stop and review! You have completed the outline for this subunit. Study multiple-choice questions 17 through 20 beginning on page 201.

QUESTIONS
8.1 Bonds

1. This year, Nelson Industries increased earnings before interest and taxes (EBIT) by 17%. During the same period, earnings per share increased by 42%. The degree of financial leverage that existed during the year is

A. 1.70

B. 4.20

C. 2.47

D. 5.90

Answer (C) is correct.
   REQUIRED: The degree of financial leverage.
   DISCUSSION: If earnings before interest and taxes increased by 17%, and earnings per share income was up 42%, the firm is using leverage effectively. The degree of financial leverage is the percentage change in earnings per share divided by the percentage change in EBIT. Accordingly, Nelson's degree of financial leverage is 2.47 (.42 ÷ .17).

2. Short-term interest rates are

A. Usually lower than long-term rates.

B. Usually higher than long-term rates.

C. Lower than long-term rates during periods of high inflation only.

D. Not significantly related to long-term rates.

Answer (A) is correct.
   REQUIRED: The true statement about short-term interest rates.
   DISCUSSION: Historically, a facet of the term structure of interest rates (the relationship of yield and time to maturity) is that short-term interest rates ordinarily have been lower than long-term rates. One reason is that less risk is involved in the short run. Moreover, future expectations about interest rates affect the term structure. Most economists believe that a long-term interest rate is an average of future expected short-term interest rates. For this reason, the yield curve will (1) slope upward if future rates are expected to rise, (2) slope downward if interest rates are anticipated to fall, and (3) remain flat if investors think the rate is stable. Future inflation is incorporated into this relationship. Another consideration is liquidity preference. Investors in an uncertain world accept lower rates on short-term investments because of their greater liquidity.
   Answer (B) is incorrect. Short-term rates are usually lower than long-term rates. Answer (C) is incorrect. Short-term rates are more likely to be greater than long-term rates if current levels of inflation are high. Answer (D) is incorrect. Long-term rates may be viewed as short-term rates adjusted by a risk factor.

3. If Brewer Corporation's bonds are currently yielding 8% in the marketplace, why is the firm's cost of debt lower?

   A. Market interest rates have increased.

   B. Additional debt can be issued more cheaply than the original debt.

   C. There should be no difference; cost of debt is the same as the bonds' market yield.

   D. Interest is deductible for tax purposes.

Answer (D) is correct.
   REQUIRED: The reason a firm's cost of debt is lower than its current market yield.
   DISCUSSION: Because interest is deductible for tax purposes, the actual cost of debt capital is the net effect of the interest payment and the offsetting tax deduction. The actual cost of debt equals the interest rate times the difference of 1 minus the marginal tax rate. Thus, if a firm with an 8% market rate is in a 40% tax bracket, the net cost of the debt capital is 4.8% [8% × (1.0 − .40)].
   Answer (A) is incorrect. The tax deduction always causes the market yield rate to be higher than the cost of debt capital. Answer (B) is incorrect. Additional debt may or may not be issued more cheaply than earlier debt, depending upon the interest rates in the market place. Answer (C) is incorrect. The cost of debt is less than the yield rate given that bond interest is tax deductible.

4.

Interest Rate %

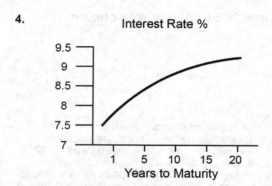

Years to Maturity

The yield curve shown implies that the

   A. Credit risk premium of corporate bonds has increased.

   B. Credit risk premium of municipal bonds has increased.

   C. Long-term interest rates have a higher annualized yield than short-term rates.

   D. Short-term interest rates have a higher annualized yield than long-term rates.

Answer (C) is correct.
   REQUIRED: The implication of the yield curve.
   DISCUSSION: The term structure of interest rates is the relationship between yield to maturity and time to maturity. This relationship is depicted by a yield curve. Assuming the long-term interest rate is an average of expected future short-term rates, the curve will be upward sloping when future short-term interest rates are expected to rise. Furthermore, the normal expectation is for long-term investments to pay higher rates because of their higher risk. Thus, long-term interest rates have a higher annualized yield than short-term rates.
   Answer (A) is incorrect. The yield curve does not reflect the credit risk premium of bonds. Answer (B) is incorrect. The yield curve does not reflect the credit risk premium of bonds. Answer (D) is incorrect. Long-term interest rates should be higher than short-term rates.

5. If a $1,000 bond sells for $1,125, which of the following statements are true?

I. The market rate of interest is greater than the coupon rate on the bond.

II. The coupon rate on the bond is greater than the market rate of interest.

III. The bond sells at a premium.

IV. The bond sells at a discount.

   A. I and III.

   B. I and IV.

   C. II and III.

   D. II and IV.

Answer (C) is correct.
   REQUIRED: The true statements about a bond that sells at more than its face value.
   DISCUSSION: The excess of the price over the face value is a premium. A premium is paid because the coupon rate on the bond is greater than the market rate of interest. Thus, because the bond is paying a higher rate than other similar bonds, its price is bid up by investors.
   Answer (A) is incorrect. If a bond sells at a premium, the market rate of interest is less than the coupon rate. Answer (B) is incorrect. A bond sells at a discount when the price is less than the face amount. Answer (D) is incorrect. A bond sells at a discount when the price is less than the face amount.

8.2 Equity

6. Each share of nonparticipating, 8%, cumulative preferred stock in a company that meets its dividend obligations has all of the following characteristics **except**

A. Voting rights in corporate elections.

B. Dividend payments that are not tax deductible by the company.

C. No principal repayments.

D. A superior claim to common stock equity in the case of liquidation.

Answer (A) is correct.

REQUIRED: The item not characteristic of nonparticipating, cumulative preferred stock.

DISCUSSION: Dividends on cumulative preferred stock accrue until declared. That is, the carrying amount of the preferred stock increases by the amount of any undeclared dividends. Participating preferred stock participates with common shareholders in excess earnings of the firm. Accordingly, 8% participating preferred stock might pay a dividend each year greater than 8% when the corporation is extremely profitable. Thus, nonparticipating preferred stock will receive no more than what is stated on the face of the stock. Preferred shareholders rarely have voting rights. Voting rights are exchanged for preferences regarding dividends and liquidation of assets.

Answer (B) is incorrect. A corporation does not receive a tax deduction for making dividend payments on any type of stock. Answer (C) is incorrect. Preferred stock normally need not be redeemed as long as the corporation remains in business. Answer (D) is incorrect. Preferred shareholders do have priority over common shareholders in a liquidation.

7. In general, it is more expensive for a company to finance with equity capital than with debt capital because

A. Long-term bonds have a maturity date and must therefore be repaid in the future.

B. Investors are exposed to greater risk with equity capital.

C. Equity capital is in greater demand than debt capital.

D. Dividends fluctuate to a greater extent than interest rates.

Answer (B) is correct.

REQUIRED: The reason equity financing is more expensive than debt financing.

DISCUSSION: Providers of equity capital are exposed to more risk than are lenders because the firm is not obligated to pay them a return. Also, in case of liquidation, creditors are paid before equity investors. Thus, equity financing is more expensive than debt because equity investors require a higher return to compensate for the greater risk assumed.

Answer (A) is incorrect. The obligation to repay at a specific maturity date reduces the risk to investors and thus the required return. Answer (C) is incorrect. The demand for equity capital is directly related to its greater cost to the issuer. Answer (D) is incorrect. Dividends are based on managerial discretion and may rarely change; interest rates, however, fluctuate daily based upon market conditions.

8. Preferred and common stock differ in that

A. Failure to pay dividends on common stock will not force the firm into bankruptcy, while failure to pay dividends on preferred stock will force the firm into bankruptcy.

B. Common stock dividends are a fixed amount, while preferred stock dividends are not.

C. Preferred stock has a higher priority than common stock with regard to earnings and assets in the event of bankruptcy.

D. Preferred stock dividends are deductible as an expense for tax purposes, while common stock dividends are not.

Answer (C) is correct.

REQUIRED: The difference between preferred and common stock.

DISCUSSION: In the event of bankruptcy, the claims of preferred shareholders must be satisfied before common shareholders receive anything. The interests of common shareholders are secondary to those of all other claimants.

Answer (A) is incorrect. Failure to pay dividends will not force the firm into bankruptcy, whether the dividends are for common or preferred stock. Only failure to pay interest will force the firm into bankruptcy. Answer (B) is incorrect. Preferred dividends are fixed. Answer (D) is incorrect. Neither common nor preferred dividends are tax deductible.

9. Unless the shares are specifically restricted, a holder of common stock with a preemptive right may share proportionately in all of the following **except**

A. The vote for directors.

B. Corporate assets upon liquidation.

C. Cumulative dividends.

D. New issues of stock of the same class.

Answer (C) is correct.

REQUIRED: The item not a right of common shareholders.

DISCUSSION: Common stock does not have the right to accumulate unpaid dividends. This right often is attached to preferred stock.

Answer (A) is incorrect. Common shareholders have the right to vote (although different classes of shares may have different privileges). Answer (B) is incorrect. Common shareholders have the right to share proportionately in corporate assets upon liquidation (but only after other claims have been satisfied). Answer (D) is incorrect. Common shareholders have the right to share proportionately in any new issues of stock of the same class (the preemptive right).

10. The following excerpt was taken from a company's financial statements: " . . . 10% convertible participating . . . $10,000,000." What is most likely being referred to?

    A. Bonds.

    B. Common stock.

    C. Stock options.

    D. Preferred stock.

Answer (D) is correct.
    REQUIRED: The securities that most likely are convertible participating.
    DISCUSSION: Preferred shareholders have priority over common shareholders in the assets and earnings of the enterprise. If preferred dividends are cumulative, any past preferred dividends must be paid before any common dividends. Preferred stock also may be convertible into common stock, and it may be participating. For example, 10% fully participating preferred stock will receive additional distributions at the same rates as other shareholders if dividends paid to all shareholders exceed 10%.
    Answer (A) is incorrect. Bonds normally have a coupon yield stated in percentage and may be convertible but are not participating. Answer (B) is incorrect. Common stock is not described as convertible or participating on the financial statements. Answer (C) is incorrect. Common stock options are not participating and do not have a stated yield rate.

8.3 Measures of Solvency

11. The relationship of the total debt to the total equity of a corporation is a measure of

    A. Liquidity.

    B. Profitability.

    C. Creditor risk.

    D. Break even.

Answer (C) is correct.
    REQUIRED: The characteristic measured by the relationship of total debt to total equity.
    DISCUSSION: The debt-to-equity ratio is a measure of risk to creditors. It indicates how much equity is available to absorb losses before the interests of debt holders are impaired. The less leveraged the firm, the safer the creditors' interests.
    Answer (A) is incorrect. Liquidity relates to how quickly cash can be made available to pay debts as they come due. Answer (B) is incorrect. The debt-to-equity ratio evaluates a firm's capital structure and is not oriented toward the balance sheet. It does not measure the use (profits) made of assets. Answer (D) is incorrect. Breakeven relates to profitability, not financing.

12. If the ratio of total liabilities to equity increases, a ratio that must also increase is

    A. Times interest earned.

    B. Total liabilities to total assets.

    C. Return on equity.

    D. The current ratio.

Answer (B) is correct.
    REQUIRED: The ratio that increases if the ratio of total liabilities to equity increases.
    DISCUSSION: Because total assets equal the sum of liabilities and equity, a factor that increases the liabilities-to-equity ratio also increases the liabilities-to-assets ratio.
    Answer (A) is incorrect. No determination can be made of the effect on interest coverage without knowing the amounts of income and interest expense. Answer (C) is incorrect. The return on equity may be increased or decreased as a result of a factor that increases in the liabilities-to-equity ratio. Answer (D) is incorrect. The current ratio equals current assets divided by current liabilities, and additional information is necessary to determine whether it is affected. For example, an increase in current liabilities from short-term borrowing increases the liabilities-to-equity ratio but decrease the current ratio.

8.4 Component Costs of Capital

13. Global Company Press has $150 par-value preferred stock with a market price of $120 a share. The organization pays a $15 per share annual dividend. Global's current marginal tax rate is 40%. Looking to the future, the company anticipates maintaining its current capital structure. What is the component cost of preferred stock to Global?

    A. 4%

    B. 5%

    C. 10%

    D. 12.5%

Answer (D) is correct.
    REQUIRED: The cost of preferred stock.
    DISCUSSION: The component cost of preferred stock is the dividend divided by the market price (also called the dividend yield). No tax adjustment is necessary because dividends are not deductible. Given that the market price is $120 when the dividend is $15, the component cost of preferred capital is 12.5% ($15 ÷ $120).
    Answer (A) is incorrect. The preferred stock dividend is not deductible for tax purposes. Answer (B) is incorrect. The preferred stock dividend is not deductible for tax purposes. Answer (C) is incorrect. The denominator is the market price, not the par value.

14. Maloney, Inc.'s $1,000 par-value preferred stock paid its $100 per share annual dividend on April 4 of the current year. The preferred stock's current market price is $960 a share on the date of the dividend distribution. Maloney's marginal tax rate (combined federal and state) is 40%, and the firm plans to maintain its current capital structure. The component cost of preferred stock to Maloney would be closest to

A. 6%

B. 6.25%

C. 10%

D. 10.4%

Answer (D) is correct.
REQUIRED: The component cost of preferred stock in the firm's capital structure.
DISCUSSION: The component cost of preferred stock is equal to the dividend yield, i.e., the cash dividend divided by the market price of the stock. (Dividends on preferred stock are not deductible for tax purposes; therefore, there is no adjustment for tax savings.) The annual dividend on preferred stock is $100 when the price of the stock is $960. The result is a cost of capital of about 10.4% ($100 ÷ $960).
Answer (A) is incorrect. Preferred dividends are not tax deductible. Answer (B) is incorrect. Preferred dividends are not tax deductible. Answer (C) is incorrect. The denominator is the current market price, not the par value.

15. What is the after-tax cost of preferred stock that sells for $5 per share and offers a $0.75 dividend when the tax rate is 35%?

A. 5.25%

B. 9.75%

C. 10.50%

D. 15%

Answer (D) is correct.
REQUIRED: The cost of preferred stock.
DISCUSSION: The component cost of preferred stock is the dividend yield, i.e., the cash dividend divided by the market price of the stock ($.75 ÷ $5.00 = 15%). Preferred dividends are not deductible for tax purposes.
Answer (A) is incorrect. The figure of 5.25% results from incorrectly multiplying the cost by the tax rate. Answer (B) is incorrect. The figure of 9.75% results from incorrectly multiplying the cost by the tax rate, which is not appropriate. Preferred dividends are not deductible for tax purposes. Answer (C) is incorrect. The figure of 10.50% is based on the assumption of a 30% tax rate and deductibility of dividends.

16. Cox Company has sold 1,000 shares of $100 par, 8% preferred stock at an issue price of $92 per share. Stock issue costs were $5 per share. Cox pays taxes at the rate of 40%. What is Cox's cost of preferred stock capital?

A. 8.00%

B. 8.25%

C. 8.70%

D. 9.20%

Answer (D) is correct.
REQUIRED: The cost of preferred equity.
DISCUSSION: Because the dividends on preferred stock are not deductible for tax purposes, the effect of income taxes is ignored. Thus, the relevant calculation is to divide the $8 annual dividend by the quantity of funds received from the issuance. In this case, the funds received equal $87 ($92 proceeds – $5 issue costs). Thus, the cost of capital is 9.2% ($8 ÷ $87).
Answer (A) is incorrect. The figure of 8.00% results from using the par value rather than the selling price and failing to subtract the issue costs. Answer (B) is incorrect. The figure of 8.25% results from adding the issue costs rather than subtracting them. Answer (C) is incorrect. The figure of 8.70% results from failing to subtract the issue costs.

8.5 Weighted-Average Cost of Capital

17. An accountant for Stability, Inc., must calculate the weighted-average cost of capital of the corporation using the following information.

		Component Cost
Accounts payable	$35,000,000	-0-
Long-term debt	10,000,000	8%
Common stock	10,000,000	15%
Retained earnings	5,000,000	18%

What is the weighted average cost of capital of Stability?

A. 6.88%

B. 8.00%

C. 10.25%

D. 12.80%

Answer (D) is correct.
REQUIRED: The weighted-average cost of capital.
DISCUSSION: Because the effect of income taxes is ignored in this situation, the stated rate on the firm's long-term debt is considered to be its effective rate. The weighted-average cost of capital (WACC) can thus be calculated as follows:

	Carrying Amount	Weight		Cost of Capital		Weighted Cost
Long-term debt	$10,000,000	40%	×	8%	=	3.2%
Common stock	10,000,000	40%	×	15%	=	6.0%
Retained earnings	5,000,000	20%	×	18%	=	3.6%
Totals	$25,000,000	100%				12.8%

Answer (A) is incorrect. The figure of 6.88% results from improperly ignoring the weighted cost of common stock. Answer (B) is incorrect. The figure of 8.00% is the component cost of debt. Answer (C) is incorrect. The figure of 10.25% results from improperly performing a simple average on the four balance sheet items listed.

18. Scrunchy-Tech, Inc., has determined that it can minimize its weighted-average cost of capital (WACC) by using a debt-equity ratio of 2/3. If the firm's cost of debt is 9% before taxes, the cost of equity is estimated to be 12% before taxes, and the tax rate is 40%, what is the firm's WACC?

    A. 6.48%

    B. 7.92%

    C. 9.36%

    D. 10.80%

Answer (C) is correct.
    REQUIRED: The firm's weighted-average cost of capital.
    DISCUSSION: A firm's weighted-average cost of capital (WACC) is derived by weighting the (after-tax) cost of debt of 5.4% [9% × (1 – 40%)] and cost of equity of 12%. The tax rate does not affect the cost of equity. Scrunchy-Tech's WACC can be calculated as follows:

Component	Weight		Component Cost		Totals
Debt	40%	×	5.4%	=	2.16%
Equity	60%	×	12.0%	=	7.20%
	100%				9.36%

    Answer (A) is incorrect. Improperly subtracting the effect of taxes from the cost of equity results in 6.48%. Answer (B) is incorrect. Improperly subtracting the effect of taxes from equity, but not from debt, results in 7.92%. Answer (D) is incorrect. Improperly using the before-tax cost of debt results in 10.80%.

19. Thomas Company's capital structure consists of 30% long-term debt, 25% preferred stock, and 45% common equity. The cost of capital for each component is shown below.

Long-term debt   8%
Preferred stock   11%
Common equity   15%

If Thomas pays taxes at the rate of 40%, what is the company's after-tax weighted-average cost of capital?

    A. 7.14%

    B. 9.84%

    C. 10.94%

    D. 11.90%

Answer (C) is correct.
    REQUIRED: Calculation of the weighted-average cost of capital.
    DISCUSSION: The effective rate for Thomas' debt is the after-tax cost [8% × (1.0 – .40 tax rate) = 4.8%]. The weighted-average cost of capital (WACC) can thus be calculated as follows:

	Weight		Cost of Capital		Weighted Cost
Long-term debt	30%	×	4.8%	=	1.44%
Preferred stock	25%	×	11.0%	=	2.75%
Common equity	45%	×	15.0%	=	6.75%
Totals	100%				10.94%

    Answer (A) is incorrect. The figure of 7.14% results from improperly applying the tax effect to the rates on preferred stock and common equity. Answer (B) is incorrect. The figure of 9.84% results from improperly applying the tax effect to the rate on preferred stock. Answer (D) is incorrect. The figure of 11.90% results from failing to adjust the rate on debt for the tax effect.

20. Osgood Products has announced that it plans to finance future investments so that the firm will achieve an optimum capital structure. Which one of the following corporate objectives is consistent with this announcement?

    A. Maximize earnings per share.

    B. Minimize the cost of debt.

    C. Maximize the net worth of the firm.

    D. Minimize the cost of equity.

Answer (C) is correct.
    REQUIRED: The consistent corporate objective.
    DISCUSSION: Financial structure is the composition of the financing sources of the assets of a firm. Traditionally, the financial structure consists of current liabilities, long-term debt, retained earnings, and stock. For most firms, the optimum structure includes a combination of debt and equity. Debt is cheaper than equity, but excessive use of debt increases the firm's risk and drives up the weighted-average cost of capital.
    Answer (A) is incorrect. The maximization of EPS may not always suggest the best capital structure. Answer (B) is incorrect. The minimization of debt cost may not be optimal; as long as the firm can earn more on debt capital than it pays in interest, debt financing may be indicated. Answer (D) is incorrect. Minimizing the cost of equity may signify overly conservative management.

STUDY UNIT NINE
WORKING CAPITAL I: CASH AND RECEIVABLES

(12 pages of outline)

All firms must hold a certain amount of current assets to operate day-to-day. Because of different types of inventory, manufacturers and distributors often hold as much as 50% of their total assets in the form of current assets. Thus, careful management of current assets is crucial to a firm's efficient operation.

All entities finance daily operations with capital from outside sources. These sources include (1) spontaneous financing in the form of trade credit offered by vendors (accounts payable) and (2) bank loans (notes payable).

Working capital management is the process of determining the optimal level and mix of these assets and liabilities. The measures used to assess the success achieved are also addressed.

9.1 WORKING CAPITAL MANAGEMENT

1. **Working capital**, as used by accountants, is calculated as follows:

   Working capital = Current assets − Current liabilities

   a. Liquidity is a firm's ability to pay its current obligations as they come due and thus remain in business in the short run. Liquidity measures the ease with which assets can be converted to cash.

   b. **Current assets** are the most liquid assets. They are expected to be converted to cash, sold, or consumed within 1 year or the operating cycle, whichever is longer. Accordingly, ratios involving current assets measure a firm's ability to continue operating in the short run.

      1) Current assets include, in descending order of liquidity, (a) cash and equivalents, (b) marketable securities, (c) receivables, (d) inventories, and (e) prepaid items.

   c. **Current liabilities** are the liabilities with the earliest due dates. They are expected to be settled or converted to other liabilities within 1 year or the operating cycle, whichever is longer.

      1) Current liabilities include (a) accounts payable, (b) notes payable, (c) current maturities of long-term debt, (d) unearned revenues, (e) taxes payable, (f) wages payable, and (g) other accruals.

2. **Permanent and Temporary Working Capital**

   a. In principle, current assets should be financed with current liabilities. But this approach oversimplifies the requirements of working capital management.

      1) Some liquid current assets must be maintained to meet the firm's long-term minimum needs regardless of the firm's level of activity or profitability. This working capital is **permanent**.

      2) As the firm's needs for current assets change on a seasonal basis, **temporary** working capital is increased or decreased.

b.   Both elements tend to increase with the growth of the firm.

Working Capital

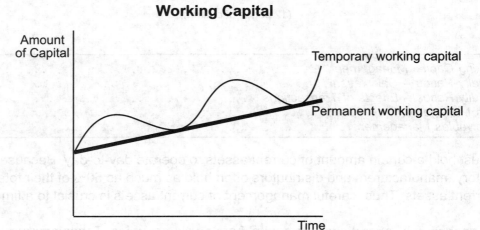

Figure 9-1

3.   **Spontaneous Financing**

   a.   Financing is spontaneous when current liabilities, such as trade payables and accruals, occur naturally in the ordinary course of business.

   b.   Trade credit is created when a firm is offered credit terms by its suppliers.

EXAMPLE of Spontaneous Financing

A vendor has delivered goods and charged the firm $160,000 on terms of net 30. The firm effectively has received a 30-day interest-free $160,000 loan.

---

   c.   Accrued expenses, such as (1) salaries, (2) wages, (3) interest, (4) dividends, and (5) taxes payable, are another source of (interest-free) spontaneous financing.

      1)   For example, employees work 5, 6, or 7 days a week but are paid only every 2 weeks. Thus, employee salaries are paid periodically in lump sums, not on a perpetual basis with daily remittances, allowing the company to receive value that has not yet been paid for. Another periodic expense directly related to labor is the remittance of federal income taxes on a quarterly basis even though the firm operates continuously.

      2)   Accruals have the additional advantage of fluctuating directly with operating activity, satisfying the matching principle.

   d.   The response to capital needs that cannot be satisfied spontaneously must be carefully planned.

4.   **Short-Term vs. Long-Term Financing**

   a.   The firm's temporary working capital usually cannot be financed by spontaneous financing alone. Thus, the firm must decide whether to use short-term or long-term financing.

      1)   The interest rate on long-term debt is higher than the interest rate on short-term debt. Consequently, long-term financing is more expensive.

      2)   However, the shorter the maturity schedule of a firm's debt obligations, the greater the risk that the firm will be unable to make principal and interest payments.

   b.   In general, short-term financing is more risky and less expensive than long-term financing.

   c.   The appropriate financing of the firm's working capital depends on management's attitude toward the tradeoff between profitability and risk.

5. **Maturity Matching**

   a. A firm ideally should offset each element of its temporary working capital with a short-term liability with the same maturity. For example, a short-term loan could be obtained before the winter season and repaid with the collections from holiday sales.

      1) This ideal practice is maturity matching or hedging. It is rarely achievable because of uncertainty.

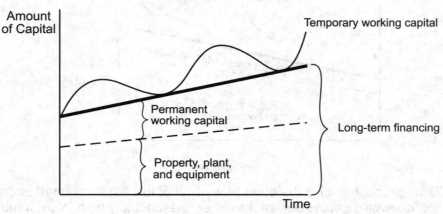

Figure 9-2

6. **Conservative Policy**

   a. A firm that adopts a conservative financing policy seeks to minimize liquidity risk by financing its temporary working capital mostly with long-term debt.

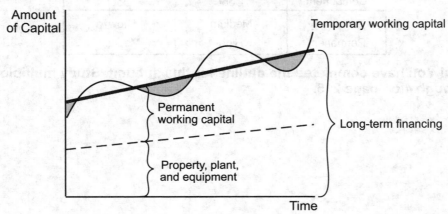

Figure 9-3

   b. This approach takes advantage of the certainty inherent in long-term debt.

      1) The locked-in interest rate mitigates interest rate risk (the risk that rates will rise in the short run).

         a) The long-term maturity date mitigates liquidity risk (the inability to repay a current obligation when due).

   c. The disadvantages are that

      1) Working capital is idle during periods when it is not needed, as represented by the shaded areas in Figure 9-3. This inefficiency is mitigated in part by investing in short-term securities.

      2) Long-term debt is more expensive.

7.   **Aggressive Policy**

    a.   To increase profits, an aggressive financing policy reduces liquidity and accepts a higher risk of short-term cash flow shortages.

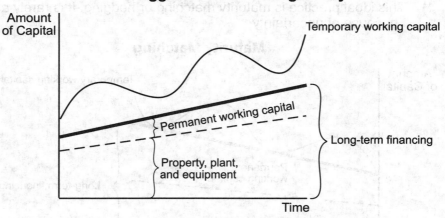

Aggressive Financing Policy

Figure 9-4

    b.   This approach avoids the opportunity cost of idle funds incurred under the conservative policy. But it risks either unexpectedly high interest rates or the total unavailability of financing in the short run.

8.   **Summary**

Risk in Relation to Financing

Working Capital Component	Financed with	
	Short-Term Debt	Long-Term Debt
Temporary	Medium	Low
Permanent	High	Medium

Stop and review! You have completed the outline for this subunit. Study multiple-choice questions 1 through 4 on page 215.

9.2 LIQUIDITY RATIOS -- CALCULATION

1. **Liquidity**

    a. Liquidity is a firm's ability to pay its current obligations as they come due and remain in business in the short run. Liquidity measures the ease with which assets can be converted to cash.

    b. Liquidity ratios measure this ability by relating a firm's liquid assets to its current liabilities.

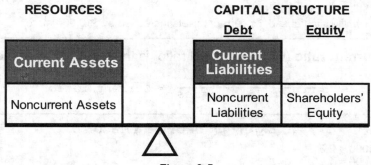

Figure 9-5

EXAMPLE

RESOURCES			FINANCING		
CURRENT ASSETS:	**Year 2**	**Year 3**	**CURRENT LIABILITIES:**	**Year 2**	**Year 3**
Cash and equivalents	$ 275,000	$ 325,000	Accounts payable	$ 75,000	$ 150,000
Available-for-sale securities	145,000	165,000	Notes payable	50,000	50,000
Accounts receivable (net)	115,000	120,000	Accrued interest on note	5,000	5,000
Notes receivable	40,000	55,000	Current maturities of L.T. debt	100,000	100,000
Inventories	55,000	85,000	Accrued salaries and wages	10,000	15,000
Prepaid expenses	5,000	10,000	Income taxes payable	35,000	70,000
Total current assets	**$ 635,000**	**$ 760,000**	**Total current liabilities**	**$ 275,000**	**$ 390,000**
NONCURRENT ASSETS:			**NONCURRENT LIABILITIES:**		
Equity-method investments	$ 115,000	$ 120,000	Bonds payable	$ 600,000	$ 500,000
Property, plant, and equipment	900,000	1,000,000	Long-term notes payable	60,000	90,000
Minus: Accum. depreciation	(55,000)	(85,000)	Employee-related obligations	10,000	15,000
Goodwill	5,000	5,000	Deferred income taxes	5,000	5,000
Total noncurrent assets	**$ 965,000**	**$1,040,000**	**Total noncurrent liabilities**	**$ 675,000**	**$ 610,000**
			Total liabilities	**$ 950,000**	**$1,000,000**
			SHAREHOLDERS' EQUITY:		
			Preferred stock, $50 par	$ 0	$ 120,000
			Common stock, $1 par	500,000	500,000
			Additional paid-in capital	100,000	110,000
			Retained earnings	50,000	70,000
			Total shareholders' equity	**$ 650,000**	**$ 800,000**
Total assets	**$1,600,000**	**$1,800,000**	**Total liabilities and shareholders' equity**	**$1,600,000**	**$1,800,000**

A candidate should know the formulas used to calculate the various financial ratios and be able to analyze the results. Numerous CPA exams have included questions on both the calculation and analysis of financial ratios. However, the numbers necessary to calculate a ratio often are not given directly. You may have to determine these numbers using information given in the question and then calculate the ratio.

NOTE: This Tip also applies to Study Unit 10, Subunits 2, 3, and 4.

2.   **Liquidity Ratios**

a.   **Net working capital** equals the resources the firm must have to continue operating in the short run if it must liquidate all of its current liabilities.

$$Current\ assets - Current\ liabilities$$

EXAMPLE of Net Working Capital
Year 2: $635,000 − $275,000 = $360,000 Year 3: $760,000 − $390,000 = $370,000
Although the firm's current liabilities increased, its current assets increased by $10,000 more.

b.   The **current ratio** (working capital ratio) is the most common measure of liquidity.

$$\frac{Current\ assets}{Current\ liabilities} = Current\ ratio$$

EXAMPLE of Current Ratio
Year 2: $635,000 ÷ $275,000 = 2.31 Year 3: $760,000 ÷ $390,000 = 1.95
Although working capital increased in absolute terms ($10,000), current assets now provide less proportional coverage of current liabilities than in the prior year.

1)   A low current ratio indicates a possible lack of liquidity. An overly high ratio indicates that management may not be investing idle assets productively. This varies by industry, but often a 2:1 ratio is desirable.

c.   The **quick (acid-test) ratio** excludes inventories and prepaid items from the numerator. Such assets are difficult to liquidate at their carrying amounts. The quick ratio is therefore a more conservative measure than the current ratio.

$$\frac{Cash\ and\ equivalents + Marketable\ securities + Net\ receivables}{Current\ liabilities} = Quick\ ratio$$

EXAMPLE of Quick Ratio
Year 2:   ($275,000 + $145,000 + $115,000 + $40,000) ÷ $275,000 = 2.09 Year 3:   ($325,000 + $165,000 + $120,000 + $55,000) ÷ $390,000 = 1.71
Despite its increase in total working capital, the firm's position in its most liquid assets deteriorated significantly.

1)   This ratio measures the firm's ability to pay its short-term debts easily. It also avoids the problem of inventory valuation.

2)   The higher the quick ratio, the more favorable for the firm. Maintaining a quick ratio of at least 1:1 is desirable.

3)   If cash is classified as a compensating balance per a loan agreement, with no contractual agreement that restricts the use of the cash, the compensating balance can be reported as part of cash and cash equivalents.

Ratio Value	Current Ratio	Quick Ratio
1/2	Indicates the firm has less current assets than current liabilities. This typically means that a firm may be losing money, at least in the short run. To satisfy current liabilities, the firm would have to sell long-term debt to satisfy its current liabilities, if possible.	Indicates the firm would not have adequate funds to pay current liabilities if the firm liquidated its current assets. In this situation, a firm would have to sell long-term liabilities to satisfy its current liabilities, if possible.
1/1	Indicates the firm would have adequate funds to pay current liabilities if the firm liquidated its current assets.	Indicates the firm would have adequate funds to pay current liabilities if the firm liquidated its current assets.
2/1	Indicates the firm has more current assets than current liabilities. It typically indicates the firm is profitable, at least in the short run. Moreover, the firm would have more funds than necessary to pay current liabilities if the firm liquidated its current assets.	Indicates the firm would have more funds than necessary to pay current liabilities if the firm liquidated its current assets.

Stop and review! You have completed the outline for this subunit. Study multiple-choice questions 5 through 8 beginning on page 216.

9.3 LIQUIDITY RATIOS -- EFFECTS OF TRANSACTIONS

1. **Effects of Transactions**

   a. If a ratio is less than 1.0, the numerator is lower than the denominator.

      1) A transaction that causes equal changes in the numerator and denominator has a proportionally greater effect on the numerator, resulting in a change in the ratio in the same direction.

         a) If the current (or quick) ratio is less than 1.0, paying a current liability with current (or quick) assets decreases the numerator and the denominator by the same amount. The effect is to **decrease** the ratio, which means less liquidity.

         EXAMPLE: $\frac{3-1}{4-1} = \frac{2}{3}$ and $\frac{3}{4} > \frac{2}{3}$

   b. If a ratio is equal to 1.0, the numerator and denominator are the same.

      1) A transaction that causes equal changes in the numerator and denominator does not affect the ratio, which does not affect liquidity.

         EXAMPLE: $\frac{4-1}{4-1} = \frac{3}{3}$ and $\frac{4}{4} = \frac{3}{3}$

    c.   If a ratio is greater than 1.0, the numerator is higher than the denominator.

        1)   A transaction that causes equal changes in the numerator and denominator has a proportionally greater effect on the denominator, resulting in a change in the ratio in the opposite direction, which means the firm is more liquid.

            a)   If the current (or quick) ratio is greater than 1.0, paying a current liability with current (or quick) assets decreases the numerator and denominator by the same amount. The effect is to **increase** the ratio, which means the firm is more liquid.

$$\text{EXAMPLE:} \quad \frac{4-1}{3-1} = \frac{3}{2} \quad \text{and} \quad \frac{4}{3} < \frac{3}{2}$$

    d.

Ratio range	Effect on ratio of equal increase of numerator and denominator	Effect on ratio of equal decrease of numerator and denominator
< 1.0	Increase – more liquid	Decrease – less liquid
= 1.0	No effect	No effect
> 1.0	Decrease – less liquid	Increase – more liquid

Stop and review! You have completed the outline for this subunit. Study multiple-choice questions 9 through 12 beginning on page 217.

9.4 CASH MANAGEMENT

Background

Too *much* cash can create a finance challenge. During the summer of 2011, large U.S. firms held large amounts of cash. They were unwilling to spend in the highly uncertain economic environment, and banks had huge U.S. dollar deposits. This sudden influx of cash greatly increased the banks' interest payouts and made them subject to more stringent ratio and reserve requirements. To compensate, Bank of New York Mellon, the largest custody bank, announced that it would start charging fees to clients whose cash balances exceeded $50 million.

---

    1.   **Managing the Level of Cash**

        a.   The three motives for holding cash are to

            1)   Purchase or use as a medium of exchange (transactional motive).
            2)   Provide for unexpected contingencies (precautionary motive).
            3)   Take advantage of unexpected opportunities (speculative motive).

        b.   The goal of cash management is to maintain the firm's **optimal** cash balance.

            1)   The optimal balance is rarely the largest. Because cash does not earn a return, only the amount needed to pay current obligations as they come due should be held.

        c.   The firm's optimal level of cash should be determined by a cost-benefit analysis.

            1)   The three motives for holding cash must be balanced against the opportunity cost of missed investments in marketable securities, or purchasing inventory when commodity prices are low.

        d.   A **compensating balance** is a minimum amount that a bank requires the firm to keep in its demand (checking) account.

            1)   This balance compensates the bank for services rendered, such as unlimited check writing.
            2)   The funds are unavailable for short-term investment and incur an opportunity cost.

2. **Speeding Cash Collections**

    a.   The period of time from when a payor puts a check in the mail to the availability of the funds in the payee's bank is called float. Firms attempt to decrease float for receipts and increase float for payments.

    b.   A **lockbox** system expedites the receipt of funds from cashing checks.

        1)   Customers submit their payments to a post office box. Bank personnel remove the envelopes from the mailbox and immediately deposit the checks in the firm's account. The remittance advices then must be transferred to the firm for entry into the accounts receivable system. The bank generally charges a flat monthly fee for this service.

        2)   For firms doing business nationwide, a lockbox network is appropriate. The country is divided into regions according to customer population patterns. A lockbox arrangement then is established with a bank in each region.

    c.   A firm using a lockbox network also participates in concentration banking. The regional banks that provide lockbox services automatically transfer their daily collections to the firm's principal bank, where they can be used for payments and short-term investment.

3. **Slowing Cash Payments**

    a.   A **draft** is a three-party instrument in which one person (the drawer) orders a second person (the drawee) to pay money to a third person (the payee).

        1)   A **check** is the most common form of draft. It is an instrument payable on demand by a drawee bank. Consequently, a draft can be used to delay the outflow of cash.

            a)   EXAMPLE: Customer (drawer) writes a check to Service Company (payee) from his bank account (drawee).

        2)   A draft dated on the due date of an invoice is not processed by the drawee until that date. Thus, the outflow is delayed until the check clears the drawee bank. By contrast, an electronic funds transfer (EFT) eliminates float.

    b.   A **zero-balance account** has a balance of $0. At the end of each processing day, the bank transfers just enough from the firm's master account to cover all checks presented against the zero-balance account that day.

        1)   This practice allows the firm to maintain higher balances in the master account from which short-term investments can be made. The bank generally charges a fee for this service.

    c.   **Disbursement float** is the period of time from when the payor puts a check in the mail to withdrawal of the funds from the payor's account. To increase disbursement float, a firm may mail checks to its vendors despite uncertainty about whether funds suffice to pay them all (e.g., a firm deposited a check and is waiting for it to clear, yet still writes a vendor a check assuming their deposit will clear).

        1)   For these situations, some banks offer overdraft protection. The bank guarantees (for a fee) to cover any shortage with a transfer from the firm's master account.

        2)   If a customer's check does not clear, the company may find it does not have sufficient funds to cover the checks it has issued. The same is true for EFT transfers.

4. **Idle Cash and Its Uses**

    a.   Idle cash incurs an opportunity cost. To offset this cost, firms invest their idle cash in marketable securities.

b.   Firms invest their temporary surpluses of cash in the market for short-term investments (the money market).

1)   Money market instruments include the following:

a)   **U.S. Treasury obligations** are the safest investment. They are exempt from state and local taxation and are highly liquid.

b)   **Repurchase agreements** (repos) are a means for dealers in government securities to finance their portfolios.

c)   **Federal agency securities** are backed (1) by the full faith and credit of the U.S. government or (2) only by the issuing agency.

d)   **Bankers' acceptances** are drafts drawn by a nonfinancial firm on deposits at a bank. Acceptance by the bank is a guarantee of payment at maturity.

e)   **Commercial paper** consists of short-term, unsecured notes payable issued in large denominations ($100,000 or more) by large corporations with high credit ratings.

f)   **Certificates of deposit** (CDs) are savings deposits that cannot be withdrawn before maturity without a high penalty.

g)   **Eurodollars** are time deposits of U.S. dollars in banks located abroad.

h)   Money-market **mutual funds** invest in short-term, low-risk securities. In addition to paying interest, these funds allow investors to write checks on their balances.

i)   **State and local** governments issue short-term securities exempt from taxation.

Stop and review! You have completed the outline for this subunit. Study multiple-choice questions 13 through 17 beginning on page 218.

9.5 RECEIVABLES MANAGEMENT

Background
In 1969, in a desperate attempt to increase sales, the department store chain W.T. Grant drastically lowered its credit standards. As a result, sales boomed. However, during the economic downturn of 1970-71, cash inflows dried up as customer accounts began to turn delinquent. The firm finally went bankrupt in 1974. Grant's creditors were completely unaware because its accrual-basis income statement reported consistently positive results, and Grant never stopped paying a dividend. The inadequacy of the traditional income statement for assessing liquidity was made obvious by the Grant bankruptcy. This incident was one of the reasons for the FASB's requirement of a statement of cash flows.

1.   **Overview**

a.   The goal of receivables management is to offer the **terms of credit** that maximize profits, not sales.

1)   Maximizing sales is easily done by raising discount percentages, offering longer payment periods, and accepting riskier customers. But this strategy could lead to cash flow shortages.

2)   Default risk can be minimized by raising credit standards, but the effect is loss of sales. Thus, the firm must achieve the proper balance.

b.   Credit terms are expressed in these terms: "Discount percentage"/"Pay by date to receive discount rate," net "Balance must be paid by date." The most common credit term is 2/10, net 30. This term means that the customer may either (1) subtract 2% of the invoice amount if it is paid within 10 days or (2) pay the entire balance by the 30th day.

    c.   **Factoring** is an arrangement in which a firm sells its accounts receivable at a discount to a factor, an entity that specializes in collections.

        1)   The seller receives cash and eliminates bad debts. Also, the seller need not maintain a credit department and an accounts receivable staff.

        2)   Visa is an example of a factor. Visa remits the cash proceeds to the seller minus a typical fee in the range of 1.5%-4%. Visa assumes the risk that purchasers may not pay their credit card bills.

2.   **Receivables Ratios**

EXAMPLE

The following is from an income statement:

	Year 3	Year 2
Net sales	$1,800,000	$1,400,000
Cost of goods sold	(1,650,000)	(1,330,000)
Gross profit	$ 150,000	$ 70,000

The following balance sheet is used in this subunit.

RESOURCES			FINANCING		
CURRENT ASSETS:	Year 3	Year 2	**CURRENT LIABILITIES:**	Year 3	Year 2
Cash and equivalents	$ 325,000	$ 275,000	Accounts payable	$ 150,000	$ 75,000
Available-for-sale securities	165,000	145,000	Notes payable	50,000	50,000
Accounts receivable (net)	120,000	115,000	Accrued interest on note	5,000	5,000
Notes receivable	55,000	40,000	Current maturities of L.T. debt	100,000	100,000
Inventories	85,000	55,000	Accrued salaries and wages	15,000	10,000
Prepaid expenses	10,000	5,000	Income taxes payable	70,000	35,000
Total current assets	**$ 760,000**	**$ 635,000**	**Total current liabilities**	**$ 390,000**	**$ 275,000**
NONCURRENT ASSETS:			**NONCURRENT LIABILITIES:**		
Equity-method investments	$ 120,000	$ 115,000	Bonds payable	$ 500,000	$ 600,000
Property, plant, and equipment	1,000,000	900,000	Long-term notes payable	90,000	60,000
Minus: Accum. depreciation	(85,000)	(55,000)	Employee-related obligations	15,000	10,000
Goodwill	5,000	5,000	Deferred income taxes	5,000	5,000
Total noncurrent assets	**$1,040,000**	**$ 965,000**	**Total noncurrent liabilities**	**$ 610,000**	**$ 675,000**
			Total liabilities	**$1,000,000**	**$ 950,000**
			SHAREHOLDERS' EQUITY:		
			Preferred stock, $50 par	$ 120,000	$ 0
			Common stock, $1 par	500,000	500,000
			Additional paid-in capital	110,000	100,000
			Retained earnings	70,000	50,000
			Total shareholders' equity	**$ 800,000**	**$ 650,000**
Total assets	**$1,800,000**	**$1,600,000**	**Total liabilities and shareholders' equity**	**$1,800,000**	**$1,600,000**

---

    a.   The **accounts receivable turnover ratio** is the number of times in a year the total balance of receivables is converted to cash. In other words, the accounts receivable turnover ratio measures how often a business collects its average accounts receivable per year.

        1)   Thus, if the accounts receivable turnover ratio equals 2.3, it means that the firm receives an amount of cash equal to 2.3 times its average accounts receivable.

        2)   Alternatively, one can also view the accounts receivable turnover ratio as the number of times per year the accounts receivable account turns over. In this regard, the accounts receivable turnover ratio indicates how efficient the firm is at obtaining cash from credit sales.

3) Therefore, the accounts receivable turnover ratio also provides insight on how liquid a firm is because the higher the accounts receivable turnover ratio, the easier it is for the firm to generate cashflow and indicates fewer credit sales are written off.

$$Accounts\ receivable\ turnover = \frac{Net\ credit\ sales}{Average\ balance\ in\ receivables}$$

EXAMPLE of Accounts Receivable Turnover

In the example presented on the previous page, all of the firm's sales are on credit. Net trade receivables at the balance sheet date for Year 1 were $105,000.

Year 3: $1,800,000 ÷ [($120,000 + $115,000) ÷ 2] = 15.3 times
Year 2: $1,400,000 ÷ [($115,000 + $105,000) ÷ 2] = 12.7 times

The firm turned over its trade receivables balance 2.6 more times during Year 3, even as receivables increased. Thus, the firm's collection effectiveness improved.

---

b. The **average collection period (days' sales in receivables)** measures the average number of days between the time of sale and receipt of payment. This indicates how well and how quickly a firm converts a credit sale into cash.

1) The lower the ratio, the quicker the firm receives cash and is able to take advantage of the time value of money. On the other hand, the higher the ratio, the longer it takes a firm to receive the cash from a credit sale and, consequently, the firm is not able to take advantage of the time value of money (i.e., loses the ability to earn interest on cash on hand).

2) This ratio also provides insight on the amount of credit sales written off. The more credit sales written off, the higher this ratio will become.

$$Days'\ sales\ in\ receivables = \frac{Days\ in\ year}{Accounts\ receivable\ turnover\ ratio}$$

EXAMPLE of Days' Sales in Receivables

Year 3: 365 days ÷ 15.3 times = 23.9 days
Year 2: 365 days ÷ 12.7 times = 28.7 days

The denominator (calculated in the preceding example) increased, and the numerator is a constant. Thus, days' sales necessarily decrease. In addition to improving its collection practices, the firm may have better assessed the creditworthiness of potential customers. Some firms (and CPA questions) use a business year of 12 months at 30 days per month for a total of 360 days per year.

	Accounts Receivable Turnover Ratio	Average Collection Period
Higher	More Liquid	Less Liquid
Lower	Less Liquid	More Liquid

Stop and review! You have completed the outline for this subunit. Study multiple-choice questions 18 through 20 on page 220.

QUESTIONS

9.1 Working Capital Management

1. As a company becomes more conservative in its working capital policy, it tends to have a(n)

- A. Decrease in its acid-test ratio.
- B. Increase in the ratio of current liabilities to noncurrent liabilities.
- C. Increase in the ratio of current assets to current liabilities.
- D. Increase in funds invested in common stock and a decrease in funds invested in marketable securities.

Answer (C) is correct.

REQUIRED: The effect of a more conservative working capital policy.

DISCUSSION: A conservative working capital policy minimizes liquidity risk by increasing net working capital (current assets – current liabilities). The result is that the company forgoes the potentially higher returns available from using the additional working capital to acquire long-term assets. A conservative working capital policy is characterized by a higher current ratio (current assets ÷ current liabilities) and acid-test ratio (quick assets ÷ current liabilities). Thus, the firm will increase current assets or decrease current liabilities. A conservative policy finances assets using long-term or permanent funds rather than short-term sources.

Answer (A) is incorrect. A decrease in the acid-test ratio suggests an aggressive policy. A conservative firm wants a higher acid-test ratio, that is, more liquid assets relative to liabilities. Answer (B) is incorrect. A conservative firm wants working capital to be financed from long-term sources. Answer (D) is incorrect. A conservative firm seeks more liquid (marketable) investments.

2. Which one of the following provides a spontaneous source of financing for a firm?

- A. Accounts payable.
- B. Mortgage bonds.
- C. Accounts receivable.
- D. Debentures.

Answer (A) is correct.

REQUIRED: The spontaneous source of financing.

DISCUSSION: Trade credit is a spontaneous source of financing because it exists automatically as part of a purchase transaction. Because of its ease in use, trade credit is the largest source of short-term financing for many firms, both large and small.

Answer (B) is incorrect. Mortgage bonds and debentures do not arise automatically as a result of a purchase transaction. Answer (C) is incorrect. The use of receivables as a financing source requires an extensive factoring arrangement and often involves the creditor's evaluation of the credit ratings of the borrower's customers. Answer (D) is incorrect. Mortgage bonds and debentures do not arise automatically as a result of a purchase transaction.

3. Net working capital is the difference between

- A. Current assets and current liabilities.
- B. Fixed assets and fixed liabilities.
- C. Total assets and total liabilities.
- D. Shareholders' investment and cash.

Answer (A) is correct.

REQUIRED: The definition of net working capital.

DISCUSSION: Net working capital is defined by accountants as the difference between current assets and current liabilities. Working capital is a measure of liquidity.

Answer (B) is incorrect. Working capital refers to the difference between current assets and current liabilities; fixed assets are not a component. Answer (C) is incorrect. Total assets and total liabilities are not components of working capital; only current items are included. Answer (D) is incorrect. Shareholders' equity is not a component of working capital; only current items are included in the concept of working capital.

4. Determining the appropriate level of working capital for a firm requires

- A. Changing the capital structure and dividend policy of the firm.
- B. Maintaining short-term debt at the lowest possible level because it is generally more expensive than long-term debt.
- C. Offsetting the benefit of current assets and current liabilities against the probability of technical insolvency.
- D. Maintaining a high proportion of liquid assets to total assets in order to maximize the return on total investments.

Answer (C) is correct.

REQUIRED: The requirement for determining the appropriate level of working capital.

DISCUSSION: Working capital finance addresses the determination of the optimal level, mix, and use of current assets and current liabilities. The objective is to minimize the cost of maintaining liquidity while guarding against the possibility of technical insolvency. Technical insolvency is the inability to pay debts as they come due.

Answer (A) is incorrect. Capital structure and dividends relate to capital structure finance, not working capital finance. Answer (B) is incorrect. Short-term debt is usually less expensive than long-term debt. Answer (D) is incorrect. Liquid assets do not ordinarily earn high returns relative to long-term assets, so holding the former will not maximize the return on total assets.

9.2 Liquidity Ratios -- Calculation

Questions 5 through 7 are based on the following information.

Tosh Enterprises reported the following account information:

Accounts receivable	$400,000	Inventory	$800,000
Accounts payable	260,000	Land	500,000
Bonds payable, due in 10 years	600,000	Short-term prepaid expense	80,000
Cash	200,000		
Interest payable, due in 3 months	20,000		

5. The current ratio for Tosh Enterprises is

A. 1.68

B. 2.14

C. 5.00

D. 5.29

Answer (D) is correct.
REQUIRED: The current ratio.
DISCUSSION: The current ratio equals current assets divided by current liabilities. Current assets consist of accounts receivable, cash, inventory, and prepaid expenses, a total of $1,480,000 ($400,000 + $200,000 + $800,000 + $80,000). Current liabilities consist of accounts payable and interest payable, a total of $280,000 ($260,000 + $20,000). Hence, the current ratio is 5.29 ($1,480,000 ÷ $280,000).
Answer (A) is incorrect. The figure of 1.68 includes long-term bonds payable among the current liabilities. Answer (B) is incorrect. The figure of 2.14 is the quick ratio. Answer (C) is incorrect. The figure of 5.00 excludes prepaid expenses from current assets.

6. What is Tosh Enterprises' quick (acid-test) ratio?

A. 0.68

B. 1.68

C. 2.14

D. 2.31

Answer (C) is correct.
REQUIRED: The quick ratio.
DISCUSSION: The quick ratio equals quick assets divided by current liabilities. For Tosh, quick assets consist of cash ($200,000) and accounts receivable ($400,000), a total of $600,000. Current liabilities consist of accounts payable ($260,000) and interest payable ($20,000), a total of $280,000. Thus, the quick ratio is 2.14 ($600,000 ÷ $280,000).
Answer (A) is incorrect. The figure of 0.68 includes long-term bonds payable among the current liabilities. Answer (B) is incorrect. The figure of 1.68 includes long-term bonds payable among the current liabilities and inventory and short-term prepaid expenses among the quick assets. Answer (D) is incorrect. The figure of 2.31 excludes interest payable from the current liabilities.

7. Tosh Enterprises' amount of working capital is

A. $600,000

B. $1,120,000

C. $1,200,000

D. $1,220,000

Answer (C) is correct.
REQUIRED: The amount of working capital.
DISCUSSION: Working capital equals current assets minus current liabilities. For Tosh Enterprises, current assets consist of accounts receivable, cash, inventory, and prepaid expenses, a total of $1,480,000 ($400,000 + $200,000 + $800,000 + $80,000). Current liabilities consist of accounts payable and interest payable, a total of $280,000 ($260,000 + $20,000). Accordingly, working capital is $1,200,000 ($1,480,000 − $280,000).
Answer (A) is incorrect. The amount of $600,000 includes long-term bonds payable among the current liabilities. Answer (B) is incorrect. The amount of $1,120,000 excludes prepaid expenses from current assets. Answer (D) is incorrect. The amount of $1,220,000 excludes interest payable from current liabilities.

8. Given an acid-test ratio of 2.0, current assets of $5,000, and inventory of $2,000, the value of current liabilities is

A. $1,500

B. $2,500

C. $3,500

D. $6,000

Answer (A) is correct.

REQUIRED: The value of current liabilities given the acid-test ratio, current assets, and inventory.

DISCUSSION: The acid-test, or quick, ratio equals the ratio of the quick assets (cash, net accounts receivable, and marketable securities) divided by current liabilities. Current assets equal the quick assets plus inventory and prepaid expenses. This question assumes that the entity has no prepaid expenses. Given current assets of $5,000, inventory of $2,000, and no prepaid expenses, the quick assets must be $3,000. Because the acid-test ratio is 2.0, the quick assets are double the current liabilities. Current liabilities therefore are equal to $1,500 ($3,000 quick assets ÷ 2.0).

Answer (B) is incorrect. Dividing the current assets by 2.0 results in $2,500. Current assets includes inventory, which should not be included in the calculation of the acid-test ratio. Answer (C) is incorrect. Adding inventory to current assets rather than subtracting it results in $3,500. Answer (D) is incorrect. Multiplying the quick assets by 2 instead of dividing by 2 results in $6,000.

9.3 Liquidity Ratios -- Effects of Transactions

9. Peters Company has a 2-to-1 current ratio. This ratio would increase to more than 2 to 1 if

A. A previously declared stock dividend were distributed.

B. The company wrote off an uncollectible receivable.

C. The company sold merchandise on open account that earned a normal gross margin.

D. The company purchased inventory on open account.

Answer (C) is correct.

REQUIRED: The transaction increasing a current ratio greater than one.

DISCUSSION: The current ratio is current assets divided by current liabilities. Thus, an increase in current assets or a decrease in current liabilities, by itself, increases the current ratio. The sale of inventory at a profit increases current assets without changing liabilities. Inventory decreases, and receivables increase by a greater amount. Thus, total current assets and the current ratio increase.

Answer (A) is incorrect. The distribution of a stock dividend affects only shareholders' equity accounts (debit common stock dividend distributable and credit common stock). Answer (B) is incorrect. Writing off an uncollectible receivable does not affect total current assets. The allowance account absorbs the bad debt. Thus, the balance of net receivables is unchanged. Answer (D) is incorrect. The purchase of inventory increases current assets and current liabilities by the same amount. The transaction reduces a current ratio in excess of 1.0 because the numerator and denominator of the ratio increase by the same amount.

10. Rice, Inc., uses the allowance method to account for uncollectible accounts. An account receivable that was previously determined uncollectible and written off was collected during May. The effect of the collection on Rice's current ratio and total working capital is

	Current Ratio	Working Capital
A.	None	None
B.	Increase	Increase
C.	Decrease	Decrease
D.	None	Increase

Answer (A) is correct.

REQUIRED: The effect on the current ratio and working capital of collecting an account previously written off.

DISCUSSION: The entry to record this transaction is to debit receivables, credit the allowance, debit cash, and credit receivables. The result is to increase both an asset (cash) and a contra asset (allowance for bad debts). These appear in the current asset section of the balance sheet. Thus, the collection changes neither the current ratio nor working capital because the effects are offsetting. The credit for the journal entry is made to the allowance account on the assumption that another account will become uncollectible. The firm had previously estimated its bad debts and established an appropriate allowance. It then (presumably) wrote off the wrong account. Accordingly, the journal entry reinstates a balance in the allowance account to absorb future uncollectibles.

11. Bond Corporation has a current ratio of 2 to 1 and a (acid test) quick ratio of 1 to 1. A transaction that would change Bond's quick ratio but **not** its current ratio is the

A. Sale of inventory on account at cost.

B. Collection of accounts receivable.

C. Payment of accounts payable.

D. Purchase of a patent for cash.

Answer (A) is correct.
REQUIRED: The transaction affecting the quick ratio but not the current ratio.
DISCUSSION: The quick ratio is determined by dividing the sum of cash, short-term marketable securities, and accounts receivable by current liabilities. The current ratio is equal to current assets divided by current liabilities. The sale of inventory (a nonquick current asset) on account increases accounts receivable (a quick asset), changing the quick ratio. The sale of inventory on account, however, replaces one current asset with another, and the current ratio is unaffected.
Answer (B) is incorrect. Neither ratio is changed. Answer (C) is incorrect. The current, not the quick, ratio changes. Answer (D) is incorrect. Both ratios decrease.

12. Windham Company has current assets of $400,000 and current liabilities of $500,000. Windham Company's current ratio will be increased by

A. The purchase of $100,000 of inventory on account.

B. The payment of $100,000 of accounts payable.

C. The collection of $100,000 of accounts receivable.

D. Refinancing a $100,000 long-term loan with short-term debt.

Answer (A) is correct.
REQUIRED: The transaction increasing a current ratio less than 1.0.
DISCUSSION: The current ratio equals current assets divided by current liabilities. An equal increase in both the numerator and denominator of a current ratio less than 1.0 causes the ratio to increase. Windham Company's current ratio is .8 ($400,000 ÷ $500,000). The purchase of $100,000 of inventory on account would increase the current assets to $500,000 and the current liabilities to $600,000, resulting in a new current ratio of .83.
Answer (B) is incorrect. The payment of $100,000 of accounts payable decreases the current ratio. Answer (C) is incorrect. The current ratio is unchanged. Answer (D) is incorrect. Refinancing a $100,000 long-term loan with short-term debt decreases the current ratio.

9.4 Cash Management

13. According to John Maynard Keynes, the three major motives for holding cash are for

A. Transactional, psychological, and social purposes.

B. Speculative, fiduciary, and transactional purposes.

C. Speculative, social, and precautionary purposes.

D. Transactional, precautionary, and speculative purposes.

Answer (D) is correct.
REQUIRED: The three major motives for holding cash.
DISCUSSION: John Maynard Keynes, founder of Keynesian economics, concluded that there were three major motives for holding cash: for transactional purposes as a medium of exchange, precautionary purposes to provide a cushion for unexpected contingencies, and speculative purposes to take advantage of unexpected opportunities.

14. A consultant recommends that a company hold funds for the following two reasons:

Reason #1: Cash needs can fluctuate substantially throughout the year.

Reason #2: Opportunities for buying at a discount may appear during the year.

The cash balances used to address the reasons given above are correctly classified as

	Reason #1	Reason #2
A.	Speculative balances	Speculative balances
B.	Speculative balances	Precautionary balances
C.	Precautionary balances	Speculative balances
D.	Precautionary balances	Precautionary balances

Answer (C) is correct.
REQUIRED: The classifications of the reasons for a firm to hold cash.
DISCUSSION: The three motives for holding cash are as a medium of exchange, as a precaution, and as a speculation. Reason #1 can be classified as a precaution, and Reason #2 can be classified as holding cash for speculation.
Answer (A) is incorrect. Reason #1 is fulfilled by precautionary balances. Answer (B) is incorrect. This combination results from reversing the correct balances. Answer (D) is incorrect. Reason #2 is fulfilled by speculative balances.

15. A lockbox system

A. Reduces the need for compensating balances.

B. Provides security for late night deposits.

C. Reduces the risk of having checks lost in the mail.

D. Accelerates the inflow of funds.

Answer (D) is correct.
   REQUIRED: The true statement about a lockbox system.
   DISCUSSION: A lockbox system is one strategy for expediting the receipt of funds. Customers submit their payments to a mailbox controlled by the bank rather than to the firm's offices. Bank personnel remove the envelopes from the mailbox and deposit the checks to the firm's account immediately. The remittance advices must then be sent to the company for entry into the accounts receivable system. The bank generally charges a flat monthly fee for this service.
   Answer (A) is incorrect. A lockbox system is not related to compensating balances; a compensating balance may be required by a covenant in a loan agreement that requires a company to maintain a specified balance during the term of the loan. Answer (B) is incorrect. A lockbox system is a process by which payments are sent to a bank's mailbox, which is checked during normal post office hours. Answer (C) is incorrect. The use of a lockbox system entails sending checks through the mail to a post office box. Thus, it does not reduce the risk of losing checks in the mail.

16. A compensating balance

A. Compensates a financial institution for services rendered by providing it with deposits of funds.

B. Is used to compensate for possible losses on a marketable securities portfolio.

C. Is a level of inventory held to compensate for variations in usage rate and lead time.

D. Is the amount of prepaid interest on a loan.

Answer (A) is correct.
   REQUIRED: The true statement about compensating balances.
   DISCUSSION: A compensating balance is a minimum amount that the bank requires the firm to keep in its demand account. Compensating balances are noninterest-bearing and are meant to compensate the bank for various services rendered, such as unlimited check writing. These funds are obviously unavailable for short-term investment and thus incur an opportunity cost.
   Answer (B) is incorrect. In financial accounting, a valuation allowance is used to reflect losses on marketable securities. Answer (C) is incorrect. Safety stock is held for such purposes. Answer (D) is incorrect. Interest deducted in advance is discount interest.

17. A working capital method that delays the outflow of cash is

A. Factoring.

B. A draft.

C. A lockbox system.

D. Electronic funds transfer.

Answer (B) is correct.
   REQUIRED: The working capital method that delays the outflow of cash.
   DISCUSSION: A draft is a three-party instrument in which one person (the drawer) orders a second person (the drawee) to pay money to a third person (the payee). A check is the most common form of draft. It is an instrument payable on demand in which the drawee is a bank. Consequently, a draft can be used to delay the outflow of cash. A draft can be dated on the due date of an invoice and will not be processed by the drawee until that date, thereby eliminating the necessity of writing a check earlier than the due date or using an EFT. Thus, the outflow is delayed until the check clears the drawee bank.
   Answer (A) is incorrect. Factoring is the sale of receivables and therefore applies to cash inflows, not outflows. Answer (C) is incorrect. A lockbox system is a means of accelerating cash inflows. Answer (D) is incorrect. An EFT results in an immediate reduction of the payor's bank balance, eliminating float.

9.5 Receivables Management

18. Aaron Co's vendor will be offering discounts next year. Which of the following credit terms offered by the vendor is most beneficial to Aaron?

A. 2/10, net 60.

B. 3/15, net 30.

C. 5/20, net 45.

D. 5/20, net 60.

Answer (D) is correct.

REQUIRED: The most favorable credit term.

DISCUSSION: Credit terms are expressed in these terms: "Discount percentage"/ "Pay by date to receive discount rate," net "Balance must be paid by date." The term 5/20, net 60 means that the customer may either (1) subtract 5% of the invoice amount if it is paid within 20 days or (2) pay the entire balance by the 60th day. This credit term offers the greatest discount percentage and longest payment period among the four options. Thus, 5/20, net 60 is the best choice.

Answer (A) is incorrect. This credit term means the customer may either (1) subtract 2% of the invoice amount if it is paid within 10 days or (2) pay the entire balance by the 60th day. Answer (B) is incorrect. This credit term means the customer may either (1) subtract 3% of the invoice amount if it is paid within 15 days or (2) pay the entire balance by the 30th day. Answer (C) is incorrect. This credit term means the customer may either (1) subtract 5% of the invoice amount if it is paid within 20 days or (2) pay the entire balance by the 45th day.

19. An organization would usually offer credit terms of 2/10, net 30 when

A. The organization can borrow funds at a rate exceeding the annual interest cost.

B. The organization can borrow funds at a rate less than the annual interest cost.

C. The cost of capital approaches the prime rate.

D. Most competitors are offering the same terms, and the organization has a shortage of cash.

Answer (D) is correct.

REQUIRED: The reason for offering credit terms of 2/10, net 30.

DISCUSSION: Because these terms involve an annual interest cost of over 36%, a company would not offer them unless it desperately needed cash. Also, credit terms are typically somewhat standardized within an industry. Thus, if most companies in the industry offer similar terms, a firm will likely be forced to match the competition or lose market share.

Answer (A) is incorrect. If the company does not need cash, it would not offer cash discounts, regardless of its cost of capital, unless required to match competition. Answer (B) is incorrect. The ability to borrow at a lower rate is a reason for not offering cash discounts. Answer (C) is incorrect. The relationship between the cost of capital and the prime rate may not be relevant if the firm cannot borrow at the prime rate.

20. The main reason that a firm would strive to reduce the number of days sales outstanding is to increase

A. Accounts receivable.

B. Cash.

C. Cost of goods sold.

D. Contribution margin.

Answer (B) is correct.

REQUIRED: The effect the number of days sales outstanding (accounts receivable collection period) has on other accounts.

DISCUSSION: A low days sales outstanding value means that it takes a company fewer days to collect accounts receivables. A company that collects accounts receivables quickly will have an increase in cash.

Answer (A) is incorrect. A low days sales outstanding value means that it takes a company fewer days to collect accounts receivables. Thus, accounts receivables will decrease, not increase. Answer (C) is incorrect. Days sales outstanding is a measure of the average number of days that it takes for a company to collect revenue after a sale has been made. Cost of goods sold is not used in the calculation of days sales outstanding. Answer (D) is incorrect. Days sales outstanding is a measure of the average number of days that it takes for a company to collect revenue after a sale has been made. Contribution margin is not used in the calculation of days sales outstanding.

STUDY UNIT TEN
WORKING CAPITAL II: INVENTORY
AND SHORT-TERM FINANCING

(13 pages of outline)

All firms must hold a certain amount of current assets to operate day-to-day. Because of different types of inventory, manufacturers and distributors often hold as much as 50% of their total assets in the form of current assets. Thus, the proper management of current assets is crucial to a firm's efficient operation.

All entities finance daily operations with capital from outside sources. These sources include (1) spontaneous financing in the form of trade credit offered by vendors and (2) bank loans.

Working capital management is the process of determining the optimal level and mix of these assets and liabilities. The measures used to assess the success achieved also are addressed.

10.1 INVENTORY MANAGEMENT -- METHODS

1. **Overview**

    a. Minimizing the total cost of inventory involves constant evaluation of the tradeoffs among the four components of total cost.

    Purchase costs + Carrying costs + Ordering costs + Stockout costs

    1) **Purchase costs** are the actual invoice amounts charged by suppliers. It is the investment in inventory.

    2) **Carrying costs** is a broad category. It consists of all costs associated with holding inventory: (a) storage, (b) insurance, (c) security, (d) depreciation or rent of facilities, (e) interest, (f) obsolescence, (g) spoilage, and (h) the opportunity cost of funds invested in inventory (percentage investment in inventory).

    3) **Ordering costs** are the fixed costs of placing an order with a vendor. They are not affected by the number of units ordered. If units are manufactured internally, **setup costs** for production lines are calculated instead.

    4) **Stockout costs** are the opportunity costs of not being able to fill customer orders. They also include the costs of expediting special shipments required because of insufficient inventory.

    b. Minimization of total inventory cost is difficult because of the following factors:

    1) Stockout costs can be minimized only by incurring higher carrying costs.

    2) Carrying costs can be minimized only by incurring the high fixed costs of placing many small orders.

    3) Ordering costs can be minimized only by incurring the higher carrying costs of larger inventories.

2.   **Inventory Replenishment Factors**

a.   **Lead time** is the time between placing an order and receipt of goods from the supplier.

1)   When lead time is known and demand is uniform, the goods can be timed to arrive just as inventory is eliminated. This is the basis of the just-in-time model discussed later in this subunit.

b.   **Safety stock** is inventory held as a hedge against contingencies.

1)   Determining the appropriate safety stock requires a probabilistic calculation that balances the variability of demand with the risk of stockouts the firm is willing to accept.

c.   The **reorder point** is the inventory amount indicating that a new order should be placed. It is calculated using the following equation:

(Average daily demand × Lead time in days) + Safety stock

3.   **The Economic Order Quantity Model**

a.   The economic order quantity (EOQ) model determines the order quantity that minimizes the sum of ordering costs and carrying costs.

$$EOQ = \sqrt{\frac{2OD}{C}}$$

If: O =   ordering cost per purchase order
       D =   periodic demand in units/usage of units
       c =   periodic carrying costs per unit

Inventory Management

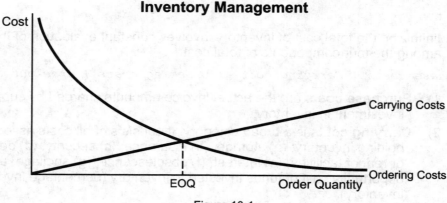

Figure 10-1

b.   The assumptions underlying the EOQ model are that

1)   Demand or production is uniform.
2)   Order (setup) costs and carrying costs are constant.
3)   No quantity discounts are allowed.

    c.   A change in any variable changes the EOQ. If demand or ordering costs increase, each order must contain more units. If carrying costs increase, each order contains fewer units.

EXAMPLE -- EOQ Calculation

A firm plans to use 2,500 inventory units (D) during the 180-day period. The ordering cost per order is $30 (O). The carrying costs per inventory unit is $15 (c). In order to minimize the total inventory cost for the 180-day period, the firm should order 100 inventory units (EOQ) in each order.

$$EOQ = \sqrt{\frac{2 \times 2,500 \times \$30}{\$15}} = 100$$

The firm should make 25 orders during that period (2,500 ÷ 100).

---

4.   **Periodic Inventory Systems**

    a.   Under a periodic system, inventory and cost of goods sold are updated only when physical inventory counts are made.

        1)   Physical inventory counts are time-consuming and costly, so inventory counts are usually performed only annually or quarterly.

            a)   Firms with relatively inexpensive and homogeneous items, such as wheat dealers, that have no need to continuously monitor their inventory and cost of goods sold generally use this system.

5.   **Perpetual Inventory Systems**

    a.   Under a perpetual system, every item received is individually recorded in the tracking system. Inventory and cost of goods sold are updated after every sale.

        1)   A perpetual system is used by a firm that requires accurate inventory information at all times.

        2)   However, even in a perpetual system, a full count must be made at least annually to (a) correct errors in the tracking system and (b) determine an ending balance for financial reporting.

            a)   There could also be shrinkage as a result of theft or breakage.

        3)   A perpetual system requires intensive bookkeeping. But the rapid, continuous increases in computer storage and processing power have made such systems more feasible, if not necessary, in a competitive environment.

    b.   A perpetual system makes replenishment models such as EOQ more practicable.

        1)   Under a periodic system, determining the optimal reorder point is difficult. Item quantities are not continuously monitored, and reordering can be unsystematic.

        2)   But the continuous monitoring inherent in a perpetual system allows reorder points for all items to be preprogrammed. The system then can initiate a reorder automatically. Safety stocks and stockout costs can be minimized simultaneously.

    c.   Thus, the added expense of a perpetual inventory system is offset by the reduced order and carrying costs made possible by modern technology.

6.   **Just-in-Time Inventory**

    a.   In a just-in-time (JIT) inventory system, the moving, handling, and storage of inventory are treated as nonvalue-adding activities.

        1)   Not just safety stock but all materials inventories (and their associated carrying costs) are reduced or eliminated entirely. Binding agreements with suppliers ensure that materials arrive exactly when they are needed and not before.

        2)   JIT is a **pull** system that is demand-driven. In a manufacturing environment, production of goods does not begin until an order has been received. In this way, finished goods inventories also are eliminated.

        3)   The purpose of the JIT inventory system is to minimize the cost associated with inventory control and maintenance by reducing the lag time between inventory's arrival and use.

    b.   A **backflush costing system** often is used in a JIT environment. Entries to inventory may be delayed until as late as the end of the period.

        1)   Conventional accounting systems track raw materials, work-in-process, and finished goods in sequence. The system provides comprehensive inventory control information and enables the calculation of manufacturing variances. However, a JIT system maintains minimal inventory and is demand-driven (sales volumes and productions are almost equal). Thus, there is no need to present a detailed view of inventory under a JIT system.

        2)   A backflush costing system eliminates the traditional sequential tracking of costs and calculation of manufacturing variances. More specifically, dispatch of goods, manufacture of goods, and use of raw materials are only recorded at the end of the period based on standard costing. It is cheaper to run, simplifies the accounting process, and addresses the need under a JIT system.

        3)   Disadvantages of a backflush costing system include that it

            a)   Is not suitable for long production processes and high inventory levels and
            b)   Lacks a sequential audit trail.

7.   **Kanban**

    a.   Another method of improving inventory flow is the kanban system developed by Toyota.

        1)   Kanban means ticket. Tickets (also described as cards or markers) control the flow of production or parts so that they are produced or obtained in the needed amounts at the needed times.

    b.   Kanban is essentially a visual workflow management system.

        1)   A kanban is an authorization to a worker to release inventory to the next step. Work cannot move to the next stage until a kanban indicates that stage is ready for it.

        2)   A basic kanban system includes (a) a withdrawal kanban that states the quantity that a later process should withdraw from its predecessor; (b) a production kanban that states the output of the preceding process; and (c) a vendor kanban that tells a vendor what, how much, where, and when to deliver.

        3)   For example, the Kanban card contains quantity, type of parts, and other product information. When the bin on the factory floor becomes empty, the empty bin and the Kanban card are sent to the factory store. The factory store replaces the empty bin with a filled bin and returns the bin along with the Kanban card to the factory floor. The factory store then informs the supplier and sends the empty bin with the factory store's Kanban card to the supplier. The supplier fills the empty bin with parts and delivers the filled bin with its Kanban card to the factory store, so the factory store has inventory for when the factory floor needs supplies. By producing only what is deliverable, Kanban prevents overproduction and reduces waste effectively.

8. **MRP and MRP II**

    a. Materials requirements planning (MRP) is a computerized system for moving materials through a production process according to a predetermined schedule.

        1) MRP is a **push** system. The demand for materials is driven by the forecasted demand for the final product as programmed into the system.

            a) MRP, in effect, creates schedules of when items of inventory are needed in the production departments.

            b) If an outage of a given item is projected, the system automatically generates a purchase order on the proper date (considering lead times) so that deliveries arrive on time.

        2) MRP consists of three essential components:

            a) The master production schedule (MPS) is a table of the projected demand for end products along with the dates they are needed.

            b) The bill of materials (BOM) is a table of every component part required by every end product (and by every subassembly).

            c) Perpetual inventory records must be used to ensure that a true count of every component, subassembly, and finished good is available at all times.

        3) In essence, MRP embodies the principle of dependent demand (also called derived demand).

            a) Demand-dependent goods are components of other goods. Their demand is driven by the demand for the final goods of which they are a part.

    b. MRP is a common function contained in enterprise resource planning (ERP) software systems.

        1) Although ERP and MRP are similar, they are not interchangeable. ERP includes many functions not included in MRP.

            a) For example, an ERP system allows a firm to determine what hiring decisions need to be made or whether it should invest in new capital assets.

                i) A firm that only needs to control materials should implement MRP.

        2) An ERP outline is in Study Unit 12, Subunit 5.

    c. Manufacturing resource planning (MRP II) does not replace, but extends the scope of, an MRP system.

        1) MRP is based on programmed demand, regardless of capacity considerations or changes in the market for the end product.

        2) MRP II is a closed-loop system that adds a feedback loop to allow analysis of capacity, market changes, and other variables.

Stop and review! You have completed the outline for this subunit. Study multiple-choice questions 1 through 7 beginning on page 234.

10.2 INVENTORY MANAGEMENT -- RATIOS

1. **Inventory Ratios**

    a. Two ratios measure the efficiency of the management of inventory.

        1) **Inventory turnover** is the number of times in a year the total balance of inventory is converted to cash or receivables.

            a) Inventory turnover is affected by two departments: purchasing and sales.

                i) The purchasing department is responsible for ensuring that the firm either has product to sell or to use in manufacturing. Typically, a firm wants to minimize the amount of inventory without being detrimental to operations. Generally, the higher the inventory turnover rate, the more efficient the inventory management.

                ii) The sales department also needs to meet or exceed the sales budget so that the firm is not holding excess inventory longer than budgeted (or expected).

                iii) A high inventory turnover may imply that the firm is **not** carrying excess inventory or that the inventory is **not** obsolete. Thus, inventory turnover can be an indication of how well the firm's departments are interoperating.

$$Inventory\ turnover = \frac{Cost\ of\ goods\ sold}{Average\ balance\ in\ inventory}$$

            b) If business is seasonal, a simple average of beginning and ending balances is inadequate. The monthly balances should be averaged instead.

            c) Because cost of goods sold is in the numerator, higher sales (and a higher cost of goods sold) without an increase in inventory results in higher turnover.

                i) Because inventory is in the denominator, reducing inventory results in a higher turnover ratio.

            d) The ratio of a firm that uses LIFO may not be comparable with that of a firm with a higher inventory measurement, such as FIFO or Average Methods.

EXAMPLE -- Inventory Turnover

The following is from an income statement:

	Year 3	Year 2
Net sales	$1,800,000	$1,400,000
Cost of goods sold	(1,650,000)	(1,330,000)
Gross profit	$ 150,000	$ 70,000

The following balance sheet is used in this subunit and in Subunit 10.3.

RESOURCES			FINANCING		
CURRENT ASSETS:	Year 3	Year 2	CURRENT LIABILITIES:	Year 3	Year 2
Cash and equivalents	$ 325,000	$ 275,000	Accounts payable	$ 150,000	$ 75,000
Available-for-sale securities	165,000	145,000	Notes payable	50,000	50,000
Accounts receivable (net)	120,000	115,000	Accrued interest on note	5,000	5,000
Notes receivable	55,000	40,000	Current maturities of L.T. debt	100,000	100,000
Inventories	85,000	55,000	Accrued salaries and wages	15,000	10,000
Prepaid expenses	10,000	5,000	Income taxes payable	70,000	35,000
Total current assets	$ 760,000	$ 635,000	Total current liabilities	$ 390,000	$ 275,000
NONCURRENT ASSETS:			NONCURRENT LIABILITIES:		
Equity-method investments	$ 120,000	$ 115,000	Bonds payable	$ 500,000	$ 600,000
Property, plant, and equipment	1,000,000	900,000	Long-term notes payable	90,000	60,000
Minus: Accum. depreciation	(85,000)	(55,000)	Employee-related obligations	15,000	10,000
Goodwill	5,000	5,000	Deferred income taxes	5,000	5,000
Total noncurrent assets	$1,040,000	$ 965,000	Total noncurrent liabilities	$ 610,000	$ 675,000
			Total liabilities	$1,000,000	$ 950,000
			SHAREHOLDERS' EQUITY:		
			Preferred stock, $50 par	$ 120,000	$ 0
			Common stock, $1 par	500,000	500,000
			Additional paid-in capital	110,000	100,000
			Retained earnings	70,000	50,000
			Total shareholders' equity	$ 800,000	$ 650,000
Total assets	$1,800,000	$1,600,000	Total liabilities and shareholders' equity	$1,800,000	$1,600,000

The balance in inventories and net accounts receivable at the balance sheet date of Year 1 were $45,000 and $105,000.

Year 3: $1,650,000 ÷ [($85,000 + $55,000) ÷ 2] = 23.6 times
Year 2: $1,330,000 ÷ [($55,000 + $45,000) ÷ 2] = 26.6 times

The firm did not turn over its inventories as many times during Year 3. This result is expected during a period of increasing sales (and increased inventory). Accordingly, lower turnover does not necessarily indicate poor inventory management.

2)   **Days' sales in inventory** measures the average number of days between the acquisition of inventory and its sale. It also indicates how many days the firm's current inventory level will last before stockout.

a)   Days' sales in inventory is important because it signifies the age of the firm's inventory. The older the inventory, the greater risk of it being obsolete (especially if the firm is in the consumer electronics industry).

i)   In addition, the lower the days' sales in inventory, the easier it is for the firm to generate sales and turn inventory into cash. This is beneficial to liquidity and working capital.

ii)   A lower days' sales in inventory also means the firm's inventory is liquid and, if necessary, creditors could liquidate it easily in a bankruptcy scenario.

$$Days'\ sales\ in\ inventory = \frac{Days\ in\ year}{Inventory\ turnover\ ratio}$$

EXAMPLE -- Days' Sales in Inventory

Year 3:   365 days ÷ 23.6 times = 15.5 days
Year 2:   365 days ÷ 26.6 times = 13.7 days

The numerator is a constant. Thus, the decreased inventory turnover means that days' sales in inventory increased. This phenomenon is common during a period of increasing sales.

	Inventory Turnover	Days' Sales in Inventory
Higher	Good – More Liquid	Bad – Less Liquid
Lower	Bad – Less Liquid	Good – More Liquid

Stop and review! You have completed the outline for this subunit. Study multiple-choice questions 8 and 9 on page 236.

10.3 THE OPERATING CYCLE AND CASH CONVERSION CYCLE

1.   **Operating Cycle**

a.   A firm's **operating cycle** is the time between the acquisition of inventory and the collection of cash for its sale. The operating cycle dictates cash flow.

1)   The length of the operating cycle provides information on the company's need for liquidity. The longer the operating cycle, the greater the need for liquidity.

a)   A company with a short operating cycle is able to quickly recover its investments in inventory.

b)   A company with a long operating cycle will have less cash available to meet short-term needs, which can result in increased borrowing.

$$Operating\ cycle = Days'\ sales\ in\ receivables + Days'\ sales\ in\ inventory$$

EXAMPLE -- Operating Cycle

Year 3:   23.9 days + 15.5 days = 39.4 days
Year 2:   28.7 days + 13.7 days = 42.4 days

The firm has reduced its operating cycle while increasing sales and inventories.

The days' sales in receivables for Year 3 (23.9 days) and Year 2 (28.7 days) are calculated in Study Unit 9, Subunit 5.

---

b. The following diagram depicts the phases of the operating cycle:

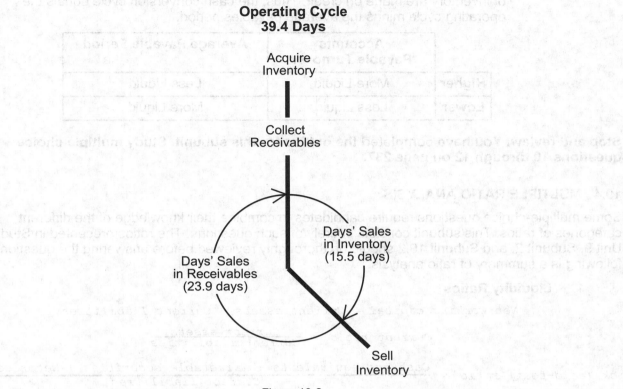

Figure 10-2

2. Cash Conversion Cycle

a. A firm's cash conversion cycle is the time between the payment of cash for inventory and the collection of cash from its sale. This describes the efficacy of the firm's investment in operations. Firms with highly demanded products that are well run by management have lower cash conversion cycles than other firms.

Cash conversion cycle = Average collection period +
Days' sales in inventory – Average payables period

1) The accounts payable turnover ratio is the number of times during a period that the firm pays its accounts payable.

a) The higher the accounts payable turnover, the more frequently a firm is able to pay all of its accounts payable.

b) When a firm attempts to obtain credit from suppliers or banks, accounts payable turnover is used to determine whether credit should be extended.

$$Accounts\ payable\ turnover = \frac{Cost\ of\ goods\ sold}{Average\ balance\ in\ accounts\ payable}$$

2) The average payables period (payables turnover in days or payables deferral period) is the average time between the purchase of inventory and the payment of cash. This ratio provides insight on how often a firm can settle its average accounts payable per year.

$$Average\ payable\ period = \frac{Days\ in\ year}{Accounts\ payable\ turnover}$$

a) This ratio is used by creditors to determine a firm's liquidity, so a lower value is advantageous.

b.   The operating cycle and the cash conversion cycle differ because the firm's purchases of inventory are made on credit. Thus, the cash conversion cycle equals the operating cycle minus the average payables period.

	Accounts Payable Turnover	**Average Payable Period**
Higher	More Liquid	Less Liquid
Lower	Less Liquid	More Liquid

Stop and review! You have completed the outline for this subunit. Study multiple-choice questions 10 through 12 on page 237.

10.4 MULTIPLE RATIO ANALYSIS

Some multiple-choice questions require candidates to combine their knowledge of the different categories of ratios. This subunit consists entirely of such questions. The ratios presented in Study Unit 9, Subunit 2, and Subunit 10.2 should be thoroughly reviewed before answering the questions. The following is a summary of ratio analysis:

1.   **Liquidity Ratios**

$$Net\ working\ capital = Current\ assets - Current\ liabilities$$

$$Current\ ratio = \frac{Current\ assets}{Current\ liabilities}$$

$$Quick\ (acid\text{-}test)\ ratio = \frac{Cash\ and\ equivalents + Marketable\ securities + Net\ receivables}{Current\ liabilities}$$

2.   **Receivable Ratios**

$$Accounts\ receivable\ turnover = \frac{Net\ credit\ sales}{Average\ balance\ in\ receivables}$$

$$Days'\ sales\ in\ receivables = \frac{Days\ in\ year}{Accounts\ receivable\ turnover\ ratio}$$

3.   **Inventory Ratios**

$$Inventory\ turnover = \frac{Cost\ of\ goods\ sold}{Average\ balance\ in\ inventory}$$

$$Days'\ sales\ in\ inventory = \frac{Days\ in\ year}{Inventory\ turnover\ ratio}$$

4.   **Operating Performance Ratios**

$$Operating\ cycle = Days'\ sales\ in\ receivables + Days'\ sales\ in\ inventory$$

$$Cash\ conversion\ cycle = Average\ collection\ period + Days'\ sales\ in\ inventory - Average\ payables\ period$$

$$Accounts\ payable\ turnover = \frac{Cost\ of\ goods\ sold}{Average\ balance\ in\ accounts\ payable}$$

$$Average\ payable\ period = \frac{Days\ in\ year}{Accounts\ payable\ turnover}$$

Stop and review! You have completed the outline for this subunit. Study multiple-choice questions 13 through 16 beginning on page 238.

10.5 SHORT-TERM FINANCING

1. Firms often need short-term financing to meet their needs in cases where working capital management was not optimally mixed or during times of slow sales.

2. **Spontaneous Financing -- Trade Credit**

   a. A supplier may offer an early payment discount. For example, payment terms may be 2/10, n/30. These terms provide a 2% discount if payment is within 10 days. Otherwise, the entire balance is due in 30 days (an interest-free 30-day loan). Taking the discount ordinarily is advantageous. The annualized cost of **not** taking a discount can be calculated using the following formula:

$$\frac{Discount\ \%}{100\% - Discount\ \%} \times \frac{Days\ in\ year}{Total\ payment\ period - Discount\ period}$$

EXAMPLE -- Trade Credit

A vendor has sold goods to a firm on terms of 2/10, net 30. The firm has chosen to pay on day 30. The effective annual rate paid by forgoing the discount is calculated as follows (using a 360-day year):

$$
\begin{aligned}
\text{Cost of not taking discount} &= [2\% \div (100\% - 2\%)] \times [360\ \text{days} \div (30\ \text{days} - 10\ \text{days})] \\
&= (2\% \div 98\%) \times (360\ \text{days} \div 20\ \text{days}) \\
&= 2.0408\% \times 18 \\
&= 36.73\%
\end{aligned}
$$

Only firms with extreme cash-flow problems are willing to pay a 36.73% rate.

---

3. **Formal Financing Arrangements**

   a. Commercial banks offer short-term loans and lines of credit.

      1) A **term loan**, such as a note, must be repaid by a definite time.
      2) A **line of credit** allows the firm to reborrow amounts continuously up to a maximum amount if minimum payments are made each month. This arrangement is similar to a consumer's credit card.

4. **Simple Interest Short-Term Loans**

   a. Interest on a simple interest loan is paid at the end of the loan term. The amount to be paid is based on the nominal (stated) rate and the principal of the loan (amount needed).

$$Interest\ expense = Principal\ of\ loan \times Stated\ rate \times Time$$

EXAMPLE -- Simple Interest

A firm obtained a short-term bank loan of $15,000 at an annual interest rate of 8%. The interest expense on the loan is $1,200 ($15,000 × 8% × 1) per year.

The stated rate of 8% also is the effective rate.

---

b.   The **effective rate** of any financing arrangement is the ratio of the amount the firm must pay to the amount it can use. Often there are fees associated with loans, and the face value of the loan is not received.

$$Effective\ interest\ rate = \frac{Interest\ expense\ (interest\ to\ be\ paid)}{Usable\ funds\ (net\ proceeds)}$$

EXAMPLE -- Effective Interest Rate

A firm obtained a short-term bank loan of $15,000 at an annual interest rate of 8%. The bank charges a loan origination fee of $500.

Effective rate = Interest paid ÷ Net proceeds
              = ($15,000 × 8%) ÷ ($15,000 − $500)
              = $1,200 ÷ $14,500
              = 8.28%

The effective interest rate (8.28%) is higher than the stated interest rate (8%) because the net proceeds are lower than the principal.

---

5.   **Discounted Loans**

a.   For a discounted loan, the interest and finance charges are paid at the beginning of the loan term.

$$Total\ borrowings = \frac{Amount\ needed}{(1.0 - Stated\ rate)}$$

EXAMPLE -- Discounted Loan Total Borrowings

A firm needs to pay a $90,000 debt. Its bank has offered to extend this amount at an 8% nominal rate on a discounted basis. How much does the firm need to borrow to pay the $90,000 debt?

Total borrowings = Amount needed ÷ (1.0 − Stated rate)
               = $90,000 ÷ (100% − 8%)
               = $90,000 ÷ 92%
               = $97,826

---

b.   Because the interest expenses are deducted from the face amount, the borrower can only use a smaller amount. Thus, the effective rate on a discounted loan is higher than its nominal rate.

EXAMPLE -- Effective Rate Discounted Loan

A firm has an outstanding loan of $90,000 on a discount basis at 10%.

Effective rate = Net interest expense (annualized) ÷ Usable funds
              = (Face amount × Discount rate) ÷ [Face amount × (1 − Discount rate)]
              = ($90,000 × 10%) ÷ [$90,000 × (1 − 10%)]
              = $9,000 ÷ $81,000
              = 11.111%

---

c.   In all financing arrangements, the effective rate can be calculated without dollar amounts.

$$Effective\ rate\ on\ discounted\ loan = \frac{Stated\ rate}{(1.0 - Stated\ rate)}$$

EXAMPLE -- Effective Interest Rate Discounted Loan

The firm calculates the effective rate on this loan without dollar amounts.

Effective rate = Stated rate ÷ (1.0 − Stated rate)
              = 8% ÷ (100% − 8%)
              = 8% ÷ 92%
              = 8.696%

6. Loans with Compensating Balances

a. Banks may require a borrower to maintain a compensating balance during the term of a financing arrangement to reduce risk and increase their returns.

$$Total\ borrowings = \frac{Amount\ needed}{(1.0 - Compensating\ balance\ \%)}$$

EXAMPLE -- Total Borrowing with Compensatory Balance

A firm has received a loan of $120,000 with terms of 2/10, net 30. The firm's bank will lend the necessary amount for 20 days. Thus, the discount can be taken on the 10th day at a nominal annual rate of 6% and a compensating balance of 10%.

Total borrowings = Amount needed ÷ (1.0 − Compensated balance %)
= ($120,000 × 98%) ÷ (100% − 10%)
= $117,600 ÷ 90%
= $130,667

---

b. Because the bank requires a compensating balance, the borrower can use a smaller amount than the face amount of the loan and therefore pays an effective rate higher than the nominal rate.

EXAMPLE -- Effective Rate with Compensatory Balance

A firm has an outstanding loan of $130,667 at a stated interest rate of 6%. The firm is required to maintain $13,067 as a minimum compensating balance.

Effective rate = Net interest expense (annualized) ÷ Usable funds
= (Principal × Interest rate) ÷ (Principal − Compensating balances)
= ($130,667 × 6%) ÷ ($130,667 − $13,067)
= $7,840 ÷ $117,600
= 6.667%

The effective interest rate (6.667%) is higher than the stated interest rate (6%) because the face amount is reduced by the compensating balance, resulting in smaller usable funds.

---

c. Again, the effective rate can be determined without dollar amounts.

$$Effective\ rate\ with\ compensatory\ balance = \frac{Stated\ rate}{(1.0 - Compensating\ balance\ \%)}$$

EXAMPLE -- Effective Interest Rate with Compensatory Balance

Effective rate = Stated rate ÷ (1.0 − Compensating balance %)
= 6% ÷ (100% − 10%)
= 6% ÷ 90%
= 6.667%

Stop and review! You have completed the outline for this subunit. Study multiple-choice questions 17 through 21 beginning on page 239.

QUESTIONS

10.1 Inventory Management -- Methods

1. Which changes in costs are most conducive to switching from a traditional inventory ordering system to a just-in-time ordering system?

	Cost per Purchase Order	Inventory Unit Carrying Costs
A.	Increasing	Increasing
B.	Decreasing	Increasing
C.	Decreasing	Decreasing
D.	Increasing	Decreasing

Answer (B) is correct.
REQUIRED: The changes in costs most conducive to switching to a JIT ordering system.
DISCUSSION: A JIT system is intended to minimize inventory. Thus, if inventory carrying costs are increasing, a JIT system becomes more cost-effective. Moreover, purchases are more frequent in a JIT system. Accordingly, a decreasing cost per purchase order is a reason to switch to a JIT system.

2. Stewart Co. uses the economic order quantity (EOQ) model for inventory management. A decrease in which one of the following variables would increase the EOQ?

A. Annual sales.

B. Cost per order.

C. Safety stock level.

D. Carrying costs.

Answer (D) is correct.
REQUIRED: The decrease in a variable that increases the EOQ.
DISCUSSION: The EOQ model minimizes the total of ordering and carrying costs. The EOQ is calculated as follows:

$$\sqrt{\frac{2 \times Periodic\ demand \times Ordering\ costs\ per\ order}{Carrying\ costs\ per\ unit}}$$

Increases in the numerator (demand or ordering costs) increase the EOQ, but decreases in the numerator decrease the EOQ. Also, a decrease in the denominator (carrying costs) increases the EOQ.
   Answer (A) is incorrect. A decrease in demand (annual sales), which is in the numerator, decreases the EOQ. Answer (B) is incorrect. A decrease in ordering costs, which is in the numerator, encourages more orders, or a decrease in the EOQ. Answer (C) is incorrect. A decrease in safety stock does not affect the EOQ, although it might lead to a different ordering point.

3. Which of the following assumptions is associated with the economic order quantity formula?

A. The carrying cost per unit will vary with quantity ordered.

B. The cost of placing an order will vary with quantity ordered.

C. Periodic demand is known.

D. The purchase cost per unit will vary based on quantity discounts.

Answer (C) is correct.
REQUIRED: The assumption associated with the EOQ formula.
DISCUSSION: The economic order quantity (EOQ) model is a mathematical tool for determining the order quantity that minimizes the sum of ordering costs and carrying costs. The following assumptions underlie the EOQ model: (1) Demand is uniform, (2) order (setup) costs and carrying costs are constant, and (3) no quantity discounts are allowed.
   Answer (A) is incorrect. An assumption of the EOQ model is that the carrying cost per unit is constant. Answer (B) is incorrect. The cost of placing an order is constant when using the EOQ formula. Answer (D) is incorrect. An assumption of the EOQ model is that no quantity discounts are allowed.

4. In inventory management, the safety stock will tend to increase if the

A. Carrying cost increases.

B. Cost of running out of stock decreases.

C. Variability of the lead time increases.

D. Variability of the usage rate decreases.

Answer (C) is correct.
REQUIRED: The factor that increases safety stock.
DISCUSSION: A firm maintains safety stock to protect itself against the losses caused by stockouts. These can take the form of lost sales or lost production time. Safety stock is necessary because of the variability in lead time and usage rates. As the variability in lead time increases, a firm tends to carry larger safety stock.
   Answer (A) is incorrect. An increase in inventory carrying costs makes carrying safety stock less efficient. Answer (B) is incorrect. If the cost of stockouts declines, the incentive to carry large safety stock is reduced. Answer (D) is incorrect. A decline in the variability of usage makes planning easier and safety stock less necessary.

5. The following information regarding inventory policy was assembled by the TKF Corporation. The company uses a 50-week year in all calculations.

Sales	12,000 units per year
Order quantity	4,000 units
Safety stock	1,500 units
Lead time	5 weeks

The reorder point is

A. 5,500 units.

B. 2,700 units.

C. 1,200 units.

D. 240 units.

Answer (B) is correct.
   REQUIRED: The level of inventory at which an order should be placed.
   DISCUSSION: The reorder point is the inventory level at which an order should be placed. It can be quantified using the following equation:

Reorder point = (Average weekly demand × Lead time) + Safety stock
   = [(12,000 units ÷ 50 weeks) × 5 weeks] + 1,500 units
   = 1,200 units + 1,500 units
   = 2,700 units

   Answer (A) is incorrect. The amount of 5,500 units equals the order size plus the safety stock. Answer (C) is incorrect. The amount of 1,200 units omits safety stock. Answer (D) is incorrect. The average weekly usage is 240 units.

6. A company serves as a distributor of products by ordering finished products once a quarter and using that inventory to accommodate the demand over the quarter. If it plans to ease its credit policy for customers, the amount of products ordered for its inventory every quarter will be

A. Increased to accommodate higher sales levels.

B. Reduced to offset the increased cost of carrying accounts receivable.

C. Unaffected if safety stock is part of the current quarterly order.

D. Unaffected if the JIT inventory control system is used.

Answer (A) is correct.
   REQUIRED: The effect on the quantity of products ordered as a result of relaxing credit policy.
   DISCUSSION: Relaxing the credit policy for customers leads to increased sales because more people are eligible for more credit. As sales increase, the amount ordered on each purchase order increases to accommodate the higher sales.
   Answer (B) is incorrect. Inventory should be increased to accommodate higher sales levels. Answer (C) is incorrect. Safety stock is based on expected sales, which are expected to rise. Answer (D) is incorrect. A just-in-time system is not used when a company orders inventory once a quarter.

7. Which of the following methods is a push system used to control inventory and minimize total inventory costs?

I. Just-in-time (JIT) system
II. Kanban method
III. Materials requirements planning
IV. Manufacturing resource planning

A. I and II only.

B. I, III, and IV only.

C. III and IV only.

D. II and III only.

Answer (C) is correct.
   REQUIRED: The push inventory control system(s).
   DISCUSSION: A push inventory system is a system that controls inventory based on forecasted demand. Materials requirements planning (MRP) is a push system. The demand for materials is driven by the forecasted demand for the final product as programmed into the system. MRP, in effect, creates schedules of when items of inventory are needed in the production departments and thus reduces unnecessary inventory costs. Manufacturing resource planning (MRP II) is an advanced MRP system that extends the scope of an MRP system. Thus, both MRP and MRP II are push systems.
   JIT is a pull system that is demand-driven. In a manufacturing environment, production of goods does not begin until an order has been received. In this way, finished goods inventories also are eliminated. Kanban is also a pull system. It uses tickets to control the flow of production or parts so that they are produced or obtained in the needed amounts at the needed times.
   Answer (A) is incorrect. Both JIT and Kanban are pull systems, not push systems. Answer (B) is incorrect. A JIT system is a pull system, not a push system. Answer (D) is incorrect. A Kanban system is a pull system, not a push system. Both materials requirements planning and manufacturing resource planning are push systems.

10.2   Inventory Management -- Ratios

8. The selected information below (in thousands) pertains to Devlin Company.

	December 31	
	Year 2	Year 1
Assets		
Current assets		
Cash	$ 45	$ 38
Trading securities	30	20
Accounts receivable (net)	68	48
Inventory	90	80
Prepaid expenses	22	30
Total current assets	$255	$216
Net sales	$480	$460
Costs and expenses		
Costs of goods sold	330	315
Selling, general, and administrative	52	51
Interest expense	8	9
Income before taxes	$ 90	$ 85
Income taxes	36	34
Net income	$ 54	$ 51

Devlin Company's inventory turnover for Year 2 was

A. 3.67 times.

B. 3.88 times.

C. 5.33 times.

D. 5.65 times.

Answer (B) is correct.
REQUIRED: The inventory turnover.
DISCUSSION: Inventory turnover equals cost of goods sold divided by the average balance in inventory. Thus, the inventory turnover is 3.88 times per year {$330 COGS ÷ [($90 + $80) ÷ 2]}.
Answer (A) is incorrect. The ratio of 3.67 times is based on ending inventory. Answer (C) is incorrect. The ratio of 5.33 times equals sales divided by ending inventory. Answer (D) is incorrect. The ratio of 5.65 times is based on sales, not cost of goods sold.

9. Selected information (in thousands) from the statement of financial position for King Products Corporation for the fiscal years ended December 31, Year 2, and Year 1, is presented below. Net credit sales and cost of goods sold for Year 2 were $600,000 and $440,000, respectively.

	December 31	
	Year 2	Year 1
Cash	$ 60	$ 50
Marketable securities (at market)	40	30
Accounts receivable (net)	90	60
Inventories (at lower of cost or market)	120	100
Prepaid items	30	40
Total current assets	$340	$280

King Products Corporation's inventory turnover ratio for Year 2 was

A. 3.7

B. 4.0

C. 4.4

D. 6.0

Answer (B) is correct.
REQUIRED: The inventory turnover ratio for Year 2.
DISCUSSION: The inventory turnover ratio equals cost of goods sold divided by the average balance in inventory. Consequently, the inventory turnover is 4 times per year {$440,000 ÷ [($120,000 + $100,000) ÷ 2]}.
Answer (A) is incorrect. The ratio of 3.7 is based on year-end inventory. Answer (C) is incorrect. The ratio of 4.4 is based on beginning inventory. Answer (D) is incorrect. The ratio of 6.0 is based on sales and beginning inventory.

10.3 The Operating Cycle and Cash Conversion Cycle

10. The following computations were made from Bruckner Co.'s current-year books:

Number of days' sales in inventory	55
Number of days' sales in trade accounts receivable	26

What was the number of days in Bruckner's current-year operating cycle?

A. 26

B. 40.5

C. 55

D. 81

Answer (D) is correct.
REQUIRED: The number of days in the operating cycle.
DISCUSSION: The operating cycle is the time needed to turn cash into inventory, inventory into receivables, and receivables back into cash. It is equal to the sum of the number of days' sales in inventory (average number of days to sell inventory) and the number of days' sales in receivables (the average collection period). The number of days' sales in inventory is given as 55 days. The number of days' sales in receivables is given as 26 days. Hence, the number of days in the operating cycle is 81 (55 + 26).
Answer (A) is incorrect. The number of days' sales in receivables is 26. Answer (B) is incorrect. The figure of 40.5 equals the sum of the number of days' sales in inventory and the number of days' sales in receivables, divided by 2. Answer (C) is incorrect. The number of days' sales in inventory is 55.

11. To determine the operating cycle for a retail department store, which one of the following pairs of items is needed?

A. Days' sales in accounts receivable and average merchandise inventory.

B. Cash turnover and net sales.

C. Accounts receivable turnover and inventory turnover.

D. Asset turnover and return on sales.

Answer (C) is correct.
REQUIRED: The pair of items needed to determine the operating cycle for a retailer.
DISCUSSION: The operating cycle is the time needed to turn cash into inventory, inventory into receivables, and receivables back into cash. For a retailer, it is the time from purchase of inventory to collection of cash. Thus, the operating cycle of a retailer is equal to the sum of the number of days' sales in inventory and the number of days' sales in receivables. Inventory turnover equals cost of goods sold divided by average inventory. The days' sales in inventory equals 365 (or another period chosen by the analyst) divided by the inventory turnover. Accounts receivable turnover equals net credit sales divided by average receivables. The days' sales in receivables equals 365 (or other number) divided by the accounts receivable turnover.
Answer (A) is incorrect. Cost of sales must be known to calculate days' sales in inventory. Answer (B) is incorrect. These items are insufficient to permit determination of the operating cycle. Answer (D) is incorrect. These items are insufficient to permit determination of the operating cycle.

12. A company purchases inventory on terms of net 30 days and resells to its customers on terms of net 15 days. The inventory conversion period averages 60 days. What is the company's cash conversion cycle?

A. 15 days.

B. 45 days.

C. 75 days.

D. 105 days.

Answer (B) is correct.
REQUIRED: The length of the company's cash conversion cycle.
DISCUSSION: A firm's cash conversion cycle is the amount of time that passes between the actual outlay of cash for inventory purchases and the collection of cash from the sale of that inventory. Accordingly, the cash conversion cycle is equal to the average collection period plus days' sales in inventory minus the average payables period. Per the formula, the company's cash conversion cycle is 45 days (15 days average collection period + 60 days' sales in inventory – 30 days average payables period).
Answer (A) is incorrect. The period of 15 days is the average collection period, not the cash collection cycle. Answer (C) is incorrect. The period of 75 days is the company's operating cycle, not the cash conversion cycle. Answer (D) is incorrect. The period of 105 days results from adding the average payables period to the company's operating cycle instead of subtracting it.

10.4 Multiple Ratio Analysis

13. Which of the following ratios would most likely be used by management to evaluate short-term liquidity?

    A. Return on total assets.

    B. Sales to cash.

    C. Accounts receivable turnover.

    D. Acid-test ratio.

Answer (D) is correct.
    REQUIRED: The ratio most likely used by management to evaluate short-term liquidity.
    DISCUSSION: Liquidity is a firm's ability to pay its current obligations as they come due. Liquidity ratios relate a firm's liquid assets to its current liabilities. The current ratio is the most common measure of short-term liquidity. It is calculated by dividing current assets by current liabilities. The acid-test (quick) ratio equals the sum of (1) cash and cash equivalents, (2) marketable securities, and (3) net receivables, divided by current liabilities. It is a more conservative short-term liquidity ratio. It excludes inventories and prepayments (recognized as assets) from the numerator.
    Answer (A) is incorrect. Return on total assets measures corporate performance. Answer (B) is incorrect. The sales to cash ratio measures the effectiveness of credit and collection policies. Answer (C) is incorrect. Accounts receivable turnover measures effectiveness in collecting accounts receivable.

14. Selected data from Sheridan Corporation's year-end financial statements are presented below. The difference between average and ending inventory is immaterial.

Current ratio	2.0
Quick ratio	1.5
Current liabilities	$120,000
Inventory turnover	
(based on cost of goods sold)	8 times
Gross profit margin	40%

Assuming no prepaid expenses are included in current assets, Sheridan's net sales for the year were

    A. $800,000

    B. $480,000

    C. $1,200,000

    D. $240,000

Answer (A) is correct.
    REQUIRED: The net sales for the year.
    DISCUSSION: Net sales can be calculated indirectly from the inventory turnover ratio and the other ratios given. If the current ratio is 2.0, and current liabilities are $120,000, current assets must be $240,000 (2.0 × $120,000). Similarly, if the quick ratio is 1.5, the total quick assets must be $180,000 (1.5 × $120,000). The difference between quick assets and current assets is that inventory is not included in the quick assets. Consequently, ending inventory must be $60,000 ($240,000 – $180,000). The inventory turnover ratio (COGS ÷ average inventory) is 8. Thus, cost of goods sold must be 8 times average inventory, or $480,000, given no material difference between average and ending inventory. If the gross profit margin is 40%, the cost of goods sold percentage is 60%, cost of goods sold equals 60% of sales, and net sales must be $800,000 ($480,000 ÷ 60%).
    Answer (B) is incorrect. Cost of goods sold is $480,000. Answer (C) is incorrect. The amount of $1,200,000 is based on a 60% gross profit margin. Answer (D) is incorrect. Current assets equal $240,000.

15. On July 14, Avila Co. collected a receivable due from a major customer. Which of the following ratios is increased by this transaction?

    A. Inventory turnover ratio.

    B. Receivable turnover ratio.

    C. Current ratio.

    D. Quick ratio.

Answer (B) is correct.
    REQUIRED: The ratio increased by collection of a receivable.
    DISCUSSION: The accounts receivable turnover is equal to net credit sales divided by the average accounts receivable. Collection of a receivable decreases the denominator and increases the ratio.
    Answer (A) is incorrect. The inventory turnover ratio equals the cost of goods sold divided by the average inventory. Collection of a receivable does not affect it. Answer (C) is incorrect. A decrease in a receivable and an equal increase in cash have no effect on the current ratio. Answer (D) is incorrect. A decrease in a receivable and an equal increase in cash have no effect on the quick ratio.

16. Which of the following ratios, if any, are useful in assessing a company's ability to meet currently maturing or short-term obligations?

	Acid-Test Ratio	Debt-to-Equity Ratio
A.	No	No
B.	No	Yes
C.	Yes	Yes
D.	Yes	No

Answer (D) is correct.
REQUIRED: The ratios, if any, useful in assessing a company's ability to meet currently maturing obligations.
DISCUSSION: Liquidity ratios measure the ability of a company to meet its short-term obligations. A commonly used liquidity ratio is the acid-test, or quick, ratio, which equals quick assets (net accounts receivable, current marketable securities, and cash) divided by current liabilities. The debt-to-equity ratio is a leverage ratio. Leverage ratios measure the impact of debt on profitability and risk.
Answer (A) is incorrect. The acid-test ratio is useful in assessing a company's ability to meet currently maturing or short-term obligations. Answer (B) is incorrect. The acid-test ratio is useful in assessing a company's ability to meet currently maturing or short-term obligations, but the debt-to-equity ratio does not exclude long-term obligations. Answer (C) is incorrect. The debt-to-equity ratio includes long-term obligations.

10.5 Short-Term Financing

17. A company obtained a short-term bank loan of $250,000 at an annual interest rate of 6%. As a condition of the loan, the company is required to maintain a compensating balance of $50,000 in its checking account. The checking account earns interest at an annual rate of 2%. Ordinarily, the company maintains a balance of $25,000 in its account for transaction purposes. What is the effective interest rate of the loan?

A. 6.44%
B. 7.00%
C. 5.80%
D. 6.66%

Answer (A) is correct.
REQUIRED: The effective interest rate on a loan that requires a compensating balance above the normal working balance.
DISCUSSION: The $50,000 compensating balance requirement is partially satisfied by the practice of maintaining a $25,000 balance for transaction purposes. Thus, only $25,000 of the loan is not available for current use. At 6% interest, the $250,000 loan requires an interest payment of $15,000 per year. This amount is partially offset by the 2% interest earned on the $25,000 incremental balance, or $500. Subtracting the $500 interest earned from the $15,000 of expense results in net interest expense of $14,500 for the use of $225,000 ($250,000 − $25,000). Dividing $14,500 by $225,000 produces an effective interest rate of 6.44%.
Answer (B) is incorrect. The percentage of 7.00% fails to consider that the $25,000 currently being maintained counts toward the compensating balance requirement. Answer (C) is incorrect. The percentage of 5.80% fails to consider the compensating balance requirement. Answer (D) is incorrect. The percentage of 6.66% fails to consider the interest earned on the incremental balance being carried.

18. If a firm purchases raw materials from its supplier on a 2/10, net 40, cash discount basis, the equivalent annual interest rate (using a 360-day year) of forgoing the cash discount and making payment on the 40th day is

A. 2%
B. 18.37%
C. 24.49%
D. 36.73%

Answer (C) is correct.
REQUIRED: The equivalent annual interest charge for not taking the discount.
DISCUSSION: The buyer could satisfy the $100 obligation by paying $98 on the 10th day. By choosing to wait until the 40th day, the buyer is effectively paying a $2 interest charge for the use of $98 for 30 days (40-day credit period − 10-day discount period). The annualized cost of not taking this discount can be calculated as follows:

$$\frac{Discount\ \%}{100\% - Discount\ \%} \times \frac{Days\ in\ year}{Total\ payment\ period - Discount\ period}$$

Cost of not taking discount = [2% ÷ (100% − 2%)] ×
[360 days ÷ (40 days − 10 days)]
= (2% ÷ 98%) × (360 days ÷ 30 days)
= 2.0408% × 12
= 24.49%

Answer (A) is incorrect. The discount rate is 2%. Answer (B) is incorrect. The percentage of 18.37% is based on the 40-day credit period. Answer (D) is incorrect. The percentage of 36.73% is based on a 20-day credit period.

Questions 19 through 21 are based on the following information. Skilantic Company needs to pay a supplier's invoice of $60,000 and wants to take a cash discount of 2/10, net 40. The firm can borrow the money for 30 days at 11% per annum plus a 9% compensating balance.

19. The amount Skilantic Company must borrow to pay the supplier within the discount period and cover the compensating balance is

   A. $60,000

   B. $65,934

   C. $64,615

   D. $58,800

Answer (C) is correct.
   REQUIRED: The amount to borrow to pay the supplier within the discount period and cover the compensating balance requirement.
   DISCUSSION: Skilantic's total borrowings on this loan can be calculated as follows:

$$
\begin{aligned}
\text{Total borrowings} &= \text{Amount needed} \div \\
&\quad (1.0 - \text{Compensating balance \%}) \\
&= (\$60,000 \times 98\%) \div (100\% - 9\%) \\
&= \$58,800 \div 91\% \\
&= \$64,615
\end{aligned}
$$

   Answer (A) is incorrect. The amount of $60,000 is the invoice amount. Answer (B) is incorrect. The amount of $65,934 assumes the amount paid to the supplier is $60,000. Answer (D) is incorrect. The amount of $58,800 is the amount to be paid to the supplier.

20. Assuming Skilantic Company borrows the money on the last day of the discount period and repays it 30 days later, the effective interest rate on the loan is

   A. 11%

   B. 10%

   C. 12.09%

   D. 9.90%

Answer (C) is correct.
   REQUIRED: The effective interest rate when borrowing to take a discount.
   DISCUSSION: Skilantic's effective rate on this loan can be calculated as follows:

$$
\begin{aligned}
\text{Effective rate} &= \text{Stated rate} \div (1.0 - \text{Compensating balance \%}) \\
&= 11\% \div (100\% - 9\%) \\
&= 11\% \div 91\% \\
&= 12.09\%
\end{aligned}
$$

   Answer (A) is incorrect. The contract rate is 11%. Answer (B) is incorrect. The effective rate is greater than the contract rate. The usable funds are less than the face amount of the note. Answer (D) is incorrect. The effective rate is greater than the contract rate. The usable funds are less than the face amount of the note.

21. Skilantic fails to take the discount and pays on the 40th day. Assuming a 360-day year, what effective rate of annual interest does it pay the vendor?

   A. 2%

   B. 24%

   C. 24.49%

   D. 36.73%

Answer (C) is correct.
   REQUIRED: The effective interest rate paid when a discount is not taken.
   DISCUSSION: By failing to take the discount, Skilantic is essentially borrowing $58,800 for 30 days. Thus, at a cost of $1,200, it acquires the use of $58,800, resulting in a rate of 2.0408% ($1,200 ÷ $58,800) for 30 days. Assuming a 360-day year, the effective annual rate is 24.49% [2.0408% × (360 days ÷ 30 days)].
   Answer (A) is incorrect. The discount rate for a 30-day period is 2%. Answer (B) is incorrect. The percentage of 24% assumes that the available funds equal $60,000. Answer (D) is incorrect. The percentage of 36.73% assumes a 20-day discount period.

STUDY UNIT ELEVEN
CAPITAL BUDGETING

(14 pages of outline)

Firms retain some of their net income and use this plus other financing to expand production, develop new products, enter new business markets through acquisition or internal development, or make speculative investments. Firms must decide whether to invest in new product lines or means of production. This process involves (1) identifying investments, (2) determining the resources required, (3) projecting the expected amounts and timing of returns, and (4) ranking the identified investments.

11.1 CAPITAL BUDGETING -- BASICS

1. **Capital Budgeting**

   a. Capital budgeting is the process of planning and controlling investments for long-term projects.

      1) Most financial and management accounting topics, such as calculating the allowance for doubtful accounts or accumulating product costs, require reporting activity for a single accounting or reporting cycle, such as 1 month or 1 year.

      2) Capital projects affect multiple accounting periods and limit the firm's future financial planning. Thus, capital budgeting decisions tend to be relatively permanent and inflexible.

   b. A capital project usually involves substantial expenditures and financing. Planning is important because of uncertainties about capital markets, inflation, interest rates, and the money supply.

   c. The following are capital budgeting applications:

      1) Buying equipment
      2) Building facilities
      3) Acquiring a business
      4) Developing a product or product line
      5) Expanding into new markets
      6) Replacing equipment

2. **Relevant Cash Flows**

   a. The first step in assessing a potential capital project is to identify the relevant cash flows (future revocable cash flows).

      1) Relevant cash flows do **not** include sunk costs, those already paid or irrevocably committed to be paid.

b. The following are relevant cash flows for capital budgeting:

1) Cost of new equipment
2) Annual after-tax cash savings or inflows
3) Proceeds from disposal of old equipment (residual or salvage value)
4) Adjustment for depreciation expense on new equipment (the depreciation tax shield that reduces taxable income and cash outflows for tax expense)

EXAMPLE of Relevant Cash Flows

A firm's annual recurring operating cash income from a new machine is $100,000. The annual depreciation expense on this machine is $20,000. The effective tax rate is 40%. To calculate the after-tax annual cash flows, the impact of annual depreciation expense on tax payments must be considered.

Operating cash inflow	$100,000	Taxable income	$80,000
Depreciation expense	(20,000)	Effective tax rate	× 40%
Annual taxable income	$ 80,000	Income tax payment	$32,000
Operating cash inflow	$100,000		
Income tax payment	(32,000)		
After-tax cash flow	$ 68,000		

After-tax cash flow also can be calculated as follows:

Operating cash flow net of taxes [$100,000 × (1.0 − .40)]	$60,000
Depreciation tax shield [$20,000 × 40%]	8,000
Annual after-tax cash flow	$68,000

NOTE: Depreciation expense affects cash flows only because it reduces tax payments.

---

3. **Accounting Rate of Return**

a. The accounting rate of return is used to assess potential capital projects. It ignores the time value of money.

$$\text{Accounting rate of return} = \frac{\text{Annual increase in GAAP net income}}{\text{Required investment}} = \frac{\text{Annual cash inflow} - \text{Depreciation}}{\text{Initial investment}}$$

1) The accounting rate of return is based on readily available GAAP numbers and is easy to calculate and understand.

EXAMPLE of Accounting Rate of Return

A manufacturer considers the purchase of a new machine. It costs $250,000 and will decrease annual after-tax cash payments by $40,000. The machine is expected to have a 10-year useful life, have no salvage value, and be depreciated on the straight-line basis. The accounting rate of return on this machine is calculated as follows:

Annual cash savings	$ 40,000
Minus: Annual depreciation expense ($250,000 ÷ 10 years)	(25,000)
Annual increase in accounting net income	$ 15,000
Divided by: Purchase price of new equipment	÷ 250,000
Accounting rate of return	6%

---

b. However, certain characteristics of the accounting rate of return limit its usefulness for selecting capital projects.

1) The accounting rate of return is affected by the accounting methods chosen.

a) Accountants must choose which expenditures to capitalize and which to expense immediately. They also choose how quickly to depreciate capitalized assets.

b) A project's true rate of return cannot be dependent on such decisions.

c) The accounting rate of return does not take into account the time value of money.

d) The accounting rate of return is not useful for projects in which the investments are made in multiple installments at different times.

e) The accounting rate of return fails to consider increased risk of long-term projects. For example, a project with a 10% return earned in 10 years is preferred over a project with an 8% return earned in 3 years.

f) Another distortion occurs when comparing a single project's accounting rate of return with the total return for all of the firm's capital projects.

g) The decreasing book value of a depreciable investment implies the ROA increases over the life of the investment.

The AICPA has tested the accounting rate of return by asking for its calculation. Questions also have asked for the components of the accounting rate of return.

Stop and review! You have completed the outline for this subunit. Study multiple-choice questions 1 through 3 on page 255.

11.2 CAPITAL BUDGETING -- PAYBACK METHODS

1. **Payback Period**

   a. The payback period is the number of years required for the net cash savings or inflows to equal the original investment, i.e., the time necessary for an investment to pay for itself. It is the break-even point expressed as time.

      1) Firms using the payback method set a maximum length of time within which projects must pay for themselves to be acceptable.

   b. If the cash flows are constant, the formula is

   $$Payback\ period = \frac{Initial\ investment}{Annual\ after\text{-}tax\ savings\ (cash\ inflow)}$$

      1) This method ignores the time value of money.

EXAMPLE of Constant Cash Flows

Aspen Company performs a 4-year payback period test on all capital projects. Aspen is considering a project requiring an initial cash outlay of $200,000 that will save a total of $260,000 of after-tax costs. These savings will be in equal amounts for each of the next 5 years.

The first step in the payback method is to determine the annual after-tax cash flow. In this example, it is $52,000 ($260,000 ÷ 5 years).

Payback period = $200,000 ÷ $52,000 = 3.846 years

Judged by this criterion, the project is acceptable because its payback period is less than Aspen's maximum.

c.   If the cash flows are not constant, the calculation must be in cumulative form.

EXAMPLE of Variable Cash Flows

Assume that Aspen's initial investment is $160,000 and that the project's cash flows are expected to vary as shown below. The payback period is calculated as follows:

End of Year	Cash Savings	Initial Investment to be Recovered
Initial investment	$ --	$160,000
Year 1	48,000	112,000
Year 2	54,000	58,000
Year 3	54,000	4,000
Year 4	60,000	--

The project is acceptable because its payback period is between 3 and 4 years and is less than Aspen's maximum.

---

d.   The advantage of the payback method is its simplicity.

   1)   The payback period measures the risk and liquidity of an investment. The longer the period, the more risky the investment and the less liquid it is.

e.   The payback method has the following significant disadvantages:

   1)   Weighting all cash flows equally disregards the time value of money.
   2)   All cash inflows after the payback cutoff date are disregarded. Applying a single cutoff date to every project results in potentially accepting marginal projects and rejecting good ones.
   3)   Overall profitability is ignored.
   4)   It assumes cash flows occur evenly throughout the year.

2.   **Discounted Payback**

a.   The discounted payback method is sometimes used to overcome the major disadvantage of the basic payback method. The only difference between the two methods is that the discounted payback method takes into account the time value of money.

   1)   The net cash flows in the denominator are discounted to calculate the period required to recover the initial investment.

EXAMPLE of Discounted Payback

Orion Company has a 12% cost of capital.

Period	Cash Savings		12% PV Factor		Discounted Cash Savings	Initial Investment to be Recovered
Initial investment	$ --		--		$ --	$160,000
Year 1	48,000	×	0.89286	=	42,857	117,143
Year 2	54,000	×	0.79719	=	43,048	74,095
Year 3	54,000	×	0.71178	=	38,436	35,659
Year 4	60,000	×	0.63552	=	38,131	--

The project is acceptable because its discounted payback period is between 3 and 4 years and is less than Orion's maximum.

If the firm wants to determine the discounted payback periods in years and assumes that the cash flows are earned evenly throughout each year, the discounted payback period in years is calculated as follows:

   1)   Full payback occurs sometime in Year 4. The remaining investment at the beginning of Year 4 is $35,659.
   2)   The following is the percentage of Year 4 at which the amount of $35,659 is recovered:

$$\frac{\$35,659}{\$38,131} = 0.935$$

   3)   The discounted payback period in years is **3.935 years** (3 + 0.935), or 3 years, 11 months, and 7 days.

---

    b.   The **breakeven time** is the time required for the discounted cash flows of an investment to equal its initial cost.

    c.   The discounted payback method's advantage is that it reflects the time value of money.

        1)   Its disadvantages are (a) its greater complexity and (b) not considering cash flows after the arbitrary cutoff date.

Stop and review! You have completed the outline for this subunit. Study multiple-choice questions 4 through 6 on page 256.

11.3 CAPITAL BUDGETING -- NET PRESENT VALUE (NPV)

1.   **Discounted Cash Flow Analysis**

    a.   A more sophisticated method for evaluating potential capital projects than the accounting rate of return is discounted cash flow analysis. It discounts the relevant cash flows to present value using the required rate of return as the discount rate. (This discount rate also is called the **hurdle rate** or **opportunity cost of capital**.)

        1)   A hurdle rate is the minimum acceptable rate when choosing to invest in a project. There is a wide range of approaches to determine the hurdle rate. In practice, firms begin with their weighted-average cost of capital (WACC) and then adjust this interest rate in relation to other risks. For the CPA exam, the hurdle rate will be provided.

        2)   A firm could also use another rate as the discount rate to reflect the risk specific to or risks for a project.

2.   **Considerations for the Required Rate of Return or the Hurdle Rate**

    a.   Adjusting for Inflation

        1)   In an inflationary environment, future cash inflows consist of inflated dollars. To compensate for this decline in purchasing power, hurdle rates must be adjusted upward.

    b.   Adjusting for Risk

        1)   Particularly risky projects may be assigned higher hurdle rates to ensure that only those whose potential returns are proportionate to their risks are accepted.

    c.   Division-Specific Rates of Return

        1)   When the divisions of a large, complex firm have specific risk attributes and capital costs, using a single firm-wide hurdle rate may result in bad decisions.

            a)   The managers of high-risk divisions may over-invest in new projects, and managers of low-risk divisions may under-invest.

                i)   Thus, compared with the firm-wide average, high-risk divisions should have slightly higher hurdle rates, and low-risk divisions should have slightly lower hurdle rates.

3.   **NPV**

a.   A capital project's NPV is the difference between (1) the present value of the net cash savings or inflows expected over the life of the project and (2) the required investment. It is the expected increase in value of the firm (assuming all underlying assumptions are true).

1)   If the difference is

a)   **Positive**, the project should be **accepted**.
b)   **Negative**, the project should be **rejected**.

EXAMPLE of NPV with Salvage Value

Badger Corporation is planning to invest $100,000 in new equipment. The equipment is expected to create savings in cash operating expenses of $80,000 in the first year and $60,000 in the second year. The equipment's estimated useful life is 2 years, and Badger expects to resell it at the end of its useful life (salvage value) for $15,000. The IRS Code requires straight-line depreciation. The equipment is depreciated for tax purposes at a rate of 50% each year. Badger's internal rate of return is 12%, and its effective tax rate is 40%. The present value of $1 for one period at 12% is 0.8929, and the present value of $1 for two periods at 12% is 0.7972. Badger calculates the NPV of this potential investment as follows:

Annual depreciation shield for Years 1 and 2

Asset's cost	$100,000
Minus salvage value	(15,000)
Depreciable amount	$ 85,000
Tax rate	× 40%
Depreciation tax shield (reduction of taxes paid)	$ 34,000
Number of years	÷ 2
Annual tax shield	$ 17,000

Resale of equipment (salvage value)

Expected proceeds	$ 15,000
Tax basis of equipment	-- (because fully depreciated)
Gain on expected disposal	$ 15,000
Tax expense ($15,000 × 40%)	(6,000)
Expected cash inflow after taxes	$ 9,000

Net annual cash savings

	Year 1	Year 2
Annual savings (cash inflow)	$ 80,000	$60,000
Tax expense	− 40%	− 40%
Net annual savings (cash inflow) after taxes	$ 48,000	$36,000

NPV

	Year 0	Year 1	Year 2
Initial investment in equipment	$(100,000)		
Net annual savings (cash inflow)		$ 48,000	$36,000
Depreciation tax shield		17,000	17,000
Inflow from resale (salvage value)			9,000
After-tax net expected cash flows	$(100,000)	$ 65,000	$62,000
Discount rate (rounded PV factor at 12%)	× 1	× 0.8929	× 0.7972
NPV	$(100,000) +	$ 58,039 +	$49,426 = $7,465

The positive NPV indicates that the project should be accepted.

NPV can easily be calculated without using present value tables. If you encounter an NPV problem in a simulation, you can use the spreadsheet function to calculate NPV. This is actually more accurate because the present value tables are rounded.

$$NPV = \left[-1 \times \begin{array}{c} \text{Amount of} \\ \text{initial investment} \end{array} \right] + \left[\frac{\text{Cash flow Year 1}}{(1 + r)^1} + \frac{\text{Cash flow Year 2}}{(1 + r)^2} + \frac{\text{Cash flow Year 3}}{(1 + r)^3} + \cdots \right]$$

| Cash outflow (negative value) | Cash inflow (positive value) |

Using the information from the previous example, NPV is calculated as follows:

$$NPV = (\$100{,}000 \times -1) + [\$65{,}000 \div (1 + .12)^1] + [\$62{,}000 \div (1 + .12)^2]$$
$$NPV = -\$100{,}000 + \$58{,}036 + \$49{,}426$$
$$NPV = \$7{,}462^*$$

Positive → Accept Investment

*The difference between $7,465 and $7,462 is the rounding difference associated with using PV factors. This second method is always exact.

EXAMPLE of NPV with No Salvage Value

Lumen Corporation is considering the purchase of a machine for $250,000 that has a useful life of 10 years and no residual (salvage) value. The machine is expected to generate an annual operating cash savings of $60,000 over its useful life. It will be depreciated on the straight-line basis, resulting in annual depreciation expense of $25,000 ($250,000 ÷ 10 years). Lumen's internal rate of return is 12%, and its effective tax rate is 40%.

The present value of $1 for 10 periods at 12% is 0.322, and the present value of an ordinary annuity of $1 for 10 periods at 12% is 5.650. Lumen calculates the NPV of this investment as follows:

Present value of cash savings		
Annual operating savings (cash inflow)		$ 60,000
Annual tax expense:		
Tax expense ($60,000 × 40%)	$(24,000)	
Depreciation tax shield ($25,000 × 40%)	10,000	(14,000)
After-tax net annual savings (cash inflow)		$ 46,000
Times: PV factor for an ordinary annuity		× 5.650
Present value of net savings (cash inflow)		$259,900
Required investment		
Cost of new equipment		$250,000
NPV of investment		
Present value of net savings (cash inflow)		$259,900
Minus: Required investment		(250,000)
NPV of investment		$ 9,900

The positive NPV indicates that the project should be accepted.

b.   Use of the NPV method implicitly assumes cash flows are reinvested at the firm's **required rate of return**.

Stop and review! You have completed the outline for this subunit. Study multiple-choice questions 7 through 9 on page 257.

11.4 CAPITAL BUDGETING -- NPV CALCULATIONS

This subunit consists entirely of questions that require the candidate to perform the detailed calculations involved in applying the NPV method. Please review Subunit 11.3 thoroughly before answering the questions.

Stop and review! You have completed the outline for this subunit. Study multiple-choice questions 10 through 12 beginning on page 258.

11.5 CAPITAL BUDGETING -- INTERNAL RATE OF RETURN (IRR)

1. **IRR**

    a. The IRR of a project is the discount rate at which the investment's NPV equals zero. Thus, the IRR equates the present value of the expected cash inflows with the present value of the expected cash outflows.

        1) If the IRR is higher than the hurdle rate (required rate of return), the investment is accepted. If the IRR is lower, the project should be rejected.

        $$IRR > Hurdle\ rate \rightarrow Accept\ project$$

        $$IRR < Hurdle\ rate \rightarrow Reject\ project$$

EXAMPLE

Cork Company has a hurdle rate of 12% for all capital projects. Cork is considering a project with an initial cash outlay of $200,000 that will save $52,000 of after-tax cash costs in each of the next 5 years. The applicable present value factor is 3.846 ($200,000 ÷ $52,000). According to a table of present value factors for an ordinary annuity for five periods, this factor is between 9% and 10%. Because a rate below 10% is less than the hurdle rate, the project should be rejected.

NOTE: 3.846 is also the payback period.

---

2. **Comparing Cash Flow Patterns**

    a. A decision maker may need to choose between two mutually exclusive projects, one with high initial cash flows and one with relatively constant cash flows.

        1) The higher the hurdle rate, the more quickly a project must be profitable.
        2) Firms with low hurdle rates prefer a steady payback.

EXAMPLE of Two Project Comparisons

The following are the net cash flows of two projects with the same initial investment:

	Initial Investment	Year 1	Year 2	Year 3	Year 4
Project K	$(200,000)	$140,000	$100,000	–	–
Project L	(200,000)	65,000	65,000	$65,000	$65,000

A graph of the two projects at various discount rates illustrates the factors a decision maker must consider.

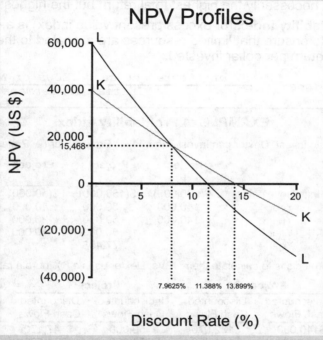

Figure 11-1

Project K's IRR is 13.899%. Project L's is 11.388%.

The NPV profile helps a manager to determine how sensitive a project's profitability is to changes in the discount rate.

- At a hurdle rate of **exactly** 7.9625%, a decision maker is **indifferent** between the two projects. The NPV of both K and L is $15,468 at that discount rate.
- At hurdle rates **below** 7.9625%, the project whose **inflows last longer** into the future is the better investment (L).
- At hurdle rates **above** 7.9625%, the project whose **inflows are received more quickly** is the better choice (K).

Stop and review! You have completed the outline for this subunit. Study multiple-choice questions 13 through 15 beginning on page 259.

11.6 RANKING CAPITAL PROJECTS

1. **Profitability Index**

   a. When sufficient resources are available, every project with a positive NPV should be accepted.

      1) However, few firms have the resources to accept every capital project with a return exceeding the hurdle rate.

      2) Under **capital rationing**, management determines which investments provide not necessarily the highest total return but the highest per dollar invested.

   b. The **profitability index** (or excess present value index) is a method for ranking projects to ensure that limited resources are allocated to the investments with the highest return per dollar invested.

$$\text{Profitability index} = \frac{\text{PV of future net cash flows or NPV of project}}{\text{Initial investment}}$$

EXAMPLE of Profitability Index

Dexter Company has $200,000 to invest. Dexter can invest either in (1) Project F or (2) Projects G and H:

	Project F	Project G	Project H
Initial investment	$(200,000)	$(150,000)	$(50,000)
Year 1	140,000	50,000	40,000
Year 2	140,000	50,000	30,000
Year 3		50,000	10,000
Year 4		77,453	

The first step in ranking these projects is to calculate their NPVs. Dexter uses a 6% hurdle rate.

	Project F Undiscounted Cash Flows	Project F Discounted Cash Flows	Project G Undiscounted Cash Flows	Project G Discounted Cash Flows	Project H Undiscounted Cash Flows	Project H Discounted Cash Flows
Year 1	$140,000	$132,076	$ 50,000	$ 47,170	$40,000	$37,736
Year 2	140,000	124,600	50,000	44,500	30,000	26,700
Year 3			50,000	41,980	10,000	8,396
Year 4			77,453	61,350		
PV of cash inflows		$256,676		$195,000		$72,832
Initial investment	(200,000)	(200,000)	(150,000)	(150,000)	(50,000)	(50,000)
NPV		$ 56,676		$ 45,000		$22,832

Each project's profitability index now can be calculated. Although the profitability indexes are different, the ranking is the same for PV or NPV in the numerator.

PV of cash inflows in numerator	NPV in numerator
Project F: $256,676 ÷ $200,000 = 1.283	Project F: $56,676 ÷ $200,000 = 0.283
Project G: $195,000 ÷ $150,000 = 1.300	Project G: $45,000 ÷ $150,000 = 0.300
Project H: $72,832 ÷ $50,000 = 1.457	Project H: $22,832 ÷ $50,000 = 0.457

Project H provides the highest profitability index, and Project G has the next highest. Thus, the initial decision is to accept Projects G and H.

---

   c. When the initial investment is the same, the independent project with the higher NPV is the project with the higher profitability index.

Stop and review! You have completed the outline for this subunit. Study multiple-choice questions 16 through 18 beginning on page 260.

11.7 COMPARISON OF CAPITAL BUDGETING METHODS

1. Some CPA exam questions involve selecting the best capital budgeting method for a given set of facts rather than the mechanics of the calculation.

2. NPV is the value today of all future cash flows.

3. IRR is the rate at which the NPV of all cash flows from an investment equal zero. It is the hurdle rate at the breakeven point.

4. **Comparing NPV and IRR**

   a. The NPV and IRR methods give the same accept or reject decision if projects have unrelated cash flows (are independent). Thus, all acceptable, independent projects can be chosen.

      1) However, if projects are **mutually exclusive** (i.e., only one project can be accepted for investment), the NPV and IRR methods may rank them differently if

         a) The cost of one project is greater than the cost of another.

         b) The timing, amounts, and directions of cash flows differ among projects.

         c) The projects have different useful lives.

         d) The cost of capital or desired rate of return varies over the life of a project. The NPV can be determined easily using different desired rates of return for different periods. The IRR determines one rate for the project.

         e) Multiple investments are involved in a project. NPV amounts are cumulative; IRR rates are not. The IRR for the whole is not the sum of the IRRs for the parts.

   b. The reinvestment rate is an important factor in choosing between the NPV and IRR methods. NPV assumes the cash flows from the investment can be reinvested at the project's **required rate of return**.

      1) The IRR method assumes reinvestment is at the **IRR**. Thus, IRR is only an accurate representation of a project's annual return when the reinvestment is at the actual IRR or when the project generates no interim cash flows.

         a) Interim cash flows are the cash flows of each year except the first and last years.

      2) If the project's funds are not reinvested at the IRR, the ranking calculations obtained may be in error.

         a) The NPV method provides a better understanding of the problem in many decision situations because reinvestment is assumed to be at the required rate of return.

         b) When a project has IRR that is close to the company's reinvestment rate (e.g., required rate of return), the annual return is less distorted by the IRR calculation. If the IRRs are 10% or more above the reinvestment rate, annual return may be significantly distorted.

            i) To avoid these distortions, companies may use a **modified internal rate of return (MIRR)** that is close to the reinvestment rate. The best assumption is to set the MIRR at the required rate of return (the company's cost of capital).

ii) Two projects with identical IRRs can generate different annual returns if different reinvestment rates are applied. The example below compounds each interim cash flow and forwards them at different reinvestment rates. Time value of money is used to calculate cash flows.

EXAMPLE of IRR vs. MIRR

Project A and project B are two mutually exclusive projects with identical cash flows, duration, and IRR values of 70%. Managers would be indifferent in selecting the two projects. However, if the reinvestment rate of project B can only be redeployed at 30% of the cost of capital, project A is clearly preferable because it generates a greater annual return.

Project A (IRR = 70%)

Year	0	1	2	3	4	5
Cash flow($S)	-20	15	15	15	15	15

Project B (IRR = 70%)

Year	0	1	2	3	4	5
Cash flow($S)	-20	15	15	15	15	15

Project A, reinvestment rate = IRR = 70%

Year	Amount
0	$(20)
1	$15 @ 70%
2	$15 @ 70%
3	$15 @ 70%
4	$15 @ 70%
5	$15 + $26 + $43 + $74 + $125 = $283

Project B, reinvestment rate = cost of capital = MIRR = 30%

Year	Amount
0	$(20)
1	$15 @ 30%
2	$15 @ 30%
3	$15 @ 30%
4	$15 @ 30%
5	$15 + $20 + $25 + $33 + $43 = $136

EXAMPLE Comparing NPV and IRR

	Initial Investment	Year 1	NPV	IRR
Project A	−$10,000	$25,000	$12,174.21	150%
Project B	−$25,000	$50,000	$19,718.79	100%
Hurdle rate	8.00%			

- If the projects are independent, both projects could be invested because both IRRs exceed the hurdle rate and the NPVs are positive.
- If the projects are mutually exclusive, the IRR method prefers project A, whereas the NPV method prefers project B.
- The question for the firm is whether to risk $10,000 to earn $15,000 or to risk $25,000 to earn $25,000.
  - There is no correct answer because the decision is up to the decision maker's preference on risks and, therefore, which model to use: NPV or IRR.

Summary

	Accounting Rate of Return	Payback Method	Discounted Payback Method	NPV	IRR
Reflects time value of money?	No	No	Yes	Yes	Yes
Considers breakeven point?	No	Yes	Yes	No	Yes
Considers all cash flows (including beyond breakeven point)?	No	No	No	Yes	Yes

Summary

	ACCOUNTING RATE OF RETURN	PAYBACK METHOD	DISCOUNTED PAYBACK METHOD	NET PRESENT VALUE	INTERNAL RATE OF RETURN
A D V A N T A G E S	1. Based on GAAP 2. Easily understood 3. Simple to calculate	1. Simplicity 2. Measures more risk than accounting rate of return because the longer the period to achieve a payback, the riskier the investment 3. Focuses on assessing liquidity of a project	1. Takes into account the TVM 2. Focuses on assessing risk and liquidity of a project	1. Takes into account the TVM with all cash flows including cash flows after the payback period 2. Indicates the quality of an investment by quantifying its risk in the form of a dollar value	1. Takes into account the TVM with all cash flows including cash flows after the payback period 2. Indicates the efficiency or quality of an investment by quantifying its risk in the form of an interest rate
D I S A D V A N T A G E S	1. Manipulated by accounting choices such as capitalization and depreciation 2. Does not take into account TVM 3. Distorts investments made at multiple installments 4. Fails to consider increased risk of long-term projects	1. Weighting all cash flows equally disregards the TVM 2. All cashflows after the payback date are disregarded 3. Ignores long-term profitability	1. Greater complexity than the payback method 2. All cash flows after the payback date are disregarded 3. Ignores overall profitability	1. Assumes the cash flows are reinvested at the firm's required rate of return, which is not necessarily always true 2. Creates difficulty when comparing two projects of different sizes because only dollar amounts are used	1. Assumes the cash flows are reinvested at the IRR, which is not necessarily true 2. Generates multiple IRR when the cash flow changes between positive and negative more than once

For both the NPV and IRR, expect to see questions asking for calculation of these values as well as an understanding of the underlying theory.

Stop and review! You have completed the outline for this subunit. Study multiple-choice questions 19 through 21 on page 261.

11.8 LEASING VERSUS BUYING

1. **Overview of Leasing**

   a. A lease is a long-term contract in which the owner of property (the lessor) allows another party (the lessee) the right to use the property for a stated period in exchange for a stated payment.

      1) The basic issue is whether the lease is (a) a purchase-and-financing arrangement (a capital lease) or (b) a long-term rental contract (an operating lease).

   b. Discounting a lease's cash flows to determine its present value allows a firm to determine the most favorable lease.

   c.   Lease financing is analyzed by comparing the cost of owning with the cost of leasing. Leasing also provides tax and other benefits.

      1)   If leases are not accounted for as installment purchases (capital leases), they are a form of off-balance-sheet financing. Thus, under an operating lease, the lessee need **not** record an asset or a liability, and rent expense is recognized.

2.   **Types of Leases**

   a.   A **sale-leaseback** is an alternate method of raising capital. It allows firms to acquire capital from the sale of an asset while retaining the use of the asset.

   b.   **Service or operating leases** usually include both financing and maintenance services.

   c.   **Financial leases**, which do not provide for maintenance services, are noncancelable and fully amortize the cost of the leased asset over the term of the basic lease contract. They are installment purchases.

3.   **Lease Classification**

   a.   A **capital lease** is, in substance, the purchase of an asset and should thus be treated as a purchase. For a lease to be classified as a capital lease, it must meet at least one of the following four criteria:

      1)   Title passes to the lessee at the end of the lease.
      2)   The lease contains a bargain purchase option.
      3)   The present value of the minimum lease payments during the lease term equals 90% or more of the fair value of the leased property.
      4)   The lease term is 75% or more of the useful economic life of the property.

   b.   An **operating lease** (off-balance-sheet financing) is a rental contract and is accounted for as such.

      1)   No accounting entry is made to record the lease. Lease payments are expensed as incurred.
      2)   Expense is recognized as the services are used. If lease payments are not reasonably aligned with the services obtained, accruals or deferrals must be used.

4.   **Buying Considerations**

   a.   Analyze the cost of leasing versus purchasing by using one of the following methods or another acceptable analysis model:

      1)   **Net present value (NPV).** A capital project's NPV is the difference between the present value of the net cash savings or inflows expected over the life of the project and the required investment.
      2)   **Internal rate of return (IRR).** The IRR of a project is the discount rate at which the investment's NPV equals zero. Thus, the IRR equates the present value of the expected cash inflows with the present value of the expected cash outflows.
      3)   **Discounted cash flow analysis.** This method discounts the relevant cash flows using the required rate of return as the rate. (This rate also is called the hurdle rate or opportunity cost of capital.)

   b.   The analysis compares the cost of each alternative by considering the timing of the payments, tax benefits, interest rate on a loan, the lease rate, and other financial arrangements.

   c.   To evaluate a lease, first find the net cash outlay in each year of the lease term. Then discount each year's net cash outlay to take into account the time value of money. This discounting provides the present value of each amount.

   d.   To evaluate the purchase, the economic life of the equipment, salvage value, and depreciation must be determined.

Stop and review! You have completed the outline for this subunit. Study multiple-choice questions 22 through 24 on page 262.

QUESTIONS

11.1 Capital Budgeting -- Basics

1. Of the following decisions, capital budgeting techniques would **least** likely be used in evaluating the

A. Acquisition of new aircraft by a cargo company.

B. Design and implementation of a major advertising program.

C. Trade for a star quarterback by a football team.

D. Adoption of a new method of allocating nontraceable costs to product lines.

Answer (D) is correct.
　REQUIRED: The decision least likely to be evaluated using capital budgeting.
　DISCUSSION: Capital budgeting is the process of planning expenditures for investments on which the returns are expected to occur over a period of more than 1 year. Thus, capital budgeting applies to the acquisition or disposal of long-term assets and the financing ramifications of such decisions. The adoption of a new method of allocating nontraceable costs to product lines has no effect on a firm's cash flows, the acquisition of long-term assets, and financing. Thus, capital budgeting is irrelevant to such a decision.
　Answer (A) is incorrect. A new aircraft is a long-term investment in a capital good. Answer (B) is incorrect. A major advertising program is a high cost investment with long-term effects. Answer (C) is incorrect. A star quarterback is a costly asset who is expected to have a substantial effect on the team's long-term profitability.

2. Which of the following is irrelevant in projecting the cash flows of the final year of a capital project?

A. Cash devoted to use in project.

B. Disposal value of equipment purchased specifically for project.

C. Depreciation tax shield generated by equipment purchased specifically for project.

D. Historical cost of equipment disposed of in the project's first year.

Answer (D) is correct.
　REQUIRED: The irrelevant information in projecting the cash flows for the final year of a capital project.
　DISCUSSION: After disposal of an old piece of equipment, its historical cost no longer affects a firm's cash flows.
　Answer (A) is incorrect. The recovery of working capital devoted to a capital project is a relevant cash flow in the final year. Answer (B) is incorrect. The disposal value of equipment acquired for the project is relevant in the final year. Answer (C) is incorrect. The depreciation tax shield generated by equipment acquired for the project is relevant to the final year.

3. Which one of the following items is **least** likely to directly impact an equipment replacement capital expenditure decision?

A. The net present value of the equipment that is being replaced.

B. The depreciation rate that will be used for tax purposes on the new asset.

C. The amount of additional accounts receivable that will be generated from increased production and sales.

D. The sales value of the asset that is being replaced.

Answer (A) is correct.
　REQUIRED: The item least likely to directly affect an equipment replacement capital expenditure decision.
　DISCUSSION: The only relevant valuation of existing equipment is its salvage value at the time of the decision.
　Answer (B) is incorrect. The depreciation rate for tax purposes on the new asset will determine the depreciation tax shield. Answer (C) is incorrect. The additional working capital associated with the new equipment is relevant to the decision. Answer (D) is incorrect. The salvage value of the existing equipment is relevant to the decision.

11.2 Capital Budgeting -- Payback Methods

4. A characteristic of the payback method (before taxes) is that it

A. Incorporates the time value of money.

B. Neglects total project profitability.

C. Uses accrual accounting inflows in the numerator of the calculation.

D. Uses the estimated expected life of the asset in the denominator of the calculation.

Answer (B) is correct.
REQUIRED: The characteristic of the payback method.
DISCUSSION: The payback method calculates the number of years required to complete the return of the original investment. This measure is determined by dividing the net investment required by the average expected cash flow to be generated, resulting in the number of years required to recover the original investment. Payback is easy to calculate but has two principal problems: (1) It ignores the time value of money, and (2) it does not consider returns after the payback period. Thus, it ignores total project profitability.
Answer (A) is incorrect. The payback method does not incorporate the time value of money. Answer (C) is incorrect. The payback method uses the net investment in the numerator of the calculation. Answer (D) is incorrect. Payback uses the net annual cash inflows in the denominator of the calculation.

5. Jasper Company has a payback goal of 3 years on new equipment acquisitions. A new sorter is being evaluated that costs $450,000 and has a 5-year life. Straight-line depreciation will be used; no salvage is anticipated. Jasper is subject to a 40% income tax rate. To meet the company's payback goal, the sorter must generate reductions in annual cash operating costs of

A. $60,000

B. $100,000

C. $150,000

D. $190,000

Answer (D) is correct.
REQUIRED: The cash savings that must be generated to achieve a targeted payback period.
DISCUSSION: Given a periodic constant cash flow, the payback period is calculated by dividing cost by the annual after-tax cash inflows, or cash savings. To achieve a payback period of 3 years, the annual increment in net cash inflow generated by the investment must be $150,000 ($450,000 ÷ 3-year targeted payback period). This amount equals the total reduction in cash operating costs minus related taxes. Depreciation is $90,000 ($450,000 ÷ 5 years). Because depreciation is a noncash deductible expense, it shields $90,000 of the cash savings from taxation. Accordingly, $60,000 ($150,000 – $90,000) of the additional net cash inflow must come from after-tax net income. At a 40% tax rate, $60,000 of after-tax income equals $100,000 ($60,000 ÷ 60%) of pre-tax income from cost savings, and the outflow for taxes is $40,000. Thus, the annual reduction in cash operating costs required is $190,000 ($150,000 additional net cash inflow required + $40,000 tax outflow).
Answer (A) is incorrect. The amount of $60,000 is after-tax net income from the cost savings. Answer (B) is incorrect. The amount of $100,000 is the pre-tax income from the cost savings. Answer (C) is incorrect. The amount of $150,000 ignores the impact of depreciation and income taxes.

6. Whatney Co. is considering the acquisition of a new, more efficient press. The cost of the press is $360,000, and the press has an estimated 6-year life with zero salvage value. Whatney uses straight-line depreciation for both financial reporting and income tax reporting purposes and has a 40% corporate income tax rate. In evaluating equipment acquisitions of this type, Whatney uses a goal of a 4-year payback period. To meet Whatney's desired payback period, the press must produce a minimum annual before-tax operating cash savings of

A. $90,000

B. $110,000

C. $114,000

D. $150,000

Answer (B) is correct.
REQUIRED: The minimum annual before-tax operating cash savings yielding a specified payback period.
DISCUSSION: Payback is the number of years required to complete the return of the original investment. Given a periodic constant cash flow, the payback period equals net investment divided by the constant expected periodic after-tax cash flow. The desired payback period is 4 years, so the constant after-tax annual cash flow must be $90,000 ($360,000 ÷ 4). Assuming that the company has sufficient other income to permit realization of the full tax savings, depreciation of the machine will shield $60,000 ($360,000 ÷ 6) of income from taxation each year, an after-tax cash savings of $24,000 ($60,000 × 40%). Thus, the machine must generate an additional $66,000 ($90,000 – $24,000) of after-tax cash savings from operations. This amount is equivalent to $110,000 [$66,000 ÷ (1.0 – .4)] of before-tax operating cash savings.
Answer (A) is incorrect. The amount of $90,000 is the total desired annual after-tax cash savings. Answer (C) is incorrect. The amount of $114,000 results from adding, not subtracting, the $24,000 of tax depreciation savings to determine the minimum annual after-tax operating savings. Answer (D) is incorrect. The amount of $150,000 assumes that depreciation is not tax deductible.

11.3 Capital Budgeting -- Net Present Value (NPV)

7. The NPV of a project has been calculated to be $215,000. Which one of the following changes in assumptions would decrease the NPV?

A. Decrease the estimated effective income tax rate.

B. Decrease the initial investment amount.

C. Extend the project life and associated cash inflows.

D. Increase the discount rate.

Answer (D) is correct.
REQUIRED: The change in assumption that decreases the NPV.
DISCUSSION: An increase in the discount rate, a decrease in cash flows, or an increase in the initial investment lowers the NPV.
Answer (A) is incorrect. A decrease in the tax rate would decrease tax expense, thus increasing cash flows and the NPV. Answer (B) is incorrect. A decrease in the initial investment amount would increase the NPV. Answer (C) is incorrect. An extension of the project life and associated cash inflows would increase the NPV.

8. Assume that the interest rate is greater than zero. Which of the following cash-inflow streams should you prefer?

	Year 1	Year 2	Year 3	Year 4
A.	$400	$300	$200	$100
B.	$100	$200	$300	$400
C.	$250	$250	$250	$250
D.	Any of these, since they each sum to $1,000.			

Answer (A) is correct.
REQUIRED: The cash flows that are most advantageous.
DISCUSSION: The concept of present value gives greater value to inflows received earlier than later. Thus, the declining inflows are superior to increasing inflows or even inflows.
Answer (B) is incorrect. The cash flow shown does not produce the greatest present value. Answer (C) is incorrect. The cash flow shown does not produce the greatest present value. Answer (D) is incorrect. Present value of the cash flows must be considered.

9. For capital budgeting purposes, management would select a high hurdle rate of return for certain projects because management

A. Wants to use equity funding exclusively.

B. Believes too many proposals are being rejected.

C. Believes bank loans are riskier than capital investments.

D. Wants to factor risk into its consideration of projects.

Answer (D) is correct.
REQUIRED: The reason for selecting a high hurdle rate for certain projects.
DISCUSSION: Risk analysis measures the likelihood of the variability of future returns from the proposed investment. Risk can be incorporated into capital budgeting decisions in various ways, one of which is to use a hurdle rate (desired rate of return) higher than the firm's cost of capital, that is, a risk-adjusted discount rate. This method adjusts the interest rate used for discounting upward as an investment becomes riskier. The expected flow from the investment must be relatively larger, or the increased discount rate will generate a negative NPV, and the proposed acquisition will be rejected.
Answer (A) is incorrect. The nature of the funding may not be a sufficient reason to use a risk-adjusted rate. The type of funding is just one factor affecting the risk of a project. Answer (B) is incorrect. A higher hurdle will result in rejection of more projects. Answer (C) is incorrect. A risk-adjusted high hurdle rate is used for capital investments with greater risk.

11.4 Capital Budgeting -- NPV Calculations

10. The Hopkins Company has estimated that a proposed project's 10-year annual net cash benefit, received each year end, will be $2,500 with an additional terminal benefit of $5,000 at the end of the 10th year.

Information on present value factors is as follows:

Present value of $1 at 8% at the end of
   10 periods   .463
Present value of an ordinary annuity of $1
   at 8% for 10 periods   6.710

Assuming that these cash inflows satisfy exactly Hopkins' required rate of return of 8%, what is the initial cash outlay?

   A. $16,775

   B. $19,090

   C. $25,000

   D. $30,000

Answer (B) is correct.
   REQUIRED: The initial cash outlay.
   DISCUSSION: If the 8% return exactly equals the present value of the future flows (the NPV is zero), the present value of the future inflows equals the initial cash outlay. Thus, the initial cash outlay is $19,090 [($2,500)(present value of an ordinary annuity at 8% for 10 periods) + ($5,000)(present value of a single amount at 8% for 10 periods = ($2,500)(6.710) + ($5,000)(.463)].
   Answer (A) is incorrect. The amount of $16,775 failed to include the present value of the $5,000 terminal benefit. Answer (C) is incorrect. The amount of $25,000 is not a result of using present value analysis. Answer (D) is incorrect. The amount of $30,000 is not a result of using present value analysis.

Question 11 is based on the following information. Jorelle Company's financial staff has been requested to review a proposed investment in new capital equipment. Applicable financial data is presented below. There will be no salvage value at the end of the investment's life and, due to realistic depreciation practices, it is estimated that the salvage value and net book value are equal at the end of each year. All cash flows are assumed to take place at the end of each year. For investment proposals, Jorelle uses a 12% after-tax target rate of return.

Investment Proposal

Year	Purchase Cost and Book Value	Annual Net After-Tax Cash Flows	Annual Net Income
0	$250,000	$ 0	$ 0
1	168,000	120,000	35,000
2	100,000	108,000	39,000
3	50,000	96,000	43,000
4	18,000	84,000	47,000
5	0	72,000	51,000

Discounted Factors for a 12% Rate of Return

Year	Present Value of $1.00 Received at the End of Each Period	Present Value of an Annuity of $1.00 Received at the End of Each Period
1	.89	.89
2	.80	1.69
3	.71	2.40
4	.64	3.04
5	.57	3.61
6	.51	4.12

11. The net present value for the investment proposal is

   A. $106,160

   B. $(97,970)

   C. $356,160

   D. $96,560

Answer (A) is correct.
   REQUIRED: The NPV.
   DISCUSSION: The NPV is the sum of the present values of all cash inflows and outflows associated with the proposal. If the NPV is positive, the proposal should be accepted. The NPV is determined by discounting each expected cash flow using the appropriate 12% interest factor for the present value of $1. Thus, the NPV is $106,160 [(.89 × $120,000) + (.80 × $108,000) + (.71 × $96,000) + (.64 × $84,000) + (.57 × $72,000) − (1.00 × $250,000)].
   Answer (B) is incorrect. The amount of $(97,970) is based on net income instead of cash flows. Answer (C) is incorrect. The amount of $356,160 excludes the purchase cost. Answer (D) is incorrect. The amount of $96,560 equals average after-tax cash inflow times the interest factor for the present value of a 5-year annuity, minus $250,000.

12. Jackson Corporation uses net present value techniques in evaluating its capital investment projects. The company is considering a new equipment acquisition that will cost $100,000, fully installed, and have a zero salvage value at the end of its 5-year productive life. Jackson will depreciate the equipment on a straight-line basis for both financial and tax purposes. Jackson estimates $70,000 in annual recurring operating cash income and $20,000 in annual recurring operating cash expenses. Jackson's desired rate of return is 12% and its effective income tax rate is 40%.

The present value factors for 12% are as follows:

Present value of $1 at the end of five periods   .567
Present value of an ordinary annuity of $1 for
  five periods   3.605

What is the net present value of this investment on an after-tax basis?

A. $28,840

B. $8,150

C. $36,990

D. $80,250

Answer (C) is correct.
REQUIRED: The NPV on an after-tax basis.
DISCUSSION: Annual cash outflow for taxes is $12,000 {[$70,000 inflows – $20,000 cash operating expenses – ($100,000 ÷ 5) depreciation] × 40%}. The annual net cash inflow is therefore $38,000 ($70,000 – $20,000 – $12,000). The present value of these net inflows for a 5-year period is $136,990 ($38,000 × 3.605 present value of an ordinary annuity for 5 years at 12%), and the NPV of the investment is $36,990 ($136,990 – $100,000 investment).
Answer (A) is incorrect. The amount of $28,840 is the present value of the depreciation tax savings. Answer (B) is incorrect. The amount of $8,150 ignores the depreciation tax savings. Answer (D) is incorrect. The amount of $80,250 ignores taxes.

11.5 Capital Budgeting -- Internal Rate of Return (IRR)

13. What is the approximate IRR for a project that costs $50,000 and provides cash inflows of $20,000 for 3 years?

Rate of Return	Present Value of an Annuity of $1 Received at the End of 3 Years
6%	2.673
8%	2.577
10%	2.487
12%	2.402

A. 10%

B. 12%

C. 22%

D. 27%

Answer (A) is correct.
REQUIRED: The approximate IRR.
DISCUSSION: The applicable factor is 2.5, which is found just below 10% on the 3-year line of an annuity table.
Answer (B) is incorrect. Discounting the cash inflows at 12% would not produce a NPV of zero. Answer (C) is incorrect. Discounting the cash inflows at 22% would not produce a NPV of zero. Answer (D) is incorrect. Discounting the cash inflows at 27% would not produce a NPV of zero.

14. Brown and Company uses the internal rate of return (IRR) method to evaluate capital projects. Brown is considering four independent projects with the following IRRs:

Project	IRR
I	10%
II	12%
III	14%
IV	15%

Brown's cost of capital is 13%. Which one of the following project options should Brown accept based on IRR?

A. Projects I and II only.

B. Projects III and IV only.

C. Project IV only.

D. Projects I, II, III and IV.

Answer (B) is correct.
REQUIRED: The acceptable projects given a certain cost of capital.
DISCUSSION: When sufficient funds are available, any capital project whose IRR exceeds the firm's cost of capital should be accepted.
Answer (A) is incorrect. Projects I and II have rates of return lower than the company's cost of capital. Answer (C) is incorrect. The rate of return for Project III also exceeds the company's cost of capital. Answer (D) is incorrect. Projects I and II should be rejected; their rates of return are lower than the company's cost of capital.

15. Pena Company is considering a project that calls for an initial cash outlay of $50,000. The expected net cash inflows from the project are $7,791 for each of 10 years.

Rate of Return	Present Value of an Annuity of $1 Received at the End of 10 Years
6%	7.360
8%	6.710
9%	6.418
10%	6.145
12%	5.650

What is the IRR of the project?

A. 6%

B. 7%

C. 8%

D. 9%

Answer (D) is correct.

REQUIRED: The IRR.

DISCUSSION: The IRR can be calculated by equating the initial cash outlay with the present value of the net cash inflows:

$7,791 × PV at i for 10 periods = $50,000
                                 = 6.418

Using the present value table, 6.418 is PV at 9% for 10 periods. Answer (A) is incorrect. Discounting the cash inflows at 6% would not produce a NPV of zero. Answer (B) is incorrect. Discounting the cash inflows at 7% would not produce a NPV of zero. Answer (C) is incorrect. Discounting the cash inflows at 8% would not produce a NPV of zero.

11.6 Ranking Capital Projects

16. Wood, Inc., is considering four independent investment proposals. Wood has $3 million available for investment during the present period. The investment outlay for each project and its projected net present value (NPV) is presented below.

Project	Investment Cost	NPV
I	$ 500,000	$ 40,000
II	900,000	120,000
III	1,200,000	180,000
IV	1,600,000	150,000

Which of the following project options should be recommended to Wood's management?

A. Projects I, II, and III only.

B. Projects I, II, and IV only.

C. Projects II, III, and IV only.

D. Projects III and IV only.

Answer (A) is correct.

REQUIRED: The acceptable capital projects given NPV.

DISCUSSION: When available funds are limited, potential projects should be ranked by profitability index. The indexes for the potential projects can be calculated as follows:

Project	NPV		Investment Cost		Profitability Index
I	$ 40,000	÷	$ 500,000	=	0.080
II	120,000	÷	900,000	=	0.133
III	180,000	÷	1,200,000	=	0.150
IV	150,000	÷	1,600,000	=	0.094

Ranked in order of desirability, they are III, II, IV, and I. Because only $3 million is available for funding, only III, II, and I will be selected.

Answer (B) is incorrect. Project III is more desirable than Project IV. Answer (C) is incorrect. Project IV is more desirable than Project I, but funding is not sufficient. Answer (D) is incorrect. Projects I and II also are desirable, and sufficient funding is available.

17. The profitability index approach to investment analysis

A. Fails to consider the timing of project cash flows.

B. Considers only the project's contribution to net income and does not consider cash flow effects.

C. Always yields the same accept/reject decisions for independent projects as the net present value method.

D. Always yields the same accept/reject decisions for mutually exclusive projects as the net present value method.

Answer (C) is correct.

REQUIRED: The true statement about the profitability index.

DISCUSSION: The profitability index is the ratio of a discounted cash flow amount to the initial investment. It is a variation of the net present value (NPV) method and facilitates the comparison of different-sized investments. Because it is based on the NPV method, the profitability index yields the same decision as the NPV for independent projects. However, decisions may differ for mutually exclusive projects of different sizes.

Answer (A) is incorrect. The profitability index, like the NPV method, discounts cash flows based on the cost of capital. Answer (B) is incorrect. The profitability index is cash based. Answer (D) is incorrect. The NPV and the profitability index may yield different decisions if projects are mutually exclusive and of different sizes.

18. Mesa Company is considering an investment to open a new banana processing division. The project involves an initial investment of $45,000, and cash inflows of $20,000 can be expected in each of the next 3 years. The hurdle rate is 10%. The present value of an ordinary annuity of 1 discounted at 10% for 3 periods is 2.487. The present value of 1 due in 3 periods discounted at 10% is .751. What is the profitability index for the project?

    A. 1.0784

    B. 1.1053

    C. 1.1379

    D. 1.1771

Answer (B) is correct.
    REQUIRED: The profitability index.
    DISCUSSION: At a 10% hurdle rate, the present value of the future cash inflows is $49,740 (20,000 × 2.487). The NPV for the project is $4,740 ($49,740 – $45,000). The profitability index is therefore 1.1053 ($49,740 ÷ $45,000).

11.7 Comparison of Capital Budgeting Methods

19. Which limitation is common to the calculations of the payback period, discounted payback, internal rate of return (IRR), and net present value (NPV)?

    A. They do not consider the time value of money.

    B. They require multiple trial and error calculations.

    C. They require knowledge of a firm's cost of capital.

    D. They rely on forecasts of future data.

Answer (D) is correct.
    REQUIRED: The limitation common to the calculations of the given capital budgeting evaluation methods.
    DISCUSSION: The long-term aspect of capital budgeting presents the accountant with specific challenges. A firm must forecast accurately future changes in demand to have the necessary production capacity when demand increases. But it must avoid excess idle capacity when demand decreases. Because capital budgeting requires choosing among investment proposals, a ranking procedure is needed. The ranking procedure also requires reliable estimates of future cost savings or revenues to calculate the estimated cash flows.
    Answer (A) is incorrect. Discounted cash flow, IRR, and NPV all consider the time value of money. Answer (B) is incorrect. Multiple trial and error calculations only are required for determining the IRR. Answer (C) is incorrect. The payback period calculation does not require knowledge of the cost of capital.

20. The method that divides a project's annual after-tax net income by the average investment cost to measure the estimated performance of a capital investment is the

    A. Internal rate of return method.

    B. Accounting rate of return method.

    C. Payback method.

    D. Net present value (NPV) method.

Answer (B) is correct.
    REQUIRED: The capital budgeting method that divides annual after-tax net income by the average investment cost.
    DISCUSSION: The accounting rate of return uses undiscounted net income (not cash flows) to determine a rate of profitability. Annual after-tax net income is divided by the average carrying amount (or the initial value) of the investment in assets.
    Answer (A) is incorrect. The IRR is the rate at which the project's NPV is zero. Answer (C) is incorrect. The payback period is the time required to recover the original investment. This method does not consider the time value of money or returns after the payback period. Answer (D) is incorrect. The NPV method calculates the discounted present value of future cash inflows to determine whether it is greater than the initial cash outflow.

21. The technique that measures the number of years required for the after-tax cash flows to recover the initial investment in a project is called the

    A. Net present value method.

    B. Payback method.

    C. Profitability index method.

    D. Accounting rate of return method.

Answer (B) is correct.
    REQUIRED: The capital budgeting method that measures the number of years required for the after-tax cash flows to recover the initial investment.
    DISCUSSION: The usual payback formula divides the initial investment by the constant net annual cash inflow. The payback method is unsophisticated because it ignores the time value of money. But it is widely used because of its simplicity and emphasis on recovery of the initial investment.
    Answer (A) is incorrect. The NPV method first discounts the future cash flows to their present value. Answer (C) is incorrect. The profitability index method divides the present value of the future net cash inflows by the initial investment. Answer (D) is incorrect. The accounting rate of return divides the annual net income by the average investment in the project.

11.8 Leasing Versus Buying

22. Neary Company has entered into a contract to lease computers from Baldwin Company starting on January 1. Relevant information pertaining to the lease is provided below.

Lease term	4 years
Useful life of computers	5 years
Present value of future lease payments	$100,000
Fair value of leased asset on date of lease	$105,000
Baldwin's implicit rate	10%

At the end of the lease term, ownership of the asset transfers from Baldwin to Neary. Neary has properly classified this lease as a capital lease on its financial statements and uses straight-line depreciation on comparable assets. At January 1, the leased equipment would be reported on Neary's books as a(n)

- A. Asset only.
- B. Asset and a liability.
- C. Liability only.
- D. Expense and a liability.

Answer (B) is correct.
REQUIRED: The proper classification of leased equipment.
DISCUSSION: A capital lease is, in substance, the purchase of an asset. Thus, the leased asset and the related liability are reported in the balance sheet.
Answer (A) is incorrect. Neary also will report the lease liability. Answer (C) is incorrect. Neary also will report the computers under assets. Answer (D) is incorrect. Neary also will report the computers under assets.

23. If a company uses off-balance-sheet financing, assets have been acquired

- A. For cash.
- B. With operating leases.
- C. With financing leases.
- D. With a line of credit.

Answer (B) is correct.
REQUIRED: The nature of off-balance-sheet financing.
DISCUSSION: No liability is reported on the balance sheet for an operating lease other than for the next rental payment.
Answer (A) is incorrect. No liability arises if the assets were paid for with cash. Answer (C) is incorrect. The long-term liability for financing leases must be reported on the balance sheet. Answer (D) is incorrect. The liability associated with a line of credit is reported on the balance sheet.

24. Lease A does not contain a bargain purchase option, but the lease term is equal to 90% of the estimated economic life of the leased property. Lease B does not transfer ownership of the property to the lessee by the end of the lease term, but the lease term is equal to 75% of the estimated economic life of the leased property. How should the lessee classify these leases?

	Lease A	Lease B
A.	Operating lease	Capital lease
B.	Operating lease	Operating lease
C.	Capital lease	Capital lease
D.	Capital lease	Operating lease

Answer (C) is correct.
REQUIRED: The proper classification of leases.
DISCUSSION: For a lease to be classified as a capital lease by the lessee, any one of four criteria must be met. One of these criteria is that the lease term equal 75% or more of the estimated remaining economic life of the leased property. Both leases meet the 75% criterion and should be properly classified as capital leases.

Online is better! To best prepare for the CPA exam, access **thousands** of exam-emulating MCQs and TBSs through Gleim CPA Review online courses with SmartAdapt technology. Learn more at www.gleimcpa.com or contact our team at 800.874.5346 to upgrade.

STUDY UNIT TWELVE
IT ROLES, SYSTEMS, AND PROCESSING

(16 pages of outline)

While the use of information technology (IT) was once restricted to financial applications, it has permeated every area of the modern organization over the last 40 years. No entity, whether for-profit or not-for-profit, can fulfill its mission without the use of sophisticated electronic technologies and their accompanying procedures.

This study unit describes the various broad categories of information systems and the functions they perform, the standardized modes of processing transactions, and standardized phases of processing.

12.1 ROLE OF INFORMATION SYSTEMS IN THE MODERN ORGANIZATION

1. **Overview**

   a. Information technology (IT) is an all-encompassing term that refers to the electronic storage, retrieval, and manipulation of data; its conversion into human-usable form (i.e., information); and its transmission from one point to another.

      1) The Information Technology Association of America has defined IT as "the study, design, development, application, implementation, support or management of computer-based information systems."

   b. For the purposes of the CPA exam, IT is a synonym for computers, computer networks, and the use of computer programs (i.e., software).

Block Diagram of Information Technology

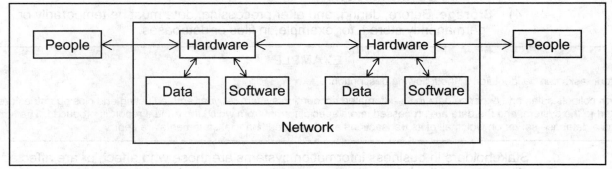

Figure 12-1

2. **Definitions**

   a. **Hardware** is any physical item that comprises a computer system. This could refer to the monitor, keyboard, mouse, microchips, disk drives, etc. In other words, hardware is anything in information technology that can be touched.

   b. **Software** is a combination of computer programs that manipulate data and instruct the hardware on what to do. Software provides instructions to the computer hardware and may also serve as input to other pieces of software. Software is intangible and is anything in the computer system that is not hardware. Examples are Microsoft Word, CCH's TaxWise, or IDEA Data Analysis Software.

    c.   **Network** is a collection of hardware devices that are interconnected so they can communicate among themselves. This allows different hardware to share software and communicate data. The Internet is an example of a network, but many offices have intranets where office computers can communicate with other office computers.

    d.   **Data** are information, not instructions, that are stored in hardware. Data may be financial sales data or could be calculations provided by a software program.

    e.   **People** refers to anyone who uses hardware (i.e., a computer). This could be an IT professional, an accountant, or a young adult who is surfing the Internet.

3.   **Business Information Systems (BIS)**

    a.   A business information system is any combination of hardware, software, data, people, and procedures employed to pursue an organizational objective.

        1)   The first generation of business information systems served the finance and accounting functions, since computing lends itself so readily to quantitative tasks.

        2)   Business information systems have evolved to serve the needs of users at all levels of the organizational hierarchy and, with the advent of fast telecommunications, even users outside the organization.

    b.   Business information systems have three strategic roles:

        1)   Support business processes and operations, such as creating purchase orders.

        2)   Support decision making, such as creating an accounts receivable aging report so a manager can ascertain if a customer's credit is still acceptable.

        3)   Support managers in planning for the future, such as the development of long-range planning and strategies.

    c.   Any information system performs four major tasks:

        1)   **Input.** The system must acquire (capture) data from within or outside of the entity.

        2)   **Processing/Transformation.** Raw materials (data) are converted into knowledge useful for decision making (information).

        3)   **Output.** The ultimate purpose of the system is communication of results to internal or external users.

        4)   **Storage.** Before, during, and after processing, data must be temporarily or permanently stored, for example, in files or databases.

EXAMPLE

All four tasks can be identified in the following description:

A firm collects sales and expense data in its automated accounting system. At year end, adjusting and closing entries are added to the system, and the data are processed into a special format from which the annual report is produced. The firm owns a database server on which all of its transactions and formatted financial statements are kept.

---

    d.   Stakeholders in business information systems are those who affect, or are affected by, the output of the information system. They have an interest in the system's effective and efficient functioning.

        1)   Hence, they include users such as managers, employees, suppliers, and customers.

4.   **Electronic Communication (Networks)**

    a.   Computer-based systems have been woven into almost every facet of the modern organization, from back-office functions, such as human resources and payroll, to instantaneous customer order placement over the Internet.

b. The use of high-speed communication networks, such as the Internet, has enabled the growth of the truly global organization.

1) Markets can be tapped in any part of the globe.

2) Customer support and supply chain functions can be performed around the clock by personnel located on different continents.

c. Organizations can make use of social networking sites, such as **Facebook** and **Twitter**, to disseminate information and gather customer feedback.

d. **RSS**, which stands for rich site summary, allows the content of a website that changes often to be downloaded and stored automatically to a user's computer. This saves the user the need to constantly revisit the site to get the latest information.

e. The newest stage of evolution is **cloud computing**, where organizations are relieved of the need to manage the storage of both applications and data since all the software and data they need are located on the Internet.

1) Cloud computing is defined as a standardized IT capability (services, software, infrastructure) delivered via the Internet in a pay-per-use, self-service way.

2) Advantages of cloud computing include lower infrastructure investments and maintenance costs, increased mobility, and lower personnel and utility costs.

3) Disadvantages of cloud computing include less control than there would be over an internal IT department, more difficulty ensuring data security and privacy, and less compatibility with existing tools and software.

Stop and review! You have completed the outline for this subunit. Study multiple-choice question 1 on page 278.

12.2 IT GOVERNANCE – VISION AND STRATEGY

1. **Overview**

a. Information systems (IS) and information technology (IT) are vital to ensure the successful implementation of an organization's strategy. IS strategy should be driven by the business needs and not by the functions of available technology when formulating a plan to achieve goals.

1) Individual departments may function well in terms of their own goals but still not serve the goals of the organization.

2) IS infrastructure purchases need to be implemented in accordance with the IS strategic plan to ensure business needs are met.

3) Business owners, employees, customers, and financers such as banks have a vested interest in the strategy.

b. An IS strategic plan incorporates the organization's vision and mission to ensure the strategy includes the needs of the business.

1) The vision statement defines in a few sentences the organization's main purpose.

2) The mission statement expands on the vision statement by communicating the organization's goals.

a) The goals should provide guidance for the IT infrastructure to create a detailed strategic plan for achieving those goals.

b) Systems to provide information for decision-making purposes can be implemented to ensure the organization's vision and mission are adhered to.

2. Organizations generally develop strategies at three different levels.

    a. **Corporate-level strategy** is concerned with market definition (i.e., business and markets to focus resources).

    b. **Business-level strategy** applies to organizations that have independent business units that each develop their own strategy.

    c. **Functional-level strategy** concentrates on a specific functional area of the organization such as treasury, information systems, human resources, and operations.

3. Strategic drivers are the critical elements that help determine the success or failure of an organization's strategy. IS has become a strategic driver in most, if not all, organizations.

    a. New technologies create opportunities for improvement and competitive advantage.

    b. **Customer relationship management (CRM)** is a term that refers to practices, strategies, and technologies that companies use to manage and analyze customer interactions and data throughout the customer lifecycle. CRM

        1) Has a goal of improving business relationships with customers, assisting in customer retention, and driving sales growth.

        2) Is designed to compile information on customers across different channels or points of contact between the customer and the company.

        3) Should manage customer relationships on a long-term basis in order to add value.

4. Business **IS strategy** and business **IT strategy** differ as follows:

    a. Business IS strategy is focused on determining what IT must be provided to accomplish the goals of the business strategy.

    b. Business IT strategy

        1) Concentrates on information needs and ensures the IS strategy aligns with the business strategy.

        2) Develops and explains the information architecture that will provide the best return for the organization, i.e., the

            a) Data, process, information, organizational network, and stakeholders
            b) Information technology trends and opportunities
            c) Technology to support the business aims of the organization

    c. Business IT strategy is focused on determining what technology and technological systems development are needed for realizing the business IS strategy.

        1) IT strategy concentrates on how to provide the information.

5. Samples of strategic analysis approaches include the following:

    a. **SWOT analysis** is a structured planning method that evaluates the strengths, weaknesses, opportunities, and threats of a project or business venture. It

        1) Specifies the objective of the business venture or project and

        2) Identifies internal and external factors that are favorable and unfavorable to achieve that objective.

            a) Strategic fit is the degree to which the internal environment of the firm matches the external environment.

    b. **Porter's five forces analysis** is a framework that analyzes the level of competition within an industry and business strategy development.

        1) According to this framework, five forces determine the competitive intensity and attractiveness of an industry.

            a) Three forces are from "horizontal" competition: the threat of substitute products or services, the threat of established rivals, and the threat of new entrants.

             b)   Two forces are from "vertical" competition: the bargaining power of suppliers and the bargaining power of customers.

        2)   Attractiveness, in this context, refers to the overall industry profitability. An unattractive industry is one in which the combination of these five forces acts to drive down overall profitability. A very unattractive industry would be one approaching pure competition.

    c.   **Environmental scanning with the use of the Internet** is a process that systematically surveys and interprets relevant data to identify external opportunities and threats. An organization gathers information about the external world, its competitors, and itself. Examples of environmental scanning with the use of the Internet include

        1)   Innovative blogs, which can be a good source for early discussion of emerging trends and cutting-edge ideas

        2)   Web-crawlers or text mining software systems that scan the Internet automatically in search of emerging innovations and trends

    d.   **Big data and analytics** is an evolving term that describes a voluminous amount of structured, semi-structured, and unstructured data that can be mined to reveal relationships and dependencies or to predict outcomes and behaviors. (Big data and analytics are covered in greater detail in Study Unit 14, Subunit 4.)

Stop and review! You have completed the outline for this subunit. Study multiple-choice questions 2 and 3 beginning on page 278.

12.3 TRANSACTION PROCESSING

    1.   **Overview**

        a.   The most common type of system used in the business information systems (BIS) environment is a **transaction processing system (TPS)**.

            1)   A transaction is a single discrete event that can be stored in an information system.

            2)   Examples include the movement of raw materials from storage to production, the issuance of a purchase order, the recording of a new employee's personal data, or the sale of merchandise.

        b.   A TPS captures the fundamental data that reflect the economic life of an organization. An example of a TPS is an **accounting information system (AIS)**.

    2.   **Two Modes of Transaction Processing**

        a.   The phrase "transaction processing modes" refers to the way in which a system is updated with new data. The methods in use can be classified into one of two categories: batch or online.

        b.   **Batch Processing**

            1)   In this mode, transactions are accumulated and submitted to the computer as a single "batch." In the early days of computers, this was the only way a set of transactions could be processed.

            2)   Inherent in batch processing is a time delay between the batching of the transactions and the updating of the records. Sometimes this delay can be as long as overnight.

                a)   Thus, errors in a batch processing system caused by incorrect programs or data may not be detected immediately.

c.   **Online Processing or Interactive Processing**

1)   In this mode, the computer processes each transaction individually as the user enters it. The user is in direct communication with the computer and gets **immediate processing/feedback** on whether the transaction was accepted.

a)   A common example is an accounts payable system in which a payables clerk can enter each individual invoice as (s)he verifies the paperwork.

2)   In online systems, having the latest information available at all times is crucial so that users can make immediate decisions. A common example is an airline reservation system, which is constantly updated from moment to moment and must be available all the time.

a)   These are called **real-time systems**. A thermostat is another example, constantly monitoring the temperature in the room and engaging the heating or cooling system accordingly.

d.   Many applications use combined batch and online modes.

1)   In such systems, users continuously enter transactions in online mode throughout the workday, collecting them in batches. The computer can then take advantage of the efficiencies of batch mode overnight when there are fewer users logged on to the system.

e.   The use of batch processing tends to be restricted to TPSs and systems that get their input from TPSs. Systems that support decision making are almost always of the online type.

3.   **IT Infrastructure**

a.   Centralization. During the early days of computer processing, computers were very large and expensive, and only organizations such as large banks and governmental agencies could afford them.

1)   As a result, all processing and systems development were done at a single, central location. Users connected to the mainframe via "dumb terminals," i.e., simple monitor-and-keyboard combinations with no processing power of their own.

2)   Since hardware, information security, and data integrity functions were located in one office, economies of scale were achieved and controls were strong.

b.   Decentralization. As the data processing industry evolved, computers became smaller (so-called minicomputers), and branch offices of large organizations could have their own.

1)   **Distributed processing** involves the decentralization of processing tasks and data storage and the assignment of these functions to multiple computers, often in separate locations. **Cooperative processing**, a form of distributed processing, involves the splitting of an application into tasks performed on separate computers. Physical connectivity can occur via a direct channel connection, a local-area network (LAN), a peer-to-peer communication link, or a master/slave link. The application software can exist in a distributed processing environment, but this is not a requirement.

a)   Advantages of distributed processing:

i)   Data are dispersed to match business requirements.

ii)   Data access is much faster because users use only a subset of company data.

iii)   Data processing speed improves because processing occurs at multiple sites.

iv)   New sites can be added to the network without affecting operations at other sites.

        v)   Communications become easier to manage because local sites are smaller and closer to customer operations.

       vi)   It is easier and more cost-effective to add workstations to a network than to upgrade or add another mainframe to the network.

      vii) The chance of a single-point failure is minimized because processing and/or data storage is distributed. For example, if a workstation goes down, its processing and data storage can be picked up by other workstations with minimal disruption.

    b) Disadvantages of distributed processing:

        i)   Database management activities become more complex to manage because data and processing are dispersed over different computers at different locations.

        ii)   Control and data anomalies, as well as security, backup, and recovery procedures, must be coordinated and issues resolved with minimal disruption.

Centralization Advantages	Decentralization Advantages
• Better and more efficient security • Consistent processing because it occurs at a set time in one location	• Remote locations have increased accountability over their data and processes • Remote locations can get data without concern of bottlenecks of traffic over networks

Stop and review! You have completed the outline for this subunit. Study multiple-choice questions 4 through 6 on page 279.

12.4 APPLICATION PROCESSING PHASES

This subunit explains how data are entered into a transaction processing system (TPS), specifically the accounting information system (AIS). CPAs hold a license with the ability to perform an audit and will need to understand how data are entered into a TPS (especially the AIS) as well as how the data in a TPS are processed.

1.   **Data Capture**

    a. Data capture is the process of entering data into an information system. Two methods of capture are identical to their respective processing modes, discussed in item 2. in the previous subunit.

       1) **Batch entry** involves loading a group of records at one time.

       2) **Online entry** involves entering single records, usually in an interactive environment where the user gets immediate feedback.

    b. One type of online entry for capturing input is the optical scanner, such as that used in retail checkout lines (called **point-of-sale**, or POS, transactions). Besides instant updating of accounting and inventory records, POS transaction systems can help management

       1) Identify and respond to trends,

       2) Make sales forecasts,

       3) Determine which products are or are not in demand,

       4) Improve customer service,

       5) Target products and promotions to customers with different demographic traits, and

       6) Evaluate the effects of promotions, including coupons.

2. **Processing**

   a. Processing is the act of converting raw data into usable information. This is performed by the combination of hardware and software that makes up the organization's IT infrastructure.

3. **Types of Data Files**

   a. An understanding of the application processing phases requires an explanation of the two types of computer data files, **master files** and **transaction files**. These types are applicable whether the files are stored on tape, disk, flash drive, or other media and whether they are "flat" files or structured databases.

   b. A master file may be fairly static or very volatile.

      1) An example of a **fairly static master file** is an authorized vendor file containing each vendor's number, name, and address.

EXAMPLE

Authorized Vendor Master File

vendor_num	vendor_name	address_1	city	state	zip	credit_limit	last_updated
0187634	Neyland's Nuts	101 Dandridge Av	Knoxville	TN	37915	$10,000	01/19/2018
1264428	Basic Barbecue	2224 Blossom St	Columbia	SC	29201	$50,000	06/25/2016
4552170	Bayou Bakery	10118 Florida St	Baton Rouge	LA	70801	$15,000	03/04/2016
5006321	Bulldog Barcoding	9085 Old West Point Rd	Starkville	MS	39759	$5,000	10/01/2015
8981463	Razorback Restaurant Supply	3510 West Maple St	Fayetteville	AR	72701	$20,000	07/01/2017

---

      2) An example of a **volatile master file** is a general ledger file, which at any given moment holds the balances of all accounts in the ledger.

EXAMPLE

General Ledger Master File

account_num	account_name	balance	last_transaction_posted
A1209	Cash	$89,580.22	01/10/2018
G6573	Accounts Receivable	$72,024.57	01/10/2018
J0226	Accounts Payable	$(15,156.89)	01/10/2018
K4411	Sales	$(100,558.60)	01/10/2018
M2020	Cost of Goods Sold	$70,005.64	01/10/2018
Y3577	Administrative Expenses	$21,110.33	01/10/2018

---

      3) Volatility is the relative frequency with which the records in a file are added, deleted, or changed during a period.

   c. A transaction file contains the data that reflect ongoing business activity, such as individual purchases from vendors or general journal entries.

	EXAMPLE				
	General Journal Transaction File				
transaction	transaction_date	debit_acct	debit_amt	credit_acct	credit_amt
GL5261904	01/10/2018	A1209	$1,001.56	G6573	$(1,001.56)
GL5261905	01/10/2018	G6573	$660.48	K4411	$(660.48)
GL5261906	01/10/2018	G6573	$898.15	K4411	$(898.15)
GL5261907	01/10/2018	Y3577	$150.75	J0226	$(150.75)

    d.   Transaction files and master files are constantly interacting.

        1)   Before an invoice can be paid, the payables transaction file must be matched against the vendor master file to see whether the vendor really exists.

        2)   The general ledger balance file must be updated every day by posting from the general journal transaction file.

  4.   **REA (Resources, Events, Agents) Processing**

    a.   REA contrasts with the traditional TPS that uses double entry (debit and credit) by using single entry.

    b.   It uses a relational database to store and process transactions.

    c.   Each transaction (event) is stored in a table chronologically and linked to other tables with the details of the transaction (resources, agents, or other attributes). For example, a sales event would be recorded in the sales table and linked to a customer table, inventory table, salesperson table, etc.

    d.   Processing is accomplished through queries to the tables. Examples include calculating (1) the sales for a period by summing the amounts in the sales table from the beginning of the period to the end of the period and (2) the accounts receivable balance for a period end by summing all sales from the sales table and subtracting the sum of all receipts from the accounts receivable cash collections table.

    e.   Advantages include the following:

        1)   Debits and credits are not considered.

        2)   No general ledger is maintained since all balances are calculated through queries.

        3)   Ad hoc reports are easily produced. For example, a report listing all customers who purchased a particular product between certain dates can be produced with a simple query.

    f.   A major disadvantage is implementation cost because it is usually so high that it is prohibitive. Reasons for this include the following:

        1)   Considerable computer storage and processing power are needed.

        2)   Many accountants and auditors are not familiar with REA, so training costs are high and acceptance may be low.

  5.   **Reporting**

    a.   **Reporting in General**

        1)   The term "report" in this context does not necessarily refer to a printed hard copy. Advances in technology allow for report viewing on a computer screen or mobile device with the option of printing granted to the user.

    b.   **Periodic Routine Reports**

        1)   Certain reports are required at regular intervals. Examples are monthly trial balances and ledger summaries to assist in closing the books.

    c.   **On-Demand and Ad Hoc Reports**

       1)   Systems can be designed so that users can generate reports at times they specify. An on-demand report is one whose design is programmed into the system. The user specifies the date and time the report is run.

       2)   Advances in processing power and software have given users the ability to design their own reports "on the fly."

          a)   These ad hoc (sometimes called "quick-and-dirty") reports can be designed to the user's own specifications without the involvement of IT personnel. Database queries are a common example.

    d.   **Exception Reports (also called error listing)**

       1)   It is a common practice after daily processing to generate reports of transactions or activities that lie outside predefined boundaries. The appropriate personnel can then follow up and determine the reasons for these exceptions.

       2)   Examples are batches whose debits and credits do not match and instances of multiple unsuccessful attempts to access the network (which may indicate hacking).

    e.   **Electronic Distribution of Reports**

       1)   The advent of email and other forms of digital communication has greatly enhanced the ability of organizations to distribute reports. Rather than wait for paper copies to be hand delivered, reports can be sent digitally to the appropriate personnel. This is sometimes referred to as **push reporting**.

    f.   **Audit Trail**

       1)   An audit trail of activities is a crucial part of monitoring security over a system. The audit trail includes not only the reports described above, but also such reports as logs of system sign-in and sign-out times to monitor who was doing what on the system.

Stop and review! You have completed the outline for this subunit. Study multiple-choice questions 7 through 11 beginning on page 280.

12.5 SYSTEMS THAT SUPPORT ROUTINE PROCESSES

This subunit introduces other types of business information systems (BISs) used in the corporate environment to perform transaction type processes. The knowledge level of many CPA candidates is most likely highest with the accounting information systems (AIS). However, there are many other types of information systems that comprise the BIS and help corporations perform their day-to-day activities. CPAs hold a license with the ability to perform an audit and will need to understand how each of these transaction information systems work and how they interrelate to each other and BISs.

    1.   **Management Information System (MIS)**

       a.   A MIS typically receives input from a transaction processing system, aggregates it, then reports it in a format useful to middle management in running the business. For this reason, MISs are often classified by function or activity, such as the following:

          1)   Accounting: general ledger, accounts receivable, accounts payable, payroll processing, fixed asset management, and tax accounting; other aspects of accounting information systems are described in item 2. on the following page.

          2)   Finance: capital budgeting, operational budgeting, and cash management

          3)   Manufacturing: production planning, cost control, and quality control

          4)   Logistics: inventory management and transportation planning

          5)   Marketing: sales analysis and forecasting

          6)   Human resources: projecting payroll, projecting benefits obligations, employment-level planning, and employee evaluation tracking

b. These single-function systems, often called stovepipe systems because of their limited focus, are gradually being replaced by integrated systems that link multiple business activities across the enterprise. The most comprehensive integrated system is termed an enterprise resource planning (ERP) system (discussed in item 3. below and on the next page).

2. **Accounting Information System (AIS)**

   a. An AIS is a subsystem of a MIS that processes routine, highly structured financial and transactional data relevant to managerial as well as financial accounting. An AIS is concerned with

   1) Transactions with external parties (e.g., customers, suppliers, governments, owners, and creditors) reflected in financial statements prepared in conformity with GAAP, and

   2) The internal activities recorded in the cost accounting system and the preparation of related reports and analyses (e.g., production reports, pro forma financial statements, budgets, and cost-volume-profit analyses).

3. **Enterprise Resource Planning (ERP)**

   a. ERP is the latest phase in the development of computerized systems for managing organizational resources. ERP is intended to integrate enterprise-wide information systems by creating one database linked to all of an organization's applications.

   1) ERP subsumes traditional MISs.

   2) Figure 12-2 contrasts the less integrated MIS with the more integrated ERP system.

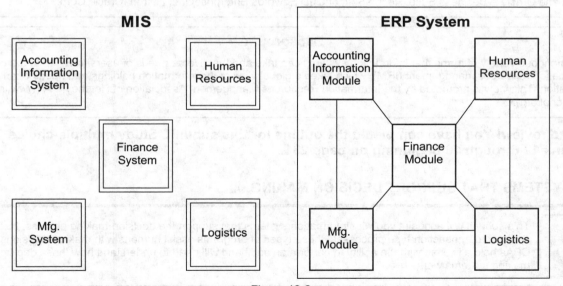

Figure 12-2

b. In the traditional ERP system, subsystems share data and coordinate their activities. Thus, if sales receives an order, it can quickly verify that inventory is sufficient to notify shipping to process the order.

   1) Otherwise, production is notified to manufacture more of the product, with a consequent automatic adjustment of output schedules.

   2) If materials are inadequate for this purpose, the system will issue a purchase order.

   3) If more labor is needed, human resources will be instructed to reassign or hire employees.

   4) The foregoing business processes (and others) should interact seamlessly in an ERP system.

    c.   The subsystems in a traditional ERP system are internal to the organization. Hence, they are often called **back-office functions**. The information produced is principally (but not exclusively) intended for **internal** use by the organization's managers.

    d.   The current generation of ERP software has added **front-office functions**. These connect the organization with customers, suppliers, owners, creditors, and strategic allies (e.g., the members of a trading community or other business association).

        1)   Moreover, the current generation of ERP software also provides the capability for smooth (and instant) interaction with the business processes of **external** parties.

        2)   A newer ERP system's integration with the firm's back-office functions enables supply-chain management (SCM), customer relationship management (CRM), and partner relationship management (PRM).

    e.   The disadvantages of ERP are its extent and complexity, which make implementation difficult and costly.

    f.   Companies with legacy ERP systems are moving to cloud-based ERP systems. Advantages include

        1)   Flexibility and agility of the cloud ERP's centralized data storage
        2)   Sharing of data-processing tasks
        3)   Internet-based access to services and resources

Background

Because ERP software is costly and complex, it is usually installed only by the largest enterprises, although mid-size organizations are increasingly likely to buy ERP software. Major ERP packages include SAP ERP Central Component from SAP SE and Oracle e-Business Suite, PeopleSoft, and JD Edwards EnterpriseOne, all from Oracle Corp.

Background

The tremendous variety of forms that information systems can take and the diverse needs of users have led to the concept of information resources management (IRM), which takes a global view of the information holdings and needs of an organization. This view is promoted by the Information Resources Management Association of Hershey, PA (www.irma-international.org).

Stop and review! You have completed the outline for this subunit. Study multiple-choice questions 12 through 16 beginning on page 281.

12.6 SYSTEMS THAT SUPPORT DECISION MAKING

 This subunit will acquaint you with information systems that support the decision-making process. In contrast to transaction-type processes, these types of programs assist humans with making decisions. CPAs hold a license with the ability to perform an audit and will need to understand how these decision-making systems work.

    1.   **Data Warehouse**

        a.   A data warehouse is a central database for transaction-level data from more than one of the organization's transaction processing systems (TPS).

            1)   A data warehouse is strictly a query-and-reporting system. It is not used to carry on the enterprise's routine operations.

            2)   Rather, a data warehouse gets its input from the various TPSs in the organization.

b. Data warehouses store a large quantity of data and require that the transaction records be converted to a standard format.

   1) The ability of the data warehouse to relate data from multiple systems makes it a very powerful tool for ad hoc queries.

   2) The data warehouse can also be accessed using analytical and graphics tools, a technique called **online analytical processing (OLAP)**.

      a) An important component of OLAP is drill-down analysis, in which the user is first presented with the data at an aggregate level and then can display successive levels of detail for a given date, region, product, etc., until finally reaching the original transactions.

   3) The following technologies are replacing OLAP:

      a) **In-memory analytics** is an approach that queries data when it resides in a computer's random access memory (RAM), as opposed to querying data that is stored on physical disks. This results in shortened query response times and allows business intelligence and analytic applications to support faster business decisions.

      b) **Search engine technology** stores data at a document/transaction level, and data is not pre-aggregated like it would be when contained in an OLAP or in-memory technology application. Users are able to have full access to their raw data and create the aggregations themselves.

c. A data warehouse enables **data mining**, i.e., the search for unexpected relationships among data.

   1) The classic example of the use of data mining was the discovery by convenience stores that diapers and beer often appeared on the same sales transaction in the late evening.

Data Warehouse and Data Mining

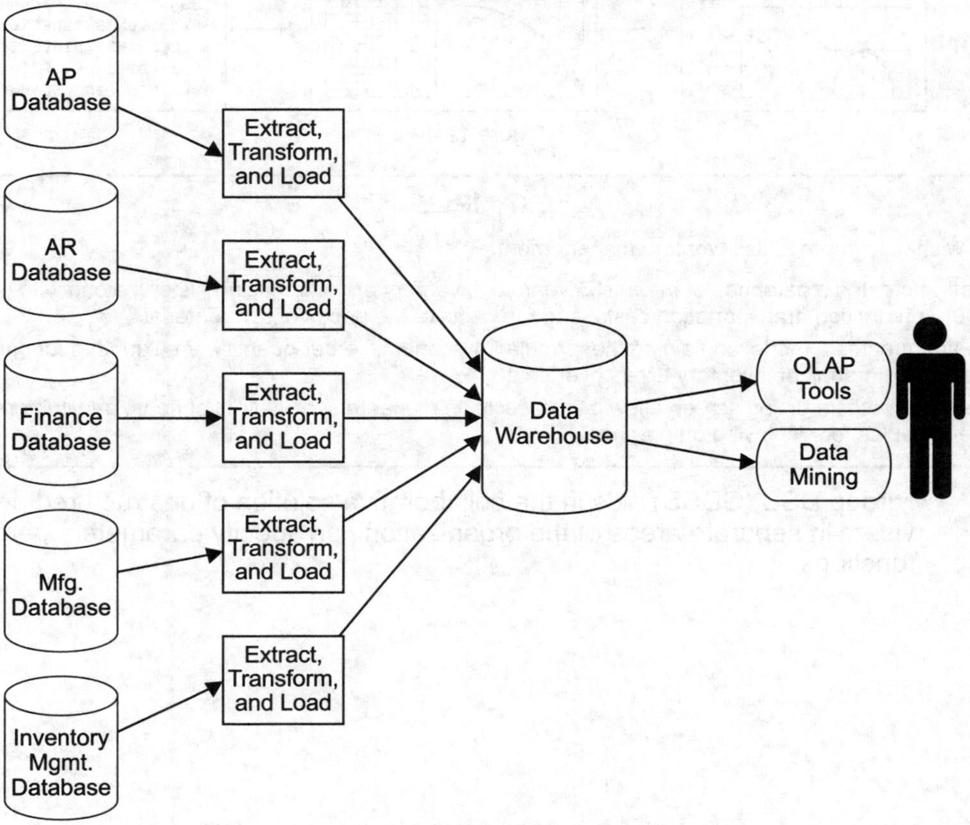

Figure 12-3

2.   **Decision Support System (DSS)**

    a.   A DSS is an interactive system that is useful in solving semistructured problems, that is, those with a structured portion (which the computer can solve) and an unstructured portion (which requires the manager's insight and judgment).

        1)   This point requires emphasis: A DSS does not automate a decision. It examines the relevant data and presents a manager with choices between alternative courses of action.

    b.   A DSS has three basic components:

        1)   The **database** consists of the raw data that are relevant to the decision. In this context, a data warehouse is very useful. The data can come from both within and outside of the organization.

        2)   The **model** is the set of equations, comparisons, graphs, conditions, assumptions, etc., into which the data will be fed.

        3)   The **dialog** is the user interface that allows the user to specify the appropriate model and the particular set of data to which the model should be applied.

Decision Support System

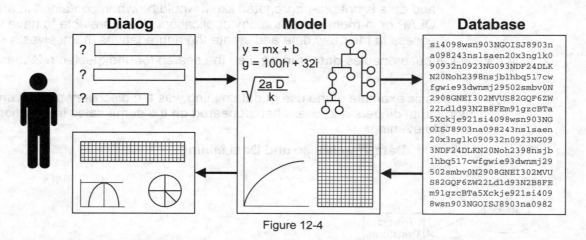

Figure 12-4

EXAMPLE

A manufacturer wishes to improve its inventory management.

- The firm creates a database of the past 5 years of inventory and purchasing history, along with projections for future production, transportation costs, and forecasts of the prices of raw materials.
- The firm creates a model containing the formula for economic order quantity, an algorithm for calculating safety stock, and graphs of inventory levels over time.
- The firm creates a dialog screen allowing the decision maker to specify time periods, particular products, and the variables for displaying on graphs.

---

    c.   A group DSS (GDSS) aids in the collaborative solution of unstructured problems. Users in separate areas of the organization can specify parameters pertinent to their functions.

3. **Artificial Intelligence (AI)**

    a. AI is computer software designed to perceive, reason, and understand.

        1) Historically, computer software works through a series of if/then conditions in which every operation has exactly two possible outcomes (yes/no, on/off, true/false, one/zero).

            a) Human reasoning, on the other hand, is extremely complex, based on deduction, induction, intuition, emotion, and biochemistry, resulting in a range of possible outcomes.

        2) AI attempts to imitate human decision making, which hinges on this combination of knowledge and intuition (i.e., remembering relationships between variables based on experience).

        3) The advantage of AI in a business environment is that IT systems

            a) Can work 24 hours a day

            b) Will not become ill, die, or be hired away

            c) Are extremely fast processors of data, especially if numerous rules (procedures) must be evaluated

    b. There are several types of AI:

        1) **Neural networks** are a collection of processing elements working together to process information much like the human brain, including learning from previous situations and generalizing concepts.

        2) **Case-based reasoning systems** use a process similar to that used by humans to learn from previous, similar experiences.

        3) **Rule-based expert systems** function on the basis of set rules to arrive at an answer. These cannot be changed by the system itself. They must be changed by an outside source (i.e., the computer programmer).

        4) **Intelligent agents** are programs that apply a built-in or learned knowledge base to execute a specific, repetitive, and predictable task, for example, showing a computer user how to perform a task or searching websites for particular financial information.

        5) An **expert system** is an interactive system that attempts to imitate the reasoning of a human expert in a given field. It is useful for addressing unstructured problems when there is a local shortage of human experts.

4. **Executive Support System (ESS)**

    a. At the strategic level, high-level decision makers get the information they need to set, and monitor progress toward, the organization's long-term objectives from an ESS, also called an executive information system (EIS).

        1) An ESS assists senior management in making nonroutine decisions, such as identifying problems and opportunities.

        2) An ESS also provides information about the activities of competitors.

    b. The information in an ESS comes from sources both within and outside the organization, including information from nontraditional computer sources.

        1) An ESS should have the ability to provide overviews, often in graphical format, or to drill down to the detailed data.

        2) An ESS can be used on computers of all sizes.

5.   **Business Intelligence (BI)**

   a.   Business intelligence is what gives upper management the information it needs to know where the organization is and how to steer it in the intended direction. BI gives an executive immediate information about an organization's critical success factors.

   1)   BI is replacing the older ESS model.

   b.   BI tools display information about the organization as bar graphs, pie charts, columnar reports, or any other format considered appropriate to upper management's decision making. These displays are sometimes grouped by a particular executive's needs into what is termed a **digital dashboard**.

   1)   Stock price trends, sales by region and date, on-time delivery performance, instantaneous cash balances, and profitability by customer are possible metrics to be included.

   c.   BI tools use data both from within and outside the organization.

Stop and review! You have completed the outline for this subunit. Study multiple-choice questions 17 through 20 beginning on page 283.

QUESTIONS

12.1   Role of Information Systems in the Modern Organization

1. The four major tasks that any system must perform are

   A.   Input, transformation, output, and storage.

   B.   Input, backup, output, and storage.

   C.   Input, transformation, output, and maintenance.

   D.   Input, transformation, storage, and feedback.

Answer (A) is correct.
   REQUIRED: The four major tasks that any system must perform.
   DISCUSSION: The four major tasks that any system must perform are input, transformation, output, and storage.

12.2   IT Governance – Vision and Strategy

2. Information systems (IS) strategy is determined by

   A.   Business needs.

   B.   Individual department needs.

   C.   The technology available.

   D.   Competitors' strategies.

Answer (A) is correct.
   REQUIRED: The item that determines information systems strategy formulation.
   DISCUSSION: IS and information technology (IT) are vital to the successful implementation of an organization's strategy. IS strategy should be driven by the business needs and not by the functions of available technology when formulating a plan to achieve goals.
   Answer (B) is incorrect. Individual departments may function well in terms of their own goals but still not serve the goals of the organization. Answer (C) is incorrect. Technology is vital to the successful implementation of an organization's strategy. IS infrastructure purchases need to be implemented in accordance with the IS strategic plan to ensure business needs are met. Answer (D) is incorrect. Although being familiar with the strategies of competitors is useful, strategy should be driven by the business's needs. Competitors' strengths and weaknesses may differ from those of the business.

3. Which of the following is (are) a type(s) of business strategy(ies)?

- A. Corporate-level strategy.
- B. Business-level strategy.
- C. Functional-level strategy.
- D. All are types of strategies.

Answer (D) is correct.
REQUIRED: The item(s) that is (are) a type of business strategy.
DISCUSSION: Organizations generally develop strategies at three different levels. Corporate-level strategy is concerned with market definition (i.e., business and markets to focus resources). Business-level strategy applies to organizations that have independent business units that each develop their own strategy. Functional-level strategy concentrates on a specific functional area of the organization such as treasury, information systems, human resources, and operations.

12.3 Transaction Processing

4. An interactive system environment is best characterized by

- A. Data files with records arranged sequentially.
- B. The processing of groups of data at regular intervals.
- C. Sorting the transaction file before processing.
- D. The processing of data immediately on input.

Answer (D) is correct.
REQUIRED: The characteristic of an interactive system environment.
DISCUSSION: In an interactive (inquiry) system, users employ interactive devices to converse directly with the system. The system is characterized by online entry and processing, direct access, and time sharing.
Answer (A) is incorrect. An interactive system requires direct-access files. Answer (B) is incorrect. An interactive system permits immediate, online processing of single transactions. Answer (C) is incorrect. The transaction file need not be sorted before processing.

5. Information processing made possible by a network of computers dispersed throughout an organization is called

- A. Online processing.
- B. Interactive processing.
- C. Time sharing.
- D. Distributed data processing.

Answer (D) is correct.
REQUIRED: The method of information processing by dispersed computers.
DISCUSSION: Distributed processing is characterized by a merger of computer and telecommunications technology. Distributed systems permit not only remote access to a computer but also the performance of local processing at local sites. The result is greater flexibility in systems design and the possibility of an optimal distribution of processing tasks.
Answer (A) is incorrect. Online processing is a method of processing data that permits both immediate posting (updating) and inquiry of master files as transactions occur. Answer (B) is incorrect. Interactive processing is a method of processing data immediately upon input. Answer (C) is incorrect. Time sharing is the processing of a program by the CPU until an input or output operation is required. In time sharing, the CPU spends a fixed amount of time on each program.

6. An insurance company that has adopted cooperative processing is planning to implement new standard software in all its local offices. The new software has a fast response time, is very user friendly, and was developed with extensive user involvement. The new software captures, consolidates, edits, validates, and finally transfers standardized transaction data to the headquarters server. Local managers, who were satisfied with existing locally written personal computer applications, opposed the new approach because they anticipated

- A. Increased workloads.
- B. Centralization of all processing tasks.
- C. More accountability.
- D. Less computer equipment.

Answer (C) is correct.
REQUIRED: The reason for opposing introduction of new software.
DISCUSSION: Cooperative processing implies a tighter coupling than previously existed between the personal computers and the server. The result may threaten the managers' perceived autonomy by increasing the control exercised by headquarters and therefore the accountability of local managers.
Answer (A) is incorrect. Given that only existing systems would be converted, the transaction volume would likely remain relatively constant. Answer (B) is incorrect. In a cooperative processing environment, different computers execute different parts of an application. Answer (D) is incorrect. Compared with mainframe-only processing, cooperative processing typically requires more computer equipment at distributed locations.

12.4 Application Processing Phases

7. At a remote computer center, management installed an automated scheduling system to load data files and execute programs at specific times during the day. The best approach for verifying that the scheduling system performs as intended is to

A. Analyze job activity with a queuing model to determine workload characteristics.

B. Simulate the resource usage and compare the results with actual results of operations.

C. Use library management software to track changes to successive versions of applications programs.

D. Audit job accounting data for file accesses and job initiation/termination messages.

Answer (D) is correct.

REQUIRED: The best approach for verifying that the scheduling system performs as intended.

DISCUSSION: Job accounting data analysis permits programmatic examination of job initiation and termination, record counts, and processing times. Auditing job accounting data for file accesses and job initiation/termination messages will reveal whether the right data files were loaded/dismounted at the right times and the right programs were initiated/terminated at the right times.

Answer (A) is incorrect. Analyzing job activity with a queuing model to determine workload characteristics gives information about resource usage but does not verify that the system actually functioned as intended. Answer (B) is incorrect. A simulation helps management characterize the workload but does not verify that the system actually functioned as intended. Answer (C) is incorrect. Using library management software to track changes to successive versions of application programs permits control of production and test versions but does not verify that the system actually functioned as intended.

8. A commonly used measure of the activity in a master file during a specified time period is

A. Volatility.

B. The index ratio.

C. The frequency ratio.

D. The volume ratio.

Answer (A) is correct.

REQUIRED: The commonly used measure of the activity in a master file.

DISCUSSION: File volatility is the relative frequency with which records are added, deleted, or changed during a specified period.

9. Management is concerned that data uploaded from a personal computer to the company's server may be erroneous. Which of the following controls would best address this issue?

A. Server data should be backed up on a regular basis.

B. Two persons should be present at the personal computer when it is uploading data.

C. The data uploaded to the server should be subject to the same edits and validation routines that online data entry would require.

D. The users should be required to review a random sample of processed data.

Answer (C) is correct.

REQUIRED: The best control to prevent uploading erroneous data from a personal computer to the company's mainframe system in batch processing.

DISCUSSION: Data that are uploaded or downloaded are subject to significant risk. Personal computers are more vulnerable than servers to unauthorized access, and uploaded or downloaded data are subject to alteration on the personal computer. Furthermore, an uploaded file may replace an existing file without being subjected to standard edit and validation procedures.

Answer (A) is incorrect. This practice is a good control, but it does not address the issue of data-upload integrity. Backups cannot prevent or detect data-upload problems. They can only help correct data errors caused by a poor upload. Answer (B) is incorrect. This control may be somewhat helpful in preventing fraud in data uploads, but it is of little use in preventing errors. Answer (D) is incorrect. The error already could have caused erroneous reports and management decisions. Having users try to find errors in uploaded data is costly.

10. Using standard procedures developed by information center personnel, staff members download specific subsets of financial and operating data as they need it. The staff members analyze the data on their own personal computers and share results with each other. Over time, the staff members learn to modify the standard procedures to get subsets of financial and operating data that were not accessible through the original procedures. The greatest risk associated with this situation is that

    A. The data obtained might be incomplete or lack currency.

    B. The data definition might become outdated.

    C. The server data might be corrupted by staff members' updates.

    D. Repeated downloading might fill up storage space on staff members' personal computers.

Answer (A) is correct.
    REQUIRED: The risk associated with downloading additional subsets of financial data.
    DISCUSSION: Staff members may not be aware of how often they need to download data to keep it current, or whether their queries, especially the ones they modified, obtain all the necessary information. Users may employ faulty parameters or logic. Poorly planned queries may also use computing resources inefficiently.
    Answer (B) is incorrect. Downloading data does not affect the data definitions. Answer (C) is incorrect. Staff members are downloading, not uploading, so the staff members are unlikely to corrupt server data. Answer (D) is incorrect. The downloading procedures could replace previously downloaded files on the staff members' personal computers.

11. Advanced electronic point-of-sale (POS) systems allow instant capture and transmission of information for which purposes?

    I. Instant updating of accounting records
    II. Accumulation of marketing information
    III. Tracking of information about specific customers
    IV. Facilitation of warehousing

    A. I and II only.

    B. III and IV only.

    C. I, II, and III only.

    D. I, II, III, and IV.

Answer (D) is correct.
    REQUIRED: The functions of an electronic POS system.
    DISCUSSION: An electronic POS system may update and analyze the perpetual inventory records for each outlet. It may also perform other accounting tasks, such as crediting revenue accounts and debiting cash, accounts receivable, and cost of goods sold. Moreover, a POS system may (1) provide marketing information to identify and respond to trends; (2) make sales forecasts; (3) determine which products are in demand; (4) improve customer service; (5) target products and promotions to customers with different demographic traits; and (6) evaluate the effects of promotions, including coupons. Another function of a POS system is to record personal and transactional information about specific customers, including tracking of warranties, deposits, rentals, progressive discounts, and special pricing. Still another function is use of bar coding in association with the stocking and warehousing functions to reduce the costs of data entry, including the effects of human error.

12.5 Systems that Support Routine Processes

12. An accounting information system (AIS) must include certain source documents in order to control purchasing and accounts payable. For a manufacturing organization, the best set of documents should include

    A. Purchase requisitions, purchase orders, inventory reports of goods needed, and vendor invoices.

    B. Purchase orders, receiving reports, and inventory reports of goods needed.

    C. Purchase orders, receiving reports, and vendor invoices.

    D. Purchase requisitions, purchase orders, receiving reports, and vendor invoices.

Answer (D) is correct.
    REQUIRED: The best set of documents to be included in an AIS to control purchasing and accounts payable.
    DISCUSSION: An AIS is a subsystem of a management information system that processes financial and transactional data relevant to managerial and financial accounting. The AIS supports operations by collecting and sorting data about an organization's transactions. An AIS is concerned not only with external parties but also with the internal activities needed for management decision making at all levels. An AIS is best suited to solve problems when reporting requirements are well defined. A manufacturer has well-defined reporting needs for routine information about purchasing and payables. Purchase requisitions document user department needs, and purchase orders provide evidence that purchase transactions were appropriately authorized. A formal receiving procedure segregates the purchasing and receiving functions and establishes the quantity, quality, and timeliness of goods received. Vendor invoices establish the liability for payment and should be compared with the foregoing documents.
    Answer (A) is incorrect. Receiving reports should be included. Answer (B) is incorrect. Requisitions and vendor invoices should be included. Answer (C) is incorrect. Purchase requisitions should be included.

13. Which one of the following statements about an accounting information system (AIS) is **false**?

A. AIS supports day-to-day operations by collecting and sorting data about an organization's transactions.

B. The information produced by AIS is made available to all levels of management for use in planning and controlling an organization's activities.

C. AIS is best suited to solve problems where there is great uncertainty and ill-defined reporting requirements.

D. AIS is often referred to as a transaction processing system.

Answer (C) is correct.
REQUIRED: The false statement about an accounting information system (AIS).
DISCUSSION: An AIS is a subsystem of a management information system that processes financial and transactional data relevant to managerial and financial accounting. The AIS supports operations by collecting and sorting data about an organization's transactions. An AIS is concerned not only with external parties, but also with the internal activities needed for management decision making at all levels. An AIS is best suited to solve problems when reporting requirements are well defined. A decision support system is a better choice for problems in which decision making is less structured.

14. In a traditional ERP system, the receipt of a customer order may result in

I.   Customer tracking of the order's progress
II. Automatic replenishment of inventory by a supplier
III. Hiring or reassigning of employees
IV. Automatic adjustment of output schedules

A. I, II, and IV only.
B. I and III only.
C. III and IV only.
D. I, II, III, and IV.

Answer (C) is correct.
REQUIRED: The possible effects of receipt of a customer order by a traditional ERP system.
DISCUSSION: The traditional ERP system is one in which subsystems share data and coordinate their activities. Thus, if sales receives an order, it can quickly verify that inventory is sufficient to notify shipping to process the order. Otherwise, production is notified to manufacture more of the product, with a consequent automatic adjustment of output schedules. If materials are inadequate for this purpose, the system will issue a purchase order. If more labor is needed, human resources will be instructed to reassign or hire employees. However, the subsystems in a traditional ERP system are internal to the organization. Hence, they are often called back-office functions. The information produced is principally (but not exclusively) intended for internal use by the organization's managers.
The current generation of ERP software (ERP II) has added front-office functions. Consequently, ERP II but not traditional ERP is capable of customer tracking of the order's progress and automatic replenishment of inventory by a supplier.

15. A principal advantage of an ERP system is

A. Program-data dependence.
B. Data redundancy.
C. Separate data updating for different functions.
D. Centralization of data.

Answer (D) is correct.
REQUIRED: The principal advantage of an ERP system.
DISCUSSION: An advantage of an ERP system is the elimination of data redundancy through the use of a central database. In principle, information about an item of data is stored once, and all functions have access to it. Thus, when the item (such as a price) is updated, the change is effectively made for all functions. The result is reliability (data integrity).
Answer (A) is incorrect. An ERP system uses a central database and a database management system. A fundamental characteristic of a database is that applications are independent of the physical structure of the database. Writing programs or designing applications to use the database requires only the names of desired data items, not their locations. Answer (B) is incorrect. An ERP system eliminates data redundancy. Answer (C) is incorrect. An ERP system is characterized by one-time data updating for all organizational functions.

16. Enterprise resource planning (ERP) software packages, such as SAP ERP Central Component and Oracle e-Business Suite, are all-inclusive systems that attempt to provide entity-wide information. ERP systems provide advantages to an organization's auditors because they

    A. Have proven difficult for some firms to install.

    B. Typically require firms to reduce the division of duties and responsibilities found in traditional systems.

    C. Typically have built-in transaction logs and ability to produce a variety of diagnostic reports.

    D. Have been installed by smaller firms so, to date, few auditors have encountered them.

Answer (C) is correct.
    REQUIRED: The advantage of an ERP for the auditor.
    DISCUSSION: ERP systems have a variety of controls and report generation functions that allow auditors to abstract and monitor data collected and processed. Some ERP systems have built-in audit functions.
    Answer (A) is incorrect. The difficulty of installing ERP systems is a disadvantage for the auditors. Answer (B) is incorrect. ERP systems often require the client to depart from the traditional functional division of duties, such as accounting, finance, marketing, etc. The result is increased audit risk. Answer (D) is incorrect. ERP systems are very costly and therefore usually have been implemented by large organizations. However, the trend is for more and more organizations to install these systems.

12.6 Systems that Support Decision Making

17. Which of the following is the best example of the use of a decision support system (DSS)?

    A. A manager uses a personal-computer-based simulation model to determine whether one of the company's ships would be able to satisfy a particular delivery schedule.

    B. An auditor uses a generalized audit software package to retrieve several purchase orders for detailed vouching.

    C. A manager uses the query language feature of a database management system (DBMS) to compile a report showing customers whose average purchase exceeds $2,500.

    D. An auditor uses a personal-computer-based word processing software package to modify an internal control questionnaire for a specific audit engagement.

Answer (A) is correct.
    REQUIRED: The best example of the use of a decision support system.
    DISCUSSION: A decision support system (DSS) assists middle- and upper-level managers in long-term, nonroutine, and often unstructured decision making. The system contains at least one decision model, is usually interactive, dedicated, and time-shared, but need not be real-time. It is an aid to decision making, not the automation of a decision process. The personal-computer-based simulation model is used to provide interactive problem solving (i.e., scheduling) assistance, the distinguishing feature of a DSS.
    Answer (B) is incorrect. The generalized audit software package does not provide interactive problem solving assistance in retrieving the purchase orders and thus is not a DSS. Answer (C) is incorrect. The query feature of a DBMS does not provide interactive problem solving assistance in compiling the report and thus is not a DSS. Answer (D) is incorrect. The word processing software package does not provide interactive problem solving assistance to the auditor and thus is not a DSS.

18. The processing in expert systems is characterized by

    A. Algorithms.

    B. Deterministic procedures.

    C. Heuristics.

    D. Simulations.

Answer (C) is correct.
    REQUIRED: The characteristic of processing in knowledge-based systems.
    DISCUSSION: Knowledge-based (expert) systems contain a knowledge base for a limited domain of human expertise and inference procedures for the solution of problems. They use symbolic processing based on heuristics rather than algorithms. A heuristic procedure is an exploratory problem-solving technique that uses self-education methods, e.g., the evaluation of feedback, to improve performance. These systems are often very interactive and provide explanations of their problem-solving behavior.
    Answer (A) is incorrect. Algorithms are defined procedures used in typical computer programs. Answer (B) is incorrect. Deterministic procedures are procedures used in computer programs that permit no uncertainty in outcomes. Answer (D) is incorrect. Simulations are computer programs that permit experimentation with logical and mathematical models.

19. For which of the following applications would the use of a fuzzy logic system be the most appropriate artificial intelligence (AI) choice?

    A. Assigning airport gates to arriving airline flights.

    B. Forecasting demand for spare auto parts.

    C. Performing indoor climate control.

    D. Diagnosing computer hardware problems.

Answer (C) is correct.

REQUIRED: The most appropriate use for fuzzy logic.

DISCUSSION: Fuzzy logic is a superset of conventional (Boolean) logic that has been extended to handle the concept of partial truth. Because they use nonspecific terms (membership functions) characterized by well-defined imprecision, fuzzy logic systems can create rules to address problems with many solutions. For example, applying fuzzy logic to indoor climate control may require defining in impressionistic terms and weighting functions such as indoor and outdoor temperature, humidity, and wind conditions. Thus, definitions (e.g., hot, warm, normal, cool, or cold, stated in temperature ranges) may overlap. The resulting rules describe actions to be taken when certain combinations of conditions exist. Fuzzy logic can be used when values are approximate or subjective, objects belong to multiple sets, membership in a set is a matter of degree, and data are incomplete or ambiguous.

Answer (A) is incorrect. Assigning airport gates to arriving airline flights requires an expert system that uses precise data for quick and consistent decisions. Answer (B) is incorrect. Neural networks provide the technology to undertake sophisticated forecasting and analysis. They emulate the processing patterns of the brain and therefore can learn from experience. Answer (D) is incorrect. Diagnosing problems with computer hardware could be accomplished by an expert system.

20. Business intelligence (BI) has all of the following characteristics **except**

    A. Focusing on strategic objectives.

    B. Giving immediate information about an organization's critical success factors.

    C. Displaying information in graphical format.

    D. Providing advice and answers to top management from a knowledge-based system.

Answer (D) is correct.

REQUIRED: The item that is not a characteristic of business intelligence (BI).

DISCUSSION: BI serves the needs of top management for managerial control and strategic planning. BI focuses on strategic (long-range) objectives and gives immediate information about a firm's critical success factors. BI is not a program for providing top management with advice and answers from a knowledge-based (expert) system.

Answer (A) is incorrect. BI does focus on strategic objectives. Answer (B) is incorrect. BI gives immediate information about an organization's critical (strategic) success factors. Answer (C) is incorrect. BI often displays information in graphical format.

STUDY UNIT THIRTEEN
IT SOFTWARE, DATA, AND CONTINGENCY PLANNING

(19 pages of outline)

A computer's software consists of the sets of instructions, often called programs, that are executed by the hardware. Programs and data are stored in a computer in a series of ones and zeros, called binary code. The binary code is grouped into larger units of fields, records, and files. Files can be integrated into a database. When an organization acquires a new system, either by buying it or by creating it internally, a series of steps must be carefully followed to ensure that the system is stable and cost-effective. Business information systems are crucial to the continued existence of the modern organization; therefore, every entity must plan how it will continue processing in the case of an interruption to normal processing.

13.1 SOFTWARE

1. **Overview**

   a. Software refers to the programs (i.e., sets of computer instructions) that are executed by the hardware.

   b. Software can be described from two perspectives: (1) systems vs. application software and (2) the programming language in which the software is written.

2. **Systems Software**

   a. Performs the fundamental tasks needed to manage computer resources. The three most common pieces of systems software are

      1) The **operating system**, which is the "traffic cop" of any computer system

         a) The operating system negotiates the conversation between the computer's hardware, the application the user is running, and the data that the application is working with.

         b) Examples are Linux, OS X, and Windows.

      2) **Utility programs**, which perform basic functions that are not particular to a certain application, such as anti-virus, file management, and network utilities

      3) **Device driver programs**, which operate or control a particular type of device that is attached to the computer

3. **Application Software**

   a. Programs designed to help people perform an activity that can manipulate text, numbers, graphics, or a combination of these elements.

      1) Examples of applications found on personal computers include word processors, spreadsheets, graphics, and databases.

      2) Applications found on dedicated servers are payroll, human resources, purchasing, accounts payable, general ledger, treasury, etc.

4.   **Programming Languages**

a.   Software is written in languages that can be processed by the computer. The following is a description of types and development of computer languages.

b.   **First-generation languages** (also called machine languages) are written in binary code (a combination of ones and zeros discussed in detail in Subunit 13.2) unique to each type of computer. Because they are in binary code, first-generation languages are understood directly by the computer.

c.   **Second-generation languages** (also called assembly languages) are a grouping of programming languages that can be written symbolically, using English words, and are subsequently converted into machine language by software termed an assembler.

d.   **Third-generation languages** (many of which are termed procedural or programming languages) consist of English-like words and phrases that represent multiple machine language instructions, making these languages much easier to learn. These languages must be converted to machine language either by compilation (the whole program is converted at once, then executed) or interpretation (the program is converted and executed one line at a time). Third-generation languages have been deployed for decades with tremendous success. The following is a list of some of the better-known ones:

1)   COBOL (COmmon Business-Oriented Language) was designed in 1959 to be easy to read and maintain, and the standard has been extensively revised and updated over the years. Vast lines of COBOL are still in use.

2)   BASIC (Beginner's All-purpose Symbolic Instruction Code) was developed to teach programming but is not used in large business application processing. Visual BASIC provides a graphical user interface to develop Microsoft Windows applications from code written in BASIC.

3)   C and C++ have been very popular languages since their introduction. C++ enhances C by adding features like support for object-oriented programming.

4)   Java is a high-level, object-oriented programming language developed by Sun Microsystems (which has since been acquired by Oracle Corporation) that, among other things, is used to write programs embedded in World Wide Web documents.

a)   Thus, software is stored on the network, and the user need not be concerned about compatibility of the software with the computer platform.

b)   Java is platform independent because if each computer has it incorporated into a browser, it can run on the platform. Java programs that run in a web browser are called **applets**, and Java programs that run on a web server are called **servlets**.

e.   **Fourth-generation languages** (also called problem-oriented or nonprocedural languages) provide still further simplification of programming. These interactive, English-like languages permit a nonspecialized user to describe the problem to, and receive guidance from, the computer instead of specifying a procedure.

1)   Generalized audit software (GAS), also known as computer-assisted audit techniques (CAAT), involves the use of computer software packages that may allow not only parallel simulation but also a variety of other processing functions, such as extracting sample items, verifying totals, developing file statistics, and retrieving specified data fields. Audit Command Language (ACL) and Interactive Data Extraction and Analysis (IDEA) are the leading CAAT packages.

2) Hypertext markup language (HTML) is the authoring software language commonly used to create and link websites.

3) Extensible markup language (XML) is an open standard language usable with many programs and platforms.

4) Extensible business reporting language (XBRL) is the specification developed by an AICPA-led consortium for commercial and industrial entities that report in accordance with U.S. GAAP. The language is XML-based and uses the XML syntax and related technologies designed to exchange financial information over the World Wide Web. The SEC requires firms to report using XBRL.

f. **Fifth-generation languages** (also called constraint-based programming) consist of programming languages built on the premise that a problem can be solved, and an application built to solve it, by providing constraints to the program, rather than specifying algorithmically how the problem is to be solved (imperative programming).

1) PROLOG (acronym for PROgramming LOGic) is an example of a logical programming language. It uses a form of mathematical logic (predicate calculus) to solve queries or a programmer-given database of facts and rules.

5. **Machine Learning**

a. A form of artificial intelligence that enables computers, when exposed to new data, to learn, grow, change, and develop by themselves.

b. The ability to adapt to new data by learning from previous computations and identifying trends in order to produce reliable results. Examples include

1) Friend suggestions on Facebook based on connections with other friends.
2) Hulu listing movies and shows the user might like based on viewing patterns.
3) Amazon listing purchase suggestions based on previous purchase behavior.

6. **Automation**

a. Technology that enables processes or procedures to be performed without human assistance.

b. Smart machines are representative of automation technology.

1) Generally, smart machine technology characteristics include but are not limited to (a) learn and operate on their own, (b) adapt their behavior based on experience (learning), and (c) be able to generate unanticipated results. Smart machines include

a) Self-driving cars
b) Robots
c) Self-service checkout counters at a supermarket

7. **Blockchain**

a. Digital ledger of economic transactions that is transparent and continually updated by countless users.

1) A block is the current part of a blockchain, which records some or all of the recent transactions and goes into the blockchain as a permanent database.

2) Each time a block gets completed, a new one is generated in chronological order.

a) This provides the capability for market participants to track digital currency transactions without central recordkeeping.

3) Each node (a computer connected to the network) automatically downloads a copy of the blockchain.

    b.   A blockchain is primarily used to verify financial transactions within digital currencies (i.e., cryptocurrency transactions) though it is possible to digitize, code, and insert practically any document into the blockchain.

        1)   **Cryptocurrency** is a digital asset designed to work as a medium of exchange using cryptography (encryption) to secure the transactions, control the creation of additional units of the currency, and verify the transfer of funds.

    c.   The blockchain enables each coin owner to transfer an amount of currency directly to any other party connected to the same network without the need for a financial institution to mediate the exchange.

        1)   The blockchain is like a full history of a financial institution's transactions, and each block is like an individual bank statement.

Stop and review! You have completed the outline for this subunit. Study multiple-choice questions 1 through 3 on page 304.

13.2 NATURE OF BINARY DATA STORAGE

1.   **Binary Storage**

    a.   Digital computers store all information in binary format, that is, as a pattern of ones and zeros. This makes arithmetic operations and true/false decisions on the lowest level extremely straightforward.

    b.   A **bit** is either 0 or 1 (off or on) in binary code. Bits can be strung together to form a binary (i.e., base 2) number.

EXAMPLE of a Bit

0

---

    c.   A **byte** is a group of bits, most commonly eight. A byte can be used to signify a character (a number, letter of the alphabet, or symbol, such as a question mark or asterisk).

EXAMPLE of an 8-Bit Byte Representing the Capital Letter P

01010000

---

        1)   Quantities of bytes are measured with the following units:

$$1,024 \ (2^{10}) \text{ bytes} = \textbf{1 kilobyte} = 1 \text{ KB}$$
$$1,048,576 \ (2^{20}) \text{ bytes} = \textbf{1 megabyte} = 1 \text{ MB}$$
$$1,073,741,824 \ (2^{30}) \text{ bytes} = \textbf{1 gigabyte} = 1 \text{ GB}$$
$$1,099,511,627,776 \ (2^{40}) \text{ bytes} = \textbf{1 terabyte} = 1 \text{ TB}$$

Author's Note: Please do not memorize these numbers. The intent is to demonstrate the difference in size for each unit to help you better grasp these terms.

    d.   A **field**, also called a data item, is a group of bytes. The field contains a unit of data about some entity, e.g., a composer's name.

EXAMPLE of a Field

Paul Hindemith

---

e. A **record** is a group of fields. All the fields contain information pertaining to an entity, e.g., a specific performance of an orchestral work.

EXAMPLE of a Record				
Paul Hindemith	Violin Concerto	Chicago Symphony	Claudio Abbado	Josef Suk

1) Some field or combination of fields on each record is designated as the **key**. The criterion for a key is that it contains enough information to uniquely identify each record; i.e., there can be no two records with the same key.

    a) The designation of a key allows records to be sorted and managed with much greater efficiency. If all the records are sorted in the order of the key, searching for a particular one becomes much easier.

    b) In the previous example, the key is the combination of the first two fields.

        i) The first field alone is not enough because there could be several works by each composer. The second field alone is likewise not enough since there could be many pieces with the same title.

        ii) The combination of the composer's name and title uniquely identify each piece of music.

f. A **file** is a group of records. All the records in the file contain the same pieces of information about different occurrences, e.g., performances of several orchestral works.

EXAMPLE of a File				
Paul Hindemith	Violin Concerto	Chicago Symphony	Claudio Abbado	Josef Suk
Gustav Mahler	Das Lied von der Erde	New York Philharmonic	Leonard Bernstein	Dietrich Fischer-Dieskau
Bela Bartok	Piano Concerto No. 2	Chicago Symphony	Sir Georg Solti	Etsko Tazaki
Arnold Schoenberg	Gurrelieder	Boston Symphony	Seiji Ozawa	James McCracken
Leos Janacek	Sinfonietta	Los Angeles Philharmonic	Simon Rattle	None
Dmitri Shostakovich	Symphony No. 6	San Francisco Symphony	Kazuhiro Koizumi	None
Carl Orff	Carmina Burana	Berlin Radio Symphony	Eugen Jochum	Gundula Janowitz

Stop and review! You have completed the outline for this subunit. Study multiple-choice questions 4 through 6 beginning on page 304.

13.3 FILE ORGANIZATION AND DATABASES

1. **Flat Files**

    a. The oldest file structure is the flat file, in which all records are stored sequentially, one after the other, as on a reel of magnetic tape.

        1) To find a certain record, every record on the tape has to be searched and bypassed until the desired one is found.

        2) Also, the ways in which a user can perform a search on a flat file are extremely limited.

    b. As computers became more powerful, new ways of storing data became possible that permitted much more flexibility in searching and updating.

        1) Databases allow companies to save information (data) in one place instead of having hundreds of specific files with similar information.

2. **Hierarchical Databases**

    a. The hierarchical, or tree, database model was a major development in file organization. Instead of the records being strung out one after the other, they form "branches" and "leaves" extending from a "root."

        1) Note that the customer's address is stored only once in a hierarchical database; in a flat file, the address had to be stored every time the customer placed an order.

        2) Another feature of the tree file structure is that every "parent" record can have multiple "child" records, but each child can have only one parent.

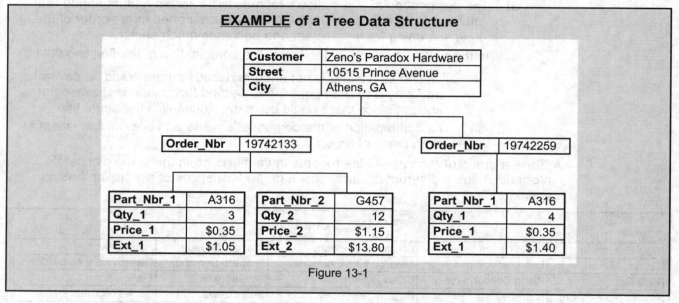

Figure 13-1

    b. One customer has many orders, but each order can only be assigned to one customer.

        1) The tree structure improves speed and storage efficiency for related data; for example, a parent record consisting of a customer may directly index the child records containing the customer's orders.

        2) However, adding new records is much more difficult than with a flat file. In a flat file, a new record is simply inserted whole in the proper place. In a tree structure, the relationships between the parent and child records must be maintained.

3. **Relational Databases**

    a. When a relational database is used, a file like the one depicted in the example on the next page is stored with every record in a single row and every column containing a value that pertains to that record.

        1) In database terminology, a file stored this way is called a table, and the columns are called attributes.

    b. Each data element is stored as few times as necessary. This reduction in data redundancy is accomplished through a process called **normalization**.

    c.   Two features that make the relational data structure stand out are cardinality and referential integrity.

        1) **Cardinality** refers to how close a given data element is to being unique.

            a) A data element that can only exist once in a given table has high cardinality. In Figure 13-2, Customer_Nbr has high cardinality in the Customer Table.

            b) A data element that is not unique in a given table but that has a restricted range of possible values is said to have normal cardinality. Order_Nbr in the Order Table is an example.

            c) A data element that has a very small range of values is said to have low cardinality. A field that can contain only male/female or true/false is an example.

        2) **Referential integrity** means that for a record to be entered in a given table, there must already be a record in some other table(s).

            a) For example, the Order Table in Figure 13-2 cannot contain a record where the part number is not already present in the Parts Table.

    d.   The tremendous advantage of a relational data structure is that searching for records is greatly facilitated.

        1) For example, a user can specify a customer and see all the parts that customer has ordered, or the user can specify a part and see all the customers who have ordered it. Such queries were extremely resource-intensive, if not impossible, under older data structures.

    e.   A group of tables built following the principles of relational data structures is referred to as a **relational database**.

        1) If the rules of cardinality, referential integrity, etc., are not enforced, a database will no longer be relational. To aid in the exceedingly challenging task of enforcing these rules, database management systems have been developed.

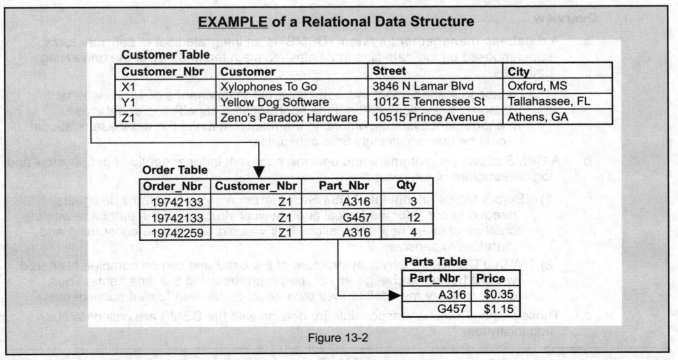

EXAMPLE of a Relational Data Structure

Customer Table

Customer_Nbr	Customer	Street	City
X1	Xylophones To Go	3846 N Lamar Blvd	Oxford, MS
Y1	Yellow Dog Software	1012 E Tennessee St	Tallahassee, FL
Z1	Zeno's Paradox Hardware	10515 Prince Avenue	Athens, GA

Order Table

Order_Nbr	Customer_Nbr	Part_Nbr	Qty
19742133	Z1	A316	3
19742133	Z1	G457	12
19742259	Z1	A316	4

Parts Table

Part_Nbr	Price
A316	$0.35
G457	$1.15

Figure 13-2

4. **Non-Relational Databases**

    a. Provide a mechanism for storage and retrieval of data other than the tabular relations used in relational databases.

        1) The data structures used by NoSQL databases do not require joining tables, which allow operations to run faster.

        2) They capture all kinds of data (e.g., structured, semi-structured, and unstructured data), which allows for a flexible database that can easily and quickly accommodate any new type of data and is not disrupted by content structure changes.

        3) They provide better "horizontal" scaling to clusters of machines, which solves the problem when the number of concurrent users skyrockets for applications that are accessible via the Web and mobile devices.

        4) Impedance mismatch between the object-oriented approach to write applications and the schema-based tables and rows of relational databases is eliminated. For instance, storing all information on one document in contrast to joining multiple tables together, resulting in less code to write, debug, and maintain.

5. **Object-Oriented Databases**

    a. An object-oriented database is a response to the need to store graphics and multimedia applications used by object-oriented programming languages such as C++ and Java.

        1) Translating this type of data into tables and rows is difficult. However, in an object-oriented database, the objects can be stored along with executable code that directs the behavior of the object.

Stop and review! You have completed the outline for this subunit. Study multiple-choice questions 7 through 9 beginning on page 305.

13.4 DATABASE MANAGEMENT SYSTEMS

1. **Overview**

    a. A **database management system** (DBMS) is an integrated set of software tools superimposed on the data files that helps maintain the integrity of the underlying database.

        1) Database management systems make the maintenance of vast relational databases practical. Without the sophisticated capabilities of database management systems, enforcing the rules that make the database relational would be overwhelmingly time-consuming.

    b. A DBMS allows programmers and designers to work independently of the physical and logical structure of the database.

        1) Before the development of DBMSs, programmers and systems designers needed to consider the logical and physical structure of the database with the creation of every new application. This was extremely time-consuming and therefore expensive.

        2) With a DBMS, the physical structure of the database can be completely altered without having to change any of the programs using the data items. Thus, different users may define their own views of the data (called subschemas).

    c. Those in the IT function responsible for dealing with the DBMS are called database administrators.

EXAMPLE

The three most prominent commercial relational database management systems are Oracle, IBM DB2, and Microsoft Access. A well-known open-source DBMS is MySQL.

2. **Aspects of a DBMS**

    a.   A particular database's design, called its **schema**, consists of the layouts of the tables and the constraints on entering new records. To a great extent, a DBMS automates the process of enforcing the schema.

    b.   Two vital parts of any DBMS are

        1)   A **data definition language**, which allows the user to specify how the tables will look and what kinds of data elements they will hold, and

        2)   A **data manipulation language**, with which the DBMS retrieves, adds, deletes, or modifies records and data elements.

            a)   Both of these roles are commonly fulfilled in the current generation of database management systems by Structured Query Language (SQL) or one of its many variants.

    c.   The **data dictionary** contains the physical and logical characteristics of every data element in a database. The data dictionary contains the size, format, usage, meaning, and ownership of every data element as well as what persons, programs, reports, and functions use the data element.

    d.   A DBMS can maintain a **distributed database**, meaning one that is stored in two or more physical sites.

        1)   In the **replication**, or **snapshot**, technique, the DBMS duplicates the entire database and sends it to multiple locations. Changes are periodically copied and similarly distributed.

        2)   In the **fragmentation**, or **partitioning**, method, specific records are stored where they are most needed. For example, a financial institution may store a particular customer's data at the branch where (s)he usually transacts his or her business. If the customer executes a transaction at another branch, the pertinent data are retrieved via communications lines.

Stop and review! You have completed the outline for this subunit. Study multiple-choice questions 10 through 12 beginning on page 306.

13.5 APPLICATION DEVELOPMENT AND MAINTENANCE

1. **Organizational Needs Assessment**

    a.   The organizational needs assessment is a detailed process of study and evaluation of how information systems can be deployed to help the organization meet its goals. The steps in the assessment are as follows:

        1)   Determine whether current systems support organizational goals

        2)   Determine needs unmet by current systems

        3)   Determine capacity of current systems to accommodate projected growth

        4)   Propose path for information systems deployment to achieve organizational goals within budgetary constraints

2. **Business Process Design**

    a.   A business process is a flow of actions performed on goods and/or information to accomplish a discrete objective.

        1)   Examples include hiring a new employee, recruiting a new customer, and filling a customer order.

    b.   Some business processes are contained entirely within a single functional area; e.g., hiring a new employee is performed by the human resources function.

        1)   Other processes cross functional boundaries. Filling a customer order requires the participation of the sales department, the warehouse, and accounts receivable.

c.   In the early days of automated system deployment, hardware and software were very expensive. Systems tended to be designed to serve a single process or even a single functional area. Tremendous gains in processing power and storage capacity have made integrated systems, i.e., those that combine multiple processes, the norm.

1)   The most advanced of these are enterprise resource planning (ERP) systems.

d.   The automation of a process, or the acquisition of an integrated system, presents the organization with an opportunity for business process reengineering.

1)   **Business process reengineering** involves a complete rethinking of how business functions are performed to provide value to customers, that is, radical innovation instead of mere improvement and a disregard for current jobs, hierarchies, and reporting relationships.

3.   **Participants in Business Process Design**

a.   The everyday functioning of a business process affects multiple stakeholder groups.

1)   Input from each group should be considered in the design of the process. However, some stakeholders will be more active participants.

b.   End-users are generally the drivers of a new or redesigned process.

1)   For example, the customers of a multi-division business may have open accounts with several of the divisions. Whenever a customer calls, the customer relations department would like the most up-to-date customer balance information for all divisions to be accessible at once.

2)   Although the motivation for the new process begins with the customer service department, personnel in various divisions as well as the central IT function will be affected.

c.   Because IT pervades every aspect of operations in a modern organization, the **IT steering committee** must study each request for a new process and either approve or deny it.

1)   Typical members of the steering committee include the chief information officer and the head of systems development from the IT function. Executive management from each division is also represented.

2)   The committee members have an understanding of the interactions of the organization's current systems and how they will affect and be affected by new or redesigned business processes.

d.   Once a new process or system has been approved, a project team is assembled, consisting of representatives of the end-users who requested it and the IT personnel who will design and build the software components that will support it.

e.   Upper management supports process design by making sufficient resources available to ensure successful implementation of the new process.

f.   If the new process or system crosses organizational boundaries, as is the case with electronic data interchange (EDI) systems, external parties, such as representatives of the vendor or customer businesses, are participants.

4.   **Build or Buy**

a.   When an organization acquires a new system by purchasing from an outside vendor, contract management personnel oversee the process. The future end-users of the system as well as IT personnel are also involved, drawing up specifications and requirements.

1)   However, when a new system is to be created in-house, planning and managing the development process is one of the IT function's most important tasks.

2)   The needs of the end-users must be balanced with budget and time constraints; the decision to use existing hardware vs. the purchase of new platforms must be weighed.

b.   Extensive time and resources are devoted to the creation of a new application, and generally, the more important the business function being automated, the more complex the application is. Thus, having a well-governed methodology for overseeing the development process is vital.

c.   Both the end-users who specified the new system's functionality and IT management who are overseeing the development process must approve progress toward the completion of the system at the end of each of the stages described below and on the following pages. This requirement for ongoing review and approval of the project is a type of implementation control.

5.   **Systems Development Life Cycle (SDLC)**

> The AICPA has asked many questions concerning the systems development life cycle (SDLC). One of their favorite questions asks candidates to select the correct phase to which an activity belongs. Be sure you know each of the phases and the activities that occur in each.

a.   The SDLC approach is the traditional methodology applied to the development of large, highly structured application systems. A major advantage of the life-cycle approach is enhanced management and control of the development process. SDLC consists of the following five steps:

1)   **Systems strategy**, which requires understanding the organization's needs.

2)   **Project initiation** is the process by which systems proposals are assessed.

3)   **In-house development** is generally chosen for unique information needs.

4)   **Commercial packages** are generally chosen for common needs rather than developing a new system from scratch.

5)   **Maintenance and support** involves ensuring the system accommodates changing user needs.

b.   Once the need for a new system has been recognized, the five steps (each with multiple steps) of the SDLC proceed as depicted in the diagram below (portions of the phases can overlap).

Systems Development Life Cycle

Figure 13-3

c.   Note that the feedback gathered during the maintenance of a system provides information for developing the next generation of systems, hence the name **life cycle**.

6.   The **phases and component steps of the traditional SDLC** can be described as follows:

a.   **Initiation, Feasibility, and Planning**

1)   The SDLC begins with recognizing there is a need for a new system, gaining an understanding of the situation to determine whether it is feasible to create a solution, and formulating a plan.

b.   **Requirements Analysis and Definition**

1)   A formal proposal for a new system is submitted to the IT steering committee, describing the need for the application and the business function(s) that it will affect.

2) Feasibility studies are conducted to determine

    a) What technology the new system will require

    b) What economic resources must be committed to the new system

    c) How the new system will affect current operations

3) The steering committee gives its go-ahead for the project.

c. **System Design**

1) Logical design consists of mapping the flow and storage of the data elements that will be used by the new system and the new program modules that will constitute the new system.

    a) Data flow diagrams and structured flowcharts are commonly used in this step.

    b) Some data elements may already be stored in existing databases. Good logical design ensures that they are not duplicated.

2) Physical design involves planning the specific interactions of the new program code and data elements with the hardware platform (existing or planned for purchase) on which the new system will operate.

    a) Systems analysts are heavily involved in these two steps.

d. **Build and Development**

1) The actual program code and database structures that will be used in the new system are written.

2) Hardware is acquired and physical infrastructure is assembled.

e. **Testing and Quality Control**

1) Testing is performed during system development with the intent of identifying errors or other defects. The job of testing is an iterative process because when one error is corrected, it can illuminate other errors or even create new ones. Testing determines whether the system

    a) Meets the requirements that guided its design and development.

    b) Responds correctly to all kinds of inputs.

    c) Performs its functions within an acceptable time.

    d) Achieves the general result its stakeholders desire.

2) Although the number of possible tests to apply is almost limitless, developers cannot test everything. All testing uses strategy to select tests that are feasible for the available time and resources.

    a) Combinatorial test design identifies the minimum number of tests needed to get the coverage developers want.

3) The following are various methods available to test systems:

    a) **Static testing** examines the program's code and its associated documentation through reviews, walkthroughs, or inspections but does not require the program to be executed.

    b) **Dynamic testing** involves executing programmed code with a given set of test cases.

    c) **White-box testing** tests internal structures or workings of a program, as opposed to the functionality exposed to the end-user.

    d) **Black-box testing** treats the software as a "black box," examining functionality without any knowledge of the source code.

    e) **Gray-box testing** involves having knowledge of internal data structures and algorithms for purposes of designing tests, while executing those tests at the user, or black-box, level.

4) There are four levels of tests:

    a) **Unit testing** refers to tests that verify (1) the functionality of a specific section of code and (2) the handling of data passed between various units or subsystems components.

    b) **Integration testing** is any type of software testing that seeks to verify the interfaces between components against a software design. Integration testing works to expose defects in the interfaces and interaction between integrated components (modules).

    c) **System testing**, or end-to-end testing, tests a completely integrated system to verify that the system meets its requirements.

    d) **Acceptance testing** is conducted to determine whether the systems meets the organization's needs and is ready for release.

f. **Acceptance, Installation, and Implementation**

1) User acceptance testing is the final step before placing the system in live operation.

    a) IT must demonstrate to the users that submitted the original request that the system performs the desired functionality.

    b) Once the users are satisfied with the new system, they acknowledge formal acceptance and implementation begins.

2) Four strategies for converting to the new system can be used.

    a) With **parallel** operation, the old and new systems both are run at full capacity for a given period.

        i) This strategy is the safest since the old system is still producing output (in case there are major problems with the new system), but it is also the most expensive and time-consuming.

    b) With **direct cutover** conversion, the old system is shut down and the new one takes over processing at once.

        i) This is the least expensive and time-consuming strategy, but it is also the riskiest.

    c) Under **pilot** conversion, one branch, department, or division at a time is fully converted to the new system.

        i) Experience gained from each installation is used to benefit the next one. One disadvantage of this strategy is the extension of the conversion time.

    d) In some cases, **phased** conversion is possible. Under this strategy, one function of the new system at a time is placed in operation.

        i) For instance, if the new system is an integrated accounting application, accounts receivable could be installed, then accounts payable, cash management, materials handling, etc.

        ii) The advantage of this strategy is allowing the users to learn one part of the system at a time.

3) Training and documentation are critical.

    a) The users must feel comfortable with the new system and have plenty of guidance available, either hard copy or online.

    b) Documentation consists of more than just operations manuals for the users. Layouts of the program code and database structures must also be available for the programmers who must modify and maintain the system.

    g.   **Operations and Maintenance**

        1)   After a system becomes operational, the system should be monitored to ensure ongoing performance and continuous improvement.

        2)   Systems follow-up or post-audit evaluation is a subsequent review of the efficiency and effectiveness of the system after it has operated for a substantial time (e.g., 1 year).

7.   **Program Change Control**

    a.   Over the life of an application, users are constantly asking for changes. The process of managing these changes is referred to as systems maintenance, and the relevant controls are called **program change controls**.

    b.   Once a change to a system has been approved, the programmer should save a copy of the production program in a test area of the computer, sometimes called a "sandbox."

        1)   Only in emergencies, and then only under close supervision, should a change be made directly to the production version of a computer program.

        2)   The IT function must be able to revert back to a prior version immediately if unexpected results are encountered during an emergency change.

    c.   The programmer makes the necessary changes to this copy of the program's source code.

    d.   The programmer transforms the changed program into a form that the computer can execute. The resulting machine-ready program is referred to as object code, or more precisely, executable code.

    e.   Once the programmer has the executable version of the changed program, (s)he tests it to see if it performs the new task as expected.

        1)   This testing process absolutely must not be run against production data. A special set of test data must be available for running test programs.

    f.   The programmer demonstrates the new functionality for the user who made the request.

        1)   Either the user accepts the new program or the programmer goes back and makes further changes.

    g.   Once the program is in a form acceptable to the user, the programmer moves it to a holding area.

        1)   Programmers (except in emergencies) should never be able to put programs directly into production.

    h.   The programmer's supervisor reviews the new program, approves it, and authorizes its move into production, which is generally carried out by operations personnel.

        1)   The compensating control is that operators generally lack the programming knowledge to put fraudulent code into production.

8.   **Rapid Application Development**

    a.   **Prototyping** is an alternative approach to application development. Prototyping involves creating a working model of the system requested, demonstrating it for the user, obtaining feedback, and making changes to the underlying code.

        1)   This process repeats through several iterations until the user is satisfied with the system's functionality.

        2)   Formerly, this approach was derided as being wasteful of resources and tending to produce unstable systems, but with vastly increased processing power and high-productivity development tools, prototyping can, in some cases, be an efficient means of systems development.

     b. **Computer-aided software engineering (CASE)** applies the computer to software design and development.

        1) It provides the capacity to (a) maintain on the computer all of the system documentation, e.g., data flow diagrams, data dictionaries, and pseudocode (structured English); (b) develop executable input and output screens; and (c) generate program code in at least skeletal form.

        2) Thus, CASE facilitates the creation, organization, and maintenance of documentation and permits some automation of the coding process.

9.   **End-User vs. Centralized Computing**

     a. End-user computing (EUC) involves user-created or user-acquired systems that are maintained and operated outside of traditional information systems controls.

        1) Certain environmental control risks are more likely in EUC. They include copyright violations that occur when unauthorized copies of software are made or when software is installed on multiple computers.

        2) Unauthorized access to application programs and related data is another concern. EUC lacks physical access controls, application-level controls, and other controls found in mainframe or networked environments.

        3) Moreover, EUC may not have adequate backup, recovery, and contingency planning. The result may be an inability to recreate the system or its data.

     b. Program development, documentation, and maintenance also may lack the centralized control found in larger systems.

        1) The risk of allowing end-users to develop their own applications is decentralization of control. These applications may not be reviewed by independent outside systems analysts and are not created using a formal development methodology. They also may not be subject to appropriate standards, controls, and quality assurance procedures.

        2) When end-users create their own applications and files, private information systems in which data are largely uncontrolled may proliferate. Systems may contain the same information, but EUC applications may update and define the data in different ways. Thus, determining the location of data and ensuring data consistency become more difficult.

        3) The auditor should determine that EUC applications contain controls that allow users to rely on the information produced. Identification of applications is more difficult than in a traditional centralized computing environment because few people know about and use them. There are three steps that the auditor should take:

           a) The first step is to discover their existence and their intended functions. One approach is to take an organization-wide inventory of major EUC applications. An alternative is for the auditors and the primary user (a function or department) to review major EUC applications.

           b) The second step is risk assessment. EUC applications that represent high-risk exposures are chosen for audit, for example, because they support critical decisions or are used to control cash or physical assets.

           c) The third step is to review the controls included in the applications chosen in the risk assessment.

     c. In a personal computer setting, the user is often the programmer and operator. Thus, the protections provided by segregation of duties are eliminated.

     d. The audit trail is diminished because of the lack of history files, incomplete printed output, etc.

     e. In general, available security features for stand-alone machines are limited compared with those in a network.

Stop and review! You have completed the outline for this subunit. Study multiple-choice questions 13 through 17 beginning on page 307.

13.6 CONTINGENCY PLANNING

1. **Overview**

   a. The information security goal of data availability is primarily the responsibility of the IT function.

   b. Contingency planning is the name commonly given to this activity.

      1) **Disaster recovery** is the process of resuming normal information processing operations after the occurrence of a major interruption.

      2) **Business continuity** is the continuation of business by other means during the period in which computer processing is unavailable or less than normal. **Business Continuity Management (BCM)** prepares the organization for IT failures through planning.

   c. Plans must be made for two major types of contingencies: those in which the data center is physically available and those in which it is not.

      1) Examples of the first type of contingency are (a) power failure; (b) random intrusions, such as viruses; and (c) deliberate intrusions, such as hacking incidents. The organization's physical facilities are sound, but immediate action is required to continue normal processing.

      2) The second type of contingency is much more serious. It is caused by disasters, such as floods, fires, hurricanes, or earthquakes. An occurrence of this type requires an alternate processing facility.

2. **Backup and Rotation**

   a. Periodic backup and offsite rotation of computer files is the most basic part of any disaster recovery or business continuity plan.

   b. An organization's data are more valuable than its hardware.

      1) Hardware can be replaced for a price, but each organization's data are unique and indispensable to operations. If they are destroyed, they cannot be replaced. For this reason, periodic backup and rotation are essential.

   c. A typical backup routine duplicates all data files and application programs. The frequency with which backups are created should depend on how often the data changes and the value of the data.

   d. The offsite location must be temperature- and humidity-controlled and guarded against physical intrusion. Just as important, it must be far enough away from the site of main operations not to be affected by the same natural disaster. Adequate backup is useless if the files are not accessible or have been destroyed.

3. **Risk Assessment Steps**

   a. Identify and prioritize the organization's critical applications.

      1) Not all of an organization's systems are equally important. The firm must decide which vital applications it simply cannot do business without and in what order they should be brought back into operation.

   b. Determine the minimum recovery time frames and minimum hardware requirements.

      1) How long will it take to reinstall each critical application, and what platform is required? If the interruption has been caused by an attack, such as a virus or hacker, how long will it take to isolate the problem and eliminate it from the system?

   c. Develop a recovery plan.

4. **Disaster Recovery Plan (DRP)**

   a. Disaster recovery is the process of regaining access to data (e.g., hardware, software, and records), communications, work areas, and other business processes.

   b. Thus, a DRP that is established and tested must be developed in connection with the business continuity plan. It should describe IT recovery strategies, including details about procedures, vendors, and systems.

      1) Detailed procedures must be updated when systems and business processes change. The following are examples of items addressed by the DRP:

         a) Data center
         b) Applications and data needed
         c) Servers and other hardware
         d) Communications
         e) Network connections
         f) IT infrastructure (e.g., log-on services and software distribution)
         g) Remote access services
         h) Process control systems
         i) File rooms
         j) Document management systems

   c. The following are considerations for choosing DRP strategies:

      1) The DRP should be based on the business impact analysis.
      2) The recovery abilities of critical service providers must be assessed.
      3) The recovery of IT components often must be combined to recover a system.
      4) Service providers (internal and external) must furnish recovery information, such as their (a) responsibilities, (b) limitations, (c) recovery activities, (d) recovery time and point objectives, and (e) costs.
      5) Strategies for components may be developed independently. The objective is the best, most cost-effective solution that (a) allows user access and (b) permits components to work together, regardless of where systems are recovered.
      6) Security and compliance standards must be considered.

5. **Contingencies with Data Center Available**

   a. The purchase of backup electrical generators protects against power failures. These can be programmed to begin running automatically as soon as a dip in electric current is detected. This practice is widespread in settings such as hospitals, where 24-hour availability is crucial.

   b. Attacks such as viruses and denial-of-service require a completely different response. The system must be brought down "gracefully" to halt the spread of the infection. The IT staff must be well trained in the nature of the latest virus threats to know how to isolate the damage and bring the system back to full operation.

6. **Contingencies with Data Center Unavailable**

   a. The most extreme contingency is a disaster that makes the organization's main facility uninhabitable. To prepare for these cases, organizations contract for alternate processing facilities.

   b. An **alternate processing facility** is a physical location maintained by an outside contractor for the purpose of providing processing facilities for customers in case of disaster.

      1) The recovery center, like the off-site storage location for backup files, must be far enough away from the main facility that it is not affected by the same natural disaster. Usually, organizations contract for backup facilities in another city.

      2) Once processing is no longer possible at the principal site, the backup files are retrieved from the secure storage location and taken to the recovery center.

    c.   Recovery centers include hot sites, warm sites, and cold sites. Organizations determine which facility is best by calculating the tradeoff between the cost of the contract and the cost of downtime.

        1) A **hot site** is a fully operational processing facility that is immediately available. The organization generally contracts with a service provider.

            a) For a fee, the service provider agrees to have a hardware platform and communications lines substantially identical to the organization's ready for use 24 hours a day, 365 days a year.

            b) This solution is the least risky and most expensive.

            c) Any contract for a hot site must include a provision for periodic testing.

               i) The service provider agrees to a window of time in which the organization can declare a fake disaster, load its backup files onto the equipment at the hot site, and determine how long it takes to resume normal processing.

        2) A **cold site** is a shell facility with sufficient electrical power, environmental controls, and communications lines to permit the organization to install its own newly acquired equipment.

            a) On an ongoing basis, this solution is much less expensive.

            b) However, the time to procure replacement equipment can be weeks or months. Also, emergency procurement from equipment vendors can be very expensive.

        3) A **warm site** is a compromise between a cold and hot site, combining features of both.

            a) Resources are available at the site but may need to be configured to support the production system.

            b) Some data may need to be restored.

            c) Typical recovery time may range from several days to a week.

7. **Other Technologies for Restoration of Processing**

    a.   Fault-tolerant computer systems (formerly called fail-soft systems) have additional hardware and software as well as a backup power supply. A fault-tolerant computer has additional processing capability and disk storage. This technology is used for mission-critical applications that cannot afford to suffer downtime.

        1) The technology that permits fault tolerance is the redundant array of inexpensive (or independent) disks, or RAID. It is a group of multiple hard drives with special software that allows for data delivery along multiple paths. If one drive fails, the other disks can compensate for the loss.

    b.   High-availability computing is used for less critical applications because it provides for a short recovery time rather than the elimination of recovery time.

8. **Elements of BCM**

    a. **Management Support**

        1) Management must assign adequate resources to preparing, maintaining, and practicing a business continuity plan.

    b. **Risk Assessment and Mitigation**

        1) The entity must (a) define credible risk events (threats), (b) assess their effects, and (c) develop risk mitigation strategies.

c. **Business Impact Analysis**

1) This analysis identifies business processes necessary to functioning in a disaster and determines how soon they should be recovered.

2) The organization (a) identifies critical processes, (b) defines the recovery time objective and the recovery point objective for processes and resources, and (c) identifies the other parties (e.g., vendors and other divisions of the organization) and physical resources (e.g., critical equipment and records) needed for recovery.

   a) A recovery time objective is the duration of time and service level within which a process must be restored. A recovery point objective is the amount of data the organization can afford to lose.

   b) The cost of a recovery solution ordinarily increases as either objective decreases.

d. **Business Recovery and Continuity Strategy**

1) A crucial element of business recovery is the existence of a comprehensive and current disaster recovery plan, which addresses the actual steps, people, and resources required to recover a critical business process. (Disaster recovery plans were discussed in greater detail earlier.)

2) The organization plans for

   a) **Alternative staffing** (e.g., staff remaining at the site, staff at another site, or staff of another organization),

   b) **Alternative sourcing** (e.g., use of nonstandard products and services, use of diverse suppliers, outsourcing to organizations that provide standard services, or reciprocal agreements with competitors),

   c) **Alternative work spaces** (e.g., another organization facility, remote access with proper security, or a commercial recovery site), and

   d) The **return to normal operations** (e.g., entry of manually processed data, resolution of regulatory and financial exceptions, return of borrowed equipment, and replenishment of products and supplies).

e. **Awareness, Exercises, and Maintenance**

1) Education and awareness (including training exercises) are vital to BCM and execution of the business continuity plan.

2) The BCM capabilities and documentation must be maintained to ensure that they remain effective and aligned with business priorities.

Stop and review! You have completed the outline for this subunit. Study multiple-choice questions 18 through 20 on page 309.

QUESTIONS

13.1 Software

1. Fourth-generation computer programming languages are represented by

A. Procedure-oriented languages, which describe processing procedures.

B. Query languages, which allow direct access to a computer database.

C. Symbolic languages, which allow direct access to a stored database.

D. Machine languages, which describe processing procedures.

Answer (B) is correct.

REQUIRED: The fourth-generation computer programming languages.

DISCUSSION: Fourth-generation languages are intended to simplify programming. They are not intended to express a procedure as a specific algorithm. These interactive, English-like languages permit the user to describe the problem to and receive guidance from the computer. Query languages are most often used with databases. They permit reading and reorganization of data but not its alteration.

Answer (A) is incorrect. Procedure-oriented languages are third-generation languages that require translation into multiple machine-level instructions. Fourth-generation languages are nonprocedural languages. Answer (C) is incorrect. Symbolic languages are second-generation languages. Answer (D) is incorrect. Machine (first-generation) languages are far from the fourth-generation software development stage.

2. XML

A. Is focused on the content of the data.

B. Has become less important as new languages on the Internet are developed.

C. Uses standardized tags.

D. Is useful to display highly unstructured data.

Answer (A) is correct.

REQUIRED: The true statement about XML.

DISCUSSION: XML (eXtensible Markup Language) is useful for putting structured data into a text file. It can be used to extract and tag structured information from a database for transmission and subsequent use in other applications, e.g., display on the Internet or importation into a spreadsheet.

Answer (B) is incorrect. XML has become very popular for use on the Internet. Information tagged in XML can be integrated into HTML and other presentations. Answer (C) is incorrect. XML is very flexible and allows the user to design customized (extensible) tags. Answer (D) is incorrect. The data must conform to a structure to be properly tagged.

3. A computer program processes payrolls. The program is a(n)

A. Operating system.

B. Application program.

C. Report generator.

D. Utility program.

Answer (B) is correct.

REQUIRED: The term associated with a computer program used to perform a business function.

DISCUSSION: Application programs are written to solve specific user problems; that is, they perform the ultimate computer functions required by system users. Thus, a program designed to process payroll is an application program.

Answer (A) is incorrect. An operating system is a set of programs used by the CPU to control operations. Answer (C) is incorrect. A report generator is a component of a database management system that produces customized reports using data stored in the database. Answer (D) is incorrect. Utility programs are standardized subroutines that can be incorporated into other programs.

13.2 Nature of Binary Data Storage

4. Computers understand codes that represent letters of the alphabet, numbers, or special characters. These codes require that data be converted into predefined groups of binary digits. Such chains of digits are referred to as

A. Registers.

B. ASCII code.

C. Input.

D. Bytes.

Answer (D) is correct.

REQUIRED: The term for the chains of digits that a computer is capable of understanding.

DISCUSSION: A byte is a grouping of bits that can define one unit of data, such as a letter or an integer.

Answer (A) is incorrect. A register is a location within the CPU where data and instructions are temporarily stored. Answer (B) is incorrect. ASCII (American Standard Code for Information Interchange) is the coding convention itself. Answer (C) is incorrect. Input is the data placed into processing (noun) or the act of placing the data into processing (verb).

5. Based only on the database file excerpt presented below, which one of the fields or combinations of fields is eligible for use as a key?

Column I	Column II	Column III	Column IV	Column V	Column VI
Florida	Sopchoppy	G9441	6	02/06/2017	$1823.65
Georgia	Hahira	H5277	2	02/06/2017	$412.01
Iowa	Clear Lake	B2021	1	02/06/2017	$6606.53
Iowa	Clear Lake	C2021	14	02/06/2017	$178.90
Kansas	Lawrence	A1714	2	02/06/2017	$444.28
Georgia	Milledgeville	A1713	1	02/06/2017	$195.60

- A. Column I and Column II in combination.
- B. Column I and Column V in combination.
- C. Column III alone.
- D. Column IV and Column V in combination.

Answer (C) is correct.
REQUIRED: The field or combination thereof that could be used as a key.
DISCUSSION: Some field or combination of fields on each record is designated as the key. The essence of a key is that it contains enough information to uniquely identify each record; i.e., there can be no two records with the same key. Of the choices presented, only Column III by itself uniquely identifies each record.
Answer (A) is incorrect. Column I and Column II in combination do not uniquely identify each record. Answer (B) is incorrect. Column I and Column V in combination do not uniquely identify each record. Answer (D) is incorrect. Column IV and Column V in combination do not uniquely identify each record.

6. Which one of the following correctly depicts the hierarchy of storage commonly found in computerized databases, from least complex to most complex?

- A. Byte, field, file, record.
- B. Byte, field, record, file.
- C. Field, byte, record, file.
- D. Field, byte, file, record.

Answer (B) is correct.
REQUIRED: The correct hierarchy in computerized databases.
DISCUSSION: A byte is a group of bits (binary 1s and 0s). A field is a group of bytes. A record is a group of fields. A file is a group of records.
Answer (A) is incorrect. A record is less complex than a file. Answer (C) is incorrect. A byte is less complex than a field. Answer (D) is incorrect. A byte is less complex than a field, and a record is less complex than a file.

13.3 File Organization and Databases

7. Of the following, the greatest advantage of a database (server) architecture is that

- A. Data redundancy can be reduced.
- B. Conversion to a database system is inexpensive and can be accomplished quickly.
- C. Multiple occurrences of data items are useful for consistency checking.
- D. Backup and recovery procedures are minimized.

Answer (A) is correct.
REQUIRED: The greatest advantage of a database architecture.
DISCUSSION: Data organized in files and used by the organization's various application programs are collectively known as a database. In a database system, storage structures are created that render the applications programs independent of the physical or logical arrangement of the data. Each data item has a standard definition, name, and format, and related items are linked by a system of pointers. The programs therefore need only specify data items by name, not by location. A database management system handles retrieval and storage. Because separate files for different application programs are unnecessary, data redundancy can be substantially reduced.
Answer (B) is incorrect. Conversion to a database is often costly and time-consuming. Answer (C) is incorrect. A traditional flat-file system, not a database, has multiple occurrences of data items. Answer (D) is incorrect. Given the absence of data redundancy and the quick propagation of data errors throughout applications, backup and recovery procedures are just as critical in a database as in a flat-file system.

8. A database is

A. Essential for the storage of large data sets.

B. A collection of related files.

C. A real-time system.

D. A network of computer terminals.

Answer (B) is correct.
    REQUIRED: The true statement about a database.
    DISCUSSION: The use of a database system significantly reduces redundancy of stored data in a system. Data in a standardized form are ideally entered once into integrated files and then used for any and all related applications. The database is usually built to serve multiple applications. Consequently, the data are independent of particular applications and greater flexibility in meeting unanticipated demands is possible. The database approach also allows for better access by users and for more rapid updating of information.
    Answer (A) is incorrect. The need for a database arises more from the multiplicity of applications than from the quantity of data stored. Answer (C) is incorrect. A database system need not provide immediate (real-time) responses. Answer (D) is incorrect. A database is an integrated, centralized group of files.

9. A database has three record types: (1) for suppliers, a type that contains a unique supplier number, a supplier name, and a supplier address; (2) for parts, a type that contains a unique part number, a part name, a description, and a location; and (3) for purchases, a type that contains a unique supplier number referencing the supplier number in the supplier record, a part number referencing the part number in the part record, and a quantity. This database has a

A. Single flat-file structure.

B. Hierarchical structure.

C. Relational structure.

D. Network structure.

Answer (C) is correct.
    REQUIRED: The structure of the described database.
    DISCUSSION: A relational structure organizes data in conceptual tables. One relation (a table or file) can be joined with (related to) another by the DBMS without pointers or linked lists if each contains one or more of the same fields (also known as columns or attributes). This database has a relational structure because it includes no links that are not contained in the data records themselves.
    Answer (A) is incorrect. Each record type corresponds to a flat file, but there are multiple structures rather than a single flat-file structure. Answer (B) is incorrect. A hierarchical structure would have a tree structure with embedded links instead of explicit data values. Answer (D) is incorrect. A network structure would have bidirectional pointers instead of explicit data values.

13.4 Database Management Systems

10. One advantage of a database management system (DBMS) is

A. Each organizational unit takes responsibility and control for its own data.

B. The cost of the data processing department decreases as users are now responsible for establishing their own data handling techniques.

C. A decreased vulnerability as the database management system has numerous security controls to prevent disasters.

D. The independence of the data from the application programs, which allows the programs to be developed for the user's specific needs without concern for data capture problems.

Answer (D) is correct.
    REQUIRED: The advantage of a DBMS.
    DISCUSSION: A fundamental characteristic of databases is that applications are independent of the database structure; when writing programs or designing applications to use the database, only the name of the desired item is necessary. Programs can be developed for the user's specific needs without concern for data capture problems. Reference can be made to the items using the data manipulation language, after which the DBMS takes care of locating and retrieving the desired items. The physical or logical structure of the database can be completely altered without having to change any of the programs using the data items. Only the schema requires alteration.
    Answer (A) is incorrect. Each organizational unit develops programs to use the elements of a broad database. Answer (B) is incorrect. Data handling techniques are still the responsibility of the data processing department. It is the use of the data that is departmentalized. Answer (C) is incorrect. The DBMS is not necessarily safer than any other database system.

11. Which of the following is a **false** statement about a database management system application environment?

A. Data are used concurrently by multiple users.

B. Data are shared by passing files between programs or systems.

C. The physical structure of the data is independent of user needs.

D. Data definition is independent of any one program.

Answer (B) is correct.

REQUIRED: The false statement about data in a DBMS environment.

DISCUSSION: In this kind of system, applications use the same database. There is no need to pass files between applications.

Answer (A) is incorrect. The advantage of a DBMS is that data can be used concurrently by multiple users. Answer (C) is incorrect. When a DBMS is used, the physical structure of the data is independent of user needs. Answer (D) is incorrect. When a DBMS is used, the data are defined independently of the needs of any one program.

12. The function of a data dictionary is to

A. Mark the boundary between two consecutive transactions.

B. Describe and share information about objects and resources.

C. Specify systems users.

D. Specify privileges and security rules for objects and resources.

Answer (B) is correct.

REQUIRED: The function of a data dictionary.

DISCUSSION: A data dictionary is an organized and shared collection of information about the objects and resources used by the information system (IS) organization to deliver or exchange information internally and externally.

Answer (A) is incorrect. The database management system log contains checkpoint records that mark the boundary between two consecutive transactions. Answer (C) is incorrect. Specification of system users is a function of the security features of a DBMS. Answer (D) is incorrect. The data control language specifies privileges and security rules for objects and resources.

13.5 Application Development and Maintenance

13. An insurance firm that follows the systems development life cycle concept for all major information system projects is preparing to start a feasibility study for a proposed underwriting system. Some of the primary factors the feasibility study should include are

A. Possible vendors for the system and their reputation for quality.

B. Exposure to computer viruses and other intrusions.

C. Methods of implementation, such as parallel or cutover.

D. Technology and related costs.

Answer (D) is correct.

REQUIRED: The primary factors the feasibility study should include.

DISCUSSION: The feasibility study should consider the activity to be automated, the needs of the user, the type of equipment required, the cost, and the potential benefit to the specific area and the company in general. Thus, technical feasibility and cost are determined during this stage.

Answer (A) is incorrect. Possible vendors for the system and their reputation for quality would be determined after the feasibility study. Answer (B) is incorrect. Exposure to computer viruses and other intrusions is part of the information requirements phase. Answer (C) is incorrect. Methods of implementation, such as parallel or cutover, would be determined during the implementation and operations stage.

14. Two phases of systems planning are project definition and project initiation. All of the following are steps in the project initiation phase **except**

A. Preparing the project proposal.

B. Informing managers and employees of the project.

C. Assembling the project team.

D. Training selected personnel.

Answer (A) is correct.

REQUIRED: The step not a part of the project initiation phase of systems planning.

DISCUSSION: The project initiation phase includes promptly informing managers and employees about the project, assembling the project team (possibly including systems analysts, programmers, accountants, and users), training selected personnel to improve necessary skills and enhance communication among team members, and establishing project controls (e.g., by implementing a project scheduling technique such as PERT). Preparing the project proposal is a part of the project definition phase, as are conducting feasibility studies, determining project priority, and submitting the proposal for approval.

Answer (B) is incorrect. Informing managers and employees of the project is a component of the project initiation phase. Answer (C) is incorrect. Assembling the project team is a component of the project initiation phase. Answer (D) is incorrect. Training selected personnel is a component of the project initiation phase.

15. The process of learning how the current system functions, determining the needs of users, and developing the logical requirements of a proposed system is referred to as

    A. Systems maintenance.

    B. Systems analysis.

    C. Systems feasibility study.

    D. Systems design.

Answer (B) is correct.

REQUIRED: The term referring to the process of learning how a system functions, determining the needs of users, and developing the logical requirements of a proposed system.

DISCUSSION: A systems analysis requires a survey of the existing system, the organization itself, and the organization's environment to determine (among other things) whether a new system is needed. The survey results determine not only what, where, how, and by whom activities are performed but also why, how well, and whether they should be done at all. Ascertaining the problems and informational needs of decision makers is the next step. The systems analyst must consider the entity's key success variables (factors that determine its success or failure), the decisions currently being made and those that should be made, the factors important in decision making (timing, relation to other decisions, etc.), the information needed for decisions, and how well the current system makes those decisions. Finally, the systems analysis should establish the requirements of a system that will meet user needs.

Answer (A) is incorrect. Maintenance is the final stage of the life cycle in that it continues throughout the life of the system; maintenance includes the redesign of the system and programs to meet new needs or to correct design flaws. Answer (C) is incorrect. The systems feasibility study does not involve the process of learning how the current system works. Answer (D) is incorrect. Systems design is the process of developing a system to meet specified requirements.

16. The process of monitoring, evaluating, and modifying a system as needed is referred to as

    A. Systems analysis.

    B. Systems feasibility study.

    C. Systems maintenance.

    D. Systems implementation.

Answer (C) is correct.

REQUIRED: The term for the process of monitoring, evaluating, and modifying a system.

DISCUSSION: Systems maintenance must be undertaken by systems analysts and applications programmers continuously throughout the life of a system. Maintenance is the redesign of the system and programs to meet new needs or to correct design flaws. Ideally, these changes should be made as part of a regular program of preventive maintenance.

Answer (A) is incorrect. Systems analysis is the process of determining user problems and needs, surveying the organization's present system, and analyzing the facts. Answer (B) is incorrect. A feasibility study determines whether a proposed system is technically, operationally, and economically feasible. Answer (D) is incorrect. Systems implementation involves training and educating system users, testing, conversion, and follow-up.

17. A benefit of using computer-aided software engineering (CASE) technology is that it can ensure that

    A. No obsolete data fields occur in files.

    B. Users become committed to new systems.

    C. All programs are optimized for efficiency.

    D. Data integrity rules are applied consistently.

Answer (D) is correct.

REQUIRED: The benefit of CASE.

DISCUSSION: CASE is an automated technology (at least in part) for developing and maintaining software and managing projects. A benefit of using CASE technology is that it can ensure that data integrity rules, including those for validation and access, are applied consistently across all files.

Answer (A) is incorrect. Obsolete data fields must be recognized by developers or users. Once recognized, obsolete data fields can be treated consistently in CASE procedures. Answer (B) is incorrect. Using CASE will not ensure user commitment to new systems if they are poorly designed or otherwise do not meet users' needs. Answer (C) is incorrect. Although it has the potential to accelerate system development, CASE cannot ensure that all programs are optimized for efficiency. In fact, some CASE-developed modules may need to be optimized by hand to achieve acceptable performance.

13.6 Contingency Planning

18. Which of the following best describes the primary reason that organizations develop contingency plans for their computer-based information systems operations?

A. To ensure that they will be able to process vital transactions in the event of a disaster.

B. To ensure the safety of important records.

C. To help hold down the cost of insurance.

D. To plan for sources of capital for recovery from any type of disaster.

Answer (A) is correct.
REQUIRED: The primary reason that organizations develop contingency plans for their IS operations.
DISCUSSION: Contingency plans must be drafted so that the organization will be able to resume normal processing following a disaster.
Answer (B) is incorrect. The safety of records is a secondary reason. Answer (C) is incorrect. The reduction of insurance costs is a secondary reason. Answer (D) is incorrect. Planning for sources of capital is seldom included in disaster recovery planning.

19. Which of the following procedures would an entity most likely include in its computer disaster recovery plan?

A. Develop an auxiliary power supply to provide uninterrupted electricity.

B. Store duplicate copies of critical files in a location away from the processing facility.

C. Maintain a listing of all entity passwords with the network manager.

D. Translate data for storage purposes with a cryptographic secret code.

Answer (B) is correct.
REQUIRED: The most likely procedure to follow in a computer disaster recovery plan.
DISCUSSION: Off-site storage of duplicate copies of critical files protects them from a fire or other disaster at the computing facility. The procedure is part of an overall disaster recovery plan.
Answer (A) is incorrect. The use of an uninterruptible power supply ensures continued processing rather than recovery from a disaster. Answer (C) is incorrect. Maintaining a safeguarded copy of passwords protects against loss of passwords by personnel. Answer (D) is incorrect. Encrypting stored data files protects them from unauthorized use.

20. If High Tech Corporation's disaster recovery plan requires fast recovery with little or no downtime, which of the following backup sites should it choose?

A. Hot site.

B. Warm site.

C. Cold site.

D. Quick site.

Answer (A) is correct.
REQUIRED: The type of backup facility that has fast recovery and little or no downtime.
DISCUSSION: A company uses a hot site backup when fast recovery is critical. The hot site includes all software, hardware, and other equipment necessary for a company to carry out operations. Hot sites are expensive to maintain and may be shared with other organizations with similar needs.
Answer (B) is incorrect. A warm site provides an intermediate level of backup and causes more downtime than a hot site. Answer (C) is incorrect. A cold site is a shell facility suitable for quick installation of computer equipment. Disaster recovery would take more time in a cold site than a hot site. Answer (D) is incorrect. There is no backup site called a quick site.

STUDY UNIT FOURTEEN
IT NETWORKS AND ELECTRONIC COMMERCE

(14 pages of outline)

Huge gains in productivity have resulted from the networking of computers. The traditional ways of carrying on business have found new channels through electronic networking. Now, the use of encryption is required to make messages sent electronically secure. As a licensed CPA, you will need to know how computers communicate over networks so you can ascertain their vulnerability. This study unit introduces you to the types of communications between computers. The next study unit focuses on how to assess and quantify information risks.

14.1 NETWORKS AND THE INTERNET

1. **Mainframe Communication**

    a. Large mainframe computers dominated the electronic data processing field in its first decades. Mainframes were arranged so that all processing and data storage were done in a single, centralized location.

    b. Communication with the mainframe was accomplished with the use of dumb terminals, simple keyboard-and-monitor combinations with no processing power (i.e., no CPU) of their own.

2. **Increasing Decentralization**

    a. Improvements in technology have led to the increasing decentralization of information processing.

    1) The mainframe-style computer was the only arrangement available in the early days of data processing. International Business Machines (IBM) dominated the marketplace.

    2) Mainframes are still in use at large institutions, such as governments, banks, insurance companies, and universities. However, remote connections to them are usually through personal computers rather than through dumb terminals. This is known as terminal emulation.

    3) As minicomputers evolved, the concept of distributed processing arose.

        a) **Distributed processing** involves the decentralization of processing tasks and data storage and assigning these functions to multiple computers, often in separate locations.

        b) This allowed for a drastic reduction in the amount of communications traffic because data needed locally could reside locally.

    b. During the 1980s, personal computers and the knowledge needed to build information systems became widespread.

    1) In the early part of this period, the primary means of moving data from one computer to another was through the laborious process of copying the data to a diskette and physically carrying it to the destination computer.

    2) It was clear that a reliable way of wiring office computers together would lead to tremendous gains in productivity.

3. Local Area Networks (LANs)

a. The need to increase productivity led to the development of the local area network (LAN). A LAN is any interconnection between devices in a single office or building.

    1) Very small networks with few devices can be connected using a peer-to-peer arrangement, where every device is connected directly to every other. Peer-to-peer networks become increasingly difficult to administer with each added device.

b. The most cost-effective and easy-to-administer arrangement for LANs uses the client-server model.

    1) Client-server networks differ from peer-to-peer networks in that the devices play more specialized roles. Client processes (initiated by the individual user) request services from server processes (maintained centrally).

    2) In a client-server arrangement, servers are centrally located and devoted to the functions that are needed by all network users.

        a) Examples include mail servers (to handle electronic mail), application servers (to run application programs), file servers (to store databases and make user inquiries more efficient), Internet servers (to manage access to the Internet), and web servers (to host websites).

        b) Whether a device is classified as a server is not determined by its hardware configuration, but rather by the function it performs. A simple personal computer can be a server.

    3) Technically, a client is any object that uses the resources of another object. Thus, a client can be either a device or a software program.

        a) In common usage, however, "client" refers to a device that requests services from a server. This understanding of the term encompasses anything from a powerful graphics workstation to a personal mobile device.

        b) A client device normally displays the user interface and enables data entry, queries, and the receipt of reports. Moreover, many applications, e.g., word processing and spreadsheet software, run on the client computer.

    4) The key to the client-server model is that it runs processes on the platform most appropriate to that process while attempting to minimize traffic over the network.

        a) This is commonly referred to as the three-tiered architecture of **client**, **application**, and **database**.

        b) Because of the specialized roles, client-server systems are often assembled with equipment from multiple vendors.

    5) Security for client-server systems may be more difficult than in a highly centralized system because of the numerous access points.

c. Along with the increased convenience and flexibility of decentralization came new security risks.

    1) Unauthorized software can be easily installed on the network from a desktop computer. This exposes the organization to both viruses and liability for copyright violation.

    2) Important files stored on a local computer may not be backed up properly by the user.

    3) Applications written by users of local computers may not adhere to the standards of the organization, making data sharing difficult.

4. **Classifying Networks by Geographical Extent and Function**

    a. The range of networking has expanded from the earliest form (two computers in the same room) to the global reach of the Internet.

    b. A **local area network (LAN)** connects devices within a single office or home or among buildings in an office park. The key aspect here is that a LAN is owned entirely by a single organization.

        1) The LAN is the network familiar to office workers all over the world. In its simplest conception, it can consist of a few personal computers and a printer.

    c. A **wide area network (WAN)** consists of a conglomerate of LANs over widely separated locations. The key aspect here is that a WAN can be either publicly or privately owned.

        1) One advantage of a WAN is the possibility of spreading the cost of ownership among multiple organizations.

            a) WANs come in many configurations. In its simplest conception, it can consist of a lone personal computer using a slow dial-up line to connect to an Internet service provider.

        2) Publicly owned WANs, such as the public telephone system and the Internet, are available to any user with a compatible device. The assets of these networks are paid for by means other than individually imposed user fees.

            a) Public-switched networks use public telephone lines to carry data. This arrangement is economical, but the quality of data transmission cannot be guaranteed and security is highly questionable.

        3) Privately owned WANs are profit-making enterprises. They offer fast, secure data communication services to organizations that do not wish to make their own large investments in the necessary infrastructure.

            a) **Value-added networks (VANs)** are private networks that provide their customers with reliable, high-speed secure transmission of data.

                i) To compete with the Internet, these third-party networks add value by providing their customers with error detection and correction services, electronic mailbox facilities for electronic data interchange (EDI) purposes, EDI translation, and security for email and data transmissions.

            b) **Virtual private networks (VPNs)** emerged as a relatively inexpensive way to solve the problem of the high cost of leased lines.

                i) A company connects each office or LAN to a local Internet service provider and routes data through the shared, low-cost public Internet.

                ii) The success of VPNs depends on the development of secure encryption products that protect data while in transit.

        4) Intranets and extranets are types of WANs.

            a) An **intranet** permits sharing of information throughout an organization by applying Internet connectivity standards and Web software (e.g., browsers) to the organization's internal network.

                i) An intranet addresses the connectivity problems faced by organizations that have many types of computers. Its use is restricted to those within the organization.

            b) An **extranet** consists of the linked intranets of two or more organizations, for example, of a supplier and its customers. It typically uses the public Internet as its transmission medium but requires a password for access.

5.   **The Internet**

   a.   The Internet is a network of networks all over the world.

Background

The Internet is descended from the original ARPANet, a product of the Defense Department's Advanced Research Projects Agency (ARPA), introduced in 1969. The idea was to have a network that could not be brought down during an enemy attack by bombing a single central location. ARPANet connected computers at universities, corporations, and government. In view of the growing success of the Internet, ARPANet was retired in 1990.

---

   b.   The Internet facilitates inexpensive communication and information transfer among computers, with gateways allowing servers to interface with personal computers.

   1)   Very high-speed Internet connections (termed the Internet backbone) carry signals around the world and meet at network access points.

   c.   Most Internet users obtain connections through **Internet service providers** (ISPs) that in turn connect either directly to a gateway or to a larger ISP with a connection to a gateway.

   1)   The topology of the backbone and its interconnections may once have resembled a spine with ribs connected along its length, but it is now more like a fishing net wrapped around the world with many circular paths.

   d.   TCP/IP (Transmission Control Protocol/Internet Protocol) is a term candidates should be familiar with. It is defined as a suite of communications protocols (rules or standards) used to connect computers to the Internet. It is also built into network operating systems.

6.   **Aspects and Terminology of the Internet**

   a.   The Internet was initially restricted to email and text-only documents. **Hypertext markup language** (HTML) allows users to click on a word or phrase (a hyperlink) on their screens and have another document automatically be displayed.

   b.   **Hypertext transfer protocol** (HTTP) allows hyperlinking across the Internet rather than on just a single computer. A browser allows users to read HTML from any brand of computer. This system became known as the World Wide Web (often simply called "the Web").

   1)   As the use of HTML and its successor languages spread, it became possible to display rich graphics and stream audio and video in addition to text.

   2)   **Extensible markup language** (XML) was developed by an international consortium and released in 1998 as an open standard (e.g., not owned or controlled by any one entity) usable with many programs and platforms.

   a)   XML codes all information in such a way that a user can determine not only how it should be presented but also what it is; i.e., all computerized data may be tagged with identifiers.

   b)   Unlike HTML, XML uses extensible codes. Thus, if an industry can agree on a set of codes, software for the industry can be written that incorporates those codes.

   c.   Every resource on the Web has a unique address, made up of alphanumeric characters, periods, and forward slashes, called a **uniform resource locator** (URL). A URL is recognizable by any web-enabled device. An example is https://www.gleim.com/.

   1)   However, just because the address is recognizable does not mean its content is accessible to every user. Security is a major feature of any organization's website.

7. **Cloud Computing**

   a. Cloud computing ("the cloud") is a popular term relating to on-demand access to resources that are accessed on the Internet and shared by others.

   b. Advantages of using cloud computing include fast access to software, a reduced need for investment in IT infrastructure, and the ability to use "pay as you go" services.

   c. IT security in the cloud is potentially more difficult due to the convenience and ease of access to sensitive data provided by cloud computing services.

   d. There are four primary cloud services:

      1) **Data-as-a-Service (DaaS)**
      2) **Infrastructure-as-a-Service (IaaS)**
      3) **Platform-as-a-Service (PaaS)**
      4) **Software-as-a-Service (SaaS)**

   e. Cloud computing has also benefited from the rise of smartphones and tablets.

      1) Because these devices have limited memory, personal data (e.g., pictures, contacts, etc.) may be stored on the cloud to be retrieved later so that available memory can be used for application software.

Stop and review! You have completed the outline for this subunit. Study multiple-choice questions 1 through 5 beginning on page 324.

14.2 ELECTRONIC COMMERCE

1. **Overview**

   a. **E-business** is an umbrella term referring to all methods of conducting business electronically.

      1) This can include strictly internal communications as well as nonfinancial dealings with outside parties (e.g., contract negotiations).

   b. **E-commerce** is a narrower term referring to the conduct of financial transactions with outside parties electronically (e.g., the purchase and sale of goods and services).

      1) E-commerce introduces a new set of efficiencies into business relationships. Where orders previously were placed using a combination of phone calls and either mailed or faxed hard copy documents, e-commerce allows such transactions to take place entirely over the Internet.

      2) There are six basic types of e-commerce:

         a) Business-to-Business (B2B)
         b) Business-to-Consumer (B2C)
         c) Consumer-to-Consumer (C2C)
         d) Consumer-to-Business (C2B)
         e) Business-to-Administration (B2A)
         f) Consumer-to-Administration (C2A)

      3) E-business and e-commerce are sometimes considered to be synonymous.

   c. An extranet is one means of carrying on e-commerce.

      1) Extranets rely on the established communications protocols of the Internet. Thus, the expensive, specialized equipment needed for electronic data interchange (EDI) is unnecessary.

      2) Firewalls, which can be hardware- or software-based, provide security.

      3) The extranet approach is based on less formal agreements between the trading partners than in EDI and requires the sending firm to format the documents into the format of the receiving firm.

2.   **Security and Reliability of E-Commerce**

   a.   Because of the reduced level of human involvement in e-commerce, new security and reliability concerns arise.

   b.   Specific concerns include the following:

      1)   The transacting parties must be correctly identified, a process known as **authentication**. IDs and passwords are the most common tools for authentication.

      2)   The circumstances in which a binding agreement can be made must be agreed to; in other words, who (or what system) is authorized to place (or promise to fill) an order? This is especially important in B2B applications, when entire production runs and large amounts of money are at stake.

      3)   The confidentiality and integrity of information transmitted electronically must be maintained. Encryption is the most useful tool for this purpose.

      4)   A reliable record of the transaction must be preserved such that disputes can be resolved and audits can be performed.

      5)   Potential customers must be able to trust listed prices and discounts.

      6)   Payment data must be verifiable.

      7)   Both parties' systems must be robust; i.e., they are up and running at all times.

3.   **Business-to-Business (B2B) E-Commerce**

   a.   B2B can be used to speed up the order and fulfillment process.

      1)   A manufacturer in need of raw materials can initiate the transaction using the Internet or the vendor's extranet.

      2)   The process can be further automated by establishing an EDI arrangement, in which the buyer's purchasing system automatically places an order with the vendor when inventories reach a predetermined level.

         a)   The partners must have (1) a common electronic document format and (2) a pre-existing agreement under which such orders will be accepted and filled without human intervention.

   b.   **Benefits of B2B** include

      1)   Reduced purchasing costs

         a)   Purchasing products online saves time, and electronically processing an order simplifies the ordering process.

      2)   Increased market efficiency

         a)   By using the Internet, companies have easy access to price quotes from various suppliers. Buyers are more likely to get a better price, given the increased number of suppliers.

      3)   Greater market intelligence

         a)   B2B provides producers with better insights into the demand levels in any given market.

      4)   Decreased inventory levels

         a)   Companies can make better use of their inventory and raw materials. The Internet allows companies using just-in-time (JIT) manufacturing techniques to achieve better control of their operations, for example, by more precise coordination of delivery of raw materials. It also allows companies to use less working capital to do the same amount of work, which allows those funds to be invested elsewhere.

    c.   The overriding principle of online B2B is that it can make companies more efficient.

         1)   Increased efficiency means lower costs, which is a goal that interests every company. Thus, the potential of B2B online commerce is enormous.

4.   Business-to-Consumer (B2C) E-Commerce

    a.   B2C is one of the fastest growing segments of the economy. Consumers can order a vast array of merchandise from the comfort of their homes or from mobile devices.

         1)   B2C is almost exclusively conducted via the Internet.

         2)   Traditional retailers have expanded their reach with B2C, and some firms, notably Amazon.com, use the Internet as their sole communication channel with customers.

    b.   Many of the same benefits accrue to businesses as in the B2B model with reduced costs and increased efficiency.

         1)   Many of the same security issues, such as authorization, also apply, but on a smaller scale. Also, the vendor need not concern itself with the IT infrastructure on the customer's end.

5.   Social Media

    a.   Social media is the interaction among people in virtual communities where they can share information and ideas.

         1)   People access these virtual communities via platforms, apps, and websites that facilitate user interaction.

              a)   Examples include Twitter, Facebook, LinkedIn, Instagram, and Snapchat.

         2)   The sharing and advancement of personal information over a virtual platform allows people to remain in contact, even if they are not physically close to each other.

    b.   The spread and advancement of mobile technology has allowed people to stay regularly connected to their social networks.

         1)   By embracing social media, many companies have been able to connect with their customers and the market on a more personal basis, increasing the rate of growth of B2C.

              a)   This can be done in the form of special coupons, promotional videos, etc.

         2)   Social media has also facilitated the growth of **consumer-to-consumer (C2C)** e-commerce.

    c.   Laws and customs regarding privacy and ownership of material posted on social media websites are developing.

6.   Electronic Funds Transfer (EFT)

    a.   EFT is an e-commerce application provided by financial institutions worldwide that enables the transfer of funds via an access device, such as an ATM or POS terminal, telephone, computer, or chip (e.g., credit, debit, and check cards).

         1)   A typical consumer application of EFT is the direct deposit of payroll checks in employees' accounts or the automatic withdrawal of payments for cable and telephone bills, mortgages, etc.

         2)   EFT transaction costs are lower than for manual systems because documents and human intervention are eliminated from the transaction process. Moreover, transfer customarily requires less than a day.

         3)   Another significant advantage is that the opportunities for clerical errors are greatly reduced.

b. The most important application of EFT is check collection. To reduce the enormous volume of paper involved, the check-collection process has been computerized.

1) The result has been to reduce the significance of paper checks because EFT provides means to make payments and deposit funds without physical transfer of negotiable instruments. Thus, wholesale EFTs among financial institutions and businesses (commercial transfers) are measured in the trillions of dollars.

2) The two major systems for these "wire" or nonconsumer transfers are Fedwire (formerly known as the Federal Reserve Wire Network) and CHIPS (Clearing House Interbank Payment System). Private systems are also operated by large banks.

7. **EFT vs. Electronic Money**

a. EFT differs from the use of electronic money, which may someday supplant traditional currency and coins.

b. **Smart cards** contain computer chips rather than magnetized stripes. A smart card, therefore, can store data and security programs. It not only stores value but also authenticates transactions, such as by means of its digital signature.

c. A disadvantage of electronic money is that most types are not covered by the insurance offered by the Federal Deposit Insurance Corporation (FDIC). Federal Reserve rules concerning EFT also do not extend to electronic money.

d. Methods other than providing a credit card number or using electronic money may be used to make electronic payments.

1) One such method is an online payment system, such as PayPal. A buyer makes a payment by a customary method to the online payment system, which then notifies the seller that payment has been made. The final step is to transfer the money to the seller's account.

Stop and review! You have completed the outline for this subunit. Study multiple-choice questions 6 through 10 beginning on page 326.

14.3 ELECTRONIC DATA INTERCHANGE (EDI)

 The AICPA has frequently tested the topic of EDI on recent exams. Questions have addressed such areas as the advantages of EDI and internal control and security for EDI transactions.

1. **Overview**

a. Electronic data interchange (EDI) is the leading method of carrying on B2B e-commerce.

1) EDI involves the communication of data in a format agreed to by the parties directly from a computer in one entity to a computer in another entity, for example, to order goods from a supplier or to transfer funds.

b. EDI was the first step in the evolution of e-business.

1) Successful EDI implementation begins with mapping the work processes and flows that support achievement of the organization's objectives.

2) EDI was developed to enhance JIT inventory management.

    c.   Advantages of EDI include the following:

        1)   Reduction of clerical errors

        2)   Increased speed of transactions

        3)   Elimination of repetitive clerical tasks, such as document preparation, processing, and mailing

        4)   Use of digital rather than physical record storage

    d.   Disadvantages of EDI include the following:

        1)   Information may be insecure.

            a)   Thus, end-to-end data encryption should be used to protect data during EDI.

        2)   Data may be lost.

        3)   Transmissions to trading partners may fail.

        4)   EDI is more complex and more costly than simpler B2B arrangements.

            a)   In simpler B2B, each transaction is initiated over the Internet, with XML as the mediating language.

            b)   EDI requires programming expertise and leased telephone lines or the use of a value-added or third-party network, whereas XML is simple and easy to understand.

2.   **Costs of EDI**

    a.   Specialized Software

        1)   The software needed to convert data into the agreed-upon EDI format must be either purchased or developed in-house.

    b.   Dedicated Hardware

        1)   High-availability servers and high-speed communications devices must be available.

    c.   Legal Costs

        1)   Contracts with current trading partners must be negotiated when entering into an EDI arrangement.

    d.   Process Reengineering

        1)   Since existing procedures are being replaced, EDI arrangements may require significant changes to current internal processes. This also involves the cost of employee retraining.

    e.   Enhanced Security and Monitoring

        1)   EDI transactions are subject to the same risks as all electronic communications that cross organizational boundaries.

3.   **Terms and Components of EDI**

    a.   **Standards** concern procedures to convert written documents into a standard electronic document-messaging format to facilitate EDI.

        1)   The current standards are ANSI X12 in the U.S. or UN/EDIFACT in Europe and most of the rest of the world.

        2)   An alternative approach is XML language, which is not a standard at all. XML enables the creation of electronic business documents in a more flexible way, one that is not bound by the strict rules of data location.

    b.   **Conventions** are the procedures for arranging data elements in specified formats for various accounting transactions, e.g., invoices, materials releases, and advance shipment notices.

    c.   A **data dictionary** prescribes the meaning of data elements, including specification of each transaction structure.

    d.   **Transmission protocols** are rules used to determine how each electronic envelope is structured and processed by the communications devices.

        1)   Normally, a group of accounting transactions is combined in an electronic envelope and transmitted into a communications network.

        2)   Rules are required for the separation and transmission of envelopes.

    e.   A crucial element of any EDI arrangement is the exchange of network and sender/recipient acknowledgment messages.

        1)   Acknowledgments serve as a nonrepudiation tool; i.e., one party cannot claim that a particular message was not received by a certain time or date.

4.   **Methods of Communication between EDI Computers**

    a.   A point-to-point system requires the use of dedicated computers by all parties.

        1)   Each computer must be designed to be compatible with the other(s). This system is very similar to a network within one company. Dedicated lines or modems are used.

    b.   Value-added networks (VANs) are private, third-party providers of common interfaces between organizations.

        1)   Subscribing to a VAN eliminates the need for one organization to establish direct computer communication with a trading partner. VANs also eliminate the need for dedicated computers waiting for incoming messages.

5.   **EDI Implications for Control**

    a.   EDI eliminates the paper documents, both internal and external, that are the traditional basis for many controls, including internal and external auditing.

    b.   Moreover, an organization that has reengineered its processes to take full advantage of EDI may have eliminated even the electronic equivalents of paper documents.

        1)   For example, the buyer's point-of-sale (POS) system may directly transmit information to the seller, which delivers on a JIT basis. Purchase orders, invoices, and receiving reports are eliminated and replaced with

            a)   A long-term contract establishing quantities, prices, and delivery schedules;

            b)   Evaluated receipts settlements (authorizations for automatic periodic payment);

            c)   Production schedules;

            d)   Advance ship notices; and

            e)   Payments by EFT.

Stop and review! You have completed the outline for this subunit. Study multiple-choice questions 11 through 14 beginning on page 327.

14.4 BIG DATA AND ANALYTICS

1.   **Overview**

    a.   Big data is an evolving term that describes any voluminous amount of structured, semi-structured, or unstructured data that has the potential to be mined for information.

        1)   **Structured data** refers to data with a high level of organization (i.e., relational database).

2) **Semi-structured data** does not conform with the formal structure of data models associated with relational databases or other forms of data tables, however, there exists some aspect of formatting of records and fields within the data.

3) **Unstructured data** refers to information that is not organized in a pre-defined manner (i.e., text-heavy facts, dates, numbers, and images).

  b. Big data includes information collected from social media, data from Internet-enabled devices, machine data, videos, and voice recordings. The information collected is converted from low-density data into high-density data (data that has value).

  c. Data are processed with analytic and algorithmic tools to reveal meaningful information.

2. Big data is often characterized by the "4 Vs."

  a. **Volume**

    1) The term is used to describe the extreme amount of data captured over time.

      a) Depending on the amount of data required to be captured, the number of servers required could range from a single server to thousands of servers.

    2) Real-time sensors used in the Internet of things (IoT) have become one of the top sources of data.

      a) IoT is a system of interrelated computing devices, mechanical and digital machines, objects, animals, or people that are provided with real-time sensors and with the ability to transfer data over a network without requiring human-to-human or human-to-computer interaction.

  b. **Variety**

    1) Data exists in a wide variety of file types.

      a) Structured data file types are generally maintained by Structured Query Language (SQL), which are used for managing relational databases and performing various operations on the data in them.

      b) Unstructured data file types (i.e., streaming data from sensors, text, audio, images, and videos) are maintained by non-relational databases (i.e., NoSQL).

  c. **Velocity**

    1) The term refers to the speed at which big data must be analyzed.

      a) Analysts must have a detailed understanding of the available data and possess some sense of what answer(s) they are looking for.

      b) The computing power required to quickly process huge volumes and varieties of data can overwhelm a single server or multiple servers. Organizations must apply adequate computing power to big data tasks to achieve the desired velocity.

      c) Businesses are hesitant to invest in an extensive server and storage infrastructure that might only be used occasionally to complete big data tasks. As a result, cloud computing has emerged as a primary source for hosting big data projects.

  d. **Veracity**

    1) The term refers to the trustworthiness of the data (inherent discrepancies in the data collected).

      a) Can the user rely on the fact the data is representative?

3. The "5th V"

  a. More and more businesses are using big data because of the **value** of the information resulting from the culmination of analyzing large information flows and identifying opportunities for improvement.

    1) Use of big data is only as valuable as the business outcomes it makes possible. It is how businesses make use of data that allows full recognition of its true value and potential to improve decision-making capabilities and enhance positive business outcomes.

      a) **Volume-based value.** The more data businesses have on the customers, both recent and historical, the greater the insights. This leads to generating better decisions around acquiring, retaining, increasing, and managing those customer relationships.

      b) **Variety-based value.** In the digital era, capability to acquire and analyze varied data is extremely valuable. This in turn provides deep insights into successfully developing and personalizing customer platforms for businesses to be more engaged and aware of customer needs and expectations.

      c) **Velocity-based value.** The faster businesses process data, the more time they will have to ask the right questions and seek answers. Rapid analysis capabilities provide businesses with the right data in time to achieve their customer relationship management goals.

      d) **Veracity-based value.** Once data is validated, the data transforms to "smart data." Collecting large amounts of statistics and numbers is of little value if they cannot be relied upon and used.

  b. Big data uses inductive statistics and concepts from nonlinear system identification (i.e., output is not directly proportional to the input) to infer laws from large sets of data to reveal relationships and dependencies, or to perform predictions of outcomes and behaviors.

    1) It can be used to analyze data to identify opportunities that include but are not limited to (a) cost reductions, (b) time reductions, (c) new product development and optimized offerings, and (d) new customers.

    2) Big data analytics tools complete missing pieces through **data fusion**, which is the process of integration of multiple data and knowledge representing the same real-world object into a consistent, accurate, and useful representation.

4. Key Technologies

  a. **Data management.** Data need to be high quality and well-governed before they can be reliably analyzed. Thus, businesses need to

    1) Establish repeatable processes to build and maintain standards for data quality.
    2) Establish a master data management program.

  b. **Data mining.** Data mining examines large amounts of data to discover patterns in the data.

    1) Sift through all the chaotic and repetitive noise in data, pinpoint what is relevant, use that information to assess likely outcomes, and then accelerate the pace of making informed decisions.

    c.   **Hadoop.** Open source software framework that stores large amounts of data and runs applications on clusters of commodity hardware.

    d.   **In-memory analytics.** Analyze data from system memory instead of secondary storage.

        1)   Derive immediate results by removing data preparation and analytical processing delays.

        2)   Enables iterative and interactive analytic scenarios more efficiently.

    e.   **Predictive analytics.** Technology that uses data, statistical algorithms, and machine-learning techniques to identify the likelihood of future outcomes based on historical data.

    f.   **Text mining.** Analyze text data from the Web, comment fields, books, and other text-based sources through the use of machine learning or natural language processing technology.

        1)   Identify new topics and term relationships.

Stop and review! You have completed the outline for this subunit. Study multiple-choice questions 15 and 16 beginning on page 328.

14.5 ELECTRONIC TRANSMISSION SECURITY

   1.   **Encryption Technology**

    a.   Encryption technology is vital for the security and therefore the success of electronic commerce, especially with regard to transactions carried out over public networks.

        1)   The sender's encryption program encodes the data prior to transmission. The recipient's program decodes it at the other end. Unauthorized users may be able to intercept the data, but without the encryption key, they will be unable to decode it.

    b.   Encryption performed by physically secure hardware is inherently more secure than encryption performed by software.

    c.   The use of encryption increases system overhead. A certain amount of system resources must be used to execute the machine instructions necessary to encrypt and decrypt data.

   2.   **Public-Key vs. Symmetric Encryption**

    a.   With public-key (asymmetric) encryption, the communicating parties create mathematically related pairs of keys. One of the keys in the pair is made public, and the other is kept secret.

        1)   The sending party uses the public key to encrypt the message. Since only the intended recipient has access to the private key that relates to that public key, only that party will be able to decrypt the message.

    b.   With symmetric encryption, the communicating parties agree on a single (private) key for use in that session.

        1)   Its strength comes from its length. The longer the key (measured in bits), the more resistant it is to decrypting by unauthorized parties.

        2)   However, the parties must have a secure way of sharing the key.

3. **Digital Certificates**

    a. Digital certificates are data files created by trusted third parties called certificate authorities (e.g., VeriSign, Thawte, GoDaddy).

        1) An entity who wishes to engage in e-commerce first establishes a relationship with a certificate authority, who verifies that party's identity.

        2) The certificate authority then creates a coded electronic certificate that contains (a) the holder's name, (b) its public key, (c) a serial number, and (d) an expiration date. The certificate authority makes its own public key widely available.

        3) A party wishing to do business over the Internet with the certificate holder seeks the holder's certificate on the authority's server and uses the authority's public key to decrypt it.

        4) The sender obtains the recipient's public key from the certificate, encodes the message, and sends it. The recipient uses its private key to decrypt the message.

    b. This system, called the public-key infrastructure, relieves the parties from the need to establish their own pairs of keys when they want to communicate securely.

        1) The public-key infrastructure allows buyers to securely exchange credit card numbers with Internet vendors.

4. **Digital Signatures**

    a. A digital signature is a means of authenticating an electronic document such as a purchase order, acceptance of a contract, or financial information.

        1) The sender uses its private key to encode all or part of the message, and the recipient uses the sender's public key to decode it. Hence, if that key decodes the message, the sender must have written it.

Stop and review! You have completed the outline for this subunit. Study multiple-choice questions 17 through 20 beginning on page 329.

QUESTIONS

14.1 Networks and the Internet

1. Appropriate uses of an organization's internal communications network, or intranet, include all of the following **except**

A. Making the human resources policy manual available to employees.

B. Informing potential investors about company operations and financial results.

C. Providing senior management with access to the executive support system.

D. Enabling a project team that crosses departments to collaborate.

Answer (B) is correct.
  REQUIRED: The item not one of the basic purposes of an organization's internal communications network.
  DISCUSSION: An intranet permits sharing of information throughout an organization by applying Internet connectivity standards and Web software (e.g., browsers) to the organization's internal network. An intranet addresses the connectivity problems faced by organizations that have many types of computers. Its use is restricted to those within the organization.
  Answer (A) is incorrect. Making the human resources policy manual available to employees is an appropriate use of an organization's internal communications network. Answer (C) is incorrect. Providing senior management with access to the executive support system is an appropriate use of an organization's internal communications network. Answer (D) is incorrect. Enabling a project team that crosses departments to collaborate is an appropriate use of an organization's internal communications network.

2. A local area network (LAN) is best described as a(n)

A. Computer system that connects computers of all sizes, workstations, terminals, and other devices within a limited proximity.

B. System to allow computer users to meet and share ideas and information.

C. Electronic library containing millions of items of data that can be reviewed, retrieved, and analyzed.

D. Method to offer specialized software, hardware, and data-handling techniques that improve effectiveness and reduce costs.

Answer (A) is correct.
REQUIRED: The best description of a LAN.
DISCUSSION: A LAN is a local distributed computer system, often housed within a single building. Computers, communication devices, and other equipment are linked by cable. Special software facilitates efficient data communication among the hardware devices.

3. Which one of the following network configurations is distinguished by the possibility of spreading the cost of ownership among multiple organizations?

A. Value-added network.

B. Baseband network.

C. Wide area network.

D. Local area network.

Answer (C) is correct.
REQUIRED: The network configuration that spreads its cost among multiple organizations.
DISCUSSION: Wide area networks consist of a conglomerate of local area networks (LANs) over widely separated locations. The key aspect here is that a WAN can be either publicly or privately owned.
Answer (A) is incorrect. A value-added network is a private network. Answer (B) is incorrect. Baseband refers to the signal-carrying capacity of a network, not the ownership of its hardware devices. Answer (D) is incorrect. All the equipment in a local area network (LAN) is owned by one organization.

4. Which of the following control risks is more likely with personal computers than in a mainframe environment with dedicated terminals?

A. Copyright violations due to the use of unauthorized copies of purchased software.

B. Applications written by one department that cannot share data with existing organization-wide systems.

C. Lack of data availability due to inadequate data retention policies.

D. All of the answers are correct.

Answer (D) is correct.
REQUIRED: The control risk(s) likely in a personal computer environment.
DISCUSSION: When personal computers are used, likely control risks include copyright violations that occur when unauthorized copies of software are made or software is installed on multiple computers; locally written applications that do not adhere to the organization's standards; and inadequate backup, recovery, and contingency planning.
Answer (A) is incorrect. Copyright violations are a common risk with personal computers. Answer (B) is incorrect. Locally written applications that do not adhere to the organization's standards are a common risk with personal computers. Answer (C) is incorrect. Failure to follow proper backup procedures is a common risk with personal computers.

5. A company has abandoned the large array of dedicated servers it formerly used to store and provide access to its database. The company has entered into a contract with a provider who will guarantee storage of the database at its own location along with access over the Internet. This arrangement is an example of

A. Distributed computing.

B. Cloud computing.

C. Wide area network.

D. Ethernet.

Answer (B) is correct.
REQUIRED: The type of arrangement described in the question.
DISCUSSION: Cloud computing is a popular term relating to on-demand access to resources that are accessed on the Internet and shared by others. The entity has the ability to choose and pay for only the applications needed from the array (cloud) of resources, reducing the need for a large investment in IT infrastructure.
Answer (A) is incorrect. Distributed processing involves the decentralization of processing tasks and data storage and assigning these functions to multiple computers, often in separate locations. Answer (C) is incorrect. A wide area network (WAN) consists of a conglomerate of local area networks over widely separated locations. Answer (D) is incorrect. Ethernet is a local area network transmission protocol.

14.2 Electronic Commerce

6. An employee uses her company-issued ID and password to log into her employer's human resources system from home and change her choices of benefits. This is an example of

A. E-business.

B. Data warehouse.

C. Transmission protocol.

D. Extensible markup language.

Answer (A) is correct.

REQUIRED: The term for the transaction described.

DISCUSSION: E-business is an umbrella term referring to all methods of conducting business electronically. This can include strictly internal communications as well as nonfinancial dealings with outside parties (e.g., contract negotiations).

Answer (B) is incorrect. A data warehouse is a central database for transaction-level data from more than one of the organization's transaction processing systems. Answer (C) is incorrect. A transmission protocol is a necessary component of this transaction but does not describe the transaction itself. Answer (D) is incorrect. Extensible markup language (XML) is a way of coding information in such a way that a user can determine not only how it should be presented but also what it is; i.e., all computerized data may be tagged with identifiers.

7. Which of the following represents the greatest exposure to the integrity of electronic funds transfer data transmitted from a remote terminal?

A. Poor physical access controls over the data center.

B. Network viruses.

C. Poor system documentation.

D. Leased telephone circuits.

Answer (D) is correct.

REQUIRED: The greatest exposure to the integrity of EFT data transmitted from a remote terminal.

DISCUSSION: Leased telephone circuits represent a direct exposure to the risk of breached data integrity. They use public lines that can be easily identified and tapped.

Answer (A) is incorrect. Poor physical access controls represent a secondary exposure for compromise of remote data communications lines. Answer (B) is incorrect. Network viruses represent a secondary exposure for compromise of remote data communications lines. Answer (C) is incorrect. Poor system documentation represents a secondary exposure for compromise of remote data communications lines.

8. Which of the following risks is **not** greater in an electronic funds transfer (EFT) environment than in a manual system using paper transactions?

A. Unauthorized access and activity.

B. Duplicate transaction processing.

C. High cost per transaction.

D. Inadequate backup and recovery capabilities.

Answer (C) is correct.

REQUIRED: The risk not greater in an EFT environment than in a manual system using paper transactions.

DISCUSSION: EFT is a service provided by financial institutions worldwide that is based on EDI technology. EFT transaction costs are lower than for manual systems because documents and human intervention are eliminated from the transaction process.

Answer (A) is incorrect. Unauthorized access and activity is a risk specific to EFT. Answer (B) is incorrect. Inaccurate transaction processing (including duplication) is a risk specific to EFT. Answer (D) is incorrect. Inadequate backup and recovery capabilities is a risk specific to EFT.

9. Which one of the following is **not** a reason for a company to use EFT with an EDI system?

A. To take advantage of the time lag associated with negotiable instruments.

B. To allow the company to negotiate discounts with EDI vendors based upon prompt payment.

C. To improve its cash management program.

D. To reduce input time and input errors.

Answer (A) is correct.

REQUIRED: The item not a reason for using EFT.

DISCUSSION: The time lag between transmittal of a check (a negotiable instrument) and its clearance through regular banking channels is called float. Float is eliminated by EFT.

Answer (B) is incorrect. Payment schedules may be based on the time required to process invoices, prepare checks, and transmit checks. Using EFT, payment is instantaneous, and payment schedules can be based on other criteria, e.g., discounts for prompt payment. Answer (C) is incorrect. EFT allows for more effective control of payments and transfers among accounts. Answer (D) is incorrect. Integration of EDI and EFT eliminates manual input of transaction data, a process that introduces errors into the accounting system.

10. Which of the following significantly encouraged the development of electronic funds transfer (EFT) systems?

I. Response to competition
II. Cost containment
III. Advances in information technology

    A. I and II.

    B. I and III.

    C. II only.

    D. I, II, and III.

Answer (D) is correct.
    REQUIRED: The items that most significantly encouraged the development of EFTs.
    DISCUSSION: Competition has been a strong motivator in the financial services industry in the development of EFT systems, which are an application of EDI. Furthermore, containing costs in a highly competitive industry can be aided by leveraging information technology. Finally, advances in information technology, especially the wide acceptance of telecommunications standards and protocols, have made EFT systems possible.
    Answer (A) is incorrect. Advances in information technology also significantly encouraged the development of EFT. Answer (B) is incorrect. Cost containment also significantly encouraged the development of EFT. Answer (C) is incorrect. Competitive forces and advances in information technology also significantly encouraged the development of EFT.

14.3 Electronic Data Interchange (EDI)

11. A system that permits suppliers and buyers to have direct access to portions of each others' databases, including inventory data, to enhance service and deliveries is

    A. Electronic mail.

    B. Interactive processing.

    C. Electronic data interchange.

    D. Distributed processing.

Answer (C) is correct.
    REQUIRED: The system giving suppliers and buyers direct access to portions of each others' databases.
    DISCUSSION: Electronic data interchange (EDI) is the communication of electronic documents directly from a computer in one entity to a computer in another entity. For example, a buyer's computer will issue a purchase order to a seller's computer. EDI was developed to enhance JIT inventory management. The advantages of EDI include reduction of clerical errors, increased speed of transactions, elimination of repetitive clerical tasks, and elimination of document preparing, processing, and mailing costs.
    Answer (A) is incorrect. Electronic mail is the computer-to-computer exchange of messages. Answer (B) is incorrect. Interactive processing does not permit access to another company's database. Answer (D) is incorrect. Distributed processing distributes work among computers linked by a communications network.

12. Electronic data interchange (EDI) offers significant benefits to organizations, but it is not without certain major obstacles. Successful EDI implementation begins with which of the following?

    A. Mapping the work processes and flows that support the organization's goals.

    B. Purchasing new hardware for the EDI system.

    C. Selecting reliable vendors for translation and communication software.

    D. Standardizing transaction formats and data.

Answer (A) is correct.
    REQUIRED: The initial phase of EDI implementation.
    DISCUSSION: Marked benefits arise when EDI is tied to strategic efforts that alter, not mirror, previous practices. Applying EDI to an inefficient process results in continuing to do things the wrong way, only faster. Hence, the initial phase of EDI implementation includes understanding the organization's mission and an analysis of its activities as part of an integrated solution to the organization's needs.
    Answer (B) is incorrect. The prerequisite for EDI success is an understanding of the mission of the business and the processes and flows that support its goals, followed by cooperation with external partners. Purchasing new hardware is a subsequent step. Answer (C) is incorrect. Before applying EDI technology to the business, EDI must be viewed as part of an overall integrated solution to organizational requirements. Answer (D) is incorrect. EDI is not a solution by itself. Instead of considering how to transmit and receive transactions, a company must first analyze the entire process.

13. Which of the following is an accepted example of electronic data interchange (EDI)?

   A. Request for an airline reservation by a travel agent.

   B. Withdrawal of cash from an automated teller by a bank's customer.

   C. Transfer of summary data from a local area network to a centralized mainframe.

   D. Placement of order entry transactions from a customer to its supplier.

Answer (D) is correct.
   REQUIRED: The accepted example of electronic data interchange.
   DISCUSSION: EDI is the communication of electronic documents directly from a computer in one entity to a computer in another entity. Placement of order entry transactions from a customer to its supplier is an accepted use of EDI between trading partners.
   Answer (A) is incorrect. A request for an airline reservation requires an online, real-time reservations system. Answer (B) is incorrect. Withdrawal of cash from an automated teller is accomplished via online transactions to copies of master files. Answer (C) is incorrect. The transfer of summary data to headquarters may be accomplished with point-to-point communications, known as distributed computing.

14. Before sending or receiving electronic data interchange (EDI) messages, a company should

   A. Execute a trading partner agreement with each of its customers and suppliers.

   B. Reduce inventory levels in anticipation of receiving shipments.

   C. Demand that all its suppliers implement EDI capabilities.

   D. Evaluate the effectiveness of its use of EDI transmissions.

Answer (A) is correct.
   REQUIRED: The process to be performed before sending or receiving EDI messages.
   DISCUSSION: Before sending or receiving EDI messages, a company should execute a trading partner agreement with its customers and suppliers. All parties should understand their responsibilities, the messages each will initiate, how they will interpret messages, the means of authenticating and verifying the completeness and accuracy of messages, the moment when the contract between the parties is effective, the required level of security, etc.
   Answer (B) is incorrect. The company may intend to reduce inventory levels, but that intention is unrelated to the timing of its first EDI messages. Answer (C) is incorrect. The company may want to demand or encourage all its customers and suppliers to implement EDI capabilities, but that request is independent of sending and receiving messages. Answer (D) is incorrect. It is not possible to evaluate the effectiveness of EDI transmissions until after they occur.

14.4 Big Data and Analytics

15. All of the following are correct statements regarding big data **except**

   A. Big data is an evolving term that describes any voluminous amount of structured, semi-structured, and unstructured data that has the potential to be mined for information.

   B. Big data includes information collected from social media, data from Internet-enabled devices, machine data, video, and voice recordings. The information collected is converted from high-density data into low-density data.

   C. Big data is often characterized by the "4 Vs" - volume, variety, velocity, and veracity.

   D. Big data processes data with analytic and algorithmic tools to reveal meaningful information.

Answer (B) is correct.
   REQUIRED: Knowledge of the general concepts of big data.
   DISCUSSION: Big data includes information collected from social media, data from Internet-enabled devices, machine data, video, and voice recordings. The information collected is converted from low-density data into high-density data. Thus, the statement regarding big data is not correct.

16. All of the following are correct statements regarding businesses deciding to utilize cloud computing for big data projects **except**

    A. Businesses are hesitant to invest in an extensive server and storage infrastructure that might only be used occasionally to complete big data tasks.

    B. Businesses only pay for the storage and computing time actually used.

    C. A public cloud provider can store petabytes of data and scale up thousands of servers just long enough to accomplish the big data project.

    D. Analysts are not required to have a detailed understanding of the available data and possess some sense of what answer(s) they're looking for.

Answer (D) is correct.
    REQUIRED: Knowledge of the general concepts of big data.
    DISCUSSION: Analysts are not required to have a detailed understanding of the available data and possess some sense of what answer(s) they're looking for is an incorrect statement. Analysts must have a detailed understanding of the available data and possess some sense of the answers they are looking for. The value of data is only as valuable as the business outcomes it makes possible. It is how businesses make use of data that allows full recognition of its true value and the potential to improve decision-making capabilities and measure them against the results of positive business outcomes.

14.5 Electronic Transmission Security

17. A client communicates sensitive data across the Internet. Which of the following controls will be most effective to prevent the use of the information if it were intercepted by an unauthorized party?

    A. A firewall.

    B. An access log.

    C. Passwords.

    D. Encryption.

Answer (D) is correct.
    REQUIRED: The most effective control for preventing the use of intercepted information.
    DISCUSSION: Encryption technology converts data into a code. Encoding data before transmission over communications lines makes it more difficult for someone with access to the transmission to understand or modify its contents.
    Answer (A) is incorrect. A firewall prevents access from specific types of traffic to an internal network. After an unauthorized user has obtained information from the site, a firewall cannot prevent its use. Answer (B) is incorrect. An access log only records attempted usage of a system. Answer (C) is incorrect. Passwords prevent unauthorized users from accessing the system. If information has already been obtained, a password cannot prevent its use.

18. Which of the following IT developments poses the **least** risk to organizational security?

    A. Adoption of wireless technology.

    B. Use of public-key encryption.

    C. Outsourcing of the IT infrastructure.

    D. Enterprise-wide integration of functions.

Answer (B) is correct.
    REQUIRED: The least risky IT developments.
    DISCUSSION: Encryption is essential when electronic commerce is conducted over public networks, such as the Internet. Thus, the use of public-key encryption is a response to risk, not a source of risk.
    Answer (A) is incorrect. Adoption of wireless technology increases the risk that communications will be intercepted. Answer (C) is incorrect. Outsourcing of the IT infrastructure means that ineffective controls over the outside service provider's operations could compromise the security of the organization's information. Answer (D) is incorrect. Enterprise-wide integration of functions, for example, in an ERP system with an organization-wide database, increases the difficulty of assuring the integrity of information. In an organization with discrete, closed functional subsystems, compromising one subsystem does not affect the others. In an ERP system, however, a breach of security may affect the entire organization.

19. Which of the following is an encryption feature that can be used to authenticate the originator of a document and ensure that the message is intact and has not been tampered with?

    A. Heuristic terminal.

    B. Perimeter switch.

    C. Default settings.

    D. Digital signatures.

Answer (D) is correct.

    REQUIRED: The encryption feature used to authenticate the originator of a document and ensure that the original message is intact.

    DISCUSSION: A digital signature is a means of authenticating an electronic document, such as a purchase order, acceptance of a contract, or financial information. Because digital signatures use public-key encryption, they are a highly secure means of ensuring security over the Internet.

    Answer (A) is incorrect. The term "heuristic terminal" is not meaningful in this context. Answer (B) is incorrect. The term "perimeter switch" is not meaningful in this context. Answer (C) is incorrect. In a computer program, a default setting is a value that a parameter will automatically assume unless specifically overridden.

20. To ensure privacy in a public-key encryption system, knowledge of which of the following keys is required to decode the received message?

    I. Private
    II. Public

    A. I only.

    B. II only.

    C. Both I and II.

    D. Neither I nor II.

Answer (A) is correct.

    REQUIRED: The key(s) required to decode messages in a public-key system to ensure privacy.

    DISCUSSION: In a public-key system, the public key is used to encrypt the message prior to transmission. The private key is needed to decrypt (decode) the message.

    Answer (B) is incorrect. The private key, not the public key, is needed to decrypt (decode) the message. Answer (C) is incorrect. The public key is needed to encode, not decode, the message. Answer (D) is incorrect. The private key is needed to decrypt (decode) the message.

STUDY UNIT FIFTEEN
IT SECURITY AND CONTROLS

(14 pages of outline)

The goals of a business information system are the same regardless of whether the system is manual or computerized; the risks of a computer-based system, however, are quite different.

The material included in this study unit overlaps with the internal control and information technology topic on the Blueprint for the Auditing and Attestation (AUD) section of the exam. We have attempted to include here those issues that are more likely to be tested on the Business Environment and Concepts (BEC) section of the exam. Many of these issues should be familiar for candidates who have already studied AUD.

15.1 RISKS ASSOCIATED WITH BUSINESS INFORMATION SYSTEMS

1. **Overview**

   a. Organizations need to be aware of the unique risks associated with a computer-based business information system.

   b. IT security (or **cybersecurity**) is information security applied to computer hardware, software, and computer networks.

   c. Safe computing can be achieved by using carefully crafted policies and procedures in conjunction with antivirus and access control software.

   d. The most comprehensive indicator of an information system's compliance with prescribed procedures is the control the system has over the data. This includes the capacity and complexity of the system, as well as the accessibility of the data to the end-user.

2. **System Availability**

   a. The ability to make use of any computer-based system is dependent on

      1) An uninterrupted flow of electricity

      2) Protection of computer hardware from environmental hazards (e.g., fire and water)

      3) Protection of software and data files from unauthorized alteration

      4) Preservation of functioning communications channels between devices

3. **Volatile Transaction Trails**

   a. In any computer-based environment, a complete trail useful for audit purposes might exist for only a short time or in only computer-readable form. In online and real-time systems, data are entered directly into the computer, eliminating portions of the audit trail traditionally provided by source documents.

4. **Decreased Human Involvement**

   a. Because employees who enter transactions may never see the final results, the potential for detecting errors is reduced. Also, output from a computer system often carries a mystique of infallibility, reducing the incentive of system users to closely examine reports and transaction logs.

5. **Uniform Processing of Transactions**

   a. Computer processing uniformly subjects like transactions to the same processing instructions, therefore, virtually eliminating clerical error. Thus, it permits consistent application of predefined business rules and the performance of complex calculations in high volume.

   b. However, programming errors (or other similar systematic errors in either the hardware or software) will result in all like transactions being processed incorrectly.

6. **Unauthorized Access**

   a. When accounting records were kept in pen-and-ink format, physical access to them was the only way to carry out an alteration. Once they are computer-based, however, access may be gained by parties both internal and external to the organization.

   b. Security measures, such as firewalls and user ID-and-password combinations, are vital to maintaining security over data in an automated environment.

7. **Data Vulnerability**

   a. Destruction of hardware devices or units of storage media could have disastrous consequences if they contain the only copies of crucial data files or application programs.

   b. For this reason, it is vital that an organization's computer files be duplicated and stored offsite periodically.

8. **Reduced Segregation of Duties**

   a. Many functions once performed by separate individuals may be combined in an automated environment.

EXAMPLE

Receiving cash, issuing a receipt to the payor, preparing the deposit slip, and preparing the journal entry may once have been performed by separate individuals. In a computer-based system, the receipt, deposit slip, and journal entry may be automatically generated by the computer. If the same employee who receives the cash is also responsible for entering the relevant data into the system, the potential for fraud or error is increased.

---

9. **Reduced Individual Authorization of Transactions**

   a. Certain transactions may be initiated automatically by a computer-based system. This is becoming ever more widespread as an increasing number of business processes become automated.

EXAMPLE

An enterprise resource planning system at a manufacturing concern may automatically generate a purchase order when raw materials inventory reaches a certain level. If the company shares an EDI system with the vendor, the purchase order may be sent to the vendor electronically without any human intervention.

---

   b. This reduced level of oversight for individual transactions requires careful coding to ensure that computer programs accurately reflect management's goals for business processes.

      1) Independent verification of transactions is an important compensating control in the absence of segregation of duties and reduced individual authorization. A third party performs the verification to ensure that the transactions were appropriately processed.

10. **Malicious Software (Malware)**

   a. Malware is a term describing any program code that enters a computer system that has the potential to degrade that system. Common forms of malware include the following:

      1) A **Trojan horse** is an apparently innocent program (e.g., a spreadsheet) that includes a hidden function that may do damage when activated.

2)   A **virus** is a program that copies itself from file to file. The virus may destroy data or programs. A common way of spreading a virus is by email attachments and downloads.

   a)   **Logic bombs** are a type of virus triggered by a predetermined event (such as Friday the 13th, April Fool's day, etc.).

3)   A **worm** copies itself not from file to file but from computer to computer, often very rapidly. Repeated replication overloads a system by depleting memory or overwhelming network traffic capacity.

4)   A **denial-of-service (DOS) attack** is an attempt to overload a system (e.g., a network or Web server) with messages so that it cannot function (a system crash).

   a)   A distributed DOS attack comes from multiple sources, for example, the machines of innocent parties infected by Trojan horses. When activated, these programs send messages to the target and leave the connection open.

5)   **Phishing** is a method of electronically obtaining confidential information, such as a password or credit card number, through deceit. The perpetrator sets up a website that appears to be legitimate but actually serves no other purpose than to obtain the victim's information.

   a)   Phishing scams are often initiated through email spoofing, in which the perpetrator sends out emails that appear to be from a real financial institution. When the victim clicks on the link to what (s)he thinks is the institution's website, the victim is unknowingly redirected to the perpetrator's website.

6)   A **back door** is a program that allows unauthorized access to a system and bypasses the normal login procedures (front door).

Stop and review! You have completed the outline for this subunit. Study multiple-choice question 1 on page 345.

15.2   COBIT -- A FRAMEWORK FOR IT

1.   **Overview**

   a.   COBIT is the best-known control and governance framework that addresses information technology.

   1)   In its original version, COBIT was focused on controls for specific IT processes.

   2)   Over the years, information technology has gradually pervaded every facet of the organization's operations. IT can no longer be viewed as a function distinct from other aspects of the organization.

   a)   The evolution of COBIT has reflected this change in the nature of IT within the organization.

Background

When originally published in 1996, COBIT was an acronym for *Control Objectives for Information and Related Technology*. COBIT 5, the most recent version, was published in April 2012 by ISACA (formerly known as the Information Systems Audit and Control Association). The COBIT 5 framework document, which describes the five key principles for IT governance and management, is available as a free download at www.isaca.org/COBIT/Pages/Product-Family.aspx.

---

2.   **Information Criteria**

   a.   **Effectiveness** deals with information's relevance to the business process and receipt in a timely, correct, consistent, and usable manner.

   b. **Efficiency** concerns the provision of information through the optimal (most productive and economical) use of resources.

   c. **Confidentiality** concerns the protection of sensitive information from unauthorized disclosure.

   d. **Integrity** relates to the accuracy and completeness of information, as well as to its validity in accordance with business values and expectations.

   e. **Availability** relates to information being available when required by the business process now and in the future. It also concerns the safeguarding of necessary resources and associated capabilities.

   f. **Compliance** deals with complying with the laws, regulations, and contractual arrangements to which the business process is subject, i.e., externally imposed business criteria as well as internal policies.

   g. **Reliability** relates to the provision of appropriate information for management to operate the entity and exercise its fiduciary and governance responsibilities.

  3. **IT Governance Focus Areas**

   a. **Strategic alignment** focuses on ensuring the linkage of business and IT plans; defining, maintaining, and validating the IT value proposition; and aligning IT operations with enterprise operations.

   b. **Value delivery** is about executing the value proposition throughout the delivery cycle, ensuring that IT delivers the promised benefits against the strategy, concentrating on optimizing costs, and proving the intrinsic value of IT.

   c. **Resource management** is about the optimal investment in, and the proper management of, critical IT resources.

   d. **IT Risk** is the business risk associated with the use, ownership, operation, involvement, influence, and adaption of IT within an enterprise or organization.

   e. **Risk management** involves risk awareness by senior corporate officers, understanding of compliance requirements, transparency about the significant risks to the enterprise, and embedding of risk management responsibilities into the organization.

   f. **Performance measurement** tracks and monitors strategy implementation, project completion, resource usage, process performance, and service delivery.

  4. COBIT defines IT activities in a generic process model within four processes:

   a. **Plan and Organize** - Provides direction to solution delivery and service delivery.

   b. **Acquire and Implement** - Solutions need to be identified, developed, or acquired and integrated into the business process.

   c. **Deliver and Support** - Provides instruction for the management of security and continuity, service support for users, and management of data and operational facilities.

   d. **Monitor and Evaluate** - Processes need to be regularly assessed over time for their quality and compliance with control requirements.

  5. **IT Resources**

   a. **Applications** are the automated user systems and manual procedures that process the information.

   b. **Information** is the data, in all their forms, input, processed, and output by the information systems in whatever form is used by the business.

   c. **Infrastructure** is the technology and facilities that enable the processing of the applications.

   d. **People** are the personnel required to plan, organize, acquire, implement, deliver, support, monitor, and evaluate the information systems.

6.   **COBIT 5 -- Five Key Principles**

a.   **Principle 1: Meeting Stakeholder Needs**

1)   COBIT 5 asserts that value creation is the most basic stakeholder need. Thus, the creation of stakeholder value is the fundamental goal of any enterprise, commercial or not.

a)   Value creation in this model is achieved by balancing three components:

i)   Realization of benefits
ii)   Optimization (not minimization) of risk
iii) Optimal use of resources

2)   COBIT 5 also recognizes that stakeholder needs are not fixed. They evolve under the influence of both internal factors (e.g., changes in organizational culture) and external factors (e.g., disruptive technologies).

a)   These factors are collectively referred to as stakeholder drivers.

3)   In response to the identified stakeholder needs, enterprise goals are established.

a)   COBIT 5 supplies 17 generic enterprise goals that are tied directly to the balanced scorecard model.

b)   Next, IT-related goals are drawn up to address the enterprise goals.

c)   Finally, enablers are identified that support pursuit of the IT-related goals. An enabler is broadly defined as anything that helps achieve objectives.

d)   COBIT 5 refers to the process described above as the goals cascade.

b.   **Principle 2: Covering the Enterprise End-to-End**

1)   COBIT 5 takes a comprehensive view of all of the enterprise's functions and processes. Information technology pervades them all; it cannot be viewed as a function distinct from other enterprise activities.

a)   Thus, IT governance must be integrated with enterprise governance.

2)   IT must be considered enterprise-wide and end-to-end, i.e., all functions and processes that govern and manage information "wherever that information may be processed."

c.   **Principle 3: Applying a Single, Integrated Framework**

1)   In acknowledgment of the availability of multiple IT-related standards and best practices, COBIT 5 provides an overall framework for enterprise IT within which other standards can be consistently applied.

2)   COBIT 5 was developed to be an overarching framework that does not address specific technical issues; i.e., its principles can be applied regardless of the particular hardware and software in use.

d.   **Principle 4: Enabling a Holistic Approach**

1)   COBIT 5 describes seven categories of enablers that support comprehensive IT governance and management:

a)   Principles, policies, and frameworks
b)   Processes
c)   Organizational structures
d)   Culture, ethics, and behavior
e)   Information
f)   Services, infrastructure, and applications
g)   People, skills, and competencies

2)   The last three of these enablers are also classified as resources, the use of which must be optimized.

3)   Enablers are interconnected because they (a) need the input of other enablers to be fully effective and (b) deliver output for the benefit of other enablers.

e.   **Principle 5: Separating Governance from Management**

1)   The complexity of the modern enterprise requires governance and management to be treated as distinct activities.

a)   In general, governance is the setting of overall objectives and monitoring progress toward those objectives. COBIT 5 associates governance with the board of directors.

i)   Within any governance process, three practices must be addressed: evaluate, direct, and monitor.

b)   Management is the carrying out of activities in pursuit of enterprise goals. COBIT 5 associates these activities with executive management under the leadership of the CEO.

i)   Within any management process, four responsibility areas must be addressed: plan, build, run, and monitor.

Background

In addition to the framework itself, the COBIT product family includes three other documents that can be purchased separately: enabler guides, which describe enabling processes (i.e., anything that can help to achieve enterprise objectives); professional guides, which provide guidance for the implementation of COBIT, as well as for such specific topics as information security, assurance, and risk; and an online environment allowing simultaneous participation and collaboration by interested parties.

Stop and review! You have completed the outline for this subunit. Study multiple-choice question 2 on page 345.

15.3 INFORMATION SECURITY

1.   **Overview**

a.   Information security encompasses not only computer hardware and software but all of an organization's information, no matter what medium it resides on. It involves far more than just user IDs and passwords.

1)   The importance of a broad definition of information security becomes clear in light of recent incidents of firms accidentally disposing of documents containing confidential customer information with their regular trash.

b.   Organizations have three principal goals for their information security programs: data confidentiality, data availability, and data integrity.

1)   **Confidentiality** is protecting data from disclosure to unauthorized persons.

2)   **Availability** is ensuring that the organization's information systems are up and running so that employees and customers are able to access the data they need.

3)   **Integrity** is ensuring that data accurately reflect the business events underlying them and are not subject to tampering or destruction.

2.   **Steps in Creating an Information Security Plan**

a.   Identify the threats to the organization's information, i.e., events that can potentially compromise an organization's information infrastructure.

1)   Threats to confidentiality include the improper disposal of customer records, threats to availability include viruses and denial-of-service attacks, and threats to integrity include employee errors and sabotage.

b.   Identify the risks that these threats entail.

1)   Risk analysis encompasses determining the likelihood of the identified threats and the level of damage that could potentially be done should the threats materialize.

2)   For example, an organization may conclude that, while the potential damage from sabotage is very high, its likelihood may be quite low.

c.   Design the controls that will compensate for the risks.

1)   Controls are designed based on the combination of likelihood and potential damage determined in the risk analysis.

d.   Incorporate the controls into a coherent, enterprise-wide information security plan.

1)   The plan lists the controls that will be put in place and how they will be enforced.

e.   Set forth policies with expectations of all persons, both employees and external users, with access to the organization's systems.

1)   The single most important policy is that which governs the information resources to which individuals have access and how the level of access will be tied to their job duties.

a)   Carrying out such a policy requires the organization's systems to be able to tie data and program access to individual system IDs.

b)   One provision of the policy must be for the immediate removal of access to the system by terminated employees.

3.   **Preventive-Detective-Corrective Control Model**

a.   IT controls can also be classified according to the traditional three-way division of internal controls.

b.   **Preventive controls** prevent errors from entering the system. Preventive controls are often highly visible and are considered better than other forms of control because they stop problems before they occur.

1)   Examples of physical preventive controls include fences, locked doors, security guards, and a segregation of duties policy.

2)   Examples of logical preventive controls are the input controls described later in this study unit.

c.   **Detective controls** call attention to errors that have already entered the system before an error causes a negative outcome.

1)   Examples of detective accounting controls are petty cash counts and physical inventory counts.

a)   An important detective control in IT is examination of system logs. These logs are reports automatically generated by the system of actions that require scrutiny, such as repeated failed login attempts and the use of powerful utility programs.

2)   Examples in an automated systems context are the output controls described later in this study unit.

d.   **Corrective controls** correct errors after they have been detected.

1)   Examples include correcting errors reported on error listings, isolating and removing viruses, and restarting from system crashes.

4.   **Broad Controls**

a.   The two broad groupings of information systems control activities are **general controls** and **application controls** discussed in the next two subunits.

Stop and review! You have completed the outline for this subunit. Study multiple-choice questions 3 through 5 beginning on page 345.

15.4 GENERAL CONTROLS

1.   **General controls** are the umbrella under which the IT function operates. They affect the organization's entire processing environment and commonly include controls over (a) data center and network operations; (b) systems software acquisition, change, and maintenance; (c) access security; and (d) application system acquisition, development, and maintenance.

2.   IT Administration Controls Over Operations

   a.   A modern organization should recognize information technology as a separate function with its own set of management and technical skills. An organization that allows every functional area to acquire and administer its own systems in isolation is not serious about proper control.

   b.   Treating IT as a separate functional area of the organization involves the designation of a chief information officer (CIO) or chief technology officer (CTO) and the establishment of an information systems steering committee to set a coherent direction for the organization's systems and prioritize information technology projects.

3.   **Segregation of duties** is vital because a separation of functions (authorization, recording, and access to assets) may not be feasible in an IT environment. For example, a computer may print checks, record disbursements, and generate information for reconciling the account balance. These activities customarily are segregated in a manual system. Segregation of duties within the IT function is discussed in Subunit 15.6.

4.   Controls over software acquisition, change, and maintenance include

   a.   **Controls over systems software,** which ensure that operating systems, utilities, and database management systems are acquired and changed only under close supervision and that vendor updates are routinely installed.

   b.   **Controls over application software,** which ensure that programs used for transaction processing (e.g., payroll and accounts receivable) are cost-effective and stable.

5.   **Hardware controls** are built into the equipment by the manufacturer. They ensure the proper internal handling of data as they are moved and stored.

   a.   They include parity checks, echo checks, read-after-write checks, and any other procedure built into the equipment to ensure data integrity.

6.   **Physical controls** limit physical access and environmental damage to computer equipment, data, and important documents.

   a.   **Access Controls**

      1)   Access controls prevent improper use or manipulation of data files and programs. They ensure that only those persons with a bona fide purpose and authorization have access.

      2)   No persons except operators should be allowed unmonitored access to the processing facility. This can be accomplished through the use of a guard desk, a keypad, or a magnetic card reader.

      3)   **Passwords and ID numbers.** The use of passwords and identification numbers (for example, a PIN used for an ATM) is an effective control in an online system to prevent unauthorized access to files. Lists of authorized persons are maintained online. To avoid unauthorized access, the entity may combine (a) the entry of passwords or identification numbers; (b) a prearranged set of personal questions; and (c) the use of badges, magnetic cards, optically scanned cards, or biometric attributes.

      4)   **Device authorization table.** This control grants access only to those physical devices that should logically need access. For example, because it is illogical for anyone to access the accounts receivable file from a manufacturing terminal, the device authorization table will deny access even when a valid password is used.

      5) **System access log.** This log records all uses and attempted uses of the system. The date and time, codes used, mode of access, data involved, and interventions by operators are recorded.

      6) **Encryption.** Encoding data before transmission over communication lines makes it more difficult for someone with access to the transmission to understand or modify its contents. Encryption technology converts data into a code. Unauthorized users may still be able to access the data but, without the encryption key, will be unable to decode the information.

      7) **Callback.** This feature requires the remote user to call, give identification, hang up, and wait for a call to an authorized number. This control ensures acceptance of data only from authorized modems. However, a call-forwarding device may thwart this control by transferring access from an authorized to an unauthorized number.

      8) **Controlled disposal of documents.** One method of enforcing access restrictions is to destroy data when they are no longer in use. Thus, paper documents may be shredded, and magnetic media may be erased.

      9) **Biometric technologies.** These are automated methods of establishing an individual's identity using physiological or behavioral traits. These characteristics include fingerprints, retina patterns, hand geometry, signature dynamics, speech, and keystroke dynamics.

      10) **Automatic log-off.** The disconnection of inactive data terminals may prevent the viewing of sensitive data on an unattended work station.

      11) **Security personnel.** An entity may hire security specialists. For example, (a) developing an information security policy for the entity, (b) commenting on security controls in new applications, and (c) monitoring and investigating unsuccessful access attempts are appropriate duties of the information security officer.

  b. **Environmental Controls**

      1) The processing facility should be equipped with both a cooling and heating system (to maintain a year-round constant level of temperature and humidity) and a fire-suppression system.

7. **Logical controls** are established to limit access in accordance with the principle that all persons should have access only to those elements of the organization's information systems that are necessary to perform their job duties. Logical controls have a double focus, authentication and authorization.

  a. **Authentication** is the act of ensuring that the person attempting to access the system is in fact who (s)he says (s)he is. The most widespread means of achieving this is through the use of IDs and passwords.

  b. The elements of user account management are as follows:

      1) Anyone attempting access to one of the organization's systems must supply a unique identifier (e.g., the person's name or other series of characters) and a password that is known only to that person and is not stored anywhere in the system in unencrypted format.

         a) Not even information security personnel should be able to view unencrypted passwords. Security personnel can change passwords, but the policy should require that the user immediately change it to something secret.

      2) The organization's systems should force users to change their passwords periodically, e.g., every 90 days.

      3) The policy should prohibit employees from leaving their IDs and passwords written down in plain view.

     c.   **Authorization** is the practice of ensuring that, once in the system, the user can only access those programs and data elements necessary for his or her job duties.

        1)   In many cases, users should be able to view the contents of some data fields but not be able to change them.

        2)   An example is an accounts receivable clerk who can view customers' credit limits but cannot change them. This same clerk can, however, change a customer's outstanding balance by entering or adjusting an invoice.

        3)   To extend the example, only the head of the accounts receivable department should be able to execute the program that updates the accounts receivable master balance file. An individual clerk should have no such power.

8.   A **firewall** is a combination of hardware and software that separates an internal network from an external network (e.g., the Internet) and prevents passage of traffic deemed suspicious. Two principal types of firewalls are network firewalls and application firewalls.

     a.   **Network firewalls** regulate traffic to an entire network, such as an organization's LAN.

        1)   The firewall examines each query and, depending on the rules set up by the network security administrator, denies entry to the network based on the source, destination, or other data in the header.

        2)   Queries from a particular source address that repeatedly fail to gain access to the network might indicate a penetration attempt. The firewall can notify network security personnel who can then investigate.

     b.   **Application firewalls** regulate traffic to a specified application, such as email or file transfer.

        1)   An application firewall is based on proxy server technology. The firewall becomes a proxy, or intermediary, between the computer actually sending the packet and the application in question. This arrangement allows for a high level of security over the application but at the cost of slowing down communications.

        2)   Since an application firewall only provides security for a single application, it is not a substitute for a network firewall.

     c.   A firewall alone is not an adequate defense against computer viruses. Specialized antivirus software is a must.

Stop and review! You have completed the outline for this subunit. Study multiple-choice questions 6 through 10 beginning on page 346.

15.5 APPLICATION CONTROLS

 CPA exam questions concerning application controls often give a description of a control, then ask for the name of it.

1.   **Application Controls**

     a.   Are built into each application (payroll, accounts payable, inventory management, etc.).

     b.   Are designed to ensure that only correct, authorized data enter the system and that the data are processed and reported properly.

     c.   Include input, processing, and output controls.

2. **Input Controls**

    a. Input controls provide reasonable assurance that data submitted for processing are (1) authorized, (2) complete, and (3) accurate. These controls vary depending on whether input is entered in online or batch mode.

    b. The most basic input control is thus authorization; e.g., a batch of accounts payable transactions must be authorized by the AP supervisor before being submitted for recording.

    c. Many input controls take the form of **edit routines**, i.e., controls programmed into the software that prevent certain types of errors from entering into the system.

      1) Preformatting. To avoid data entry errors in online systems, a preformatted screen may be designed to look exactly like the corresponding paper document.

      2) Edit (field) checks. Some data elements can only contain certain characters, and any transaction that attempts to use an invalid character is halted.

        a) A typical example is a Social Security number, which is not allowed to contain letters.

      3) Limit (reasonableness) and range checks. Based on known limits for given information, certain entries can be rejected by the system.

        a) For example, hours worked per week cannot exceed 80 without a special override by management, date of birth of an employee cannot be any date within the last 15 years, etc.

      4) Validity checks. In order for a transaction to be processed, some other record must already exist in another file.

        a) For example, for the system to accept a transaction requesting payment of a vendor invoice, the vendor must already have a record on the vendor master file.

      5) Sequence checks. Processing efficiency is greatly increased when files are sorted on some designated field(s), called the "key," before operations such as matching.

        a) For instance, the accounts payable transaction file and master file should both be sorted according to vendor number before the matching operation is attempted. If the system discovers a record out of order, it may indicate that the files were not properly prepared for processing.

      6) Closed-loop verification. Inputs by a user are transmitted to the computer, processed, and displayed back to the user for verification.

      7) Check-digit verification (self-checking digits). An algorithm is applied to, for instance, a product number and incorporated into the number. This reduces keying errors, such as dropped and transposed digits.

EXAMPLE

A box of detergent has the product number 4187604. The last digit is actually a derived number, arrived at by applying the check-digit algorithm to the other digits.

In this example, the check digit is calculated by starting with the last position of the base product number (418760) and multiplying each successive digit to the left by 2, then by 1, then by 2, etc., and adding the results: $(0 \times 2) + (6 \times 1) + (7 \times 2) + (8 \times 1) + (1 \times 2) + (4 \times 1) = 0 + 6 + 14 + 8 + 2 + 4 = 34$. The last digit of this result becomes the check digit.

When the clerk enters 4187604 into the terminal, the system performs an immediate calculation and determines that this is a valid product number.

---

      8) Zero-balance checks. The system will reject any transaction or batch thereof in which the sum of all debits and credits does not equal zero.

d.   **Batch input controls** can be used when data are grouped for processing.

1)   **Management release.** A batch is not released for processing until a manager reviews and approves it.

2)   **Record count.** A batch is not released for processing unless the number of records in the batch, as reported by the system, matches the number calculated by the user.

3)   **Financial total.** A batch is not released for processing unless the sum of the dollar amounts of the individual items as reported by the system matches the amount calculated by the user.

4)   **Hash total.** The arithmetic sum of a numeric field, which has no meaning by itself, can serve as a check that the same records that should have been processed were processed. An example is the sum of all department numbers.

3.   **Processing Controls**

a.   Processing controls provide reasonable assurance that (1) all data submitted for processing are processed and (2) only approved data are processed. These controls are built into the application code by programmers during the systems development process.

b.   Some processing controls repeat the steps performed by the **input controls**, such as limit checks and batch controls.

c.   **Validation.** Identifiers are matched against master files to determine existence. For example, any accounts payable transaction in which the vendor number does not match a number on the vendor master file is rejected.

d.   **Completeness.** Any record with missing data is rejected.

e.   **Arithmetic controls.** Cross-footing compares an amount with the sum of its components. Zero-balance checking adds the debits and credits in a transaction or batch to ensure that their sum is zero.

f.   **Sequence check.** Computer effort is expended most efficiently when data are processed in a logical order, such as by customer number. This check ensures the batch is sorted in the proper order before processing begins.

g.   **Run-to-run control totals.** The controls associated with a given batch are checked after each stage of processing to ensure all transactions have been processed.

h.   **Key integrity.** A record's key is the group of values in designated fields that uniquely identify the record. No application process should be able to alter the data in these key fields.

4.   **Output Controls**

a.   Output controls provide assurance that the processing result (such as account listings or displays, reports, files, invoices, or disbursement checks) is accurate and that only authorized personnel receive the output.

b.   These procedures are performed at the end of processing to ensure that all transactions the user expected to be processed were actually processed.

1)   **Transaction Logs**

a)   Every action performed in the application is logged along with the date, time, and ID in use when the action was taken.

2)   **Error Listings**

a)   All transactions rejected by the system are recorded and distributed to the appropriate user department for resolution.

3) **Record Counts**

   a) The total number of records processed by the system is compared to the number the user expected to be processed.

4) **Run-to-Run Control Totals**

   a) The new financial balance should be the sum of the old balance plus the activity that was just processed.

Stop and review! You have completed the outline for this subunit. Study multiple-choice questions 11 through 16 beginning on page 347.

15.6 ROLES AND RESPONSIBILITIES WITHIN THE IT FUNCTION

In the early days of computing, maintaining a rigid segregation of duties was a simple matter because the roles surrounding a mainframe computer were so specialized. As IT became more and more decentralized over the years, clear lines that once separated jobs such as systems analyst and programmer became blurred and then disappeared.

Recent CPA exams have contained questions regarding the duties and responsibilities of various IT personnel, as well as the segregation of duties within the IT function. Understand the responsibilities of IT personnel from the standpoint of duty segregation.

1. **Segregation of Duties -- IT Function**

  a. Organizational controls concern the proper segregation of duties and responsibilities within the information systems department.

  b. Controls should ensure the efficiency and effectiveness of IT operations. They include proper segregation of the duties within the IT environment. Thus, the responsibilities of systems analysts, programmers, operators, file librarians, the control group, and others should be assigned to different individuals, and proper supervision should be provided.

  c. Segregation of duties is vital because a traditional segregation of responsibilities for authorization, recording, and access to assets may not be feasible in an IT environment.

    1) For example, a computer may print checks, record disbursements, and generate information for reconciling the account balance, which are activities customarily segregated in a manual system.

      a) If the same person provides the input and receives the output for this process, a significant control weakness exists. Accordingly, certain tasks should not be combined.

      b) Thus, compensating controls may be necessary, such as library controls, effective supervision, and rotation of personnel. Segregating test programs makes concealment of unauthorized changes in production programs more difficult.

2. **Responsibilities of IT Personnel**

  a. **Database administrators** (DBAs) are responsible for developing and maintaining the organization's databases and for establishing controls to protect their integrity.

    1) Thus, only the DBA should be able to update data dictionaries.

    2) In small systems, the DBA may perform some functions of a database management system (DBMS). In larger applications, the DBA uses a DBMS as a primary tool.

    b.   **Network technicians** maintain the bridges, hubs, routers, switches, cabling, and other devices that interconnect the organization's computers. They are also responsible for maintaining the organization's connection to other networks, such as the Internet.

    c.   The **webmaster** is responsible for the content of the organization's website. (S)he works closely with programmers and network technicians to ensure that the appropriate content is displayed and that the site is reliably available to users.

    d.   **Computer operators** are responsible for the day-to-day functioning of the data center, whether the organization runs a mainframe, servers, or anything in between.

        1)   Operators load data, mount storage devices, and operate the equipment. Operators should not be assigned programming duties or responsibility for systems design. Accordingly, they also should have no opportunity to make changes in programs and systems as they operate the equipment.

            a)   Ideally, computer operators should not have programming knowledge or access to documentation not strictly necessary for their work.

    e.   **Librarians** maintain control over and accountability for documentation, programs, and data storage media.

    f.   **Systems programmers** maintain and fine-tune the operating systems on the organization's medium- and large-scale computers. The operating system is the core software that performs three of a computer's four basic tasks, i.e., input, output, and storage.

        1)   Programmers, as well as analysts, may be able to modify programs, data files, and controls. Thus, they should have no access to the data center operations or to production programs or data.

    g.   **Applications programmers** design, write, test, and document computer programs according to specifications provided by the end users.

    h.   A **systems analyst** uses his or her detailed knowledge of the organization's databases and applications programs to determine how an application should be designed to best serve the users' needs. These duties are often combined with those of applications programmers.

        1)   Systems analysts should not have access to data center operations, production programs, or data files.

    i.   **Help desk personnel** log problems reported by users, resolve minor difficulties, and forward more difficult problems to the appropriate person, such as a database administrator or the webmaster. Help desk personnel are often called on to resolve such issues as desktop computers crashing or problems with email.

    j.   **Information security officers** are typically in charge of developing information security policies, commenting on security controls in new applications, and monitoring and investigating unsuccessful login attempts.

    k.   **End users** must be able to change production data but not programs.

Stop and review! You have completed the outline for this subunit. Study multiple-choice questions 17 through 20 beginning on page 349.

QUESTIONS

15.1 Risks Associated with Business Information Systems

1. Which of the following statements most accurately describes the impact that automation has on the controls normally present in a manual system?

A. Transaction trails are more extensive in a computer-based system than in a manual system because a one-for-one correspondence always exists between data entry and output.

B. Responsibility for custody of information assets is more concentrated in user departments in a computer-based system than it is in a manual system.

C. Controls must be more explicit in a computer-based system because many processing points that present opportunities for human judgment in a manual system are eliminated.

D. The quality of documentation becomes less critical in a computer-based system than it is in a manual system because data records are stored in machine-readable files.

Answer (C) is correct.

REQUIRED: The impact that automation has on the controls normally present in a manual system.

DISCUSSION: Using a computer does not change the basic concepts and objectives of control. However, the use of computers may modify the control techniques used. The processing of transactions may be combined with control activities previously performed separately, or control functions may be combined within the information system activity.

Answer (A) is incorrect. The audit trail is less extensive in an information system. Combining processing and controls within the system reduces documentary evidence. Answer (B) is incorrect. Information assets are more likely to be under the control of the information system function. Answer (D) is incorrect. Documentation is more important in an information system. Information is more likely to be stored in machine-readable form than in hard copy.

15.2 COBIT -- A Framework for IT

2. Which of the following statements is **inconsistent** with the key principles of the COBIT 5 framework?

A. Enterprise governance and management are treated as the same activity.

B. The needs of stakeholders are the focus of all organizational activities.

C. Information technology controls are considered to be intertwined with those of the organization's everyday operations.

D. COBIT 5 can be applied even when other IT-related standards have been adopted.

Answer (A) is correct.

REQUIRED: The statement inconsistent with the key principles of the COBIT 5 framework.

DISCUSSION: Under the COBIT 5 framework, the complexity of the modern enterprise requires governance and management to be treated as distinct activities.

Answer (B) is incorrect. COBIT 5 asserts that the creation of stakeholder value is the fundamental goal of any enterprise. Answer (C) is incorrect. COBIT 5 takes a comprehensive view of all of the enterprise's functions and processes. Information technology pervades them all; it cannot be viewed as a function distinct from other enterprise activities. Answer (D) is incorrect. In acknowledgment of the availability of multiple IT-related standards and best practices, COBIT 5 provides an overall framework for enterprise IT within which other standards can be applied.

15.3 Information Security

3. A client installed the sophisticated controls using the biometric attributes of employees to authenticate user access to the computer system. This technology most likely replaced which of the following controls?

A. Use of security specialists.

B. Reasonableness tests.

C. Passwords.

D. Virus protection software.

Answer (C) is correct.

REQUIRED: The control most likely replaced by biometric technologies.

DISCUSSION: The use of passwords is an effective control in an online system to prevent unauthorized access to computer systems. However, biometric technologies are more sophisticated and difficult to compromise.

Answer (A) is incorrect. Biometric technologies do not eliminate the need for specialists who evaluate and monitor security needs. Answer (B) is incorrect. Reasonableness tests are related to input controls, not access controls. Answer (D) is incorrect. Virus protection software prevents damage to data in a system, not access to a system.

4. Spoofing is one type of malicious online activity. Spoofing is

A. Trying large numbers of letter and number combinations to access a network.

B. Eavesdropping on information sent by a user to the host computer of a website.

C. Accessing packets flowing through a network.

D. Identity misrepresentation in cyberspace.

Answer (D) is correct.
REQUIRED: The nature of spoofing.
DISCUSSION: Passwords, user account numbers, and other information may be stolen through spoofing. Spoofing is identity misrepresentation in cyberspace, for example, by using a false website to obtain information about visitors.
Answer (A) is incorrect. A brute-force attack uses password cracking software to try large numbers of letter and number combinations to access a network. Answer (B) is incorrect. Sniffing is the use of software to eavesdrop on information sent by a user to the host computer of a website. Answer (C) is incorrect. A man-in-the-middle attack takes advantage of network packet sniffing and routing and transport protocols to access packets flowing through a network.

5. Attacks on computer networks may take many forms. Which of the following uses the computers of innocent parties infected with Trojan horse programs?

A. A distributed denial-of-service attack.

B. A man-in-the-middle attack.

C. A brute-force attack.

D. A password-cracking attack.

Answer (A) is correct.
REQUIRED: The attack on a network that uses the computers of innocent parties infected with Trojan horse programs.
DISCUSSION: A denial-of-service (DOS) attack is an attempt to overload a system (e.g., a network or Web server) with false messages so that it cannot function (a system crash). A distributed DOS attack comes from multiple sources, for example, the machines of innocent parties infected by Trojan horses.
Answer (B) is incorrect. A man-in-the-middle attack takes advantage of network packet sniffing and routing and transport protocols to access packets flowing through a network. Answer (C) is incorrect. A brute-force attack uses password cracking software to try large numbers of letter and number combinations to access a network. Answer (D) is incorrect. Password-cracking software accesses a network by trying many letter and number combinations.

15.4 General Controls

6. One of the major problems in a computer system is that incompatible functions may be performed by the same individual. One compensating control is the use of

A. Echo checks.

B. A check digit system.

C. Computer-generated hash totals.

D. A computer log.

Answer (D) is correct.
REQUIRED: The control compensating for inadequate segregation of duties in a computer system.
DISCUSSION: A computer (console) log is a record of computer and software usage usually produced by the operating system. Proper monitoring of the log is a compensating control for the lack of segregation of duties. For instance, the log should list operator interventions.
Answer (A) is incorrect. Echo checks are hardware controls used to determine if the correct message was received by an output device. Answer (B) is incorrect. A check digit system is an input control that tests identification numbers. Answer (C) is incorrect. Hash totals are control totals used to check for losses or inaccuracies arising during data movement.

7. The two broad groupings of information systems control activities are general controls and application controls. General controls include controls

A. Relating to the correction and resubmission of faulty data.

B. For developing, modifying, and maintaining computer programs.

C. Designed to assure that only authorized users receive output from processing.

D. Designed to ensure that all data submitted for processing have been properly authorized.

Answer (B) is correct.
REQUIRED: The general controls.
DISCUSSION: General controls are policies and procedures that relate to the entity's overall IT environment. They support the effective functioning of application controls by helping to ensure the continued proper operation of information systems. General controls include controls over (1) data center and network operations; (2) systems software acquisition and maintenance; (3) access security; and (4) application systems acquisition, development, and maintenance.
Answer (A) is incorrect. Control over correction of input errors is an application control. Answer (C) is incorrect. Control over report distribution (output) is an application control. Answer (D) is incorrect. Control over authorization of input is an application control.

8. The significance of hardware controls is that they

A. Ensure the proper execution of machine instructions.

B. Reduce the incidence of user input errors in online systems.

C. Ensure accurate programming of operating system functions.

D. Ensure that run-to-run totals in application systems are consistent.

Answer (A) is correct.
    REQUIRED: The significance of hardware controls.
    DISCUSSION: Hardware controls are built into the equipment by the manufacturer to detect and control errors arising from the use of the equipment. Examples include parity checks, read-after-write checks, and echo checks.
    Answer (B) is incorrect. Use of input screens, limit tests, self-checking digits, and other input controls can reduce the incidence of input errors in online systems. Answer (C) is incorrect. Programmers and/or analysts must correct errors in computer programs. Answer (D) is incorrect. Run-to-run totals ensure the completeness of update in an online system by accumulating separate totals for all transactions processed throughout a period. This total is compared with the total of items accepted for processing.

9. Authentication is the process by which the

A. System verifies that the user is entitled to enter the transaction requested.

B. System verifies the identity of the user.

C. User identifies himself or herself to the system.

D. User indicates to the system that the transaction was processed correctly.

Answer (B) is correct.
    REQUIRED: The definition of authentication.
    DISCUSSION: Identification is the process of uniquely distinguishing one user from all others. Authentication is the process of determining that individuals are who they say they are. For example, a password may identify but not authenticate its user if it is known by more than one individual.
    Answer (A) is incorrect. Authentication involves verifying the identity of the user. This process does not necessarily confirm the functions the user is authorized to perform. Answer (C) is incorrect. User identification to the system does not imply that the system has verified the identity of the user. Answer (D) is incorrect. This procedure is an application control for accuracy of the transaction.

10. When a user enters a certain entity's system, a series of questions is asked of the user, including a name and mother's birth date. These questions are primarily intended to provide

A. Authorization for processing.

B. Access control to computer hardware.

C. Authentication of the user.

D. Data integrity control.

Answer (C) is correct.
    REQUIRED: The purpose of requiring a user to enter his or her name and mother's birth date.
    DISCUSSION: Requiring specified information allows the computer to identify the user. This access control is intended to limit access to data and programs and the nature of that access.
    Answer (A) is incorrect. Such names and questions are intended to identify the user entering the system. Answer (B) is incorrect. Access to the computer has already taken place. Questions and names do not prevent access to the hardware. Answer (D) is incorrect. Such questions have no effect on the integrity of data.

15.5 Application Controls

11. An employee in the receiving department keyed in a shipment from a remote terminal and inadvertently omitted the purchase order number. The best systems control to detect this error is

A. Completeness test.

B. Sequence check.

C. Reasonableness test.

D. Compatibility test.

Answer (A) is correct.
    REQUIRED: The control to detect the omission of a purchase order number keyed in from a remote terminal.
    DISCUSSION: A completeness test checks that all data elements are entered before processing. An interactive system can be programmed to notify the user to enter the number before accepting the receiving report.
    Answer (B) is incorrect. A sequence check tests for the ordering, not omission, of records. Answer (C) is incorrect. A limit or reasonableness test checks the values of data items against established limits. Answer (D) is incorrect. A compatibility test (field check) determines whether characters are appropriate to a field.

12. Which of the following computerized control procedures is most effective in ensuring that files of data uploaded from personal computers to a server are complete and that **no** additional data are added?

- A. Self-checking digits to ensure that only authorized part numbers are added to the database.
- B. Batch control totals, including control totals and hash totals.
- C. Passwords that effectively limit access to only those authorized to upload the data to the server.
- D. Field-level edit controls that test each field for alphanumerical integrity.

Answer (B) is correct.

REQUIRED: The most effective computerized control procedure.

DISCUSSION: Batch control totals for the data transferred can be reconciled with the batch control totals in the existing file. This comparison provides information on the completion of the data transfer. Batch totals may include record counts, totals of certain critical amounts, or hash totals. A hash total is a control total without a defined meaning, such as the total of employee numbers or invoice numbers, that is used to verify the completeness of data. Thus, the hash total for the employee listing by the personnel department could be compared with the total generated during the payroll run.

Answer (A) is incorrect. Self-checking digits detect inaccurate identification numbers. They are an effective control to ensure that the appropriate part has been identified but not that data transfer is complete. Answer (C) is incorrect. Passwords help ensure that only authorized personnel make the transfer, not that data transfer is complete. Answer (D) is incorrect. Field checks are effective input controls, but they do not ensure completeness of data transfer.

13. In an automated payroll processing environment, a department manager substituted the time card for a terminated employee with a time card for a fictitious employee. The fictitious employee had the same pay rate and hours worked as the terminated employee. The best control to detect this action using employee identification numbers is a

- A. Reasonableness test.
- B. Record count.
- C. Hash total.
- D. Financial total.

Answer (C) is correct.

REQUIRED: The best control technique to detect the action.

DISCUSSION: A hash total is a control total without a defined meaning, such as the total of employee numbers or invoice numbers, that is used to verify the completeness of data. Thus, the hash total for the employee listing by the personnel department could be compared with the total generated during the payroll run.

Answer (A) is incorrect. A reasonableness test is based on known limits for given information. Answer (B) is incorrect. A record count is a control total of the number of records processed during the operation of a program. Answer (D) is incorrect. Financial totals summarize dollar amounts in an information field in a group of records.

14. Certain payroll transactions were posted to the payroll file but were not uploaded correctly to the general ledger file on the main server. The best control to detect this type of error would be

- A. A standard method for uploading mainframe data files.
- B. An appropriate edit and validation of data.
- C. A record or log of items rejected during processing.
- D. Balancing totals of critical fields.

Answer (D) is correct.

REQUIRED: The best control to detect failure to upload correctly to the general ledger certain payroll transactions.

DISCUSSION: Balancing totals should be used to ensure completeness and accuracy of processing. For example, comparing totals of critical fields generated before processing with output totals for those fields tests for missing or improper transactions.

Answer (A) is incorrect. A standard method for uploading data may not include the controls necessary to detect errors in the uploading process. Answer (B) is incorrect. Edit and validation checks are typically designed to identify errors in data entry rather than in processing. Answer (C) is incorrect. A record or log of rejected items is a control for monitoring the subsequent correction and processing of the items.

15. Which of the following errors most likely would be detected by batch financial totals?

- A. A transposition error on one employee's paycheck on a weekly payroll run.
- B. A missing digit in an invoice number in a batch of daily sales.
- C. A purchase order mistakenly entered into two different batches.
- D. Malfeasance resulting from a receivable clerk's pocketing of a customer's payment and altering of the related records.

Answer (A) is correct.

REQUIRED: The error that will likely be detected by batch financial totals.

DISCUSSION: Batch financial totals compare the sum of the dollar amounts of the individual items as reported by the system, with the amount calculated by the user. Thus, batch financial totals would most likely detect a transposition error on an employee's paycheck.

Answer (B) is incorrect. Batch financial totals give information about the total dollar amounts of the invoices within the batch but do not detect errors in the digits of the invoice numbers themselves. Answer (C) is incorrect. Batch financial totals are not capable of detecting errors that are made in two separate batches. Answer (D) is incorrect. Batch financial totals alone are not capable of detecting the alteration of records or the theft of payment.

16. A systems engineer is developing the input routines for a payroll system. Which of the following methods validates the proper entry of hours worked for each employee?

    A. Check digit.

    B. Sequence check.

    C. Capacity check.

    D. Reasonableness check.

Answer (D) is correct.
    REQUIRED: An understanding of application controls and their uses.
    DISCUSSION: Reasonableness checks are performed based on known limits for given information. Certain entries can be rejected by the system due to the reasonable limits. If the employee hours are within reasonable limits, then they are validated.
    Answer (A) is incorrect. Check digit verification is used to reduce keying errors such as dropped and transposed digits. Answer (B) is incorrect. A sequence check ensures the batch is sorted in the proper order before processing begins. Answer (C) is incorrect. A capacity check ensures that the selected storage has the capacity to store the quantity necessary.

15.6 Roles and Responsibilities within the IT Function

17. The risks created by rapid changes in IT have **not** affected which concepts of internal control?

    I.   Cost-benefit analysis
    II. Control environment
    III. Reasonable assurance
    IV. Management's responsibility

    A. I and II only.

    B. III and IV only.

    C. II, III, and IV only.

    D. I, II, III, and IV.

Answer (D) is correct.
    REQUIRED: The concepts of control not affected by rapid IT change.
    DISCUSSION: Internal control objectives remain essentially the same although technology, risks, and control methods change. Thus, many concepts of control (management's responsibility, the role of the control environment, reasonable assurance, monitoring, and cost-benefit analysis) are relevant regardless of IT changes.
    Answer (A) is incorrect. IT control processes and procedures must provide reasonable assurance that objectives are achieved and risks are reduced. Moreover, management continues to be responsible for control and for coordinating activities to achieve objectives. Answer (B) is incorrect. Cost-benefit analysis remains an essential tool for determining which controls mitigate identified risks at an acceptable cost. Furthermore, the control environment in an IT setting reflects the tone of the organization, influences control consciousness, and provides a foundation for the other components of control. Answer (C) is incorrect. Cost-benefit analysis remains an essential tool for determining which controls mitigate identified risks at an acceptable cost.

18. In the organization of the information systems function, the most important segregation of duties is

    A. Not allowing the data librarian to assist in data processing operations.

    B. Assuring that those responsible for programming the system do not have access to data processing operations.

    C. Having a separate information officer at the top level of the organization outside of the accounting function.

    D. Using different programming personnel to maintain utility programs from those who maintain the application programs.

Answer (B) is correct.
    REQUIRED: The most important segregation of duties.
    DISCUSSION: Segregation of duties is a general control that is vital in a computerized environment. Some segregation of duties common in noncomputerized environments may not be feasible in an IT environment. However, certain tasks should not be combined. Systems analysts and programmers should be segregated from computer operators. Both programmers and analysts may be able to modify programs, files, and controls, and should therefore have no access to the data center operations or to production programs or data. Operators should not be assigned programming duties or responsibility for systems design, and should have no opportunity to make changes in programs and systems.
    Answer (A) is incorrect. Librarians maintain control over documentation, programs, and data files; they should have no access to equipment, but they can assist in data processing operations. Answer (C) is incorrect. A separate information officer outside of the accounting function would not be as critical a segregation of duties as that between programmers and processors. Answer (D) is incorrect. Programmers usually handle all types of programs.

19. Which of the following should **not** be the responsibility of a database administrator?

A. Design the content and organization of the database.

B. Develop applications to access the database.

C. Protect the database and its software.

D. Monitor and improve the efficiency of the database.

Answer (B) is correct.

REQUIRED: The choice not a responsibility of a database administrator.

DISCUSSION: The database administrator (DBA) is the person who has overall responsibility for developing and maintaining the database. One primary responsibility is to design the content of the database. Another responsibility of the DBA is to protect and control the database. A third responsibility is to monitor and improve the efficiency of the database. The responsibility of developing applications to access the database belongs to systems analysts and programmers.

Answer (A) is incorrect. Designing the content and organization of the database is a responsibility of the database administrator. Answer (C) is incorrect. Protecting the database and its software is a responsibility of the database administrator. Answer (D) is incorrect. Monitoring and improving the efficiency of the database is a responsibility of the database administrator.

20. If a payroll system continues to pay employees who have been terminated, control weaknesses most likely exist because

A. Procedures were not implemented to verify and control the receipt by the computer processing department of all transactions prior to processing.

B. There were inadequate manual controls maintained outside the computer system.

C. Programmed controls such as limit checks should have been built into the system.

D. Input file label checking routines built into the programs were ignored by the operator.

Answer (B) is correct.

REQUIRED: The reason control weaknesses most likely exist.

DISCUSSION: The authorization to pay employees comes from outside the computer department. Thus, inadequate controls external to the computer processing department are most likely the cause of allowing the payments to terminated employees to continue without detection.

Answer (A) is incorrect. Batch totals constitute adequate controls over properly authorized transactions but provide no control over unauthorized transactions. Answer (C) is incorrect. A limit check tests the reasonableness of a particular transaction but not whether it was authorized. Answer (D) is incorrect. Paying proper attention to input file labels (header labels) will not detect unauthorized transactions.

Online is better! To best prepare for the CPA exam, access **thousands** of exam-emulating MCQs and TBSs through Gleim CPA Review online courses with SmartAdapt technology. Learn more at www.gleimcpa.com or contact our team at 800.874.5346 to upgrade.

STUDY UNIT SIXTEEN
PERFORMANCE MEASUREMENT
AND PROCESS MANAGEMENT

(17 pages of outline)

Responsibility accounting allows each component of the organization to be judged based on the achievement of its own objectives. The performance of a responsibility center must be evaluated using appropriate criteria. Such criteria includes financial and nonfinancial performance measures. The balanced scorecard is a tool used for implementing the organization's strategies towards achieving its objectives.

Much practical and theoretical innovation has occurred in business processes and the ways of monitoring their efficiency. Quality is a special area of management scrutiny. Its costs can be quantified, and frameworks have been developed for systematizing the pursuit of quality.

16.1 RESPONSIBILITY CENTERS

1. **Decision Making and Decentralization**

    a. The primary distinction between centralized and decentralized organizations is in the degree of freedom of decision making by managers.

        1) In a centralized organization, decision making is consolidated so that activities may be more effectively coordinated from the top.

        2) In a decentralized organization, decision making is at the lowest level possible. The premise is that the local manager can make more informed decisions than a manager farther from the decision.

2. **Responsibility Centers**

    a. A decentralized organization is divided into **responsibility centers** (also called **strategic business units**, or SBUs) to facilitate local decision making. Four types of responsibility centers are generally recognized.

        1) A **cost center**, e.g., a maintenance department, is responsible for costs only.

            a) Cost drivers are the relevant performance measures.

            b) A disadvantage of a cost center is the potential for cost shifting, for example, replacement of variable costs for which a manager is responsible with fixed costs for which (s)he is not.

                i) Another disadvantage is that long-term issues may be disregarded when the emphasis is on, for example, annual costs.

            c) Allocation of service department costs to cost centers is another issue. Service centers provide specialized support to other organizational subunits. They are usually operated as cost centers.

2)   A **revenue center**, e.g., a sales department, is responsible for revenues only.

   a)   Revenue drivers are the relevant performance measures. They are factors that influence unit sales, such as (1) changes in prices and products, (2) customer service, (3) marketing efforts, and (4) delivery terms.

3)   A **profit center**, e.g., an appliance department in a retail store, is responsible for revenues and expenses.

4)   An **investment center**, e.g., a branch office, is responsible for revenues, expenses, and invested capital.

   a)   The performance of an investment center can be compared with that of other responsibility centers or other potential investments on a return on investment (ROI) basis. ROI measures the effectiveness of asset usage.

3.   **Performance Measures and Manager Motivation**

   a.   In a responsibility center, a logical group of operations is directed by one manager.

      1)   Measures are designed for every responsibility center to monitor performance.

   b.   **Controllability.** The performance measures on which the manager's compensation is based should be, to the extent practicable, under the manager's influence.

      1)   Controllable factors are those a manager can influence in a given period.

         a)   But some costs, for example, the costs of central administration, cannot be traced to particular activities or responsibility centers.

         b)   Most costs, revenues, etc., are not wholly controlled by one manager. They may be influenced by (1) factors external to the organization (e.g., prices of materials), (2) a team of managers, or (3) a person with no authority over incurrence of the cost (e.g., a purchasing manager with expert knowledge of price changes).

      2)   Controllable cost is not synonymous with variable cost. Often, this classification depends on the level of the organization.

         a)   For example, the fixed cost of depreciation may not be controllable by the manager of a revenue center. But it is controllable by the division vice president to which that manager reports.

   c.   **Goal congruence.** Performance measures must be designed so that they relate directly to accomplishment of the organization's goals.

      1)   Suboptimization results when the goals of segments of the organization differ from the organization's goals.

4.   **Common Costs**

   a.   Common costs are the costs of products, activities, facilities, services, or operations shared by two or more cost objects. Joint costs are the common costs of a single process that yields two or more joint products.

      1)   The costs of service centers and central administration are examples.

   b.   Because common costs are indirect, identification of a direct cause-and-effect relationship with the actions of the cost object to which it is allocated can be difficult.

      1)   Such a relationship promotes acceptance of common cost allocation by managers who perceive the fairness of the procedure.

5.   **Management Reporting**

   a.   Relevance is the most important attribute of management reporting. Relevance is determined by whether a revenue or cost element depends on a manager's decision.

Stop and review! You have completed the outline for this subunit. Study multiple-choice questions 1 and 2 on page 368.

16.2 PERFORMANCE MEASUREMENT -- FINANCIAL AND NONFINANCIAL MEASURES

1. **Financial vs. Nonfinancial Measures**

   a. The appropriate financial performance measures vary with the type of responsibility center.

      1) Cost centers -- Variable costs, total costs
      2) Revenue centers -- Gross sales, net sales
      3) Profit centers -- Sales, gross margin, operating income
      4) Investment centers

         a) Return on investment, residual income

         b) Return on assets, return on equity, return on common equity, economic rate of return on common stock, economic value added

   b. Nonfinancial performance measures are not standardized and thus can take any appropriate form.

      1) Product quality -- measures include returns and allowances and the number and types of customer complaints.

      2) Manufacturing systems -- measures include throughput time (i.e., the time required to convert raw materials into finished goods), the ratio of equipment setup time to total production time, and the ratio of reworked units to completed units.

2. **Return on Investment and Residual Income**

   a. The return provided to a corporation's owners most often is assessed using one of two measures:

      1) Return on investment, stated in percentage terms
      2) Residual income, stated in dollar terms

   b. These measures allow an investor to assess how effectively and efficiently the firm is using assets to obtain a return.

   c. Operating income equals earnings before interest and tax.

3. **Return on Investment -- Basic Version**

   a. ROI is calculated as follows if the investment is defined as assets:

$$\text{Return on investment (ROI)} = \frac{\text{Operating income}}{\text{Average invested capital}} = \frac{\text{Operating income}}{\text{Total assets}}$$

      1) If the firm's ROI is higher than its cost of capital, its activities are adding to shareholder value.

EXAMPLE

A firm had the following information for the year just ended:

Sales	$100,000
Operating expenses	58,000
Invested capital (total assets)	800,000

Invested capital at the previous year end was $600,000. ROI for the year can be calculated as follows:

Return on investment (ROI) = Operating income ÷ Average invested capital
= ($100,000 − $58,000) ÷ [($800,000 + $600,000) ÷ 2]
= $42,000 ÷ $700,000
= 6%

4.   **Return on Investment -- Component View**

   a.   ROI can be viewed as the product of two component ratios.

Return on Investment		**Profit Margin**		**Capital (Asset) Turnover**
$\dfrac{Operating\ income}{Average\ invested\ capital}$	=	$\dfrac{Operating\ income}{Sales}$	×	$\dfrac{Sales}{Average\ invested\ capital}$

EXAMPLE

Invested capital at the previous year end was $600,000. ROI for the year can be calculated as follows:

   Profit margin*:   Operating income ÷ Sales   = $42,000 ÷ $100,000 = 42%
   Capital turnover: Sales ÷ Average invested capital = $100,000 ÷ $700,000 = .143 times

The calculation can be checked by recombining the two ratios to generate ROI.

   Return on investment: Profit margin × Capital turnover = 42% × .143 = 6%

*Profit margin also is known as return on sales (ROS).

---

5.   **Residual Income**

   a.   Residual income is calculated as follows:

   Residual income = Operating income − Target return on invested capital

      1)   The target return amount equals average invested capital times an imputed interest rate.

EXAMPLE

The firm's capital has an imputed interest rate of 5.5%.

         Residual income = Operating income − Target return on invested capital
                  = $42,000 − ($700,000 × 5.5%)
                  = $42,000 − $38,500
                  = $3,500

---

6.   **Comparison of ROI and Residual Income**

   a.   ROI is a percentage, and residual income is a monetary amount.
   b.   ROI is widely used because it facilitates comparison with other percentage-based measures, such as the firm's cost of capital and the ROIs of competitors.

      1)   But a disadvantage of ROI is the potential rejection of projects that decrease the ROI despite increasing shareholder value.

EXAMPLE

A firm assesses divisional performance based solely on ROI. If a division with a current ROI of 12% is considering a project that is estimated to return only 10%, management might reject it because divisional ROI would decrease.

Nevertheless, if the project has a positive NPV, it should be accepted because it increases shareholder value.

---

   c.   The example above indicates why residual income often is preferable.

      1)   The distinction between ROI and residual income is similar to that between internal rate of return (IRR), a percentage, and net present value (NPV), a monetary amount.

         a)   A percentage identifies the highest return per dollar invested. But the firm ultimately is most interested in the total monetary amount of the return.

> The AICPA has frequently asked questions about the determination of ROI and residual income as well as questions requiring their comparison.

7. **Return on Assets**

    a. Return on assets (ROA) is an alternative to return on investment.

$$Return\ on\ assets\ (ROA) = \frac{Net\ income}{Average\ total\ assets}$$

EXAMPLE

A firm reports the following information for the year just ended:

Operating income	$ 90,000
Income taxes	27,000
Total assets	400,000

Total assets at the previous year end were $500,000. ROA for the year is calculated as follows:

$$
\begin{aligned}
Return\ on\ assets\ (ROA) &= Net\ income \div Average\ total\ assets \\
&= (\$90{,}000 - \$27{,}000) \div [(\$400{,}000 + \$500{,}000) \div 2] \\
&= \$63{,}000 \div \$450{,}000 \\
&= 14\%
\end{aligned}
$$

---

8. **Earnings per Share (EPS) and Return on Equity (ROE/ROCE)**

    a. EPS is a ratio of interest to common shareholders. It is a profitability ratio that measures the amount of current-period earnings that can be associated with a single share of common stock.

$$EPS = \frac{Net\ income - Preferred\ dividends}{Common\ shares\ outstanding}$$

        1) The numerator also is known as income available to common shareholders.

    b. Return on equity (ROE) measures the amount of net income returned in relation to shareholder equity.

$$ROE = \frac{Net\ income}{Average\ shareholder's\ equity}$$

    c. Return on common equity (ROCE) measures the amount of income earned per dollar invested by the common shareholders.

$$ROCE = \frac{Net\ income - Preferred\ dividends}{Average\ common\ equity}$$

    d. The price-earnings (P-E) ratio measures the amount that investors are willing to pay for $1 of earnings.

$$P\text{-}E = \frac{P}{E} = \frac{Market\ price\ of\ share}{EPS}$$

        1) Generally, the higher the ratio, the more confidence the market has in the firm's ability to provide higher returns to investors.

9. **Economic Rate of Return on Common Stock**

    a. The economic rate of return on common stock measures the amount of shareholder value generated during a period in relation to the investment.

$$\frac{Dividends\ paid + Change\ in\ share\ price}{Beginning\ share\ price}$$

10. **Economic Value Added**

   a. Economic value added (EVA) is the formula for residual income adjusted for the opportunity cost of capital.

   b. The following is the basic formula:

   EVA = After-tax operating income − (Initial investment × Weighted average cost of capital[1])

   [1]The weighted average cost of capital (WACC) is defined in Study Unit 8, Subunit 5.

EXAMPLE

A firm invested $200,000 in a new operating segment. Its current-year net income was $21,000. The WACC is 9%.

Net income	$21,000
Investment × Cost of capital ($200,000 × 9%)	(18,000)
EVA	$ 3,000

The EVA is positive. Thus, the investment increased shareholder value.

---

   c. EVA represents a business unit's true economic profit primarily because it is determined by subtracting the cost of equity capital.

   1) The cost of equity is an opportunity cost, i.e., the return on the best alternative investment of similar risk.

   2) Accordingly, EVA measures the marginal benefit obtained by using resources in a specific way.

   d. EVA also differs from accounting income because it results from certain other adjustments.

   1) For example, R&D costs may be capitalized and amortized over 5 years for EVA purposes, and true economic depreciation rather than the amount used for accounting or tax purposes may be recognized. Adjustments vary from firm to firm.

 A candidate should know the formulas used to calculate the various financial ratios and also should be able to analyze the results. Numerous CPA exams have included questions on both the calculation and analysis of financial ratios. However, the numbers necessary to calculate a ratio often are not given directly.

NOTE: This tip also applies to Study Unit 9, Subunit 3, and Study Unit 10, Subunit 2.

Stop and review! You have completed the outline for this subunit. Study multiple-choice questions 3 through 5 beginning on page 368.

16.3 PERFORMANCE MEASUREMENT -- BALANCED SCORECARD

1. **Critical Success Factors (CSFs)**

   a. The trend in performance evaluation is the balanced scorecard approach to managing the implementation of the firm's strategy. This includes multiple performance measures.

   1) The balanced scorecard is an accounting report that connects the firm's CSFs with measurements of its performance.

   b. The balanced scorecard is a goal congruence tool that informs managers about the nonfinancial factors that upper management believes to be important.

   1) Measures on the balanced scorecard may be financial or nonfinancial, internal or external, and short-term or long-term.

   2) The balanced scorecard facilitates best practice analysis. Best practices are methods of performing a business function that are superior to all other known methods.

    c.   CSFs are specific, measurable financial and nonfinancial, internal and external, short-term and long-term elements of performance that are vital to competitive advantage.

        1)   Multiple measures of performance determine whether a manager is achieving certain objectives but not others that may be more important. For example, an improvement in operating results at the expense of new product development is apparent using a balanced scorecard.

2. **SWOT Analysis**

    a.   A firm identifies its CSFs by means of a SWOT analysis that addresses internal factors (its **S**trengths and **W**eaknesses) and external factors (its **O**pportunities and **T**hreats).

3. **Measures**

    a.   Specific measures for each CSF should be relevant to the success of the firm and reliably stated.

        1)   Thus, the balanced scorecard varies with the strategy adopted by the firm.

    b.   The scorecard should include **lagging** indicators (such as output and financial measures) and **leading** indicators (such as many types of nonfinancial measures, e.g., customer satisfaction, returns, and repeat customers).

        1)   The latter should be used only if they are predictors of ultimate financial performance.

    c.   The scorecard should permit a determination of whether certain objectives are being achieved at the expense of others.

        1)   For example, reduced spending on customer service may improve short-term financial results at a significant cost that is revealed by a long-term decline in customer satisfaction measures.

4. **Possible CSFs and Measures**

    a.   A typical balanced scorecard classifies objectives into one of four perspectives:

        1)   **Financial**

Possible CSF	Possible Measure
Sales	New Product Sales
FV of Firm's Stock	Price-Earnings Ratio
Profitability	Return on Investment
Liquidity	Quick Ratio, current ratio, days payables or receivables.

        2)   **Customer Satisfaction**

CSF	Financial Measure	Nonfinancial Measure
Customer Satisfaction	Trends in dollar amounts of returns	Market share
Dealer and Distributor Relationships	Trends in dollar amounts of discounts taken	Lead time
Marketing and Selling Performance	Trends in dollar amounts of sales	Market research results
Prompt Delivery	Trends in delivery expenses	On-time delivery rate
Quality	Dollar amounts of defects	Rate of defects

3) Internal Business Processes

CSF	Financial Measure	Nonfinancial Measure
Quality	Scrap costs	Rate of scrap and rework
Productivity	Change in company revenue/ change in company costs	Units produced per machine hour
Flexibility of Response to Changing Conditions	Cost to repurpose machine for new use	Time to repurpose machine for new use
Operating Readiness	Set-up costs	Downtime
Safety	Dollar amount of injury claims	Number and type of injury claims

4) Learning and Growth

CSF	Financial Measure	Nonfinancial Measure
Development of New Products	R&D costs	Number of new patents applied for
Promptness of Their Introduction	Lost revenue (from slow introduction of new product to market)	Length of time to bring a product to market
Human Resource Development	Recruiting costs	Personnel turnover
Morale	Orientation/team-building costs	Personnel complaints
Competence of Work Force	Training/retraining costs	Hours of training

5. **Development**

    a.   The active participation of senior management is essential.

        1)   This involvement ensures the cooperation of lower-level managers in the identification of objectives, appropriate measures, targeted results, and methods of achieving the results.

    b.   The scorecard should contain measures at the detail level that permits everyone to understand how his or her efforts affect the firm's results.

        1)   The scorecard and the strategy it represents must be communicated to all managers and used as a basis for compensation decisions.

6. **Functionality**

    a.   Each objective is associated with one or more measures that permit the organization to measure progress toward the objective.

        1)   The organization should identify a cause-and-effect relationship between an action taken (or avoided), that affects a CSF.

            a)   For example, if the R&D budget increases, the number of new patents applied for increases.

        2)   Achievement of the objectives in one perspective makes it possible to achieve the objectives in other perspectives.

        3)   A **strategy map** relates objectives and perspectives.

    b.   To achieve its objectives, the organization must establish relevant

        1)   Criteria to measure outcomes
        2)   Performance drivers

The AICPA has tested the balanced scorecard approach by asking for the perspective related to either measures or CSFs.

EXAMPLE of a Balanced Scorecard

OBJECTIVES	PERFORMANCE MEASURES	TARGETS	INITIATIVES
PERSPECTIVE: Financial			
Increase sales	Gross revenues	Increase 15%	• Expand into new markets • Improve same-store sales
PERSPECTIVE: Customer Satisfaction			
Reduce returns	Number of returns	Decrease 10%	• Reduce number of defects • Determine customer needs prior to sale
PERSPECTIVE: Internal Business Processes			
Reduce scrap	Costs of scrap	Decrease 5%	• Employee training • Seek higher quality materials
PERSPECTIVE: Learning and Growth			
Reduce personnel turnover	Length of time employed	Increase 50%	• Improve hiring practices • Reevaluate compensation plan

Stop and review! You have completed the outline for this subunit. Study multiple-choice questions 6 and 7 on page 369.

16.4 PROCESS MANAGEMENT

1. **Performance-Improving Processes**

   a. The Process-Management-Driven Business

      1) Management emphasizes the effective and efficient performance of predefined business processes.

      2) Well-designed processes lead to the accomplishment of the organization's goals.

   b. Shared Services

      1) Shared services are centralized but with a nontraditional focus.

      2) The shared services model involves designing the service center so that its employees are motivated to be flexible and responsive to customer needs.

      3) Centralizing a firm's internal services at a single location may delay services.

   c. Outsourcing

      1) Processes such as human resources, payroll, and information services may not be core competencies of an organization.

         a) Contracting with outside service providers who specialize in these functions may result in cost savings. The organization also is not affected by knowledge loss when key employees leave.

      2) Potential disadvantages include (a) loss of core knowledge, (b) loss of control over the outsourced function, (c) unexpected costs, and (d) the challenges of contract management.

   d. Off-Shore Operations

      1) Cost advantages (lower taxes, lower wages, and less strict environmental and occupational safety regulations) can be gained by moving operations to foreign countries.

      2) The effects of currency exchange rate fluctuations and the possibility of political instability must be considered.

2. **Business Process Reengineering (BPR)**

    a. BPR is the complete, bottom-up revision of the way an organization performs a business process.

    b. Organizations undertaking BPR ignore how the process currently is performed.

    c. BPR is **not**

        1) A gradual, incremental streamlining of existing procedures (kaizen);
        2) Computerization of manual processes (automation); or
        3) A change in the nature of the business itself (paradigm shift).

    d. The goals of BPR are usually stated in terms of increased efficiency or elimination of redundant jobs. These goals eventually can be stated in terms of cost savings.

    e. But BPR often does not provide the promised benefits.

        1) Business processes routinely cross organizational boundaries.

            a) Redesigning the process of one department often requires the cooperation of other departments that may be reluctant to reduce their autonomy.

        2) Upper management may have begun other strategic initiatives, such as total quality management or Six Sigma, that conflict with either the goals of, or the resources necessary for, BPR.

            a) Any BPR program must be closely aligned with the overall organizational strategy.

3. **Lean Operation**

    a. The ultimate goal of lean operation is a smooth, rapid flow of work through the system. To achieve this ultimate goal, three supporting goals are constantly pursued.

        1) Elimination of Disruptions

            a) A disruption is anything that interrupts the smooth flow of work, e.g., line stoppages, materials shortages, and excessive defects.

        2) System Flexibility

            a) A flexible system can be adapted to changes in product mix or quantities without creating a disruption.

        3) Elimination of Waste

            a) Waste is any unproductive use of resources. In accordance with a just-in-time philosophy, inventory is considered waste.

4. **Demand Flow Technology (DFT)**

    a. Demand flow technology is a mathematically based approach devised in the 1980s by operations management expert John Costanza.

    b. DFT combines knowledge of materials and work-in-process inventory levels with customer demand to maximize use of the firm's productive capacity, i.e., to maintain continuous production flow.

        1) In contrast with the forecast-push model used by MRP described in Study Unit 10, Subunit 1, DFT is a pull system driven by customer demand.

5. **Theory of Constraints (TOC)**

    a. The theory of constraints is a system to improve human thinking about problems. It has been greatly extended to include manufacturing operations.

        1) The basic premise of TOC as applied to business is that improving any process is best done not by trying to maximize efficiency in every part of the process but by focusing on a limiting factor, called the constraint (or bottleneck operation).

          2)   Increasing the efficiency of processes that are not constraints merely creates backup in the system.

    b.   The following are the steps in a TOC analysis:

          1)   Identify the constraint.
          2)   Determine the most profitable product mix given the constraint.
          3)   Maximize the flow through the constraint.
          4)   Increase capacity at the constraint.
          5)   Redesign the manufacturing process for greater flexibility and speed.

    c.   A basic principle of TOC analysis is that short-term profit maximization requires maximizing the contribution margin through the constraint (throughput contribution).

          1)   Thus, the product with the highest output should be the one with the highest throughput contribution per unit, not necessarily the highest contribution margin per unit.

    d.   To determine the most profitable use of the bottleneck operation, a manager calculates the throughput contribution per unit of time spent in the constraint.

          1)   Profits are maximized by maximizing the flow through the bottleneck operation of the product with the highest throughput contribution per unit of time.

6. **Six Sigma**

    a.   Six Sigma is a quality improvement approach. The goal is to reduce the number of defects in a mass-production process.

          1)   The name Six Sigma (sometimes written 6σ) is derived from statistics and probability theory. In a normal distribution (i.e., a bell curve), six standard deviations encompass 99.99966% of the items in the distribution.
          2)   Because of the importance of statistical analysis in any Six Sigma program, accurate and verifiable data are a necessity.

    b.   A Six Sigma program also involves role-filling by specific individuals in the organization. (The color coding system is based on martial arts belt rankings).

          1)   The executive level must demonstrate its commitment to the Six Sigma program and must empower those in the other roles with enough authority and resources to implement the program successfully.
          2)   Champions have responsibility for oversight of the implementation of the Six Sigma program across the organization.
          3)   Master black belts assist the champions in implementing the program.
          4)   Black belts, like champions and master black belts, devote all of their time to the Six Sigma program. They oversee specific projects.
          5)   Green belts and yellow belts do Six Sigma work in addition to their regular duties. They are closest to the production processes to be improved.

Stop and review! You have completed the outline for this subunit. Study multiple-choice questions 8 through 10 on page 370.

16.5 TOOLS FOR PROCESS MANAGEMENT

 Past exam questions have asked for identification of the methods used to measure process performance.

1. **Statistical Process Control (SPC)**

    a. SPC is a method of quality control that uses statistical methods.
    b. Results of an operation are monitored to determine whether it is within certain limits or at certain capacities.
    c. SPC can be applied to any process in which a conforming product can be measured.
    d. The information learned from SPC should be used in planning and budgeting.

2. **Statistical Control Charts**

    a. Statistical control charts are graphic aids for monitoring the status of any process subject to acceptable or unacceptable variations during repeated operations.

        1) They also have applications of direct interest to auditors and accountants, for example, (a) unit cost of production, (b) direct labor hours used, (c) ratio of actual expenses to budgeted expenses, (d) number of calls by sales personnel, or (e) total accounts receivable.

    b. A control chart consists of three lines plotted on a horizontal time scale.

        1) The center line represents the overall mean or average range for the process being controlled. The other two lines are the upper control limit (UCL) and the lower control limit (LCL).
        2) The processes are measured periodically, and the values (X) are plotted on the chart.

            a) If the value falls within the control limits, no action is taken.
            b) If the value falls outside the limits, the result is abnormal, the process is considered out of control, and an investigation is made for possible corrective action.

    c. Another advantage of the chart is that it makes trends and cycles visible.

        1) A disadvantage of the chart is that it does not indicate the cause of the variation.

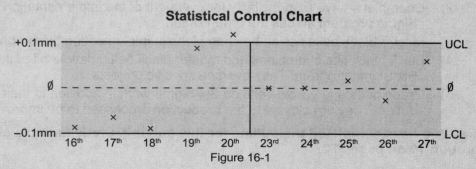

EXAMPLE

The chart below depicts 2 weeks of production by a manufacturer who produces a single precision part each day. To be usable, the part can vary from the standard by no more than +/– 0.1 millimeter.

Statistical Control Chart

Figure 16-1

The part produced on the 20th had to be scrapped, and changes were made to the equipment to return the process to the controlled state for the following week's production.

3.   **Pareto Diagrams**

   a.   A Pareto diagram is a bar chart that assists managers in quality control analysis.

      1)   In the context of quality control, managers optimize their time by focusing their effort on the relatively few sources of the most defects.

         a)   The independent variable, plotted on the x axis, is the factor selected by the manager as the subject of interest, e.g., a department, time period, or geographical location. The frequency of occurrence of the defect (dependent variable) is plotted on the y axis.

         b)   The occurrences of the independent variable are ranked from highest to lowest, allowing the manager to observe the sources of the most defects.

EXAMPLE

The chief administrative officer wants to know which departments are generating the most travel vouchers that have to be returned to the submitter because of incomplete documentation.

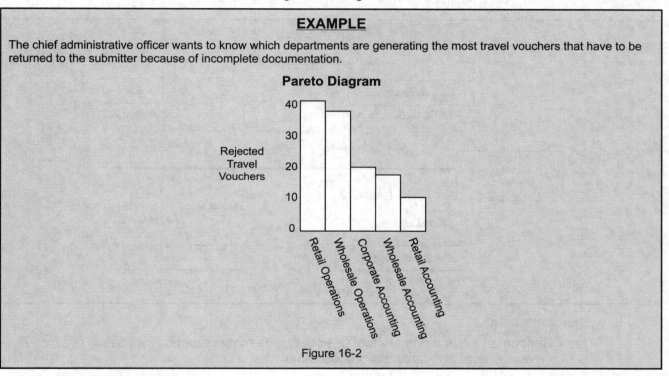

Figure 16-2

---

4.   **Histograms**

   a.   A histogram is similar to a Pareto diagram. The major distinction is that histograms display a continuum for the independent variable.

EXAMPLE

The CAO wants to know the amount of a typical rejected travel voucher.

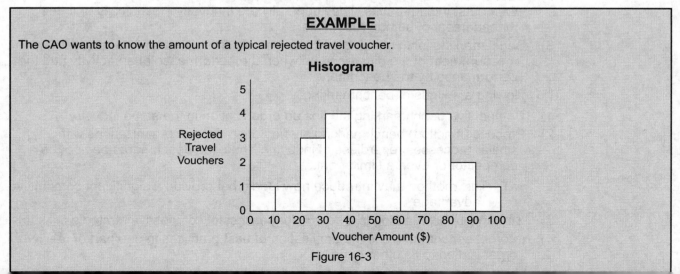

Figure 16-3

5.   **Fishbone Diagrams**

   a.   A fishbone diagram (also called a cause-and-effect diagram) is a total quality management process improvement method that is useful in studying causation (why the actual and desired situations differ).

   1)   The diagram organizes the analysis of causation and helps to identify possible interactions among causes.

   2)   The head of the skeleton represents the statement of the problem.

   3)   The principal classifications of causes are represented by lines (bones) drawn diagonally from the heavy horizontal line (the spine).

   4)   Smaller horizontal lines are added in their order of probability in each classification.

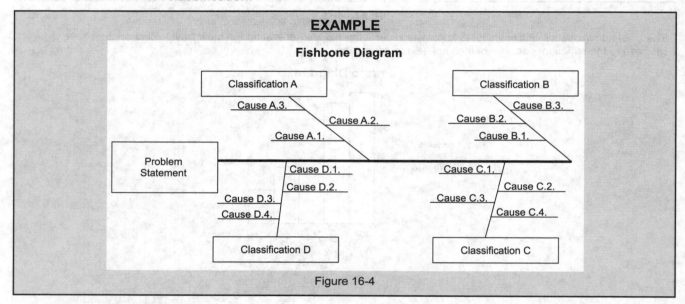

EXAMPLE

Fishbone Diagram

Figure 16-4

6.   **Benchmarking**

   a.   Benchmarking is a primary tool used in quality management. It applies to productivity management and business process analysis.

   1)   Benchmarking involves analysis and measurement of key outputs against those of the best organizations. This procedure also identifies the underlying key actions and causes that contribute to the performance difference.

   2)   Best practices are recognized by authorities in the field and by customers for their outstanding results. They generally are innovative technically or in the management of human resources.

   3)   Benchmarking is an ongoing process that requires quantitative and qualitative measurement of the difference between the performance of an activity and the performance by the benchmark.

   b.   The following are kinds of benchmarking:

   1)   Competitive benchmarking studies an organization in the same industry.

   2)   Process (function) benchmarking studies operations of organizations with similar processes regardless of industry. Thus, the benchmark need not be a competitor or even a similar entity.

   a)   This method may introduce new ideas that provide a significant competitive advantage.

   3)   Strategic benchmarking is a search for successful competitive strategies.

   4)   Internal benchmarking is the application of best practices in one part of the organization to its other parts.

EXAMPLE

A team from an airline company charged with improving its aircraft ground turnaround time (refueling, maintenance, and service) might consider the benchmark of auto racing's pit stops and determine the applicability of their best practices.

---

7. **Gamification**

    a.   This method of problem solving involves thinking of business goals as if they were goals in a game, such as achieving a higher return on investment.

        1)   Rewards are given to players who achieve certain goals.

             a)   **Scores** can be published so that players are encouraged to compete.

             b)   Due to the possibility that increased competition could lead to unethical behavior, the game should be monitored.

Stop and review! You have completed the outline for this subunit. Study multiple-choice questions 11 through 14 beginning on page 370.

16.6 COSTS OF QUALITY

1. **Costs of Quality**

    a.   The costs of quality must be assessed in terms of relative costs and benefits. Thus, an organization should attempt to optimize its total cost of quality.

        1)   Moreover, nonquantitative factors also must be considered. For example, an emphasis on quality improves competitiveness, enhances employee expertise, and generates goodwill.

2. **Categories**

    a.   **Conformance costs** include costs of prevention and costs of appraisal, which are financial measures of internal performance.

        1)   **Prevention** attempts to avoid defective output. These costs include (a) preventive maintenance, (b) employee training, (c) review of equipment design, and (d) evaluation of suppliers.

        2)   **Appraisal** includes such activities as statistical quality control programs, inspection, and testing.

    b.   **Nonconformance costs** include internal failure costs (a financial measure of internal performance) and external failure costs (a financial measure of customer satisfaction).

        1)   **Internal failure costs** occur when defective products are detected before additional costs are incurred on defective products. Examples are scrap, rework, tooling changes, and downtime.

        2)   **External failure costs**, e.g., warranty costs, product liability costs, and loss of customer goodwill, result when problems occur after shipment.

             a)   Environmental costs also are external failure costs, e.g., fines for nonadherence to environmental law and loss of customer goodwill.

EXAMPLE

Conformance costs:	
Prevention costs	$35,000
Appraisal costs	5,000
Nonconformance costs:	
Internal failure costs	17,500
External failure costs	9,500
Total costs of quality	**$67,000**

Stop and review! You have completed the outline for this subunit. Study multiple-choice questions 15 through 17 on page 372.

16.7 TQM AND THE ISO FRAMEWORK

1. **Total Quality Management (TQM) Defined**

   a. TQM is the continuous pursuit of quality in every aspect of organizational activities through (1) a philosophy of doing it right the first time, (2) employee training and empowerment, (3) promotion of teamwork, (4) improvement of processes, and (5) attention to satisfaction of internal and external customers.

      1) TQM emphasizes the supplier's relationship with the customer and identifies customer needs. It also recognizes that everyone in a process is at some time a customer or supplier of someone else, either within or outside the organization.

      2) Thus, TQM (a) begins with external customer requirements, (b) identifies internal customer-supplier relationships and requirements, and (c) establishes requirements for external suppliers.

      3) Organizations tend to be vertically organized, but TQM requires strong horizontal linkages.

Background

TQM was developed in the mid-1940s by statistician W. Edwards Deming, who aided Japanese industry in its recovery from World War II. The Deming Prize is awarded by the Union of Japanese Scientists and Engineers for outstanding contributions to the study or application of TQM (www.juse.or.jp/deming_en). While Deming was praised and deeply respected in Japan, it took 30 years for his principles to be applied in the U.S.

---

   b. TQM treats the pursuit of quality as a basic organizational function that is as important as production or marketing.

   c. TQM recognizes that quality improvement can increase revenues and decrease costs significantly. The following are TQM's core principles or critical factors:

      1) Emphasis on the customer

         a) Satisfaction of external customers
         b) Satisfaction of internal customers
         c) Requirements for external suppliers
         d) Requirements for internal suppliers

      2) Continuous improvement as a never-ending process, not a destination

      3) Engaging every employee in the pursuit of total quality

         a) Avoidance of defects in products or services and satisfaction of external customers requires that all internal customers be satisfied.

   d. The management of quality is not limited to quality management staff, engineers, and production personnel. It extends to everyone in the organization.

2. **Implementation**

   a. Implementation of TQM cannot be accomplished by application of a formula, and the process is lengthy and difficult. The following phases are typical:

      1) Establishing an executive-level quality council of senior managers with strong involvement by the CEO.

      2) Providing quality training programs for senior managers.

      3) Conducting a quality audit to evaluate the success of the process for gathering background information to develop the strategic quality improvement plan.

         a) The quality audit also may identify the best improvement opportunities and the organization's strengths and weaknesses compared with its benchmarked competitors.

    4) Preparing a gap analysis to determine what is necessary to close the gap between the organization and the quality leaders in its industry and to establish a database for the development of the strategic quality improvement plan.

    5) Developing strategic quality improvement plans for the short and long term.

    6) Conducting employee communication and training programs.

    7) Establishing quality teams, which ensure that goods and services conform to specifications.

    8) Creating a measurement system and setting goals.

    9) Revising compensation, appraisal, and recognition systems.

    10) Reviewing and revising the entire effort periodically.

3. **The ISO Standards**

    a. In 1987, the International Organization for Standardization (ISO) introduced ISO 9000, a group of 11 standards and technical reports that provide guidance for establishing and maintaining a **quality management system** (QMS). The ISO's rules specify that its standards be revised every 5 years to reflect technological and market developments.

Background

ISO is not an acronym. It means equal, suggesting that entities certified under ISO standards have equal quality. For specific and up-to-date information, see the ISO's website (www.iso.org).

---

    b. The intent of the standards is to ensure the quality of the process, not the product. The marketplace determines whether a product is good or bad.

      1) For this reason, the ISO deems it unacceptable for phrases referring to ISO certification to appear on individual products or packaging.

    c. Basic Requirements of an ISO QMS

      1) Key processes affecting quality must be identified and included.

        a) A process management approach must be used. It manages the entity as a set of linked processes that are controlled for continuous improvement.

      2) General requirements. The entity must have a quality policy and quality goals. It also must design a QMS to control process performance. Quality goals are measurable and specific.

        a) The QMS is documented in the (1) quality policy, (2) quality manual, (3) procedures, (4) work instructions, and (5) records.

      3) Management responsibility. Management (a) reviews the quality policy, (b) analyzes data about QMS performance, and (c) assesses opportunities for improvement and the need for change.

        a) Management ensures that systems exist to determine and satisfy customer requirements.

      4) Resource management. The resources needed to improve the QMS and satisfy customer requirements must be provided.

      5) Product realization processes result in products or services received by customers. These processes must be planned and controlled. Issues are (a) means of control, (b) objectives, (c) documentation and records needed, and (d) acceptance criteria.

      6) Measurement, analysis, and improvement. The entity must have processes for (a) inspection, (b) testing, (c) measurement, (d) analysis, and (e) improvement.

Stop and review! You have completed the outline for this subunit. Study multiple-choice questions 18 through 20 beginning on page 372.

QUESTIONS

16.1 Responsibility Centers

1. A segment of an organization is referred to as a profit center if it has

A. Authority to make decisions affecting the major determinants of profit including the power to choose its markets and sources of supply.

B. Authority to make decisions affecting the major determinants of profit including the power to choose its markets and sources of supply and significant control over the amount of invested capital.

C. Authority to make decisions over the most significant costs of operations including the power to choose the sources of supply.

D. Authority to provide specialized support to other units within the organization.

Answer (A) is correct.

REQUIRED: The definition of a profit center.

DISCUSSION: A profit center is responsible for both revenues and expenses. For example, the perfume department in a department store is a profit center. The manager of a profit center usually has the authority to make decisions affecting the major determinants of profit, including the power to choose markets (revenue sources) and suppliers (costs).

Answer (B) is incorrect. An investment center, not a profit center, has control over invested capital. Answer (C) is incorrect. A cost center manager has authority over all significant costs but not of revenues or investments. Answer (D) is incorrect. A service center supports other organizational units.

2. Managers are most likely to accept allocations of common costs based on

A. Cause and effect.

B. Ability to bear.

C. Percent of revenues earned.

D. Top management decisions.

Answer (A) is correct.

REQUIRED: The criterion most likely to result in acceptable allocations of common costs.

DISCUSSION: The difficulty with common costs is that they are indirect costs whose allocation may be arbitrary. A direct cause-and-effect relationship between a common cost and the actions of the cost object to which it is allocated is desirable. Such a relationship promotes acceptance of the allocation by managers who perceive the fairness of the procedure, but identification of cause and effect may not be feasible.

Answer (B) is incorrect. Allocation using an ability-to-bear criterion punishes successful managers and rewards underachievers. Answer (C) is incorrect. Allocations based on the percentage of revenues earned use an ability-to-bear approach. Answer (D) is incorrect. Top management decisions on cost allocation tend to be arbitrary.

16.2 Performance Measurement -- Financial and Nonfinancial Measures

3. Which one of the following statements pertaining to the return on investment (ROI) as a performance measurement is **false**?

A. When the average age of assets differs substantially across segments of a business, the use of ROI may not be appropriate.

B. ROI relies on financial measures that are capable of being independently verified, while other forms of performance measures are subject to manipulation.

C. The use of ROI may lead managers to reject capital investment projects that can be justified by using discounted cash flow models.

D. The use of ROI can make it undesirable for a skillful manager to take on troubleshooting assignments such as those involving turning around unprofitable divisions.

Answer (B) is correct.

REQUIRED: The false statement about ROI as a performance measure.

DISCUSSION: ROI is calculated by dividing a segment's income by the invested capital. Thus, ROI can be manipulated by falsifying income or invested capital.

Answer (A) is incorrect. ROI can be misleading when the quality of the investment base differs among segments. Answer (C) is incorrect. Managers may reject projects that are profitable (a return greater than the cost of capital) but decrease ROI. For example, the manager of a segment with a 15% ROI may not want to invest in a new project with a 10% ROI, even though the cost of capital might be only 8%. Answer (D) is incorrect. The use of ROI does not reflect the relative difficulty of tasks undertaken by managers.

4. Charlie's Service Co. is an automobile service center. For the month of June, Charlie's had the following operating statistics:

Sales	$750,000
Operating income	50,000
Net profit after taxes	6,000
Total assets available	700,000
Shareholders' equity	300,000
Cost of capital	8%

Charlie's has a

A. Return on investment of 6.67%.

B. Residual income of $(6,000).

C. Return on investment of 8%.

D. Residual income of $(10,000).

Answer (B) is correct.

REQUIRED: The true statement about operating performance.

DISCUSSION: Residual income is the excess of operating income (a pretax amount) over a targeted amount equal to an imputed interest charge on invested capital. Using total assets available as the investment base, Charlie's targeted amount is $56,000 ($700,000 total assets × 8% cost of capital). Subtracting this amount from operating income results in residual income of $(6,000).

Answer (A) is incorrect. The return on sales is 6.67% ($50,000 ÷ $750,000). Answer (C) is incorrect. The cost of capital is 8%. Answer (D) is incorrect. Residual income of $(10,000) results from improperly subtracting weighted sales rather than weighted assets.

5. Avionics Industrials reported at year end that operating income before taxes for the year equaled $2,400,000. The firm's weighted-average cost of capital (WACC) is 7.24%. The carrying amount of debt is $1,300,000, and the carrying amount of equity capital is $8,800,000. The income tax rate for Avionics is 30%. What is the economic value added (EVA)?

A. $731,240

B. $948,760

C. $1,668,760

D. $1,680,000

Answer (B) is correct.

REQUIRED: The EVA.

DISCUSSION: EVA equals after-tax operating income minus the product of the weighted-average cost of capital (WACC) and the investment base. After-tax operating income equals operating income multiplied by 1 minus the tax rate, or $1,680,000 [$2,400,000 × (1 – .3)]. The investment base is $10,100,000, consisting of $1,300,000 of debt and $8,800,000 of equity. Thus, EVA equals $948,760 [$1,680,000 – ($10,100,000 × 0.0724)].

Answer (A) is incorrect. The cost of capital is $731,240. Answer (C) is incorrect. Income taxes must be subtracted from operating income to compute EVA. Answer (D) is incorrect. The after-tax operating income is $1,680,000.

16.3 Performance Measurement -- Balanced Scorecard

6. Using the balanced scorecard approach, an organization evaluates managerial performance based on

A. A single ultimate measure of operating results, such as residual income.

B. Multiple financial and nonfinancial measures.

C. Multiple nonfinancial measures only.

D. Multiple financial measures only.

Answer (B) is correct.

REQUIRED: The nature of the balanced scorecard approach.

DISCUSSION: The trend in managerial performance evaluation is the balanced scorecard approach. Multiple measures of performance permit a determination as to whether a manager is achieving certain objectives at the expense of others that may be equally or more important. These measures may be financial or nonfinancial and usually include items with four perspectives: (1) financial; (2) customer satisfaction; (3) internal business processes; and (4) learning and growth.

7. On a balanced scorecard, which is more of an internal process measure than an external-based measure?

A. Cycle time.

B. Profitability.

C. Customer satisfaction.

D. Market share.

Answer (A) is correct.

REQUIRED: The measure more internal-process related on a balanced scorecard.

DISCUSSION: Cycle time is the manufacturing time to complete an order. Thus, cycle time is strictly related to internal processes. Profitability is a combination of internal and external considerations. Customer satisfaction and market share are related to how customers perceive a product and how competitors react.

Answer (B) is incorrect. Profitability is a measure that includes external considerations. Answer (C) is incorrect. Customer satisfaction is a measure that includes external considerations. Answer (D) is incorrect. Market share is a measure that includes external considerations.

16.4 Process Management

8. System flexibility, elimination of waste, and elimination of disruptions are characteristic goals of which business process?

    A. Lean operation.

    B. Six Sigma.

    C. Delphi technique.

    D. Monte Carlo technique.

Answer (A) is correct.

    REQUIRED: The business process with the characteristic goals of system flexibility, elimination of waste, and elimination of disruptions.

    DISCUSSION: The three supporting goals of lean operation are (1) elimination of disruptions, (2) system flexibility, and (3) elimination of waste. Inventory is considered a waste.

    Answer (B) is incorrect. The goal of Six Sigma is to reduce the number of defects per million opportunities in a mass-production process to 3.4. Answer (C) is incorrect. The Delphi technique is a system for forecasting based on identifying a consensus among experts. Answer (D) is incorrect. Monte Carlo is a system for using random variables for forecasting in an environment of uncertainty.

9. Increasing the efficiency of all phases of a given process is specifically discouraged by which of the following models?

    A. Lean operation.

    B. Theory of constraints.

    C. Six Sigma.

    D. Demand flow technology.

Answer (B) is correct.

    REQUIRED: The business process model that specifically discourages increasing the efficiency of all phases.

    DISCUSSION: Under the theory of constraints, increasing the efficiency of processes that are not constraints (bottlenecks) merely creates backup in the system.

    Answer (A) is incorrect. Lean operation does not specifically discourage increasing the efficiency of all phases. Answer (C) is incorrect. Six Sigma does not specifically discourage increasing the efficiency of all phases. Answer (D) is incorrect. Demand flow technology does not specifically discourage increasing the efficiency of all phases. It is based on a set of applied mathematical tools that help connect processes in a flow to daily changes in demand.

10. Which of the following is a characteristic of business process reengineering?

    A. Gradual, incremental streamlining of existing procedures.

    B. The movement of manual processes to computers.

    C. A change in the nature of the business itself.

    D. The bottom-up revision of the way the organization carries out a particular business process.

Answer (D) is correct.

    REQUIRED: The characteristic of business process reengineering.

    DISCUSSION: Business process reengineering (BPR) is the complete, bottom-up revision of the way an organization carries out a particular business process. Organizations undertaking BPR totally rethink how a particular business function should be carried out, without regard to how it is currently performed.

    Answer (A) is incorrect. Gradual, incremental streamlining of existing procedures (kaizen) is specifically rejected by business process reengineering. Answer (B) is incorrect. Simply moving manual processes to computers (automation) is not a characteristic of business process engineering. Answer (C) is incorrect. A change in the nature of the business itself (paradigm shift) is not a characteristic of business process reengineering.

16.5 Tools for Process Management

11. The director of sales asks for a count of customers grouped in descending numerical rank by (1) the number of orders they place during a single year and (2) the dollar amounts of the average order. The visual format of these two pieces of information is most likely to be a(n)

    A. Fishbone diagram.

    B. Cost of quality report.

    C. Kaizen diagram.

    D. Pareto diagram.

Answer (D) is correct.

    REQUIRED: The appropriate process measurement tool.

    DISCUSSION: A Pareto diagram displays the values of an independent variable such that managers can quickly identify the areas most in need of attention.

    Answer (A) is incorrect. A fishbone diagram is useful for determining the unknown causes of problems, not for stratifying quantifiable variables. Answer (B) is incorrect. The contents of a cost of quality report are stated in monetary terms. This report is not helpful for determining when to adjust machinery. Answer (C) is incorrect. Kaizen diagram is not a meaningful term in this context.

12. Which of the following statements regarding benchmarking is **false**?

A. Benchmarking involves continuously evaluating the practices of best-in-class organization and adapting processes to incorporate the best of these practices.

B. Benchmarking, in practice, usually involves formation of benchmarking teams.

C. Benchmarking is an ongoing process that involves quantitative and qualitative measurement of the difference between the organization's performance of an activity and the performance by the best in the world or the best in the industry.

D. The benchmarked organization against which a firm is comparing itself must be a direct competitor.

Answer (D) is correct.
REQUIRED: The false statement about benchmarking.
DISCUSSION: Benchmarking is an ongoing process that involves quantitative and qualitative measurement of the difference between the organization's performance of an activity and the performance by a best-in-class organization. The benchmarked organization need not be a direct competitor. The important consideration is that it be an outstanding performer in its industry.
Answer (A) is incorrect. Benchmarking involves continuously evaluating the practices of best-in-class organization and adapting company processes to incorporate the best of these practices. Answer (B) is incorrect. Benchmarking, in practice, usually involves a formation of benchmarking teams. Answer (C) is incorrect. Benchmarking is an ongoing process that involves quantitative and qualitative measurement of the difference between the organization's performance of an activity and the performance by the best in the world or the best in the industry.

13. A company, which has many branch stores, has decided to benchmark one of its stores for the purpose of analyzing the accuracy and reliability of branch store financial reporting. Which one of the following is the most likely measure to be included in a financial benchmark?

A. High turnover of employees.

B. High level of employee participation in setting budgets.

C. High amount of bad debt write-offs.

D. High number of suppliers.

Answer (C) is correct.
REQUIRED: The most likely measure to be included in a financial benchmark.
DISCUSSION: High bad debt write-offs could indicate fraud, which compromises the accuracy and reliability of financial reports. Bad debt write-offs may result from recording fictitious sales.
Answer (A) is incorrect. Turnover of employees is not a financial benchmark. Answer (B) is incorrect. Employee participation in setting budgets is not a financial benchmark. Answer (D) is incorrect. The number of suppliers is not a financial benchmark.

14. A manufacturer that wants to improve its staging process compares its procedures against the check-in process for a major airline. Which of the following tools is the manufacturer using?

A. Total quality management.

B. Statistical process control.

C. Economic value added.

D. Benchmarking.

Answer (D) is correct.
REQUIRED: The tool that the manufacturer is using in comparing its procedures to the check-in process of a major airline.
DISCUSSION: Benchmarking is a primary tool used in quality management. It is a means of helping organizations with productivity management and business process analysis. Benchmarking involves analysis and measurement of key outputs against those of the best organizations. This procedure also involves identifying the underlying key actions and causes that contribute to the performance difference. The benchmark need not be a competitor or even a similar entity. Process (function) benchmarking studies operations of organizations with similar processes regardless of industry. Thus, a comparison to procedures against the check-in process for a major airline is an example of benchmarking.
Answer (A) is incorrect. Total quality management is the continuous pursuit of quality in every aspect of organizational activities through a philosophy of doing it right the first time, employee training and empowerment, promotion of teamwork, improvement of processes, and attention to satisfaction of both internal and external customers. This tool is not helpful in comparing the processes of two companies in different industries. Answer (B) is incorrect. Statistical process control is used to monitor and measure the manufacturing process in real time. This tool is not helpful in comparing the processes of two companies in different industries. Answer (C) is incorrect. Economic value added is calculated using monetary amounts and is thus a financial performance measure. It is not a helpful tool in improving the staging process of a company.

16.6 Costs of Quality

15. An example of an internal failure cost is

    A. Maintenance.

    B. Inspection.

    C. Rework.

    D. Product recalls.

Answer (C) is correct.
    REQUIRED: The example of an internal failure cost.
    DISCUSSION: In a quality management system, one of the costs of product nonconformance is internal failure cost, the cost of discovering, after appraisal but before shipment, that a completed product does not meet quality standards. An example is the cost of reworking the product.
    Answer (A) is incorrect. A maintenance cost is a prevention cost. Answer (B) is incorrect. Inspection is an appraisal cost. Answer (D) is incorrect. Product recalls are external failure costs.

16. The cost of statistical quality control in a product quality cost system is categorized as a(n)

    A. Internal failure cost.

    B. Training cost.

    C. External failure cost.

    D. Appraisal cost.

Answer (D) is correct.
    REQUIRED: The cost category that includes statistical quality control.
    DISCUSSION: The four categories of quality costs are (1) prevention, (2) appraisal, (3) internal failure, and (4) external failure (lost opportunity). Appraisal costs include quality control programs, inspection, and testing. However, some authorities regard statistical quality and process control as preventive activities. They not only detect faulty work but also allow for adjustment of processes to avoid future defects.
    Answer (A) is incorrect. Internal failure costs are incurred after poor quality has been found before shipment. Statistical quality control is designed to detect quality problems. Answer (B) is incorrect. Statistical quality control is not a training cost. Answer (C) is incorrect. External failure costs are incurred after the product has been shipped, including the costs associated with (1) warranties, (2) product liability, and (3) loss of customer goodwill.

17. The four categories of costs associated with product quality costs are

    A. External failure, internal failure, prevention, and carrying.

    B. External failure, internal failure, prevention, and appraisal.

    C. Warranty, product liability, training, and appraisal.

    D. Warranty, product liability, prevention, and appraisal.

Answer (B) is correct.
    REQUIRED: The categories of product quality costs.
    DISCUSSION: The four categories of quality costs are (1) prevention, (2) appraisal, (3) internal failure, and (4) external failure. Costs of prevention include attempts to avoid defective output, such as (1) employee training, (2) review of equipment design, (3) preventive maintenance, and (4) evaluation of suppliers. Appraisal includes quality control programs, inspection, and testing. Internal failure costs are incurred when detection of defective products occurs before shipment. They include costs of (1) scrap, (2) rework, (3) tooling changes, and (4) downtime. External failure costs are incurred after the product has been shipped. They include the costs associated with warranties, product liability, and loss of customer goodwill.
    Answer (A) is incorrect. Carrying cost is an inventory cost. Answer (C) is incorrect. All training costs are not quality control related. Also, internal failure costs should be included. Answer (D) is incorrect. Internal failure costs should be included.

16.7 TQM and the ISO Framework

18. Which statement best describes total quality management (TQM)?

    A. TQM emphasizes reducing the cost of inspection.

    B. TQM emphasizes participation by all employees in the decision-making process.

    C. TQM implementation is quick and easy.

    D. TQM is the continuous pursuit of quality.

Answer (D) is correct.
    REQUIRED: The best description of TQM.
    DISCUSSION: TQM is the continuous pursuit of quality in every aspect of organizational activities through (1) a philosophy of doing it right the first time, (2) employee training and empowerment, (3) promotion of teamwork, (4) improvement of processes, and (5) attention to satisfaction of customers, both internal and external.
    Answer (A) is incorrect. Reducing the cost of inspection helps achieve the lowest overall business cost. Answer (B) is incorrect. Participative management emphasizes participation by all employees in the decision-making process. Answer (C) is incorrect. TQM implementation is often lengthy and difficult.

19. If a company is customer-centered, its customers are defined as

A. Only people external to the company who have purchased something from the company.

B. Only people internal to the company who directly use its product.

C. Anyone external to the company and those internal who rely on its product to get their job done.

D. Everybody external to the company who is currently doing, or may in the future do, business with the company.

Answer (C) is correct.

REQUIRED: The definition of customers if a firm is customer-centered.

DISCUSSION: One of the principles of TQM is customer orientation, whether the customer is internal or external. An internal customer is a member of the organization who relies on another member's work to accomplish his or her task.

20. Which statement best describes the emphasis of total quality management (TQM)?

A. Reducing the cost of inspection.

B. Implementing better statistical quality control techniques.

C. Doing each job right the first time.

D. Encouraging cross-functional teamwork.

Answer (C) is correct.

REQUIRED: The emphasis of TQM.

DISCUSSION: The basic principles of TQM include (1) doing each job right the first time, (2) being customer-oriented, (3) committing the organizational culture to continuous improvement, and (4) promoting teamwork and employee empowerment.

Answer (A) is incorrect. Reducing the cost of inspection is a detail of the TQM emphasis. Answer (B) is incorrect. Implementing better statistical quality control is a detail of the TQM emphasis. Answer (D) is incorrect. Encouraging cross-functional teamwork is a detail of the TQM emphasis.

CANDIDATES L♥VE GLEIM CPA REVIEW

Check out the stories of some of the millions who have succeeded with Gleim.

> From first hand experience, practicing the multiple-choice questions with Gleim will give you enough confidence and knowledge to pass each section. Using Gleim will have you well-prepared and conditioned for the exam.
>
> *- Thomas Najarian, CPA*

> The Gleim program was the answer I'd been looking for to finally conquer the exam. I've used other programs before and none of them compared to the step by step process Gleim used, which truly prepared me to conquer all four parts on my first try.
>
> *– Eric Murphy, CPA*

> The testing components simulate the actual exam, so I was completely comfortable with the exam setup when I took the actual exams.
>
> *- Tracy Caisse, CPA*

> Due to passing the exam, I was able to secure an excellent new job as a controller at a large company! Thank you, Gleim, as your products have changed my life!
>
> *– Kent Kellenberger, CPA, CIA*

> I cannot say enough good things about the counselors and the structure of the Gleim system. The structure of the Gleim program keeps you focused and on task.
>
> *– Angela Brinley, CPA*

> I am so glad that I made the decision to take the jump and purchase Gleim. It was so well developed that it didn't feel like I was giving up my entire life just to study.
>
> *– Holly Fowler, CPA*

> The most important piece of advice I can give is follow the order that is laid out in the review material. There is a reason the Gleim Team chose the sequence they did: IT WORKS!
>
> *– Benjamin Ziccardy, CPA*

> In taking all 4 parts, I felt totally confident during the exams because I knew the Gleim products had me prepared!
>
> *– Larvizo Wright, CPA, MBA*

STUDY UNIT SEVENTEEN
BUDGET COMPONENTS

(11 pages of outline)

A modern organization needs an integrated, entity-wide budget. To be effective, a budget must be based on reasonably determined standard costs. The preparation of a comprehensive budget has two stages: the operating budget and the financial budget. A flexible budget is prepared for better analysis of budget variances.

17.1 THE MASTER BUDGET AND ITS COMPONENTS

1. **The Master Budget Process -- Sequence**

    a. The **master budget** (also called the comprehensive budget, static budget, or annual profit plan) encompasses the organization's operating and financial plans for a specified period (ordinarily a year or single operating cycle).

    b. The master budget consists of the **operating budget** and the **financial budget**. Both consist of inputs from interrelated sub-budgets.

        1) For example, the production budget cannot be prepared until after completion of the sales budget. The direct materials budget and the direct labor budget cannot be prepared until after completion of the production budget.

2. **The Operating Budget**

    a. In the operating budget, the emphasis is on obtaining and using current resources. It contains the following components:

        1) Sales budget
        2) Production budget
        3) Direct materials budget
        4) Direct labor budget
        5) Manufacturing overhead budget
        6) Cost of goods sold budget
        7) Nonmanufacturing budget

            a) Research and development budget
            b) Selling and administrative budget

                i) Design budget
                ii) Marketing budget
                iii) Distribution budget
                iv) Customer service budget
                v) Administrative budget

        8) Pro forma income statement

3.   The Financial Budget

a.   In the financial budget, the emphasis is on obtaining the funds needed to purchase operating assets. It contains the following components:

    1)   Capital budget

    2)   Cash budget

        a)   Projected cash collection schedule

        b)   Projected cash disbursement schedule

    3)   Pro forma balance sheet

    4)   Pro forma statement of cash flows

4.   Master Budget Process -- Graphical Depiction

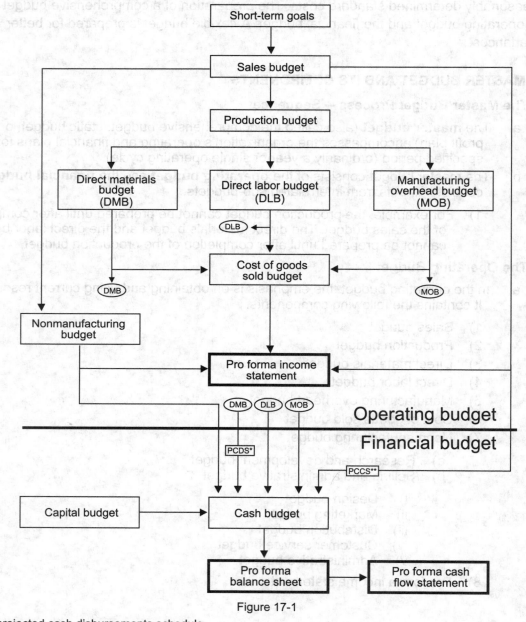

Figure 17-1

* PCDS = projected cash disbursements schedule

** PCCS = projected cash collection schedule

Stop and review! You have completed the outline for this subunit. Study multiple-choice questions 1 through 5 beginning on page 386.

17.2 STANDARD COSTS

1. **Standard Costs**

   a. Standard costs are **predetermined expectations** about how much a unit of input, a unit of output, or a given activity should cost.

      1) The use of standard costs in budgeting allows the standard-cost system to alert management when the actual costs of production differ significantly from the standard.

$$\begin{array}{c}\text{Standard cost of input} \\ \text{per unit of output}\end{array} = \begin{array}{c}\text{Units of input per} \\ \text{single unit of output}\end{array} \times \begin{array}{c}\text{Price per} \\ \text{unit of input}\end{array}$$

   b. A standard cost is not just an average of past costs but is an **objectively determined estimate** of what a cost should be. Standards may be based on accounting, engineering, or statistical quality control studies.

Standard costs have been tested by asking for the calculation of a cost for a standard unit of input. Candidates may be asked to explain the use of standard costs.

---

2. **Ideal vs. Attainable Standards**

   a. **Ideal (theoretical) standards** are standard costs that are set for production under optimal conditions. For this reason, they also are called perfection or maximum efficiency standards.

      1) They are based on the work of the most skilled workers **with no allowance** for spoilage, waste, machine breakdowns, or other downtime.

      2) Often called tight standards, they can have positive behavioral effects if workers are motivated to strive for excellence. However, they are not in wide use because they can have negative effects if the standards are impossible to attain.

      3) Ideal standards ordinarily are replaced by **attainable (practical) standards** for cash budgeting, product costing, and budgeting departmental performance. Otherwise, accurate financial planning is impossible.

   b. Attainable (practical) standards are the results expected to be achieved by reasonably well-trained workers **with an allowance** for normal spoilage, waste, and downtime.

      1) Compared to ideal standards, attainable standards serve as a better motivating target for manufacturing personnel.

3. **Activity Analysis**

   a. Activity analysis identifies, describes, and evaluates the activities and resources needed to produce a particular output. This process aids in the development of standard costs.

   b. Each operation requires a unique set of inputs and preparations. Activity analysis describes what these inputs are and who performs these preparations.

      1) Inputs include the amounts and kinds of equipment, facilities, materials, and labor. Engineering analysis, cost accounting, time-and-motion study, and other approaches may be useful.

   c. Historical data, adjusted for current conditions, may be used to set standards if an entity lacks the resources to engage in the complex task of activity analysis.

Stop and review! You have completed the outline for this subunit. Study multiple-choice questions 6 through 8 on page 387.

17.3 THE OPERATING BUDGET

1. **Sales Budget**

   a. The sales budget (also called the revenue budget) is the starting point for the cycle that produces the annual profit plan (the master budget).

   b. The sales budget is based on the sales forecast. The forecast reflects (1) recent sales trends, (2) overall conditions in the economy and industry, (3) market research, (4) activities of competitors, and (5) credit and pricing policies.

   c. The sales budget must specify both projected unit sales and dollar revenues.

EXAMPLE of a Sales Budget

	April	Ref.
Projected sales in units	1,000	SB1
Selling price	× $400	
Projected total sales	$400,000	SB2

---

2. **Production Budget**

   a. The production budget follows directly from the sales budget. The production budget is stated in units only. Product pricing is ignored because the purpose is only to plan output and inventory levels and the necessary manufacturing activity.

   b. To minimize finished goods carrying costs and obsolescence, the levels of production are dependent upon the projections in the sales budget.

EXAMPLE of a Production Budget

Finished goods beginning inventory consists of 100 units at $125 cost per unit (a total of $12,500), and the desired finished goods ending inventory is 120 units.

	Source	April	Ref.
Projected sales in units	SB1	1,000	
Plus: Desired ending inventory		120	
Minus: Beginning inventory		(100)	
Units to be produced		1,020	PB

---

   c. The **purchases budget** for a retailer is prepared after projected sales are estimated.

   1) It is prepared on a monthly or even a weekly basis.

   2) Purchases can be planned so that stockouts are avoided.

   3) Inventory should be at an appropriate level to avoid unnecessary carrying costs while acting as a "shock absorber."

   4) It is similar to the production budget example above. However, the units are purchased rather than produced.

Questions asked by the AICPA about budgeting often require calculations. Always read and think through the scenario very carefully. For example, you may encounter a question regarding budgeted materials required for a time period. If it asks for the budgeted number of legs necessary for tables produced, be sure to calculate the amount using the appropriate number of legs per table.

3. **Direct Materials Budget**

   a. The direct materials budget reflects both units and input prices. (Direct materials is defined in Study Unit 18.)

      1) Two dollar amounts are calculated in the direct materials budget: (a) the cost of materials actually **used** in production and (b) the total cost of materials **purchased**.

EXAMPLE of a Direct Materials Budget

Materials beginning inventory is 1,000 units at $18 cost per unit, and the desired materials ending inventory is 980 units.

Materials Used (Quantity)	Source	April	Ref.
Finished units to be produced	PB	1,020	
Times: Materials per finished product		× 4	
Total units needed for production		4,080	DMB1

Materials Purchased	Source	April	Ref.
Units needed for production	DMB1	4,080	
Plus: Desired units in ending inventory		980	
Minus: Beginning inventory		(1,000)	
Materials to be purchased		4,060	
Times: Materials cost per unit*		× $20	
Cost of materials to be purchased		$81,200	DMB2

Materials Used ($)	Source	April	Ref.
Beginning inventory (1,000 × $18)		$18,000	
Plus: Purchases of material	DMB2	81,200	
Minus: Desired ending inventory (980 × $20)		(19,600)	
Cost of materials used in production		$79,600	DMB3

*For the month of April.

---

4. **Direct Labor Budget**

   a. The direct labor budget depends on wage rates, amounts and types of production, numbers and skill levels of employees to be hired, etc.

   b. In addition to the regular wage rate, the total direct labor cost per hour also may include employer FICA taxes, health insurance, life insurance, and pension contributions. (Direct labor is explained in detail in Study Unit 18.)

EXAMPLE of a Direct Labor Budget

The Human Resources department has determined that the total cost per labor hour is $18.

	Source	April	Ref.
Units to be produced	PB	1,020	
Times: Direct labor hours per unit		× 2	
Projected total direct labor hours		2,040	DLB1
Times: Direct labor cost per hour		× $18	
Total projected direct labor cost		$36,720	DLB2

5.   **Manufacturing Overhead Budget**

a.   The manufacturing overhead budget has variable and fixed components because overhead is a mixed cost. (Mixed costs are defined in Study Unit 18.)

$$Total\ costs = Fixed\ costs + (Variable\ Cost\ Each\ Item \times Quantity\ Used)$$
$$TC = FC + (VC_{EA} \times Q)$$

b.   Variable overhead contains elements that vary with the level of production.

1)   Indirect materials
2)   Some indirect labor
3)   Variable factory operating costs (e.g., electricity)
4)   Depreciation using the units-of-production method

a)   EXAMPLE: Miles on a motor vehicle.

EXAMPLE of a Variable Overhead Budget

Variable overhead is applied to production on the basis of direct labor hours.

	Source	April	Ref.
Projected total direct labor hours	DLB1	2,040	
Variable OH rate per direct labor hour		× $3	
Projected variable overhead		$6,120	MOB1

---

c.   Fixed overhead contains elements that do **not** change regardless of the level of production.

1)   Real estate taxes
2)   Insurance
3)   Depreciation using the straight line method

EXAMPLE of a Fixed Overhead Budget

	April	Ref.
Projected fixed overhead	$9,000	MOB2

---

6.   **Cost of Goods Sold Budget**

a.   The cost of goods sold budget combines the projections for the three major inputs (materials, labor, and overhead). The result directly affects the pro forma income statement. Cost of goods sold is the largest cost for a manufacturer.

EXAMPLE of a Cost of Goods Sold Budget

	Source	April		Ref.
Beginning finished goods inventory			$ 12,500	
Manufacturing costs:				
Direct materials used	DMB3	$79,600		
Direct labor used	DLB2	36,720		
Variable overhead	MOB1	6,120		
Fixed overhead	MOB2	9,000		
Cost of goods manufactured			131,440	
Cost of goods available for sale			$143,940	
Ending finished goods inventory				
(120 units × $129*)			(15,480)	
Cost of goods sold			$128,460	CGSB

*Rounded to the nearest whole number (131,440 COGM ÷ 1,020 units to be produced)

7. Nonmanufacturing Budget

a. The nonmanufacturing budget consists of the individual budgets for (1) R&D, (2) design, (3) marketing, (4) distribution, (5) customer service, and (6) administrative costs. The development of separate budgets for these functions is based on a value chain approach.

   1) An alternative is to prepare a single budget for selling and administrative (S&A) costs of nonproduction functions.

b. The variable and fixed portions of selling and administrative costs must be treated separately.

   1) Some S&A costs vary directly and proportionately with the level of sales. As more products are sold, sales representatives must travel more miles and serve more customers.

   2) Other S&A expenses, such as sales support staff, are fixed. They must be paid at any level of sales.

8. Pro Forma Income Statement

a. The pro forma income statement is prepared after the operating budget process.

   1) Financial statements are pro forma when they report projected, not actual, results.

b. The pro forma income statement is used to decide whether the budgeted activities will result in an acceptable level of income. If the initial projection is a loss or otherwise unacceptable, adjustments can be made to the components of the master budget.

EXAMPLE of a Pro Forma Income Statement

Manufacturing Company
Pro Forma Statement of Income
Month of April

Sales	$400,000
Cost of goods sold	(128,460)
Gross margin	$271,540
Minus: Selling and administrative expenses	(82,000)
Operating income	$189,540
Minus: Other revenues, expenses, gains, and losses	(15,000)
Earnings before interest and taxes	$174,540
Minus: Interest expense	(45,000)
Earnings before income taxes	$129,540
Minus: Income taxes (40%)	(51,816)
Net income	$ 77,724

Stop and review! You have completed the outline for this subunit. Study multiple-choice questions 9 through 12 beginning on page 388.

17.4 THE FINANCIAL BUDGET

1. **Capital Budget**

   a. The preparation of the capital budget is separate from the operating budget cycle.

   b. The capital budget, which often must be approved by the board of directors, addresses financing of major expenditures for long-term assets. It therefore must have a multi-year perspective. Productive assets must be acquired to enable the entity to achieve its projected levels of output.

   c. A procedure for ranking projects according to their risk and return characteristics is necessary because every organization has finite resources. [These procedures (net present value, internal rate of return, etc.) are covered in Study Unit 11.]

   d. The capital budget is a direct input to the cash budget and the pro forma balance sheet and statement of cash flows.

      1) Principal and interest on debt acquired to finance capital purchases require regular **cash outflows**. The acquired debt also appears in the liabilities section of the pro forma balance sheet.

      2) The output produced by new productive assets generates regular **cash inflows**. The new assets also appear in the assets section of the pro forma balance sheet.

2. **Cash Budget**

   a. The cash budget is the part of the financial budget cycle that connects all the schedules from the operating budget. A cash budget projects cash flows for planning and control purposes. Thus, it helps prevent not only cash emergencies but also excessive idle cash.

      1) A cash budget is vital because an organization must have adequate cash at all times. Almost all organizations, regardless of size, prepare a cash budget.

         a) Even with plenty of other assets, an organization with a temporary shortage of cash can become bankrupt.

      2) Proper planning can help prevent financial difficulty. Thus, cash budgets are prepared not only for annual and quarterly periods but also for monthly and weekly periods.

         a) They are particularly important for organizations operating in seasonal industries.

         b) The factors needed to prepare a cash forecast include all other elements of the budget preparation process plus consideration of (1) collection policies, (2) bad debt estimates, and (3) changes in the economy.

      3) Credit and purchasing policies directly affect the cash budget.

         a) Loose customer credit policies delay cash receipts.
         b) Use of purchase discounts accelerates cash payments.

   b. The cash budget process begins with preparation of a **projected cash collection schedule**. It forecasts the inflows of cash from customer payments.

EXAMPLE of a Cash Collection Schedule for April

Sales are made on credit.

	February Sales (Actual)	March Sales (Actual)	Source	April Sales (Projected)	Totals	Ref.
Sales	$180,000	$220,000	SB2	$400,000		
Projection of collection in April	× 30%	× 50%		× 15%		
From 2nd prior-month sales	$ 54,000				$ 54,000	
From prior-month sales		$110,000			110,000	
From current-month sales				$ 60,000	60,000	
Total cash collections from sales					$224,000	PCCS

c. The next step is preparation of a **projected cash disbursements schedule**.

EXAMPLE of a Cash Disbursements Schedule for April

Materials purchases are the only purchases made on credit.

	March Purchases (Actual)	Source	April Purchases (Projected)	Totals	Ref.
Cost of materials purchased	$72,000	DMB2	$81,200		
Projection of payments in April	× 40%		× 60%		
For prior-month purchases	$28,800			$28,800	
For current-month purchases			$48,720	48,720	
Total cash disbursements for materials				$77,520	PCDS

---

d. The **cash budget** is the key element of the financial budget.

1) A comprehensive statement of the sources and uses of the entity's cash flows combines the operating budget and the cash flow schedules.

2) The cash budget can be used to plan financing activities. For example, if the budget projects a cash deficit, the entity can plan to borrow the necessary funds or sell stock.

3) Dividend policy can also be planned using the cash budget. For example, dividend payment dates should correspond to a time when the entity has excess cash. For publicly held companies, dividends are usually paid quarterly.

EXAMPLE of a Cash Budget

The bottom line is the expected cash surplus or the financing required.

	Source	April
Beginning cash balance		$100,000
Cash collections from sales	PCCS	224,000
Cash available for disbursement		$324,000
Cash disbursements:		
For materials	PCDS	$ 77,520
For direct labor	DLB2	36,720
For variable overhead	MOB1	6,120
For fixed overhead	MOB2	9,000
For nonmanufacturing costs		26,000
For equipment purchases		110,000
Total disbursements		(265,360)
Excess of cash available over disbursements		$ 58,640
Desired ending cash balance		100,000
Short-term financing required		$ 41,360

---

3. **Pro Forma Balance Sheet and Cash Flow Statement**

a. The **pro forma balance sheet** is prepared using the cash and capital budgets and the pro forma income statement.

1) The pro forma balance sheet is the beginning-of-the-period balance sheet updated for projected changes in cash, receivables, payables, inventory, etc.

2) If the balance sheet indicates that a contract may be breached, the budgeting process must be repeated.

a) For example, some loan agreements require that (1) owners' equity be maintained at some percentage of total debt or (2) current assets be maintained at a given multiple of current liabilities.

b. The **pro forma statement of cash flows** classifies cash flows depending on whether they are from operating, investing, or financing activities.

c. The pro forma statements are interrelated. For example, the pro forma cash flow statement includes anticipated borrowing. The interest on this borrowing appears in the pro forma income statement.

Stop and review! You have completed the outline for this subunit. Study multiple-choice questions 13 through 17 beginning on page 389.

17.5 FLEXIBLE BUDGETING AND VARIANCE ANALYSIS

1. **Flexible Budget**

    a. A flexible budget is an annual profit plan prepared for various levels of production or sales. It reports the operating income for each level.

        1) A flexible budget can be used for any component of the budget process that varies with the level of activity. Examples are (a) sales revenue, (b) direct labor and materials, (c) marketing expenses, and (d) sales and administrative expenses.

2. **Static vs. Flexible Budgeting**

    a. The **static (master) budget** is prepared before the period begins and is not changed. The static budget is based on only one level of **expected activity** (output planned at the beginning of the period).

EXAMPLE of a Static Budget

The following static (master) budget for the upcoming month is based on production and sales of 1,000 units:

Sales revenue ($400 per unit)	$400,000
Minus: Variable costs ($160 per unit)	(160,000)
Contribution margin	$240,000
Minus: Fixed costs	(200,000)
Operating income	$ 40,000

---

b. The **flexible budget** is prepared

    1) Based on the **actual output** sold (produced) during the period.
    2) Using the same drivers as those used to prepare the master budget.
    3) After the end of the period when all actual results are known.

EXAMPLE of a Flexible Budget

	Flexible Budget Based on 800 Units	Static Budget Based on 1,000 Units
Sales revenue ($400 per unit)	$320,000	$400,000
Minus: Variable costs ($160 per unit)	(128,000)	(160,000)
Contribution margin	$192,000	$240,000
Minus: Fixed costs	(200,000)	(200,000)
Operating income	$ (8,000)	$ 40,000

---

3. **Variance Analysis Using Flexible Budgeting**

    a. The most common use of the flexible budget is for analysis of budget variances.

        1) Variance analysis helps management in monitoring and measuring performance.

b. A variance is the difference between the actual results for the period and a budgeted amount for the period.

1) A **favorable** variance (F) occurs when actual revenues are greater than standard (budgeted) or actual costs are less than standard (budgeted), i.e., income increases.

2) An **unfavorable** variance (U) occurs when actual revenues are less than standard (budgeted) or actual costs are greater than standard (budgeted), i.e., income decreases.

EXAMPLE of Budget Variances

Actual results for the month were as follows:

Sales revenue	$342,000 (800 units × $427.50 price per unit)
Variable costs	$153,000
Fixed costs	$220,000

	Actual Results	Budget Variances	Master Budget
Sales revenue	$342,000	$(58,000) U	$400,000
Minus: Variable costs	(153,000)	7,000 F	(160,000)
Contribution margin	$189,000	$(51,000) U	$240,000
Minus: Fixed costs	(220,000)	(20,000) U	(200,000)
Operating income (loss)	$ (31,000)	$(71,000) U	$ 40,000

---

c. To analyze performance for the period, the budget variances should be subdivided into sales-volume variances and flexible budget variances.

1) **Sales-volume** variances result from inaccurate forecasting of the output sold for the period. They are measured as the difference between the flexible budget and the static (master) budget amounts.

2) **Flexible budget** variances report the differences between (a) the actual revenues and costs for the period and (b) the amounts that should have been earned and expended given the achieved level of production.

a) **Flexible budget** variances are measured as the difference between the actual results and the flexible budget. More extensive analysis of flexible budget variances can be made by using standard costing. (This topic is covered in detail in Study Unit 20.)

EXAMPLE of a Flexible Budget and Sales-Volume Variances

	Actual Results	Flexible Budget Variances	Flexible Budget Based on Actual Sales of 800 Units	Sales-Volume Variances	Master (Static) Budget
Sales revenue	$342,000	$ 22,000 F	$320,000	$(80,000) U	$400,000
Minus: Variable costs	(153,000)	(25,000) U	(128,000)	32,000 F	(160,000)
Contribution margin	$189,000	$ (3,000) U	$192,000	$(48,000) U	$240,000
Minus: Fixed costs	(220,000)	(20,000) U	(200,000)	– –	(200,000)
Operating income (loss)	$ (31,000)	$(23,000) U	$ (8,000)	$(48,000) U	$ 40,000

The net of the two variances equals the difference between the master budget and the actual results, the **static budget variance**.

Flexible budget variance	$(23,000) U	Actual results	$(31,000)
Sales volume variance	(48,000) U	Master (static) budget	40,000
Static budget variance	$(71,000) U	Static budget variance	$(71,000) U

Stop and review! You have completed the outline for this subunit. Study multiple-choice questions 18 through 21 beginning on page 390.

QUESTIONS

17.1 The Master Budget and Its Components

1. In an organization that plans by using comprehensive budgeting, the master budget is

   A. A compilation of all the separate operational and financial budget schedules of the organization.

   B. The booklet containing budget guidelines, policies, and forms to use in the budgeting process.

   C. The current budget updated for operations for part of the current year.

   D. A budget of a not-for-profit organization after it is approved by the appropriate authoritative body.

Answer (A) is correct.
   REQUIRED: The nature of the master budget.
   DISCUSSION: The overall budget, often called the master or comprehensive budget, encompasses the organization's operating and financial plans for a specified period (ordinarily a year). Thus, all other budgets are subsets of the master budget.
   Answer (B) is incorrect. The booklet containing budget guidelines, policies, and forms to use in the budgeting process is the budget manual. Answer (C) is incorrect. The current budget updated for operations for part of the current year is a continuous budget. Answer (D) is incorrect. A master budget may be prepared by a for-profit entity.

2. Pro forma financial statements are part of the budgeting process. Normally, the **last** pro forma statement prepared is the

   A. Capital expenditure plan.

   B. Income statement.

   C. Statement of cost of goods sold.

   D. Statement of cash flows.

Answer (D) is correct.
   REQUIRED: The last pro forma financial statement prepared.
   DISCUSSION: The statement of cash flows is usually the last of the listed items prepared. All other elements of the budget process must be completed before it can be developed.
   Answer (A) is incorrect. The capital expenditure plan must be prepared before the cash budget. Cash may be needed to pay for capital purchases. Answer (B) is incorrect. The income statement must be prepared before the statement of cash flows, which reconciles net income and net operating cash flows. Answer (C) is incorrect. Cost of goods sold is included in the income statement, which is an input to the statement of cash flows.

3. Wilson Company uses a comprehensive planning and budgeting system. The proper order for Wilson to prepare certain budget schedules would be

   A. Cost of goods sold, balance sheet, income statement, and statement of cash flows.

   B. Income statement, balance sheet, statement of cash flows, and cost of goods sold.

   C. Statement of cash flows, cost of goods sold, income statement, and balance sheet.

   D. Cost of goods sold, income statement, balance sheet, and statement of cash flows.

Answer (D) is correct.
   REQUIRED: The order in which budget schedules should be prepared.
   DISCUSSION: The cost of goods sold budget is an input for the pro forma income statement. The entire operating budget process must be completed before the pro forma balance sheet and statement of cash flows can be prepared.
   Answer (A) is incorrect. The balance sheet should not precede the income statement. Answer (B) is incorrect. The income statement cannot precede cost of goods sold. Answer (C) is incorrect. The statement of cash flows cannot precede the cost of goods sold. The latter is an input of the former.

4. The cash budget must be prepared before completing the

   A. Capital expenditure budget.

   B. Sales budget.

   C. Forecasted balance sheet.

   D. Production budget.

Answer (C) is correct.
   REQUIRED: The budget element prepared after the cash budget.
   DISCUSSION: The pro forma balance sheet is the balance sheet for the beginning of the period updated for projected changes in cash, receivables, inventories, payables, etc. Accordingly, it cannot be prepared until after the cash budget is completed because cash is a current asset reported on the balance sheet.
   Answer (A) is incorrect. The capital expenditure budget is an input necessary for the preparation of a cash budget. Answer (B) is incorrect. The sales budget is usually the first budget prepared. Answer (D) is incorrect. A production budget is normally prepared before the cash budget is started.

5. Many companies use comprehensive budgeting in planning for the next year's activities. When both an operating budget and a financial budget are prepared, which one of the following is correct concerning the financial budget?

	Included in the Financial Budget		
	Capital Budget	Pro Forma Balance Sheet	Cash Budget
A.	Yes	No	Yes
B.	No	Yes	No
C.	Yes	Yes	Yes
D.	No	No	No

Answer (C) is correct.
REQUIRED: The true statement concerning the financial budget.
DISCUSSION: In the financial budget, the emphasis is on obtaining the funds needed to purchase operating assets. It contains the capital budget, projected cash disbursement schedule, projected cash collection schedule, cash budget, pro forma balance sheet, and pro forma statement of cash flows.
Answer (A) is incorrect. The pro forma balance sheet is part of the financial budget. Answer (B) is incorrect. The capital budget and cash budget are part of the financial budget. Answer (D) is incorrect. The capital budget, pro forma balance sheet, and cash budget are part of the financial budget.

17.2 Standard Costs

6. The best basis upon which cost standards should be set to measure controllable production inefficiencies is

A. Engineering standards based on ideal performance.

B. Normal capacity.

C. Recent average historical performance.

D. Engineering standards based on attainable performance.

Answer (D) is correct.
REQUIRED: The best basis upon which cost standards should be set.
DISCUSSION: Standards must be accepted by those who will carry them out if they are to have maximum effectiveness. Subordinates should believe that standards are both fair and achievable. Otherwise, they may tend to sabotage, ignore, or circumvent them.
Answer (A) is incorrect. Employees may not cooperate with standards based on ideal performance. Attainable standards are usually better for motivational purposes. Answer (B) is incorrect. Normal capacity may not suffice to control production inefficiencies. Answer (C) is incorrect. Historical performance may not always be a guide to future performance, and standards should be based on anticipated future conditions.

7. When compared with ideal standards, practical standards

A. Produce lower per-unit product costs.

B. Result in a less desirable basis for the development of budgets.

C. Incorporate very generous allowance for spoilage and worker inefficiencies.

D. Serve as a better motivating target for manufacturing personnel.

Answer (D) is correct.
REQUIRED: The correct statement regarding practical standards when compared to ideal standards.
DISCUSSION: Practical standards, also called attainable standards, are more likely to be accepted by workers than standards based on an unachievable ideal.
Answer (A) is incorrect. The effect of one type of standard over another cannot guarantee lower costs. Answer (B) is incorrect. Practical standards are more appropriate in most cases than ideal standards in the development of budgets. Answer (C) is incorrect. An acceptance of high levels of spoilage and worker inefficiencies cannot be overcome through the use of standards.

8. After performing a thorough study of Michigan Company's operations, an independent consultant determined that the firm's labor standards were too tight. Which of the following is **inconsistent** with the consultant's conclusion?

A. A review of performance reports revealed the presence of many unfavorable efficiency variances.

B. Michigan's budgeting process was based on a top-down (authoritative) philosophy.

C. Management noted that minimal incentive bonuses have been paid in recent periods.

D. Production supervisors found several significant fluctuations in manufacturing volume, with short-term increases in output being followed by rapid, sustained declines.

Answer (D) is correct.
REQUIRED: The statement inconsistent with the consultant's conclusion.
DISCUSSION: The situation described is indicative of rush jobs being too common, which is a result of poor production planning, not tight labor standards.
Answer (A) is incorrect. Many unfavorable efficiency variances indicate standards are too tight. Answer (B) is incorrect. A budgeting process based on a top-down (authoritative) philosophy is more likely than a bottom-up approach to set standards that are too tight. Answer (C) is incorrect. The widespread failure to earn expected bonuses indicates standards are too tight.

17.3 The Operating Budget

9. When budgeting, the items to be considered by a manufacturing firm in going from a sales quantity budget to a production budget would be the

A. Expected change in the quantity of work-in-process inventories.

B. Expected change in the quantity of finished goods and work-in-process inventories.

C. Expected change in the quantity of finished goods and raw material inventories.

D. Expected change in the availability of raw material without regard to inventory levels.

Answer (B) is correct.
REQUIRED: The items to be considered in developing a production budget from a sales quantity budget.
DISCUSSION: Production quantities are not identical to sales because of changes in inventory levels. Both finished goods and work-in-process inventories may change during a period, necessitating an analysis of both inventory levels before the production budget can be set.
Answer (A) is incorrect. Finished goods inventories cannot be ignored. Answer (C) is incorrect. Work-in-process inventory should be considered. Answer (D) is incorrect. Existing inventories determine production levels.

Questions 10 and 11 are based on the following information. Paradise Company budgets on an annual basis for its fiscal year. The following beginning and ending inventory levels (in units) are planned for the fiscal year of July 1 through June 30:

	July 1	June 30
Direct material*	40,000	50,000
Work-in-process	10,000	20,000
Finished goods	80,000	50,000

* Two units of direct material are needed to produce each unit of finished product.

---

10. If Paradise Company plans to sell 480,000 units during the fiscal year, the number of units it will have to manufacture during the year is

A. 440,000 units.

B. 480,000 units.

C. 510,000 units.

D. 450,000 units.

Answer (D) is correct.
REQUIRED: The number of units to be manufactured at a given sales level.
DISCUSSION: Projected sales of 480,000 units, plus the ending finished goods inventory of 50,000 units, minus the beginning finished goods inventory of 80,000 units equals the units to be produced of 450,000 units.
Answer (A) is incorrect. The calculation need not be adjusted for the change in work-in-process. Only finished goods are being discussed. Answer (B) is incorrect. The amount to be sold is 480,000 units. Answer (C) is incorrect. The number of 510,000 units equals sales, plus beginning inventory, minus ending inventory.

11. If 500,000 complete units were to be manufactured during the fiscal year by Paradise Company, the number of units of direct materials to be purchased is

A. 1,000,000 units.

B. 1,020,000 units.

C. 1,010,000 units.

D. 990,000 units.

Answer (C) is correct.
REQUIRED: The number of units of materials to be purchased at a given production level.
DISCUSSION: The total materials needed for production will be 1,000,000 units (500,000 units × 2 units of materials). Because Paradise Company planned to have beginning direct materials inventory (July 1) of 40,000 units and ending direct materials inventory (June 30) of 50,000 units, materials inventory is expected to increase by 10,000 units. Thus, materials purchases will be 1,010,000 units.
Answer (A) is incorrect. The total needed for production is 1,000,000 units. Answer (B) is incorrect. The number of units in materials is not doubled. Answer (D) is incorrect. The number of 990,000 units is less than the amount used in production.

12. Superior Industries' sales budget shows quarterly sales for the next year as follows:

Quarter	Units
1	10,000
2	8,000
3	12,000
4	14,000

Company policy is to have a finished goods inventory at the end of each quarter equal to 20% of the next quarter's sales. Budgeted production for the second quarter of the next year would be

A. 7,200 units.

B. 8,000 units.

C. 8,800 units.

D. 8,400 units.

Answer (C) is correct.

REQUIRED: The budgeted production for the second quarter given ending inventory for each quarter.

DISCUSSION: The finished units needed for sales (8,000), plus the units desired for ending inventory (12,000 units to be sold in the third quarter × 20% = 2,400), minus the units in beginning inventory (8,000 units to be sold in the second quarter × 20% = 1,600) equals budgeted production for the second quarter of 8,800 units.

Answer (A) is incorrect. Subtracting the beginning inventory twice results in 7,200 units. Answer (B) is incorrect. Assuming no change in inventory results in 8,000 units. Answer (D) is incorrect. Including the beginning inventory for the first quarter, not the second quarter, in the calculation results in 8,400 units.

17.4 The Financial Budget

13. Which one of the following is the best characteristic concerning the capital budget? The capital budget is a(n)

A. Plan to ensure that there are sufficient funds available for the operating needs of the company.

B. Exercise that sets the long-range goals of the company including the consideration of external influences caused by others in the market.

C. Plan that results in the cash requirements during the operating cycle.

D. Plan that assesses the long-term needs of the company for plant and equipment purchases.

Answer (D) is correct.

REQUIRED: The true statement about the capital budget.

DISCUSSION: Capital budgeting is the process of planning expenditures for long-lived assets. It involves choosing among investment proposals using a ranking procedure. Evaluations are based on various measures involving the IRR.

Answer (A) is incorrect. Capital budgeting involves long-term investment needs, not immediate operating needs. Answer (B) is incorrect. Establishing long-term goals in the context of relevant factors in the environment is strategic planning. Answer (C) is incorrect. Cash budgeting determines operating cash flows. Capital budgeting evaluates the rate of return on specific investment alternatives.

14. Which one of the following items would have to be included for a company preparing a schedule of cash receipts and disbursements for Calendar Year 1?

A. A purchase order issued in December Year 1 for items to be delivered in February Year 2.

B. Dividends declared in November Year 1 to be paid in January Year 2 to shareholders of record as of December Year 1.

C. The amount of uncollectible customer accounts for Year 1.

D. The borrowing of funds from a bank on a note payable taken out in June Year 1 with an agreement to pay the principal and interest in June Year 2.

Answer (D) is correct.

REQUIRED: The item included in a cash budget for Year 1.

DISCUSSION: A schedule of cash receipts and disbursements (cash budget) should include all cash inflows and outflows during the period without regard to the accrual accounting treatment of the transactions. Thus, it should include all checks written and all sources of cash, including borrowings. A borrowing from a bank in June Year 1 should appear as a cash receipt for Year 1.

Answer (A) is incorrect. The cash disbursement presumably will not occur until Year 2. Answer (B) is incorrect. The cash flow will not occur until dividends are paid in Year 2. Answer (C) is incorrect. Bad debt expense is a noncash item.

15. Which one of the following may be considered an independent item in the preparation of the annual master budget?

    A. Ending inventory budget.

    B. Capital investment budget.

    C. Pro forma income statement.

    D. Pro forma statement of financial position.

Answer (B) is correct.
    REQUIRED: The independent item in the preparation of the annual master budget.
    DISCUSSION: The capital investment budget may be prepared more than a year in advance, unlike the other elements of the master budget. Because of the long-term commitments that must be made for some types of capital investments, planning must be done far in advance and is based on needs in future years as opposed to the current year's needs.
    Answer (A) is incorrect. The ending inventory budget is based on the current production budget. Answer (C) is incorrect. The pro forma income statement is based on the sales budget, expense budgets, and all other elements of the current master budget. Answer (D) is incorrect. The pro forma balance sheet is based on the other elements of the current master budget.

16. Trumbull Company budgeted sales on account of $120,000 for July, $211,000 for August, and $198,000 for September. Collection experience indicates that 60% of the budgeted sales will be collected the month after the sale, 36% will be collected the second month, and 4% will be uncollectible. The cash receipts from accounts receivable that should be budgeted for September would be

    A. $169,800

    B. $147,960

    C. $197,880

    D. $194,760

Answer (A) is correct.
    REQUIRED: The budgeted cash receipts for September.
    DISCUSSION: The budgeted cash collections for September equal $169,800.

July:	$120,000 × .36 =	$ 43,200
August:	211,000 × .60 =	126,600
		$169,800

    Answer (B) is incorrect. Reversing the percentages for July and August results in $147,960. Answer (C) is incorrect. Using the wrong months (August and September) and reversing the percentages results in $197,880. Answer (D) is incorrect. The amount of $194,760 assumes collections were for August and September.

17. Whopper, Inc., budgeted sales on account of $150,000 for July, $210,000 for August, and $198,000 for September. Collection experience indicates that 60% of the budgeted sales will be collected the month after the sale, 36% the second month, and 4% will be uncollectible. The cash receipts from accounts receivable that should be budgeted for September equal

    A. $180,000

    B. $165,600

    C. $194,400

    D. $198,000

Answer (A) is correct.
    REQUIRED: The budgeted cash receipts from sales on account for September.
    DISCUSSION: The budgeted cash collections for September equal $180,000.

July:	$150,000 × .36 =	$ 54,000
August:	210,000 × .60 =	126,000
		$180,000

    Answer (B) is incorrect. Reversing the percentages for July and August results in $165,600. Answer (C) is incorrect. Budgeted collections for October equal $194,400. Answer (D) is incorrect. The amount of $198,000 equals September sales.

17.5 Flexible Budgeting and Variance Analysis

18. The use of the master budget throughout the year as a constant comparison with actual results signifies that the master budget is also a

    A. Flexible budget.

    B. Capital budget.

    C. Zero-based budget.

    D. Static budget.

Answer (D) is correct.
    REQUIRED: The type of budget that is used throughout the year for comparison with actual results.
    DISCUSSION: If an unchanged master budget is used continuously throughout the year for comparison with actual results, it must be a static budget, that is, one prepared for just one level of activity.
    Answer (A) is incorrect. A flexible budget can be used in conjunction with standard costs to provide budgets for different activity levels. Answer (B) is incorrect. A capital budget addresses only long-term investments. Answer (C) is incorrect. A zero-based budget is one that requires its preparer to fully justify every item in the budget for each period.

19. Which one of the following statements regarding the difference between a flexible budget and a static budget is true?

A. A flexible budget primarily is prepared for planning purposes, while a static budget is prepared for performance evaluation.

B. A flexible budget provides cost allowances for different levels of activity, whereas a static budget provides costs for one level of activity.

C. A flexible budget includes only variable costs, whereas a static budget includes only fixed costs.

D. A flexible budget is established by operating management, while a static budget is determined by top management.

Answer (B) is correct.
REQUIRED: The difference between a flexible and a static budget.
DISCUSSION: A flexible budget provides cost allowances for different levels of activity, but a static budget provides costs for only one level of activity. Thus, a flexible budget conceptually is a series of budgets prepared for many different levels of activity.
Answer (A) is incorrect. Both budgets are prepared for both planning and performance evaluation purposes. Answer (C) is incorrect. Both budgets include both fixed and variable costs. Answer (D) is incorrect. Either budget can be established by any level of management.

20. RedRock Company uses flexible budgeting for cost control. RedRock produced 10,800 units of product during October, incurring indirect materials costs of $13,000. Its master budget for the year reflected indirect materials costs of $180,000 at a production volume of 144,000 units. A flexible budget for October production would reflect indirect materials costs of

A. $13,000

B. $13,500

C. $13,975

D. $11,700

Answer (B) is correct.
REQUIRED: The flexible budget amount of indirect materials cost for the month.
DISCUSSION: The cost of indirect materials for 144,000 units was expected to be $180,000. Consequently, the unit cost of indirect materials is $1.25 ($180,000 ÷ 144,000). Multiplying the $1.25 unit cost times the 10,800 units produced results in an expected total indirect materials cost of $13,500.
Answer (A) is incorrect. The actual cost of indirect materials in October is $13,000. Answer (C) is incorrect. The amount of $13,975 is not the flexible budget cost for indirect materials. Answer (D) is incorrect. The amount of $11,700 is not the flexible budget cost for indirect materials.

21. Flexible budgets

A. Provide for external factors affecting company profitability.

B. Are used to evaluate capacity use.

C. Are budgets that project costs based on anticipated future improvements.

D. Accommodate changes in activity levels.

Answer (D) is correct.
REQUIRED: The true statement about flexible budgets.
DISCUSSION: A flexible budget conceptually is a series of budgets prepared for various levels of activity. A flexible budget adjusts the master budget for changes in activity so that actual results can be compared with meaningful budget amounts.
Answer (A) is incorrect. Flexible budgets address external factors only to the extent that activity is affected. Answer (B) is incorrect. A flexible budget essentially restates variable costs for different activity levels within the relevant range. Thus, a flexible budget variance does not address capacity use. An output level (production volume) variance is a fixed cost variance. Answer (C) is incorrect. By definition, flexible budgets address differences in activity levels only within the relevant range.

STUDY UNIT EIGHTEEN
COSTING FUNDAMENTALS

(12 pages of outline)

Management accounting has specialized terminology that should be understood before the other outlines are read. This study unit also covers the most fundamental cost calculations and measurements. It also addresses decisions involving marginal (incremental or differential) costs. The final subunits in this study unit apply to cost-volume-profit analysis, a method for determining the effects of changes in unit sales, sales price, unit variable cost, fixed cost, and product mix.

18.1 COST MEASUREMENT TERMINOLOGY

1. **Manufacturing vs. Nonmanufacturing**

   a. The costs of manufacturing a product can be classified as one of two types: direct and indirect.

      1) Direct costs would be eliminated if the product was eliminated.

         a) **Direct materials** are tangible inputs to the manufacturing process that can feasibly be traced to the product, e.g., sheet metal welded together for a piece of heavy equipment.

            i) All costs of bringing materials to the production line, e.g., transportation-in, are included in the cost of direct materials.

         b) **Direct labor** is the cost of human labor that can feasibly be traced to the product, e.g., the wages of the welder.

      2) Indirect costs would not be eliminated if the product was eliminated.

         a) **Manufacturing overhead** consists of all costs of manufacturing that **are not direct** materials or direct labor.

            i) **Indirect materials** are tangible inputs to the manufacturing process that cannot feasibly be traced to the product, e.g., the welding compound used to put together a piece of heavy equipment.

            ii) **Indirect labor** is the cost of human labor connected with the manufacturing process that cannot feasibly be traced to the product, e.g., the wages of assembly line supervisors and janitorial staff.

            iii) Other manufacturing costs include utilities expense, real estate taxes, insurance, and depreciation on factory equipment.

   b. Manufacturing costs also may be classified as follows:

      1) **Prime cost** – costs directly attributable to a product (equals direct materials plus direct labor).

      2) **Conversion cost** – costs of converting materials into the finished product (equals direct labor plus manufacturing overhead).

    c.   A manufacturer incurs **nonmanufacturing costs (operating costs)**.

        1)   Selling (marketing) costs are incurred while getting the product to the consumer, e.g., sales personnel salaries and product transportation.

        2)   Administrative expenses are not directly related to producing or marketing the product, e.g., executive salaries and depreciation on the administration building.

2.   **Direct vs. Indirect**

    a.   Costs can be classified by how they are assigned to cost objects.

        1)   **Direct costs** can be traced to a cost object in an economically feasible way.

            a)   Examples are direct materials and direct labor inputs.

        2)   **Indirect costs**, such as indirect materials and indirect labor, cannot be traced to a cost object in an economically feasible way. Thus, they must be allocated.

            a)   To simplify allocation, indirect costs often are collected in cost pools.

                i)   A cost pool is an account in which similar cost elements with a common cause (cost driver) are accumulated.

                ii)   Manufacturing overhead is a commonly used cost pool in which various indirect costs of manufacturing are accumulated prior to allocation.

3.   **Product vs. Period**

    a.   An important issue in management accounting is whether to **capitalize** costs in inventory or to **expense** them in the period incurred.

        1)   Product costs (inventoriable costs) are capitalized as part of inventory. They eventually become components of cost of goods sold.

        2)   Period costs are expensed as incurred and are therefore excluded from cost of goods sold and inventory.

    b.   This distinction is crucial because of the required treatment of manufacturing costs for external financial reporting purposes.

        1)   Under GAAP, all manufacturing costs (direct materials, direct labor, variable overhead, and fixed overhead) must be recognized as product costs. All selling and administrative (S&A) costs are period costs, which affects ratios and decisions.

            a)   This approach is **absorption costing** (full costing).

        2)   For internal reporting, operational planning and control may be facilitated by treating only variable manufacturing costs as product costs. All other costs (variable S&A and the fixed portion of both production and S&A expenses) are period costs.

            a)   This approach is **variable costing** (direct costing).

            b)   Variable costing is covered in Study Unit 19, Subunit 1.

        3)   The following table summarizes absorption and variable costing:

	Absorption Costing (Required under GAAP)	Variable Costing (For Internal Reporting Only)
Product Costs (Included in Cost of Goods Sold)	Variable production costs	
	Fixed production costs	
Period Costs		Fixed production costs
	Variable S&A expenses	
(Excluded from Cost of Goods Sold)	Fixed S&A expenses	

c. **Gross margin** (gross profit) is an intermediate component of operating income under absorption (full) costing. It is the excess of sales over cost of goods sold that consists of variable and fixed manufacturing costs.

1) Only costs directly associated with manufacturing the product may be subtracted.

2) GAAP require this calculation.

Gross profit ratio = Gross profit ÷ Sales

d. **Contribution margin** is the intermediate component under variable costing. It is the excess of sales over the sum of variable manufacturing and selling and administrative costs.

1) Contribution margin is the amount available to cover fixed costs.

2) This calculation often is used for internal (managerial) reporting purposes.

Stop and review! You have completed the outline for this subunit. Study multiple-choice questions 1 through 4 on page 405.

18.2 BASIC COST CALCULATIONS

1. **Cost of Goods Sold and Cost of Goods Manufactured**

a. Cost of goods sold is a straightforward computation for **retailers** because they have only one class of inventory.

```
  Beginning inventory
+ Purchases
- Ending inventory
= Cost of goods sold
```

b. The calculation is more complex for **manufacturers** because they have three classes of inventory.

1) Cost of goods manufactured is an intermediate component of cost of goods sold. It is similar to a retailer's purchases account.

```
  Beginning work-in-process inventory
+ Total manufacturing costs
- Ending work-in-process inventory
= Cost of goods manufactured
```

c. A comparison of these computations in full is as follows:

Cost of goods sold for a manufacturer:

Beginning direct materials inventory		$ 2,000
Plus: Purchases	$ 4,000	
Minus: Returns and discounts	(1,000)	
Net purchases	$ 3,000	
Plus: Freight-in	1,000	4,000
Direct materials available for use		$ 6,000
Minus: Ending direct materials inventory		(1,000)
Direct materials used in production		$ 5,000
Direct labor costs		5,000
Manufacturing overhead costs		4,000
Total manufacturing costs for the period		**$14,000**
Plus: Beginning work-in-process inventory		5,000
Minus: Ending work-in-process inventory		(4,000)
Cost of goods manufactured		**$15,000**
Plus: Beginning finished goods inventory		6,000
Goods available for sale		**$21,000**
Minus: Ending finished goods inventory		(11,000)
Cost of goods sold		**$10,000**

Cost of goods sold for a retailer:

Beginning inventory		$10,000
Plus: Purchases	$15,000	
Minus: Returns and discounts	(1,000)	
Net purchases	**$14,000**	
Plus: Freight-in	1,000	15,000
Goods available for sale		**$25,000**
Minus: Ending inventory		(5,000)
Cost of goods sold		**$20,000**

2. **Relevant vs. Sunk**

a. Relevant costs are future costs that change depending on the action taken. All other costs are assumed to be constant and are irrelevant to the decision.

1) An example is tuition that must be spent to attend a fourth year of college.

b. Sunk costs already have been incurred or irrevocably committed to be incurred. Because they are unavoidable and do not vary with the option chosen, they are not relevant to future decisions.

1) An example is 3 years of tuition already paid. The previous 3 years of tuition do not affect the decision to attend a fourth year.

3. **Additional Cost Concepts**

a. **Value-adding costs** cannot be eliminated without reducing the quality, responsiveness, or quantity of the output required.

b. **Incremental (differential or marginal) cost** is the difference in total cost between two decisions. Incremental cost never includes fixed costs or sunk costs.

c. **Opportunity cost** is the maximum benefit forgone by using a scarce resource for a given purpose.

Stop and review! You have completed the outline for this subunit. Study multiple-choice questions 5 through 8 beginning on page 406.

18.3 OTHER COST MEASUREMENT CONCEPTS

1. **Variable vs. Fixed**

a. Variable cost **per unit** is constant in the short run regardless of the level of production. But variable costs **in total** vary directly and proportionally with changes in volume. Typical variable costs are direct materials, direct labor, and manufacturing supplies.

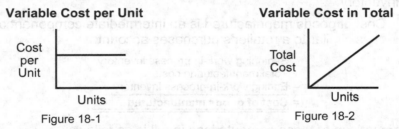

Figure 18-1   Figure 18-2

EXAMPLE

One unit of direct materials is to be used in each unit of a finished good.

Number of Units Produced		Cost per Unit		Total Cost of Units
0	×	$10	=	$ 0
100	×	$10	=	$ 1,000
1,000	×	$10	=	$ 10,000
5,000	×	$10	=	$ 50,000
10,000	×	$10	=	$100,000

b.   Fixed costs **in total** are unchanged in the short run regardless of production level. Accordingly, the amount paid for an assembly line is the same even if nothing is produced. But fixed cost **per unit** varies indirectly with the activity level. Typical fixed costs are rent, depreciation, and insurance.

Fixed Costs in Total

Figure 18-3

Fixed Cost per Unit

Figure 18-4

EXAMPLE

The historical cost of an assembly line is fixed, but its cost per unit decreases as production increases.

Cost of Assembly Line		Number of Units Produced		Per-Unit Cost of Assembly Line
$1,000,000	÷	1	=	$1,000,000
$1,000,000	÷	100	=	$ 10,000
$1,000,000	÷	1,000	=	$ 1,000
$1,000,000	÷	5,000	=	$ 200
$1,000,000	÷	10,000	=	$ 100

---

c.   **Mixed (semivariable) costs** combine fixed and variable elements, e.g., rental of a car for a flat fee per month plus an additional fee for each mile driven.

Mixed Cost

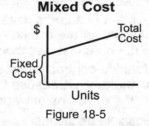

Figure 18-5

EXAMPLE

A piece of machinery is rented to improve the efficiency of a production line. The rent is $150,000 per year plus $1 for every unit produced.

Number of Units Produced	Fixed Cost of Extra Machine		Variable Cost of Extra Machine		Total Cost of Extra Machine
0	$150,000	+	$ 0	=	$150,000
100	$150,000	+	$ 100	=	$150,100
1,000	$150,000	+	$ 1,000	=	$151,000
5,000	$150,000	+	$ 5,000	=	$155,000
10,000	$150,000	+	$10,000	=	$160,000

---

1)   The fixed and variable portions of a mixed cost can be estimated using the high-low method (this method is covered in Study Unit 7, Subunit 2).

2.   **Relevant Range**

a.   Relevant range is the **expected** range of activity.

b.   Within the relevant range, per-unit variable costs and fixed costs do not change. It is synonymous with the **short run** because all costs are variable in the long run.

1)   The relevant range is established by the efficiency of current manufacturing operations, agreements with labor unions and suppliers, etc.

a)   Investment in more efficient equipment may result in higher total fixed costs and lower total and per-unit variable costs.

3. **Spoilage and Scrap**

   a. **Normal spoilage** occurs under normal, efficient operating conditions. It is essentially uncontrollable in the short run. Thus, it is accounted for as a product cost and included in the cost of the good output (predicted and unavoidable).

   b. **Abnormal spoilage** is **not** expected to occur under normal, efficient operating conditions. It is accounted for as a period cost (a loss).

   c. **Scrap** consists of materials left over from making a product. No cost is recognized for scrap, and it is not classified as normal or abnormal. Scrap also may be reused or discarded.

      1) If scrap is **common** to all jobs or **process costing** is used, the proceeds of sale **reduce manufacturing overhead**.

      2) If **job costing** is used, the proceeds **reduce work-in-process**.

Stop and review! You have completed the outline for this subunit. Study multiple-choice questions 9 through 12 beginning on page 407.

18.4 DECISION COSTING

1. **Relevant vs. Irrelevant Factors**

   a. Decision making should focus only on relevant revenues and costs. To be relevant, they must

      1) Be **expected** to be earned or incurred, respectively, in the **future**.

         a) Costs already incurred or to which the organization is committed (sunk costs) do not affect current decisions.

         b) EXAMPLE: A manufacturer is considering the purchase of new equipment. The amounts paid for the existing equipment are sunk costs. They are irrelevant to the purchase decision.

         c) EXAMPLE: A union contract may require 6 months of wage continuance after a plant shutdown. Because the occurrence of a plant shutdown is a future event, the 6 months of wages represent relevant costs.

      2) Differ among the possible decisions.

      3) Be avoidable.

         a) A cost is avoidable if it can be eliminated by choosing a specific option. Avoidable costs may include variable materials costs or direct labor costs.

         b) An unavoidable cost must be incurred regardless of whether a specific option is chosen.

            i) For example, rent under a long-term lease on a building is not eliminated by closing the business in that building. Thus, the rent is an unavoidable cost.

   b. Marginal (incremental or differential) analysis relates to relevance.

      1) For example, throughout the relevant range, the marginal cost of an additional unit of output is usually the same. However, beyond a certain output, current production capacity is insufficient and additional fixed costs must be incurred.

      2) The basic decision model is, if marginal revenue exceeds marginal costs (i.e., the contribution margin is positive), accept the project.

EXAMPLE

The following unit costs of a product are incurred:

Direct materials	$2.00
Direct labor	3.00
Variable overhead	.50
Fixed overhead	.50
Total cost	$6.00

The product normally sells for $10 per unit. Marginal analysis is necessary if a buyer, who has never before been a customer, offers to pay $5.60 per unit for a special order of the product. One possibility is to reject the offer because the selling price is less than the average cost of production.

However, marginal analysis results in a different decision. Assuming idle capacity is available, the only marginal costs are for direct materials, direct labor, and variable overhead. No additional fixed overhead costs are incurred. Because marginal revenue (the $5.60 selling price) exceeds marginal costs ($2 materials + $3 labor + $.50 variable OH = $5.50 per unit), accepting the special order is profitable (i.e., the contribution margin is positive: $5.60 – $5.50 = $0.10 per unit).

---

2.   **Add-or-Drop-a-Segment Decisions**

   a.   Disinvestment decisions involve discontinuing an operation, product or product line, business segment, branch, or major customer.

   1)   In general, if the marginal cost of a project exceeds the marginal revenue, the firm should disinvest.

   b.   A firm making a disinvestment decision should

   1)   Identify fixed costs that will be eliminated, e.g., insurance on equipment used.

   2)   Determine the revenue that justifies continuing operations. In the short run, this amount should at least equal the variable cost of production or continued service.

   3)   Establish the opportunity cost of alternatives.

   4)   Determine whether the carrying amount of the assets equals their economic value. If not, the decision should be evaluated using current fair value.

   c.   When a firm disinvests, excess capacity may exist unless it is used immediately by another project. The cost of idle capacity is a relevant cost.

3.   **Special Orders When Excess Capacity Exists**

   a.   When a manufacturer has excess production capacity, accepting a special order has no opportunity cost.

   1)   The order should be accepted if the minimum price for the product is equal to or greater than the variable costs.

   2)   A special order might be rejected if acceptance affects the price of regular sales.

EXAMPLE

The following price and cost data are available for two products:

	X		Z	
Selling price		$250		$300
Variable costs:				
Direct materials	$110		$125	
Direct labor	20		25	
Variable overhead	55		50	
Variable S&A	5	(190)	5	(205)
Unit contribution margin (UCM)		$ 60		$ 95

A special, one-time order for 2,000 units of X has been received. Sufficient unused capacity exists. The order can be accepted at a price of at least $190 (unit variable cost) per unit of X.

---

4. **Special Orders in the Absence of Excess Capacity**

    a. When a manufacturer lacks excess production capacity, the marginal costs of accepting the order must be considered.

        1) Besides the variable costs of the production run, the firm must consider the opportunity cost of redirecting productive capacity away from (possibly more profitable) products.

EXAMPLE

A special order for 2,000 units of X has been received, but the firm is operating at full capacity. All 24,000 machine hours available to produce Z are being used.

Each unit of X requires 4 hours to produce, and each unit of Z requires 6 hours. The firm must divert 8,000 hours (2,000 units of X × 4 hours per unit) to produce the special order.

The opportunity cost of these hours is the contribution margin (CM) earned by producing Z. X has a CM of $15 per machine hour ($60 ÷ 4 hours), and Z has a CM of $15.83 per machine hour ($95 ÷ 6 hours).

Hours needed	8,000	Units of Z forgone	$	1,333
Hours per unit of Z	÷ 6	Z's UCM	×	95
Units of Z forgone	1,333	Opportunity cost		$126,635

For the special order to be profitable, the firm must recover (1) the opportunity cost of not producing 1,333 units of Z and (2) the variable costs of the production run.

Z's total CM forgone (opportunity costs)	$ 126,635
Variable costs of special order (2,000 units × $190)	380,000
Total cost to be recovered	$ 506,635
Units in the special order	÷ 2,000
Minimum price per unit	$ 253.32 (rounded)

---

5. **Make-or-Buy Decisions (Insourcing vs. Outsourcing)**

    a. The firm should use available resources as efficiently as possible before outsourcing.

        1) If the total relevant costs of production are **less** than the costs to buy the item, it should be made in-house.

        2) If the total relevant costs of production are **more** than the costs to buy the item, it should be bought (outsourced).

    b. As with a special order, the manager considers only the costs relevant to the investment decision. The key variable is total relevant costs, not all total costs.

        1) Sunk costs are irrelevant.

        2) Costs that do not differ between two alternatives should be ignored because they are not relevant to the decision being made.

        3) Opportunity costs must be considered when idle capacity (additional capacity) is not available. Opportunity cost is important because it represents the forgone opportunities of the firm.

            a) In some situations, a firm may decide to stop processing one product in order to free up capacity for another product, reducing relevant costs, and affecting the decision to make or buy.

    c. The firm also should consider the qualitative aspects of the decision.

        1) Will the product quality be as high if a component is outsourced rather than produced internally?

        2) How reliable are the suppliers?

        3) Will workers acquire new skills or efficiencies?

6. **Make-or-Buy Decisions When Available Capacity Exists**

    a. When there is available capacity, fixed costs are **irrelevant** in deciding whether to make or buy the product because they will not change.

EXAMPLE

Luna must determine whether to make or buy an order of 1,000 frames. Luna can purchase the frames for $13 or choose to make them in-house. Luna currently has adequate available capacity. Cost information for the frames is as follows:

Total variable costs	$10
Allocable fixed costs	5
Total unit costs	$15

Since there is available capacity, the allocable fixed costs are not relevant. The total relevant costs of $10 are less than the $13 cost to purchase; therefore, Luna should make the frames.

---

7. **Make-or-Buy Decisions in the Absence of Available Capacity**

    a. When there is no available capacity, the differential (marginal or incremental) costs of accepting the order must be considered.

        1) This means that the revenue, variable costs, and direct fixed costs related to reduced production of existing product lines are **relevant** in deciding whether to make or buy the product.

EXAMPLE

Luna has received another special order for 1,000 frames, but this month there is no available capacity.

Since there is no available capacity, the allocable fixed costs are relevant. The total relevant costs of $15 are more than the $13 cost to purchase; therefore, Luna should purchase the frames.

Stop and review! You have completed the outline for this subunit. Study multiple-choice questions 13 through 18 beginning on page 409.

18.5 COST-VOLUME-PROFIT ANALYSIS -- BASICS

1. Cost-volume-profit (CVP) analysis (also called **breakeven analysis**) explains the effects of changes in assumptions about cost behavior and the relevant ranges in which those assumptions are valid. These changes may affect the relationships among revenues, variable costs, and fixed costs at different output levels.

    a. Thus, CVP analysis determines the probable effects of changes in unit sales, sales price, unit variable cost, fixed cost, and product mix.

2. **Simplifying Assumptions**

    a. Cost and revenue relationships are predictable and linear. They are true over the relevant range of activity and specified time span.

    b. Unit selling prices and market conditions are constant.

    c. Changes in inventory are insignificant in amount. Thus, production equals sales.

    d. Total variable costs change proportionally with volume, but unit variable costs are constant over the relevant range.

        1) Direct materials and direct labor are variable costs.

    e. Fixed costs are constant over the relevant range, but unit fixed costs vary indirectly with activity.

3. **Breakeven Point in Units**

   a. The **breakeven point** is the output at which all fixed costs and cumulative variable costs have been covered. It is the output at which operating income is zero.

      1) Each additional unit produced above the breakeven point generates operating profit equal to the UCM. UCM equals unit selling price minus unit variable cost.

   b. The simplest calculation for breakeven in units is to divide fixed costs by the UCM.

$$\text{Breakeven point in units} = \frac{Fixed\ costs}{UCM}$$

      1) Breakeven point in units should always be rounded up to the next unit. For example, 3333.34 units should be rounded up to 3334 units.

EXAMPLE

A product has a unit sales price of $0.60 and a unit variable cost of $0.20. Fixed costs are $10,000.

Unit selling price	$0.60
Minus: Unit variable costs	(0.20)
UCM	$0.40

Breakeven point in units = Fixed costs ÷ UCM
= $10,000 ÷ $0.40
= 25,000 units

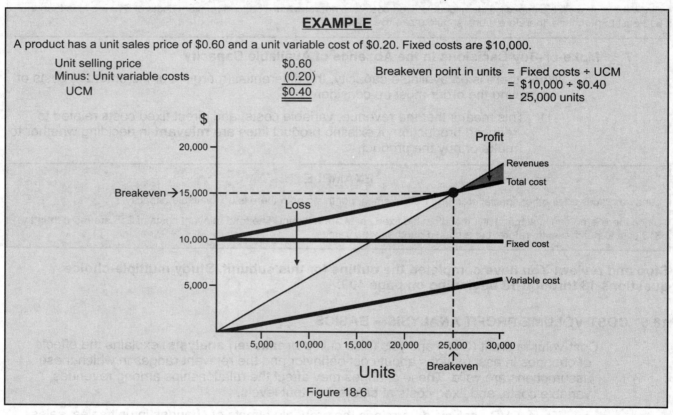

Figure 18-6

---

4. **Breakeven Point in Dollars**

   a. The breakeven point in sales dollars equals fixed costs divided by the contribution margin ratio (CMR). CMR is the ratio of contribution margin to sales price on either a total or per-unit basis.

$$\text{Breakeven point in dollars} = \frac{Fixed\ costs}{CMR}$$

   b. The breakeven point in sales dollars also equals the breakeven point in units multiplied by the selling price.

EXAMPLE

The contribution margin ratio is 66.667% ($0.40 ÷ $0.60).

Breakeven point in dollars = Fixed costs ÷ CMR
= $10,000 ÷ .66667
= $15,000

Stop and review! You have completed the outline for this subunit. Study multiple-choice questions 19 through 21 on page 411.

18.6 COST-VOLUME-PROFIT ANALYSIS -- ADVANCED

1. **Margin of Safety**

   a. The margin of safety is the excess of sales over breakeven sales. It is the amount by which sales can decline before losses occur.

   b. The margin of safety can be expressed as either a dollar amount or a percentage of sales.

$$\text{Margin of safety in dollars = Total sales in dollars - Breakeven point in dollars}$$

$$\text{Margin of safety (\%)} = \frac{\text{Margin of safety (in dollars)}}{\text{Total sales (in dollars)}}$$

2. **Target Operating Income**

   a. An amount of operating income, either in dollars or as a percentage of sales, can be calculated by treating target income as an additional fixed cost (e.g., financing costs or required profits to keep the stock price from falling). The necessary sales can be expressed in either units or dollars.

$$\text{Target units} = \frac{\text{Fixed costs + Target operating income}}{\text{UCM}}$$

$$\text{Target sales in dollars} = \frac{\text{Fixed costs + Target operating income}}{\text{Contribution margin ratio}}$$

   b. Other problems involving target income require use of the standard equation for operating income.

$$\text{Sales - Variable costs - Fixed costs = Operating income}$$

EXAMPLE

Fixed costs are $150,000, and variable costs are 85% of the selling price. The dollar amount of sales needed for a 10% return on sales (profit margin) is calculated as follows:

$$\text{Sales - Variable costs - Fixed costs = Target operating income}$$
$$\text{Sales - (.85)Sales - \$150,000 = (.1)Sales}$$
$$\text{(.15)Sales - \$150,000 = (.1)Sales}$$
$$\text{(.05)Sales = \$150,000}$$
$$\text{Sales = \$3,000,000}$$

Alternatively, it can be calculated as follows:

$$\text{Sales - Variable costs - Fixed costs - Target operating income = 0}$$
$$\text{Sales - (.85)Sales - \$150,000 - (.10)Sales = 0}$$
$$\text{Sales(1.00 - .85 - .10) - \$150,000 = 0}$$
$$\text{Sales(.05) = \$150,000}$$
$$\text{Sales = \$3,000,000}$$

   1) The unit selling price is not necessary for this calculation.

EXAMPLE

Assuming that target operating income is $25,000, unit sales are calculated as follows:

$$\text{Target units = (Fixed costs + Target operating income) ÷ UCM}$$
$$= \text{(\$10,000 + \$25,000) ÷ \$0.40}$$
$$= \text{\$35,000 ÷ \$.40}$$
$$= \text{87,500 units}$$

3. **Target Net Income**

a. A problem may ask for net income (an after-tax amount) instead of operating income (a pretax amount).

$$\text{Net income} = \text{Operating income} - (\text{Operating income} \times \text{Tax rate})$$
$$= \text{Operating income} \times (1 - \text{Tax rate})$$
$$\text{Operating income} = \text{Net income} \div (1 - \text{Tax rate})$$

1) The calculation of unit sales or sales dollars for a given target net income is based on the same equations used for target operating income. The difference is that net income is substituted for target operating income.

$$\text{Target units} = \frac{\text{Fixed costs} + [\text{Target net income} \div (1.0 - \text{tax rate})]}{UCM}$$

EXAMPLE

Assuming that target net income is $30,000 and the effective tax rate is 20%, unit sales are calculated as follows:

$$\text{Target units} = \{\text{Fixed costs} + [\text{Target net income} \div (1.0 - .20)]\} \div UCM$$
$$= [\$10,000 + (\$30,000 \div .80)] \div \$.40$$
$$= 118,750 \text{ units}$$

---

4. **Multiple Products**

a. CVP analysis can be adapted to problems involving multiple products. The assumption is that the product mix is constant over the relevant range.

1) The composite UCM is the weighted average of the UCMs of the products.

EXAMPLE

Two products have the following selling prices and variable costs:

	Q	Y
Unit selling price	$100	$130
Unit variable cost	85	95
UCM	$15	$35
UCM Ratio	15/100	35/130
	15%	26.92%

Five units of Q are sold for every four units of Y. Total annual fixed costs are $80,600. The problem is to determine how many units of each product must be sold to earn $100,000 of operating income.

The UCMs of the two products are $15 ($100 – $85) and $35 ($130 – $95), respectively. The sales mix consists of a composite unit of five units of Q and four units of Y. Thus, the number of composite units that must be sold is calculated using the composite (weighted-average) UCM.

$$\text{Target units} = (\text{Target operating income} + \text{Fixed costs}) \div \text{Composite (weighted-average) UCM}$$
$$= (\$100,000 + \$80,600) \div [(5 \times \$15) + (4 \times \$35)]$$
$$= \$180,600 \div (\$75 + \$140)$$
$$= \$180,600 \div \$215$$
$$= 840 \text{ composite units}$$

$$840 \times 9 = 7,560 \text{ total units of Q and Y sold}$$
$$Q: \ 7,560 \times (5 \div 9) = 4,200 \text{ units}$$
$$Y: \ 7,560 \times (4 \div 9) = 3,360 \text{ units}$$

Total contribution margin of $180,600 [(4,200 × $15) + (3,360 × $35)] equals the sum of fixed costs ($80,600) and target operating income ($100,000).

 Proficiency in using the CVP equations is needed to determine the information required by questions. The multiple-choice questions in the Gleim materials provide an opportunity to practice and improve proficiency in working with these equations.

Stop and review! You have completed the outline for this subunit. Study multiple-choice questions 22 through 25 beginning on page 412.

QUESTIONS

18.1 **Cost Measurement Terminology**

1. If a product required a great deal of electricity to produce, and crude oil prices increased, which of the following costs most likely increased?

    A. Direct materials.

    B. Direct labor.

    C. Prime costs.

    D. Conversion costs.

Answer (D) is correct.
    REQUIRED: The costs that most likely increase if overhead increases.
    DISCUSSION: Conversion costs consist of direct labor and manufacturing overhead. Overhead includes the costs of utilities, such as electricity. An increase in the price of crude oil, which is used to generate electricity, therefore, is likely to increase conversion costs.
    Answer (A) is incorrect. Direct materials are tangible inputs to the manufacturing process that can practically be traced to the product. Electricity is not a direct material. Answer (B) is incorrect. Direct labor is the cost of labor that can feasibly be traced to the product. Electricity is not direct labor. Answer (C) is incorrect. Prime costs equal direct materials plus direct labor. Because electricity is neither a direct material nor direct labor, electricity is not a prime cost.

2. Inventoriable costs

    A. Include only the prime costs of manufacturing a product.

    B. Include only the conversion costs of manufacturing a product.

    C. Are expensed when products become part of finished goods inventory.

    D. Are regarded as assets before the products are sold.

Answer (D) is correct.
    REQUIRED: The true statement about inventoriable costs.
    DISCUSSION: Product (inventoriable) costs are capitalized as part of inventory. But period costs are expensed as they are incurred and are not capitalized as assets. Under an absorption costing system, inventoriable costs include variable and fixed costs of production. Under variable costing, inventoriable costs include only variable production costs.
    Answer (A) is incorrect. Overhead costs and prime costs (direct materials and labor) are included in inventory. Answer (B) is incorrect. Materials costs also are included. Answer (C) is incorrect. Inventory costs are expensed when the goods are sold, not when they are transferred to finished goods.

3. The unit costs for direct materials, machining, and assembly of a manufactured product represent

    A. Conversion costs.

    B. Separable costs.

    C. Committed costs.

    D. Prime costs.

Answer (D) is correct.
    REQUIRED: The type of cost represented by direct materials, machining, and assembly.
    DISCUSSION: Prime costs are a manufacturer's direct cost. Direct materials and direct labor (such as machining and assembly) are examples.
    Answer (A) is incorrect. Conversion costs consist of direct labor and overhead. Answer (B) is incorrect. Separable costs are incurred beyond the point at which jointly produced items become separately identifiable. Answer (C) is incorrect. Committed costs result when an entity holds fixed assets. Examples of committed costs include long-term lease payments and depreciation.

4. In cost terminology, conversion costs consist of

    A. Direct and indirect labor.

    B. Direct labor and direct materials.

    C. Direct labor and factory overhead.

    D. Indirect labor and variable factory overhead.

Answer (C) is correct.
    REQUIRED: The components of conversion costs.
    DISCUSSION: Conversion costs consist of direct labor and manufacturing overhead. They are the costs of converting materials into a finished product.
    Answer (A) is incorrect. All manufacturing overhead is included in conversion costs, not just indirect labor. Answer (B) is incorrect. Direct materials are not an element of conversion costs. They are a prime cost. Answer (D) is incorrect. Direct labor is also an element of conversion costs.

18.2 Basic Cost Calculations

Questions 5 and 6 are based on the following information. The estimated unit costs for Cole Co. using absorption (full) costing and planning to produce and sell at a level of 12,000 units per month are as follows:

Cost Item	Estimated Unit Cost
Direct materials	$32
Direct labor	20
Variable manufacturing overhead	15
Fixed manufacturing overhead	6
Variable selling	3
Fixed selling	4

5. Cole's estimated conversion costs per unit are

   A. $35
   B. $41
   C. $48
   D. $67

Answer (B) is correct.
   REQUIRED: The estimated conversion costs per unit.
   DISCUSSION: Conversion costs are incurred in transforming direct materials into finished products. They include direct labor and manufacturing overhead. Thus, unit conversion costs equal $41 ($20 direct labor + $15 variable overhead + $6 fixed overhead).
   Answer (A) is incorrect. Direct labor plus variable manufacturing overhead equals $35. It should include the $6 of fixed overhead. Answer (C) is incorrect. Including period costs of $3 in variable selling costs and $4 in fixed selling costs results in $48. Answer (D) is incorrect. The amount of $67 includes $32 in direct materials and excludes $6 fixed overhead.

6. Cole's estimated prime costs per unit are

   A. $73
   B. $32
   C. $67
   D. $52

Answer (D) is correct.
   REQUIRED: The estimated prime costs per unit.
   DISCUSSION: The direct costs of manufacturing, also called prime costs, are the costs of direct materials and direct labor. They are costs that can be directly associated with the finished product. Thus, direct manufacturing costs per unit are $52 ($32 direct materials + $20 direct labor).
   Answer (A) is incorrect. The amount of $73 includes $15 variable manufacturing overhead and $6 fixed manufacturing overhead. Answer (B) is incorrect. Not including $20 direct labor results in $32. Answer (C) is incorrect. Including $15 variable manufacturing overhead results in $67.

Questions 7 and 8 are based on the following information.

Jackson Products
Schedule of Cost of Goods Manufactured
For the Year Ended December 31 (in thousands)

Direct materials:		
Beginning inventory	$17,000	
Purchases of direct materials	70,000	
Cost of direct materials available for use	$87,000	
Ending inventory	(9,000)	
Direct materials used		$ 78,000
Direct manufacturing labor		9,000
Indirect manufacturing costs:		
Indirect manufacturing labor	$ 8,000	
Supplies	1,000	
Heat, light, and power	4,000	
Depreciation -- plant building	2,000	
Depreciation -- plant equipment	3,000	
Miscellaneous	2,000	20,000
Manufacturing costs incurred during the period		$107,000
Add: Beginning work-in-process inventory		11,000
Total manufacturing costs to account for		$118,000
Minus: Ending work-in-process inventory		(7,000)
Cost of goods manufactured (to Income Statement)		$111,000

7. What are Jackson's direct manufacturing costs for the year?

A. $20,000

B. $79,000

C. $87,000

D. $98,000

Answer (C) is correct.
REQUIRED: The total of prime costs.
DISCUSSION: Prime costs are all direct manufacturing costs. They equal the direct materials cost ($78,000) plus direct manufacturing labor cost ($9,000), or $87,000.
Answer (A) is incorrect. Overhead is $20,000. Answer (B) is incorrect. Using the cost of material purchases instead of materials used results in $79,000. Answer (D) is incorrect. Using overhead instead of direct labor results in $98,000.

8. What are Jackson's conversion costs for the year?

A. $4,000

B. $20,000

C. $29,000

D. $98,000

Answer (C) is correct.
REQUIRED: The total conversion costs.
DISCUSSION: Conversion costs are all manufacturing costs other than direct material costs. Conversion costs equal direct manufacturing labor cost ($9,000) plus indirect manufacturing costs ($20,000), or $29,000.
Answer (A) is incorrect. The difference between the beginning and ending work-in-process inventories is $4,000. Answer (B) is incorrect. The amount of $20,000 is indirect manufacturing costs only and excludes direct labor. Answer (D) is incorrect. Including direct materials and excluding direct labor results in $98,000.

18.3 Other Cost Measurement Concepts

9. In manufacturing its products for the month just ended, Elk Co. incurred normal spoilage of $10,000 and abnormal spoilage of $12,000. How much spoilage cost should Elk charge as a period cost for the month?

A. $22,000

B. $12,000

C. $10,000

D. $0

Answer (B) is correct.
REQUIRED: The spoilage charged as a period cost.
DISCUSSION: Normal spoilage occurs under efficient operating conditions and is therefore a product cost. Abnormal spoilage is not expected to occur under efficient operating conditions. It is accounted for as a period cost. Thus, the amount of spoilage charged as a period cost is the $12,000 related to abnormal spoilage.
Answer (A) is incorrect. The amount of $22,000 includes the normal spoilage ($10,000), which is a product cost. Answer (C) is incorrect. The $10,000 normal spoilage is a product cost. Answer (D) is incorrect. The abnormal spoilage ($12,000) is a period cost.

Questions 10 and 11 are based on the following information. The estimated unit costs for Cole Co. using absorption (full) costing and planning to produce and sell at a level of 12,000 units per month are as follows:

Cost Item	Estimated Unit Cost
Direct materials	$32
Direct labor	20
Variable manufacturing overhead	15
Fixed manufacturing overhead	6
Variable selling	3
Fixed selling	4

10. Cole's estimated total variable costs per unit are

A. $38

B. $70

C. $52

D. $18

Answer (B) is correct.
REQUIRED: The estimated total variable costs per unit.
DISCUSSION: Variable costs vary in direct proportion to production. Total unit variable costs are $70 ($32 direct materials + $20 direct labor + $15 variable overhead + $3 variable selling costs).
Answer (A) is incorrect. The amount of $38 does not include $32 direct materials. Answer (C) is incorrect. The amount of $52 does not include $15 variable overhead and $3 variable selling costs. Answer (D) is incorrect. The amount of $18 does not include $32 direct materials and $20 direct labor.

11. Estimated total costs that Cole would incur during a month with a production level of 12,000 units and a sales level of 8,000 units are

A. $692,000

B. $960,000

C. $948,000

D. $932,000

Answer (C) is correct.
REQUIRED: The estimated total costs incurred during a month with given production and sales levels.
DISCUSSION: Manufacturing costs at a production level of 12,000 units are $73 per unit ($32 + $20 + $15 + $6). Total estimated manufacturing costs are therefore $876,000 (12,000 units × $73). Fixed selling costs are expected to be $48,000 (12,000 units × $4). The anticipated total variable selling costs are $24,000 (8,000 units × $3). Thus, the total estimated costs are $948,000 ($876,000 + $48,000 + $24,000).
Answer (A) is incorrect. Total estimated costs are $948,000 [(12,000 × $73) + (12,000 × $4) + (8,000 × $3)]. Answer (B) is incorrect. Using 12,000 units to determine variable selling costs instead of 8,000 results in $960,000. Answer (D) is incorrect. Using 8,000 units to determine fixed selling costs instead of 12,000 results in $932,000.

12. Dahl Co. uses a standard costing system in connection with the manufacture of a "one size fits all" article of clothing. Each unit of finished product contains 2 yards of direct materials. However, a 20% direct materials spoilage calculated on input quantities occurs during the manufacturing process. The cost of the direct materials is $3 per yard. The standard direct materials cost per unit of finished product is

A. $4.80

B. $6.00

C. $7.20

D. $7.50

Answer (D) is correct.
REQUIRED: The standard direct materials cost per unit of finished product.
DISCUSSION: If 2 yards remain in each unit after spoilage of 20% of the direct materials input, the total per unit input must have been 2.5 yards (2.0 ÷ 80%). The standard unit direct materials cost is therefore $7.50 (2.5 yards × $3).
Answer (A) is incorrect. The 2 yards of good output should be divided (not multiplied) by 80% to determine the standard yards of material per unit. Answer (B) is incorrect. The cost per unit before spoilage is added is $6.00. Answer (C) is incorrect. Adding 20% of the materials of the finished product as spoilage and then multiplying by the $3.00 cost per yard results in $7.20 [(2.00 × 1.20) × $3.00].

18.4 Decision Costing

13. Clay Co. has considerable excess manufacturing capacity. A special job order's cost sheet includes the following applied manufacturing overhead costs:

Fixed costs	$21,000
Variable costs	33,000

The fixed costs include a normal $3,700 allocation for in-house design costs, although no in-house design will be done. Instead, the job will require the use of external designers costing $7,750. What is the total amount to be included in the calculation to determine the minimum acceptable price for the job?

- A. $36,700
- B. $40,750
- C. $54,000
- D. $58,050

Answer (B) is correct.
REQUIRED: The total amount to be included in the calculation to determine the minimum acceptable price.
DISCUSSION: Given excess capacity, neither increased fixed costs nor opportunity costs are incurred by accepting the special order. Thus, the marginal cost of the order (the minimum acceptable price) is $40,750 ($33,000 variable costs + $7,750 cost of external design).
Answer (A) is incorrect. The amount of $36,700 equals variable costs plus the in-house design costs. Answer (C) is incorrect. The amount of $54,000 equals the fixed costs plus the variable costs. Answer (D) is incorrect. The amount of $58,050 equals the fixed costs, plus the variable costs, minus the in-house design costs, plus the external design costs.

14. Based on potential sales of 500 units per year, a new product has estimated traceable costs of $990,000. What is the target price to obtain a 15% profit margin on sales?

- A. $2,329
- B. $2,277
- C. $1,980
- D. $1,935

Answer (A) is correct.
REQUIRED: The target price.
DISCUSSION: Costs of the product must be 85% of sales to achieve a 15% profit on sales. Thus, sales must be $1,164,706 ($990,000 ÷ .85). The price per unit is $2,329 ($1,164,706 ÷ 500).
Answer (B) is incorrect. The amount of $2,277 results from multiplying $990,000 by 1.15 and dividing by 500 units. Answer (C) is incorrect. The cost per unit is $1,980 ($990,000 ÷ 500 units). Answer (D) is incorrect. The amount of $1,935 is 85% of $2,277.

15. Mili Co. plans to discontinue a division with a $20,000 contribution to overhead. Overhead allocated to the division is $50,000, of which $5,000 cannot be eliminated. The effect of this discontinuance on Mili's pretax income would be an increase of

- A. $5,000
- B. $20,000
- C. $25,000
- D. $30,000

Answer (C) is correct.
REQUIRED: The effect of discontinuing a division.
DISCUSSION: This disinvestment decision eliminates $45,000 of overhead ($50,000 – $5,000) and the $20,000 contribution to overhead. The net effect on pretax income is therefore a $25,000 increase ($45,000 – $20,000).
Answer (A) is incorrect. The overhead allocated to the division, which cannot be eliminated, is $5,000. The net effect is a $25,000 increase in pretax income ($45,000 overhead that can be eliminated – $20,000 contribution to overhead). Answer (B) is incorrect. The contribution to overhead is $20,000. Answer (D) is incorrect. The $5,000 of overhead that cannot be eliminated from the $50,000 overhead allocated should be subtracted.

16. In a make-versus-buy decision, the relevant costs include variable manufacturing costs as well as

- A. Factory management costs.
- B. General office costs.
- C. Avoidable fixed costs.
- D. Depreciation costs.

Answer (C) is correct.
REQUIRED: The relevant costs in a make-versus-buy decision.
DISCUSSION: The relevant costs in a make-versus-buy decision are those that differ between the two decision choices. These costs include any variable costs plus any avoidable fixed costs. Avoidable fixed costs will not be incurred if the "buy" decision is selected.
Answer (A) is incorrect. Factory management costs are unlikely to differ regardless of which decision is selected. Answer (B) is incorrect. General office costs are unlikely to differ regardless of which decision is selected. Answer (D) is incorrect. Depreciation costs are unlikely to differ regardless of which decision is selected.

Questions 17 and 18 are based on the following information. Whitehall Corporation produces chemicals used in the cleaning industry. During the previous month, Whitehall incurred $300,000 of joint costs in producing 60,000 units of AM-12 and 40,000 units of BM-36. Whitehall uses the units-of-production method to allocate joint costs. Currently, AM-12 is sold at split-off for $3.50 per unit. Flank Corporation has approached Whitehall to purchase all of the production of AM-12 after further processing. The further processing will cost Whitehall $90,000.

17. Concerning AM-12, which one of the following alternatives is most advantageous?

A. Whitehall should process further and sell to Flank if the total selling price per unit after further processing is greater than $3.00, which covers the joint costs.

B. Whitehall should continue to sell at split-off unless Flank offers at least $4.50 per unit after further processing, which covers Whitehall's total costs.

C. Whitehall should process further and sell to Flank if the total selling price per unit after further processing is greater than $5.00.

D. Whitehall should process further and sell to Flank if the total selling price per unit after further processing is greater than $5.25, which maintains the same gross profit percentage.

Answer (C) is correct.
REQUIRED: The most advantageous processing and selling alternative.
DISCUSSION: The unit price of the product at the split-off point is known to be $3.50, so the joint costs are irrelevant. The additional unit cost of further processing is $1.50 ($90,000 ÷ 60,000 units). Consequently, the unit price must be at least $5.00 ($3.50 opportunity cost + $1.50).
Answer (A) is incorrect. The joint costs are irrelevant. Answer (B) is incorrect. The unit price must cover the $3.50 opportunity cost plus the $1.50 of additional costs. Answer (D) is incorrect. Any price greater than $5 will provide greater profits, in absolute dollars, even though the gross profit percentage declines.

18. Assume that Whitehall Corporation agreed to sell AM-12 to Flank Corporation for $5.50 per unit after further processing. During the first month of production, Whitehall sold 50,000 units with 10,000 units remaining in inventory at the end of the month. With respect to AM-12, which one of the following statements is true?

A. The operating profit last month was $50,000, and the inventory value is $15,000.

B. The operating profit last month was $50,000, and the inventory value is $45,000.

C. The operating profit last month was $125,000, and the inventory value is $30,000.

D. The operating profit last month was $200,000, and the inventory value is $30,000.

Answer (B) is correct.
REQUIRED: The operating profit and inventory value after specified sales of a product.
DISCUSSION: Joint costs are allocated based on units of production. Accordingly, the unit joint cost allocated to AM-12 is $3.00 [$300,000 ÷ (60,000 units of AM-12 + 40,000 units of BM-36)]. The unit cost of AM-12 is therefore $4.50 [$3.00 joint cost + ($90,000 additional cost ÷ 60,000 units)]. Total inventory value is $45,000 (10,000 units × $4.50), and total operating profit is $50,000 [50,000 units sold × ($5.50 unit price – $4.50 unit cost)].
Answer (A) is incorrect. The $3 unit joint cost should be included in the inventory value. Answer (C) is incorrect. The $1.50 unit additional cost should be included in total unit cost. Answer (D) is incorrect. The $3 unit joint cost should be included in the cost of goods sold, and inventory should include the $1.50 unit additional cost.

18.5 Cost-Volume-Profit Analysis -- Basics

19. The following information pertains to Sisk Co.:

Sales (25,000 units)	$500,000
Direct materials and direct labor	150,000
Factory overhead:	
Variable	20,000
Fixed	35,000
Selling and general expenses:	
Variable	5,000
Fixed	30,000

Sisk's breakeven point in number of units is

A. 4,924

B. 5,000

C. 6,250

D. 9,286

Answer (B) is correct.

REQUIRED: The breakeven point in units.

DISCUSSION: The breakeven point in units equals the fixed costs divided by the unit contribution margin (UCM). The fixed costs are $65,000 ($35,000 manufacturing overhead + $30,000 SG&A). The UCM is calculated as follows:

	Dollars		Units		Per Unit
Sales	$500,000	÷	25,000	=	$20.00
Variable costs:					
Prime costs	$150,000				
Variable overhead	20,000				
Variable SG&A	5,000				
Total var. costs	$175,000	÷	25,000	=	(7.00)
Contribution margin					$13.00

Thus, the breakeven point in units is 5,000 ($65,000 fixed costs ÷ $13 UCM).

Answer (A) is incorrect. The amount of 4,924 does not include the variable selling and general expenses in the unit contribution margin calculation. Answer (C) is incorrect. The amount of 6,250 includes the unit fixed manufacturing overhead and unit fixed selling and general expenses in the unit contribution margin. Answer (D) is incorrect. The amount of 9,286 results from using the total variable costs of $7 rather than the contribution margin of $13.

20. The breakeven point in units sold for Tierson Corporation is 44,000. If fixed costs for Tierson are equal to $880,000 annually and variable costs are $10 per unit, what is the contribution margin per unit for Tierson Corporation?

A. $0.05

B. $20.00

C. $44.00

D. $88.00

Answer (B) is correct.

REQUIRED: The contribution margin per unit.

DISCUSSION: The breakeven point in units is equal to the fixed costs divided by the unit contribution margin (UCM).

$$\text{Fixed costs} \div \text{UCM} = \text{Breakeven point in units}$$
$$\$880,000 \div \text{UCM} = 44,000 \text{ units}$$
$$\text{UCM} = \$20$$

Answer (A) is incorrect. The amount of $.05 results from inverting the numerator and denominator in the calculation. Answer (C) is incorrect. The amount of $44.00 results from using variable cost as part of the calculation. Answer (D) is incorrect. The amount of $88.00 results from dividing by an erroneous denominator.

21. The breakeven point in units increases when unit costs

A. Increase and sales price remains unchanged.

B. Decrease and sales price remains unchanged.

C. Remain unchanged and sales price increases.

D. Decrease and sales price increases.

Answer (A) is correct.

REQUIRED: The event that causes the breakeven point in units to increase.

DISCUSSION: A BEP ratio can be increased either by raising the numerator or lowering the denominator. The breakeven point in units is calculated by dividing fixed costs by the unit contribution margin. If selling price is constant and costs increase, the unit contribution margin decreases. The effect is to decrease the denominator and increase the ratio.

Answer (B) is incorrect. A decrease in costs decreases the breakeven point. The unit contribution margin increases. Answer (C) is incorrect. An increase in the selling price also increases the unit contribution margin, resulting in a lower breakeven point. Answer (D) is incorrect. The unit contribution margin is increased by a cost decrease and a sales price increase, resulting in a lower breakeven point.

18.6 Cost-Volume-Profit Analysis -- Advanced

22. During Year 1, Thor Lab supplied hospitals with a comprehensive diagnostic kit for $120. At a volume of 80,000 kits, Thor had fixed costs of $1 million and a profit before income taxes of $200,000. Because of an adverse legal decision, Thor's Year 2 liability insurance increased by $1.2 million over Year 1. Assuming the volume and other costs are unchanged, what should the Year 2 price be if Thor is to make the same $200,000 profit before income taxes?

A. $120.00

B. $135.00

C. $150.00

D. $240.00

Answer (B) is correct.

REQUIRED: The price charged to earn a specified pretax profit.

DISCUSSION: CVP analysis can be used to restate the equation for operating income to determine the required level of unit sales:

$$Target\ unit\ volume = \frac{Fixed\ costs\ +\ Target\ operating\ income}{UCM}$$

Thor's Year 1 unit variable cost (UVC) can thus be calculated as follows:

$$80,000\ units = (\$1,000,000 + \$200,000) \div (\$120 - UVC)$$
$$80,000 \times (\$120 - UVC) = \$1,200,000$$
$$\$120 - UVC = \$15$$
$$UVC = \$105$$

The Year 2 unit selling price (USP) can now be derived:

$$80,000\ units = (\$1,000,000 + \$200,000 + \$1,200,000) \div (USP - \$105)$$
$$80,000 \times (USP - \$105) = \$2,400,000$$
$$USP - \$105 = \$30$$
$$USP = \$135$$

Answer (A) is incorrect. The Year 1 unit price was $120.00. Answer (C) is incorrect. The amount of $150.00 assumes that the unit variable cost is $120. Answer (D) is incorrect. The amount of $240.00 assumes that the price must double, given that the sum of fixed costs and targeted profit has doubled.

23. The following information pertains to Clove Co. for the month just ended:

Budgeted sales	$1,000,000
Breakeven sales	700,000
Budgeted contribution margin	600,000
Cash flow breakeven	200,000

Clove's margin of safety is

A. $300,000

B. $400,000

C. $500,000

D. $800,000

Answer (A) is correct.

REQUIRED: The margin of safety.

DISCUSSION: The margin of safety measures the amount by which sales may decline before losses occur. It is the excess of budgeted or actual sales over the breakeven sales. Given that the budgeted sales are $1,000,000 and the breakeven sales are $700,000, the margin of safety is $300,000 ($1,000,000 – $700,000).

Answer (B) is incorrect. The budgeted sales minus the budgeted contribution margin is $400,000. Answer (C) is incorrect. The breakeven sales minus the cash flow breakeven is $500,000. Answer (D) is incorrect. The budgeted sales minus the cash flow breakeven is $800,000.

24. Wren Co. manufactures and sells two products with selling prices and variable costs as follows:

	A	B
Selling price	$18.00	$22.00
Variable costs	12.00	14.00

Wren's total annual fixed costs are $38,400. Wren sells four units of A for every unit of B. If operating income last year was $28,800, what was the number of units Wren sold?

A. 5,486

B. 6,000

C. 9,600

D. 10,500

Answer (D) is correct.

REQUIRED: The number of units sold.

DISCUSSION: The contribution margins of the two products are $6 and $8, respectively ($18 – $12 and $22 – $14). The units sold can be calculated as follows:

Target unit volume = (Fixed costs + Target operating income) ÷ Weighted UCM
$$= (\$38,400 + \$28,800) \div (\$6A + \$8B)$$
$$\$6A + \$8B = \$67,200$$
$$\$6(4B) + \$8B = \$67,200$$
$$\$32B = \$67,200$$
$$B = 2,100\ units$$

Because 4 units of A are sold for every unit of B, the volume of A was 8,400 units (2,100 × 4). Thus, the total number of units sold was 10,500 (8,400A + 2,100B).

Answer (A) is incorrect. The amount of 5,486 units equals the fixed costs divided by the contribution margin from product B. Answer (B) is incorrect. The amount of 6,000 units does not include the operating income of $28,800 in the calculation. Answer (C) is incorrect. The operating income plus the fixed costs are divided by the contribution margin for product B, giving the number of units sold of 9,600.

25. In using cost-volume-profit analysis to calculate expected unit sales, which of the following should be added to fixed costs in the numerator?

    A. Predicted operating loss.

    B. Predicted operating income.

    C. Unit contribution margin.

    D. Variable costs.

Answer (B) is correct.
    REQUIRED: The addition to fixed costs when calculating expected unit sales.
    DISCUSSION: CVP analysis can be used to restate the equation for target net income to determine the required level of unit sales.

$$Target\ unit\ volume = \frac{Fixed\ costs\ +\ Target\ operating\ income}{UCM}$$

    Answer (A) is incorrect. Predicted operating loss is subtracted from fixed costs, not added. Answer (C) is incorrect. Unit contribution margin is the denominator. Answer (D) is incorrect. Variable costs are a component of unit contribution margin.

414   *Notes*

STUDY UNIT NINETEEN
COSTING METHODS

(10 pages of outline)

The difference between absorption and variable costing is in the treatment of fixed manufacturing overhead. **Absorption costing** includes **all** manufacturing costs, variable and fixed, in product cost. This method is required under GAAP. **Variable costing** includes **only** variable manufacturing costs in product cost. It is not permitted for external reporting, but it is useful for managerial purposes.

Cost allocation is necessary when separate products are produced by a manufacturing process from a common input. The outputs are **joint products**. Joint costs must be allocated to the various products but normally are not allocated to by-products. **By-products** are of relatively small total value and are produced simultaneously from a common process with products of greater value and quantity (joint products).

Job-order costing and process costing are the fundamental methods for assigning costs to products. **Job-order costing** assigns costs to specific units, lots, or batches. It is appropriate when products have unique characteristics, such as custom-made furniture. **Process costing** assigns costs to large numbers of homogeneous products with costs accumulated by processes, departments, or cost centers. Process costing is covered in Study Unit 20.

Overhead consists of indirect costs that cannot be traced feasibly to final products. They consist primarily of indirect materials, indirect labor, and indirect operating costs such as utilities and depreciation. Overhead is accumulated in one or more cost pools and applied using a standard rate.

19.1 ABSORPTION COSTING AND VARIABLE COSTING -- THEORY

1. **Absorption Costing**

    a. Absorption (full) costing includes the fixed portion of manufacturing overhead in product cost.

        1) Product cost includes all manufacturing costs (fixed and variable).

        2) Sales minus absorption-basis cost of goods sold equals **gross profit** (gross margin).

        3) **Operating income** equals gross profit minus total selling and administrative expenses (fixed and variable).

        4) This method is required under GAAP for external reporting purposes and under the Internal Revenue Code for tax purposes. The justification is that, for external reporting, product cost should include any and all costs to bring the product to the point of sale.

2. **Variable Costing**

    a.   Variable costing includes only variable manufacturing costs in product cost. Variable costing is preferable for internal reporting. It better satisfies management's needs for operational planning and control information because it excludes arbitrary allocations of fixed costs.

        1)   Furthermore, variable-costing net income varies directly with sales and is not affected by changes in inventory levels.

    b.   **Contribution margin** equals sales minus variable cost of goods sold and the variable portion of selling and administrative expenses.

        1)   This amount (sales – total variable costs) is an important element of the variable costing income statement. It is the amount available for covering fixed costs (fixed manufacturing, fixed selling, and administrative).

EXAMPLE

Beginning inventory is 0, 100 units are produced, and 80 units are sold. The following costs were incurred:

Direct materials	$1,000
Direct labor	2,000
Variable overhead	1,500
Manufacturing costs for variable costing	$4,500 (a)
Fixed overhead	3,000 (b)
Manufacturing costs for absorption costing	$7,500

The following are the effects on the financial statements of using absorption or variable costing:

	Manufacturing costs	Divided by: Units produced	Equals: Per-unit cost	Times: Units in ending inventory	Equals: Cost of ending inventory
Absorption costing	$7,500	100	$75	20	$1,500 (e)
Variable costing	4,500	100	45	20	900 (f)

The per-unit selling price of the finished goods was $100, and $200 (c) of variable selling and administrative expenses and $600 (d) of fixed selling and administrative expenses were incurred.

The following are partial income statements prepared using the two methods:

		Absorption Costing (Required under GAAP)	Variable Costing (Internal reporting only)
	Sales	$ 8,000	$ 8,000
	Beginning inventory	$ 0	$ 0
Product Costs	Plus: Variable manufacturing costs	4,500 (a)	4,500 (a)
	Plus: Fixed manufacturing costs	3,000 (b)	
	Goods available for sale	$7,500	$4,500
	Minus: Ending inventory	(1,500) (e)	(900) (f)
	Cost of goods sold	$(6,000)	$(3,600)
	Minus: Variable S&A expenses		(200) (c)
	Gross profit (abs.) or contribution margin (var.)	$ 2,000	$ 4,200
Period Costs	Minus: Fixed manufacturing costs		(3,000) (b)
	Minus: Variable S&A expenses	(200) (c)	
	Minus: Fixed S&A expenses	(600) (d)	(600) (d)
	Operating income	$ 1,200	$ 600

Given no beginning inventory, the difference in operating income ($1,200 – $600 = $600) is the difference between the ending inventory amounts ($1,500 – $900 = $600).

Under the absorption method, 20% of the fixed overhead costs ($3,000 × 20% = $600) is recorded as an asset because 20% of the month's production (100 units available – 80 units sold = 20 units) is still in inventory.

3.   **Effects on Operating Income**

CPA candidates must know how to calculate the various income statement components under the absorption and variable costing methods. The AICPA has frequently tested this topic, focusing especially on the differences between the amounts, such as operating income, determined by each method.

a.   As production and sales change, the two methods have varying effects on operating income.

b.   When production and sales are equal for a period, the two methods report the same operating income.

1)   Total fixed costs for the period are expensed during the period under both methods.

c.   When production and sales are not equal for a period, the two methods report different operating incomes as illustrated below:

When production △△△△△△△ **exceeds sales,** △△△	When production △△△ **is less than sales,** △△△△△△△
ending inventory increases. ↑↑↑↑↑↑↑↑↑↑↑↑↑↑	**ending inventory decreases.** ↓↓↓↓↓↓
Under absorption costing, some fixed manufacturing costs are included in ending inventory, reducing COGS.	**Under absorption costing,** fixed manufacturing costs included in beginning inventory are expensed, increasing COGS.
Under variable costing, all fixed costs of the current period are expensed. No fixed costs are included in ending inventory.	**Under variable costing,** all fixed costs of the current period are expensed. No fixed costs are included in ending inventory.
Operating income is higher under <u>absorption</u> costing.	**Operating income is higher under <u>variable</u> costing.**

Figure 19-1

Stop and review! You have completed the outline for this subunit. Study multiple-choice questions 1 through 4 beginning on page 425.

19.2 ABSORPTION COSTING AND VARIABLE COSTING -- CALCULATIONS

CPA candidates can expect questions that require quantifying the difference between absorption and variable costing. This subunit consists entirely of such questions. Please review Subunit 19.1 before answering these questions.

Stop and review! You have completed the outline for this subunit. Study multiple-choice questions 5 through 8 beginning on page 426.

19.3 JOINT PRODUCT AND BY-PRODUCT COSTING

1. **Joint Product Costing**

   a. Joint products are separate products resulting from a common manufacturing process. They have high sales values compared with the sales values of other outputs.

      1) **Joint costs** are incurred up to the split-off point where the products become separately identifiable. They include direct materials, direct labor, and manufacturing overhead.

         a) Because joint costs are incurred before products can be identified separately, they must be allocated.

   b. Costs incurred after split-off are separable costs.

      1) Separable costs can be identified with a specific joint product.

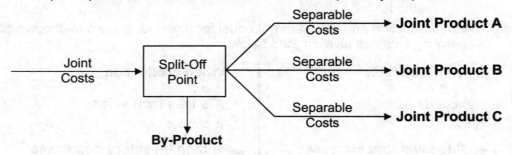

Figure 19-2

   c. The decision to **sell or process further** is made based on whether the incremental revenue from further processing exceeds the incremental cost. The joint cost of the product is irrelevant because it is a sunk cost.

2. **By-Product Costing**

   a. By-products are one or more products of relatively small total value that are produced simultaneously from a common manufacturing process with products of greater value.

      1) Whether the benefits of further processing and sale exceed the costs must be determined.

> Selling price
> − Additional processing costs
> − Selling costs
> = **Net realizable value**

      2) If the net realizable value (NRV) is zero or negative, the by-products should be sold at the split-off point or discarded as scrap if they cannot be sold.

   b. The value of a by-product may be recognized when (1) production is complete or (2) the by-product is sold.

      1) If recognized when production is completed, the amount equals the expected net proceeds from its sale (or its expected NRV if the by-product is subject to further processing to be salable). Thus, by-product inventory is recognized.

   c. Any proceeds (revenue) from the sale of a by-product are recognized either as (1) a reduction of the cost of goods sold of the joint products or (2) a revenue.

      1) Cost of goods sold is not recognized for by-products.

   d. Regardless of the timing of their recognition in the accounts, by-products usually do not receive an allocation of joint costs. The cost of this accounting treatment ordinarily exceeds the benefit.

Stop and review! You have completed the outline for this subunit. Study multiple-choice questions 9 through 13 beginning on page 427.

19.4 JOINT COST ALLOCATION METHODS

1. **Physical-Quantity Method**

   a. The physical-quantity method uses a physical measure such as volume or weight.

      1) Joint production costs are allocated to each product based on its relative proportion of the measure selected.

EXAMPLE

Processing 1,000 barrels of crude oil costs $100,000. The process results in the following outputs:

	Barrels	Selling price per barrel at a split-off point	Separable costs	Selling price per barrel after additional process
Asphalt	300	$ 60	$1,000	$ 70
Fuel oil	300	180	1,000	200
Diesel fuel	200	160	1,000	180
Kerosene	100	80	2,000	90
Gasoline	100	180	2,000	190

Under the physical-quantity method, the joint costs up to split-off are allocated as follows:

Asphalt	$100,000 × (300 barrels ÷ 1,000 barrels) =	$ 30,000
Fuel oil	$100,000 × (300 barrels ÷ 1,000 barrels) =	30,000
Diesel fuel	$100,000 × (200 barrels ÷ 1,000 barrels) =	20,000
Kerosene	$100,000 × (100 barrels ÷ 1,000 barrels) =	10,000
Gasoline	$100,000 × (100 barrels ÷ 1,000 barrels) =	10,000
Joint costs allocated		$100,000

---

   b. The physical-quantity method's simplicity is an advantage, but it does not match costs with the individual products' revenues.

2. **Market-Based Method**

   a. A market-based method assigns a proportionate amount of the total cost to each product on a quantitative basis. These allocations are **not** based on units sold because the joint costs were incurred for all units produced, not just those sold. The following are common methods of allocation:

      1) The **sales-value at split-off method** is based on the relative sales values of the separate products at split-off.

EXAMPLE

The five outputs can be sold for the following prices at split-off:

Asphalt	300 barrels × $ 60 per barrel	=	$ 18,000
Fuel oil	300 barrels × $180 per barrel	=	54,000
Diesel fuel	200 barrels × $160 per barrel	=	32,000
Kerosene	100 barrels × $ 80 per barrel	=	8,000
Gasoline	100 barrels × $180 per barrel	=	18,000
Total sales value at split-off			$130,000

The total sales value for the production run at split-off is $130,000. For each product, total joint cost to be allocated is multiplied by the proportion of the sales of each product:

Asphalt	$100,000 × ($18,000 ÷ $130,000) =	$ 13,846
Fuel oil	$100,000 × ($54,000 ÷ $130,000) =	41,538
Diesel fuel	$100,000 × ($32,000 ÷ $130,000) =	24,616
Kerosene	$100,000 × ($ 8,000 ÷ $130,000) =	6,154
Gasoline	$100,000 × ($18,000 ÷ $130,000) =	13,846
Joint costs allocated		$100,000

---

2)   The estimated **net realizable value (NRV) method** allocates joint costs based on the relative market values of the products after additional processing.

a)   NRV at split-off equals the sale price at the point of sale minus the cost to complete after split-off (separable costs).

b)   Under the estimated NRV method, all separable costs necessary to make the product salable are subtracted before the allocation.

EXAMPLE

The following are the final estimated sales prices:

Asphalt	300 barrels × $ 70 per barrel =	$21,000
Fuel oil	300 barrels × $200 per barrel =	60,000
Diesel fuel	200 barrels × $180 per barrel =	36,000
Kerosene	100 barrels × $ 90 per barrel =	9,000
Gasoline	100 barrels × $190 per barrel =	19,000

From these amounts, separable costs are subtracted (these costs are given):

Asphalt	$21,000 − $1,000 =	$ 20,000
Fuel oil	$60,000 − $1,000 =	59,000
Diesel fuel	$36,000 − $1,000 =	35,000
Kerosene	$ 9,000 − $2,000 =	7,000
Gasoline	$19,000 − $2,000 =	17,000
Total net realizable value		$138,000

The total NRV for the production run is $138,000. For each product, total joint cost to be allocated is multiplied by the proportion of the NRV of each product:

Asphalt	$100,000 × ($20,000 ÷ $138,000) =	$ 14,493
Fuel oil	$100,000 × ($59,000 ÷ $138,000) =	42,754
Diesel fuel	$100,000 × ($35,000 ÷ $138,000) =	25,362
Kerosene	$100,000 × ($ 7,000 ÷ $138,000) =	5,072
Gasoline	$100,000 × ($17,000 ÷ $138,000) =	12,319
Joint costs allocated		$100,000

Stop and review! You have completed the outline for this subunit. Study multiple-choice questions 14 through 18 beginning on page 429.

19.5 JOB-ORDER COSTING AND OVERHEAD APPLICATION

1.   **Uses of Job-Order Costing**

a.   Job-order costing is used when each end product is unique. Because the end products are few, tracking their costs is relatively simple.

b.   Manufacturers that use job-order costing include construction and shipbuilding. Service industries include software design and plumbing.

2.   **Accumulation of Direct Costs**

a.   The accumulation of costs in a job-order system can best be described in terms of the flow of manual documents in the process. (These functions currently are performed most often with computers rather than physical documents.)

b.   The accounting process begins when a sales order is received from a customer. Because products are custom made, no finished goods inventory is held, but production cannot begin until an order is placed. After the sales order is approved, a production order is issued.

c.   The physical inputs required for production are obtained from suppliers.

1)   For example, $100,000 of direct materials are purchased on account. The journal entry is

Materials control	$100,000	
Accounts payable		$100,000

d. A subsidiary account is created within the work-in-process ledger to track the costs for each job. The accumulation of direct costs (direct materials and direct labor) is simple.

e. Materials requisition forms request direct materials to be sent from the warehouse to the production line.

  1) For example, the production line submits a materials requisition to the warehouse for $60,000 of direct materials for Job 1015. The journal entry is

Work-in-process -- Job 1015	$60,000	
Materials control		$60,000

f. Time tickets track the direct labor by workers on various jobs.

  1) For example, workers accrue $45,000 in salaries on Job 1015. The journal entry is

Work-in-process -- Job 1015	$45,000	
Wages payable		$45,000

g. Direct costs are recorded in the general ledger at their actual amounts. Job-order costing facilitates tracing the direct costs incurred for a given job.

3. **Accumulation of Indirect Costs**

a. Accounting for overhead costs is more difficult because they are indirect costs. It is not feasible to trace them to final products. Thus, they must be accumulated in one or more indirect cost pools and allocated based on an appropriate cost driver.

  1) When one indirect cost pool is used, it is commonly called manufacturing overhead control. (Some manufacturers require a higher degree of accuracy in indirect cost assignment and use two overhead control accounts, one for variable overhead and one for fixed. For simplicity, the following examples use one pool.)

b. Manufacturing overhead consists of three main categories of costs:

  1) Indirect materials are tangible inputs to the manufacturing process that cannot feasibly be traced to the product, e.g., lubricating oil for machines.

    a) For example, the production department requisitions $4,500 of lubricating oil for a machine that was due maintenance. The journal entry is

Manufacturing overhead control	$4,500	
Materials control		$4,500

  2) Indirect labor is the labor used in the manufacturing process that cannot feasibly be traced to the product, e.g., the wages of assembly line supervisors and janitorial staff.

    a) For example, $2,000 in wages are accrued for the janitorial staff. The journal entry is

Manufacturing overhead control	$2,000	
Wages payable		$2,000

  3) Other overhead operating costs include such items as utility expense, real estate taxes, insurance, and depreciation of equipment. The actual total of these costs is not known until the end of the period.

    a) For example, $8,500 of property taxes are accrued, $1,600 of insurance costs are prepaid, and $12,000 of depreciation expense is recognized. The journal entries are

Manufacturing overhead control	$8,500	
Property taxes payable		$8,500
Manufacturing overhead control	$1,600	
Prepaid insurance		$1,600
Manufacturing overhead control	$12,000	
Accumulated depreciation -- equipment		$12,000

    c.   When an overhead control account is used, actual overhead costs do not affect work-in-process when they are incurred. The total actual overhead incurred is the debit balance in the control account.

4.   **Allocation of Indirect Costs**

    a.   Indirect costs are allocated to production using an overhead allocation rate. The first step is to estimate the total indirect costs for the next period.

        1)   The overhead application rate is best derived using estimated annual totals rather than on a monthly basis. Many overhead costs are fixed and must be incurred every month regardless of the level of production. Calculating a new rate every month may cause large variations in product costs even though the underlying cost structure does not change.

    b.   The following is the equation for the rate:

$$Overhead\ application\ rate = \frac{Estimated\ annual\ total\ overhead\ costs}{Estimated\ total\ units\ of\ allocation\ base}$$

(If more than one indirect cost pool is used, a different rate is used for each pool.)

        1)   The numerator is estimated from annual budget data.

        2)   The denominator (the allocation base) must be a cost driver that has a **direct cause-and-effect relationship** with the incurrence of overhead costs. When overhead costs change, the units of the allocation base also should change. Common allocation bases for one indirect cost pool are direct labor hours and machine hours.

            a)   For example, an estimated $350,000 in overhead costs will be incurred during the year. The best way to allocate these costs is by machine hours (budgeted at 10,000 hours). The allocation rate is determined as follows:

Overhead application rate ($350,000 ÷ 10,000) = $35 per machine hour

    c.   At the end of each month, the number of units of the allocation base expended is multiplied by the application rate to determine the amount of overhead to be applied to that month's production.

        1)   For example, Job 1015 has used 900 machine hours this month. The calculation is

Overhead applied = Units of overhead driver × Application rate
= 900 machine hours for Job 1015 × $35 per hour
= $31,500

        2)   This amount ordinarily is not credited to the control account. Instead, it is credited to manufacturing overhead applied (a contra account). The two accounts track actual and applied costs separately.

            a)   For example, overhead is applied to Job 1015. The journal entry is

Work-in-process -- Job 1015	$31,500	
Manufacturing overhead applied		$31,500

        3)   Separate tracking retains actual overhead amounts in the debit balance of the control account. It also permits comparison of actual and applied costs. The closer they are, the better the estimate.

5. **Completion of Job**

   a. When a job order is completed, all costs are transferred to finished goods.

      1) For example, when work on Job 1015 is completed, the product is prepared for sale. Total costs incurred for Job 1015 are $136,500. The journal entry is

Finished goods	$136,500	
Work-in-process -- Job 1015		$136,500

   b. When the output is sold, the sale is recorded and the appropriate portion of the cost is transferred to cost of goods sold.

      1) For example, the product created in Job 1015 is sold for $200,000 on account. The journal entry is

Accounts receivable	$200,000	
Sales		$200,000
Cost of goods sold	$136,500	
Finished goods		$136,500

6. **Cost Flows**

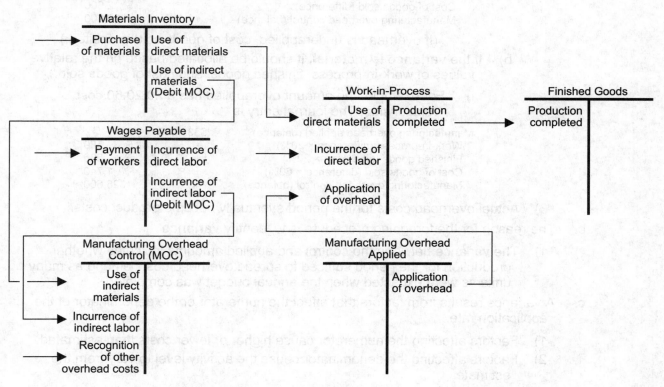

Figure 19-3

7.   **Over- and Underapplied Overhead**

    a.   At the end of the period, if the balance in the overhead control account (records actual amount incurred) is less than that in the overhead applied account (i.e., actual < applied), **overhead was overapplied**. If the balance in the overhead applied account is lower (i.e., actual > applied), **overhead was underapplied**.

        1)   For example, overhead applied was $331,500 during the period, but the amount accrued was only $328,600.

        2)   Given that more overhead was applied than was actually incurred, overhead was overapplied by $2,900.

            a)   If the **variance is immaterial**, it may be closed directly to cost of goods sold.

                i)   Overhead applied is debited and manufacturing overhead control is credited. The balancing credit is to cost of goods sold. The journal entry is

Manufacturing overhead applied (balance)	$331,500	
Cost of goods sold (difference)		$ 2,900
Manufacturing overhead control (balance)		328,600

                (If overhead is underapplied, cost of goods sold is debited.)

            b)   If the **variance is material**, it should be allocated based on the relative values of work-in-process, finished goods, and cost of goods sold.

                i)   For example, the amount overapplied has a 20:20:60 cost relationship. The journal entry is

Manufacturing overhead applied (balance)	$331,500	
Work-in-process (difference × 20%)		$ 580
Finished goods (difference × 20%)		580
Cost of goods sold (difference × 60%)		1,740
Manufacturing overhead control (balance)		328,600

        3)   Actual overhead costs for the period eventually become product costs.

    b.   The reason for the foregoing procedure is to identify **variance**.

        1)   The variance between the control and applied amounts indicates whether production for the period sufficed to spread overhead costs among as many units as were expected when the annual budget was completed.

    c.   A variance results from factors that affect the numerator or the denominator of the application rate.

        1)   Factors affecting the numerator cause higher or lower costs than estimated.

        2)   Factors affecting the denominator cause the activity level to vary from the estimate.

Stop and review! You have completed the outline for this subunit. Study multiple-choice questions 19 through 23 beginning on page 431.

QUESTIONS

19.1 Absorption Costing and Variable Costing -- Theory

1. The change in period-to-period operating income when using variable costing can be explained by the change in the

A. Unit sales level multiplied by the unit sales price.

B. Finished goods inventory level multiplied by the unit sales price.

C. Unit sales level multiplied by a constant unit contribution margin.

D. Finished goods inventory level multiplied by a constant unit contribution margin.

Answer (C) is correct.
  REQUIRED: The factor explaining the change in period-to-period operating income when using variable costing.
  DISCUSSION: In a variable costing system, only the variable costs are recorded as product costs. All fixed costs are expensed in the period incurred. Because changes in the relationship between production levels and sales levels do not cause changes in the amount of fixed manufacturing cost expensed, profits more directly follow the trends in sales, especially when the UCM (selling price per unit – variable costs per unit) is constant. Unit sales times the UCM equals the total CM, and operating income (a pretax amount) equals the CM minus fixed costs of operations. If the UCM is constant and fixed costs are stable, the change in operating income will approximate the change in the CM (unit sales × UCM).

2. The management of a company computes net income using both absorption and variable costing. This year, the net income under the variable-costing approach was greater than the net income under the absorption-costing approach. This difference is most likely the result of

A. A decrease in the variable marketing expenses.

B. An increase in the finished goods inventory.

C. Sales volume exceeding production volume.

D. Inflationary effects on overhead costs.

Answer (C) is correct.
  REQUIRED: The reason net income is greater under variable costing than absorption costing.
  DISCUSSION: Absorption costing (full costing) is the accounting method that considers all manufacturing costs as product costs. These costs include variable and fixed manufacturing costs, whether direct or indirect. However, variable costing treats fixed manufacturing overhead as a period cost instead of charging it to the product (inventory). Thus, when sales exceed production, the absorption costing method recognizes fixed manufacturing overhead inventoried in a prior period. Direct costing does not. Accordingly, net income under variable costing is greater than net income under absorption costing.
  Answer (A) is incorrect. A change in a variable period cost will affect absorption and variable costing in the same way. Answer (B) is incorrect. If the beginning inventory is less than the ending finished goods inventory, absorption costing assigns more fixed overhead costs to the balance sheet and less to the cost of goods sold on the income statement than does variable costing. Answer (D) is incorrect. Inflationary effects usually affect both absorption and variable costing in the same way.

3. When a firm prepares financial reports by using absorption costing,

A. Profits will always increase with increases in sales.

B. Profits will always decrease with decreases in sales.

C. Profits may decrease with increased sales even if there is no change in selling prices and costs.

D. Decreased output and constant sales result in increased profits.

Answer (C) is correct.
  REQUIRED: The profit relationship between output and sales under absorption costing.
  DISCUSSION: In an absorption costing system, fixed overhead costs are included in inventory. When sales exceed production, more overhead is expensed under absorption costing because fixed overhead is carried over from the prior inventory. If sales exceed production, more than one period's fixed overhead is recognized as expense. Accordingly, if the increase in fixed overhead expensed is greater than the contribution margin of the increased units sold, less profit may result from an increased level of sales.
  Answer (A) is incorrect. Profit is a function of both sales and production, so profit may not increase with increases in sales. Answer (B) is incorrect. Profit is a function of both sales and production, so profit may not decrease with decreases in sales. Answer (D) is incorrect. Decreased output will increase the unit cost of items sold. Fixed overhead per unit will increase.

4. In the application of variable costing as a cost-allocation process in manufacturing,

A. Variable direct costs are treated as period costs.

B. Nonvariable indirect costs are treated as product costs.

C. Variable indirect costs are treated as product costs.

D. Nonvariable direct costs are treated as product costs.

Answer (C) is correct.

REQUIRED: The true statement about variable costing.

DISCUSSION: Variable costing considers only variable manufacturing costs to be product costs. Variable indirect costs included in variable overhead are therefore treated as inventoriable. Fixed costs are considered period costs and are expensed as incurred.

Answer (A) is incorrect. Variable manufacturing costs, whether direct (direct materials and direct labor) or indirect (variable overhead), are accounted for as product costs, not period costs. Answer (B) is incorrect. Nonvariable indirect costs are treated as period costs in variable costing. Answer (D) is incorrect. In variable costing, nonvariable direct costs are treated as period costs, not product costs.

19.2 Absorption Costing and Variable Costing -- Calculations

Questions 5 and 6 are based on the following information. At the end of its fiscal year, C.G. Manufacturing recorded the data below:

Prime cost	$800,000
Variable manufacturing overhead	100,000
Fixed manufacturing overhead	160,000
Variable selling and other expenses	80,000
Fixed selling and other expenses	40,000

5. If C.G. uses variable costing, the inventoriable costs for the fiscal year are

A. $800,000

B. $900,000

C. $980,000

D. $1,060,000

Answer (B) is correct.

REQUIRED: The inventoriable costs using variable costing.

DISCUSSION: The only costs capitalized are the variable costs of manufacturing. Prime costs (direct materials and direct labor) are variable.

Prime costs (direct materials and direct labor)	$800,000
Variable manufacturing overhead	100,000
Total inventoriable costs	$900,000

Answer (A) is incorrect. Prime costs equal $800,000. Answer (C) is incorrect. The amount of $980,000 includes the variable selling and other expenses. Answer (D) is incorrect. Inventoriable costs under absorption costing equal $1,060,000.

6. Using absorption (full) costing, C.G.'s inventoriable costs are

A. $800,000

B. $900,000

C. $1,060,000

D. $1,080,000

Answer (C) is correct.

REQUIRED: The inventoriable costs using absorption costing.

DISCUSSION: Absorption costing is required by GAAP. It charges all costs of production to inventories. The prime costs ($800,000), variable manufacturing overhead ($100,000), and the fixed manufacturing overhead ($160,000) are included. They total $1,060,000.

Answer (A) is incorrect. Prime costs equal $800,000. Answer (B) is incorrect. Inventoriable costs under variable costing equal $900,000. Answer (D) is incorrect. The amount of $1,080,000 includes the fixed and variable selling and other expenses.

Questions 7 and 8 are based on the following
information. Presented are Valenz Company's
records for the current fiscal year ended
November 30:

Direct materials used	$300,000
Direct labor	100,000
Variable manufacturing overhead	50,000
Fixed manufacturing overhead	80,000
Selling and admin. costs -- variable	40,000
Selling and admin. costs -- fixed	20,000

7. If Valenz Company uses variable costing, the
inventoriable costs for the fiscal year are

A. $400,000

B. $450,000

C. $490,000

D. $530,000

Answer (B) is correct.
   REQUIRED: The inventoriable costs using the variable
costing.
   DISCUSSION: Under variable costing, the only costs that
are capitalized are the variable costs of manufacturing. These
include

Direct materials used	$300,000
Direct labor	100,000
Variable overhead	50,000
Total inventoriable costs	$450,000

   Answer (A) is incorrect. The amount of $400,000 does not
include $50,000 of variable overhead. Answer (C) is incorrect.
The $40,000 of variable selling and administrative costs
should not be included in the inventoriable costs. Answer (D) is
incorrect. The inventoriable cost under absorption (full) costing is
$530,000.

8. Using absorption (full) costing, inventoriable costs
for Valenz are

A. $400,000

B. $450,000

C. $530,000

D. $590,000

Answer (C) is correct.
   REQUIRED: The inventoriable costs using the absorption
costing.
   DISCUSSION: The absorption method is required for
financial statements prepared according to GAAP. It charges all
costs of production to inventories. The variable cost of materials
($300,000), direct labor ($100,000), variable overhead ($50,000),
and fixed overhead ($80,000) are included. They total $530,000.
   Answer (A) is incorrect. Not including $80,000 of fixed
overhead and $50,000 of variable overhead results in $400,000.
Answer (B) is incorrect. The inventoriable cost under variable
costing is $450,000. Answer (D) is incorrect. Selling and
administrative costs are not inventoriable using absorption (full)
costing.

19.3 Joint Product and By-Product Costing

9. For the purposes of cost accumulation, which of
the following are identifiable as different individual
products before the split-off point?

	By-Products	Joint Products
A.	Yes	Yes
B.	Yes	No
C.	No	No
D.	No	Yes

Answer (C) is correct.
   REQUIRED: The products identifiable before the split-off
point.
   DISCUSSION: In a joint production process, at the split-
off point, neither by-products nor joint products are separately
identifiable as individual products. Joint costs up to the split-off
point are usually related to both joint products and by-products.
After split-off, additional (separable) costs can be traced and
charged to the individual products. By-products usually do not
receive an allocation of joint costs.
   Answer (A) is incorrect. Neither by-products nor joint
products are separately identifiable until split-off. Answer (B) is
incorrect. By-products are also not separately identifiable until
split-off. Answer (D) is incorrect. Joint products are also not
separately identifiable until split-off.

10. Kode Co. manufactures a major product that gives rise to a by-product called May. May's only separable cost is a $1 selling cost when a unit is sold for $4. Kode accounts for May's sales by deducting the $3 net amount from the cost of goods sold of the major product. There are no inventories. If Kode were to change its method of accounting for May from a by-product to a joint product, what would be the effect on Kode's overall gross margin?

  A. No effect.

  B. Gross margin increases by $1 for each unit of May sold.

  C. Gross margin increases by $3 for each unit of May sold.

  D. Gross margin increases by $4 for each unit of May sold.

11. A lumber company produces two-by-fours and four-by-eights as joint products and sawdust as a by-product. The packaged sawdust can be sold for $2 per pound. Packaging costs for the sawdust are $.10 per pound and sales commissions are 10% of sales price. The by-product net revenue serves to reduce joint processing costs for joint products. Joint products are assigned joint costs based on board feet. Cost and production data are:

Joint processing costs	$ 50,000
Two-by-fours produced (board feet)	200,000
Four-by-eights produced (board feet)	100,000
Sawdust produced (pounds)	1,000

What is the cost assigned to two-by-fours?

  A. $32,000

  B. $32,133

  C. $32,200

  D. $33,333

12. Copeland, Inc., produces X-547 in a joint manufacturing process. The company is studying whether to sell X-547 at the split-off point or upgrade the product to become Xylene. The following information has been gathered:

I. Selling price per pound of X-547
II. Variable manufacturing costs of upgrade process
III. Avoidable fixed costs of upgrade process
IV. Selling price per pound of Xylene
V. Joint manufacturing costs to produce X-547

Which items should be reviewed when making the upgrade decision?

  A. I, II, and IV.

  B. I, II, III, and IV.

  C. All items.

  D. I, II, IV, and V.

Answer (B) is correct.
REQUIRED: The effect on gross margin (gross profit) of treating a product as a joint product rather than a by-product.
DISCUSSION: Gross margin is the difference between sales and the cost of goods sold. Subtracting the $3 net amount from cost of goods sold does not have the same effect on overall gross margin as recording the $4 sales revenue and subtracting the $1 cost. In the latter case, the $1 unit selling cost is not subtracted in arriving at the gross margin. Thus, gross margin increases by $1 for each unit of May sold.
Answer (A) is incorrect. Net income, not gross margin, is unaffected. Answer (C) is incorrect. The amount of $3 is the per-unit increase in net income using either by-product or joint-product costing. Answer (D) is incorrect. The amount of $4 is the per-unit increase in sales when switching to joint-product from by-product costing.

Answer (C) is correct.
REQUIRED: The cost assigned to a joint product when joint products and a by-product are produced.
DISCUSSION: The net revenue from sale of the by-product is $1,700 [(1,000 lb. × $2 price) – (1,000 lb. × $.10) – (1,000 lb. × $2 × .1)]. Joint processing costs to be allocated to joint products are therefore $48,300 ($50,000 – $1,700 net by-product revenue). Of this amount, $32,200 should be assigned to the two-by-fours [$48,300 × (200,000 board feet of two-by-fours ÷ 300,000 total board feet)].
Answer (A) is incorrect. The net revenue from the sale of the by-product is $1,700, not $2,000. The costs related to the packaging and selling of the by-product must be deducted. Answer (B) is incorrect. The $.10-per-pound packaging cost for the sawdust must be subtracted from the by-product revenue. Answer (D) is incorrect. The net revenue of $1,700 [1,000 lb. × ($2 sale price – $.10 packaging – $.20 sales cost)] from the by-product should be subtracted from the joint processing costs before the joint processing costs are allocated.

Answer (B) is correct.
REQUIRED: The items reviewed for a sell-or-process further decision.
DISCUSSION: Common, or joint, costs cannot be identified with a particular joint product. By definition, joint products have common costs until the split-off point. Costs incurred after the split-off point are separable costs. The decision to continue processing beyond split-off is made separately for each product. The costs relevant to the decision are the separable costs because they can be avoided by selling at the split-off point. They should be compared with the incremental revenues from processing further. Thus, items I (revenue from selling at split-off point), II (variable costs of upgrade), III (avoidable fixed costs of upgrade), and IV (revenue from selling after further processing) are considered in making the upgrade decision.
Answer (A) is incorrect. The avoidable fixed costs of the upgrade process also should be considered. Answer (C) is incorrect. The joint manufacturing costs are irrelevant. Answer (D) is incorrect. The avoidable fixed costs of the upgrade process should be reviewed, and the joint manufacturing costs should be ignored.

13. In accounting for by-products, the value of the by-product may be recognized at the time of

	Production	Sale
A.	Yes	Yes
B.	Yes	No
C.	No	No
D.	No	Yes

Answer (A) is correct.
REQUIRED: The timing of recognition of by-products.
DISCUSSION: Practice with regard to recognizing by-products in the accounts is not uniform. The most cost-effective method for the initial recognition of by-products is to account for their value at the time of sale as a reduction in the joint cost or as a revenue. The alternative is to recognize the net realizable value at the time of production, a method that results in the recording of by-product inventory.
Answer (B) is incorrect. By-products also may be recognized initially at the time of sale. Answer (C) is incorrect. By-products may be initially recognized at the time of sale or at the time of production. Answer (D) is incorrect. By-products may also be recorded in the accounts when produced.

19.4 Joint Cost Allocation Methods

Questions 14 and 15 are based on the following information.

Petro-Chem, Inc., is a small company that acquires high-grade crude oil from low-volume production wells owned by individuals and small partnerships. The crude oil is processed in a single refinery into Two Oil, Six Oil, and impure distillates. Petro-Chem does not have the technology or capacity to process these products further and sells most of its output each month to major refineries. There were no beginning inventories of finished goods or work-in-process on November 1. The production costs and output of Petro-Chem for November are shown in the next column.

Crude oil acquired and placed in production	$5,000,000
Direct labor and related costs	2,000,000
Manufacturing overhead	3,000,000

Production and sales

- Two Oil, 300,000 barrels produced; 80,000 barrels sold at $20 each
- Six Oil, 240,000 barrels produced; 120,000 barrels sold at $30 each
- Distillates, 120,000 barrels produced and sold at $15 each

14. The portion of the joint production costs assigned to Two Oil based upon the relative sales value of output is

A. $4,800,000
B. $4,000,000
C. $2,286,000
D. $2,500,000

Answer (B) is correct.
REQUIRED: The joint production costs assigned to a product based on relative sales value.
DISCUSSION: The total production costs incurred are $10,000,000, consisting of crude oil of $5,000,000, direct labor of $2,000,000, and overhead of $3,000,000. The total value of the output is as follows:

Two Oil (300,000 × $20)	$ 6,000,000
Six Oil (240,000 × $30)	7,200,000
Distillates (120,000 × $15)	1,800,000
Total sales value	$15,000,000

Because Two Oil composes 40% of the total sales value ($6,000,000 ÷ $15,000,000), it will be assigned 40% of the $10,000,000 of joint costs, or $4,000,000.
Answer (A) is incorrect. The amount of $4,800,000 is the amount that would be assigned to Six Oil. Answer (C) is incorrect. The amount of $2,286,000 is based on the relative sales value of units sold. Answer (D) is incorrect. The amount of $2,500,000 is based on the physical quantity of barrels sold.

15. The portion of the joint production costs assigned to Six Oil based upon physical output is

A. $3,636,000
B. $3,750,000
C. $1,818,000
D. $7,500,000

Answer (A) is correct.
REQUIRED: The joint production costs assigned to a product based on physical output.
DISCUSSION: The total production costs incurred are $10,000,000, consisting of crude oil of $5,000,000, direct labor of $2,000,000, and overhead of $3,000,000. The total physical output was 660,000 barrels, consisting of 300,000 barrels of Two Oil, 240,000 barrels of Six Oil, and 120,000 barrels of distillates. Thus, the allocation (rounded) is $3,636,000 {$10,000,000 × [240,000 ÷ (300,000 + 240,000 + 120,000)]}.
Answer (B) is incorrect. The amount of $3,750,000 is based on the physical quantity of units sold, not units produced. Answer (C) is incorrect. The amount of $1,818,000 is the amount that would be assigned to distillates. Answer (D) is incorrect. Six Oil does not compose 75% of the total output in barrels.

Questions 16 through 18 are based on the following information.

Atlas Foods produces the following three supplemental food products simultaneously through a refining process costing $93,000.

The joint products, Alfa and Betters, have a final selling price of $4 per pound and $10 per pound, respectively, after additional processing costs of $2 per pound of each product are incurred after the split-off point. Morefeed, a by-product, is sold at the split-off point for $3 per pound.

Alfa	10,000 pounds of Alfa, a popular but relatively rare grain supplement having a caloric value of 4,400 calories per pound
Betters	5,000 pounds of Betters, a flavoring material high in carbohydrates with a caloric value of 11,200 calories per pound
Morefeed	1,000 pounds of Morefeed, used as a cattle feed supplement with a caloric value of 1,000 calories per pound

16. Assuming Atlas Foods inventories Morefeed, the by-product, the joint cost to be allocated to Alfa using the net realizable value method is

A. $3,000

B. $30,000

C. $31,000

D. $60,000

Answer (B) is correct.
    REQUIRED: The joint cost allocated to a joint product based on net realizable values if the by-product is inventoried.
    DISCUSSION: The NRV at split-off for each of the joint products are as follows:

	Selling Price Per Pound		Additional Processing Cost Per Pound		NRV Per Unit		Units of Output		Total NRV
Alfa	$ 4	–	$2	=	$2	×	10,000 lbs.	=	$20,000
Betters	$10	–	$2	=	$8	×	50,000 lbs.	=	$40,000

The 1,000 pounds of Morefeed has a split-off value of $3 per pound, or $3,000. Assuming that Morefeed (a by-product) is inventoried (recognized in the accounts when produced) and treated as a reduction of joint costs, the allocable joint cost is $90,000 ($93,000 – $3,000). The total net realizable value of the main products is $60,000 ($20,000 Alfa + $40,000 Betters). The allocation to Alfa is $30,000 [$90,000 × ($20,000 ÷ $60,000)].
    Answer (A) is incorrect. The value of the by-product is $3,000. Answer (C) is incorrect. Failing to adjust the joint processing cost for the value of the by-product results in $31,000. Answer (D) is incorrect. The amount allocated to Betters is $60,000.

17. Assuming Atlas Foods inventories Morefeed, the by-product, and that it incurs no additional processing costs for Alfa and Betters, the joint cost to be allocated to Alfa using the gross sales value method is

A. $36,000

B. $40,000

C. $41,333

D. $50,000

Answer (B) is correct.
    REQUIRED: The joint cost allocated to a joint product using the gross sales value method if the by-product is inventoried.
    DISCUSSION: The gross sales value of Alfa is $40,000 (10,000 pounds × $4), Betters has a total gross sales value of $50,000 (5,000 pounds × $10), and Morefeed has a split-off value of $3,000. If the value of Morefeed is inventoried and treated as a reduction in joint cost, the allocable joint cost is $90,000 ($93,000 – $3,000). The total gross sales value of the two main products is $90,000 ($40,000 + $50,000). Of this total, $40,000 should be allocated to Alfa [$90,000 × ($40,000 ÷ $90,000)].
    Answer (A) is incorrect. The amount of $36,000 is based on 40%, not 4/9. Answer (C) is incorrect. Failing to adjust the joint cost by the value of the by-product results in $41,333. Answer (D) is incorrect. The joint cost allocated to Betters is $50,000.

18. Assuming Atlas Foods does not inventory Morefeed, the by-product, the joint cost to be allocated to Betters using the net realizable value method is

A. $30,000

B. $31,000

C. $52,080

D. $62,000

Answer (D) is correct.
    REQUIRED: The joint cost allocated to a joint product based on net realizable values if the by-product is not inventoried.
    DISCUSSION: The NRV of Alfa is $20,000, and the NRV of Betters is $40,000. If the joint cost is not adjusted for the value of the by-product, the amount allocated to Betters is $62,000 {$93,000 × [$40,000 ÷ ($20,000 + $40,000)]}.
    Answer (A) is incorrect. The amount allocated to Alfa when the by-product is inventoried is $30,000. Answer (B) is incorrect. The amount allocated to Alfa when the by-product is not inventoried is $31,000. Answer (C) is incorrect. Assuming that a weighting method using caloric value is used results in $52,080.

19.5 Job-Order Costing and Overhead Application

19. Felicity Corporation manufactures a specialty line of dresses using a job-order cost system. During January, the following costs were incurred in completing job J-1:

Direct materials	$27,400
Direct labor	9,600
Administrative costs	2,800
Selling costs	11,200

Overhead was applied at the rate of $50 per direct labor hour, and job J-1 required 400 direct labor hours. If job J-1 resulted in 4,000 good dresses, the cost of goods sold per unit is

A. $9.25

B. $14.25

C. $14.95

D. $17.75

Answer (B) is correct.
REQUIRED: The cost of goods sold per unit.
DISCUSSION: Cost of goods sold is based on the manufacturing costs incurred in production. It does not include selling or general and administrative expenses. Manufacturing costs consist of direct materials ($27,400), direct labor ($9,600), and overhead (400 direct labor hours × $50 per hour = $20,000). The total of these cost elements is $57,000. Dividing the $57,000 of total manufacturing costs by the 4,000 units produced results in a per-unit cost of $14.25.
Answer (A) is incorrect. Failing to include overhead results in $9.25. Answer (C) is incorrect. Including administrative costs results in $14.95. Answer (D) is incorrect. The amount of $17.75 includes selling and administrative costs.

20. Lucy Sportswear manufactures a specialty line of T-shirts using a job-order cost system. During March, the following costs were incurred in completing Job ICU2: direct materials, $13,700; direct labor, $4,800; administrative, $1,400; and selling, $5,600. Overhead was applied at the rate of $25 per machine hour, and Job ICU2 required 800 machine hours. If Job ICU2 resulted in 7,000 good shirts, the cost of goods sold per unit would be

A. $6.50

B. $6.30

C. $5.70

D. $5.50

Answer (D) is correct.
REQUIRED: The cost of goods sold per unit.
DISCUSSION: Cost of goods sold is based on the manufacturing costs incurred in production but does not include selling or general and administrative expenses. Manufacturing costs equal $38,500 [$13,700 DM + $4,800 DL + (800 hours × $25) OH]. Thus, per-unit cost is $5.50 ($38,500 ÷ 7,000 units).
Answer (A) is incorrect. The amount of $6.50 includes selling and administrative expenses. Answer (B) is incorrect. Including selling costs results in cost of goods sold per unit of $6.30. Answer (C) is incorrect. Including administrative expenses results in cost of goods sold per unit of $5.70.

21. Worley Company has underapplied overhead of $45,000 for the year. Before disposition of the underapplied overhead, selected year-end balances from Worley's accounting records were

Sales	$1,200,000
Cost of goods sold	720,000
Direct materials inventory	36,000
Work-in-process inventory	54,000
Finished goods inventory	90,000

Under Worley's cost accounting system, over- or underapplied overhead is assigned to appropriate inventories and COGS based on year-end balances. In its year-end income statement, Worley should report COGS of

A. $682,500

B. $684,000

C. $757,500

D. $765,000

Answer (C) is correct.
REQUIRED: The amount of cost of goods sold after allocation of underapplied overhead.
DISCUSSION: The assignment of underapplied overhead increases COGS. The underapplied overhead of $45,000 for the year should be assigned on a pro rata basis to work-in-process ($54,000), finished goods ($90,000), and COGS ($720,000). The sum of these three items is $864,000. Thus, $37,500 should be assigned to COGS [($720,000 ÷ $864,000) × $45,000]. COGS after assignment is $757,500 ($37,500 + $720,000). The remaining $7,500 should be assigned proportionately to work-in-process and finished goods.
Answer (A) is incorrect. The appropriate COGS balance if overhead was overapplied by $45,000 and $37,500 was assigned to COGS is $682,500. Answer (B) is incorrect. The COGS balance if overhead was overapplied by $45,000 and direct materials inventory was incorrectly included in the denominator of the ratio used to assign overhead is $684,000. Answer (D) is incorrect. Debiting the full amount of underapplied overhead ($45,000) to COGS results in $765,000.

Questions 22 and 23 are based on the following information. Hamilton Company uses job-order costing. Manufacturing overhead is applied to production at a predetermined rate of 150% of direct labor cost. Any over- or underapplied overhead is closed to the cost of goods sold account at the end of each month. Additional information is available as follows:

- Job 101 was the only job in process at January 31, with accumulated costs as follows:

Direct materials	$4,000
Direct labor	2,000
Applied manufacturing overhead	3,000
Total manufacturing costs	$9,000

- Jobs 102, 103, and 104 were started during February.
- Direct materials requisitions for February totaled $26,000.
- Direct labor cost of $20,000 was incurred for February.
- Actual manufacturing overhead was $32,000 for February.
- The only job still in process on February 28 was Job 104, with costs of $2,800 for direct materials and $1,800 for direct labor.

---

22. The cost of goods manufactured for February was

A. $77,700

B. $78,000

C. $79,700

D. $85,000

Answer (A) is correct.
REQUIRED: The cost of goods manufactured (COGM).
DISCUSSION: COGM is the sum of the costs in BWIP and all the costs incurred during the period minus the costs in EWIP. The calculation of COGM uses applied overhead ($30,000 = $20,000 DL cost × 150%). The $7,300 in EWIP includes $2,800 for direct materials, $1,800 for direct labor, and $2,700 for applied overhead (at 150% of DL cost).

BWIP	$ 9,000
Direct labor	20,000
Applied overhead	30,000
Direct materials	26,000
EWIP	(7,300)
COGM	$77,700

Answer (B) is incorrect. The amount of $78,000 does not reflect BWIP and EWIP and is based on actual manufacturing overhead. Answer (C) is incorrect. Actual manufacturing overhead of $32,000 was used. Answer (D) is incorrect. EWIP was not subtracted.

---

23. Over- or underapplied manufacturing overhead should be closed to the cost of goods sold account at February 28 in the amount of

A. $700 overapplied.

B. $1,000 overapplied.

C. $1,700 underapplied.

D. $2,000 underapplied.

Answer (D) is correct.
REQUIRED: The amount of over- or underapplied manufacturing overhead closed to COGS.
DISCUSSION: The amount of over- or underapplied overhead is the difference between the actual overhead incurred and the overhead applied. The amount of overhead applied was $30,000 ($20,000 DL cost ×150%). The amount of overhead incurred was $32,000. Consequently, underapplied overhead of $2,000 ($32,000 actual − $30,000 applied) should be closed to COGS.

Answer (A) is incorrect. The amount of $700 overapplied equals applied overhead in EWIP minus the difference between actual February overhead and overhead applied in February. Answer (B) is incorrect. The $3,000 of applied manufacturing overhead in BWIP should not be used in determining the current month's over- or underapplied overhead. Answer (C) is incorrect. The amounts of applied overhead in BWIP and EWIP should not be used in calculating the current month's over- or underapplied overhead.

Online is better! To best prepare for the CPA exam, access **thousands** of exam-emulating MCQs and TBSs through Gleim CPA Review online courses with SmartAdapt technology.
Learn more at www.gleimcpa.com or contact our team at 800.874.5346 to upgrade.

STUDY UNIT TWENTY
COSTING SYSTEMS AND VARIANCE ANALYSIS

(16 pages of outline)

Process costing is used when relatively homogeneous products are mass produced on a continuous basis (Subunits 20.1 and 20.2). Activity-based costing is used when indirect costs are high (Subunit 20.3).

A standard cost is an estimate of what a cost should be under normal operating conditions based on accounting and engineering studies. Standard costs are used to assign costs to products and control actual costs. Comparing actual and standard costs permits evaluation of managerial performance using variance analysis (Subunits 20.4 and 20.5). This analysis also can be applied to revenue amounts (Subunit 20.6).

20.1 PROCESS COSTING -- PRINCIPLES

1. **Uses of Process Costing**

    a. Process cost accounting assigns costs to inventoriable goods or services. It applies to relatively homogeneous products that are mass produced on a continuous basis (e.g., petroleum products, thread, and computer monitors).

    b. Instead of using subsidiary ledgers to track specific jobs, process costing typically uses a **work-in-process** account for each department through which the production of output passes.

    c. Process costing calculates the average cost of all units as follows:

        1) Costs are accumulated for a **cost object** that consists of a large number of similar units of goods or services,

        2) Work-in-process is stated in terms of **equivalent units produced (EUP)**, and

        3) Cost per EUP is established.

2. **Accumulation of Costs**

    a. The accumulation of costs under a process costing system is by department to reflect the continuous, homogeneous nature of the process.

    b. The physical inputs required for production are obtained from suppliers.

Materials	$XXX	
Accounts payable		$XXX

    c. Direct materials are added by the first department in the process.

Work-in-process -- Department A	$XXX	
Materials		$XXX

d. **Conversion costs** are the sum of direct labor and manufacturing overhead. The nature of process costing makes this accounting treatment more efficient. (Item 4. contains an outline of equivalent units.)

Work-in-process -- Department A	$XXX	
Wages payable (direct labor)		$XXX
Manufacturing overhead		XXX

e. Products move from one department to the next.

Work-in-process -- Department B	$XXX	
Work-in-process -- Department A		$XXX

f. The second department adds more direct materials and more conversion costs.

Work-in-process -- Department B	$XXX	
Materials		$XXX

Work-in-process -- Department B	$XXX	
Wages payable (direct labor)		$XXX
Manufacturing overhead		XXX

g. When processing is finished in the last department, all costs are transferred to finished goods.

Finished goods	$XXX	
Work-in-process -- Department B		$XXX

h. As products are sold, sales are recorded and the costs are transferred to cost of goods sold.

Accounts receivable	$XXX	
Sales		$XXX
Cost of goods sold	$XXX	
Finished goods		$XXX

i. The changes in these accounts during the period can be summarized as follows:

Materials Inventory (MI)	Work-in-Progress Inventory (WIP)	Finished Goods Inventory (FG)
Beginning MI	Beginning WIP	Beginning FG
Purchases of MI	Conversion Costs	Cost of Goods Manufactured
(Ending MI)	Materials Used	(Ending FG)
	(Ending WIP)	
Materials Used	Cost of Goods Manufactured	Cost of Goods Sold

Figure 20-1

3. Process Cost Flows

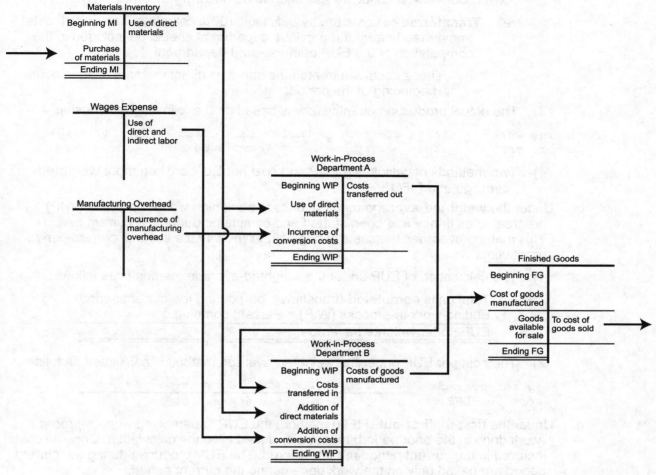

Figure 20-2

4. Equivalent Units of Production (EUP)

The AICPA frequently tests the calculation of equivalent units of production (EUP). This topic may be confusing to CPA candidates. To understand fully the calculation and use of EUP, work through the questions in the Gleim materials. Examples of how to calculate EUP are on pages 436 and 437.

a. Some units are unfinished at the end of the period. To account for their costs, the units are restated in terms of EUP. EUP equal the number of finished goods that could have been produced using the inputs consumed during the period. EUP for direct materials or conversion costs is the amount required to complete one physical unit of production.

EXAMPLE

1,000 work-in-process units, 80% complete for direct materials and 60% for conversion costs, equal 800 EUP of direct materials (1,000 × 80%) and 600 EUP of conversion costs (1,000 × 60%).

1) Determining the costs of unfinished units requires two calculations: (a) calculating the EUP and (b) calculating the cost per EUP.

2) The two calculations are made separately for direct materials and conversion costs. Conversion costs are assumed to be uniformly incurred.

     a) **Transferred-in** costs are by definition 100% complete. The units (costs) transferred in from the previous department should be included in the computation of the EUP of the second department.

         i) These costs are treated the same as direct materials added at the beginning of the period.

3) The actual production quantity flow is based on the following relationship:

$$\begin{array}{c} Beginning\ work\text{-} \\ in\text{-}process \end{array} + \begin{array}{c} Units\ started \\ this\ period \end{array} = \begin{array}{c} Units\ transferred \\ out\ (completed) \end{array} + \begin{array}{c} Ending\ work\text{-} \\ in\text{-}process \end{array}$$

4) Two methods of calculating EUP and cost per EUP are common: **weighted-average** and **FIFO**.

b. Under the **weighted-average** method, units in beginning work-in-process (WIP) are treated as if they had been started and completed during the current period. This method averages the costs of beginning WIP with the costs of current-period production.

     1) The calculation of EUP under the weighted-average method is as follows:

Total units **completed** (transferred out) during the current period
+ Ending work-in-process (WIP) × Percent completed

EUP under weighted-average

     2) The cost per EUP under the weighted-average method is calculated as follows:

$$\begin{array}{c} Weighted\text{-}average \\ cost\ per\ EUP \end{array} = \frac{Beginning\ WIP\ costs\ +\ Current\text{-}period\ costs}{Weighted\text{-}average\ EUP}$$

c. Under the **first-in, first-out (FIFO)** method, the EUP in beginning work-in-process (work done in the prior period) must be excluded from the calculation. Only the costs incurred in the current period are considered. The EUP produced during the current period are based only on the work done during the current period.

     1) The calculation of EUP under the FIFO method is as follows:

Beginning work-in-process (WIP) × Percent left to complete
+ Units **started and completed** during the current period
+ Ending work-in-process (WIP) × Percent completed

EUP under FIFO

NOTE: Units **started and completed** during the current period are equal to units started minus ending WIP (or equal to units completed minus beginning WIP).

Another version of this equation is below:

Total units completed (transferred out) this period
+ Ending work-in-process (WIP) × Percent completed
− Beginning work-in-process (WIP) × Percent completed in the prior period
------
EUP under FIFO

     2) The cost per EUP under FIFO is calculated as follows:

$$FIFO\ cost\ per\ EUP = \frac{Current\text{-}period\ costs}{FIFO\ EUP}$$

EXAMPLE of Weighted-Average vs. FIFO

	Units	Completed for Direct Materials (DM)	Completed for Conversion Costs (CC)
Beginning work-in-process (BWIP)	100	30%	40%
Units started during period	3,000		
Units completed (transferred out)	2,600		
Ending work-in-process (EWIP)	500	15%	20%
Costs to account for:		DM	CC
BWIP costs		$ 1,200	$ 2,200
Costs incurred during the period		30,000	33,000
		$31,200	$35,200

Step 1: Determine the equivalent units produced (EUP)

	Weighted-Average		FIFO	
	DM	CC	DM	CC
BWIP				
100 units × (1 – 30%)			70	
100 units × (1 – 40%)				60
Units completed	2,600	2,600		
Units started and completed				
2,600 units completed – 100 units BWIP			2,500	2,500
EWIP				
500 units × 15%	75		75	
500 units × 20%		100		100
EUP	2,675	2,700	2,645	2,660

Step 2: Determine the cost per EUP

	Weighted-Average		FIFO	
	DM	CC	DM	CC
(BWIP costs + current-period costs) ÷ EUP				
($1,200 + $30,000) ÷ 2,675 units	$11.66			
($2,200 + $33,000) ÷ 2,700 units		$13.04		
Current-period costs ÷ EUP				
$30,000 ÷ 2,645 units			$11.34	
$33,000 ÷ 2,660 units				$12.41

d. After the EUP have been calculated, the cost per EUP under each method can be determined.

   1) Under the **weighted-average method**, all direct materials and conversion costs incurred in the current period and in beginning work-in-process are averaged.

   2) Under the **FIFO method**, only the costs incurred in the current period are included in the calculation.

e. When beginning work-in-process is zero, the two methods have the same results.

Beginning inventory is subtracted in the EUP calculation only when applying FIFO. The weighted-average method treats units in beginning inventory as if they had been started and completed during the current period.

Stop and review! You have completed the outline for this subunit. Study multiple-choice questions 1 through 3 on page 449.

20.2 PROCESS COSTING -- CALCULATIONS

Process costing questions on the CPA exam test the understanding of principles and the ability to perform detailed calculations. This subunit consists entirely of the second type of question. Please review Subunit 20.1 before answering these questions.

Stop and review! You have completed the outline for this subunit. Study multiple-choice questions 4 through 7 beginning on page 450.

20.3 ACTIVITY-BASED COSTING (ABC)

1.   **Disadvantages of Volume-Based Systems**

   a.   ABC is a response to the significant increase in the incurrence of **indirect costs** resulting from the rapid advance of technology. ABC is a refinement of an existing costing system (job-order or process).

   1)   Under a **traditional (volume-based)** system, overhead is accumulated in **one cost pool** and allocated to all end products using one allocation base, such as direct labor hours or direct machine hours used.

   2)   Under **ABC**, indirect costs are assigned to **activities** and then rationally allocated to end products.

   a)   ABC may be used by manufacturing, service, or retailing firms.
   b)   ABC may be used in a job-order system or a process cost system.

   b.   The inaccurate averaging or spreading of indirect costs over products or service units that use different amounts of resources is called **peanut-butter costing**. Peanut-butter costing results in product-cost cross-subsidization. It miscosts one product and, as a result, miscosts other products.

   c.   The peanut-butter effect of using a volume-based system can be summarized as follows:

   1)   Direct labor and direct materials are traced to products or service units.

   2)   One pool of indirect costs (overhead) is accumulated for a given organizational unit.

   3)   Indirect costs from the pool are assigned using an allocative (rather than a tracing) procedure, such as using a single overhead rate for an entire department, e.g., $3 of overhead for every direct labor hour.

   a)   The effect is an averaging of costs that may result in significant inaccuracy when products or service units do not use similar amounts of resources (i.e., cost shifting).

EXAMPLE of ABC vs. Volume-Based

The effect of product-cost cross-subsidization can be illustrated as follows:

- Two products are produced. Both require 1 unit of direct materials and 1 hour of direct labor. Materials costs are $14 per unit, and direct labor is $70 per hour. Also, the manufacturer has no beginning or ending inventories.

- During the month just ended, production equaled 1,000 units of Product A and 100 units of Product B. Manufacturing overhead for the month was $20,000.

-- Continued on next page --

EXAMPLE -- Continued

Volume-Based

Using direct labor hours as the overhead allocation base, per-unit costs and profits are calculated as follows:

	Product A	Product B	Total
Direct materials	$ 14,000	$ 1,400	
Direct labor	70,000	7,000	
Overhead {$20,000 × [1,000 ÷ (1,000 + 100)]}	18,182		
Overhead {$20,000 × [100 ÷ (1,000 + 100)]}		1,818	
Total costs	$102,182	$ 10,218	$112,400
Selling price	$ 119.99	$ 139.99	
Cost per unit ($102,182 ÷ 1,000)	(102.18)		
Cost per unit ($10,218 ÷ 100)		(102.18)	
Profit per unit	$ 17.81	$ 37.81	

ABC

Overhead consists almost entirely of production line setup costs, and the two products require equal setup times. Allocating overhead on this basis has different results.

	Product A	Product B	Total
Direct materials	$14,000	$ 1,400	
Direct labor	70,000	7,000	
Overhead ($20,000 × 50%)	10,000		
Overhead ($20,000 × 50%)		10,000	
Total costs	$94,000	$18,400	$112,400
Selling price	$119.99	$139.99	
Cost per unit ($94,000 ÷ 1,000)	(94.00)		
Cost per unit ($18,400 ÷ 100)		(184.00)	
Profit (loss) per unit	$ 25.99	$ (44.01)	

Under volume-based costing, Product B appeared to be profitable. But ABC revealed that high-volume Product A has been subsidizing the setup costs for the low-volume Product B.

d. The example above assumed a single component of overhead for clarity. In reality, overhead consists of many components. The peanut-butter effect of volume-based overhead allocation is illustrated in the following diagram:

Overhead Allocation in Volume-Based Costing

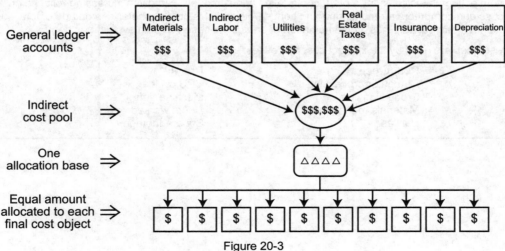

Figure 20-3

2.   **Volume-Based vs. Activity-Based**

    a.   Volume-based systems are appropriate when most manufacturing costs are homogeneously consumed. In these cases, one volume-based cost driver can be used to allocate the overhead costs. However, overhead costs do not always fluctuate with volume. ABC addresses the increasing complexity and variety of overhead costs.

    b.   Activity-based systems involve

        1)   Identifying organizational activities that incur overhead.

        2)   Assigning the costs of resources consumed by the activities.

        3)   Assigning the costs of the activities by appropriate cost drivers to final cost objects.

3.   **Step 1: Activity Analysis**

    a.   An activity is a set of work actions undertaken, and a cost pool is established for each activity.

    b.   Analysis identifies **value-adding** activities, which contribute to customer satisfaction. **Nonvalue-adding** activities should be reduced or eliminated.

    c.   Activities are classified in a hierarchy according to the level of the production process where they occur.

4.   **Step 2: Assign Resource Costs to Activities**

    a.   After activities are identified, the next step is to assign the costs of resources to the activities, a **first-stage allocation**.

    b.   Identifying resource costs is not as simple as in volume-based overhead allocation, which designates general ledger accounts to be combined in one general ledger cost pool.

        1)   A separate accounting system may be necessary to track resource costs separately from the general ledger.

    c.   After resource costs have been identified, resource drivers are designated to allocate resource costs to **activity cost pools**.

        1)   **Resource drivers** are measures of the causes of resources consumed by an activity.

EXAMPLE

A job-order system accumulates costs for a product made in various models. But given increasing reliance on robots in the production process and computers for monitoring and control, overhead is now a greater percentage of total costs, and direct labor costs have decreased. Thus, implementation of an activity-based costing system has begun.

The following resources are used by the indirect cost processes:

Resource	Driver
Computer processing	CPU cycles
Production line	Machine hours
Materials management	Hours worked
Utilities	Square footage

5. **Step 3: Allocate Costs in Activity Cost Pools to Final Cost Objects**

    a.   This final step is a **second-stage allocation**.

    b.   Costs are reassigned to final-stage cost objects on the basis of activity cost drivers.

        1)   **Activity cost drivers** are measures of the demands on an activity by next-stage cost objects (e.g., the number of parts in a product used to measure an assembly activity).

        2)   A driver is a factor that causes a change in a cost. **Cost drivers** are cost assignment bases that are used in the allocation of manufacturing overhead costs to cost objects.

    c.   Drivers (both resource and activity) must be chosen on the basis of a **cause-and-effect** relationship with the resource or activity cost allocated.

EXAMPLE

The following cost drivers have a cause-and-effect relationship with their corresponding activities:

Activity	Cost driver
Product design	Number of products
Production setup	Number of setups
Machining	Number of units produced
Inspection and testing	Number of units produced
Production orders	Number of orders

EXAMPLE

The following information pertains to current-month activities regarding the manufacture of X and Z:

Manufacturing overhead costs		Cost driver
Plant utilities and real estate taxes	$150,000	Square footage
Materials handling	40,000	Pounds of direct materials used
Inspection and testing	10,000	Number of units produced
	$200,000	

Current month activity level

	X	Z	Total
Direct labor hours	20,000	5,000	25,000
Plant square footage	400	600	1,000
Pounds of direct materials used	10,000	6,000	16,000
Number of units produced	15,000	3,000	18,000

Under a **volume-based system**, using direct labor hours as the overhead allocation base, the manufacturing overhead costs are allocated as follows:

    X: $200,000 × (20,000 ÷ 25,000) = $160,000
    Z: $200,000 × (5,000 ÷ 25,000) = $40,000

    Manufacturing overhead costs per unit of X: $160,000 ÷ 15,000 = $10.67
    Manufacturing overhead costs per unit of Z: $40,000 ÷ 3,000 = $13.33

Under an **ABC system**, the manufacturing overhead costs are allocated as follows:

	X		Z	
Plant utilities and real estate taxes	$150,000 × (400 ÷ 1,000)	= $60,000	$150,000 × (600 ÷ 1,000)	= $ 90,000
Materials handling	$40,000 × (10,000 ÷ 16,000)	= 25,000	$40,000 × (6,000 ÷ 16,000) =	15,000
Inspection and testing	$10,000 × (15,000 ÷ 18,000)	= 8,333	$10,000 × (3,000 ÷ 18,000) =	1,667
		$93,333		$106,667

    Manufacturing overhead costs per unit of X = $93,333 ÷ 15,000 = $6.22
    Manufacturing overhead costs per unit of Z = $106,667 ÷ 3,000 = $35.56

Stop and review! You have completed the outline for this subunit. Study multiple-choice questions 8 through 12 beginning on page 452.

20.4 VARIANCE ANALYSIS -- MATERIALS AND LABOR

The AICPA frequently tests variance analysis. Be certain to learn how to calculate the different variances. However, variance analysis is complex, and the terminology is not standardized.

1. **Use of Variance Analysis**

    a. Variance analysis is the basis of performance evaluation using standard costs (i.e., budgeted costs).

        1) A **favorable** variance **(F)** increases net income and occurs when actual costs are **less** than standard.

        2) An **unfavorable** variance **(U)** decreases net income and occurs when actual costs are **greater** than standard.

    b. Variance analysis enables management by exception, the practice of emphasizing significant deviations from expectations (whether favorable or unfavorable). A variance alerts management that corrective action may be needed.

2. **Framework for Variance Calculation**

    a. Variable inputs (direct materials and direct labor) can be analyzed in terms of a price (rate) variance and a quantity (efficiency) variance.

        1) **Price (rate) variances** result from a difference between (a) the actual price of resources used in production and (b) the standard price if **quantity** is constant.

        2) **Quantity (efficiency) variances** result from differences between (a) the actual resources used in production and (b) the standard amount if **price** is constant.

    b. The following abbreviations are used in the calculation of variances:

        AQP = Actual quantity of materials purchased
        AQ = Actual quantity of materials or hours
        AP = Actual price (rate) of materials or hours consumed
        SQ = Standard quantity of materials or hours for the actual production
        SP = Standard price (rate) of materials or hours

3. **Direct Materials**

    a. The **total direct materials variance** is the difference between (1) the actual materials cost of the actual units of output and (2) the standard materials cost of that output. Direct materials variances have price and quantity components.

        1) The **materials price variance** equals the actual quantity of input purchased during the period times the difference between (a) the standard price of materials and (b) the actual price.

$$\text{Direct materials price variance} = \text{Actual quantity purchased (AQP)} \times \left(\text{Standard materials price (SP)} - \text{Actual materials price (AP)} \right)$$

        2) The **materials quantity variance** (also called usage or efficiency variance) equals the standard price times the difference between (a) the standard quantity of materials and (b) the actual quantity used in production.

$$\text{Direct materials quantity variance} = \left(\text{Standard quantity of input allowed (SQ)} - \text{Actual quantity consumed (AQ)} \right) \times \text{Standard materials price (SP)}$$

EXAMPLE of Direct Materials Variances

Budgeted use is 980 tons of materials at a cost of $54 per ton. The actual amounts purchased and used during the month were 1,150 tons and 1,078 tons, respectively. The actual cost for the period was $50 per ton. If the materials price variance is recognized at purchase, variances for direct materials are calculated as follows:

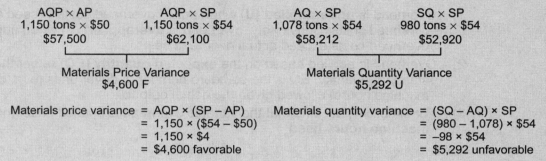

AQP × AP	AQP × SP	AQ × SP	SQ × SP
1,150 tons × $50	1,150 tons × $54	1,078 tons × $54	980 tons × $54
$57,500	$62,100	$58,212	$52,920

Materials Price Variance
$4,600 F

Materials Quantity Variance
$5,292 U

Materials price variance	= AQP × (SP − AP)	Materials quantity variance	= (SQ − AQ) × SP
	= 1,150 × ($54 − $50)		= (980 − 1,078) × $54
	= 1,150 × $4		= −98 × $54
	= $4,600 favorable		= $5,292 unfavorable

---

4. **Direct Labor**

    a. The **total variance for direct labor** is the sum of the two components below:

        1) The **labor rate variance** equals the actual number of hours worked times the difference between (a) the standard hourly wage rate and (b) the actual hourly rate.

$$\begin{array}{c} \text{Direct labor} \\ \text{rate variance} \end{array} = \begin{array}{c} \text{Actual hours} \\ \text{worked (AQ)} \end{array} \times \left(\begin{array}{c} \text{Standard hourly} \\ \text{rate (SP)} \end{array} - \begin{array}{c} \text{Actual hourly} \\ \text{rate (AP)} \end{array} \right)$$

        2) The **labor efficiency variance** equals the difference between (a) the standard number of hours allowed and (b) the actual number of hours worked, times the standard hourly wage rate.

$$\begin{array}{c} \text{Direct labor} \\ \text{efficiency variance} \end{array} = \left(\begin{array}{c} \text{Standard number} \\ \text{of hours} \\ \text{allowed (SQ)} \end{array} - \begin{array}{c} \text{Actual number} \\ \text{of hours} \\ \text{worked (AQ)} \end{array} \right) \times \begin{array}{c} \text{Standard hourly} \\ \text{rate (SP)} \end{array}$$

AQ × AP   AQ × SP   SQ × SP

Labor Rate Variance   Labor Efficiency Variance

Figure 20-4

EXAMPLE of Direct Labor Variances

Standard direct labor use was 882 hours at $17 per hour. However, 932 direct labor hours were actually worked at $18 per hour. The variances for direct labor are calculated as follows:

AQ × AP	AQ × SP	SQ × SP
932 hours × $18	932 hours × $17	882 hours × $17
$16,776	$15,844	$14,994

Labor Rate Variance
$932 U

Labor Efficiency Variance
$850 U

Labor rate variance	= AQ × (SP − AP)	Labor efficiency variance	= (SQ − AQ) × SP
	= 932 × ($17 − $18)		= (882 − 932) × $17
	= $932 unfavorable		= $850 unfavorable

Stop and review! You have completed the outline for this subunit. Study multiple-choice questions 13 through 16 beginning on page 454.

20.5 VARIANCE ANALYSIS -- OVERHEAD

1. **Variable Overhead**

   a. The amount of variable overhead (VOH) **under- or overapplied** for the period is the **variable overhead flexible-budget variance**.

      1) Overhead is **underapplied (U)** when actual overhead costs exceed applied overhead costs. Conversely, overhead is **overapplied (F)** when applied overhead costs exceed actual overhead costs.

      2) Overhead is applied based on the **expected quantity (EQ)** rather than the standard quantity. EQ is the standard number of driver units (e.g., direct machine hours) allowed given the actual output.

      3) For simplicity, assume that the variable overhead is applied based on **direct machine hours used**.

   $$VOH\ flexible\text{-}budget\ variance = Actual\ VOH\ costs\ incurred - (EQ \times SP)$$

   $$VOH\ over\text{-}\ or\ underapplied = Actual\ VOH\ costs\ incurred - VOH\ applied$$

   $$= \frac{Actual\ VOH}{incurred} - \left(\frac{Actual\ unit}{output} \times \frac{Standard\ hours\ allowed}{per\ unit\ of\ output} \times Standard\ VOH\ rate \right)$$

   b. This variance has a spending component and an efficiency component.

      1) The **VOH spending variance** is the difference between (a) the actual VOH incurred and (b) the actual number of driver units (e.g., machine hours) times the standard VOH rate.

   $$VOH\ spending\ variance = Actual\ VOH - (Actual\ number\ of\ hours\ used \times Standard\ VOH\ rate)$$

   $$= Actual\ VOH - (AQ \times SP)$$

      2) The **VOH efficiency variance** is the difference between (a) the standard number of hours allowed for actual unit output (EQ) and (b) the actual number of hours used, times the standard VOH rate.

   $$VOH\ efficiency\ variance = (EQ - AQ) \times SP$$

Variable Overhead Variances

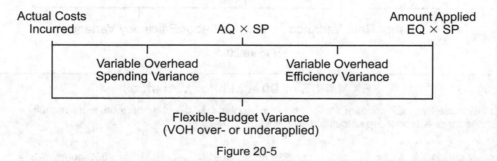

Figure 20-5

EXAMPLE of Variable Overhead Variances

Variable overhead is applied at the rate of $4 per machine hour. The use of 10 machine hours is budgeted for each unit produced. The planned output was 90 units. Actual output is 98 units. The number of machine hours used was 900, and actual variable overhead was $4,000. The variances for variable overhead are calculated as follows:

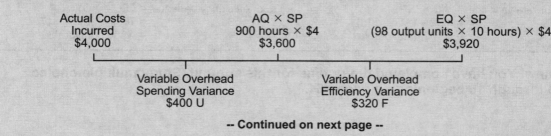

-- Continued on next page --

2. **Fixed Overhead**

   a. The amount of fixed overhead (FOH) that was under- or overapplied for the period consists of a spending component and a volume component.

$$\text{FOH over- or underapplied} = \text{Actual FOH incurred} - \text{FOH applied}$$

$$= \begin{matrix} \text{Actual FOH} \\ \text{incurred} \end{matrix} - \left(\begin{matrix} \text{Actual unit} \\ \text{output} \end{matrix} \times \begin{matrix} \text{Standard hours allowed} \\ \text{per unit of output} \end{matrix} \times \begin{matrix} \text{Standard} \\ \text{FOH rate} \end{matrix} \right)$$

   1) The **FOH spending variance** is the difference between (a) the actual costs incurred and (b) the amount budgeted.

$$\text{FOH spending variance} = \text{Actual FOH incurred} - \text{Amount budgeted}$$

$$= \begin{matrix} \text{Actual FOH} \\ \text{incurred} \end{matrix} - \left(\begin{matrix} \text{Budgeted} \\ \text{unit output} \end{matrix} \times \begin{matrix} \text{Standard hours allowed} \\ \text{per unit of output} \end{matrix} \times \begin{matrix} \text{Standard} \\ \text{FOH rate} \end{matrix} \right)$$

   2) The **FOH volume variance** is the difference between (a) the amount of fixed overhead budgeted and (b) the amount applied.

$$\text{FOH volume variance} = \text{Amount budgeted} - \text{FOH applied}$$

   b. Fixed overhead has a volume variance instead of an efficiency variance. Fixed costs by definition do not change within the relevant range of the budgeting cycle. The same amount of fixed cost is budgeted regardless of the number of driver units actually used or the actual unit output.

   1) For the same reason, the sum of the fixed overhead spending and volume variances is not flexible budget variance.

Fixed Overhead Variances

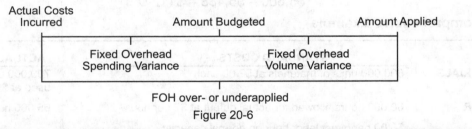

Figure 20-6

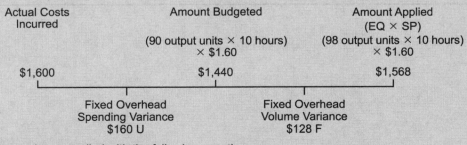

3. **Integrated Overhead Variance Analysis**

    a. **Three-way overhead variance analysis** combines the variable and fixed spending variances ($400 U + $160 U = $560 U) and reports the other two variances separately.

EXAMPLE			
Three-Way Analysis	Spending Variance	Efficiency Variance	Volume Variance
Total overhead	$560 U	$320 F	$128 F

    b. **Two-way overhead variance analysis** combines the spending and efficiency variances into one budget variance ($400 U + $160 U + $320 F = $240 U) and reports the volume variance separately.

EXAMPLE		
Two-Way Analysis	Budget Variance	Volume Variance
Total overhead	$240 U	$128 F

    1) The budget variance in two-way analysis also is called the **controllable variance**. It is the portion of the total not attributable to the volume variance.

    c. The **net overhead variance** (one-way overhead variance analysis) combines all the components into one amount ($240 U + $128 F = **$112 U**).

    1) The net overhead variance equals the difference between (a) the total actual overhead incurred of $5,600 ($4,000 actual VOH + $1,600 actual FOH) and (b) the total overhead applied of $5,488 [(98 × 10) standard hours applied to actual output produced × ($4 + $1.6) standard total overhead rate].

    $$\$5,600 - \$5,488 = \$112 \text{ U}$$

4. **Comprehensive Example**

	STANDARD COSTS	ACTUAL COSTS (AC)
DIRECT MATERIALS	600,000 units of materials at $2.00 each	700,000 units purchased and used at $1.90
DIRECT LABOR	60,000 hours allowed for actual output at $7 per hour	65,000 hours at $7.20
OVERHEAD	$8.00 per direct labor hour on normal capacity of 50,000 direct labor hours:	
	$6.00 for variable overhead	$396,000 variable
	$2.00 for fixed overhead	$130,000 fixed

MATERIALS VARIANCES

Price

$$
\begin{aligned}
\text{AQP} \times (\text{SP} - \text{AP}) &= \text{Actual quantity purchased} \times (\text{Standard price} - \text{Actual price}) \\
&= 700{,}000 \text{ units} \times (\$2.00 - \$1.90) \\
&= 700{,}000 \times \$0.10 \\
&= \$70{,}000 \text{ F}
\end{aligned}
$$

Quantity

$$
\begin{aligned}
(\text{SQ} - \text{AQ}) \times \text{SP} &= (\text{Standard quantity} - \text{Actual quantity used}) \times \text{Standard price} \\
&= (600{,}000 \text{ units} - 700{,}000 \text{ units}) \times \$2.00 \\
&= -100{,}000 \times \$2.00 \\
&= \$200{,}000 \text{ U}
\end{aligned}
$$

LABOR VARIANCES

Rate

$$
\begin{aligned}
\text{AQ} \times (\text{SP} - \text{AP}) &= \text{Actual hours} \times (\text{Standard rate} - \text{Actual rate}) \\
&= 65{,}000 \text{ hours} \times (\$7.00 - \$7.20) \\
&= 65{,}000 \times -\$0.20 \\
&= \$13{,}000 \text{ U}
\end{aligned}
$$

Efficiency

$$
\begin{aligned}
(\text{SQ} - \text{AQ}) \times \text{SP} &= (\text{Standard hours} - \text{Actual hours}) \times \text{Standard rate} \\
&= (60{,}000 \text{ hours} - 65{,}000 \text{ hours}) \times \$7.00 \\
&= -5{,}000 \times \$7.00 \\
&= \$35{,}000 \text{ U}
\end{aligned}
$$

VARIABLE OVERHEAD VARIANCES

Spending

$$
\begin{aligned}
(\text{AQ} \times \text{SP}) - \text{AC} &= (\text{Actual hours} \times \text{Standard rate}) - \text{Actual costs incurred} \\
&= (65{,}000 \times \$6.00) - \$396{,}000 \\
&= \$390{,}000 - \$396{,}000 \\
&= \$6{,}000 \text{ U}
\end{aligned}
$$

Efficiency

$$
\begin{aligned}
(\text{SQ} - \text{AQ}) \times \text{SP} &= (\text{Standard hours allowed for actual production} - \text{Actual hours}) \times \text{Standard rate} \\
&= (60{,}000 - 65{,}000) \times \$6.00 \\
&= -5{,}000 \times \$6.00 \\
&= \$30{,}000 \text{ U}
\end{aligned}
$$

Total VOH Variance

$$
\begin{aligned}
&= \text{Actual VOH incurred} - \text{VOH applied} \\
&= \$396{,}000 - (60{,}000 \times \$6.00) \\
&= \$36{,}000 \text{ U}
\end{aligned}
$$

FIXED OVERHEAD VARIANCES

Spending

$$
\begin{aligned}
\text{Flexible/Static budget} - \text{Actual costs incurred} &= (50{,}000 \text{ hours} \times \$2.00) - \$130{,}000 \\
&= \$30{,}000 \text{ U}
\end{aligned}
$$

Volume

$$
\begin{aligned}
(\text{Standard hours allowed for actual output} \times \text{Standard rate}) - \text{Flexible/Static budget} &= (60{,}000 \text{ hours} \times \$2.00) - (50{,}000 \text{ hours} \times \$2.00) \\
&= \$120{,}000 - \$100{,}000 \\
&= \$20{,}000 \text{ F}
\end{aligned}
$$

Total FOH Variance

$$
\begin{aligned}
&= \text{FOH incurred} - \text{FOH applied} \\
&= \$130{,}000 - (60{,}000 \text{ hours} \times \$2.00) \\
&= \$10{,}000 \text{ U}
\end{aligned}
$$

Stop and review! You have completed the outline for this subunit. Study multiple-choice questions 17 through 21 beginning on page 455.

20.6 SALES VARIANCES

1.   **Sales, Contribution Margin, and Operating Income**

 a.   Variance analysis is useful for evaluating not only the production function but also the selling function.

   1)   If sales differ from the amount budgeted, the difference could consist of a **sales price variance**, a **sales volume variance**, or both.

   2)   The analysis of these variances concentrates on **contribution margins** because fixed costs are assumed to be constant.

EXAMPLE

Budgeted sales of a product are 10,000 units at $17 per unit. Variable costs are expected to be $10 per unit, and fixed costs are budgeted at $50,000. The following compares budgeted and actual results:

	Budget Computation	Budget Amount	Actual Computation	Actual Amount
Sales	10,000 units × $17 per unit	$170,000	11,000 units × $16 per unit	$176,000
Variable costs	10,000 units × $10 per unit	(100,000)	11,000 units × $10 per unit	(110,000)
Contribution margin		$ 70,000		$ 66,000
Fixed costs		(50,000)		(50,000)
Operating income		$ 20,000		$ 16,000
Unit contribution margins	$70,000 ÷ 10,000 units	$ 7	$66,000 ÷ 11,000 units	$ 6

---

2.   **Sales Variances**

 a.   In the example above, sales were greater than budgeted, but the contribution margin is lower. The difference can be analyzed in terms of the sales price variance and the sales volume variance. If net income increases (decreases) the variance is favorable (unfavorable).

   1)   The **sales price variance** is the change in the contribution margin attributable solely to the change in selling price (if quantity is constant).

$$\text{Sales price variance} = \text{Actual units sold} \times \left(\begin{array}{c} \text{Actual selling} \\ \text{price per unit} \end{array} - \begin{array}{c} \text{Budgeted selling} \\ \text{price per unit} \end{array} \right)$$

   2)   In the example, the actual selling price of $16 per unit is $1 less than expected. Thus, the sales price variance is $11,000 U (11,000 actual units sold × $1).

 b.   The **sales volume variance** is the change in the contribution margin attributable solely to the difference between the actual and budgeted unit sales (if price is constant).

$$\text{Sales volume variance} = \begin{array}{c} \text{Budgeted contribution} \\ \text{margin per unit} \end{array} \times \left(\begin{array}{c} \text{Actual} \\ \text{units sold} \end{array} - \begin{array}{c} \text{Budgeted} \\ \text{units sold} \end{array} \right)$$

   1)   In the example, it equals $7,000 F (1,000 unit increase in sales × $7).

 c.   The sales price variance ($11,000 U) plus the sales volume variance ($7,000 F) equals the total change in the contribution margin ($4,000 U).

Stop and review! You have completed the outline for this subunit. Study multiple-choice question 22 on page 456.

QUESTIONS

20.1 Process Costing -- Principles

1. The units transferred in from the first department to the second department should be included in the computation of the equivalent units for the second department under which of the following methods of process costing?

	FIFO	Weighted-Average
A.	Yes	Yes
B.	Yes	No
C.	No	Yes
D.	No	No

Answer (A) is correct.

REQUIRED: The cost flow method(s) that include(s) transferred-in costs in EUP calculations.

DISCUSSION: The units transferred from the first to the second department should be included in the computation of EUP for the second department regardless of the cost flow assumption used. The transferred-in units are considered materials added at the beginning of the period.

Answer (B) is incorrect. Units transferred in also should be included in the EUP computation under the weighted-average method. Answer (C) is incorrect. Units transferred in also should be included in the EUP computation under the FIFO method. Answer (D) is incorrect. Units transferred in should be included in the EUP computation under both methods.

2. Purchased direct materials are added in the second department of a three-department process. This addition does **not** increase the number of units produced in the second department and will

A. Not change the dollar amount transferred to the next department.

B. Decrease total ending work-in-process inventory.

C. Increase the factory overhead portion of the ending work-in-process inventory.

D. Increase total unit cost.

Answer (D) is correct.

REQUIRED: The effect of adding direct materials in a subsequent department given constant production.

DISCUSSION: Adding materials to a production process without changing the number of units produced increases the unit cost. The numerator (total cost) increases while the denominator (total units) remains the same.

Answer (A) is incorrect. If purchased materials are added to the process, the cost will be added to the total cost transferred to the next department. Answer (B) is incorrect. The unit cost, and therefore the cost of EWIP, increases when materials are added. Answer (C) is incorrect. Materials cost is separate from overhead.

3. Assuming no beginning work-in-process inventory, and that the ending work-in-process inventory is 100% complete as to materials costs, the number of equivalent units as to materials costs is

A. The same as the units placed in process.

B. The same as the units completed.

C. Less than the units placed in process.

D. Less than the units completed.

Answer (A) is correct.

REQUIRED: The number of EUP as to materials costs.

DISCUSSION: Given no BWIP, whether the FIFO or weighted-average method is used is immaterial. Because EWIP is 100% complete as to materials costs, the EUP for materials costs are equal to the number of units placed in process (units in EWIP + units transferred to finished goods).

Answer (B) is incorrect. The number of EUP is equal to the units completed only if there is no EWIP. Answer (C) is incorrect. The number of EUP is less than the units placed in process when EWIP is less than 100% complete as to materials costs. Answer (D) is incorrect. The EUP must at least equal the number of units completed.

20.2 Process Costing -- Calculations

Questions 4 and 5 are based on the following information. A sporting goods manufacturer buys wood as a direct material for baseball bats. The Forming Department processes the baseball bats, and the bats are then transferred to the Finishing Department, where a sealant is applied. The Forming Department began manufacturing 10,000 "Casey Sluggers" during the month of May. There was no beginning inventory. Costs for the Forming Department for the month of May were as follows:

Direct materials	$33,000
Conversion costs	17,000
Total	$50,000

A total of 8,000 bats were completed and transferred to the Finishing Department; the remaining 2,000 bats were still in the forming process at the end of the month. All of the Forming Department's direct materials were placed in process, but, on average, only 25% of the conversion cost was applied to the ending work-in-process inventory.

4. The cost of the units transferred to the Finishing Department is

    A. $50,000

    B. $40,000

    C. $53,000

    D. $42,400

Answer (D) is correct.

    REQUIRED: The cost of the units transferred to the Finishing Department.

    DISCUSSION: The total EUP for materials equal 10,000 because all materials for the ending work-in-process had already been added to production. Thus, the materials cost per unit was $3.30 ($33,000 ÷ 10,000). For conversion costs, the total EUP equal 8,500 [8,000 completed + (2,000 in EWIP × 25%)]. Thus, the conversion cost was $2.00 per unit ($17,000 ÷ 8,500). The total cost transferred was therefore $42,400 [8,000 units × ($3.30 + $2.00)].

    Answer (A) is incorrect. A portion of the total costs is still in work-in-process. Answer (B) is incorrect. The amount of $40,000 assumes that work-in-process is 100% complete as to conversion costs. Answer (C) is incorrect. The amount of $53,000 exceeds the actual costs incurred during the period. Given no beginning inventory, the amount transferred out cannot exceed the costs incurred during the period.

5. The cost of the work-in-process inventory in the Forming Department at the end of May is

    A. $10,000

    B. $2,500

    C. $20,000

    D. $7,600

Answer (D) is correct.

    REQUIRED: The cost of the work-in-process inventory.

    DISCUSSION: The EUP for materials equal 10,000 (8,000 + 2,000) because the work-in-process is 100% complete as to materials. Thus, dividing the $33,000 by 10,000 units results in a unit cost for materials of $3.30. The EUP for conversion costs equal 8,500 units [8,000 + (2,000 units × .25)]. Dividing the $17,000 of conversion costs by 8,500 EUP results in a unit cost of $2 per bat, and the total cost of goods transferred out is $5.30, consisting of $3.30 for materials and $2 for conversion costs. Multiplying $5.30 by the 8,000 bats completed results in a total transfer of $42,400. Consequently, the cost of the ending work-in-process must have been $7,600 ($50,000 total costs incurred − $42,400).

    Answer (A) is incorrect. The amount of $10,000 assumes that work-in-process inventory is 100% complete as to conversion costs. Answer (B) is incorrect. The amount of $2,500 assumes that work-in-process inventory is 100% complete as to conversion costs and that 500 bats are in inventory. Answer (C) is incorrect. The amount of $20,000 assumes that work-in-process is 100% complete as to conversion costs and that 6,000 units were transferred out.

6. The following data pertain to a company's cracking-department operations in December:

	Units	Completion
Work-in-process, December 1	20,000	50%
Units started	170,000	
Units completed and transferred to the distilling department	180,000	
Work-in-process, December 31	10,000	50%

Materials are added at the beginning of the process, and conversion costs are incurred uniformly throughout the process. Assuming use of the FIFO method of process costing, the equivalent units of production (EUP) with respect to conversion performed during December were

A. 170,000

B. 175,000

C. 180,000

D. 185,000

Answer (B) is correct.
   REQUIRED: The EUP for conversion.
   DISCUSSION: Under the FIFO method, EUP are determined based only on work performed during the current period. Thus, units in beginning work-in-process must be excluded.

	Conversion
Units transferred out	180,000
Add: EWIP (10,000 × 50%)	5,000
Total completed units	185,000
Less: BWIP (20,000 × 50%)	(10,000)
Equivalent units of production	175,000

   Answer (A) is incorrect. The number of EUP of materials for the period is 170,000. Answer (C) is incorrect. The total amount of work done on the completed units is 180,000. Answer (D) is incorrect. The amount determined using the weighted-average method is 185,000.

7. A company employs a process cost system using the first-in, first-out (FIFO) method. The product passes through both Department 1 and Department 2 in order to be completed. Units enter Department 2 upon completion in Department 1. Additional direct materials are added in Department 2 when the units have reached the 25% stage of completion with respect to conversion costs. Conversion costs are added proportionally in Department 2. The production activity in Department 2 for the current month was as follows:

Beginning work-in-process inventory (40% complete with respect to conversion costs)	15,000
Units transferred in from Department 1	80,000
Units completed and transferred to finished goods	85,000
Ending work-in-process inventory (20% complete with respect to conversion costs)	10,000

How many equivalent units for direct materials were added in Department 2 for the current month?

A. 70,000 units.

B. 80,000 units.

C. 85,000 units.

D. 90,000 units.

Answer (A) is correct.
   REQUIRED: The EUP for direct materials added in Department 2 for the current month.
   DISCUSSION: Beginning inventory is 40% complete. Thus, direct materials have already been added. Ending inventory has not reached the 25% stage of completion, so direct materials have not yet been added to these units. Thus, the EUP for direct materials calculated on a FIFO basis are equal to the units started and completed in the current period (85,000 units completed – 15,000 units in BWIP = 70,000 units started and completed).
   Answer (B) is incorrect. The amount transferred in from Department 1 was 80,000 total units. Answer (C) is incorrect. The EUP for direct materials calculated on a weighted-average basis equals 85,000. Answer (D) is incorrect. The sum of units transferred in from Department 1 and ending work-in-process inventory equals 90,000 units.

20.3 Activity-Based Costing (ABC)

Question 8 is based on the following information.

Zeta Company is preparing its annual profit plan. As part of its analysis of the profitability of individual products, the controller estimates the amount of overhead that should be allocated to the individual product lines from the information given in the next column:

	Wall Mirrors	Specialty Windows
Units produced	25	25
Material moves per product line	5	15
Direct labor hours per unit	200	200
Budgeted materials handling costs		$50,000

8. Under a costing system that allocates overhead on the basis of direct labor hours, Zeta Company's materials handling costs allocated to one unit of wall mirrors would be

A. $1,000

B. $500

C. $2,000

D. $5,000

Answer (A) is correct.
   REQUIRED: The amount of materials handling costs allocated to one unit of wall mirrors when direct labor hours is the activity base.
   DISCUSSION: If direct labor hours are used as the allocation base, the $50,000 of costs is allocated over 400 hours of direct labor. Multiplying the 25 units of each product times 200 hours results in 5,000 labor hours for each product, or a total of 10,000 hours. Dividing $50,000 by 10,000 hours results in a cost of $5 per direct labor hour. Multiplying 200 hours times $5 results in an allocation of $1,000 of overhead per unit of product.
   Answer (B) is incorrect. The amount of $500 is the allocation based on number of material moves. Answer (C) is incorrect. The amount of $2,000 assumes that all the overhead is allocated to the wall mirrors. Answer (D) is incorrect. The amount of $5,000 assumes overhead of $250,000.

9. Pelder Products Company manufactures two types of engineering diagnostic equipment used in construction. The two products are based on different technologies, X-ray and ultrasound, but are manufactured in the same factory. Pelder has computed the manufacturing cost of the X-ray and ultrasound products by adding together direct materials, direct labor, and overhead cost applied based on the number of direct labor hours. The factory has three overhead departments that support the single production line that makes both products. Budgeted overhead spending for the departments is as follows:

Department			
Engineering design	Material handling	Setup	Total
$6,000	$5,000	$3,000	$14,000

Pelder's budgeted manufacturing activities and costs for the period are as follows:

	Product	
Activity	X-Ray	Ultrasound
Units produced and sold	50	100
Direct materials used	$5,000	$8,000
Direct labor hours used	100	300
Direct labor cost	$4,000	$12,000
Number of parts used	400	600
Number of engineering changes	2	1
Number of product setups	8	7

The budgeted cost to manufacture one ultrasound machine using the activity-based costing method is

A. $225

B. $264

C. $293

D. $305

Answer (B) is correct.
   REQUIRED: The ABC cost of a single ultrasound machine.
   DISCUSSION: Charges for direct materials and direct labor are traceable to each type of machine ($8,000 and $12,000 respectively for the ultrasound). The departmental costs must be allocated based on each machine's proportional driver level. Engineering design costs can be allocated to the ultrasound machine at a rate of 33.3% [1 ÷ (1 + 2)], material handling at a rate of 60% [600 ÷ (600 + 400)], and setup at a rate of 46.7% [7 ÷ (7 + 8)]. Pelder's cost for a single ultrasound machine can thus be calculated as follows:

	For 100 Units
Direct materials ($8,000)	$ 80
Direct labor ($12,000)	120
Engineering changes ($6,000 × 33.3%)	20
Materials handling ($5,000 × 60%)	30
Setup ($3,000 × 46.7%)	14
Total	$264

   Answer (A) is incorrect. The amount of $225 results from using X-ray direct labor rather than ultrasound direct labor. Answer (C) is incorrect. The amount of $293 results from improperly using the units of production to allocate the engineering, handling, and setup costs. Answer (D) is incorrect. The amount of $305 results from improperly using direct labor hours to allocate the engineering, handling, and setup costs.

10. A company is considering the implementation of an activity-based costing and management program. The company

A. Should focus on manufacturing activities and avoid implementation with service-type functions.

B. Would probably find a lack of software in the marketplace to assist with the related recordkeeping.

C. Would normally gain added insights into causes of cost.

D. Would likely use fewer cost pools than it did under more traditional accounting methods.

Answer (C) is correct.
REQUIRED: The most likely result of an ABC and ABM program.
DISCUSSION: One of the benefits of activity-based costing is the discovery of cost relationships that are unnoticed using traditional accounting methods.
Answer (A) is incorrect. Activity-based costing is suitable for service-type functions. Answer (B) is incorrect. Software exists to help firms implement activity-based management. Answer (D) is incorrect. Activity-based costing generally results in many more cost pools than under traditional accounting methods.

11. The Chocolate Baker specializes in chocolate baked goods. The firm has long assessed the profitability of a product line by comparing revenues to the cost of goods sold. However, Barry White, the firm's new accountant, wants to use an activity-based costing system that takes into consideration the cost of the delivery person. Listed below are activity and cost information relating to two of Chocolate Baker's major products.

	Muffins	Cheesecake
Revenue	$53,000	$46,000
Cost of goods sold	26,000	21,000
Delivery activity:		
Number of deliveries	150	85
Average length of delivery	10 minutes	15 minutes
Cost per hour for delivery	$20.00	$20.00

Using activity-based costing, which one of the following statements is correct?

A. The muffins are $2,000 more profitable.

B. The cheesecakes are $75 more profitable.

C. The muffins are $1,925 more profitable.

D. The muffins have a higher profitability as a percentage of sales and therefore are more advantageous.

Answer (C) is correct.
REQUIRED: The true statement given activity-based costing.
DISCUSSION: The first step is to calculate the gross margin on the two products:

	Muffins	Cheesecake
Revenues	$53,000	$46,000
Cost of goods sold	(26,000)	(21,000)
Gross margin	$27,000	$25,000

The next step is to calculate total delivery cost for each product:

	Muffins	Cheesecake
Number of deliveries	150	85
Times: Minutes per delivery	× 10	× 15
Total delivery minutes	1,500	1,275
Divided by: Minutes per hour	÷ 60	÷ 60
Total delivery hours	25.00	21.25
Times: Delivery cost per hour	× $20	× $20
Total delivery cost	$500	$425

The operating profits on these two products, and the difference between them, can now be determined:

Muffins	($27,000 – $500)	$26,500
Cheesecake	($25,000 – $425)	(24,575)
Excess		$ 1,925

Answer (A) is incorrect. Muffins exceed cheesecake by $2,000 only at the gross margin, not the total profitability level. Answer (B) is incorrect. The total delivery cost for muffins exceeds that of cheesecake by $75. Answer (D) is incorrect. Muffins ($26,500 ÷ $53,000 = 50.0%) have a lower profitability percentage than cheesecake ($24,575 ÷ $46,000 = 53.4%).

12. A company with three products classifies its costs as belonging to five functions: design, production, marketing, distribution, and customer services. For pricing purposes, all company costs are assigned to the three products. The direct costs of each of the five functions are traced directly to the three products. The indirect costs of each of the five business functions are collected into five separate cost pools and then assigned to the three products using appropriate allocation bases. The allocation base that will most likely be the best for allocating the indirect costs of the distribution function is

A. Number of customer phone calls.

B. Number of shipments.

C. Number of sales persons.

D. Dollar sales volume.

Answer (B) is correct.
REQUIRED: The allocation base that will most likely be the best for allocating the indirect costs of the distribution function.
DISCUSSION: The number of shipments is an appropriate cost driver. A cause-and-effect relationship may exist between the number of shipments and distribution costs.
Answer (A) is incorrect. The number of customer phone calls has little relation to distribution. It is probably more closely related to customer service. Answer (C) is incorrect. The number of sales persons is not related to distribution. It is more closely related to marketing. Answer (D) is incorrect. The dollar sales volume is not necessarily related to distribution. It is more likely related to marketing.

20.4 Variance Analysis -- Materials and Labor

13. Tub Co. uses a standard cost system. The following information pertains to direct labor for product B for the month of October:

Standard hours allowed for actual production	2,000
Actual rate paid per hour	$8.40
Standard rate per hour	$8.00
Labor efficiency variance	$1,600 U

What were the actual hours worked?

- A. 1,800
- B. 1,810
- C. 2,190
- D. 2,200

Answer (D) is correct.
REQUIRED: The actual hours worked.
DISCUSSION: The labor efficiency variance is the difference between the standard hours and the actual hours worked, times the standard wage rate.

$$
\begin{aligned}
(SQ - AQ) \times SP &= \text{Labor efficiency variance} \\
(2{,}000 \text{ hours} - AQ) \times \$8 &= -\$1{,}600 \\
\$16{,}000 - \$8AQ &= -\$1{,}600 \\
-\$8AQ &= -\$17{,}600 \\
AQ &= 2{,}200 \text{ hours}
\end{aligned}
$$

14. The standard unit cost is used in the calculation of which of the following variances?

	Materials Price Variance	Materials Usage Variance
A.	No	No
B.	No	Yes
C.	Yes	No
D.	Yes	Yes

Answer (D) is correct.
REQUIRED: The variance(s) using standard unit costs.
DISCUSSION: The materials price variance is isolated at either the time of purchase or use in production. It is calculated by multiplying the actual quantity of units purchased (or used) by the difference between actual price and standard price. The materials quantity (usage) variance is calculated by multiplying the difference between (1) the standard quantity of units (the actual output times the standard number of inputs per unit of output) and (2) the actual quantity of units consumed, times standard price. Thus, the standard unit cost is used to compute both the materials price variance and the materials quantity variance.
Answer (A) is incorrect. Standard unit cost is used in the calculation of materials price variance and materials quantity variance. Answer (B) is incorrect. Standard unit cost also is used in the calculation of the materials price variance. Answer (C) is incorrect. Standard unit cost also is used in the calculation of the materials quantity variance.

15. Information on Hanley's direct labor costs for the month of January is as follows:

Actual direct labor rate	$7.50
Standard direct labor hours allowed	11,000
Actual direct labor hours	10,000
Direct labor rate variance -- favorable	$5,500

The standard direct labor rate in January was

- A. $6.95
- B. $7.00
- C. $8.00
- D. $8.05

Answer (D) is correct.
REQUIRED: The standard direct labor rate for the month.
DISCUSSION: The labor rate variance, actual hours, and actual rate are given. Thus, the standard rate can be derived by substituting into the following formula:

$$
\begin{aligned}
AQ \times (SP - AP) &= \text{Labor rate variance} \\
10{,}000 \times (SP - \$7.50) &= \$5{,}500 \text{ F} \\
10{,}000SP - \$75{,}000 &= \$5{,}500 \\
10{,}000SP &= \$80{,}500 \\
SP &= \$8.05
\end{aligned}
$$

Answer (A) is incorrect. The amount of $6.95 treats the $.55 variance per unit as unfavorable. Answer (B) is incorrect. Actual hours, not standard hours, are used to determine the standard rate. Furthermore, the favorable variance should be added, not subtracted, in calculating the standard rate. Answer (C) is incorrect. Actual hours, not standard hours, should be used in determining the standard rate.

16. The difference between the actual labor rate multiplied by the actual hours worked and the standard labor rate multiplied by the standard labor hours is the

    A.   Total labor variance.

    B.   Labor rate variance.

    C.   Labor usage variance.

    D.   Labor efficiency variance.

Answer (A) is correct.
    REQUIRED: The variance defined by the difference between total actual labor costs and total standard costs allowed.
    DISCUSSION: The total actual labor cost equals the actual labor rate times the actual labor hours. The total standard cost for good output equals the standard rate times the standard hours allowed. The total labor rate variance is the difference between the total actual labor costs and the total standard labor costs.
    Answer (B) is incorrect. The labor rate variance is AQ × (SP − AP). Answer (C) is incorrect. The labor usage variance is (SQ − AQ) × SP. Answer (D) is incorrect. The labor efficiency variance is the same as the labor usage variance: (SQ − AQ) × SP.

20.5 Variance Analysis -- Overhead

17. During the month just ended, a department's fixed overhead standard costing system reported unfavorable spending and volume variances. The activity level selected for allocating overhead to the product was based on 80% of practical capacity. If 100% of practical capacity had been selected instead, how would the reported unfavorable spending and volume variances be affected?

	Spending Variance	Volume Variance
A.	Increased	Unchanged
B.	Increased	Increased
C.	Unchanged	Increased
D.	Unchanged	Unchanged

Answer (C) is correct.
    REQUIRED: The effects on unfavorable spending and volume variances of increasing the budgeted activity level.
    DISCUSSION: The fixed overhead spending variance equals the actual costs incurred minus the budgeted amount. Thus, the spending variance is not affected by the denominator level of the overhead application driver. However, the volume variance equals the budgeted amount minus the amount applied. Because the fixed overhead applied depends on the activity level of the driver used for application, a change in the denominator affects the volume variance. If the denominator increases, the application rate and the amount applied decrease, causing the variance to increase.

18. Which of the following variances would be useful in calling attention to a possible short-term problem in the control of overhead costs?

	Spending Variance	Volume Variance
A.	No	No
B.	No	Yes
C.	Yes	No
D.	Yes	Yes

Answer (C) is correct.
    REQUIRED: The variance(s) useful for controlling overhead costs.
    DISCUSSION: The volume variance is the difference between fixed overhead applied and fixed overhead budgeted. Thus, the volume variance has no relation to cost control because the amount of fixed costs is constant. The variance results only from a change in the level of the application base. However, the spending variance is simply a price variance for manufacturing overhead. Consequently, it is the spending variance, not the volume variance, that is useful in detecting problems in the control of overhead costs.
    Answer (A) is incorrect. The spending variance is a price variance. Answer (B) is incorrect. The spending variance, not the volume variance, is useful for calling attention to a possible short-term problem in the control of overhead costs. Answer (D) is incorrect. The volume variance does not indicate whether problems exist in the control of costs.

19. Under the three-variance method for analyzing factory overhead, the difference between the actual factory overhead and the factory overhead applied to production is the

    A.   Net factory overhead variance.

    B.   Controllable variance.

    C.   Efficiency variance.

    D.   Spending variance.

Answer (A) is correct.
    REQUIRED: The difference between the actual manufacturing overhead and the manufacturing overhead applied.
    DISCUSSION: Three-way analysis calculates spending, efficiency, and volume variances. However, regardless of whether two-, three-, or four-way analysis is used, the net manufacturing overhead variance is the difference between actual overhead and the amount applied to production.
    Answer (B) is incorrect. The controllable (budget) variance is calculated in two-way analysis. Answer (C) is incorrect. No single efficiency variance is calculated in overhead variance analysis. Answer (D) is incorrect. In three-way analysis, the spending variance is the sum of the variable overhead spending variance and the fixed overhead spending variance.

20. Union Company uses a standard cost accounting system. The following factory overhead and production data are available for August:

Standard fixed overhead rate per DLH	$1
Standard variable overhead rate per DLH	$4
Budgeted monthly DLH	40,000
Actual DLH worked	39,500
Standard DLH allowed for actual production	39,000
Overall overhead variance – favorable	$2,000

The applied factory overhead for August should be

A. $195,000

B. $197,000

C. $197,500

D. $199,500

Answer (A) is correct.
REQUIRED: The applied manufacturing overhead for the month.
DISCUSSION: The applied overhead equals the standard direct hours allowed for actual production multiplied by the total standard overhead rate per hour.

$$39,000 \times (\$4 \text{ VOH} + \$1 \text{ FOH}) = \$195,000$$

Answer (B) is incorrect. The amount of $197,000 includes the $2,000 favorable overhead variance. This variance should not be added to the $195,000 applied overhead. Answer (C) is incorrect. The actual DLH worked were used to determine the applied FO when the standard DLH allowed for actual production should have been used. Answer (D) is incorrect. The actual DLH worked were used instead of the standard DLH allowed. Furthermore, the $2,000 favorable overhead variance should not be included.

21. Jones, a department manager, exercises control over the department's costs. The following is selected information relating to the department for July:

Variable factory overhead

Budgeted based on standard hours allowed	$80,000
Actual	85,000

Fixed factory overhead

Budgeted	25,000
Actual	27,000

In a three-way analysis of variance, the department's unfavorable spending variance for July was

A. $7,000

B. $5,000

C. $2,000

D. $0

Answer (A) is correct.
REQUIRED: The amount of unfavorable spending variance.
DISCUSSION: In three-way analysis, the spending variance is the sum of the variable overhead spending variance and the fixed overhead spending variance. The variable overhead spending variance equals the actual number of units of the overhead driver consumed times the application rate minus the amount actually incurred ($80,000 – $85,000 = $5,000 unfavorable). The fixed overhead spending variance equals the budgeted amount minus the actual amount incurred ($25,000 – $27,000 = $2,000 unfavorable). The department's total unfavorable spending variance for July is thus $7,000 ($5,000 + $2,000).
Answer (B) is incorrect. The variable overhead spending variance is $5,000. Answer (C) is incorrect. The fixed overhead spending variance is $2,000. Answer (D) is incorrect. The department incurred an unfavorable spending variance for the month.

20.6 Sales Variances

22. The following data are available for July:

	Budget	Actual
Sales	40,000 units	42,000 units
Selling price	$6 per unit	$5.70 per unit
Variable cost	$3.50 per unit	$3.40 per unit

What is the sales volume variance for July?

A. $5,000 favorable.

B. $4,600 favorable.

C. $12,000 unfavorable.

D. $12,600 unfavorable.

Answer (A) is correct.
REQUIRED: The sales volume variance for a particular month.
DISCUSSION: The sales volume variance is the difference between the actual volume and the budgeted volume in units, times the budgeted contribution margin per unit.

= (Actual volume – Budgeted volume) ×
    (Selling price – Unit variable cost)
= (42,000 – 40,000) × ($6 – $3.50)
= $5,000 F

Answer (B) is incorrect. The budgeted selling price and budgeted variable cost must be used to determine the sales volume variance, not the actual selling price and actual variable cost. Answer (C) is incorrect. The budgeted variable cost must be subtracted from the selling price before multiplying by the 2,000 unit difference actually sold from budgeted sales. Answer (D) is incorrect. The sales volume variance is found by multiplying the 2,000 unit difference between actual and budgeted sales by the $2.50 budgeted contribution margin.

APPENDIX A
AICPA UNIFORM CPA EXAMINATION
BLUEPRINTS WITH GLEIM CROSS-REFERENCES

The AICPA has indicated that the Blueprints have several purposes, including to

- *Document the minimum level of knowledge and skills necessary for initial licensure.*
- *Assist candidates in preparing for the Exam by outlining the knowledge and skills that may be tested.*
- *Apprise educators about the knowledge and skills candidates will need to function as newly licensed CPAs.*
- *Guide the development of Exam questions.*

For your convenience, we have reproduced the AICPA's BEC Blueprint. We also have provided cross-references to the study units in this book that correspond to the Blueprint's coverage.

BUSINESS ENVIRONMENT AND CONCEPTS (BEC)

Area I – Corporate Governance (17-27%)

A. INTERNAL CONTROL FRAMEWORKS

1. Purpose and objectives - SU 2
2. Components and principles - SUs 1-2

B. ENTERPRISE RISK MANAGEMENT FRAMEWORKS

1. Purpose and objectives - SU 2
2. Components and principles - SU 2

C. OTHER REGULATORY FRAMEWORKS AND PROVISIONS - SU 1

Area II – Economic Concepts and Analysis (17-27%)

A. ECONOMIC AND BUSINESS CYCLES - MEASURES AND INDICATORS - SUs 3-5

B. MARKET INFLUENCES ON BUSINESS - SU 3, SU 5, SU 18

C. FINANCIAL RISK MANAGEMENT

1. Market, interest rate, currency, liquidity, credit, price and other risks - SUs 5-6
2. Means for mitigating/controlling financial risks - SUs 6-7

Area III – Financial Management (11-21%)

A. CAPITAL STRUCTURE - SU 8, SU 10

B. WORKING CAPITAL

1. Fundamentals and key metrics of working capital management - SUs 8-10
2. Strategies for managing working capital - SUs 9-10

C. FINANCIAL VALUATION METHODS AND DECISION MODELS - SUs 6-9, SU 11

Area IV – Information Technology (15-25%)

A.   INFORMATION TECHNOLOGY (IT) GOVERNANCE

    1.   Vision and strategy - SU 12
    2.   Organization - SU 13, SU 15
    3.   Risk assessments - SU 13, SU 15

B.   ROLE OF INFORMATION TECHNOLOGY IN BUSINESS - SU 12, SU 14

C.   INFORMATION SECURITY/AVAILABILITY

    1.   Protection of information - SUs 14-15
    2.   Logical and physical access controls - SU 15
    3.   System disruption/resolution - SU 13

D.   PROCESSING INTEGRITY (INPUT/PROCESSING/OUTPUT CONTROLS) - SU 13, SU 15

E.   SYSTEMS DEVELOPMENT AND MAINTENANCE - SU 13

Area V – Operations Management (15-25%)

A.   FINANCIAL AND NON-FINANCIAL MEASURES OF PERFORMANCE MANAGEMENT - SU 16

B.   COST ACCOUNTING

    1.   Cost measurement concepts, methods and techniques - SUs 18-20
    2.   Variance analysis - SU 20

C.   PROCESS MANAGEMENT

    1.   Approaches, techniques, measures, benefits to process-management driven businesses - SU 16
    2.   Management philosophies and techniques for performance improvement - SU 16

D.   PLANNING TECHNIQUES

    1.   Budgeting and analysis - SU 17
    2.   Forecasting and projection - SUs 6-7, SU 10, SUs 17-18

APPENDIX B
OPTIMIZING YOUR SCORE ON THE TASK-BASED SIMULATIONS (TBSs) AND WRITTEN COMMUNICATIONS (WCs)

Each section of the CPA exam contains multiple testlets of Task-Based Simulations. The number of TBS testlets and the number of TBSs in each testlet are the same for each exam section except BEC.

TBSs per Exam Section

	Testlet 3	Testlet 4	Testlet 5	Total
AUD	2	3	3	8
BEC	2	2	N/A*	4
FAR	2	3	3	8
REG	2	3	3	8

*Testlet 5 of BEC is Written Communications.

Task-Based Simulations are constructive response questions with information presented either with the question or in separate information tabs. Question responses may be in the form of entering amounts or formulas into a spreadsheet, choosing the correct answer from a list in a pop-up box, completing accounting or tax forms, or reviewing and completing or correcting a draft of a document. In the AUD, FAR, and REG exam sections, you will also have to complete a Research task, which requires you to research the relevant authoritative literature and cite the appropriate guidance as indicated. You will not have to complete a Research task in BEC.

In the BEC section of the exam, your last testlet will be the written communication tasks, which test your ability to logically organize and communicate information. This testlet will contain three written communication scenarios (two graded, one pretest) that you must respond to in the form of a memo by typing with a word processor.

It is not productive to practice TBSs or WCs on paper. Instead, you should use your online Gleim CPA Review Course to complete truly interactive TBSs and WCs that emulate exactly how they are tested on the CPA exam. As a CPA candidate, you must become an expert on how to approach TBSs and WCs, how to budget your time in the last three testlets, and the different types of TBSs. This appendix covers all of those topics for you and includes examples of typical TBSs and WCs. Use this appendix only as an introduction to TBSs and WCs, and then practice hundreds of exam-emulating TBSs and WCs in your Gleim CPA Review Course.

TASK-BASED SIMULATIONS

Toolbar Icons and Operations**

The following information and toolbar icons are located at the top of the testlet screen of each TBS. All screen shots are taken from the AICPA Sample Test (www.aicpa.org). The CPA exam, the Sample Test, and all screenshots are Copyright 2017 by the AICPA with All Rights Reserved. The AICPA requires all candidates to review the Sample Test and Tutorials before sitting for the CPA exam.

1. **Exam Section and Testlet Number:** The testlet number will always be 3 or 4 of 5 for the simulations in BEC.

2. **Time Remaining:** This information box displays how much time you have remaining in the entire exam. Consistently check the amount of time remaining to stay on schedule.

3. **Unsplit:** This icon, when selected, will unsplit the screen between two tabs.

4. **Split Horiz:** This icon, when selected, will split the screen horizontally between two tabs, enabling you to see, for example, both the simulation question and the help tab at the same time.

5. **Split Vertical:** This icon, when selected, will split the screen vertically between two tabs, enabling you to see, for example, both the simulation question and the help tab at the same time.

6. **Authoritative Literature:** The Authoritative Literature is available in every TBS testlet in every section, including BEC. When researching for AUD, FAR, and REG TBSs, you can use either the Table of Contents or the Search function to locate the correct guidance. Note that although the AUD, FAR, and REG Authoritative Literature will be available for BEC TBSs, you do not need it. Practically speaking, it is just a distraction on the BEC section, and you should not spend any of your valuable time looking at it.

**IMPORTANT NOTE: The AICPA has announced the launch of new, more user-friendly software for the CPA exam sometime in 2018. At time of print, the finalized interface and actual launch date had not been released. Gleim will keep candidates up-to-date on all news and will provide the most realistic emulations within our course and in an update PDF for book users as soon as they are available. Be sure to check the Gleim CPA Blog at www.gleim.com/cpablog for breaking news on this development.

7. **Spreadsheet:** The spreadsheet operates like most others and is provided as a tool for complex calculations. You may enter and execute formulas as well as enter text and numbers.

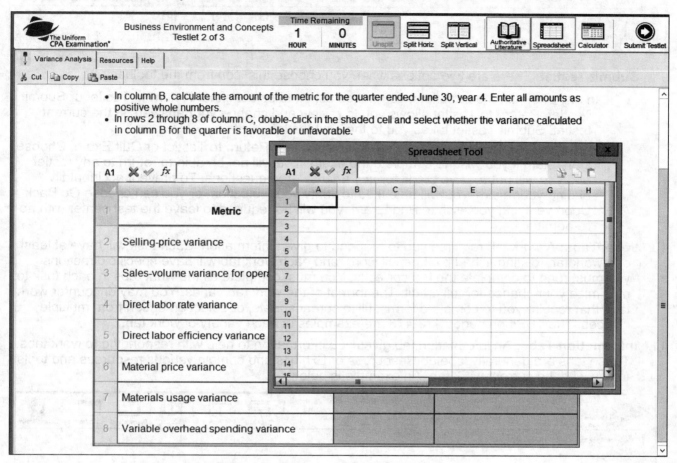

8. **Calculator:** The calculator provided is a basic tool for simple computations. It is similar to calculators used in common software programs.

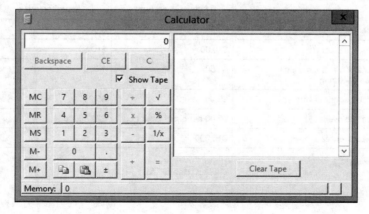

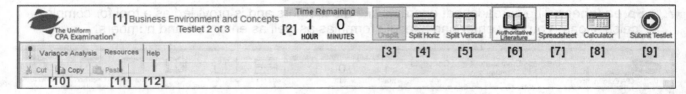

9. **Submit Testlet:** There are two options when you choose this icon from the toolbar.

   - In any of the first four testlets, you will be asked to select either Return to Testlet or Submit Testlet. Return to Testlet allows you to review and change your answers in the current testlet. Submit Testlet takes you to the next testlet.

   - In the final testlet, you will be asked to select either Return to Testlet or Quit Exam. Choose Quit Exam if you wish to complete the exam. You will not be able to return to any testlet, and you will not receive credit for any unanswered questions. To prevent accidentally ending your exam, you will be asked to verify your selection, or you can choose Go Back. Upon verifying you wish to End Exam, you will be required to leave the test center with no re-admittance.

10. **Work Tabs:** A work tab requires you to respond to given information. Each task will have at least one work tab (distinguished by a pencil icon), and each work tab will have specific directions you must read to complete the tab correctly. You must complete all the work tabs in each task to maximize your chance for full credit. The format of the work tab varies. You may encounter work tabs that require you to complete forms, fill in spreadsheets, or select an option from multiple choices. The TBSs on pages 473-478 are examples of each variety of work tab.

11. **Information Tabs:** An information tab gives you information to help with responding to work tabs. These tabs are generally labeled Resources or Exhibits and contain various resources and tools to use with the current work tab. An example is below.

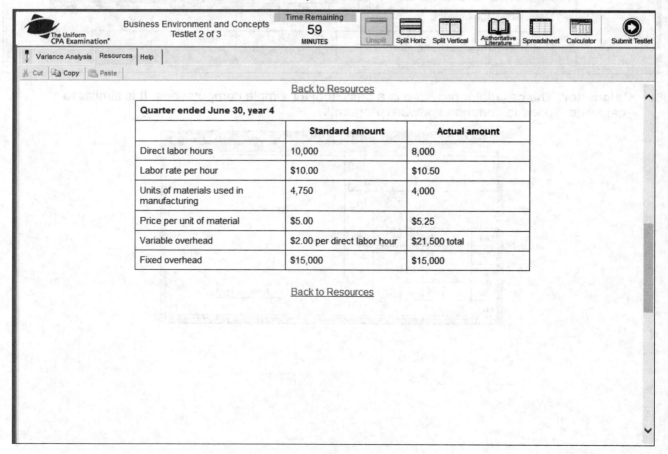

Back to Resources

Quarter ended June 30, year 4		
	Standard amount	**Actual amount**
Direct labor hours	10,000	8,000
Labor rate per hour	$10.00	$10.50
Units of materials used in manufacturing	4,750	4,000
Price per unit of material	$5.00	$5.25
Variable overhead	$2.00 per direct labor hour	$21,500 total
Fixed overhead	$15,000	$15,000

Back to Resources

12. **Help:** This tab, when selected, provides a quick review of certain functions and tool buttons specific to the type of task you are working in. It will also provide directions and general information but will not include information related specifically to the test content.

The **navigation toolbar** below appears at the bottom of every TBS screen.

Clicking on a number takes you to that TBS; hovering over the number shows the name of the TBS. Clicking on the flag under a number marks the TBS. You can use the flag as a reminder to go back and check that TBS again if you have time.

Answering Task-Based Simulations

Do not be intimidated by TBSs. Just learn the material and practice answering the different question types. Knowing **how** to work through the simulations is nearly as important as knowing what they test.

You can maximize your score on the TBS testlets of each exam section by following these suggested steps for completing Task-Based Simulations.

A. **Budget your time so you can finish before time expires.**

    1.   Allot small segments of the total testing time to each specific task. We recommend you budget 18 minutes for each TBS.

    2.   Track your progress to ensure that you will have enough time to complete all the tasks.

    3.   Use our Time Allocation Table to determine the time at which you need to start and finish each TBS testlet.

B. **Devote the first few minutes to reading the directions and scanning each TBS.**

    1.   Spend no more than 3 minutes reading the directions and previewing the TBSs you received by clicking through the navigation bar at the bottom of the screen.

    2.   You will not need to spend any time on the directions for your second TBS testlet, so you can dedicate the full time (minus a minute for scanning to preview) to responding.

    3.   You will be familiar with the layout of the TBSs if you have been practicing with Gleim TBSs under exam conditions.

C. **Answer all the tasks within the time limit for each testlet.**

    1.   Read all information tabs (e.g., financial statements, memos, etc.) associated with the tab you are working on before you attempt to answer the simulation.

        a.   We have included detailed directions on using exhibits as source documents in the next section on Document Review Simulations. Much of those instructions can also be used when answering regular TBSs that contain exhibits.

    2.   Do not skip any of the questions within a tab. Make an educated guess if you are unsure of the answer and set a reminder for yourself by clicking the flag icon under the number of the TBS in the navigation toolbar at the bottom of the screen. There is no penalty for incorrect answers, so do not move on without at least selecting your best guess.

D. **Spend any remaining time wisely to maximize your points.**

    1.   Ask yourself where you will earn the most points.

    2.   Move from task to task systematically, reviewing and completing each one. Focus specifically on any TBS you flagged.

    3.   Move on to the next TBS within the testlet or to the next testlet at the end of 18 minutes.

DOCUMENT REVIEW SIMULATIONS

Within the Task-Based Simulation testlets included in each CPA exam section, you may find a Document Review Simulation (DRS), which will be named Document Review. You are required to review various exhibits to determine the best phrasing of a particular document. The document will contain highlighted words, phrases, sentences, or paragraphs that may or may not be correct. You then must select answer choices that indicate which (if any) changes you believe should be made in the highlighted words, phrases, sentences, or paragraphs.

The DRSs always include the actual document you must review and correct, a help tab, and one or more information tabs. Information tabs vary from one DRS to the next because they contain the exhibits to be used as sources for your conclusions. For example, these exhibits may be financial statements, emails, letters, invoices, memoranda, or minutes from meetings. You must read each DRS tab so that you are always aware of the resources available.

Answering Document Review Simulations

A. **Familiarize yourself with every part of the DRS.**

Review each information tab so you know what information is available. If your subject-matter preparation has been thorough, you should be able to identify quickly the most relevant information in each part of the DRS.

B. **Address every underlined portion of text in the DRS.**

You must make an answer selection for every modifiable section of a DRS because each counts as a separate question. You will know an answer has been selected when you see that the white outline in the blue icon has changed to a white checkmark.

C. **Read the underlined section and answer choices carefully and completely.**

Each underlined portion of text may have five to seven answer choices that may include the options to revise the text, retain the original text, or delete the text. Verify that each word or amount is correct in your choice before making your final selection.

D. **Clearly understand the information in the exhibits.**

Quickly survey the various items; then analyze the most relevant facts specifically and refer to them to reduce the possible answer choices. Keep in mind that the relevant information may be presented or worded differently than the document you are revising.

E. **Double-check that you have officially responded to each underlined portion of text.**

If you have time, go through the entire DRS once more to confirm that every underlined section has a white checkmark next to it.

WRITTEN COMMUNICATIONS

Toolbar Icons and Operations**

The following information and toolbar icons are located at the top of the testlet screen of each WC. The AICPA requires all candidates to review the Sample Test and Tutorials before sitting for the CPA exam.

1. **Exam Section and Testlet Number:** The testlet number will always be 5 of 5 for the Written Communications in BEC.

2. **Time Remaining:** This information box displays to the examinee how long (s)he has remaining in the entire exam. Consistently check the amount of time remaining in order to stay on schedule for completion.

3. **Unsplit:** This icon, when selected, will unsplit the screen between two tabs.

4. **Split Horiz:** This icon, when selected, will split the screen horizontally between two tabs, enabling you to see, for example, both the written communication scenario and the help tab at the same time.

5. **Split Vertical:** This icon, when selected, will split the screen vertically between two tabs, enabling you to see, for example, both the written communication scenario and the help tab at the same time.

6. **Submit Testlet:** There are two options when you choose this icon from the toolbar.

   - In any of the first four testlets, you will be asked to select either Return to Testlet or Submit Testlet. Return to Testlet allows you to review and change your answers in the current testlet. Submit Testlet takes you to the next testlet.

   - In the final testlet, you will be asked to select either Return to Testlet or Quit Exam. Choose Quit Exam if you wish to complete the exam. You will not be able to return to any testlet, and you will not receive credit for any unanswered questions. To prevent accidentally ending your exam, you will be asked to verify your selection, or you can choose Go Back. Upon verifying you wish to End Exam, you will be required to leave the test center with no re-admittance.

**IMPORTANT NOTE: The AICPA has announced the launch of new, more user-friendly software for the CPA exam sometime in 2018. At time of print, the finalized interface and actual launch date had not been released. Gleim will keep candidates up-to-date on all news and will provide the most realistic emulations within our course and in an update PDF for book users as soon as they are available. Be sure to check the Gleim CPA Blog at www.gleim.com/cpablog for breaking news on this development.

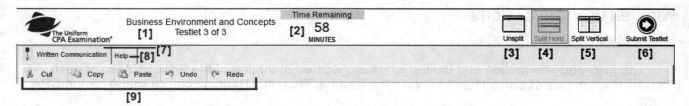

7. **Written Communication:** Each written communication work tab will contain a scenario that requires you to prepare a written memo or business letter in response.

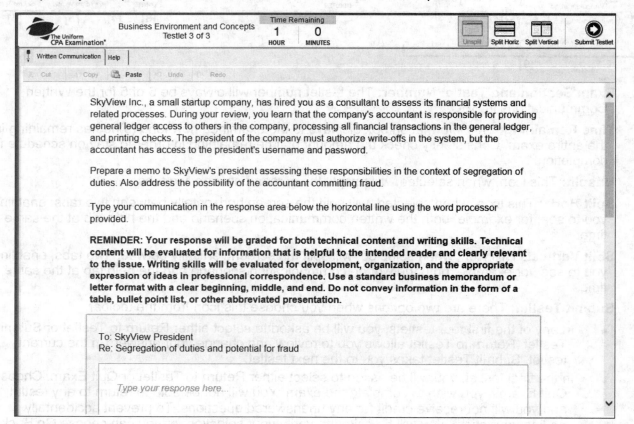

8. **Help:** This icon, when selected, provides a quick review of certain functions and tool buttons. It will also provide directions and general information but will not include information related specifically to the test content.

9. **Processor Tools:** You will be able to cut, copy, paste, undo, and redo by clicking on the appropriate icon within the response area.

Answering Written Communications

You can maximize your score on the written communications testlet by following these suggested steps for completing the WCs.

1. **Budget your time so you can finish before time expires.**

   a. Commit small segments of the total testing time to responding to each WC scenario.

   b. Monitor your time and track your progress so you have enough time to respond to all three scenarios.

   c. Use our Time Allocation Table to learn more about how to manage your time during the WCs.

2. **Read the directions in the first 2 minutes.**

   a. Do not spend too much time on the directions.

   b. If you have been studying with the Gleim Premium CPA Review System, then you will have used an exact emulation of the WCs on the CPA Exam and be comfortable with the directions already.

3. **Allocate 60 minutes to respond to the scenarios in the WC testlet in the BEC exam.**

   a. Complete each response in no more than 20 minutes.

   b. Do NOT try to guess which is the ungraded pretest scenario. Respond to each scenario as though it counts!

4. **Now that you have spent most of your time responding to the scenarios, spend your remaining 15 minutes or so perfecting your responses for maximum points.**

   a. Edit your responses to ensure they meet the writing criteria of the AICPA and that you have effectively communicated your response.

   b. Move from scenario to scenario systematically, reviewing and completing each one.

Grading Written Communications

Your score on the WCs will make up 15% of your total score. The other 85% of your total score will be the sum of your scores on the multiple-choice testlets at 50% and the TBS at 35%.

> **Your BEC Written Communications may cover topics outside the scope of the BEC Blueprint (i.e., they may relate to topics from the AUD, FAR, and/or REG Blueprints instead).** Gleim includes written communication scenarios that cover all topics from all four sections of the exam in the Gleim system to ensure you are prepared. Also, while the graders are mainly evaluating your writing ability and will overlook minor technical mistakes, they will take content into account if your response contains egregious factual errors, off-topic information, or illegal advice. Therefore, you should (1) try to respond to each Written Communication as clearly as possible and (2) ensure that your response is free from off-topic or drastically incorrect information.

In the written communication on the BEC exam, you will be graded on both technical content and writing skills. The AICPA's Sample Test states that the "technical content will be evaluated for information that is helpful to the intended reader and clearly relevant to the issue." It also states that writing skill scores will be based on three criteria from the AICPA: organization (structure, ordering of ideas, linking of ideas to one another), development (presentation of supporting evidence), and expression (use of standard business English). The AICPA advises that all responses "should provide the correct information in writing that is clear, complete, and professional. Only those writing samples that are generally responsive to the topic will be graded. If your response is off-topic, or offers advice that is clearly illegal, you will not receive any credit for the response."

Gleim has expanded the definitions of the AICPA's three writing skills criteria below. Note that the italics denote items taken from the AICPA; everything else is further clarification from Gleim.

***Organization** -- the document's structure, ordering of ideas, and linking of one idea to another*

- *Overview/thesis statement*: Inform the reader of the overall purpose of the document; i.e., name the subject about which you are attempting to provide information.
- *Unified paragraphs (topic and supporting sentences)*: Make a statement, then use the remainder of the paragraph to back up that statement.
- *Transitions and connectives*: Words such as "because," "although," "however," and "moreover" allow you to connect related topics or shift the reader's attention to a new idea.

***Development** -- the document's supporting evidence/information to clarify thoughts*

- *Details*: Simply asserting a fact, such as that debt on the balance sheet increases risk, is insufficient. The writer must describe the cause-and-effect relationship underlying this fact.
- *Definitions*: Accounting and finance terms, such as solvency and liquidity, may not be understood by the reader. The writer should explain them.
- *Examples*: The description of unfamiliar terms can be enhanced by the use of examples, such as the use of an expert system in the practice of distance medicine.
- *Rephrasing*: Stating an idea twice with different wording can also help the reader understand.

***Expression** -- the document's use of conventional standards of business English*

- *Grammar (sentence construction, subject/verb agreement, pronouns, modifiers)*: Adherence to the basic rules of English grammar is essential.
- *Punctuation (final, comma)*: A period must be used to bring a complete sentence to a close. Commas should be used to separate items in lists as well as to separate clauses within a single sentence.
- *Word usage (incorrect, imprecise language)*: Business readers expect writers to avoid ambiguity and to choose the right word for the situation; for example, not to use the word "bond" where "note" is meant.
- *Capitalization*: The first word of a sentence and all proper names must be capitalized. Concepts and measures, such as liquidity and earnings per share, are not normally capitalized.
- *Spelling*: Business readers have an expectation that writers have a grasp of standard spelling conventions.

To help you gauge your proficiency in constructing a response that excels in all of the AICPA's criteria, the Gleim CPA Review Course allows you to assign a self-grade to your written communication responses. Self-grading your responses for practice written communication tasks will make you an expert on what the AICPA is looking for, and you will be able to quickly assess your response on the actual exam because you have practiced doing so during your studies.

You will grade yourself on technical content by noting (1) if your response is on-topic, (2) if you have any significant errors in the information you give, and (3) if you give any illegal advice. You will also grade yourself on a scale of 1 to 5 on each of the AICPA's writing skills criteria (organization, development, and expression). An average response is 3. Use 4 for better than average and 5 for outstanding. Use 2 for less than average and 1 for quite poor.

MANAGING TIME ON THE TBSs and WCs

Managing your time well during the CPA exam is critical to success, so you must develop and practice your time management plan before your test date. The only help you will receive during your actual CPA exam is a countdown of the hours and minutes remaining. When there are less than 2 minutes left in an exam section, the exam clock will begin to include the seconds, but you should be doing your final review by that point.

Each of the testlets on the exam is independent, and there are no time limits on individual testlets. Therefore, you must budget your time effectively to complete all five testlets in the allotted 4 hours.

The key to success is to become proficient in answering all types of questions in an average amount of time. When you follow our system, you'll have 2-17 minutes of total extra time (depending on the section) that you will be able to allocate as needed.

Each exam will begin with three introductory screens that you must complete in 10 minutes. (Time spent in the introductory screens does not count against the 240 minutes you get for the exam itself.) Then you will have two MCQ testlets. Each testlet contains half the total number of MCQs for that section (36/testlet for AUD, 31/testlet for BEC, 33/testlet for FAR, and 38/testlet for REG.). Based on the total time of the exam and the amount of time needed for the other testlets, you should average 1.25 minutes per MCQ.

The final three testlets in AUD, FAR, and REG will have eight TBSs each: two in Testlet #3, three in Testlet #4, and three in Testlet #5. BEC will have four TBSs in two testlets, then a final testlet of three Written Communications (WCs). We suggest you allocate approximately 18 minutes to answering each TBS. On BEC, budget 25 minutes for each of the three WCs (20 minutes to answer, 5 minutes to review and perfect your response).**

To make the most of your testing time during the CPA exam, you will need to develop a time management system and commit to spending a designated amount of time on each question. To assist you, please refer to the Gleim Time Management System.

The table below shows how many minutes you should expect to spend on each testlet for each section. Remember, you cannot begin a new testlet until you have submitted a current testlet, and once you have submitted a testlet, you can no longer go back to it.

Time Allocation per Testlet (in minutes)

Testlet	Format	AUD	BEC**	FAR	REG
1	MCQ	45	38*	41*	47*
2	MCQ	45	38*	41*	47*
3	TBS	36	36	36	36
15-Minute Break					
4	TBS	54	36	54	54
5	TBS/WC	54	75	54	54
Total		234	223	226	238
Extra Time		6	17	14	2
Total Time Allowed		240	240	240	240

*Rounded down

**BEC candidates may prefer to allocate more time to the TBSs and reduce the 17 minutes of extra review time after the WCs. In this case, we suggest 20 minutes per TBS, for a total time of 40 minutes in Testlet 3 and 40 minutes in Testlet 4, leaving 9 minutes of final review after the WCs.

The exam screen will show hours:minutes remaining. Focus on how much time you have, NOT the time on your watch. Using the times on the previous page, you would start each testlet with the following hours:minutes displayed on-screen:

Completion Times and Time Remaining

	AUD	BEC**	FAR	REG
Start	4 hours 0 minutes	4 hours 0 minutes	4 hours 0 minutes	4 hours 0 minutes
After Testlet 1	3 hours 15 minutes	3 hours 22 minutes	3 hours 19 minutes	3 hours 13 minutes
After Testlet 2	2 hours 30 minutes	2 hours 44 minutes	2 hours 38 minutes	2 hours 26 minutes
After Testlet 3	1 hour 54 minutes	2 hours 8 minutes	2 hours 2 minutes	1 hour 50 minutes
15-Minute Break				
After Testlet 4	1 hour 0 minutes	1 hour 32 minutes	1 hour 8 minutes	0 hours 56 minutes
After Testlet 5	0 hours 6 minutes	0 hours 17 minutes	0 hours 14 minutes	0 hours 2 minutes

Next, develop a shorthand for hours:minutes. This makes it easier to write down the times on the noteboard you will receive at the exam center.

	AUD	BEC**	FAR	REG
Start	4:00	4:00	4:00	4:00
After Testlet 1	3:15	3:22	3:19	3:13
After Testlet 2	2:30	2:44	2:38	2:26
After Testlet 3	1:54	2:08	2:02	1:50
15-Minute Break				
After Testlet 4	1:00	1:32	1:08	0:56
After Testlet 5	0:06	0:17	0:14	0:02

**BEC candidates may prefer to allocate more time to the TBSs and reduce the 17 minutes of extra review time after the WCs. In this case, we suggest 20 minutes per TBS, for a total time of 40 minutes in Testlet 3 and 40 minutes in Testlet 4, leaving 9 minutes of final review after the WCs.

The following pages of this appendix contain the AICPA TBS directions and the following four example TBSs and three example Written Communications:

> Absorption vs. Variable Costing: Numeric Entry
> Financing Policies: Numeric Entry and Drop-Down
> IT Networks: Drop-Down
> Document Review Simulation (DRS)
> Written Communication 1
> Written Communication 2
> Written Communication 3

We have included three Written Communication scenarios and a variety of TBS types, including Drop-Down, Numeric Entry, and DRS, along with suggestions on how to approach each type. The answer key and our unique answer explanations for each TBS as well as an example response for each WC appear at the end of the appendix.

Again, do not substitute answering TBSs or WCs in your Gleim CPA Review Course with answering the ones presented here. Refer to these only for guidance on how to approach these difficult elements of the exam. It is vital that you practice answering TBSs and WCs in the digital environment of our online course so that you are comfortable with such an environment during your CPA exam.

DIRECTIONS

> Below and on the next page are reproductions of the Directions screen that appears at the beginning of each TBS and WC testlet. Take the time now to read these directions line by line so that you do not have to spend time reading this screen when you take your exam. This preparation, along with completing numerous TBSs and WCs under exam conditions in the Gleim CPA Review Course, will help you refine your answering techniques.

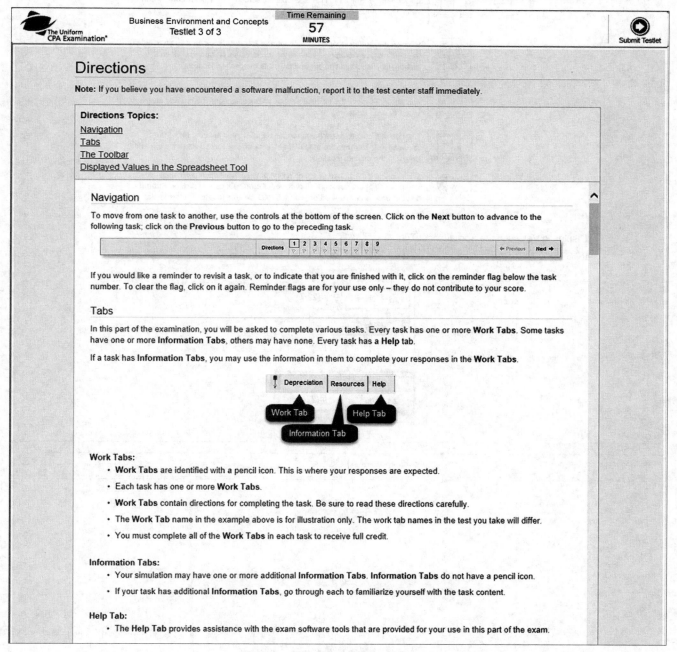

-- Continued on next page --

-- Continued

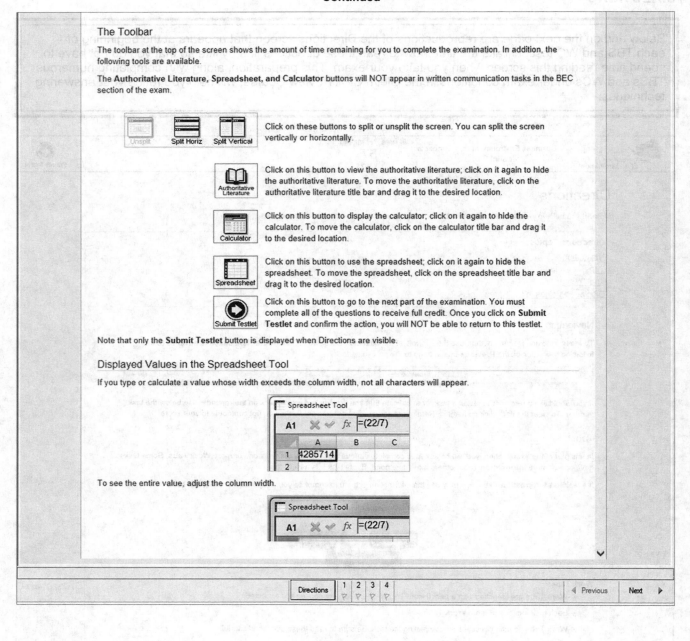

The Toolbar

The toolbar at the top of the screen shows the amount of time remaining for you to complete the examination. In addition, the following tools are available.

The **Authoritative Literature, Spreadsheet, and Calculator** buttons will NOT appear in written communication tasks in the BEC section of the exam.

Click on these buttons to split or unsplit the screen. You can split the screen vertically or horizontally.

Click on this button to view the authoritative literature; click on it again to hide the authoritative literature. To move the authoritative literature, click on the authoritative literature title bar and drag it to the desired location.

Click on this button to display the calculator; click on it again to hide the calculator. To move the calculator, click on the calculator title bar and drag it to the desired location.

Click on this button to use the spreadsheet; click on it again to hide the spreadsheet. To move the spreadsheet, click on the spreadsheet title bar and drag it to the desired location.

Click on this button to go to the next part of the examination. You must complete all of the questions to receive full credit. Once you click on **Submit Testlet** and confirm the action, you will NOT be able to return to this testlet.

Note that only the **Submit Testlet** button is displayed when Directions are visible.

Displayed Values in the Spreadsheet Tool

If you type or calculate a value whose width exceeds the column width, not all characters will appear.

To see the entire value, adjust the column width.

ABSORPTION VS. VARIABLE COSTING: NUMERIC ENTRY

> The following TBS is a Numeric Entry. This type of TBS requires that you calculate and then respond with some kind of number, e.g., an amount of currency, a ratio, etc. The spreadsheet functions much like an Excel document would. Negative numbers should be entered using a leading minus sign and will be automatically formatted with parentheses. Some Numeric Entry TBSs may also have Drop-Down type responses required. The Drop-Down TBSs are in essence multiple-choice questions.

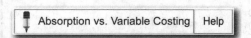 | Absorption vs. Variable Costing | Help |

Galaxy Co. is a manufacturer of a single product. During January of 20X7, variable costs per unit and total fixed costs were constant, and the entity had no beginning or ending work-in-process or spoiled units.

After considering the exhibits, calculate the following amounts using absorption costing and variable costing. Enter those amounts in the shaded cells below. Enter all amounts as positive whole numbers.

	Absorption Costing	Variable Costing
1. January manufacturing cost per unit		
2. January 31 inventory		
3. January gross profit or contribution margin		

ABSORPTION VS. VARIABLE COSTING: EXHIBITS

Subject: January production
From: Ryan Jones, Production Manager
To: Ken Thomas, VP of Operations
Date: 20X7-02-10

Dear Ken:

January was a very good month in the production department. By producing 50,000 units, we surpassed the monthly goal by approximately 10%. We also achieved our other goals of matching actual unit costs with standard unit manufacturing costs of $6 for direct materials, $10 for direct labor, and $1 for variable overhead. Barring no breakdowns of equipment, we should be able to reach or surpass our goals for this month as well.

Best regards,

Ryan

Galaxy Co.
Trial Balance (partial)
January 31, 20X7

	Debit	Credit
Sales (51,000 units)		$1,530,000
Total manufacturing overhead	$150,000	
Variable selling and administrative costs	50,000	
Fixed selling and administrative costs	200,000	

Galaxy Co.
Balance Sheet*
December 31, 20X6

Assets

Current assets

Cash		$135,000
Accounts receivable		19,000
Inventory (5,000 units)		95,000
Total current assets		249,000
Noncurrent assets		
Equipment	$76,000	
Accumulated depreciation	(24,000)	
Total noncurrent assets		52,000
Total assets		**$301,000**

Liabilities

Current liabilities

Accounts payable	$ 34,000
Accrued expenses	7,000
Total current liabilities	$ 41,000
Noncurrent liabilities	26,000
Total liabilities	**$ 67,000**

Shareholders' Equity

Retained earnings	$134,000
Common stock	100,000
Total shareholders' equity	$234,000
Total liabilities and shareholders' equity	**$301,000**

*The applicable financial reporting framework is U.S. GAAP.

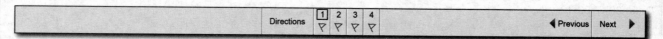

Directions 1 2 3 4   ◀ Previous   Next ▶

FINANCING POLICIES: NUMERIC ENTRY AND DROP-DOWN

> This TBS is an example of both Numeric Entry and Drop-Down type questions being asked in the same TBS.

 Financing Policies | Exhibits | Help

Use the information provided in the exhibits to answer the following questions regarding Aaron, Inc.

A. Select from the list provided the correct type of policy for each financing option. Each choice may be used once.

B. Enter the appropriate amount in each cell to indicate the correct amount of temporary working capital and permanent working capital in 20X8.

C. Select from the list provided the correct financing type for each fund. Each choice may be used once, more than once, or not at all.

A

Options	Type of Policy
1. Option 1	
2. Option 2	
3. Option 3	

Types of Policy
Conservative Policy
Moderate Policy
Aggressive Policy

B

Capital Type	Amount
4. Temporary Working Capital for 20X8	
5. Permanent Working Capital for 20X8	

C

Funds	Type of Financing
6. Mortgage bonds	
7. Debentures	
8. Preferred stock	
9. Term loan	
10. Common stock	
11. Commercial paper	
12. Retained earnings	
13. Trade credit	

Types of Financing
Long-term financing
Spontaneous financing
Short-term financing

FINANCING POLICIES: EXHIBITS

Summary of Working Capital Structure		
Aaron, Inc.		
Year	Working Capital during Slack Season	Working Capital during Peak Season
20X6	$55 million	$65 million
20X7	$55 million	$72 million
20X8	$55 million	$70 million

To: Gary Hayes, CEO
From: Juliana Hall, Controller
Date: October 6, 20X8
Subject: Financing options

Hi Gary,

I am emailing you per our previous correspondence regarding the financing options for our new project. My team has determined several possible levels of working capital that involve fundamental decisions regarding our firm's liquidity and the maturity composition of the debt portfolio.

I have listed the three financing options below. Each option has advantages and disadvantages. I will discuss further details at our next meeting.

- Option 1: $75 million equity and long-term debt against long-term assets, permanent working capital, and temporary working capital; $5 million short-term overdrafts and bank loans against temporary working capital.
- Option 2: $50 million equity and long-term debt against long-term assets and permanent working capital; $30 million short-term overdrafts and bank loans against permanent working capital and temporary working capital.
- Option 3: $65 million equity and long-term debt against long-term assets and permanent working capital; $15 million short-term overdrafts and bank loans against temporary working capital.

For your reference, I have attached a summary of our firm's working capital structure for the most recent 3 years.

Please let me know if you have any questions.

Regards,

Juliana

To: Juliana Hall, Controller
From: Frank Blake, Accounting Manager
Date: October 1, 20X8
Subject: Financing options

Hi Juliana,

As you requested, below are the current outstanding amounts of our capital funds.

Sources of funds	Dollar amount (in millions)
1. Mortgage bonds ($1,000 par, 7.5% due 2X26)	$105
2. Debentures ($1,000 par, 8% due 2X25)	215
3. Preferred stock ($100 par, 7.5%)	90
4. Term Loan (due in 11 months)	10
5. Common stock ($10 par)	100
6. Commercial paper	25
7. Retained earnings	325

Let me know if you need more information.

Frank

IT NETWORKS: DROP-DOWN

> The following TBS is a Drop-Down, which are in essence multiple-choice questions. This type of task requires that you select a response from a list of choices. Some Drop-Down TBSs may also have Numeric Entry type responses required.

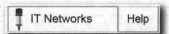

IT Networks   Help

Select from the choices provided the answer that best describes the network depicted in each item below. Each choice may be used once, more than once, or not at all.

Network	*Answer*	*Choices*
1. An entity decentralizes the processing of tasks and data storage, as well as the assignment of these functions, to multiple computers in separate locations.		Distributed processing
2. A small company uses a network arrangement to make every device directly connected.		Local area network (LAN)
3. An organization connects each office to a local Internet service provider and routes data through the shared, low-cost public Internet.		Wide area network (WAN)
4. A company uses the public Internet with password-required access to communicate with its customers.		Client-server model
5. A company uses a link between devices in its headquarters building to enhance its productivity.		Peer-to-peer arrangement
6. An organization shares information within the organization by applying Internet connectivity standards and web software to its internal network.		Value-added network (VAN)
7. A company provides its customers with a reliable, high-speed secure data transmission through a private network.		Virtual private network (VPN)
8. A network of all networks all over the world.		Intranet
9. An organization is considering using a LAN arrangement utilizing various servers.		Extranet
10. The Internet and the public telephone system are both typical examples of this kind of network.		Internet

DOCUMENT REVIEW SIMULATION (DRS)

This type of TBS requires that you analyze certain words or phrases in a document to decide whether to (1) keep the current text, (2) replace the current text with different text, or (3) delete the text. You must review various exhibits (e.g., financial statements, emails, invoices, etc.; see the second row of tabs in the image below) presented with the original document in order to find the information necessary for each response.

↕ Document Review	Exhibits	Help

📄 Futures Contract	📄 Trading Account	📄 Approval to Hedge

Using the information from the exhibits on the following pages, select the option from the list provided that corrects each underlined portion of the memo. If the underlined text is already correct in the context of the document, select *[Original Text]* from the list.

To: Howard Smith, CFO Bongo Saddle
From: Mark McElwein, Accounting Department
Date: 1/15/20X7
Re: Australian Dollar Hedge

Hi Howie:

On August 28, 20X6, we sold our 1976 Magellanic Machine to a firm in Australia. Our final payment is to be received on or about March 1, 20X7. As a result, we have a material receivable denominated in a foreign currency. <u>We are required to report any change in the exchange rate only at the final payment date.</u>

- [A] *[Original Text]* We are required to report any change in the exchange rate only at the final payment date.
- [B] We are required to report any change in the exchange rate only at year end.
- [C] We are required to report any change in the exchange rate only at year end and the final payment date.
- [D] We are required to report only the change in the exchange rate and the translation adjustments at the final payment date.

Due to potential fluctuations in the value of the Australian dollar, we decided to hedge our Australian dollar exposure. The spot rate on September 3, 20X6, was $.625 per Australian dollar. <u>We hedged the Australian dollar exposure on September 6, 20X6, when we purchased three Australian dollar futures contracts.</u>

- [A] *[Original Text]* We hedged the Australian dollar exposure on September 6, 20X6, when we purchased three Australian dollar futures contracts.
- [B] We hedged the Australian dollar exposure on September 3, 20X6, when we purchased three Australian dollar futures contracts.
- [C] We hedged the Australian dollar exposure on September 3, 20X6, when we purchased an Australian dollar futures contract.
- [D] We hedged the Australian dollar exposure on September 6, 20X6, when we purchased an Australian dollar futures contract.

At the end of 20X6, we <u>must report the changes in our foreign currency exposure and the gain or loss on the futures contracts.</u>

- [A] *[Original Text]* must report the changes in our foreign currency exposure and the gain or loss on the futures contracts.
- [B] must report only the gain or loss on the futures contracts.
- [C] must report changes only in our foreign currency exposure.
- [D] are not required to report the changes in our foreign currency exposure and gain or loss on the futures contracts.

The objective is to make these two exposures, when measured at their fair values, <u>have a beta of 0.</u>

- [A] *[Original Text]* have a beta of 0.
- [B] have a beta of +1.
- [C] have a beta of −1.
- [D] be perfectly positively correlated.
- [E] be perfectly negatively correlated.

Please let me know if you have any questions or concerns.

Best,
Mark

DRS: EXHIBITS

ACTION BY WRITTEN CONSENT OF THE BOARD OF DIRECTORS
OF
Bongo Saddle Stitching, Inc.

The undersigned, being all of the members of the Board of Directors (the "***Board***") of Bongo Saddle Stitching, Inc., a Delaware corporation (the "***Company***"), pursuant to Delaware General Corporation Law ("***DGCL***"), hereby adopt the following resolutions by executing this written consent effective this 29th day of August 20X6, for all purposes.

Approval to Hedge Foreign Currency Exposure

WHEREAS, the Board previously approved the sale of its used 1976 Magellanic Machine Model Number XST pursuant to the terms of the Purchase Agreement dated August 28, 20X6 (the "Purchase Agreement");

WHEREAS, the Company will sell its used 1976 Magellanic Machine Model Number XST to Outback Saddle, Ltd., in the amount of $1,173,957.76 Australian Dollars pursuant to the Purchase Agreement;

WHEREAS, Outback Saddle, Ltd., will make an initial deposit on September 3, 20X6, and is required to remit the remaining balance on or about March 1, 20X7, of $600,000 Australian dollars upon verified installation at Outback Saddle, Ltd., in Alice Springs, Australia, pursuant to the Purchase Agreement;

WHEREAS, the Board is aware of the material facts related to the foreign currency exposure and has had adequate opportunity to ask questions regarding, and investigate the nature of the Purchase Agreement and foreign currency exposure.

RESOLVED, that it is desirable and in the best interest of this Company that it hedge its future foreign currency exposure. The sooner the Company is able to lock in the current fair market value of the future foreign currency exposure, the better. The Company should utilize Australian Dollar Futures. Subject to compliance with all applicable federal and state securities laws, corporate officers are hereby authorized to perform on behalf of this Company any and all such acts as they deem necessary or advisable in order to comply with the applicable laws of any such states, and in connection therewith to execute and file all requisite papers and documents; and the execution by such officers of any such paper or document or the doing by them of any act in connection with the foregoing matters shall conclusively establish their authority from this Company and the approval and ratification by this Company of the papers and documents so executed and the action so taken.

Omnibus

RESOLVED FURTHER, that the appropriate officers of the Company be, and they hereby are, authorized and directed to execute and deliver on behalf of the Company such other documents, certificates, instruments and agreements, and to take such further action by and on behalf of the Company as shall be either necessary or appropriate to further the purposes of the foregoing resolutions, the necessity or propriety of such actions to be conclusively evidenced by such execution and delivery.

RESOLVED FURTHER, that any corporate action taken on or prior to the date hereof by the officers of the Company in connection with the above actions and transactions be, and they hereby are, ratified and adopted as the action of the Company effective as of the date such action was taken.

Currency
Futures Contract
December 31, 20X6

	OPEN	HI	LO	SETTLEMENT	CHANGE IN SETTLEMENT FROM YESTERDAY	
JAPANESE YEN (CME) – 12.5 million yen; $ per yen (.00)						
Mar	.9720	.9754	.9528	.9562	–	.0139
June	.9772	.9779	.9645	.9672	–	.0140
Sept	.9783	.9787	.9770	.9783	–	.0141
EU EURO (CME) – 125,000 euros; $ per euro						
Mar	.6523	.6523	.6432	.6446	–	.0067
June	.6522	.6523	.6471	.6479	–	.0067
Sept	.6512	.6514	.6511	.6513	–	.0067
CANADIAN DOLLAR (CME) – 100,000 dlrs.; $ per Can $						
Mar	.6677	.6685	.6679	.6675	–	.0002
June	.6675	.6694	.6673	.6673	–	.0003
Sept	.6682	.6699	.6677	.6681	–	.0003
BRITISH POUND (CME) – 62,500 pds.; $ per pound						
Mar	1.6376	1.6376	1.6318	1.6326	–	.0149
June	1.6290	1.6220	1.6290	1.6298	–	.0149
Sept	1.6380	1.6388	1.6381	1.6388	–	.0149
SWISS FRANC (CME) – 125,000 francs; $ per franc						
Mar	.7956	.7961	.7821	.7835	–	.0113
June	.7972	.7986	.7891	.7906	–	.0114
Sept	.7973	.7974	.7970	.7973	–	.0115
AUSTRALIAN DOLLAR (CME) – 100,000 dlrs.; $ per A. $						
Mar	.5898	.5899	.5889	.5894	+	.0011
June	.6667	.6660	.6667	.6665	+	.0013
Sept	.6723	.6720	.6729	.6728	+	.0012
MEXICAN PESO (CME) – 500,000 new Mex. peso; $ per MP						
Mar	.09372	.09492	.09268	.09312	–	.00459
June	.08900	.08980	.08870	.08865	–	.00459
Sept	.08700	.08660	.08900	.08730	–	.00357

EXCELLENT BROKERAGE COMPANY

Trading Account of
BONGO SADDLE STITCHING, INC.

Account Number
1234-5678

Trade Confirmation

BOUGHT   March 20X7 Australian Dollar Futures

				Type: Cash Trade: 9/3/20X6	Settle: 9/6/20X6
Quantity	Spot Rate	Price ($)	Principal ($)	Charges and/or Interest ($)	Total Amount ($)
3	$.625/A. dollar	$125,000	$375,000	Commission Waived	$375,000

For this security:
- Unless you have already instructed us differenty, we will: hold this security in your account.
- Unsolicited trade.
- EBC acted as your agent.

Internal Use Only: 1

WRITTEN COMMUNICATION 1

The following are three Written Communications. Respond to each scenario in a memo or other appropriate form of communication. Your response will be graded on your ability to logically organize and relay information.

NOTE: Your Written Communications on the actual CPA exam may cover topics outside the scope of the BEC Blueprint (i.e., they may relate to topics from the AUD, FAR, and/or REG Blueprints instead). Answer to the best of your ability, and remember that graders are mainly evaluating your writing ability and will overlook minor technical mistakes.

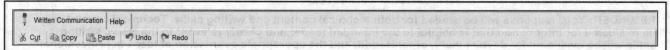

Pine Company has hired you to be its first Chief Risk Officer. As part of your job duties, you must explain the COSO Enterprise Risk Management (ERM) Framework to executive management. You have decided to use the cube model described in the COSO framework as your starting point.

Prepare a memo to executive management describing the three dimensions of the COSO ERM cube model.

Type your communication below the line in the response area below.

REMINDER: Your response will be graded for both technical content and writing skills. Technical content will be evaluated for information that is helpful to the intended reader and clearly relevant to the issue. Writing skills will be evaluated for development, organization, and the appropriate expression of ideas in professional correspondence. Use a standard business memorandum or letter format with a clear beginning, middle, and end. Do not convey information in the form of a table, bullet point list, or other abbreviated presentation.

To: Executive Management, Pine Company
Re: COSO Enterprise Risk Management (ERM) Framework

WRITTEN COMMUNICATION 2

<table>
<tr><td>⬇ Written Communication | Help</td></tr>
<tr><td>✂ Cut   📋 Copy   📋 Paste   ↶ Undo   ↷ Redo</td></tr>
</table>

The partners of Packitup Partnership are considering the decision to convert to the corporate form of business organization. During your discussions with them, you determine that they have only the vaguest ideas about the relationship between corporate debt and equity.

Prepare a memo to the partners of Packitup Partnership describing the concept of solvency, the two main components of corporate capital, and how capital structure decisions affect the risk profile of a firm.

Type your communication below the line in the response area below.

REMINDER: Your response will be graded for both technical content and writing skills. Technical content will be evaluated for information that is helpful to the intended reader and clearly relevant to the issue. Writing skills will be evaluated for development, organization, and the appropriate expression of ideas in professional correspondence. Use a standard business memorandum or letter format with a clear beginning, middle, and end. Do not convey information in the form of a table, bullet point list, or other abbreviated presentation.

To: Packitup Partnership
Re: Solvency and capital structure

Directions   1   [2]   3   ◀ Previous   Next ▶

WRITTEN COMMUNICATION 3

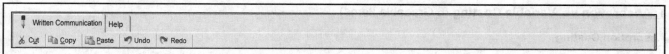

Dawn currently owns a home and uses it as her principal residence. She purchased the house and is considering moving to a more expensive home closer to her business. She has asked you to explain to her, in a memorandum-type format, the current tax law regarding sales of principal residences.

Type your communication below the line in the response area below.

REMINDER: Your response will be graded for both technical content and writing skills. Technical content will be evaluated for information that is helpful to the intended reader and clearly relevant to the issue. Writing skills will be evaluated for development, organization, and the appropriate expression of ideas in professional correspondence. Use a standard business memorandum or letter format with a clear beginning, middle, and end. Do not convey information in the form of a table, bullet point list, or other abbreviated presentation.

To: Dawn Early
Re: Sale of principal residence

TBS ANSWERS 1 OF 3

1. Absorption vs. Variable Costing (6 Gradable Items)

Absorption Costing

1. $19. (50,000 × $6) direct materials + (50,000 × $10) direct labor + (50,000 × $1) variable manufacturing overhead + [$150,000 – (50,000 × $1)] fixed manufacturing overhead = $950,000 total manufacturing cost

   $950,000 ÷ 50,000 units = $19 manufacturing cost per unit

2. $76,000. 5,000 units beginning inventory + 50,000 units manufactured – 51,000 units sold = 4,000 units ending inventory

   4,000 units ending inventory × $19 = $76,000 ending inventory

3. $561,000.

Sales (51,000 × $30)		$1,530,000
Cost of goods sold:		
Beginning inventory[1]	$ 95,000	
Cost of goods manufactured ($19 × 50,000)	950,000	
Minus: Ending inventory	(76,000)	(969,000)
Gross profit		$ 561,000

[1] The applicable financial reporting framework is U.S. GAAP. This framework requires that inventories be measured at absorption cost. The January beginning inventory equals the December ending inventory.

Variable Costing

1. $17. (50,000 × $6) direct materials + (50,000 × $10) direct labor + (50,000 × $1) variable manufacturing overhead = $850,000 total manufacturing cost

   $850,000 ÷ 50,000 units = $17 manufacturing cost per unit

2. $68,000. 5,000 units beginning inventory + 50,000 units manufactured – 51,000 units sold = 4,000 units ending inventory

   4,000 units ending inventory × $17 = $68,000 ending inventory

3. $613,000.

Sales (51,000 × $30)		$1,530,000
Minus: Variable costs		
Manufacturing ($17 × 51,000)	$867,000	
Selling and administrative	50,000	(917,000)
Contribution margin		$ 613,000

2. Financing Policies (13 Gradable Items)

1. Conservative policy. A conservative financing policy seeks to minimize liquidity risk by financing temporary working capital mostly with long-term debt and equity. Because Option 1 mainly uses long-term financing to finance long-term assets, permanent working capital, and temporary working capital, it is a conservative policy.

2. Aggressive policy. An aggressive financing policy reduces liquidity and accepts a higher risk of short-term cash shortages. Because Option 2 mainly uses short-term financing to finance temporary working capital and permanent working capital, it is an aggressive financing policy.

3. Moderate policy. Option 3 uses less long-term financing to finance temporary working capital than Option 1. But it uses more long-term financing to finance temporary working capital than Option 2. It is a moderate policy.

4. $15,000,000. As the firm's needs for working capital change on a seasonal basis, temporary working capital is increased or decreased. During the peak season, the firm requires more working capital to meet the needs of increasing sales. The temporary working capital in 20X8 is $15 million ($70 million – $55 million permanent working capital).

5. $55,000,000. Some liquid current assets must be maintained to meet the firm's long-term minimum needs regardless of the firm's level of activity or profitability. During the slack season in 20X6, 20X7, and 20X8, permanent working capital is $55 million.

TBS ANSWERS 2 OF 3

Definitions

Spontaneous financing: Financing is spontaneous when current liabilities, such as trade payable and accruals, occur naturally in the ordinary course of business. Trade credit is created when suppliers offer the firm goods and services with payment delayed for a short time.

Short-term financing: Commercial paper consists of short-term notes payable issued in large denominations by large corporations with high credit ratings to other corporations and institutional investors. Because the term loan is due in 11 months, it is short-term financing.

Long-term financing: Long-term financing includes long-term debt and equity financing. Mortgage bonds, debentures, preferred stock, common stock, and retained earnings are permanent financing.

6.   Long-term financing.

7.   Long-term financing.

8.   Long-term financing.

9.   Short-term financing.

10.   Long-term financing.

11.   Short-term financing.

12.   Long-term financing.

13.   Spontaneous financing.

3. IT Networks (10 Gradable Items)

1.   Distributed processing. Distributed processing involves the decentralization of processing tasks and data storage and assigning these functions to multiple computers, often in separate locations.

2.   Peer-to-peer arrangement. Very small networks with few devices can be connected using a peer-to-peer arrangement, in which every device is directly connected.

3.   Virtual private network (VPN). A VPN is a privately owned WAN and is a relatively inexpensive means to solve the problem of the high cost of leased lines. An entity can connect each office or LAN to a local Internet service provider and route data through the shared, low-cost public Internet. It is a privately owned WAN.

4.   Extranet. An extranet consists of the linked intranets of two or more organizations. It typically uses the public Internet as its transmission medium but requires a password to access.

5.   Local area network (LAN). A LAN is any interconnection between devices in a single office or building. The development of the LAN was caused by the need to increase productivity.

6.   Intranet. An intranet permits sharing of information throughout an organization by applying Internet connectivity standards and web software to the organization's internal network.

7.   Value-added network (VAN). A VAN is a privately owned WAN that provides its customers with reliable, high-speed secure transmission of data.

8.   Internet. The Internet is a network of networks all over the world.

9.   Client-server model. In a client-server arrangement, servers are centrally located and devoted to the functions that are needed by all network users. The client-server model is the most cost-effective and easy-to-administer arrangement for LANs.

10.   Wide area network (WAN). A WAN consists of a conglomerate of LANs over widely separated locations. It can be either publicly or privately owned. The Internet and the public telephone system are both examples of publicly owned WANs.

TBS ANSWERS 3 OF 3

4. Document Review (4 Gradable Items)

1.   A.   *[Original Text]* <u>We are required to report any change in the exchange rate only at the final payment date.</u> The receivable is denominated in a foreign currency. But it is recorded in the entity's accounts using its domestic currency. Initial measurement is at the spot rate on the transaction date. Any change in the exchange rate must be recognized not only at (1) the final payment date but also (2) any intervening financial statement date.

      B.   <u>We are required to report any change in the exchange rate only at year end.</u> Any change in the exchange rate also must be recognized at the final payment date.

      C.   **Correct:** <u>We are required to report any change in the exchange rate only at year end and the final payment date.</u> The receivable is denominated in a foreign currency. But it is recorded in the entity's domestic currency. Initial measurement is at the spot rate on the transaction date. The entity therefore must record a foreign currency transaction gain or loss for any change in the exchange rate at (1) the final payment date and (2) any intervening financing statement date.

      D.   <u>We are required to report only the change in the exchange rate and the translation adjustments at the final payment date.</u> Translation exposure results only if the receivable is recorded by a foreign subsidiary using a currency different from the parent's functional currency.

2.   A.   *[Original Text]* <u>We hedged the Australian dollar exposure on September 6, 20X6, when we purchased three Australian dollar futures contracts.</u> The hedge was effective not on the settlement date (September 6, 20X6), but on the trade date (September 3, 20X6).

      B.   **Correct:** <u>We hedged the Australian dollar exposure on September 3, 20X6, when we purchased three Australian dollar futures contracts.</u> The hedge was effective not on the settlement date (September 6, 20X6), but on the trade date (September 3, 20X6), the date that Bongo purchased three futures contracts as stated in the trade confirmation.

      C.   <u>We hedged the Australian dollar exposure on September 3, 20X6, when we purchased an Australian dollar futures contract.</u> Bongo purchased three futures contracts.

      D.   <u>We hedged the Australian dollar exposure on September 6, 20X6, when we purchased an Australian dollar futures contract.</u> Three contracts were purchased, and the hedge was effective on September 3, 20X6.

3.   A.   **Correct:** *[Original Text]* <u>must report the changes in our foreign currency exposure and the gain or loss on the futures contracts.</u> A hedge, such as a forward contract or futures contract, creates an additional asset or liability. Accordingly, Bongo must report at the financial statement date on (1) the hedged item (the receivable denominated in Australian dollars) and (2) the hedging instruments (the Australian dollar futures contracts).

      B.   <u>must report only the gain or loss on the futures contracts.</u> The entity must report the gain or loss on the hedged item and the hedging instruments. If the hedge is a cash flow hedge, the effective gain or loss is reported in other comprehensive income if the earnings effect does not occur until a future period.

      C.   <u>must report changes only in our foreign currency exposure.</u> The entity also must report the foreign currency transaction gain or loss on the receivable.

      D.   <u>are not required to report the changes in our foreign currency exposure and gain or loss on the futures contracts.</u> The entity must report at the financial statement date the gain or loss on (1) the hedged item and (2) the hedging instruments even if the transaction will not be completed until a future period.

4.   A.   *[Original Text]* <u>have a beta of 0.</u> Beta is a component of the capital asset pricing model (CAPM). Beta measures how well the value of an asset or investment security moves with the value of the market. But an effective hedge relates to correlation, not beta.

      B.   <u>have a beta of +1.</u> The issue is correlation, not beta. Also, beta is not limited to values between −1 and +1.

      C.   <u>have a beta of −1.</u> The ideal hedging instrument has a correlation (not beta) of −1 with the hedged item.

      D.   <u>be perfectly positively correlated.</u> The correlation should be negative.

      E.   **Correct:** <u>be perfectly negatively correlated.</u> Firms enter hedges to reduce risks by creating a relationship by which losses on certain positions are expected to be offset in whole or in part by gains on separate positions in another market. Consequently, an entity can offset any risk by investing (or purchasing) an asset or liability that moves in the opposite direction of the original risk. The second asset, the hedge, should be negatively correlated with the value of the first asset.

WC ANSWERS 1 OF 3

> Below and on the following pages you will find an example of responses at writing skill level 5 for each Written Communication. The Grading Written Communications section beginning on page 467 of this appendix has more information on what constitutes a level 5 response. These examples are intended to provide you with tips about how to structure sentences and state your ideas when completing Written Communications on the BEC portion. All other suggested responses provided by Gleim throughout your online courses are writing skill level 5 responses that are on-topic and contain no egregious errors or illegal advice.

Written Communication 1

To: Executive Management, Pine Company
Re: COSO Enterprise Risk Management (ERM) Framework

The COSO Enterprise Risk Management Framework depicts the interaction of the various elements of an ERM program as a matrix in the form of a cube. The four categories of objectives are on one side, the eight interrelated components are on another, and the organizational units of the entity are on a third. The organization can apply the appropriate approach to each intersection of the three elements, such as control activities for reporting objectives at the division level.

The four categories of objectives are strategic, operations, reporting, and compliance. They apply to all entities. Strategic objectives align with and support the entity's mission. Operations objectives address effectiveness and efficiency. Reporting objectives concern reliability. Compliance objectives relate to adherence to laws and regulations. These categories overlap but are distinct. They concern different needs, and different managers may be assigned responsibility for them.

The eight components of ERM are integrated with the management process and may mutually influence each other. They are the internal environment, objective setting, event identification, risk assessment, risk response, control activities, the information and communication component, and monitoring. The internal environment reflects the entity's risk management philosophy, risk appetite, integrity, ethical values, and overall environment. It sets the tone of the entity. Objective setting precedes event identification. Event identification relates to internal and external events affecting the entity. Risk assessment considers likelihood and impact as a basis for risk management. The assessment considers the inherent risk and the residual risk. Risk responses should be consistent with the organization's risk tolerances and appetite. Control activities are policies and procedures to ensure the effectiveness of risk responses. The information and communication component identifies, captures, and communicates relevant and timely information. Monitoring involves ongoing management activities or separate evaluations.

The third dimension is the enterprise's organizational units, for example, subsidiary, business unit, division, and entity level. The structure depends on the unique characteristics of the entity.

In summary, the cube provides a model demonstrating the relationship among the objectives, components, and units of the organization.

The above depicts a level 5 answer. Consult the Grading Written Communications section of this appendix for a description of the three writing skills criteria.

Self-Grade

Below, grade your response on technical content and writing skills. Bubble in the circle next to the most appropriate score for your response based on the criteria given. Your **total** score is the sum of your scores on all six items. The maximum score is 19 points.

Technical Content Evaluation

Was your response on topic?	O No [0]	O Mostly [1]	O Yes [2]
Did your response have any _significant_ errors?	O 0 errors [1]	O 1 major error [–1]	O 2 or more major errors [–2]
Did your response contain any illegal advice?	O No [1]	O Yes [0]	

Writing Skills Evaluation

	Poor	Below Average	Average	Above Average	Outstanding
Organization	O 1	O 2	O 3	O 4	O 5
Development	O 1	O 2	O 3	O 4	O 5
Expression	O 1	O 2	O 3	O 4	O 5

Disclaimer: This scoring schedule was developed by Gleim Publications as a guideline only. The AICPA has not released specific information on how the Written Communications are graded.

WC ANSWERS 2 OF 3

Written Communication 2

To: Packitup Partnership
Re: Solvency and capital structure

Solvency is a firm's ability to pay its noncurrent obligations as they come due and remain in business in the long run. It differs from liquidity, the ability to remain in business in the short run. The key ingredients of solvency are the firm's capital structure and degree of leverage. A firm's capital structure includes its sources of financing, both long- and short-term. These sources can be in the form of debt (external sources) or equity (internal sources).

Debt is the creditor interest in the firm. The firm is contractually obligated to repay debtholders. The terms of repayment (i.e., timing of interest and principal payments) are specified in the debt agreement. If the return on debt capital exceeds the amount of interest paid, debt financing is advantageous. The return is increased because interest payments on debt are tax-deductible. The tradeoff is that increased debt increases the firm's risk. Debt must be paid regardless of whether the firm is profitable. When risk reaches a certain level, either the firm will have to pay a higher interest rate than its return on debt, or creditors will refuse to lend any more money.

Equity is the ownership interest in the firm. Equity is the permanent capital of an entity, contributed by the firm's owners in expectation of a return. However, a return on equity is uncertain because equity is only a residual interest in the firm's assets. It is residual because it is the claim remaining after all debt has been satisfied. Periodic returns to owners of excess earnings are dividends. The firm may be contractually obligated to pay dividends to preferred shareholders but not to common shareholders.

Capital structure decisions affect the risk profile of a firm. For example, a firm with a higher percentage of debt capital will be riskier than a firm with a higher percentage of equity capital. Thus, when the relative amount of debt is high, equity investors will demand a higher rate of return on their investments to compensate for the greater risk. But a firm with a relatively larger proportion of equity capital will be able to borrow at lower rates because debt holders will accept lower interest in exchange for the lower risk.

The above depicts a level 5 answer. Consult the Grading Written Communications section of this appendix for a description of the three writing skills criteria.

Self-Grade

Below, grade your response on technical content and writing skills. Bubble in the circle next to the most appropriate score for your response based on the criteria given. Your **total** score is the sum of your scores on all six items. The maximum score is 19 points.

Technical Content Evaluation

Was your response on topic?	O No [0]	O Mostly [1]	O Yes [2]
Did your response have any *significant* errors?	O 0 errors [1]	O 1 major error [–1]	O 2 or more major errors [–2]
Did your response contain any illegal advice?	O No [1]	O Yes [0]	

Writing Skills Evaluation

	Poor	Below Average	Average	Above Average	Outstanding
Organization	O 1	O 2	O 3	O 4	O 5
Development	O 1	O 2	O 3	O 4	O 5
Expression	O 1	O 2	O 3	O 4	O 5

Disclaimer: This scoring schedule was developed by Gleim Publications as a guideline only. The AICPA has not released specific information on how the Written Communications are graded.

WC ANSWERS 3 OF 3

Written Communication 3

To: Dawn Early
Re: Sale of principal residence

IRC 121 allows taxpayers to exclude a portion of their gain upon the sale of a principal residence. The taxpayer can exclude up to $250,000 if filing single or $500,000 if married filing jointly. This exclusion may be used only once every 2 years. However, no loss may be recognized on the sale of such a residence.

The gain may only be excluded if the taxpayer owned and used the property as a principal residence for an aggregate of 2 years during the previous 5 years. The ownership and use times do not have to be concurrent. Short temporary absences for vacations or seasonal absences are counted for the period of use, even if the taxpayer rents out the residence during that time. An absence of an entire year is not considered a short temporary absence. Any portion of the gain that is allocable to a portion of the property that is separate from the principal residence and not used as the taxpayer's residence is not available for the exclusion. Gain must also be recognized to the extent of any depreciation adjustments with respect to the rental or business use of a principal residence after May 6, 1997.

In order for married individuals to exclude $500,000 of the gain, they must meet certain requirements. Either spouse may meet the ownership requirement, but both spouses must meet the use requirement. Additionally, neither spouse may be ineligible for the exclusion by virtue of a sale or an exchange of a residence within the last 2 years. However, if one spouse fails to meet these requirements, the other qualifying spouse is not prevented from claiming the $250,000 exclusion available to taxpayers filing single.

If the use and ownership tests are not met, or if the minimum 2-year period for claiming the full exclusion has not elapsed, the taxpayer may be able to claim a partial exclusion. However, the taxpayer's failure to meet one of the requirements must be due to either a change in the place of the taxpayer's employment, health reasons, or unforeseen circumstances. The partial exclusion is based on the ratio of months used to 24 months.

The above depicts a level 5 answer. Consult the Grading Written Communications section of this appendix for a description of the three writing skills criteria.

Self-Grade

Below, grade your response on technical content and writing skills. Bubble in the circle next to the most appropriate score for your response based on the criteria given. Your **total** score is the sum of your scores on all six items. The maximum score is 19 points.

Technical Content Evaluation

Was your response on topic?	o No [0]	o Mostly [1]	o Yes [2]
Did your response have any *significant* errors?	o 0 errors [1]	o 1 major error [–1]	o 2 or more major errors [–2]
Did your response contain any illegal advice?	o No [1]	o Yes [0]	

Writing Skills Evaluation

	Poor	Below Average	Average	Above Average	Outstanding
Organization	o 1	o 2	o 3	o 4	o 5
Development	o 1	o 2	o 3	o 4	o 5
Expression	o 1	o 2	o 3	o 4	o 5

Disclaimer: This scoring schedule was developed by Gleim Publications as a guideline only. The AICPA has not released specific information on how the Written Communications are graded.

INDEX